SOFTWARE ENGINEERING

Concepts and management

PRACTICAL SOFTWARE ENGINEERING SERIES

SOFTWARE ENGINEERING

Concepts and management

ALLEN MACRO

PRENTICE HALL

NEW YORK   LONDON   TORONTO   SYDNEY   TOKYO

First published 1990 by
Prentice Hall International (UK) Ltd
66 Wood Lane End, Hemel Hempstead
Hertfordshire, HP2 4RG
A division of
Simon & Schuster International Group

Printed and bound in Great Britain at the
University Press, Cambridge

Typeset in 9½/12pt Times
by Best-set, Hong Kong.

Library of Congress Cataloging-in-Publication Data

Macro, Allen.
  Software engineering: concepts and management/Allen Macro.
    p.   cm. — (Practical software engineering series)
  Includes bibliographical references.
  ISBN 0−13−820267−2: $64.95
  1. Software engineering. I. Title. II. Series.
    QA76.758.M25   1990
    005.1—dc20   89-23212
                                                  CIP

British Library Cataloguing in Publication Data

Macro, Allen
  Software engineering: concepts and management. −
  (Practical software engineering series)
  1. Computer systems. Software. Development. Management
  I. Title II. Series
  005.1

  ISBN 0−13−820267−2

1 2 3 4 5 94 93 92 91 90

ISBN 0-13-820267-2

CONTENTS

EDITOR'S PREFACE

The 'PSE series', five volumes on practical software engineering topics, is intended for several purposes and their appropriate audiences.

First, as a whole, the series is intended as a basis for guidelines in software engineering practice, for people who engage directly in programming computers at a non-trivial level, as the whole or a part of their work. Typically, this list will include software engineers of greater or lesser experience, amateur programmers who are generally of little (or intermittent) experience and computer scientists. They will, by and large, be involved in some or all of the activities that make up software development, such as system specification, software requirements' definition and design, implementation, testing and quality assurance.

Second, the series is intended for the comprehension of others involved in software development. In this category are managers of software engineers and the managers of these managers (and so on), commercial staff who buy or sell software, or contract for services to provide it, quality assurance people, personnel officers and operatives in associated disciplines – such as mechanical, electronic and production engineering – who may work with software development staff on composite systems.

Third, the series is intended as a text for courses in software engineering, both for academic-level and industrial/business courses in continuing education.

The breadth of this address may possibly invoke reaction, if not disfavor, for it is not immediately apparent that the third objective is compatible with the other two, certainly concerning the academic component of education as distinct from practical training courses.

A prevailing sentiment in business and industry, as we have found, seems to be that academic material is pretty irrelevant to real, everyday problems of software development. It teaches (the argument goes) computer science; it does not provide (the argument continues) for good practices in software engineering to be learned. On the other hand, academics might repost – with some justification – that software engineering in the big, wide world is in a state of such glorious shambles that the kindliest and most socially useful act that they can commit is to refrain from enabling it to be learned, and some may even opt for its prevention.

It is a lamentable state of affairs to summarize the problem as a gap between two deficiencies, for that makes three problems of it. Yet, that is the case and, seen that way,

it goes some way to justify the stated aims of this series. Whether they eventuate is another matter altogether.

We have set the series out as five, monograph-length volumes. Four of these correspond to the main activities in software development:

1. Specification and feasibility.
2. Design.
3. Implementation.
4. Software estimating and technical quality.

These are Volumes 2–5 respectively, and their authors are Michael Marcotty (Volume 4 – *Software Implementation*), Wayne Stevens (Volume 3 – *Software Design*) and Allen Macro (Volumes 2 and 5).

There is also a volume whose subjects cover matters intrinsic to all four other volumes; in that sense it is the 'orthogonal' title in the series, and is called Volume 1; it covers:

5. Software engineering; concepts and management.

The impetus to read books of this sort usually arises from some recognized need; the disincentives to do so, merits of the work apart, include a misjudgment by people of what they need to know, and what they may be likely to understand. For example it is commonplace to find software development staff, at the programming level, who think and say that they have no need to interest themselves in management matters, no wish to, and no facility anyway. Nothing could be more unwise. Practitioners may prevent good management practice, by others, if they are unaware of the scope and modalities concerned in it. Equally, it is commonplace to find managers – and others not especially knowledgeable in the subject, but involved one way or another – for whom 'software' is an uncharted territory (of the 'here be dragons' sort) and to whom 'software engineering' is an arcane – perhaps profane – art, conducted in some hermetic ritual by its initiates. To some degree this attitude is understandable, if not justified. The terminology of software and its development may seem more alien to non-practitioners than that of any other subject, and apparently changes too rapidly for a start to be made in understanding it. In fact, this conclusion is only true up to a point. A basic method in cognition is that of classification and, once the basic classes are identified in this subject, as in any other, the problems of volatile terminology are lessened.

With this understanding, and in order to be helpful (with a modest reservation about the merits of books in this series, for it is the province of readers and critics to judge), we recommend that software *practitioners* and participants on courses offering software engineering modules, should read Volumes 1 and 5 as well as their rather narrow, subject-interest topics in Volumes 3 and 4. Chapter 1 of Volume 1, being elementary, may be read for passing interest only by these populations, and for an understanding of the basic problems in comprehension that many managers, and others, have. Volume 5 (*Quality*) should be read with especial care.

The *managers* and 'others' referred to should – in our view – start with Volume 1, progress to Volume 2 and then read Volume 5 with particular acuity. Anyone in these categories who also wishes to achieve some insight into the 'arcana' of software engineering should attempt Volume 3 (*Software Design*); Volume 4 requires some prelimin-

ary grasp of computer programming considerably beyond the level of Basic on a personal computer – which is about the limit for many people in this class.

Students (in, for example, computer science) may benefit from a close acquaintance with Volumes 3 and 4. An interesting question, of considerable topicality, is what should be read by students in schools of business management, or by undergraduates in the cognate disciplines of software engineering such as electronic engineering. In the first case, we would recommend 'the management volume' 1, and Volume 5; for the cognate disciplines such as electronic, production or mechanical engineering we would recommend the whole series, to be read in sequence, with the reservation that Volumes 3 and 4 may be beyond the detailed study of many in this class, and beyond their need to do so.

One other point of our policy might give rise to speculation or adverse comment, and an explanation is owed. The examples in each volume are not harmonized across volumes nor, necessarily, even within volumes. The reason is really quite simple. No one application of reasonable size would incorporate an example set sufficient for all purposes; the priority is to demonstrate points in the text in the best way for that issue, not necessarily the most harmonized way. Also, obviously, a thematic example across volumes might be seen as counter to the modular approach of this series if, for example, one had to get Volume 2 in order to understand the examples in Volumes 3 and 4. One would not want to attract accusations of sharp commercial practice.

However, as Volume 1 is 'the orthogonal text', covering all topics synoptically at least, it has been felt right to incorporate a worked example at the end (Appendix 1). This is a 'demonstration piece' of the thematic example, used for other purposes elsewhere in this volume.

Now, all I can do as editor is to commend readers to whatever comforts they prefer – spiritous or spiritual – and hope that neither this book nor others in the series leaves them with the opinion held by Jean de Bruyère (1646–96), that:

> A man starts upon a sudden, takes Pen, Ink and Paper, and without ever having had a thought of it before, resolves within himself to write a Book; he has no Talent at Writing, but he wants Fifty Guineas.

As one late and much lamented comedian used to say: 'There's no answer to that'.

Allen Macro
Rotterdam 1989

INTRODUCTION

It would be disingenuous to claim that software engineering is not, at the present time, in a state of flux – if not outright disarray. But, then again, when was it not?

Software development – the methods and tools for it, and the artefacts they produce – proceeds like a man carrying a private crossroads around with him, to be always at, and a slough of despond into which he takes headers periodically. We are currently in such an epoch, a period of introspection and some indecision, as practitioners (and others) hear of new approaches. Some of them, not yet having grasped the old ones, are beset by the sort of doubts that lead, later and ineluctably, to that very negative certainty – a curse on them all.

However, as we have already warned, the portended changes in approach to the subject – even when justified – may confront an environment of practitioners and managers, and others as defined, who have an inexact or otherwise defective grasp of current practice and its limitations. The situation is not unlike that of a child – this is a real instance – coming upon two bogus Santa Clauses fighting for territory outside an underground station in London, some years ago. It was unarguably the season for Santa Clauses, with piles of dirty snow in the gutters, and that brooding sense that precedes a season of mandatory pleasure. But everything else in the tableau seemed strangely out of place and disturbing to the unformed mind, with its simple expectations in the matter. Why two Father Christmases when only one is required? Why fighting?

In its short history, software engineering has been through three distinct stages – growing up, one might reasonably say. If we include its 'pre-history', the fifteen years or so (*circa* 1950–65) from the inception of computer usage as we know it today, the state of our understanding has changed and then changed again.

In its infancy up to about 1965, the period of 'mewling and puking' according to Jaques in *As you like it*, we enjoyed a blissful innocence about software development when we didn't know what we didn't know, and largely didn't care. In fact, there was no software engineering at all – the term was not yet invented. We either programmed or we did not; it was a very binary world in more senses than one.

Between 1965 and (roughly) 1980, many basic questions relating to good software development practice were faced. For it was found that software usually took longer and cost more to develop than had been hoped or anticipated, and its quality – whether it worked, would go on working and could reasonably be adapted – was generally very poor.

Furthermore it was questioned whether software development was really a subject at all in the sense that it could be adequately defined and described, and that its underlying principles and the methods that depended on them could be taught.

In that decade and a half, several major approaches to better software development were put forward, of which the following three are certainly representative and, perhaps, even the most important:

1. The principles of structured programming were advanced and established, due to Dijkstra amongst others. A synoptic account of this work will be found in Section 3.2, and a fuller exposition in Volume 4 of this series.
2. Some guidelines on good design practice were enunciated by Mills, Myers, Constantine, Parnas and others (e.g. 'top down' structured design techniques and data structure methods, coherency and coupling in systems design, and information hiding). A synoptic account of these will be found in Chapter 7, and a fuller exposition in Volume 3 of this series.
3. A life cycle model of the software development process was put forward, principally by Boehm after work done by Royce and others. This is described at length in Chapter 2.

The first of these enlightenments came about mainly as a result of computer science-based investigations into the reasons why program complexity disabled program testing and maintenance, as was the case at that time – even more so than now. The second set was due, in part, to both practical experience and theoretical considerations for 'good', 'modular' design, that would provide a structured approach and produce well considered software architecture; the beneficiaries were expected to be the problems of validation and software emendation.

The third was a step in understanding the software development process by depicting it as a life cycle model, and was the outcome of practical experience, and the need to order and manage large software developments in the world of real applications. Of the three innovations cited, it is this one that is now at question.

There is a feeling in many quarters – not only academic ones either, where some of the problems associated with existing life cycle models of software development have been predicted – that a simple, serial depiction of activities, with limited iteration between sequential phases, is inadequate. It is argued that the software engineering process, to be adequate for using available tools in the course of producing software of high quality, is too complex to be simply depicted. Further, it is argued that adopting too simplistic a model is likely to be detrimental to the outcome – the quality of software artefacts produced.

This case has emerged from several sources in recent years. For example (enumerating but not limiting), there have been important papers by the following:

1. Balzer and Swartout (1982): On the inevitable intertwining of specification implementation.
2. Zave (1984) in Gehani and McGettrick (1986): The operational versus the conventional approach to software development.
3. Boehm (1986): A spiral model of software development and enhancements.

These and other references are set out in full in Appendix 4.

In the same epoch, methods have been developed for formal specification of programs

(e.g. in Gehani and McGettrick 1986) and for program proving, and metrics have been suggested for quality and complexity factors (e.g. in Conte *et al.* 1986). In addition, languages have been developed for fast prototyping, and ways suggested for producing specifications that are executable prototypes.

Some of these works are still best viewed as research, since their general utility is, as yet, by no means certain outside the problem set on which they are demonstrated. However, the ferment of relatively new suggestions, and their adoption in some areas, points, if not yet to wide-scale change in the methods of software development, to a growing consensus for change or, better, real improvement in the process of software development.

In this volume, we will begin by outlining what might be thought of as a 'classical' view of software engineering; let us get the thesis established. Then, as matters progress, the suggested developments will be introduced and discussed.

This is a deliberately cautious approach which may find disfavor in quarters where the research is being done, and in others where the benefits of change are said to have been established. Yet it is the audience in general that concerns us; those practitioners and their managers, for instance, to whom the arguments are incomprehensible through a lack of preliminary knowledge. Software development can be a most troublesome business, and nostrums to deal with it frequently take on a proportionate allure. There is a distinct danger of expecting some novelty to be a palliative, irrespective of its worth.

These dangers are very real, as we have found. The ferment of ideas is naturally very exciting, and a measure of its current vitality has entered the literature, to the effect that one hears of approaches that, by their adoption, might assist in achieving 'the last 10%' (Mathis 1986) or may even contribute to 'taming the tiger' (Levy 1987). Some people have yet to achieve the first 90 percent with any regularity; and one should first catch one's tiger, as they say. I am reminded of an old story which, I think, originally concerned a computer salesman and his client. It can be adapted for the present context.

Two intrepid males, a software engineer and a computer scientist say, were on safari in a densely overgrown and tiger-infested part of northern India. Out of food for several days, they pitched camp one evening in a clearing.

'Look here', said the computer scientist, who was used to rather cheap refectory lunches and could have eaten his boots, 'we can't possibly go on like this. My metabolism is being depleted at a most interesting rate – a negative exponential function, I believe. Anyway, we must eat and – as I think you'll agree given our mutual attitudes – cannibalism is out of the question. Now I'll tell you what we'll do.'

'Huh?' grunted his companion, furrowing a rather simian forehead in what looked like thought. The computer scientist continued, though; he hadn't got where he had by being interrupted by simian engineers.

'You stay here and make a fire – make a large fire, in fact very large. Build it this high precisely. And get the cooking pot ready. Put exactly 13.7 liters of water in it, and have it at 78 °C by the time I get back. Add nearly half a dash of salt, some peppercorns, and a sufficiency of bay leaves for flavor. These inexactitudes should please you. Also, sharpen the butcher's knife and get ready to make a nourishing stew. I propose to go out there and get some meat. The tigers are clearly eating all the other game around here so, as logic decrees, we'll eat tigers.'

He was gone for some time. Rather longer than might have been expected in fact, but

the software engineer hardly noticed as he busied himself with his tasks. It was the first time for years he had done anything without arguing, and he found the experience a novel one and exhilarating. The fire only took eight goes to get started, and he hardly cut himself at all on the knife.

After about half an hour, a terrible uproar broke out on the edge of camp, and the startled software engineer turned in time to see his learned colleague streaking across the clearing with the biggest Bengal tiger you can imagine gnashing at the seat of his corduroy trousers, and snarling dreadfully and grunting fit to freeze your blood.

'Here you are', shrieked the scholar, head back, arms pumping and generally moving well with a nice knee-action, 'you deal with this one. I can't hang around talking all day, I'm going back for the next.'

That is one side of the story. What is this tiger that needs to be tamed? Let us open the cage-door a little way, and inspect the monster. After all it may not be so fierce, and we should know as soon as possible, as a choice of instruments depends upon it. One should not be seen to take a knout to the pussy cat.

But before proceeding, I should (and will) proclaim my method in this text, and why I have adopted it. This is the 'management volume' – not only for people inexperienced in software development but for practitioners too. Without a shared vocabulary, the two parties will probably refrain from communicating at all on the subject. They may do so anyway, but assuredly this should not be the case if software development is to be actively managed.

In many cases, companies have several 'layers' or levels of staff who should be 'adding value' to a software development process, but who lack the means for this universe of discourse. I have had the privilege of devising and delivering practical orientation and vocational training courses for people at all sorts of levels, and with all sorts of back-grounds, and I have found that mutual understanding of software engineering concepts *is* possible, and meaningful discourse *can* be established between different parties in-volved in software development. The approach on offer here is, therefore, based on that premise. The material is set out much as it might be for a seven to ten days' orientation course in the subject – in fact it is effectively a course textbook for that pur-pose, and its material has been so used.

However, software engineering can be a wonderfully solemn subject, and some of its ancillaries are rather dreary in their own right. Education is not, or should not, be so. Most education programs that I have conducted have been enriched by the wit (and wisdom) of attendees, and if some of this appears in these pages it may leaven the lump a little – which will be no bad thing.

PART ONE

CONCEPTS AND DEFINITIONS

Whereof one cannot speak, thereof one must be silent
(Wittgenstein, *Tractatus Logico Philosophicus*;
Lemma 7)

He who makes a concordance of names merely . . . may think himself
lucky to avoid a lunatic asylum
(Mead, *Fragments of a Faith Forgotten, 1932*)

Part One, the first three chapters of this book, deals with elementary, but fundamentally important definitions and concepts. These range from the etymology of 'software' and 'software engineering' to a presentation of the issues for and against a life cycle model of the software development process, and a classification of software properties, including a description of work on complexity.

CHAPTER ONE

THE ETYMOLOGY: WHAT IS SOFTWARE ENGINEERING?

Software engineering is considered from the non-specialist's point of view – as on an orientation course for management staff, and others who may have done little (or no) programming even. Aspiring software engineers should read this material too, if only to provide them with the same vocabulary and conceptual models. Non-specialist's problems with some aspects of definition and of the basic etymology are dealt with, such as the fundamental misnomer (of both parts) in the term 'software engineering'. The relationship with computer science is considered, with this term also being found to be a misnomer.

1.1 ONE STEP BACKWARDS: WHAT IS SOFTWARE?

I have used the terms 'software development' and 'software engineering' without definition so far. In fact, presuming an understanding of what 'software' means, 'software development' is self-evident; the question is, can 'software development' be seen as a synonym for software engineering and, if not, what do the two terms mean in relation to each other?

In fact, software engineering is the evolution and use of helpful tools and techniques for software development and, as such, contains an implicit value component. Thus, whilst one generally speaks of software development in the unqualified sense of a process, one might ask of software engineering: 'Is the process a good, bad or indifferent one?', just as one might ask whether an artefact of another sort is 'well engineered' or not.

A firm (or person) may be doing software development but may not be engaged in software engineering in any implied positive sense of that term. When the term 'software engineering' is used in an unqualified way, its connotation is that the process has value in terms of its tools and techniques, and that this value will enhance the artefacts produced. Such is the general connotation of 'engineering'; whether or not its use is justified in this case is dealt with below.

By now, the reader of acuity will have spotted – by the superscription, and probably by the quotations at the start as much as anything – that this part of the book is about the real meaning of subject-names, and their appropriateness for the purposes. Of course,

this is a tall order. As the ancient joke ran, and it probably had the philisopher Wittgenstein choking on his meat-pie: 'Adam called the tiger "tiger" because it looked like a tiger'.

The question 'What is software?' will take us into definition, classification and description as the techniques for producing a full answer – for the simplicity of the question is deceptive, so much so that, in the beginning, a common fallacy was to think that 'software is programs', and have done with it. Furthermore, for reasons that will become apparent, we will reverse this order of play, and concern ourselves with description of properties first, then classification and finally definition.

This is by no means a sterile exercise in linguistics, and we will not be following Wittgenstein far into his wilderness. However, in conducting many education courses for general management and other non-specialists in the subject, it has become apparent to this author that one of Wittgenstein's other aphorisms 'Language disguises thought' is particularly true in this context, and many others, in software engineering.

In essence, the problem is one of knowing where to start. A person listens to words, or reads them, purporting to describe or explain an issue. But unless one has some paradigm for thought, such as a description of properties might provide, and serviceable methods of classification, the problem of meaning becomes unmanageable very quickly. (The problem for a reader is slightly less; one can always stop and think, re-read, explore other sources and so on.)

1.1.1 Coming to terms with the problem gradually

A simple example may suffice. A lecturer stands before an audience of managers and others, whose 'need to know' shines like a lamp through the room, and whose urge to 'find out' creates enough pressure to give him a nasty attack of the bends. He may begin the lecture thus:

'Hands up those who have ever programmed a computer.' There are two, perhaps three out of twenty.

'Hands up those who have used a terminal.' There are perhaps ten out of twenty; the ratio is increasing.

'Now, you are all here, ostensibly, for your interest in developing information technology products, and the problems you and your firms have with their computer components. In particular, you wouldn't be on a software engineering course if this aspect of "IT" did not concern you. Well, I share your concern. Let us begin at the beginning, as in all the best stories. Software concerns programs, and programs are expressed in languages, and these programs are translated into a basic (not Basic) language of binary notation for recognition and execution by digital circuitry within a computer. How many of you can name a computer language?'

Somebody mumbles 'Basic'; another offers Cobol but more as a question; one tragic case shouts 'Apple' and a glum silence descends.

The lecturer proceeds: 'How many would be happier, before we talk about software engineering, to get some basic terminology settled, like bit and byte, binary and hexadecimal, high level language and low level language?' (100 percent affirmative).

'Has anyone got additions to make to this list of unknowns?'

'Yes' they reply animatedly, and the pressure eases noticeably; the Apple-fellow's vitality is particularly noticeable. 'Hardware and software. What the [expletive deleted] is software?'

'But I thought I'd just told you. Software concerns programs, and programs are expressed in . . . why, what seems to be the trouble?'

'You're defining a thing we don't understand in terms of other things we don't understand. Our [perjorative] software engineers do that all the time. That's the problem. We wouldn't know a binary notation if we found one swimming for its life in our beer. If you're going to start at the beginning, have the common decency to do so.'

Just so; what exactly is this software whose engineering is to concern us? And here we come to the first small problem in cognition; there is no logical beginning to begin at. It is rather like fighting a grizzly-bear; the best one can do is jump upwards, grab the loose fur and climb.

For a start, software is funny stuff. It is difficult for many people to realize just how peculiar it is – and that includes many of the practitioners who make it. For example, is software, or is it not, intangible? This is a problem that mainly affects engineers from other disciplines – particularly mechanical, production or building engineering where some visible construction is attempted. They, and many others, tend to think that software is both tangible (because its effects are evident), and intangible because they cannot see or touch it, nor can any amplification of their senses help. These people, generally trained in entirely deterministic matters like bridge building, are most uncomfortable when this realization occurs. Software (I am told on my courses) is therefore like gravity – action, at a distance, of some intangible force.

On the other hand, others, usually electronic engineers and some computer scientists, aver that software is tangible because of the following:

1. The circuitry on which it works is tangible enough – even at the level of molecular domains in VLSI – and its behavior is determinable.
2. All programs, being expressed in a language or languages, exist in documentable form at all stages of translation down to binary bit level, the lowest level coded equivalents of the program statements in the language of their first expression.

This is as persuasive a pair of arguments as one could meet at 9.15 on a wet Monday morning but, although I should dearly like to convince my audience that software is tangible, probity requires that I must disqualify both arguments for one and the same reason. Both concern the static representation of something; the first of the hardware on which software performs; the second of programs and their documented form. Sadly for this argument, software is not a static thing. Let this, then, be our point of departure for answering the question: 'What is software?'

We have jumped and grabbed, and the loose fur in our fists just happens to be a fundamentally important property. *Software is not static; programs are.*

Software is the dynamic behavior of a program or programs, on real (and tangible) computers and ancillary equipment. Are programs, then, 'software' in any meaningful sense, in the absence of their interaction with computer and ancillary hardware? The answer is, self-evidently, 'no'. The 'software' on a floppy disk is not software but

programs. When it is loaded into the disk reader-unit, read into the computer and begins to execute (as intended, or not if it is wrong), then it becomes software by virtue of its dynamic interaction with the hardware, as the coded instructions and data making up the software activate circuitry in the computer and ancillary equipment.

The point of greatest significance about all this concerns the contrast between software and programs, and for this we need to turn our attention to what programming is about, and the properties of programs. And, lest it be thought that all this is so much fluster about mere definitions, consider the unhappy plight of somebody hoping to buy a software system of some sort, with reasonable surety of its ongoing performance, and its maintenance by the vendor. Imagine the perplexity that arises when, in response to a reasonable request for some escrow in kind and not cash, the purchaser is offered the program listing to be placed with a third party. What is this worth? Is it worth anything at all? The point is pursued in detail, as an issue in software purchasing, in Section 13.5. But the short answer here is that program listings alone are of little or no value as a guarantee for several reasons, not least amongst them being that they do not represent the dynamic behavior of software – which is the only thing at issue, not the static representation of programs.

1.1.2 Programs and programming languages

A program is a set of statements or instructions (the terms are synonymous in this context) and associated data, expressed in some language to represent logic, arithmetic or expedient operations of some sort. An understanding of the hardware, computer and ancillary equipment, on which the program is to operate as software, may be necessary as this – along with the rules of the language concerned – could limit the operations intended within a program. Typical of such equipment constraints are arithmetic rounding errors on data, where these might be critically important, and the time it takes for hardware to execute (i.e. perform) operations within a program, in cases where some synchronization of events is required.

As a simple example of an arithmetic function-statement one may find:

Distance = StartVelocity * Time + 0.5 * Acceleration * Time * Time

This represents the relationship $S = ut + at^2/2$ in dynamics. In most high level languages (n.b. the above statement would be similar in form in several 'high level' languages, such as Fortran and Modula-2), the statement would probably invoke a library routine for the exponentiation:

Distance = StartVelocity * Time + 0.5 * Acceleration * Time ** 2

Our expectation is that, if some real numeric values exist in the data stores called StartVelocity and Time, then a correct value for Distance will be computed.

Similarly, a logic statement may specify some conditions, and actions (expressed as program statements) contingent on them; typical is the IF (something) THEN (something) ELSE (something) construction. An example is given below.

As for statements of expedient operations, these are mainly to activate ancillary equipment such as disks or screen-based monitors, or to access libraries. Thus:

Writeln
Writestring ("Error message – parameter values out of range")

This will (or should) display a message with the text prescribed.

A simple 'example of examples' for arithmetic, logic and expedient statements, might well look thus:

Name: Compdist
BEGIN
   If StartVelocity < 0 THEN Writeln
                  Writestring ("Error message, negative start velocity")
                  END
         ELSE Distance = StartVelocity * Time + 0.5 * Acceleration
                    * Time ** 2
         Writeln
         Writestring ("Distance computed")
         END
END

The trivial examples given here are all in a high level language, and the statements between the BEGIN and the last END are often called a program module. Because of the many different uses made of 'module' elsewhere in computer and software terminologies, we prefer the term 'integrand' to denote a small, self-contained chunk of program that can be referenced by name. The term 'integrand' will appear with increasing frequency in this series, especially of course in Volume 4. There the topic – implementation – largely concerns the programming of integrands and (hence their name) their integration into programs, program packages, load modules and finally the software to 'run' on, i.e. interact with, the computer and its ancillary equipment.

At this point in an orientation course for managers and others, the question that surfaces is: 'Good, that shows us, up to a point, what goes on in a high level language. What happens now? We've got all these integrands lying around the place, or programs or whatever they're called, but what happens to them then?'

There are, in fact, several levels of linguistic expression in programming. The word 'levels' should be stressed since, in recent times, the concept of a language's epoch has crept into the vocabulary and we hear reference to '4GLs', or in plain English 'fourth generation languages'. Since there is no clear idea of third, second, first or any other 'generation' of languages, this term is at least questionable (and, in this author's view, undesirable).

In Table 1.1 we list the main levels at which programs can be written, albeit in the knowledge that no such scheme is so precise, with clear and generally applicable boundaries between the classes.

No one programs at level 0 nowadays, nor in octal or decimal code – the half level above; these were the means in the very early days of computing as we know it now – the period around 1945–55. In fact, most applications are attempted at level 2, in a high

TABLE 1.1 Levels of programming and quasi-programming languages

Level 0	Binary bit-strings representing coded instructions or data.
Level 1	Mnemonic codes, for instructions and decimal numbers for data, alphanumeric characters for designating parameters, and data areas. So-called assembler, or 'low level', languages.
Level 2	Limited syntax of natural language, such as imperative case of verb plus object, for logical or expedient functions. The compiler/interpreter level. So-called 'high level languages' such as Cobol, Fortran, Algol, PL1, Pascal, Ada, Basic, Modula-2.
Level 3	More extended syntax of natural language, for structuring application packages out of system components, plus some 'high level language' features. So-called 'very high level languages' such as Focus and many others (Martin and Kleinrock 1985 cite 'over 400'); job control languages (JCLs); Query by Example (QBE); database access regimes (DBMS); etc.

level language suitable for the system to be made. Thus, we find Cobol and (to a somewhat smaller extent) PL/1 used very widely for those business data processing applications with a preponderance of data storage and transfer, in the form of files and records, of textual and numeric information, and the low order transformation of numeric data through relatively simple arithmetic operations. Similarly we find a lot of Fortran programming done for large scale computational programs not so predominantly characterized by data transfer and file manipulations. Many engineers, now being used to small computers such as Apple, Commodore, the small Hewlett Packard machines and others, have become used to Basic.

However, when time criticality is involved (for example, some feature of a system must respond in an extremely short elapsed time), programs may have to be written more efficiently than a high level language will allow. Then the critical integrands are programmed in assembler (level 1 on our scheme) or a half level above, a language such as C, or an assembler with some features for defining complex statements such as a so-called macro assembler.

We are now almost ready to answer the question: 'What happens to the high level code?' But before we do so, let us dispose of another question 'Why did you start at level 2 in your earlier example; why not level 3?' Now that, as they say, is a very awkward question. One answer is that our so-called level 3 languages are so strongly application-oriented or, in the case of a database management system, oriented to a specific function, that their use here could not serve as a paradigm in the general principles for good software development practice.

Another answer is (and it's best bolted quickly like a draught of something nasty): 'Because "programming" in the "very high level" languages such as 4GLs is not really programming as we define it, but a quasi-clerical task that is only similar in *form* to programming, and that not strongly.' The difficulty with this answer is that, although true, it seems to claim a superior status for lower level programming as an intellectual activity. 'Quasi-clerical activity indeed! What cheek'. And yet, in defense of this view, consider the following extract from a question and answer debate about what industry needs, as distinct from what academia teaches:

Now for the names of languages that are important, there are something like four hundred new languages that have come into existence in the last six years or so that

aim at attempting to build applications without conventional programming. Some of the most popular names are Focus, Ramis, SAS, Natural, Ideal, Nomad, Application Factory, ADF, CNS and DMS from IBM.

Q: Of course I am trying to understand how you frame your categories.

A: Anything that relates to systems that are important in industry – where you want to try to build something that works without using Cobol, Pascal or Fortran. And you'd like to build it without using professional programmers. And you'd like to build it quickly. (James Martin, in Martin and Kleinrock 1985, report of an interview)

The third level 'languages' are not really programming at all, otherwise they would need 'professional programmers' – or, better still, software engineers – for their competent use. For some straightforward applications, mainly in the business data processing sector, very high level languages are useful for the quick construction of software systems, using access and linkage features, and building blocks suitable for that area of usage. In that respect, a 4GL will tend to be declarative – invoking already programmed features – rather than procedural, as when the operator statements of a lower level language are used to build up a function.

Other types of application are beyond the means of these limited virtues, and the programming part of software engineering goes on, mainly with the use of level 2 languages with recourse to languages at lower levels, some intermediate position which we may call 1.5, or 1 where need be.

'What's in a name' then? Apparently quite an amount of potential confusion and misdirection.

Now to our high level language program or integrand, or whatever it may be. The first thing that happens, if we are to 'run' it on the computer, is that it is taken as an operand by another computer program (part of the computer system in use), and translated by it, often as a two-pass process, into level 0 form. In such an operation, the high level statements are first translated into level 1 (assembler) instructions. For instance:

Distance = StartVelocity * Time + 0.5 * Acceleration * Time ** 2

might appear as:

```
LDQ CONST
MPY ACCL
MPY TIME
MPY TIME
STQ TEMPSTO
LDQ VELU
MPY TIME
XAQ
ADD TEMPSTO
STO DIST
```

Thus, one reasonably complex statement in a high level language translates (in this particular case) into ten assembler, mnemonic code statements. The rather baffling items in the left-hand column, e.g. LDQ, MPY, are alphabetically encoded instructions such as

'load quotient' and 'multiply', whilst XAQ exchanges the contents of an accumulator and a multiplication unit ('quotient'). Then each assembler statement is converted into an equivalent in binary number base form. Thus, LDQ CONST might be 'assembled' into a binary bit-string as follows: 01111 000 10001001.

In this simple scheme, the first five binary bits represent the instruction code, the next three are reserved for the logical address of index registers (address modifiers effectively), and the eight bit field on the right is the address of the operand in the instruction. So, LDQ is, in binary code, 01111, and CONST is at address 10001001.

On the evidence, we would say that the computer concerned has a sixteen bit architecture, or two 'bytes' since a byte is an arrangement of eight binary bits, generally to represent an alphanumeric character.

1.1.3 Translation of programs

The translation process of a high level language is called either compilation (via a compiler) or interpretation (via an interpreter); the translation process of a level 1 language is called assembly, and is via an assembler.

The difference between compiler and interpreter languages is that in the case of a compiler the whole string of statements in an integrand, or set of such (programs) presented for compilation, is translated and checked for syntactic errors and then – if grammatically correct – translated (assembled) into level 1 and then level 0 code; all this without, necessarily, trying to execute the statements. Thus compilation and execution are distinct actions and concern the whole integrand or program. In the case of interpreter languages, each statement is executed following syntax error-checking, and the statements are not necessarily translated into level 0 form. Most Basic systems are of this type. In some other cases, such as the P-machine implementation of Pascal, translation before execution takes place, into 'abstract (P) machine' code.

There are advantages and disadvantages to each approach. Compiler language programs tend to be a little cumbersome to change if the compiler requires the whole program to be recompiled; this disadvantage is absent from interpreters. On the other hand, the execution of programs under an interpreter regime tends to be slow as it is associated with the translation and syntax error-checking of each statement.

It is worthwhile, at this point, returning to our hypothetical seminar for managers and others. The two predominant question now are as follows:

1. 'What is all this business about binary bases, decimal, octal, hexadecimal and so on? We see our software people poring over the most amazing-looking stuff, like augurs pondering entrails. It makes us want to ponder their entrails!'
2. 'What is all this software already floating about in the computer, compilers and assemblers and such? How did that get into the act?' '

It is no use the recalcitrant lecturer blustering and obfuscating, and don't think I haven't tried. The audience does not yet feel itself to be on solid ground and, until it does, any attempt at progress will only result in further bewilderment. So, let us begin with the

example already cited. It is a harmless looking little pattern, but one that acts on an audience of non-initiates to stultify its senses, as does the pretty mongoose to its prey:

01111 000 10001001

In our hypothetical computer, an instruction register will exist into which the next instruction, to be excuted by the hardware, will be loaded. This register will comprise sixteen binary-state electronic units, of which the five leftmost represent the instruction code, the next three represent the logical address of an index register, and the rightmost eight represent an address in the programmable store of the computer. So, in the quoted case, the instruction code is 01111 in binary-base notation and this, we assert, represents the decimal number 15; the address field contains 10001001 and this, we claim, is the binary equivalent of 137 decimal. Now, what does all that mean?

The juggling with numbers, and diving into and out of number bases causes dismay to many people; 'Ah-ha', they think, 'the advanced mathematics – I always knew it would come to this. What time is there a 'bus out of here?'

In fact, nothing could be less advanced, for we are dealing with the most elementary *convention* in our representation of numbers. When, for example, we write down a number such as 3561 we do not specify it as a decimal-base number although, for all we know, it could be in any number-base above 6. For example, a list of integers in a septal system (i.e. base 7) would proceed: 0, 1, 2, 3, 4, 5, 6, 10, 11, 12, etc. Thus the 3561 *could* be a septal number without violating our numeric convention.

Now, what we mean when we write 3561, on the understanding that number-base 10 (decimal) is the basis of our notation, is:

$$3 \times 10^3 + 5 \times 10^2 + 6 \times 10^1 + 1 \times 10^0$$

with the special convention that a number raised to the power 0 equals 1. Precisely the same is the case in binary, octal and hexadecimal conventions, or any other number-bases we may care to use. If, indeed, 3561 had been a septal number we would no doubt have signified the fact in some way, such as 3561/7, and the number would then have represented:

$$3 \times 7^3 + 5 \times 7^2 + 6 \times 7^1 + 1 \times 7^0$$

and, had we wished to know its equivalent in decimal, the computation would have been trivial, and its answer 1,317 (i.e. $3 \times 343 + 5 \times 49 + 6 \times 7 + 1 \times 1$).

Now, the reader who is otherwise unacquainted with these arcana might like to verify that 01111 is 15 in our decimal convention, and 10001001 is 137 likewise.

Octal and hexadecimal, the bases 8 and 16 for number representation, have a special usefulness in programming. Three binary digits represent the numbers 0 to 7 in decimal, and four binary digits represent the numbers 0 to 15 in decimal. As before, readers may care to verify these assertions by checking the values of 111 and 1111 binary. Very quickly, programmers used to testing and correcting software at the low levels of language representation – levels 1 and 0 in Table 1.1 – become accustomed to binary bit-patterns in these small ranges of three or four digits; thus 010 is instantly recognized as 2 (decimal); 1001 as 9; 1011 as 11 and so on. Following from this facility is the reverse

one; that octal numbers, for instance, can be written down instantly as binary bit sequences. Thus 6 octal is 110; 1 octal is 001 and so forth.

Hexadecimal, the number-base 16, is even more popular, as in this case the facility concerns four binary digits, and this corresponds to another convention – that of representing alphanumeric and special characters as 'bytes' of information, where a byte is defined as eight binary digits. The application is obvious; a byte can be represented by two hexadecimal numbers whose binary equivalents comprise a total of eight binary digits, or 'bits'. The problem is that the hexadecimal convention lacks single symbols to represent numbers between and including 10 and 15 on the decimal scale. A hexadecimal representation of integers may start 0, 1, 2, ... and so on, and continue ..., 8, 9, but then what?

We surmount this problem by assigning the letters a to f in place of numbers 10 to 15 inclusive. So, the hexadecimal scale comprises 0, 1, 2 ... as before, and 8, 9, a, b, c, d, e, f to represent all sixteen numbers in the range 0 to 15.

Thus, our earlier example of 3561 would mean in hexadecimal:

$$3 \times 16^3 + 5 \times 16^2 + 6 \times 16^1 + 1 \times 16^0$$

with a decimal equivalent of $12,288 + 1,280 + 96 + 1 = 13,665$.

However, we may also find hexadecimal numbers of the form:

710e4b

which would represent:

$$7 \times 16^5 + 1 \times 16^4 + 0 \times 16^3 + 14 \times 16^2 + 4 \times 16^1 + 11 \times 16^0$$

or the equivalent of 7,409,227 in decimal.

Now, with a developed facility for recognizing the decimal equivalent of short strings of binary digits, programmers can slip easily in and out of binary and hexadecimal, and this is very handy when information – such as may appear in a level 0 depiction of states of programs or data – is presented as bytes.

For example, we may see in binary form a representation of some sixteen bit number, thus:

1011 0110 1101 0011

The programmer will read this, left to right or right to left, as four-bit chunks; thus (left to right), 1011 equals 11 decimal and that is b in the hexadecimal convention, and so on; arriving at the hexadecimal equivalent:

b6d3

Most experienced programmers do this elementary translation almost instantaneously. Conversely, if the programmer is confronted with (as some computer systems will produce) a hexadecimal 'dump' of the state of some storage device, e.g. the number f96a, then this can easily be written as a binary bit string:

1111 1001 0110 1010

The facility with which these manipulations are made is a very quickly acquired trait, and requires almost no numeracy at all, more a simple pattern-recognition ability for

three or four binary digits. This realization usually comes as a profound relief to non-specialists. Why binary notation is so important, in the first place, also causes little concern, as the possible bi-stable state of an electric component ('on–off') is easy to grasp, and its application to encoded information in electric circuits is obvious.

1.1.4 The 'virtual computer' concept

Now to the second question posed a few pages back, concerning the software that may (or may not) come with the computer of one's choice. How are we to view that as an adjunct to software in general, and the process of software engineering in particular? On the surface, the issue is quite simple and straightforward but attached to it is a subtlety that is instructive to reveal here.

To begin our explanation of this issue – generally known as the 'virtual computer' concept – we will adopt the position of a user of some computer system and, for this, we must have a simple classification of 'users'.

There are three kinds of computer user in general:

1. Users of already prepared software, such as applications packages and the '4GL' (language level 3) activities already noted.
2. Software engineers writing programs in level 2 languages (and, perhaps, level 1 in places).
3. Some software engineers and, it must be admitted, many 'amateur programmers', working very close to the electronic 'hardware' level of, for example, microprocessor devices, using level 1 languages and, sometimes, lower levels of access to equipment.

Of these, the first kind are generally unaware of the features of the equipment they are using, the computer languages in which facilities were coded and so forth. They know what their terminal looks like and, if the user manuals are adequate, how to access and use the program packages they need. We will call these people the 'users' as they often also specify requirements for software systems, and we will find alternative names for the other two types.

In the second category we find software engineers who program the computer, usually in a level 2 language with – perhaps – recourse to assembler code on occasion. We will call these people 'programmers' for the moment, until the distinction between programming and software engineering becomes clearer. Similarly, as a temporary measure, we will call the third category 'low level programmers' to denote the proximity of their tasks to the actual electronics of computer and ancillary devices.

Now each type of usage presumes the availability of system features, hardware and software. For instance, a 'user' requires that a computer and other ancillaries are attached to the terminal at his or her desk, and that an operating system is available in the computer to help to initiate, and to regulate, access to application packages, data, etc. So such a person might type in at a keyboard:

    *$ LOGON REQUESTED

if the user manual stipulates that format; and the 'system' may reply with a message of the following type displayed on the terminal screen:

> HELLO. YOU HAVE REQUESTED ACCESS TO 'MORON' THE USER
> SCHEDULING FEATURE OF OUR DREADFUL OPERATING SYSTEM;
> WE SYMPATHIZE!
> * TYPE IN IDENTIFICATION IF YOU HAVE AN OPEN SYSTEM-FILE
> * OTHERWISE TYPE IN: OPEN FILE/IDENTIFIER
> YOUR IDENTIFIER MUST BE IN PARENTHESES AND MAY BE ANY 20
> OR LESS CHARACTERS; THUS (FRED BLOGGS), OR (ABC 123) OR
> WHATEVER. THANK YOU, AND GOOD LUCK! YOU WILL NEED IT.

In this case, the operating system programs are 'prompting' the user in a helpful (if rather sardonic) way.

Similarly, the programmer and low level programmer will have features for accessing language translators, keying integrands and programs into store, editing programs, linking and loading programs, and executing them. These features, and others not specified here, are known collectively as the 'PSE', or programming support environment of the computer equipment concerned and its ancillaries. PSEs and their supersets Ipses (integrated project support environments) are dealt with in Section 8.5.

In the general case, users and programmers will access a so-called 'virtual computer system' in which the features and facilities named above will exist – possibly as hundreds of thousands of program statements of 'standard' software, effectively (though not physically) 'on top of' the electronic hardware. This view of 'virtual' or 'standard' software being 'on top of' the hardware is useful but not strictly accurate of course. The programs are stored as binary bit-patterns within the computer's circuitry, or on ancillary equipment such as magnetic disk storage, cassette tape and so forth. The view that it covers the hardware is substantially correct in the sense that its procedures very strongly regulate access to circuitry (or prevent it altogether), and to other 'standard software' and programmers' applications. This regimentation has caused some people, particularly electronic engineers wanting to operate in level 1 programming languages, to see computers – by which they mean the hardware – as 'silting up' with software facilities, as a river estuary does with sand.

The situation can be depicted schematically as shown in Figure 1.1. This shows, in outline, the relationship between hardware, the virtual software regimes and the total 'virtual system' visible to users and programmers. For many low level programmers, such as work on programmable microprocessors which are to be embedded as components in other electronic or electromechanical systems, the virtual computer may look very different (see Figure 1.2).

Where this is the case, the relative lack of virtual software to help development, such as 'PSE' features, may be compensated by an independent program development computer, or 'host' as it is called (see Figure 1.3). Then, the object device, such as a microprocessor, is known as the 'target' and one speaks of a hosted development on machine X, for target equipment Y.

In some former epochs, all programming was 'low level' in the sense that the number-codes at level 0 were the only ways of expressing programs; then mnemonic assemblers were invented, but still the features of operating software were very primitive. As this gradually improved over the period 1955–65, the 'virtual computer' concept came into

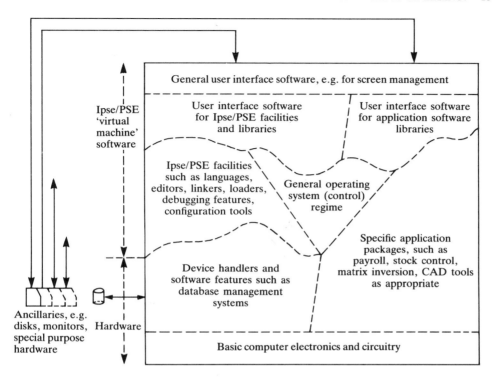

FIGURE 1.1 The virtual computer depicted as a geological section.

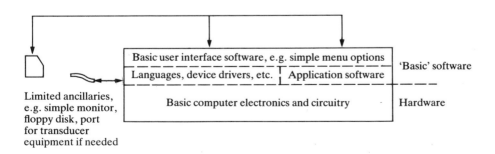

FIGURE 1.2 The 'nearly naked' micro depicted as a 'geological section'.

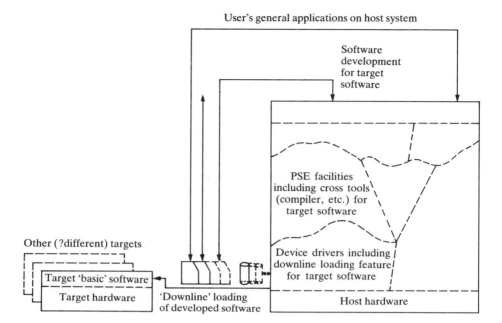

User's general applications on host system

Software
development
for target
software

PSE facilities
including cross tools
(compiler, etc.) for
target software

Device drivers including
downline loading feature
for target software

Other (?different) targets

Target 'basic' software

Target hardware

'Downline' loading
of developed software

Host hardware

FIGURE 1.3 Host/target(s) symbiosis.

being. With it – and here is the subtlety referred to earlier – the programmers' approach to implementing software systems changed. Whereas, previously, implementation – the programming and testing of programs – had to be as best possible, to make use of the limited language and few features available, now it became good practice to build software upwards from the virtual machine facilities. The effect of this, commented on elsewhere in this series, has been the great attention given to developing software tools of the PSE sort. This has had a co-lateral effect, as noted elsewhere in this series, that software implementation teams have increasingly incorporated an expert on tools and facilities available, and the software is increasingly built outwards from these facilities rather than just dumped on top of them so to speak.

1.1.5 A brief revision

By now on our mythical orientation course, even the most technology-dyslexic commercial executive or personnel officer will have grasped some of the fundamental properties of software:

1. Software is the dynamic behavior of programs when they operate on and interact with the equipment for which they were developed – computers and ancillary equipment.
2. A program is an intellectual construction expressed in a formal language, i.e. one

having a defined vocabulary and syntactic rules. The program activates equipment ('hardware') to emulate a conceptual model of some real or supposed requirement which has been specified (see Chapter 5). The hardware executes the level 0 form of the program.

3. Programs comprise algorithms (for computation, logic or data manipulation functions of some sort) and data definitions.

4. Languages for expressing programs in may be categorized as ultra-low level (e.g. binary coded depiction), low, high and very high level. Very high level programming has only a partial resemblance to lower level, or 'real', programming.

5. Programs are translated (either compiled or interpreted then assembled, or just assembled) as the means of rendering them suitable to activate the hardware.

6. Number-base transformations of program statements or data are far easier than they may seem at first sight, since they comprise no more than an understanding of the convention by which we express numbers in everyday life.

7. Usage of computer equipment may be at a very high level; for example, the use of application packages, or at lower levels such as programming and testing programs. In general, the full set of hardware, operating systems and PSE features are known as 'the virtual computer', and the behavior of this virtual computer represents a highly procedural buffer between the user and the lowest level – hardware – in the virtual system.

Our hypothetical lecturer may, at this stage, revisit his earlier question: 'Have you all now got some idea of what software is? Are there any more intimidating terms or concepts worrying you, or have you any questions concerning all this?' The likelihood is that – as has happened to me a thousand or more times – several members of the class will ask: 'But is software "soft"? You seemed to be saying, earlier, that programs are tangible but that software – in its dynamic behavior – may not be.' Now we are back, full circle, to the point of departure. Is, or is not, the etymology well considered and, of itself, useful?

1.1.6 Is software 'flexible'?

Software is, in fact, ill-named. The neologism, at the time it was coined, was intended to distinguish programs from the 'hardware' on which they operate, and the term 'hardware', if inelegant, was at least accurate in its adjectival particle; it was and is, 'hard', i.e. physically tangible in one form or another. Now these designations did not happen yesterday. 'Software' is a term from the early 1960s and 'software engineering from about 1965–8. Yet, as recently as 1985, a correspondence between two leading figures in the software engineering profession, in one of its major journals (ACM Sigsoft, Association for Computing Machinery), proceeded thus:

Bill Riddle's letter [sic] touched a responsive chord. I, too, believe that the name 'software engineering' makes our problems worse. Bill would replace 'engineering' if he could. I would replace 'software'.

> Names and metaphors do have power. While they are no substitute for thinking, good ones help us to look in profitable directions, and poor ones can mislead us. (Horning 1985)

This correspondence will be quoted again, in Section 1.2, for its conjectures on the suitability of 'engineering' as a description of the process. It goes on to cite another author, Dijkstra, as observing that the true subject-matter for programmers is not programs but the design of computations.

This observation is entirely consistent with the implementation part of the whole process, where a prime object is the design of algorithms and data structures in integrands. However, as we shall show, it draws a narrow task-description for software implementation staff as it is stated, as though programs for or design of computation functions were their only concerns and, even more narrowly, as though computations were the only sort of algorithms.

In fact, software implementation staff will – or should – generally have been involved in a variety of other software development tasks before serious programming is undertaken – specification of requirements for instance. Programming is indisputably a part of software engineering, but can one justifiably speak of 'programmers', as though of a different species from software engineers – whatever *they* are? As if this was not enough there is clearly something else amiss with the unfortunate term 'software' and, as the quoted author rightly says, such a poor designation can mislead. In this case, the first particle – 'soft' – has helped in a wide-scale accidental deception, for it is commonly believed that software is, in some rather general way, flexible.

Ah words, words! What does 'soft' mean, or 'flexible' for that matter? In the general context of engineering, these adjectives are applied to the physical properties of material, such as elasticity, malleability, rigidity, thixotropy, shearing characteristics and so on. They cannot possibly mean the same for programs, or for the dynamic state of programs as software. Why then do we speak of software being 'soft' or 'flexible', for it is terribly common to find those terms in use?

What, in fact, happens is that inexperienced people equate the apparent ease of changing programs for flexibility, and assume this to represent an ease of changing a software system if its specifications change. Consider the earlier example. If, instead of the formula

$$S = at + at^2/2$$

we had – in error – assumed

$$S = -at + at^2/2$$

We might have programmed (in a level 2 language):

Distance = 0.5 * Acceleration * Time ** 2 − StartVelocity * Time

or (in a level 1 language):

```
LDQ VELU
MPY TIME
STQ TEMPSTO
```

```
LDQ CONST
MPY ACCL
MPY TIME
MPY TIME
XAQ
SUB TEMPSTO
STO DIST
```

Now, it seems to be the easiest thing on earth to correct this error. Merely change the sign in the high level language statement or, if the function is coded in assembler, change the penultimate instruction to *ADD* TEMPSTO. In this simple example that is all, and the original error is easily corrected at the expense of a recompilation or re-assembly. In fact, we may be able to fire the change straight into the computer store, in binary code. This awful procedure is called a 'binary patch' to the object code – and should be prohibited by act of parliament, and carry with it a punitive penalty. It is exactly this facility that causes the illusion of quick, cheap and easy 'flexibility'.

In fact, nothing could be further from the truth. Simple corrections to programs are one thing, and even then must be very carefully done and thoroughly tested and documented. Complex changes to *software* are another thing entirely, and here the behavior of programs in their dynamic states may be difficult to determine.

The problem is that of an exceedingly large amount of possible permutations in the actions and interactions of parts of software with each other, with users and with the equipment – in both correct and incorrect (or faulty) modes of each. In some cases, this constitutes a 'behavior space' that is effectively infinite. That is to say that the prediction of all conditions that can occur in that behavior space may be – in fact usually is – effectively impossible. Thus, changing software is at best a hazard-fraught task and, at worst, the first step to disaster. Software, for it to be changed with safety, requires the most sedulous application of good program design and implementation, and careful management practices in both its original implementation and in the process of changing it.

For many software systems, the problems of their behavior spaces are reduced by the following:

1. Good development practices, technical and managerial, applied in the original and any subsequent implementations.
2. The progressively increasing reliability of well made software with extensive usage. This, effectively, charts many of the permutations within the behavior space of the system, although, it must be said, the natural tendency is to use the system as intended, which means that unpredictable circumstances may still project the system into parts of the behavior space never before experienced.

In effect, all efforts to construct programs, and to operate them as software within the bounds of the specifications, are efforts to retain their behavior within reasonably predictable and understandable limits. The problem may become effectively insuperable for some types of software, for example complex systems involving what may be, in effect, randomly initiated, concurrent subprocesses. When things go wrong in such

systems, for whatever reasons, faults may propagate (again, in effect, randomly) through the system. Building software systems to be defensive, i.e. to limit this propagation, is a major objective of design and implementation.

Is software soft, then? In general, an allegory from the materials sciences may be useful. Gold, for example, is a soft metal. It is malleable and ductile; in other words, it can be 'worked' easily – divided, amalgamated into alloys or bigger lumps of gold, and so forth. Software is not in the slightest bit like that, although programs are. One can do anything to a program in its static state; how it then behaves is another matter. On the other hand crystals, such as diamond, cannot be worked easily. They must be very carefully cut along the major 'grains' of the lattice or they will shatter, and fracture lines may propagate in an unordered way. Working crystalline substances requires painstaking skill applied by specialists. Software is exactly like that.

This allegory is useful as it says something, too, about the possibility of increasing functionality of an existing software system. It is, in fact, a major problem to extend software by adding features to it after the original implementation. Of course it may seem, on the surface, perfectly easy to 'graft' new features on, but the limiting consideration is the preservation of reliability – which tends to be an exceedingly fragile characteristic of most software systems. In crystals, of course, there is an immanent property (a 'program' of their morphogenical behavior in fact) that determines the only way in which they *can* grow. In effect, the same is true of a software system, and many (most) are so ill-structured that they cannot 'grow' – that is, be extended to incorporate new features – without quite catastrophic loss of reliability. In terms of our allegory, any pseudo-crystalline growth is a rogue formation, and the structure becomes non-viable, tending to shatter. In software, this is evidenced by instability, apparently capricious failure and the greatest difficulty experienced in detecting and correcting the cases of error.

The structures of crystalline lattices are mathematical in form, being regular and 'closed' in the sense that a complete mathematical statement describing a structure may be made. That suggests an approach for software design. If a complex program structure could be represented to show the mathematical properties of fractals, for example, then the viability of its growth (or contraction) could possibly be assessed as the immanent growth or contraction property of that system. To our knowledge, such notions await a researcher's attention, although complexity theory has been applied otherwise to program systems, without much conclusive result (see Section 3.2).

1.1.7 Conclusions

In summary, programs are 'soft' and tangible, and that has led us to the delusion that their dynamic behavior is the same. For the past 20 years we have called this behavior 'software' – a neologism in its time that was not only inelegant in form but also wrong in meaning. Software tends to be like a very brittle substance in its behavior, in spite of the fact that it is intangible.

Now to the term 'engineering', as that too is cause for legitimate concern. The

generally held belief that the programmable part of an electronic or electromechanical assembly is reconfigurable with greater ease than the 'hardware', has led many companies in the business of developing information technology products to incorporate computers as components for mainly this reason. What, though, if that component is – in some crucial sense such as its software – not 'engineered' to the same high standards as the rest of the assembly? There is an epigram in engineering about chains and weakest links, and it is most apposite to the quality of composite electronic products. Could not the brittle property of software be contained, or reduced, by the way it is engineered? Conversely, does not a lack of 'good engineering practice' worsen the problem of software being inherently brittle?

The earlier quotation (Horning 1985) inferred that a correspondent to the ACM journal had questioned the suitability of the second particle in 'software engineering', as we have just questioned the first. So widespread has been the impression that software is 'flexible' because it is 'soft', and so great has been the disservice due to that delusion, that we should also inspect the generic name for its development with especial care. What, then, is the situation in *this* part of the etymology?

1.2 ANOTHER STEP BACKWARDS: IS SOFTWARE DEVELOPMENT REALLY AN ENGINEERING DISCIPLINE?

Of all the authors on this subject, the best known is probably Fred Brooks. His book of wit and wisdom, based on some of the most harrowing experiences in software development, has deservedly been, by the standards of this trade, a bestseller over the past decade (Brooks 1976). Few people associated with software engineering have not heard of *The Mythical Man-month*, and most have read it by now. Elsewhere (in Gibbs and Fairley 1987), Brooks has recently written, on the distinction between a scientist and an engineer, that:

> Software engineering is concerned with building programming products and programming systems products. In other words it is proper to call it software engineering. It is indeed an engineering discipline – it focusses on building . . . .
> The scientist builds in order to learn; the engineer learns in order to build.

The aphorism in the last line of this quotation would not be seriously challenged by most scientists or engineers. However, the conclusion – that software development is an engineering discipline – is open to serious question on two major counts.

First, though, let us formulate Brook's thesis as a syllogism with a middle term (which, in his argument, he omits): 'The engineer learns in order to build; the properties of software development are . . . [enumerated]; thus software development is an engineering discipline'. Now let us inspect that middle term as, in this case, it is that which decides the fate of the conclusion. If this second premise is, in any material way, incompatible with the first one then the asserted conclusion is a *non sequitur*.

1.2.1 Software engineering, or software . . . what?

Software development can be described, in very simple terms, as comprising five main activities: specification, design, implementation, validation and operation (this last incorporating corrective maintenance, which can be legitimately viewed as ongoing development). Major emendations to a software system, for new version improvements, can be seen as a repetition of some or all of these stages, for our purposes.

Now, in two major respects, the properties of these phases require approaches that challenge the conclusion that software development is an engineering discipline. In some cases, such as the development of highly innovative constructions containing software for functions not hitherto attempted, prototypes have to be developed. These may be to investigate the requirements being specified, or the technology of solution, or both. A typical example of prototyping, to develop solution-means, might be for image processing in computer-based models for weather forecasting. One school of thought in the current epoch advances the view that all software development should be done on this basis, with the first three phases of the process comprising a highly iterative (and hopefully convergent) scheme of prototyping.

The argument for software development by prototyping is taken forward in Chapter 2, but it is sufficient here to note that the defects of software development to date have raised the proposal that all software should be created in this way. Insofar as this proposal has merit, it represents a shining example of software developers building in order to learn. Of course, engineers too build prototypes – pilot plants, prototype cars, airplanes, nuclear reactors and so forth. In doing so they are performing engineering development research (often associated with quality/safety) which, like all forms of applied research is, in itself, a scientific discipline. As Brooks would say: 'Building in order to learn'.

1.2.2 Software quality and the establishing of theories

An equally serious objection to the word 'engineering' lies in the different processes by which artefacts – physical constructions and programs – are certified for use. In general, one is concerned with three, usually mandatory, aspects of quality: *compliance*, whether the system does as required; *modifiability*, whether the system can be changed, for repair or improvement, with relative ease; and *reliability*, whether an apparently compliant system goes on being so. Other considerations such as safety, security and integrity will (or should) be subsumed within the explicit provisions of the requirements' specification – against which the compliance of a system, when constructed, may be judged.

In the case of physically engineered objects, such as bridges, ships, electronic assemblies and so forth, compliance and modifiability are usually self-evident, or straightforwardly determined by inspection and trial. It will not take me long to find out if my new car has a steering wheel or not, or whether the only way to change a rear wheel is to hack through the back seat and the trunk to get at it. As for reliability, that may have been assessed from the start, by computation of physical stresses and the strength of materials, pilot-plant prototypes or component sampling and associated determinations of their

failure rates. In that sense, as in the case of modifiability, reliability may be seen as being 'designed-in'.

As will be established at greater length in Chapter 9, and in Volume 5 of this series, the three quality criteria are precisely the same for programs in their dynamic state as software, but – importantly – the determination of these crucial properties is quite dissimiliar to that for physical constructions.

Nothing about programs can be said to be 'self-evident' or straightforwardly 'determined by inspection and trial'. This is even more so the case in their dynamic state as software, when they interact with the hardware and operating environments for which they are intended. Then, the determination of quality factors has to be by a two level process of positive demonstration and attempted falsification.

First, the programs' authors (the author-team) test the programs by static inspection, and a limited form of dynamic operation, progressively integrating parts of the system-to-be, and testing it incrementally. This process, rather simplified in this description, culminates in what is known as a benevolent, black-box alpha-test of the whole set of programs operating as software. It is said to be 'benevolent' because it is undertaken by the authors of the programs. It is said to be 'black-box' because the system is viewed as a closed entity, having an interface with the external ('exogenous') world. What goes on in 'the box' is of no concern so long as the software system is compliant, viewed against its specifications. Of course, if it fails this test, 'the box' is opened and suitable corrections are attempted.

This is the first level of positive demonstration, and when it succeeds it makes a limited statement about the quality of the programs in their operating state as software. What it lacks is any independent view of this assertion of compliance, or of those other determinants of quality, modifiability and reliability.

The second level of demonstration proceeds on the basis of independent testing (i.e. by people other than the programs' authors), including both black-box and white-box tests. The first of these attempts to *falsify* the successful alpha-test assertion of compliance. The second, 'white-box', test, seeks to provide a basis for some independent, judgmental view of modifiability. At the time of alpha-testing, modifiability is seldom an issue – almost as if it is presumed to be the case, as though the authors say (in effect): 'We made it, we can change it'. This assumption is by no means justified however, and hence the need for some objective assessment.

We call the independent tests of a software system the adversarial black-box and white-box beta-tests of the programs and their documentation. The term 'white-box' is antipodal to the term 'black-box' as previously described. The object of scrutiny here is not so much the interaction of the system as a whole with the 'exogenous' world, but more the view of it as a holistic concatenation of potentially or actually connected parts – known as the 'endogenous' world within the 'the box'. Testing or inspecting these parts ('holons') individually or in combination is – as Einstein put it, in a different context – 'opening the watch'.

It is through this two-level process of benevolent demonstration, followed by an adversarial attempt to falsify the assertions and assumptions emerging from alpha-tests, that the accretion of confidence in programs resembles most of all the development of a tenable theory in science. One postulates a hypothesis, supported (as best possible) by any

axioms we may admit, and whatever other currently accepted theories are helpful. This is then subject to a critical peer-group process, operating under the influence of a well-known dictum: 'A theory which is not refutable by any conceivable event is non scientific' (Popper 1963). The same may also seem true in physical engineering, but there the issues are usually deterministic, with prescribed numeric limits for quality criteria. What software development lacks – for either alpha- or beta-testing purposes – are metrics for the quality issues concerned, such as modifiability and reliability. It is left to the peer-group of (beta-) testers to allow the hypothesis to pass to the stage of a tenable theory that appears to fit the quality criteria.

This concept of 'fit' has been defined as 'the absence of misfit' (Alexander 1964), in dealing with design and the fitness of form. The compliance of software is the lack of categorical difference ('misfit') between its behavior and the specification of requirements for which it was made. A failure of real attempts to falsify ('refute') a software system, for example by beta-testing, leaves it in the position of a scientific theory that must, *faut de mieux*, be adopted, albeit temporarily and with inexplicit qualification. In logic, and the subject of scientific method in general, this means of establishing a positive by negating its converse is known as Scheffer's axiom:

$$P \Leftarrow -(-P)$$

or, in words: 'If not (not P), then (P)', where P is any categorical proposition.

The fact that the objects of this process, the programs, are intellectual constructions depicted in an abstract form, and that their dynamic behavior as software may represent a very large potential behavior space, take this part of software development even further from the likeness with engineering in general.

1.2.3 Conclusions

So, where do we stand with this question of whether 'engineering' is a suitable description of software development? The software engineer builds in order to learn, and so, according to Brooks, does the scientist; the software engineer (and others) validate a software system in ways remarkably analogous to scientific method applied to the 'fit' – i.e. absence of misfit – of a theory.

In this author's experience, the gerund 'engineering' applied to software development has been as misleading as the synthetic name 'software'. In particular, engineers from other disciplines, and their managers and non-software-expert colleagues, attach a significance to the term 'engineering' that cannot exactly be carried over into the process of software development. Similarities between software development and the more accepted engineering disciplines break down very rapidly, and real engineers are left confused and frustrated, suspecting that some awful inadequacy on the part of software development staff is being concealed behind a smokescreen of special pleading.

I have, in fact, found very few engineers who – if they have also developed extensive and complex software systems – support the incorporation of software 'engineering' into the corpus of real engineering subjects, except in one respect. The term 'engineering'

carries with it a strong connotation of planning and control – of managing, in fact. In this respect we have, over the past decade and a half, sought to make software development a more manageable activity. In doing so we quite justifiably construct conceptual models of the process – called 'life cycle models', for reasons explained in Section 2.2. And, again to an entirely justified extent, we force the process of software development to fit the model of the process in order to manage it.

Confronted with these models of the software engineering process, and when introduced to their significance and meaning, engineers claim them for their own subject: 'Why', they remark, 'that is exactly what we do. So, why all the special pleading about software being different? What a load of rubbish, there's some dirty work going on somewhere, there must be. We've been waiting six years for a bit of software from our "software engineers", and it won't work when we get it.'

These attitudes are thoroughly understandable, but can be catastrophic for the 'culture' within a company, particularly as a 'culture' may encourage or discourage software development groups. One finds demotivation first, then attrition in the software development sector concerned, and finally a self-reinforcing effect so that the residual and declining software group not only feels, but actually becomes, alienated from the rest of the organization. And much of this can arise through unreasonable expectations brought on by the word 'engineering' – particularly if amplified by some notions of cheap flexibility in the artefacts.

In one most distressing case of this, the author was – quite literally – asked to diagnose the causes of a 'culture-gap' between a software group and the main company comprising, in this case, engineers in telecommunication technology. The result was like whistling an aria to the deaf.

'But it's called software engineering', they cried, 'then let them *be* engineers like us'.

They were probably still chanting this mantra, and playing with bits of wire in lieu of prayer-wheels, when the firm closed down.

1.3 THE RELATIONSHIP WITH COMPUTER SCIENCE

By now we know something of software engineering, both the properties of its outcome, the software and of the process to develop it. If this was a true engineering discipline we should expect it to be supported by some science or sciences – as, for example, physics, mathematics and chemistry underpin other forms of engineering. But we (and many others) have questioned the classification of software development as 'engineering'.

1.3.1 Yet another etymological issue

What, then, is 'computer science'? Is it an endeavor without application, a 'pure' science without any engineering utility in the software development sense? This is the place where classification may turn into polemic. As one author puts it, more categorically:

the logical nature of the product ... is the major difference between software 'engineering' and 'real' engineering. Because of this ... there are few physical laws which can be used to model, describe or predict the behaviour of software. Obviously, some mathematical 'laws' are relevant to software, but these have not yet been demonstrated to fill the rôle that physical laws do in other forms of development. It is because of the lack of physical laws that the software aspect of computer science is sometimes called an artificial science – like political science, or social science – rather than a natural science like physics or chemistry. (Richardson, in Gibbs and Fairley 1987)

Then, too, in a recent article, the president of the ACM wrote a leading article in its *Communications*, on 'What is computer science?' (Abrahams 1987). In it, he concludes (the paraphrasing is my own) the following:

1. Computer science has the properties of both a scientific and an engineering discipline.
2. Mathematics is the underlying reality of computer science, as physics is of electrical and mechanical engineering.
3. Because of its mathematical substructure, computer science has particular affinity with, and effect through, computer programming; in this respect computer science concerns the microstructure of computing, whilst software engineering concerns its macrostructure.
4. 'Computer science' is probably a misnomer! The author (Abrahams) then suggests another neologism, 'computology', as being, in his view, more suitable.

What is evident at this point is the quite clear distinction of interest between computer science endeavors and those of software engineering, rather than any close and intimate connection. What is being said, in effect, and it makes eminently good sense in the world of software development, is that computer science should *behave* as a science – one that is very strongly rooted in applied mathematics and logic. Further, that software development – like some engineering subjects with their cognate sciences – should, as is the case in fact, utilize whatever applicable findings emerge from computer science.

The main area of computer science that has been of direct use to software engineering has concerned low level design of integrands and programs, their implementation, and some aspects of their validation. As will be seen, this area of main impact and influence to date makes up only a part – perhaps no more than 50 per cent – of a software engineer's task. However, this is not, by and large, quite the role for computer science as seen by its exponents.

Rather than investigating and publishing the laws that should sustain the practical endeavors in software engineering, for instance at the design and implementation levels, there is a tendency for computer scientists to prescribe them, rather than trusting that utility will ensure their adoption. It is as though physicists turned to passionate exhortation to influence construction engineers. The tendency, noted earlier, for enquiry and classification to merge into polemics is very clear, and few are exempt from it – present company included.

1.3.2 Subject education as a possible discriminator

Part of the confusion is that computer science is a curriculum subject, within the formal education systems of most countries, whereas software engineering, for the most part, is not. It is as though there were no sources of graduates for employment by engineering firms except from departments of physics, notwithstanding the requirements for mechanical, aeronautical, marine, chemical, process, electronic engineering and so on.

This is a most unnatural state of affairs, and leads to the obvious confusion of computer science with software engineering – particularly to non-practitioners of either. Perhaps the most devastating indictment of the computer business in general is that there is so little agreement existing or emerging, after three and a half decades, about the scope of theory and practice, the relationship between theory and practice, and what to teach – and how to teach it – in either computer science or software engineering. Lest the reader suspect this author of exaggeration, the proceedings of the 1986 Workshop 'Software engineering education; the educational needs of the software community' is salutory (Gibbs and Fairley 1987). There were twenty-nine participants listed – twelve university professors, thirteen doctoral level attendees from business and industry, and several high ranking officers from the military sector. The proceedings reveal a lively affair, with many interesting papers read, and a highly stimulating level of debate. However, what seems to emerge is the following:

1. *Computer science is not software engineering.* As with thermodynamics and chemical engineering, some of its basic 'laws' are fundamental to software engineering – but it does not say much about how you actually make software.
2. *Computer science education is not software engineering education, nor does it necessarily provide for that activity.*

In fairness, of course, computer scientists do not claim for their subject that which, clearly, it is not, but the point is that the confusion persists and is only made worse when the distinct nature of the endeavors is obscured.

> If you ask an academic what Software Engineering is, you will find out that it is a branch of Computer Sciences .... Some say that Software Engineering is simply the practice of engineering the software. But differences between research and practitioners are more profound. Their two camps really do not talk much to each other. Perhaps this is due to mutual arrogance or mistrust, but I think the real reason is technical. The experimental component in software engineering as it is practiced today is entirely missing. (Belady, in Conte *et al.* 1986, pp. v–vi)

Can anybody spot the tangle we are in? If Belady is right, and in my experience he is, then there is a danger that we are defining software engineering as a part of something (computer science) that the president of the ACM starts out to attempt a new definition for, and largely concludes that one cannot even define the subject, because computer science is a wrongly named activity, and should be called 'computology' instead. It is not a happy state of affairs.

As for Belady's other point, about an experimental component in software engineer-

ing, this too is a valid comment. Often the gap between computer science and software engineering prevents the trial of research results in real, large scale software systems, and both communities are impoverished consequently. At that stage, exponents of computer science may resort to assertion and exhortation, and the gap widens.

In my own view, given the misnomer of 'engineering' for software development, the practical development of programs and their validation as dynamic software should become, as Belady suggests, more scientific. However, as will be seen throughout this text, there is one major impediment to the rather cozy notion of software development seen as the evolution of a scientific theory that 'fits' the requirement 'facts'. And that major impediment is *commerce*. Could Maxwell have developed his equations for electromagnetic properties to a deadline, or Einstein his special theory or relativity, if working to a fixed price contract for it, with stringent damages for failure to supply?

To return to the question 'What is computer science?', it is (again in this author's view) a branch of applied mathematics in the part of it that affects – or should affect – the programming stage of software development. In this respect, computer science research has already played a fundamentally important role in the establishment and progress of programming. The role of computer science education as a source for practical software development is more obscure. The two are cognate up to a point in the shared aptitudes of practitioners in each. However, computer scientists may tend more to a mathematical interest than is the case with 'software engineers' and, whilst that is essential for computer science and for some applications in software development, it is not necessarily a precondition for good software engineering, where it is the aptitude for dealing with abstract processes that is required rather than an interest in mathematics. Furthermore, one would need to settle several questions of curricula for both subjects before defining their relationship. Whereas this may be relatively straightforward for computer science education, it is far from that for software engineering as a subject. The point is developed at some length in Chapter 13.

As to etymology, 'computer science' is not so wrongly designated in my view, despite Abrahams's trouble with the name. Except, possibly, that 'computer' bears a rather narrow connotation of the use of devices, hardware, electronics, etc. – rather than the much wider field of endeavor actually undertaken.

An earlier quoted reference (Horning 1985) proceeded (in the context of software engineering it should be noted): 'Dijkstra has observed that the true subject matter for programmers is not programming but the design of computations.' In fact, on inspection, we find that this is true up to a point – the major concern is design – but rather narrow in the sense that it prescribes computations rather than transformations, the latter being the general case statement of what a computer actually does to data.

Here the radical problem lies in the name 'computer' itself, which is a historical ascription from the epochs in which these devices were used mainly for large scale computations in applied science and engineering. Now, as well as numbers that are operands for calculation-based algorithms, our devices process numerically coded text and data to act as operands in logical operations. The word 'computer' is inadequate to describe this and, consequently, is inadequate as a prefix in some subject name like 'computer science'. However, like 'software engineering', the term 'computer' has such widespread currency now that we are best to leave it alone; as the French have found with *le*

hamburger, once something enters demotic speech it is too late to resist it, however unappetizing it – and its object – might be.

1.4 THE ORIGINAL QUESTION REVISITED: WHAT *IS* SOFTWARE ENGINEERING?

At a trivial level of definition, almost tautological, software engineering is the creation and construction of software that works, i.e. fits a specification of its purposes and goes on doing so, and that can be modified either for corrective maintenance or for new versions.

So far, we have used the etymological arguments as a vehicle for describing, rather than defining, the process, and have used other issues, in engineering and science, as antipodal points for this purpose. Before leaving the domain of description, we must address one further property of software engineering that has already been anticipated by earlier comments. Software development is generally done under economic constraints and, therefore, requires management. In this respect, of course, it resembles engineering amongst many other things. We will begin by considering alternative approaches to the question of allocating staff to tasks for a software development. Once more, we are describing the process through one of its attributes, rather than defining it. Purists, and the impatient, will baulk at this procrastination, but we are faced with a formidable, if imaginary, audience of non-practitioners for whom a few crisp definitions will not suffice.

1.4.1 The activity of 'software engineering'

Software engineering is, generally, an endeavor whose main subprocesses, listed below, call for distinctly different qualities in the people performing them:

1. Requirements' analysis and specification.
2. Feasibility and resources' estimating.
3. Design of a computer-based software solution (or emulation of functions) for the requirements.
4. Implementation of the design as programs, and program testing by their authors.
5. Objective quality determination of the programs as software, i.e. in their dynamic state with hardware, and of the system documentation – including that of design and implementation of the programs.

These activities are highly disparate, and require a rare combination of attributes in the people performing them. One supposed palliative for this difficulty is phase-allocation of staff. For example, 'systems analysts' to do the first part and, perhaps, the second; a species called 'designers' and one called 'programmers' for the next two; and 'testers' for the objective quality assurance stage.

This scheme is like a relay-race with the baton changing periodically. The only difference is that, in software engineering, the nature of the baton changes too. What, at

the start, exists as specifications in natural language ends up as programs in a highly specialized language, and then a complex and dynamic interaction – as software – with electronic circuitry. By and large, the relay-race approach over several populations of phase-allocated staff is not a success in software engineering. There are too many possibilities for miscommunication between people at contiguous stages; baton dropping in fact. There is the danger also that highly critical stages such as design and implementation may be viewed as 'inferior' if the phase-allocation of staff is (as is often the case) correlated with career progression. However, some well understood and fairly straightforward applications – such as for office administration systems on a small or medium sized scale – may be done, on this basis, without undue hazard.

With these things in mind, we take as our working hypothesis for software development the case when an application is complex and the technologies of solution (algorithms and data structures, and the necessary virtual computer facilities) are not obvious. In these cases very careful specification and design are required prior to substantive implementation which, too, must be exceedingly carefully done if the programs are to have any semblance of real quality. Phase allocation of staff may seem advantageous, providing different expertise at each stage, but will in fact amplify the dangers of dislocation in the process as a whole.

Another hazard of staffing that may beset the process is one that seems like a converse of the structured approach just described. In this, some wizard programmer (or a group of such) jump into a half-defined problem and turn out reams of program code which may or may not be functionally compliant, but will undoubtedly be unmaintainable and unevolvable through its lack of good design and consequent structure.

This is *premature implementation*, and is to be avoided like the plague. It is often the emphatic programming activity of what we call 'amateur programmers' – the people who, whatever their skill in the use of some programming language, and despite their possible avocation in other subjects, are generally unaware of the problems that accrue through premature implementation. This is different from deliberately creating a prototype, and must be carefully distinguished from it, except in cases where the status of a prototype is inflated beyond any reasonable claims for its quality; on these occasions a prototype may be no better than the outcome of some amateur programmer's worst efforts.

These examples of staffing problems in software engineering are treated in greater depth elsewhere, particularly in Part III. They are provided here to highlight a most important and problematical property of software engineering: the one concerning the practitioners, and their organization into effective teams. In his 'Editor's letter', the Principal of SIGSOFT, the special interest group of the ACM for software engineering, wrote (as a footnote incidentally!) that: 'Indeed, software engineering is considered by some to be primarily a management discipline'. We shall return to this point at the end of this book – in Chapter 13. In no sense is the quotation more fundamentally true than in the choice of people to undertake the process, and their dispositions. Software engineers are people who must be prepared and able to do system specification work with users and feasibility assessment, as well as program design, implementation and software validation – in which the essential (program) documentation is included in the definition of 'software'.

1.4.2 Conclusion

As for the crisp and succinct definition of software engineering that has been so long delayed by our etymological adventure, it is this:

> Software engineering is the establishment and use of sound engineering principles and good management practice, and the evolution of applicable tools and methods, and their use as appropriate, in order to obtain – within known but adequate resources limitations – software that is of high quality in an explicitly defined sense. (Marco and Buxton 1987)

To this, one can add that the determination of one aspect of quality – compliance – is closely analogous to a peer-group process in scientific method for most software systems.

Stated as a tautology, software engineering is what real software engineers do; it is misnamed and consequently misunderstood and so, again in consequence, are they. That is not special pleading so much as the problem that lies at the heart of what has been termed 'the crisis in software engineering'. For the most part, software engineers fail to realize what they should do and how they should do it, and so do their managers and others who should add value to the process.

When these problems are surmounted, the crisis in software engineering, that has dragged on now for three and a half decades, will be solvable by technical means such as the improvements currently taking place in tools and techniques. Until then all the technical means possible cannot bridge the cognition gap between exponents and their managers, and between both groups and the subject.

CHAPTER TWO

THE STATE OF SOFTWARE ENGINEERING

Software is a central issue in all aspects of information technology, of no lesser importance than hardware (electronic) engineering itself. Conceptual models of the process are considered, and the basic question 'is the life cycle model of software engineering a reasonable basis for actually doing software development?' is faced. This has taken on the dimensions, if not quality, of a 'great debate' on the issue, over the past half decade or so.

We conclude that adequate life cycle depictions of the software development process have been, are and will remain an essential tool in 'good software engineering practice'.

Some research topics are considered that are claimed to (and in some cases may) extend, or even obviate, life cycle models of software development. These are: formal means for specification; rapid prototyping; design as a 'stepwise process with enrichment'.

2.1 WHY THE STATE OF SOFTWARE ENGINEERING MATTERS

Software systems concern a quite bewildering range of applications. The 'tic-tac-toe' program on little Johnnie's computer is a rather trivial example – perhaps ten or twenty source statements of code, in a very simple high level language such as Basic. At the other end of the scale, the programs executing on computers in the attitude control apparatus of a space-probe possibly comprise a quarter of a million source statements in Ada, C and assembler code – and may represent concurrent processes with difficult issues of synchrony between parts of them. Both of these types, and innumerable ones in between and beyond, are software – part of the enormously widespread, rapidly increasing, variagated and generally ubiquitous scope of this subject. Likewise, its exponents are various in type also.

The PC-based game will advertise its author, no doubt: 'Tic-tac-toe; by Fred Bloggs of East Orange', and we may surmise that it is the result of some proud hobbyist's rapid endeavor, sold for a few dollars to the manufacturer, to enhance (or at least extend) a catalog. Our expectations of this software will not be very high. If it has an irritating, or even incompetent, screen format about which little Johnnie moans a bit – well there are ways of dealing with that at the little Johnnie level! Or if the time between keying moves in and observing a response at the screen is over three hours we may concede that the little brute

has a point, and formulate an uncomplimentary view of East Orange's least competent hobbyist as a result. But that is all; no life will be lost and very little money wasted. No writs will be issued; Fred Bloggs will not get the chop, and little Johnnie's thick ear was overdue anyway.

On the other hand, our space vehicle of earlier reference may burst on the launching-pad, fall into the sea or head off for Pluto if things go amiss. This software will have been developed to extremely exacting standards or, if not, it most assuredly should have been. A team of twenty or thirty graduate-level staff, each with at least five years' experience in developing 'real' software for the most exacting applications, may have spent perhaps three years developing it. It will have been exhaustively validated on test-bed simulators that may themselves have occupied at least as much effort to develop. These will emulate conditions that might occur – known ones and randomized 'accidents' – within the behavior space of the system. Even so, the validation will be an approximation to absolute certitude and there will be a risk, however slight and almost certainly unquantifiable, that the software may fail. Then there would be lamentation in the land and, if negligence was established, writs would be issued, contracts cancelled and staff fired with far greater facility than the launch and booster rockets.

Clearly, we cannot apply the same criteria to developing and validating a PC-based game and the attitude control features of a space-probe. To take a slightly more reasonable example, we cannot even apply the same criteria to developing and validating any non-life-critical system to those we must use when the consequences of failure might mean human injury or death.

If an incompetently made banking-transaction system allows a hobbyist (or 'hacker' as they are often called) to divert a few million units of some currency into his or her own pocket, this may be seen – when the first *frisson* of amusement has passed – as proper cause for concern; all the more so if we bank our money there. But when the computer system fails (again) at the Heathrow air-traffic control center, then circumstances for tragedy are all too evident, as laden jumbo jets skim close to each other.

However, the point that we will make immediately is that all software should be developed within a scheme of 'good software engineering practice', whatever that can be taken to mean, in which the practitioners may vary in quality (i.e. appropriateness for the task), just as the technical tools may also vary in quality, according to the limitations of supply, economic means and so on. The one thing that should not change is the 'good practice'. But to bring this about for all, or even most, of the software developments going on in the world would be a daunting task, for two reasons. Firstly, one would need a clear comprehension of what constitutes 'good practice' and, as we will show, that is far from a matter of consensus. Secondly, the sheer scale of software activity, and its rates of growth and change, militate against the assertion of good practices in general, their adoption and their further propagation.

It is difficult to measure the size of the software industry, but an 'order of magnitude' estimate may be made with fair confidence. One recent estimate puts the value in 1985 of worldwide software sales and services at 40×10^9 (Miles and Ahlberg 1985), with a compound growth-rate of 40 percent per annum. However, this figure undoubtedly contains a substantial component for sales or rentals of 'virtual' software and other packages already developed, and some of it will be for the very large 'home computer'

market,and the applications in very high level 'languages' (such as a 4GL) that are not a subject for this work. Furthermore, it does not estimate the ongoing cost of software development within users' organization and product development firms. Our main interest is to estimate the amount of real software engineering going on in the world, as this will help us to put a value on the dimension of a potential problem – how 'good practices' may be propagated and established if, and when, they are ever incontrovertably established.

In 1975, it was estimated that about 450,000 people were roughly classifiable as 'programmers' in the USA (Boehm 1975). This was before the major increases in applications and usage due to microprocessor and microcomputer technology, from about 1976 onwards. Assuming a conservative 30 percent per annum compounding growth, this number must now be in the range 7–8 million in the USA alone, and well over 10 million worldwide. If one applies some fairly stringent factor to account for the work done by 'non-professional programmers' (Martin and Kleinroch 1985), it is plausible to suppose that some 3 million people are occupied, worldwide, in 'real' software engineering – of which about 30 percent will be engaged in software development as distinct from maintenance of existing software. It is not fanciful, therefore, to see the dimension of an audience directly interested in 'good software engineering practices' as being in the order of 1 million people worldwide. This is, in fact, both the dimension and the essential nature of what has been seen, rather myopically, as 'the software engineering crisis'.

Of course, not all the 1 million (plus or minus) software engineers doing development – nor their colleagues in maintenance tasks – are proceeding without 'good software engineering practices'. Over the past ten years or so, there has been much emphasis in the literature, reflected too in the behavior of clients for software systems, and their suppliers, towards delineating and demonstrating the elements of 'good practice'. Pressed as I am at times in some educational context to estimate the penetration of these good practices (and, thereby, the degree of improvement in the profession), I would hazard an 'informed' guess of 30–40 percent in total, at this time. The problem, however, resides in the differential (if any), and in which direction it is, between the rate of propagation of approaches, tools, procedures, etc., and the growth-rate in demand for new software systems. Here, the earlier quoted figure of 40 percent (Miles and Ahlberg 1985) is perfectly plausible as a factor for *latent* growth, i.e. the rate at which the sector would be growing if unconstrained. As it is, the inability of education sources to provide the right kind of entrants, in the right numbers, probably constrains the growth-rate to nearer 30 than 40 percent per annum.

This is a very worrying picture, and one that is commonly held to be a true statement of affairs in software engineering, whether or not one agrees on the precise values assigned in the order of magnitude estimates given. If it has taken ten to fifteen years to establish good practices and propagate them to something like a 30 percent level in this sector, then any substantial growth-rate may constitute a receding target, unless the supply of new entrants is quantitatively adequate, and is properly educated in the practicalities of the subject.

That, not to obfuscate the point, is precisely what is *not* happening to a sufficient extent. The software engineering crisis *is* getting progressively worse. Obviously, there is a steady and persistent increase in the absolute numbers of 'real' software engineers who

are practicing in a highly competent manner – although much of this has come about as the result of a slow process of empirical learning, a very costly affair by and large. However, the relative proportion, viewed against growth-rate in this sector, is possibly not increasing at all, and may now be decreasing.

There is evidence of this from all countries, and one example recently in the United Kingdom is particularly clear on the issue (ACARD report on *Software – A vital key to UK competitiveness*; 1986). The generally held view is that software development and usage are crucial to an industrialized country's national prosperity; that the state of software development (in the world, and in any country you may care to name) is parlous; and that the main cause of this state of affairs lies in the lack of means (and, in some cases, the will) in the formal education sector, and in individual companies' own policies for staff training.

This topic is taken further and to greater depth in Section 13.4. It is the most radical problem we face in software engineering, and its remedy in software education is the most urgently awaited.

2.2 MODELS OF THE SOFTWARE DEVELOPMENT PROCESS

In Chapter 1 we explained the problems of defining the subject 'software engineering' as a reasonable way of beginning to grasp its elements. We have just delineated one of the consequences that might be thought to derive from this problem – namely, an inability to produce enough software engineers of adequate quality, for how can one educate or train people in something so apparently difficult to define?

Now, we turn to the process of software development itself, the stage (so to speak) on which 'software engineering' is enacted – presuming the positive value component for 'engineering' that the word normally carries with it. If the subject is so uncertain of definition, is the act itself any clearer? For there is enough software around in the world, whatever its quality, and it did not instantiate itself by an act of autogenesis. It was all developed, carefully or carelessly. Surely (a dangerous word admittedly), we can, by now, say something about the facts of this prodigious act of creation.

Since about 1970, the software engineering process has been described, quite widely, by means of schematic depictions of its main activities – models of the process represented by simple bubble and arrow diagrams. We include several examples below. Now, however, an argument has broken out about whether this is, in fact, a good idea. The year 1982 seemed a particularly fruitful one for this dispute. In the *Software engineering notes* for Sigsoft, the special interest group of ACM, we find papers entitled as follows:

1. 'Lifecycle concepts considered harmful': McCracken and Jackson (1982).
2. 'Stop the lifecycle, I want to get off': Gladden (1982).
3. 'The lifecycle – a debate over alternative models': Blum (1982).

And more recently, we find the following:

4. 'A spiral model for software development and enhancement': Boehm (1986).
5. 'Defending the lifecycle': Ledgard (1987).

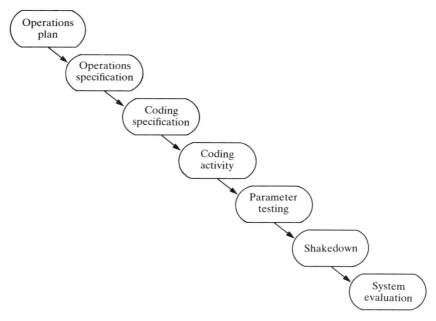

FIGURE 2.1 A 'stagewise' model. State of knowledge *circa* 1960.

The image of Santa Clauses fighting for territory on the London streets has come back to plague us.

2.2.1 Early ideas about the software development process

The ordering of essential activities in software engineering has long concerned practitioners, theoreticians and authors in this field. As early as 1956 Benington suggested 'a stagewise model' for software development terminology that was by no means widely accepted at the time and has been superseded since. (In fairness, very little could be 'widely accepted' in that distant epoch, as computing was not an extensively applied activity. Benington was a pioneer in this, and in other matters.) The early model for software development (Benington 1956) is depicted in Figure 2.1.

Part of the current criticism of life cycle models is that either they impose a standard view of the software engineering process (whereas, in fact, the objects of the process are multifarious, and the development environments are so varied that no cliché can be applied to them) or the life cycle model generally fitting all such types must be at so high a level of generality that it says little. The matter is put trenchantly on one side of the argument:

To contend that any lifecycle scheme, even with variations, can be applied to all system developments is either to fly in the face of reality, or to assume a lifecycle so general as to be vacuous. (McCracken and Jackson 1982)

This is a view from which we will differ with some vigor although, it must be said, with a twinge of conscience. There is a tendency, which we deplore, to extreme rigidity of view on this and other matters in software engineering; an inclination to standards where none exist, nor can reasonably exist. In that, we entirely agree with the authors quoted. However, that is not the critics' main point. What seems to be the burden of criticism is that, because software applications are so varied, nothing in common can be said about their development. However, that is assertion and not demonstration of the point. In fact, the question at issue does not concern the variety of applications, so much as whether there exist invariant and irreducible properties of software development that constitute a 'best way' of going about development, some eternal verities from which we could extrude guidelines for 'good software engineering practice'. They would hardly be vacuous and, in fact, that is the first merit we would assert for software life cycle models, above a trivial level of detail. However, we must first attempt to demonstrate their worth.

The virtues of 'non-vacuous' life cycle models seen as 'guidelines' or the basis for understanding, are the following:

1. They act as a shared conceptual model and are a limited, but serviceable, vocabulary of what is going on, or should be going on, in a software development.
2. They greatly facilitate the management of software development. In fact, as we intimated earlier (and is agreed by critics of life cycle models): Any form of lifecycle is a project management structure' (McCracken and Jackson 1982).

Just so. In any non-trivial context, outside the domain of research, a project management structure is *sine qua non* for an orderly development; in the world of software – with all its imponderables and hazards – the pursuit of means for an orderly development is a distinct and urgent need in most environments where software is developed.

We shall return to this argument a little later.

The early models, with their archaic terminology, such as that depicted in Figure 2.1, were clearly inadequate for a process as problematic as software development had turned out to be by 1970. Just as an example, the simple schematic and its vocabulary lack the following essential features:

1. Any notion of back-tracking in the event of additional clarification, or discovery of prior omission, or error.
2. Any anticipation of changes to the scope or detail of specifications, or need to develop prototypes to find out about them.
3. Any concept that, even after completion, the system may have to be evolved.
4. Any idea of a design stage, between specification stages and coding.
5. Any requirement for quality control and assurance, or reference to the system's documentation.

This short list is given merely to get us used to enumerating the defects of process models for software engineering. At this level, one can appreciate the criticism that such a model is vacuous; it is also seriously wrong by omission.

By 1970 it had become apparent that even the implementation part of software development – programming and testing programs – is a highly non-trivial activity, which does not contain all the activities that make up the process of software engineering. As the scope and size of programs increased, it became evident that this process of creating software systems must be put under some regulatory means if utter chaos was to be avoided.

Increasingly, managers required estimates, in which they could believe, of both effort and the time-scale over which the effort would be expended before the system was complete. Procurement officers in companies requiring a 'bespoke' software system (i.e. a 'one-off' artefact for that company alone) – generally the sort of people accustomed to shopping for large-scale mechanical or electrical systems and for their components – adopted a very crisp attitude to any putative supplier of software who equivocated about price or delivery. However unreasonable this may have seemed (after all making software *is* a bit different from building a physical object), it had its effect.

It was not the only factor bearing on the emerging profession, whose own exponents had – for themselves – noticed much that was wrong with the practice of creating and constructing software systems. A major source of trouble was that of treating the matter as though it only concerned programming and debugging programs. From this time, somewhere in the period 1965–70, emerged the main approaches which we deploy today – when and where appropriate – to 'engineer' our software. One author has listed eight such, that strike him as the major 'promising attacks', and we offer this compendium (Brooks, in Gibbs and Fairly 1987) which indicates, also, the provenance:

1. Top down design: Wirth.
2. Outside-in design; system architecture: Blaauw.
3. Incremental growth on an executable driver: Mills.
4. Information-hiding modules: Parnas.
5. Chief programmer teams: Mills.
6. Formal verification (useful, but limited by costliness): Hoare *et al*.
7. GO TO less programming (structure, yes; coding level, no): Dijkstra.
8. Structured walkthroughs.

These topics will all be elaborated elsewhere, some in this volume, others in later volumes.

It is an interesting list and, as we indicated in the introduction, shows influence from both computer science endeavors and practice. The last entry, 'structured walkthrough', is listed without provenance for exactly that reason; we all invented it as part of good software management practice and, to do so, we first produced notional activities' structures of the process; life cycles in fact.

Now, before *glasnost*, there was a joke, of the gallows-humour variety, that enjoyed a furtive sort of vogue in some Warsaw-pact countries. This wit depended on a hypothetical broadcasting station in the south of the USSR, known as 'Radio Yerevan!'. During a quiz program on this Radio Yerevan (first prize, an industrial blast furnace) a

contestant is asked: 'What are the four basic problems of Soviet agriculture?' He is desperate to get it right, and answers with trepidation (after all, the second prize might be two blast furnaces): 'Spring, summer, autumn and winter'.

Software engineering was like that in the 1960s: 'What are the four main problems of software engineering?' 'Specification, design, implementation and validation'. We began to grasp the elements of software engineering, and to get to grips with its problems, in the 1970s – as Brooks's list shows. An important element in all this was the development of management models of the process. It was clearly time to bring Benington's scheme up to date.

2.2.2 Later developments, and the value of criticism

This work was largely, but not entirely, due to Boehm who, in published papers and – finally – a rather large book (*Software Engineering Economics*; Boehm 1981), proposed a software life cycle scheme that became known as the 'cascade' or 'waterfall' model. It is simply depicted in Figure 2.2.

This is a schematic representation of life cycle activities according to Royce (1970). It answers the objections to the earlier schematic up to a point. Thus, the model shows the following:

1. Limited feedback between contiguous activities.
2. Limited recognition of the need, on occasion, to develop prototypes.
3. No clear recognition of specification changes, or evolutions of the system after completion.
4. A clear indication of design as an identifiable activity.
5. Only a very limited view of the quality issues, but a clear statement on documentation – although this is depicted as an *ex post facto* event rather than an ongoing part of development.

Of these limitations, the one most apparent was that concerning quality control and assurance throughout the process. By about 1975 Boehm had produced a 'risk management variant' of the waterfall model similar to that set out in Figure 2.3.

The use of the terms 'verification' and 'validation' needs to be attended to here, as their meanings help materially in our development of concepts and definitions. There is a certain looseness, in general, in the use of the two words in the processes of quality control and assurance. However, Boehm quite correctly distinguishes the two as follows:

> Verification: Are we building the product right?
> Validation: Are we building the right product?

In other words, the first primarily concerns the process ('software development') and the second its outcome ('software'); application of the terms at stages within the process concern that stage and its outcome. These 'outcomes' have become known as 'deliverables', and we speak of these deliverables being the object of review during 'structured walkthroughs' of the software development, a management technique described in Section 11.2.

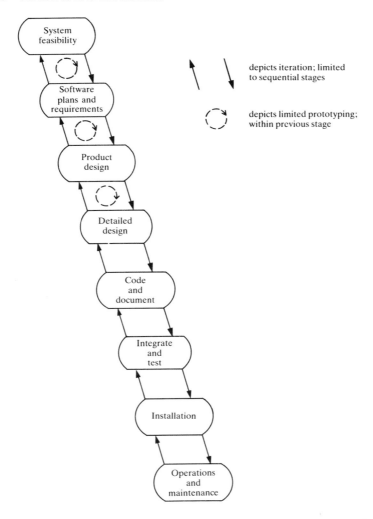

FIGURE 2.2 A 'waterfall' model of software development activities. State of knowledge *circa* 1970.

The simple schematic due to Boehm has many interesting features, and certainly could not be dismissed as 'vacuous'. No entirely vacuous model would, as Figure 2.3 does, allow us to make the following major criticisms of it:

1. Iteration is restricted to contiguous stages; in real life we often back-track over more than one.
2. Developing prototypes may be intended (as shown in Figure 2.3), but is not mentioned as a means of achieving complete specifications or adequate designs.
3. The model omits the most important of all software engineering properties – that the process does not necessarily terminate, but will probably back-track from the bottom

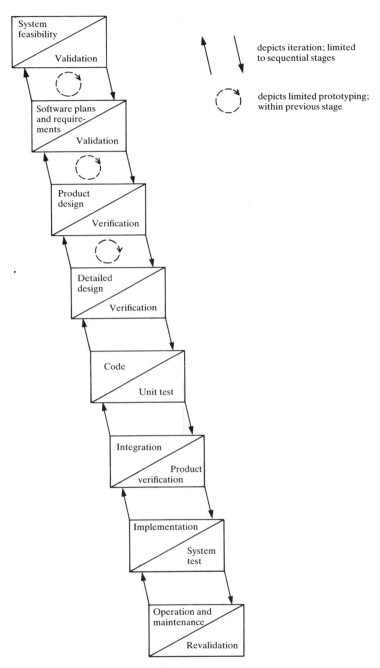

FIGURE 2.3 An evolved 'waterfall' model (after Boehm). State of knowledge *circa* 1975–80.

activity to the top in order to accommodate major changes, *post hoc*, to the original required system scope.

4. The use of terminology in the model contradicts the definitions that are attached to it (e.g. of 'verification' and 'validation'). For instance:
    (a) it is difficult to see how we can answer the question 'Are we building the right system?' at step one – what is being validated? (there is no specification prior to that step);
    (b) the same comment for 'validating' the so-called 'software plans and requirements';
    (c) there is a very interesting shift in terminology at step 3 – the model now speaks (correctly) of verifying the design process;
    (d) the terminology becomes very arbitrary around 'Coding' and 'Integration' – in fact, given its author's own definitions, the product cannot be verified, only the process can;
    (e) this last point is borne out by the use of 'revalidation' at the last step.

I have found this process of criticizing a life cycle model of the greatest use. It seems to increase the comprehension of managers, practitioners and others involved in software development of what constitutes the elements to which good software engineering tools and practices should be directed.

Between about 1976 and 1986, models of this sort proliferated, and became ubiquitous. Figures 2.4 and 2.5 give examples of the way in which life cycle models became more elaborate. The first is by the present author (Marco and Buxton 1987) and has been adapted slightly to incorporate developing prototypes more clearly. This model has been extensively used for software development and its management, and for orientation and education courses in the subject of software engineering. It has invariably carried with it the following caveats:

1. It is a somewhat ideal depiction of what is frequently a more iterative procedure, and one where parts of a software development may be done asynchronously with each other.
2. It is a model for management control purposes, and for use as a paradigm in software engineering education; as a basis for software development, the model should be viewed as a point of departure for *guidelines* and not *standards*.

Thus, both of the objections in McCracken and Jackson's paper (1982) are adequately answered. The life cycle model in Figure 2.4 is neither 'flying in the face of reality' nor 'vacuous'. A misapplied *standard* may be 'flying in the face of reality', but a basis for guidelines avoids these unseemly aerobatics.

Another representation is shown in Figure 2.5. This is by unidentified authors in a booklet produced, for purchasers of software systems, by the British National Computing Centre and the Department of Trade and Industry (*The STARTS Purchasing Handbook*, 1987). There are a few quibbles, and some more important objections, that can be made about this schematic:

1. Quality assurance should not start as low down the life cycle (in any scheme) as the 'structural software design' step, and it should continue into the post-delivery stage (see Volume 5 of this series).

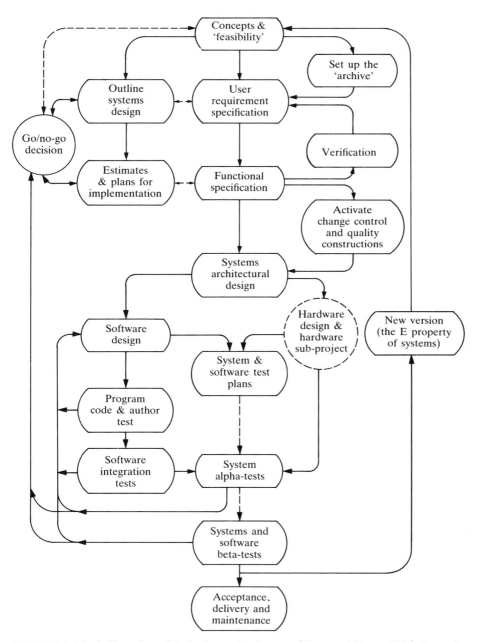

FIGURE 2.4 A basic life cycle model of software development (Marco and Buxton 1987). State of knowledge *circa* 1980–85.

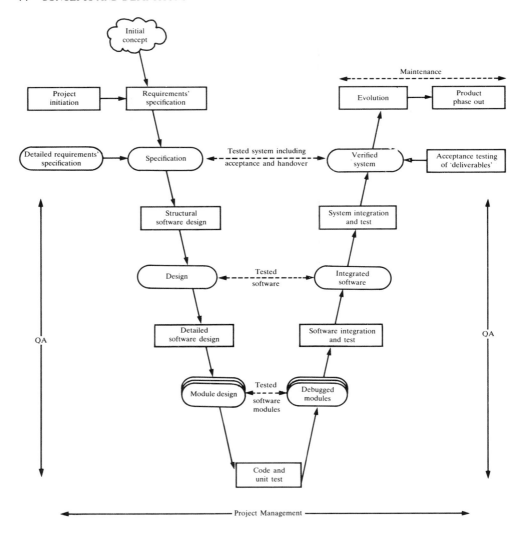

FIGURE 2.5 An alternative model for the software life cycle (STARTS Manual 1987). State of knowledge *circa* 1985–87.

2. Feasibility evaluations are missing, as are the stages where it may be necessary to do prototype developments for other purposes.
3. No indication of the best points to do estimating are given.
4. No change control mechanisms seem required.
5 No iteration or back-tracking of any sort seems possible.

As a basis for guidelines in software development, or means in its management, or as a paradigm in education, this model would be unsuitable in my view – even 'harmful' to

use the previous phrase – because it is misleading in the particulars enumerated. Life cycle models can be 'considered harmful' if they are seriously wrong by omission or otherwise.

In Chapter 4 we will propose a life cycle model (basically that depicted in Figure 2.4). Now, however, we must proceed with the debate about the life cycle concept as considered, by some, to be too limiting – or otherwise detrimental to the process of software development.

2.3 SOME RESEARCH TOPICS TO BE CONSIDERED AT THIS STAGE

In the past decade or so (post-1980, roughly speaking), several developments in software engineering methods have occurred, and claims have been for them that – in some combinations – they effectively do (or should) revolutionize the way we undertake software development. It is from these, by and large, that we see emerging the urge to dispense with life cycle models. Briefly enumerated, these developments comprise the following:

1. Specification by formal means.
2. Design as a 'stepwise process, with enrichment', seen as a sequence of linguistic transformations between 'canonical steps'.
3. Executable specification languages and rapid prototyping techniques.

It is beyond our aims to deal with any of these in detail here; accounts of the approaches will be given in other volumes of this series. For example, topic 1 is dealt with in Volume 2 (and in Volume 4 also, to some extent), 2 is an approach that is discussed in Volume 3, and topic 3 is also dealt with in Volume 2. However, it is appropriate that we give here, in a most stringent synopsis, the main features of these approaches and our summarized comments on them, in order that we can consider them for incorporation in a life cycle-based model of the software engineering process or, alternatively, amend or even discard the life cycle approach altogether. Even though quite ruthlessly summarized, the subjects might be thought too technically detailed for this relatively early part of a 'management' volume. However, we can hardly proceed without raising and settling these issues.

2.3.1 Specification by formal means

We employ the term 'means' here, as distinct from 'methods', to avoid the inference that some generally accepted utilities exist and are of demonstrated worth. This whole subject of formal specification is a major research topic in computer science.

Much confusion in this work attaches to and derives from unclarity about the everyday use of 'specification'. A usual connotation of 'specification' in the demotic speech of software engineers, their managers and others, is that it concerns users' requirements. Things like needs, wants, desires and so on are specified. Their supply or solution is

defined, designed, made and so on. Are we then, here, speaking of users' requirements and their specifications?

A cursory review of the literature is enough to show that most of the work in formal specification concerns the definition of integrands, programs or program modules, and an excellent anthology of such research papers may be found in Gehani and McGettrick (1986). Some work, again mainly at the research stage, concerns the use of formal languages for specification of systems' requirements high in the life cycle, and an example is given (after Stepney and Lord 1987) in Chapter 5. However, such approaches should not be conflated with, nor mistaken for other – and rather dominant – features of research into so-called 'specification by formal means'.

Much research work concerns the search for means, such as languages and proof-methods, suitable for the definition of integrands (or programs), their generation as code directly, even 'automatically' (that is, via other programs) from the definition, and the validation by formal proof of the resulting code. One proceeds by defining a pre-condition and a post-condition for a program or program-part (integrand). The pre-condition, S, is an assertion of the state of the program or part-program (for example, in terms of some parameter values perhaps) before its execution. The post-condition, S', is an assertion (before its execution) of the state that a program or part-program will be in after its execution, i.e. the intended post-condition state. Program (or part-program) proof is the formal demonstration that its semantics are consistent with the tranformation of pre-condition into post-condition.

This approach is clearly of relevance at and around the lowest levels of design, and for implementation (using the terminology of Figure 2.4). We might depict this part of a life cycle model schematically; see Figure 2.6.

The language concerned at this level, for definition of integrands or programs, is generally a logical notation such as that deployed in predicate calculus. This subject, which concerns the rules for operating on and transforming 'predicates' (generally noun constructions of some sort), is of clear, but limited, use in formal logic. In computer science, predicates may be complex expressions, and have either a truth or falsehood status. Thus, at a trivial level, $1 + 1 = 3$ is a predicate expression with the status, or 'value', false. A generalization of this, such as the algebraic expression $x + y = z$ is not a real predicate expression until its terms are given real (i.e. noun) values.

The use of predicate calculus as a language for formal 'specification' is due to its properties, as a notation, to express inference rules analogous to those of arithmetic, algebraic and differential calculus conventions and so on, but having – as operands – predicate expressions with a truth status. (In fact 'value' is better, as we speak of the logical correctness being 'calculated'.) Again, the suitability of predicate calculus for this purpose tends to locate its field of usefulness in software engineering at, and around, the implementation stage. The notation itself tends to make it unsuitable for activities in requirements' specification, as it is generally 'user unfriendly', and it is not particularly useful in design either (see Section 2.3.2 below). Many managers tell me that the use of abstract languages for requirements' specification is positively 'manager-bellicose', and I must agree. A specimen expression in predicate calculus might be (in this case to define an assignment statement in a program):

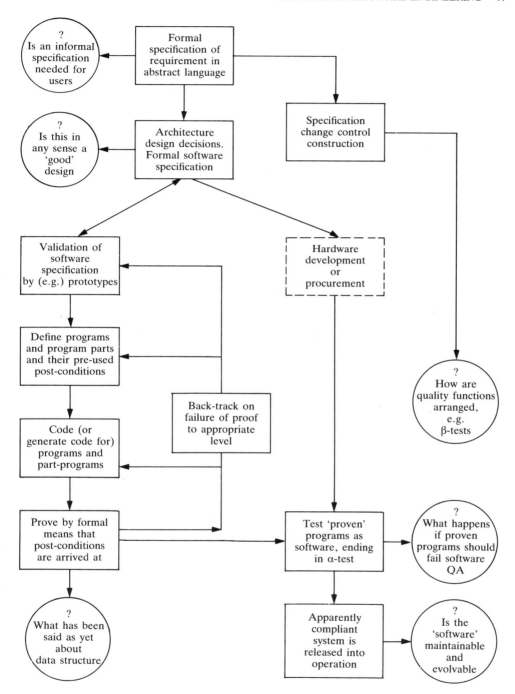

FIGURE 2.6 The questions raised by implementation with formal means. State of knowledge 1990–95?

$$\{P^V_E\}V := E\{P\}$$

for any predicate P, variable V and valid expression E.

This is an example, that is absolutely meaningless in itself outside its context of course, but also relatively meaningless even in its most exact context to anyone inexperienced in, or without facility for, this species of applied mathematics. It is the stuff of formal methods (see Gehani and McGettrick 1986).

2.3.2 Design as a stepwise process with 'enrichment'

It has long been recognized, in software engineering as in other fields of endeavor, that the design of large scale and complex constructions is a multi-step process, often iterative between steps and (hopefully) convergent to a 'good' design. Furthermore, criteria of virtue in the design may incorporate aspects of utility and modifiability, and (for some artefacts) esthetic qualities.

In software engineering we call this a *'stepwise process with refinement or enrichment'* and, as this is the strictest summary at this stage, all that we shall offer in the way of explanation, is that one generally incorporates several intuitive and therefore largely unquantifiable properties in the word 'enrichment'. The process has been further described (in Lehman *et al.* 1984) as follows:

> Software design – from 'topmost' specification down to final implementation – is viewed as a chain of uniform steps, each step being a transformation between two linguistic levels.

The authors go on to define a 'canonical step' in this process, and to assert that each canonical step contains an intuitive ('unconstrained, creative') part, and a 'calculable part, which is the actual transformation effected'. Furthermore, the design steps may result in back-tracking. Now, up to a point, this is the accepted method in design anyway – for instance in schemes of progressive decomposition of a requirements' specification, and transformation into levels of increasing detail for the solution. The languages of design may be words, algorithms, diagrams and pictures, or whatever supplies the designer's need. In software design processes, the sort of linguistic transformations referred to are between words and diagrams, and between diagrams of one sort and another.

What is meant in the quoted paper is, however, somewhat different. The aim here is to produce steps, from requirements' specification to validated programs, that are computably correct with respect to each other and, thereby, to produce a program (the final 'post-condition') that is, *a fortiori*, correct with respect to the original pre-condition (specification). Once more, as above, the language of expression is to be predicate calculus, or a near relative of it, to ensure the computability of logical correctness of transformations. Once more, the objections concern its user unfriendliness at the specification stage, and the fact that it does not help with the 'unconstrained, creative' parts of design, and may even impoverish or constrain them. This point is amply demonstrated by research into the use of formal 'specification' languages as a design tool. In a paper with that title (Guttag and Horning 1980) the authors state:

Getting the design 'right' is much more difficult than implementing the design. This assumption implies that we consider the case of demonstrating the consistency of a design specification and a program to be of secondary importance. The ease with which the design itself can be examined and manipulated is of primary importance. The key verification issue then is 'what can one prove about a design'?

This locates the work quite clearly as that part of the design process called, by Lehman[1] 'the calculable part, which is the actual transformation effected.' Research work in this field generally fails to show how the formal approach in design affects any of the most pressing problems in the design of real software systems, such as how to decompose and detail the design of systems containing concurrent operations where problems of synchrony may arise, and – importantly – how to design these systems so that they are relatively easily maintained and adapted.

These works quoted, as for much that is quoted in Section 2.3.1 for 'formal specification', are in the domain of computer science research. The useful content for practical software engineering is in the notions of canonical steps, linguistic transformations and back-tracking, and can be depicted schematically as in Figure 2.7 (after Macro and Buxton 1987).

In this scheme a 'language' is, literally, anything the designer finds useful for design. Usually it will be one of a set of more or less suitable notations (see Section 7.2), for the diagrammatic depiction of logical relationships, or flows of data, or both, for timing diagrams if necessary, and so on. The first 'base' (B_1) will be the requirements' specification and the last (B_n) will be definition of integrands prior to the implementation. However, the concept of design as somehow fitting neatly between specification and implementation assumes little interaction between life cycle 'stages' – such as those of design and implementation – and that is one of the matters at question in the present epoch. But this question of whether real-life software development should be seen as a complex interaction between activities in specification, design and programming, to the detriment (possibly terminal) of life cycle concepts, is unaffected, either way, by the present research into the use of predicate transforms to achieve a calculatedly 'correct' program, or set of programs.

Likewise, the use of formal means to 'prove' some properties of designs is not a method for doing design, and should not be confused with that issue. On the other hand, the notion of design as 'a stepwise process with enrichment, seen as a sequence of linguistic transformations', would be seriously (probably fatally) affected by excessive interaction (as via intermediate development of prototypes) between specification, design and implementation activities. This discussion proceeds below. In the meantime, more questions have arisen about the suitability of life cycle models and these, bearing as they do on the use of prototyping techniques in software development, require summarizing in their turn.

2.3.3 Executable specification languages and rapid prototyping

Over the past ten years or so, attempts have been made to develop languages that are suitable for requirements' specification and, in addition, are such that the specification

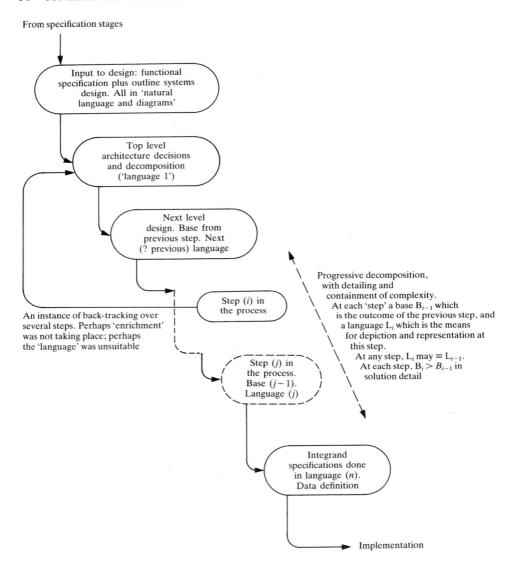

From specification stages

Input to design: functional
specification plus outline systems
design. All in 'natural
language and diagrams'

Top level
architecture decisions
and decomposition
('language 1')

Next level
design. Base from
previous step. Next
(? previous) language

Step (i) in
the process

An instance of back-tracking over
several steps. Perhaps 'enrichment'
was not taking place; perhaps
the 'language' was unsuitable

Step (j) in
the process.
Base ($j-1$).
Language (j)

Progressive decomposition,
with detailing and
containment of complexity.
At each 'step' a base B_{i-1} which
is the outcome of the previous step, and
a language L_i which is the means
for depiction and representation at
this step.
At any step, L_i may $\equiv L_{i-1}$.
At each step, $B_i > B_{i-1}$ in
solution detail

Integrand
specifications done
in language (n).
Data definition

Implementation

FIGURE 2.7 Design as a stepwise process, with enrichment, seen as a sequence of linguistic transformations.

effected can be taken as high (or very high) level language modules which, after 'compilation', can be run as a prototype solution on a computer.

The virtues of this approach are that (a) the process of developing prototypes may materially assist in clarifying, and even extracting, real requirements from the people specifying them; (b) the prototype may assist one to investigate potentially difficult parts of an implementation; and (c) the prototype may serve as a basis for a rapid implementation of the system-to-be, if the 'rapid prototype' is of sufficiently good quality as an operational system. This last qualification is a large one, but that does not detract from the other virtues of rapid prototyping. The point is that the objectives of prototyping are generally inimical, in any species of engineering, to 'good' construction (see Section 3.1).

The following general points can be made about executable specification languages:

1. They are most often application-specific; for example one may find a 'language' developed for this purpose in telephony, transaction-oriented data processing, tomography in medical science, and so on. Where there is a very well defined application, the problem of defining a suitable specification language for it becomes finite and, therefore, possible.
2. They are most often extensions of well known 'level 2' languages such as Fortran, Pascal and Cobol, so as to ease the problems of comprehension at the software engineer level, and to facilitate compilation. One exception is in telephony (in Europe at least), where a language (Chill) has been developed, and extensions of this for executable specification have appeared, as well as a design notation (CCITT-SDL). Readers interested in Chill will find an account of it in Smedema *et al.* (1985); SDL is described in Chapter 7.

For our purposes here, we shall take an example that appeared in an impressive (and rigorously fair) paper entitled: 'An operational approach to requirement specification for embedded systems' (Zave 1982). In this, the author describes a language, *Pais*ley, in which requirements may be enunciated as an explicit model of the proposed system, along with a model of the system environment in order that they may interact.

In this case, the application-specific aspect of *Pais*ley is that of systems containing concurrency, i.e. parts of the system operating at the same time, with or without synchrony of those parts. The language similarity is that *Pais*ley is somewhat like a well known, high (perhaps even 'very high') level language called APL.

The purpose of the exercise, as set out in the paper, is to enhance the process of specification and investigate some tricky aspects of concurrency. What is impressive to software engineers is the limitation placed on the approach by the author of the paper. The approach is called an 'operational' one, and is well named at that. It concerns a model of a system-to-be as derived from a statement of requirements, operational in a simulation of its environment. It is an excellent instance of prototyping at the requirements' specification level, with derived insights for implementation. The approach may be depicted – in life cycle terms – as in Figure 2.8.

In a section entitled 'Qualms about operational requirements', Zave points out with exemplary clarity the scope of the approach and its limitations. In particular, she explains that the operational model is not really a requirements' model at all but an implementation model, done at the requirements stage, that fits (or should fit) the (then) evident

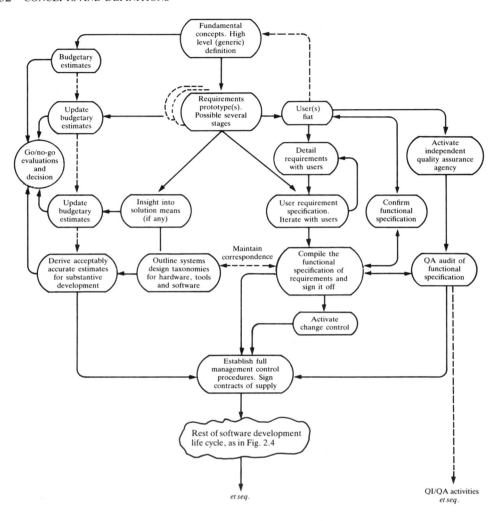

FIGURE 2.8 Specifying requirements by prototyping.

requirements, assists in their evolution and enables some design problems (e.g. in concurrency) to be investigated. This in turn raises the question, do such prototype models 'encroach on design'?

This question is at the heart of all prototyping exercises for whatever purpose. The virtues of prototyping (to adduce and even induce requirements, and to develop and evaluate technical means) are not diminished by the fact that the prototype implementations, or implementation/simulated environment, may not be well 'engineered'. So long as we use them only as prototypes, who cares? Rapid prototyping produces prototypes rapidly; it does not necessarily help with other aspects of software development – such as its quality.

2.3.4 Conclusions

This concludes our highly synoptic review of the three main developments that have been cited to cast doubt on historical life cycle models in the decade after 1978. The three are easily confused and conflated with each other, and our main concern here has been to clarify the applicable area of an approach, or field of research.

In case anyone doubts the tendency to confusion and conflation that can occur, the book *Software Specification Techniques* provides a vivid example. The compilers and editors of papers incorporated in it (Gehani and McGettrick 1986) comment that: 'The first paper by Pamela Zave indicates an approach that is radically different from the others . . .'. The reason why it is different is that it differs fundamentally in *type* as well as approach. The book purports to be about 'software specification techniques', and all its contents but one in the section on 'Particular approaches' concern matters at or around the *program* implementation level in life cycle terms, i.e. the outcome of design, coding and validation of integrands and programs. Zave's approach concerned a rapid prototyping technique for developing requirements' specification and investigating some properties of a solution. It concerns an entirely different set of issues from the work of other authors quoted in that part of the compendium.

This is a very salutory lesson, but should not be taken to detract from the work concerned as set out in the quoted reference. The problem is not with the work, but the ease with which the aims and achievements of generically different issues are conflated and generalized.

Prediction is a perilous business, but my own view is that the following, derived from the three classes of development work quoted above, are already making – or may in future make – some substantial impact on the way software development is done:

1. *Program-proving techniques*. These will be limited to the formal proof that the static properties of integrands, programs and small assemblies of program modules are categorically correct with respect to their formal definition, as this emerges at the 'bottom step' of the design process. This will be helpful, particularly when program generators are in widespread use to generate code from the specification of integrands, but the effect will be limited by the following:
   (a) The need to re-prove the relational behavior of integrands after any changes to software, possibly a major task in this scheme of things.

(b) The fact that categorical proof that something is 'correct' (integrand, program or assembly of such), with respect to its low level definition, does not allow us to infer that it is similarly correct concerning its higher level specification, such as for requirements and designs.

(c) The fact that techniques of this type either concern the static aspects of a program and not its dynamic behavior as software, or are so contingent on the environment in which the software is executed (such as compiler semantics, operating systems and the hardware itself) that the 'proof' must be heavily qualified, if it can be called real proof at all.

(d) The fact that formal proof of correctness depends for its ultimate validity on the correctness of its means – who is to prove the mechanism of proof, and how?

(e) The fact that the status of programs as 'formally proved correct' says nothing about other aspects of their quality – such as reliability and modifiability.

The largest collection of programs 'proved', to date, in this fashion is – we believe – about five thousand source statements of a high level language code. The validity of this 'proof' must remain uncertain given (b), (c) and (d) above, and its relevance to the programs in their operating state as software must be equally uncertain given points (c) and (e).

2. *Proof of design properties*. This is a more distant prospect, unless the meaning of 'design' becomes limited to whatever, below specification level and above implementation, can be expressed in a formal notation so that some precisely defined properties of algorithms, data structures and their interrelationship may be 'proved'. This circularity will limit the extension of formal proof techniques upwards, out of implementation into design proper. If the extension of formal properties requires design in formal notations, then it may even limit design as an activity!

   Other approaches, such as the use of directed graphs in complexity theory, may hold out hope for achieving more modest aims, e.g. the determination of metrics for 'good' design, rather than the formal proof of 'correctness' of design according to some defined properties. However, as is set out in Section 3.3, the value of some of this work has recently been questioned.

3. *Rapid protoype techniques*, such as executable specification languages. This prospect is with us now, and several schemes dependent on application-type have been produced. The caveats on their widespread dissemination are that:

(a) they are generally developed by, and therefore are the proprietary property of, software development companies and may, therefore, represent their commercial advantage;

(b) they accelerate a part or parts of the software engineering process only – such as requirements' specification and technical feasibility assessment – but they do not necessarily produce quality-assured software;

(c) they tend to be features of large scale computer facilities, as their ancillaries (such as features for extensive parametric modeling, whereby to test them) may require considerable computer capacity.

These views are offered as a means of clearing the decks, so to speak, for the main argument in this chapter.

For some years now, as we have already remarked, the question has been persistently raised – and a variety of answers to it have been offered – about whether or not a life cycle model of the software development process is an adequate, even competent, way to depict the complexities of the process and to allow the incorporation of concepts such as rapid prototyping and the use of formal means.

This argument has taken on the feature of a 'great debate' in and between software engineers and computer scientists. As an exponent of courses in practical software engineering, I am asked – with increasing frequency – what 'the real answer' is, as the child in the former story might turn to its appalled parent to enquire: 'Which one is the real Santa?' In the conclusion to their paper, McCracken and Jackson (1982) made their position lambently clear: 'The lifecycle concept is simply unsuited to the needs of the 1980's in developing systems'.

2.4 THE GREAT DEBATE

We are now half a decade on, and the life cycle is alive and convalescing. To trace this state of affairs, and to account for it (because surely it is unlikely that both sides are simultaneously right), let us begin with a paper from a different source, but the same year (Blum 1982). The author of this paper defines two different concepts of software development:

1. The system architecture model, for which the life cycle schematics depicted above – particularly the early ones – are a good representation. As the name implies, the process here is one of sequential planning stages such as requirements' definition, design, construction (e.g. of programs) and so on.
2. The system sculpture model, for which the life cycle schematics already shown would be a very poor representation. In this case the process does not proceed from settled (or relatively settled) requirements, but envisages the creation of a 'base-line product' as a 'dynamic' activity along with the evolution of requirements.

The author then proceeds to classify certain attributes in software engineering, and uses these to compare the two models as in Table 2.1. Now this scheme sets the debate exactly in context and, for that, it serves a most useful purpose. There are elements in it with which to disagree, and I shall return to these. However, the most instructive aspect of Table 2.1 accrues through selectively extracting from its contents. Table 2.2 demonstrates this point.

The first two items in column 1 of Table 2.2 cover a wide-ranging class of applications. Obviously one would need some agreed understanding about 'high technical risk', 'very large projects' and so on. But the gist is clear. Technically exacting software development, resulting in software systems of (say) the order of hundreds of thousands or even millions of source statements of code, seems to require the 'classical' life cycle.

There is another consideration, and that is indicated indirectly in the row named 'Test'. In many cases, software developed along 'classical' life cycle lines is done so because the management of the process is at a premium – not only because the work is

TABLE 2.1 Two models of software engineering contrasted (Blum 1982)

	System architecture	System sculpture
Life cycle model	Classical	Dynamic
High technical risk	Required	Inappropriate
High application risk	Limited utility	Preferred where tools available
Very large products	Effective	Limited applicability
Requirements	Formal, complete	Incomplete, dynamic
Tools	Traditional languages, tools	Application-oriented tools
Prototypes	To establish requirements	Base-line product
Test	Against requirements	Subjective acceptance
Maintenance	Renew cycle	Renew cycle
Response to new requirements	Slow	Fast

TABLE 2.2 Comparison based on abstracted attributes

	System architecture	System sculpture
High technical risk	Required	Inappropriate
Very large projects	Effective	Limited applicability
Test	Versus requirements	Subjective acceptance
Life cycle model	Classical	Dynamic

exacting but because the management of it must be performed within the bounds of some stringent contract of supply. Such stringency may come about through what is known as 'fixed price' supply. (Even less stringent contract forms, such as 'cost plus fixed fee' or 'time and materials', require adequate management – but a 'fixed price' contract acts as effectively as the prospect of hanging does, according to Dr Johnson, on a condemned man; it clarifies the mind remarkably.)

The key to the matter lies in the entry for Test/System sculpture: '*Subjective* acceptance'; for it is a distinct requirement in software development as distinct from experimental work, or prototype construction, that quality is determined by *objective* (if judgmental) means. Nor does the 'classical' life cycle emerge too badly from a closer inspection of other elements in Table 2.1. For example, as shown in Figure 2.8 earlier, a life cycle model is easily adapted – as management practice is also – to incorporate prototyping at the specification stage. The highest 'application risk' at the specification stage is that of incomplete requirements being informally expressed, as is usually the case in new or radically evolved computer applications. It is not, however the monopoly of some new approach, however named, to employ prototyping to evolve and fix requirements.

There are further objections to some of the elements in Table 2.1. For instance, an approach that leaves requirements 'incomplete and dynamic' will, inevitably, produce an artefact or artefacts that are prototypes. To call them 'base-line products' is either to beg the question: 'What do we do with it now?', or to run the risk that a prototype may become regarded as 'the real thing'.

Another objection concerns maintenance and new requirements ('versions') of a

software system. The 'classical' approach – to treat all emendation as a full life cycle process – is certainly slow, but it is safe, both from the viewpoint of management and that of quality in the resulting software. In fact, one of the major defects in Blum's scheme is that there is absolutely no mention whatsoever of quality. To achieve a 'fast response' to new requirements by developing 'base-line products' via a process of (rapid) prototyping emphasizes the question asked earlier: 'What do we do with it now?' In software engineering, a degree of apparent slowness can be a positive virtue when it is coupled with precision in the method, and with quality in general of the end artefact. Such 'slowness' often saves a lot of time.

It is clear from all this that we are really talking about two different things. Comparing them is invidious, and extracting a conclusion from the comparison is most likely to produce fallacy.

The so-called approach of system sculpture would seem to be no more or less than prototyping and, incidentally, should not only be to establish requirements; prototyping concerns the investigation of technical means also. In 'classical' life cycle terms, the rapid prototyping referred to by Zave can be depicted as in Figure 2.8.

The general case of prototyping at the requirements' stage, to clarify the full set of specifications for users' needs and to highlight tricky areas of a possible implementation, is shown in Figure 2.9. Any particular case of prototyping will show how dynamic this life cycle scheme really is, and every instance will have its own life cycle depiction. Where the prototyping cannot be depicted in life cycle terms, it is probably a chaotic situation in which prototypes are not being properly designated as such, nor controlled in their development.

As much of software management is based on life cycle activities' planning and control, the present picture should be completed as far as possible. Rapid prototyping tools have come into existence in the past few years, although their incorporation within programming support environments (PSE) and integrated project support environments (Ipse) is limited and, consequently, their adoption outside the development environment is slow.

So far as models of the software engineering process are concerned, the situation seems to be that the original, rather static, life cycle concept has evolved in the manner presaged above. In an earlier work (Macro and Buxton 1987), matters were represented as a scheme comprising a static, 'idealized' life cycle with, implicit in it and expressed explicitly alongside, the likely practicalities of prototyping, much as in Figure 2.9. Boehm, whose name is the one most strongly associated with the original life cycle concept, has gone further. In a paper on the subject (Boehm 1986) he has suggested a 'spiral model of software development and enhancement'. This is on view in Figure 2.10.

The spiral process is a set of repetitive steps whose iterations converge, or should do, to an 'operational prototype'. Each step begins with an adumbration of objectives for that part of the software system being developed, alternative means of implementing it, and known constraints on these means – such as 'cost, schedule, interface', to quote the paper. It is clear, even from a cursory inspection, that the 'spiral' activities are, in fact, merely an extended feasibility exercise as a prelude to a 'classical' life cycle of activities such as design, code and test.

Before offering a revised schematic to show this form of Boehm's work, another

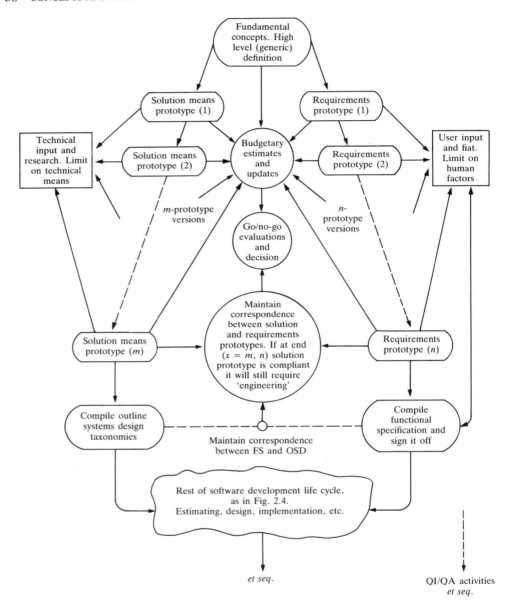

FIGURE 2.9 Multi-prototyping to explore technical means, as well as users' requirements.

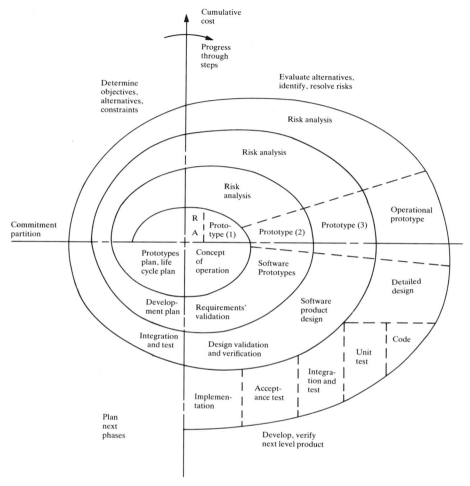

FIGURE 2.10 A 'spiral' model of the software development process (Boehm 1986), depicting sequential prototyping and risk analysis.

suggestion may be made for incorporation into software life cycle models. That is to write the 'user's manual' at whatever stage the requirements first seem to be reasonably well known and fairly stable. In an approach such as Boehm's, or the 'sculptural' scheme of Blum as already described, prototyping will tend to fix requirements as well as investigate technical means for their provision. At the exit point to Boehm's outer spiral, therefore, it is reasonable to conjecture that a user's manual could (and therefore should) be written. Figure 2.11 incorporates that notion.

In all of this, one thing is clear; life cycle models in general are far from 'unsuited to the needs of the 1980s', nor are they 'vacuous' necessarily. Boehm's claims for the spiral approach, as tried in his company (TRW), are quite properly modest and somewhat

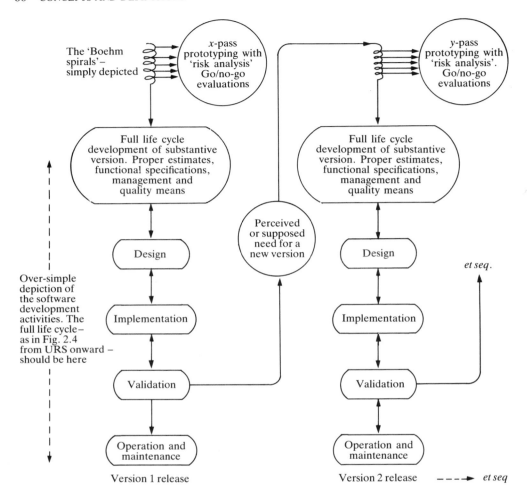

FIGURE 2.11 Precursor 'spirals' of prototype activity, with risk analysis, and substantive software development depicted as a life cycle model.

qualified. The extended feasibility and risk management aspects are appropriate only in contexts where there lacks a contractual constraint of the kind applying in procurement actions and formal contracts of supply.

Readers of acuity will recognize that here, yet again, the contractual issues are playing a role in discriminating appropriate from inappropriate life cycle models of the software engineering process. This, in turn, leads to the realization (yet again) that these models are for use as the basis for managing the software engineering process. To some, this is all a hyper-inflation of some mere bubble of quite low intellectual content and, on the face of it, that may seem true.

However, when the generic activities making up a life cycle model are expanded upon and detailed, what has merely been a gaunt framework, becomes a viable conceptual model. In no sector is this more true than that of subject education, particularly the orientation courses needed for managers, where a life cycle model plays an invaluable role in the classification of subject-material, as well as acting as a paradigm and vocabulary for the elements in software development.

As a epilog to his paper suggesting a spiral model for software development (which, as we have seen, is really a spiral model of preludal feasibility/risk containment prototyping), Boehm offers the following list of its outstanding defects, or 'challenges', at this time (my paraphrasing):

1. (As stated above.) The spiral model does not yet match the world of contract software acquisition.
2. The spiral model places much premium on the ability of software engineers to do risk assessment.
3. In general, the spiral model's process steps need further elaboration so that all the participants in the process are similarly aware of it and its modalities (the 'framework/ detailed edifice' matter already referred to).

For product development, or the development of internal systems in a company, Boehm's spiral model – attached to a 'normal' (or 'classical') life cycle management model – has merit. But it is not an alternative to the waterfall model in any way; in fact it includes and is attached to the 'classical' life cycle model – as shown in Figure 2.11 – for any software artefacts that require cautious, strongly managed stepwise progression with quality consideration. Alternatively, if the spiral merely terminates at the fourth pass, the result is a prototype.

We will deploy these concepts elsewhere in this volume, and use them in whatever context there to illuminate the issues at hand, not least as a framework for managing the process of software development.

What useful things life cycles are, to be sure!

CHAPTER THREE

THE PROPERTIES OF SOFTWARE SYSTEMS

A classification system is suggested for software artefacts comprising the following:

1. **Features (or paradigms) in the requirement – such as computation intensive, process oriented, etc.**
2. **Response requirements (batch, on-line, real-time).**
3. **Prototype, project or product; size; Lehman features, S, P or E systems.**

Software complexity is considered, and the means to contain it. Research into software complexity models is reviewed. The conclusions are that inherent, implementation and interaction complexities must be treated by the means outlined.

3.1 CLASSIFICATION OF SOFTWARE SYSTEMS

We have now seen some of the problems in etymology that afflict our subject, and have eavesdropped on the current discourse over models of the process. In arriving at this point, we have avoided any discussion on the purposes for which software systems may be made. Would such a discussion achieve anything? Is it, in fact, instructive to dwell on the types of software developed? Will it in any way inform our view of software engineering; will it make the process more manageable perhaps and, thereby, enhance the outcome in some real way – such as in its quality?

Earlier, we claimed that our excursion into the etymology of subject-names was not a sterile exercise in linguistics and we hope that, on balance, the reader would now agree. However, the classification of software systems might well become an arid task because, as a method, classification is usually only of use if it provides some insight into a property of the objects it deals with.

Take, as a simple example, a pile of leaves several kilometers to the north-east of a forest, in some region where the prevailing wind is from the south-west. We may choose to classify leaves by size, color or type and, of course, we would get three vastly different results. However, we may find it of little interest that 63.7 percent of the leaves are

yellow, 12.2 percent are red and the rest are brown; similarly, their dimensions might be equally unrevealing. On the other hand, knowing the distribution of types (oak, beech, larch, etc.) may allow us to infer something about the composition of the forest, if only in terms of its deciduous population.

Classification of software systems is tricky because there is a very obvious way to do it, and it so happens that this is the least instructive. If one begins to compile a list of computer applications, one swiftly realizes that – their usage being ubiquitous – the task is a very difficult one to complete. However, during the process the possibility arises of clustering applications under some generic types, and under other attributes altogether.

We shall consider classification of software systems under five types:

1. That of predominant, generic function – where 'predominant' may mean 'most difficult to achieve' rather than most numerous.
2. Where systems' requirement determines temporal properties, within the software or concerning its response.
3. Software system size.
4. Purpose, as distinct from specific requirement – for example, prototype.
5. Lehman's 'S, P and E' properties of requirements – as defined below.

3.1.1 Classification by predominant function

In the 1950s, computers – as distinct from tabulating and sorting equipment – were used for basically one type of purpose, that of performing the sort of extensive calculations in engineering and applied science that were beyond other means. Later, *circa* 1960 and thereafter, another major type of application arose: that in which computers were (and are) used in character-processing oriented, rather than number- and calculation-based, applications. This evolution provided us with two classes of computer usage; computation intensive and data transformation intensive.

There are in the present epoch, four main types of computer usage, into one or more of which most applications fit. The classifications themselves derive from the application types directly, but can also be seen from the approaches to programming language design which reflect, or should reflect, the basic properties within the types for which they are deemed (in fact designed to be) suitable.

Briefly stated here, the idea of a programming language suiting a particular class of applications has been forced on the computing community by the failure to date to produce a universal language, acceptable to the programming community, for any and all applications. One attempt (PL/1 = Programming Language 1) became quite widely adopted mainly because subsets of its features could be used as recognizable versions of other languages, such as Cobol and Fortran.

In the present epoch, we regard the approaches to programming language design as deriving from the application class they are due to serve, and this stance owes much to ideas concerning fitness of form in design in general (Alexander 1964).

We speak of four categories (classes, or types) of application, and thence of language design:

1. *The computation paradigm*, involving possibly high order mathematical and logical transformations on aggregates of numerical data, where the accuracy of computation may be important. Software systems for applications of this type most often contain little time-criticality and, therefore, no need for 'parallel' or 'concurrent' subprocesses within them. These terms are defined later in this section. A subclass of this type in which, to speed up computation, software routines operate concurrently, may be regarded as a part of 'process-oriented' applications (see below).

2. *The data processing paradigm*, involving low order transformations on possibly extremely high volumes of alphanumeric information, represented either as sequential files of data, or as non-sequential records with a set of logical pointers attached. Software systems for applications of this type may contain some low order time-criticality or none at all, in which cases they are known as 'on-line' or 'batch' systems respectively. These terms are defined below. Software systems of this type seldom incorporate 'parallel' or 'concurrent' subprocesses, with the following exception: a subclass of this type in which, through 'on-line' transactions, databases are accessed concurrently. These may be regarded as a part of 'process-oriented' applications.

3. *The process-oriented paradigm*, usually involving low or medium order properties of the two former types, but with high order time-criticality of the whole or parts of the system. Software for applications of this type frequently requires parts of a system to operate in parallel or, more properly, concurrently – and considerations of synchrony within the software system may have to be dealt with as a result. A prevalent type of application of this sort is commonly known as 'real-time, embedded systems' – although this is not a very useful term except to denote time-criticality and miniaturization at the hardware level.

4. *The rule-based paradigm*, probably involving properties of all three proeceding types – possibly to a high order, i.e. computation, data processing and time-critical processes – with the added complexity of heuristic adaptation, as in self-regulating systems that 'learn'.

Examples of these four types are as follows.

Computation intensive applications include such things as linear programming models for the solution of scheduling problems, Monte Carlo techniques for solving neutron transport problems in nuclear physics, CAD (computer aided design), and simulation in general, such as for modeling geological formations in oil exploration and so on. Often, much computer processing capacity is required, and even the use of parallel processing to reduce otherwise inordinate computation times.

Data processing intensive applications include such things as large scale financial transactions in banking, reservation systems, records' administration (inventories, personnel records, payroll), text processing systems, so-called expert systems and so forth. Often, the computer processing requirement is far exceeded by that for working and archival storage.

Process-oriented applications include all things in the field of signal processing, such as production plant and other types of control system (open and closed loop), detection and fire control for defense systems, telephony, navigation and so on. Often, special features

of a computer are required, such as the possibility to link telemetry equipment for direct interruption, as in the case of a priority signal. The processing and data storage requirements, whilst important perhaps, may be of far lesser importance. Many computer-based systems in this category are said to be 'embedded', as they are essentially components in a system of wider scope and greater technical variety.

Rule-based applications are currently more in the research than the development domain; they include robotics and so-called artificial intelligence systems. It is more than a little likely that these will require a non-classical (von Neumann) kind of computer and computing before more progress can be made, not to mention a rather firmer grasp of what human intelligence comprises than may be derived from present-day cognitive psychology. (Always bearing in mind the paradox that understanding the human brain might require an additional faculty, which would then itself require understanding, and so on.)

Programming languages may be correlated with these types, naturally since it is the properties of applications and their solutions, within types, that largely determine the properties of languages in which to program them. Thus, level 2 languages as defined earlier are widely in use for computation and data processing systems, e.g. Fortran, Basic, Pascal, Modula in the first case; and Cobol and PL/1 in the second.

The area of process applications is not well served, and languages such as RTL-2, Coral and Chill tend to be limited either by application (e.g. Chill in telephony/ telegraphy) or by geography. Coral – a language largely used by the British Ministry of Defence in the 1965–80 period – hardly traveled far outside the UK in terms of its usage, and RTL-2 has fared somewhat, but only a little, better in the period since 1975.

A similar experience befell Jovial in the USA; it was extensively but very locally utilized. As a result, much use is made of Pascal and Modula in this area, with descent into C (a 1½ level language) and assembler for the time-critical parts of process-based systems.

The reader may, at this stage, ask how Ada fits into this recital. Clearly, the pressure to adopt this language has been formidable over the past half-decade or so. Its major sponsor, the US Department of Defense, funded and encouraged the development of compilers and support environments for Ada – and yet its general adoption has been slow. As we will say elsewhere, there is a natural gestation period for innovations of this sort, possibly as long as fifteen years, whatever 'pressure' is applied by a major sponsor. It is currently unclear whether Ada will have particular virtues for time-critical applications, and even whether, 'pressure' apart, it will be widely adopted for either computation or data processing in cases where it is in competition with Fortran and Cobol.

The rule-based sector is served, basically, by languages that have not progressed far beyond the research domain and are not widely used for other application types. They include Prolog and Lisp, and – inevitably – a host of laboratory variants of these, as well as 'new' languages, some of which may emerge as languages of the future. One such, the modern development of Smalltalk, is based on an alternative view of systems and software development known as the 'object-oriented paradigm'; substantial claims are made for this approach and for the language, and these are discussed elsewhere in this series.

3.1.2 Classification by temporal properties

The different types of time-dependent systems have caused difficulties of definition over the years. In our own four classes defined above, we referred several terms to later description; there are in fact three types of temporal requirement for software:

1. *Batch* (or '*off-line*') software systems. These are for applications, generally in computation or data processing, that have no particular response-time requirements attaching to answers to human users, or replies to other parts of a system.

   The term 'batch' derives from the use of a scheduler within the virtual computer complex. This arrives at the next job, in a series of such, in sequence; the series is called a 'batch' of such jobs. The term 'off-line' is also used, occasionally, to denote a lack of time-criticality for a software (or other) system; it is derived from a practice of generating results on some intermediate device attached to the computer (tape or disk), and then using this as input to a free-standing device (typically a printer) to display the output.

   The turn-around time on results from batch systems (i.e. the duration between submitting the programs to be run on a computer and getting the results back) may be hours or even days. In the early days of computing as we know it today (circa 1950–60), all systems were 'batch'. Nowadays, very few are entirely thus, although many major computer facilities run a batch workload as a background task to more immediate time-critical applications of the following types.

2. *On-line* software systems. These are for applications, generally in computation (e.g. CAD) and data processing (e.g. transaction oriented), in which some system response within the duration of normal human reaction/interest is required. This time period is generally held to be between a few seconds – say three – and somewhat less than half a minute. Since about 1970, an increasing number of computation and data processing software based systems have become 'on-line', as has software development itself.

3. So-called *real-time* software systems. These are for applications, generally in the process sector as defined above, or for current research into rule-based systems, in which there is some extremely stringent requirement for system response, usually within a duration well below that of human reaction time.

   The dominant consideration of 'real'-time may be seen in the fact that a default in the time domain (event A in the computer system not completing before time T) causes a default in some event B, either in the computer system, or elsewhere in the outside world. The consequences of default may be severe, even catastrophic. For example, in areas such as signal-processing, where there may be a telemetry-based controller for closed-loop operation of a distillation process, within some petrochemical refining plant, and where an out of range parameter might require the closing of a valve, within, say, half a second. If other system considerations (signal transmission, mechanical operation, etc.) require, say, 0.872 seconds of this duration, then the software response, its execution time (or 'run-time' as it may be called), could be required not to exceed 0.128 seconds.

   Clearly, in this example much will depend on the speed with which the computer concerned executes instructions within it. However, much will also depend on the

efficiency of the programs, and languages such as level 2 'interpreter-based' (and perhaps, even, compiler-based) may be insufficiently efficient in the code they generate for this purpose. In these cases, for highly time-critical parts of a software system, programs are written in assembler, and 'optimized', i.e. improved to the necessary extent in terms of their execution time. This process of 'tuning' parts of a software system has dangers associated with it, for the subsequent testing and maintenance of the code, and should not be undertaken casually. The point is taken further in Chapters 7 and 9. Since about 1968 there have been an increasing number of 'real-time' applications, with a particular surge in the sector since the emergence (*circa* 1975) of the viable microprocessor/microcomputer.

Of all these terms, the one that tends to cause most trouble in its usage is 'real-time'. There are two reasons for this:

1. First, the term gets used in contexts more suitably described as 'on-line'.
2. Second, the term gets used to describe a set of problematical properties for which great care must be taken, in software design and implementation, and which are most often the *consequence*, in the first place, of an *application* type having real-time features.

It is the second of these inaccuracies that will concern us here, for its instructive content.

The term 'real-time' refers, as the definition demonstrates, to required system properties concerning response. Its connotations for software design and implementation can be severe, and the achievement of response time criteria can, in turn, lead to problems in software validation, maintenance, improvement, and adaptation. In this respect, descent into low level languages, and other ways of achieving run-time efficiency – such as clever programming with code and data optimization – will probably deplete the quality of software, perhaps to a limiting degree.

In designing and implementing software with real-time properties, one has a potential means available – process concurrency within the software – but several associated problems may arise; these are generically known as the problems of synchrony. These factors, along with the means and their derivative properties, are features of a design and implementation, and not necessarily of the application itself, unless the design of software mirrors the system processes exactly. Structural isomorphism between requirement and solution is seldom the requirement ; it is rather that the software performs the specified system functions compliantly. Usually, therefore, real-time properties of requirements lead to the design of systems in which problems of synchrony arise.

Therefore calling the concurrency/synchrony properties of a software system 'real-time' is to miss the point, doubly so if one may be using the same term (incorrectly) to describe applications with 'on-line' features. These seldom have a need for concurrency to be designed into the software, and the only questions of synchrony are likely to derive from updating databases, and retrieving from them, in an on-line system. The consequences of all this are that we should reserve the term 'real-time' to describe requirements (as we reserve 'on-line' and 'batch'), and preserve 'concurrency/synchrony' for the means of creating compliant software for them.

Clearly, some requirements will, in their achievement as computer-based software

TABLE 3.1 Applications, software types and languages, loosely related

	1. Batch	2. On-line	3. Real-time	4. Other (e.g. new approaches)
1. Computation	Fortran, Basic, Ada	Pascal, Modula-2		
2. Data-processing	Cobol, PL/1, Ada	Pascal (?), Ada, Modula-2 (?)		
3. Process-oriented			Modula-2, C, assemblers, Ada (?)	
4. Rule-based paradigm				Polog, Lisp, Smalltalk

systems, incorporate batch, on-line and real-time features, or some subset of two of these. We might, as a result, find ourselves working in the computation, data-processing, process and rule-based paradigms all within the same system and – derivatively – having a need for appropriate languages. What a babel this would be. Imagine: Modula-2, Cobol, C + assembler and (say) Prolog!

On the requirements' side of the affair, a typical example (within its context) would be an integrated on-board command and control system (e.g. on a ship) incorporating the administrative functions as a background system of batch processing with on-line access; an 'expert system' for target identification; an encoded telemetry system; gunnery computations; target detection via active sonar radar and, and an associated fire-control system in 'real-time'. The fact that the system is 'integrated' does not necessarily mean that it is centralized, nor that parts of it may be allowed to act autonomously. It may well be best implemented as a highly distributed, and connected, set of computers and software around the ship.

It is for such multivariate purposes that a special, high level language has been developed: Ada. It is sufficient to repeat that some ten years after its definition, and despite the impetus of its prescription by an oligarchic sponsor (the US Department of Defense), this language has been rather slow in its adoption. To date it has failed to replace old favorites such as Cobol, Fortran, Pascal and Modula, where it might have been expected to do so given a fair chance, not to mention the ubiquitous Basic, and (to purists) the unmentionable C and assemblers.

The previous review is summarized in Table 3.1, in which a matrix is constructed of application types and software systems' properties. Within the matrix elements, assigned rather judgmentally by the author, are some of the better-known computer languages and (roughly) their most likely usage. The category for rule-based applications is left open-ended, for obvious reasons.

There are, of course, many more level 2 programming languages than the ones listed, without ascending to level 3 (see Section 1.1) and the 'more than 400 4GLs' (Martin and Kleinrock 1985). RTL-2 and Chill, for instance, would fit into element (3, 3) in the matrix, expressing the matrix element as (row, column). Forth might well fit into (1, 1) and so on. It is all a matter of 'fit' as the author of a famous and much quoted text would say.

Other schemes of classification can also be mapped on to this one. Take, for instance, a reasonably well known definition of information technology (IT) due to the 'Butcher Committee' on IT skills' shortage in the United Kingdom. This defines seven kinds of IT product or product development activity, for all of which software is a major part, and for all of which, therefore, software engineering is crucial.

The classification is as follows (acknowledgments to Butcher 1984; amplified and slightly amended here). Along with it is an attribution, in each case, of a matrix element from Table 3.1:

1. *Electronic systems and consumer electronics*: generally mini- or microcomputer-based systems 'embedded' in products of a wider technological scope; e.g. a minicomputer as part of a tomography system in medicine, the controller for a washing machine and so on. These generally fit into category (3, 3) in Table 3.1.
2. *Telecommunication and radio frequency engineering*: these are, in fact, parts of the first class, and fit into category (3, 3) therefore.
3. *Computing* (software and hardware): categories (1, 1) and (1, 2) presumably.
4. *Computing services*: categories (2, 1) and (2, 2) presumably.
5. *Artificial intelligence, 'expert' and 'knowledge based' systems*: category (4, 4) as to the first, and (2, 2) as to the other two.
6. *Communications between electronic data processors*: a subject of class 2 since the digitization of telephony systems; properly, therefore, in category (3, 3), although what they are communicating might be in any other class on this list.
7. *Design and production of manufactured products*; thus CAD (computer-aided design), CAM or CAE (computer aided manufacture or engineering), and CAT (computer aided testing). Of these, CAD is in category (1, 2) generally – with some aspects of (2, 2) also; CAM is in (3, 3) and its robotics cognate is a mixture of (3, 3) and (4, 4); CAT is firmly in (3, 3).

If nothing else, this exercise should have shown that other schemes of classification are mappable. It also reveals the weaknesses of the original IT taxonomy. Not least, when the language connotations are listed from Table 3.1, it helps to clarify why some IT applications, such as integrated manufacturing design, production and product testing systems, have failed to materialize in the quantities expected.

Another way in which we can usefully classify software systems is by their size. This is particularly revealing, for it throws light on issues of staffing, team organization and management of software engineering.

3.1.3 Classification of software systems by size

In speaking of software size, the metric normally used is that of source code statements. Now this will require some explanation, as it is not a precise term and can therefore easily be misrepresented or mistaken for other, cognate issues. Nor is it a particularly good metric for either this or other use (for instance, divided by the effort to achieve it, source code size is often, wrongly, taken as a metric for productivity). The fact is, software size is not source code size at all, since there is at least a one pass translation,

TABLE 3.2 Gradation of software system size

Size	Examples
'Small', up to 2,000 source statements	Games on a PC; embedded systems of limited functionality such as the program-setting controller on a car radio
'Medium', *c.* 2,000–100,000 source statements	A very wide range of computing, data-processing and process applications, such as for matrix inversion, payroll, etc., CAD/CAE
'Large', *c.* 100,000–1,000,000 source statements	Operating systems for computers, including most 'virtual' features but not full Ipse facilities (q.v.). Extensive computation and simulation systems and full-scale administrative systems for (e.g.) banking transactions. Artificial intelligence and 'expert' systems
'Very large', over 1,000,000 source statements	Large scale command and control systems, weather forecasting, medical tomography, higher order 'AI' and expert systems SDI = 'Star Wars'

and in most cases a two pass translation to obtain computer-executable bit strings from low or high level language programs.

Nonetheless, for our purposes here, the source code size in the form of its expression (i.e. as Ada statements, assembler or whatever) is the method we choose – for reasons that will become evident. First of all, though, a classification; by statements of source code we do not mean *lines* of source code, unless the two are synonymous. For example, in assembler, the two are the same:

MPY TIME

This is a statement of source code and a line of object code. On the other hand, in high level languages one may have multi-line statements; in this case it counts as one statement. Also within an integrand or program there will be working data such as constants, and storage definition or allocation for partial results and so on. These are generally included as source code statements. Not so any in-line comments in the code, as these will be ignored by the compiler/interpreter/assembler as being not properly part of the integrand or program, so much as part of its documentation.

With these clarifications made, we can define – within rough limits of a judgmental convention – what might be a small, medium sized, large and very large software system (see Table 3.2). Remember, that we regard it as irrelevant for this purpose whether the source language is second (high) or first (low) level – although this will have a profound effect on the real software size – known as the 'object code' size, to distinguish it from the 'source code' size.

The main significance in this is, as already said, for the staffing and organization connotations that follow from task size. This aspect of software engineering is dealt with at length elsewhere in this volume (see Section 13.4). It is sufficient to note that small

systems are generally done by a single person, or a very small 'team' of two. Since we will define a viable software team size at a median value of 5 ± 1, we can say something about the resourcing of levels of software system other than that of the smallest. Medium sized software systems, on our rough scale, generally require one to three 'teams' depending on which end of the range they occupy, and the time to achieve the software as a properly validated and working system. Large scale software systems can occupy up to fifteen teams and, whereas the larger of medium sized software systems is probably achievable in a 3–4 year period, large systems may take 5–7 years to make.

Very large systems are in a class of their own, in more ways than one. 'SDI' has been estimated as requiring somewhere between 30 and 100 million source statements of program code. This daunting prospect may be expected to occupy about 300 software teams over a period of, perhaps, fifteen years – whatever the gloss placed on this prospect by advocates of the enterprise. Of course, all 'estimates' such as the one I have just done are based more on analogy than any process relating to the detail of real designs for the intended systems. The only purpose of my 'calculation' is to indicate the extreme non-linearity of staffing requirements with software size in order to preserve some semblance of control in the time domain.

If the resourcing was to be constrained (e.g. trying to do a mega-source statement system with the resources for a medium sized development), then the factors in the time domain would go wild. The reverse effect is generally even more dramatic; see Section 12.5. Then, a compression of time-scale leads to extremely non-linear increases in required effort, and very often the effect is that the job cannot be done at all on these terms. These, too, are properties of software systems, and ones that will occupy us considerably elsewhere in this volume, and in Volume 5. In the meantime the reader might like to dwell on the question: how are 15 teams of software engineers managed on a single development, let alone the glorious prospect of 300 teams for ultra-large systems? The answer must be, rather like one concerning porcupines mating, with some difficulty, and very carefully.

We now turn to other properties of software systems, such as their purpose, other than that of immediate application type; the 'version' and contract purposes. Any relief felt at leaving the intimidations of large and ultra-large team constructions will soon fade as we approach these subjects.

3.1.4 Classification by purpose

We will consider, from the viewpoint of definition only here, the following classifications for software systems:

1. Prototypes.
2. Projects.
3. Products.

Each of these will be the object of further reference elsewhere in this volume; here they will each be accorded a definitive paragraph in the order of the list.

PROTOTYPES

The issue of prototype development can be contentious, as Section 2.2 attests. We will not revisit those issues here. Simply stated, *prototype development is the process of buying information*. In particular, in software engineering, one may be buying information for one of two distinct reasons.

1. That insufficient is known about the requirements.
2. That insufficient is known about the means of solution – actually how to develop a software system to provide the requirements, given that these are sufficiently well known.

The first of these are known, obviously, as 'requirements' prototypes' – or some manifest variant of that name. The second are called 'feasibility prototypes', again for quite obvious reasons. There is far more than this to be said about each of these, and it is set out in appropriate sections elsewhere. However, there is one property of all prototypes – already mentioned in Section 2.2 – that requires as strenuous and frequent repeating as may be commensurate with good taste. That is that prototypes may be the *basis* for a dependable version of an artefact; they must never (stress 'never') be taken *for* that dependable version. I cannot speak for the reader, but I am disinclined to travel in a prototype car, or on a prototype airplane or ship; a prototype dentist's drill in my mouth would fill me with a nameless foreboding; and a prototype life-support system suggests to me a contradiction in terms. These are unsubtle hints. The author feels strongly about misclassifying and misusing prototypes.

The simple fact is that the main imperative of prototypes – that of buying information, usually at the lowest cost in effort and time – is inimical to the quality of the artefact produced. The expressions 'bread-board version', 'mock-up' and 'quick and dirty' generally apply. To trespass into the argument about iterative development, for an instant only, it is not clear how iterative prototype development, toward a compliant system (i.e. one that 'fits' requirements in all respects), will achieve real quality in other senses.

Prototypes should be labeled clearly, and software engineering that involves prototyping must be designated clearly in those part of the process. Indeed, some would agree with S. J. Perelmann, who wrote scripts for the Marx brothers; where prototypes are concerned, when the information sought and bought has been acquired and used – then, concerning the prototype itself 'Insert flap A, and throw away'.

PROJECTS

The development of either projects or products may, in principle, include prototypes, although it is in the nature of things (as will become evident) that product development is the one more likely to incorporate prototypes. In fact, in some circumstances, projects may have to exclude prototyping for reasons of contractual pressures and imperatives to deliver to a stringent time-scale. This is a problem for the hyper-modernists who claim iterative development (in effect, hopefully convergent prototyping) as a new method in software engineering. Let us see why. Projects, in the software sense, are developments undertaken for a *single, identifiable end client*. They may be part of a wider context of

development and supply, and most often involve explicit and potentially stringent contract terms between client and supplier.

Contractual matters are dealt with in greater detail elsewhere in this text; it is sufficient here to note that stringent terms of supply are often called 'contracts of fixed price and time', whereas their less exacting counterparts might be called 'time and materials supply' or 'cost plus fixed fee' or a variety of variant terms.

A software development for a single, identifiable end client, has the advantages (or should have) of a clear *source* of requirements and an equally clear agency for the acceptance, or rejection, of the final artefacts. Whoever is to do the development can interrogate the 'users' or 'users' representatives' to adduce their needs, and can later confirm with them that they have been supplied.

As will be appreciated, there is a clear difference here between circumstances under different terms of supply. In one case, say an internal 'project' development within a company, or an external 'time and materials' contract, there may be prototyping needed to identify requirements or clarify technical means. However, for the most part, software projects are done to fixed price and time-scale contracts (or some pseudonymous equivalent for internal supplies within a company), and anything but the most rudimentary prototyping – such as to define 'user interfaces' – is excluded for obvious reasons of conflict between the imponderability of prototyping, and the rigors of the 'contract'.

By the large, projects are the stuff from which the 'classical' life cycles, referred to in Section 2.2, have been built. In the contracting sense, software development projects represent a substantial proportion of work proceeding in software engineering – including some contracted project supplies within what is otherwise a product development. In some sectors, such as supply to major governmental procurement agencies (e.g. defense organizations) and large companies in the electronics and telecommunications field, fixed-price 'project' supply is increasing as a proportion of overall software procurement. No other form of software development places so high a premium on good software engineering practice, particularly management, as a 'project' does.

PRODUCTS

Products, on the other hand, are artefacts developed for a *plurality* of end clients. They may include externally (or internally) contracted supplies on a real (or pseudo-) fixed price, 'project' basis, for subsystems. They will frequently involve prototyping of both types defined above, and the premium placed on good software engineering practice will be high, especially for the management of a product development, for somewhat different reasons from that for a 'project'.

Products are mainly undertaken by companies ambitious to sell many units of the product to a defined market sector. The degree of definition of this market may be imprecise and access to it will, for a clarification of requirements, certainly not be definitive. This serves to highlight a particular requirement in product development. It is clear that no single identifiable end client is available to specify requirements, and to pass judgment (acceptance or rejection) on the product when it is finally made. The worst that can happen is that *everyone* in the product development company assumes a role in these matters, but no responsibility for them. Chaos ensues, which however innovative a chaos it is, is chaos nonetheless.

The correct way of proceeding is to nominate a 'surrogate user/client', usually from the product marketing department. This person, or small group, should then act as the agency for specification and acceptance of the product, and act at all intermediate stages as would a client for supplies from an external source or sources. In fact the supplies can be contracted by the 'surrogate' if they are to be from external sources, and can (and should) be 'pseudo-contracted' if they are from internal sources, such as the technical laboratory on the next floor.

Any prototype development within a product will require especially careful management lest that whole process become inchoate. This can quite easily happen; I have seen many instances of it, where the development seems to take on a life of its own, without clear review or decision points by which to regulate it. The existence of a 'pseudo-client' and 'pseudo-contracts' must have enough reality about them to avoid these dangers. The argument that 'we can't pseudo-contract old Fred's technical laboratory upstairs' is, or should be, specious. It is a 'happy families' argument that usually leaves two branches of the family singularly miserable – the managing director and the financial controller!

These, then, are the famous three Ps – prototypes, projects and products – about which much more will be said, progressively, in this text. There now remains one more, most useful, way to classify software systems. This scheme is due to Lehman who, some years ago, addressed himself (and colleagues) to the problem of versions of project or product software. As a result of this, there were ennunciated several 'laws' to account for software evolution (Lehman 1980), and three main types of program.

3.1.5 Lehman's classification

This classification is known generally as the 'S, P or E' property of programs with the following meanings:

1. S programs; or those derived from a fixed, formal *specification*.
2. P programs; or those derived from an inexact formulation of a real world *problem*.
3. E programs; or those whose derivation will be likely to change through their being *embedded* in a part of the real world.

A short description of each is in order. Before doing so it is useful to note that Lehman's work is very much in the domain of computer science, and explicitly concerns programs. By a slight adjustment, it is equally valid as a classification system for software, with the terms, S, P and E meaning 'specifiable', 'programmable' and 'evolvable' respectively. We proceed, on this basis, with a discussion of S, P and E software, with acknowledgement to the original work.

S systems refer to software systems that are formally specifiable and, therefore, provable; moreover their specification will be invariant, not only during development but thereafter. Typical of this class are small problems in computation of the form:

$$\sum_{i=1}^{100} X_i$$

denoting the sum of all integers from 1 to 100. This is a formal specification, and invariant. The operative term in this example is 'small'. S software systems are generally very small in source code statements; 500–1,000 source statements of code will cover most S software requirements. This is seldom the stuff of 'real' software engineering, as Table 3.2 shows. Lehman has done a service in discriminating a class of software system that is, in fact, the main province of hobbyists and people learning to program; S software systems are also the object, often, of computer scientists, serving as vehicles for demonstration.

P software systems, or programmable ones, are precisely (but not, necessarily, 'formally') specifiable at a high generic level of definition, but their means of solution will be an approximation. A typical example would be a complex scheduling or rostering system whose solution may be a 'minimax' linear programming approximation. Weather-forecasting systems are in this class, as are chess-playing systems.

Specifying the high level requirement is easy; evolving ways to do it (in software) is not. Unlike the case of S software, P systems are not invariant. However, their incidence of change is due less to variation in the specification than to improvement in the means of solution. The rate of change of this factor in P software is usually slow – five, ten and more years are not uncommon for algorithms to be in vogue. Also unlike S software, P systems are not usually small. They can be anywhere in size from the upper end of 'medium' right through to 'very large' on our rough, judgmental scale. P software is very much the stuff of software engineering, although not, perhaps, quite so manifestly thus as the last category, E software.

E or evolvable, software is both specifiable and solvable, although it does not necessarily follow that the specification will be 'formal', or that the solution will be provable as with S systems. The specification may be produced by some informal process, as described further in Chapter 5; the solution means may, or may not, involve prototypes. However, the specification is known to be a temporary one, an approximation that happens to be valid at the time but will probably change over some period. Consequently, the software 'solution' will have to be evolved from time to time. The possible reasons why requirements evolve are threefold:

1. Natural change in circumstances, such as alterations in the organization of a company that change its information-flow.
2. Changes in circumstances brought on by the E software itself, e.g. traffic patterns around a signaling system.
3. Improvements in technical means in the requirements' domain (as for P systems in the solution domain), such as the advent of word processing technology and the impact it has had on office automation.

E software systems, and to a lesser extent P software, are the stuff of software engineering. In fact, it is the E property of the object within software engineering that has caused the most furious perplexity (or just fury) over the past three decades. For the truth is that, so poorly are most software systems made, the vast majority of what should be E software artefacts are not evolvable with any degree of confidence. The reasons for this, and their remedies, are the subject of this series. E software is of any and all known forms of application (computation, data processing, process-oriented, rule-based), and

comes in all conceivable sizes on our rough scale of values. It can be project or product, and its achievement – the software engineering done to make it – can involve prototypes, with the caveat already posted about that activity.

E systems can contain P systems and vice versa; integrands can be defined as very small S systems and, within extremely strict and clear rules of inference concerning the outcome, may be totally consistent with Lehman's definition being, up to a point, capable of proof or disproof. This argument, a contentious issue at the present time, is taken forward in Volume 4 of this series.

3.1.6 Summary

In concluding this rather extensive section, it may be advisable to revise the issues. We have set up five different ways of classifying software according to its requirement characteristics as well as the immanent properties of a software system once made. There are 432 permutations within these classifications, assuming (an approximate truth only) that a software system can bear only one characteristic out of each class. The usefulness for shared discourse between parties to the process of software engineering must be obvious. In one terse sentence, the whole context of some endeavor may be conveyed: 'The job I am working on is a large, on-line system, generally of the P type, predominantly computational. I am working on a prototype for one of the algorithms; the overall system will be a project supply'. What could be clearer or more succinct? Now we know the scope and scale of what we're talking about.

Or do we?

3.2 COMPLEXITY, AND OTHER BANES

Because of the troubles people have with software being intangible and not soft, and some co-lateral problems with the process of software engineering itself, there is much discomfiture about the whole conflation of software artefacts and their development. The best and clearest examples of this are usually to be found amongst product and project development managers in suppliers of IT equipment or services. These people are usually engineers of some sort by background; electronic, mechanical or production. After some exposure to the world of software development, the impression is gained (and perhaps the foregoing chapters will not have mitigated it), that the whole issue is miasmic.

I have, over the years, been confronted by highly intelligent men and women clearly at the end of their tether about this. 'Even so', they retort after the most sedulous exposition on the real and supposed vicissitudes of software engineering, 'Even so, the whole issue is dreamlike to us. We hear the words and even understand them, but it still all seems unreal, metaphysical'. Pursued further, this problem usually separates into four distinct questions, some of which we have already faced:

1. What is software, and what is software engineering? (This is generally seen as one, conflated question.)

2. What is invisible, and what is not?
3. Are there any limits to software systems, given a finite specification?
4. Is software inherently more complex than other human creations?

Lest the reader despairs of questions like this, let me be precise. They, and their like, do not occur on a few, isolated occasions; they are the stuff of most orientation courses in software engineering for non-vocational specialists in that subject. Their occurrence is at the heart of the software engineering 'crisis' of popular reference. They are legitimate questions that redound to the credit of the enquirer, and any fault occurring is the responsibility of the hapless 'expert' who has to answer.

We shall, in the fashion of earlier chapters, take a few paragraphs for each of 2 and 3. The first question, a dyad, has been the subject (at some length) of Chapters 1 and 2. Question 4 will be the subject of the rest of this chapter, taking incidentally, far more than just a paragraph. This method too follows closely the organic development of an orientation course in the subject; there comes a time at which the phobia underlying these questions can be articulated, and that is usually after issues such as 'what is software?' and 'what is software engineering?' have been covered.

Question 2 is 'What is invisible and what is not?' This problem remorselessly recurring, causes difficulty to non-specialists. It gets confused and conflated over issues of what applies to software and what applies to software engineering. In fact, the question is exceedingly easy to answer now that the definitions and explanations in Chapter 1 are behind us.

So far as software is concerned it, being dynamic and intangible, is invisible – just as the electric current motivating your reading lamp is invisible. Its effects (like those of the lamp) may be clearly evident, but the cause itself is, nonetheless, invisible. Programs, on the other hand, being the static and linguistic expression of the software needed to produce a certain effect, are visible, e.g. as printed listings or strings of statements depicted on a VDU screen.

So, software is invisible; what then of software engineering? Here we confront a *process*, not an intangible artefact behaving dynamically, and the simple answer about invisibility is that any and all parts of the process are – within limits – as visible as one makes them. We will return to these 'limits' eventually but, in the first place, we must deal with the subsidiary question of how one makes a human-based process 'visible'. The answer is obvious in this case – by active involvement of the managers of such processes, including their direct (or commissioned) inspection of such tangible outcomes as are produced during the process. In software engineering, these 'tangible' outcomes are requirements' specifications, plans and estimates, systems and software designs, programs, test plans, tests and results, and the documentation pertaining to the developed software. All these are detailed elsewhere in this volume (see Chapter 5, etc.), and the management methods – for example 'structured walkthrough' – are described in Part III. Managing the software development process to achieve visibility *vis à vis* its 'tangible outcomes' at specific stages requires some conceptual model of the process – and this takes us back again to the issue of life cycles.

The limits to inspection are the natural and normal ones attaching to any stage that might still be in the process of completion. A person or people may not yet have

completed the requirements' specification. Or the design may be at a highly dynamic stage with only the most rudimentary visible evidence of actual achievement; or implementation staff may be creating integrands and programs by interactions with VDU equipment (or, seemingly, by just sitting and clutching a fevered brow – their own, or someone else's), and so on.

The argument that the whole process of software development is an intellectual exercise, or that some part is particularly so, and that only limited amounts of a mental process get recorded, must be countered. People are more disinclined than unable to record their mental process, believing this to be 'uncreative'. Good management of software development must combat and transcend this disinclination.

These, then, are the limitations on inspection of creative processes during the creative act. Although they are not serious limitations on the visibility of the whole process of software engineering, the question is raised of *intelligibility* of some 'deliverables' which may be inspected – *viz.* specifications, designs, programs, tests, software documentation. For – it might be thought – visibility without intelligibility may just as well be invisibility.

In truth, some of the 'tangible outcomes' during software engineering are unintelligible to a 'lay' audience (some are even a bit impenetrable for adepts, if it comes to that – depending on how well the job has been documented at that stage). Designs and programs are particular instances of this. The way round this unintelligibility, if and when it occurs, is to commission inspection by other, accredited experts in the subject. This, then, becomes visibility with derived intelligibility, and is as good as the real thing if the inspectors are real experts.

So, in summary, software is invisible but the process of developing it is largely visible, although sometimes (i.e. on occasions, to some) it may be unintelligible in parts.

Question 3 is 'Are there any limits to software systems, given a finite specification?' This is another quite fearsome problem for many people whose view of computing may fluctuate between extremes of awe ('It's the new industrial revolution') and contempt ('Did you see what that cretinous computer did to the payroll this month?'). The simple answer is that 'yes', there are limits to software, as might have been expected given the Lehman classification of P systems. These limitations are, however, sometimes not evident at the design and programming levels; they often concern the 'run-time' behavior of the software itself.

Software limitations come about, when they do occur, through the specification of requirements that are beyond available technical means to achieve. A simple and extreme example will suffice to demonstate this. We are to make a computer-based, chess-playing system that will: (a) achieve an 'Elo rating' of not less than 3,000 on that recognized scale of competence, i.e. it will regularly beat the current world champion, and (b) that it responds, by displaying its next move on a screen, within 0.1 second of the opponent's move being entered.

It will be clear in this example that there is an extreme unlikelihood that software can be developed whose execution time, for the most complex combinatorial analysis needed, will permit sufficient residual time for the display within 0.1 second. Equally, it is clear that any software would be compliant in its response time if the equipment (computer hardware, electrical coupling, screen) worked quickly enough. But that, as we have seen, is an integral aspect of software as distinct from programs. A grandmaster-

level chess-playing system would probably require the evaluation of thousands of move-permutations for each response, and this would cause the execution of, perhaps, millions of program instructions each time. It would take special hardware indeed to do all this, and display the outcome, in 0.1 second.

So, software may be limited by timing requirements on the specifications. Are there other limitations to software or to its constituent programs?

Again the answer is yes, and again the restraints are due to insufficiency in technical means to achieve some fairly (or very) stringent requirement. Thus, for instance, we may require that the chess system supposed to floor the world champion must be written on a generally available computer such as a Digital Equipment VAX, in programs not exceeding 150 statements of object (i.e. level 1) code, or occupying not more than 500 bytes of random access memory, or some such. The size aspects of computer programs are explained elsewhere (see Chapter 6), but it will already be clear that we will never make a super grandmaster-level chess program by such insufficient means.

These are extreme examples for purposes of illustration. We would say, on encountering such in real life, that they suffered from manifestly *infeasible specification*. In other, less obvious, cases, we might have to say that the specification – whilst seemingly feasible in terms of solution means – *might* prove beyond technical means. In these cases, we are confronted with indeterminacy in software development, when we cannot categorically say that a computer-based software system will be possible for the requirements.

Viewed as a formal issue in logic – the categorical, prior computation of what of the specification can be implemented on the equipment, and with the means available – most non-trivial computer applications are indeterminate. However, we usually embark on software development after some less stringent evaluation of feasibility and the adequacy of resources, effectively certain that the job concerned can be done, and that software can be made to fit the requirements' specification. In the rare instances when this is not the case, when the feasibility exercise has been wrong in fact, the prohibitions may not become clear until fairly late in the software engineering process. In life cycle terms, we may be some way into design, or even implementation, before some basic infeasibility becomes evident.

This properly of some software, that its successful implementation may be indeterminate, even after a most sedulous exercise in feasibility, is substantially different from the notion of Turing and Church that anything that can be specified, as algorithms and data, can be *programmed* given a machine and a language of suitable characteristics. For software, one must be especially careful of inherent infeasibility between specification and means – as in the case of the very extreme examples given.

So, in summary, we can say that there may be limitations to developing software for certain specifications which, however finite, contain inherent infeasibility given the prevailing means. One's inability to tell in advance (the 'decidability') whether such specifications are, or are not, feasible is often due to factors better dealt with in answer to the next question.

Question 4 is 'Is software inherently more complex than other human creations?' The simple answer here is 'probably yes', with the obvious exception of our biological generation of other humans – which is in a different category of endeavor altogether. In

fact, it is exceedingly difficult to imagine any human construction, material or conceptual, that rivals the elaborateness of a large software system. Some creations in chess resemble the determination of valid (i.e. 'winning') permutations in an extensive behavior space. Some music resembles software in its complexity, and a music score may be seen as the analog of the program. But, by and large, no other human creation rivals even a medium sized software system, in either constructional complexity or in the scope of its possible behavior space.

In fact, the complexity of software systems is, itself, many-faceted. We can identify three basic sources of complexity:

1. Complexity of intention.
2. Complexity of implementation.
3. Complexity of interaction.

We shall deal with these in turn. Complexity of intention concerns the scope of requirements that result in a computer-based software system; complexity of implementation concerns the design and programming of software systems; complexity of interaction concerns the dynamic behavior of software.

As in previous cases, we will give a numbered subsection to each item, as here we are concerned only with basic concepts and definitions, and detailed treatment of the three issues will be done in the appropriate volumes ('intention' in Volume 2; 'implementation' in Volumes 3 and 4; 'interaction' in Volume 5).

A summary of the various theoretical treatments of complexity is given in Section 3.3.

3.2.1 Complexity of intention

Complexity of intention concerns requirements' specification, and in particular how one is to apprehend the complexity of solution that attaches to a relatively simple expression of need. A simple example may be taken from the area of store-and-forward message switching, a subject in telecommunication technology.

A set of sources S_i emits messages of variable length and priority, at whatever frequency and in whatever order is the case. They are destined for, and addressed to, a set of known destinations D_j; a maximum transmission time between sources and destinations is attached. All messages are sent to a central message switching computer C, and routed from there to the destinations.

The central computer performs message validation checks on the incoming messages, and certification checks on emitted messages, as well as 'cut through' functions for rapid routing of the priority messages. To prevent chaos, all incoming messages are stored, then processed in some order (e.g. for validity, involving an ACK/NACK conversation with the source), then queued and finally transmitted – again with validation.

All this sounds so simple; we can even draw a childish diagram of it (see Figure 3.1). The complexity of a system that provides these simply stated features is, however, much more formidable than the picture shows. An idea of this complexity may be seen from the following list of elementary questions, restricted to four only here, although many more could be formulated:

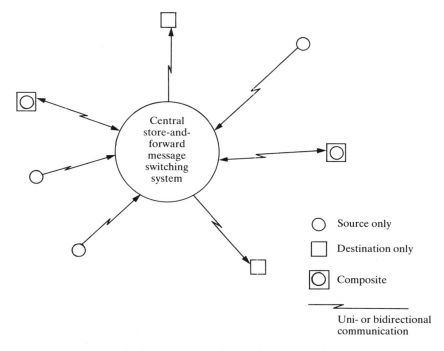

FIGURE 3.1 Example of a simply stated requirement for a store-and-forward message switching system.

1. How are first level buffers and hierarchies of overflow buffers to be arranged for incoming messages?
2. How are priorities to be handled, i.e. on an interrupt basis or by a polled signal?
3. What happens to incoming messages if the central message switch is busy with a priority message?
4. What happens if the maximum transmission time is exceeded?

These complexities may take the most elaborate system and software design to deal with, even though the specification was, on the face of it, bland.

The moral of this is that solution complexity is very easily imported by apparently harmless statements in a specification. What is more, and worse, it can be virtually impossible to realize that these consequences are present at the time of specification.

There is, effectively, no antidote to this. Once again, the suggestion may be made that early prototyping will at least show up the areas of difficult or complex implementation, and Zave's work (1982) indicates the truth of this. However, knowledge is not circumvention. The ineluctable consequences of specification may be realized before they occur but, without changing the specification, they will occur.

An essential palliative to the problem lies in a process of progressively detailing the requirements, and ordering this detail, the outcome is what we call (if done properly) a 'functional specification' of the requirements, which should be sufficiently detailed to highlight the areas of especial complexity (see Chapter 5; and Volume 2). Nonetheless,

that complexity will remain if the requirements from which it derives remain; we will merely have illuminated it – via the functional specification – early enough to evaluate (or investigate) its consequences, such as the time and resources that may be required to develop a system to meet the requirements, the feasibility of doing so, and so on.

3.2.2 Complexity of implementation

This is the tendency to unnecessary complexity of programs, and their interrelationships, and compounds the complexity due to specification defined above. It has been an area of study since the period, some twenty years ago, when program complexity became recognized as a major impediment to validation, maintenance and emendation of software systems. Consequently, several approaches were suggested for reducing complexity of designs and programs. The principal 'laws' that emerged were as follows:

1. Maximum cohesion, minimal coupling in program design.
2. Single decision in an integrand, and information hiding in order to ensure the self-containment of parts of a software system.
3. Formal structure of an integrand.

These advances were due largely to Constantine, Myers *et al.*; and Parnas; and Dijkstra, Hoare, Jackson *et al.* respectively. A brief account of each follows, and they are explained at greater length in Volumes 3 and 4.

COHESION AND COUPLING IN PROGRAM STRUCTURES
Cohesion and coupling refer to the mutual relationships of integrands within programs, and between programs themselves. The distinction is not entirely precise, since there is no 'law' that says when a piece of code is an integrand and when it is a program, nor any 'law' determining how programs are composed of integrands. We might compose one program of eight integrands, and another of two, depending on their generic similarity, authorship, etc. Similarly, there is no hard and fast rule concerning the 'packaging' of programs into what are known as program load-modules; this, too, proceeds on the basis of generic relationship and authorship, limited by considerations of size and utility.

The guidelines for good structure, in these mutual relationships between integrands or programs, were formulated along the following lines by Constantine and Yourdon (1979):

Cohesion: Level 0 – coincidental	No meaningful relationship between elements of a structure.
Level 1 – logical	All elements of a structure relate to some external, generic function in requirements, e.g. all input routines.
Level 2 – temporal	All elements of a structure are related by their sequence within the run-time systems, e.g. this before that, and then the following.
Level 3 – functional	All elements of a structure relate to a generic class of functions in the solution, e.g. all polynomial func-

	tions for computing logarithms, hyperbolic trigo-nomeric functions, and so on.
Level 4 – abstract	All elements operate on, or serve, one data structure and may then be said to be 'abstracted by data type'.
Coupling: Level 0 – direct	One element directly references others, or parts of others, without access controls or privacy rules.
Level 1 – common	Two or more elements have access to data in common data areas – a particular feature of programming languages such as Fortran.
Level 2 – block	Low level elements (e.g. integrands) refer to higher level elements in a program's block structure when composed in languages such as Algol and Pascal.
Level 3 – import/export	An element may list the names of other elements to which it will grant access and, conversely, to which it will require access – a regulatory property of some modern languages such as Ada.
Level 4 – procedure	All transformations between elements are represented as procedure calls in the programming language, and transmit only single element parameters.

Cohesion represents the strength of a structure (program or program package). Coupling concerns the logical and minimal interdependence of its components. Ideally, one designs for a clear and rational structure at the level of cohesion, and ends up with a composite of high level cohesion types; one also designs for a simple structure in terms of coupling, i.e. tending to level 4 on this scale also.

LOCALIZATION IN PROGRAM SUBSTRUCTURES

Information hiding is a concept due, principally, to Parnas. The aim is to develop a program structure in which each integrand encapsulates – or 'hides' – a single design decision. The originator of the approach advocated preparation of a list of particularly difficult design issues, or components of an overall design, that may be thought most likely to be changed after the software system had been validated and put into service. These 'difficult' and 'volatile' parts of a design then become the object of especial attention in implementation, with the design of an integrand proceeding on the basis of encapsulating the unique decision, designing the functions to be performed to arrive at the decision, and the rigorous disablement of more general functionality of an integrand through the dedication (i.e. 'hiding') of its purpose. The localization of data through the concepts of 'own' rather than global variables and parameter values, is a means to this end. This tends to make program structures easier to change, since the effects of changing an integrand are localized; in fact if they are not so, then the principle of information hiding has been violated.

CODE STRUCTURES AT THE MICROSCOPIC LEVEL

The formal structure of integrands and, thereby, programs in general, is achieved by adherence of principles of programming first enunciated by (among other) Dijkstra and

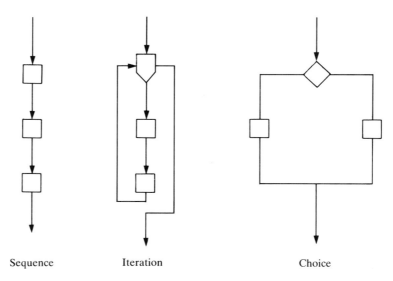

Sequence   Iteration   Choice

FIGURE 3.2 Basic constructs in structured code.

Jackson; these are widely known, at the present time, as the principles of structured programming. Being, largely, the product of computer science in the first place, structured programming has a formal definition that proceeds roughly as follows (acknowledgment to the *Dictionary off Computing*, Glaser *et al.* 1983).

Programs, or parts of programs ('integrands' in our terminology), are seen as composites of algorithms and data structures. When a program (or integrand) specification exists, an ideal machine is formulated that offers features for implementing the algorithms and data structures; this is said to be the first level of 'abstract machine'. A second level of abstract machine is then formulated on which to implement the algorithms and data structures of the first, and so on repetitively until the next formulation may conveniently by done in the chosen programming language.

The aims and means of this approach are heavily influenced by an overall objective to prove a program's correctness. At a more pragmatic level, a way of achieving relatively simple code within integrands (at the highest level of 'abstract machine' needed in the structured programing approach) depends on the use of three basic constructs which can be depicted in simple flowgraphs – as in Figure 3.2.

These coding constructs are sufficient, in combination, for any programming eventualities and – as formulated – appear strictly to avoid the use of unconditional transfers of control, of the type represented by the GO TO statement in high level languages. Each construct depicts one entry point and one exit for an integrand, and seeks to avoid the use of GO TO (and similar unconditional transfers) within integrands. In practice, code without GO TO statements is an abstraction seldom realized and widely held to be not worth inordinate effort to achieve. What is regarded as 'good programming practice' allows carefully, even minimally, utilized GO TO (or similar) unconditional transfer statements, so as to avoid a rat's nest appearance of the control flow of programs.

These, then, are the approaches for containing complexity in design and implementation: cohesion, coupling, single decision/information hiding; and the derivate of structured programming known as structured coding. Adherence to these principles ensures not that the outcome (integrands, programs, program packages, software load-modules, etc.) will lack complexity, but that the issue of program (and ultimately software) complexity will be *contained* at the level of *inherent complexity* for the application concerned, and will tend to exclude gratuitous complexity through careless design and implementation.

Failure to proceed in the ways recommended will almost certainly ensure the totally unnecessary 'complexity of design and implementation' such as befell many software systems of medium size and upwards, made in the period prior to 1980. The consequences deriving from this failure alone have been – in extreme cases – unmaintainable software. Since about 1975–80, there has been a steadily increasing, absolute, amount of 'good' programs written as a result of these precepts in design and coding. But the effect has been seriously masked by the even greater rate of increase in the total amount of software being developed by 'amateur programmers' who may be unaware of the basic principles of good design and programming practices, or operating under such limitations of time-scale and effort that 'good practice' is sacrificed.

3.2.3 Complexity of interaction

We have remarked elsewhere that software is the dynamic behavior of programs on the equipment for which they were written, and that the possible behavior of a software system in its correct, incorrect and accidental operations usually represents a large number of outcome permutations in the 'behavior space' of the system as a whole.

This, too, is an aspect of software complexity. In cases of relatively untested software systems, the behavioral complexity may be extremely severe. As if, for instance, one wrote programs amounting to (say) 20,000 source statements of Pascal code, and then without further ado – no testing of small parts in isolation and combination – fired the whole lot into the target computer, and attempted its execution.

In these circumstances, one might wander round the behavior space of the system for ever. The antidote to the problem is, of course, to test the software on some more rational basis such as component (e.g. integrand) testing and the progressive integration and testing of components. This, and the subsequent usage of a software system, performs, in effect, a controlled investigation of a part of the behavior space. As all who have ever dealt with large, complex software systems will know, that is only part of the problem. The unexplored behavior space of a software system looms like a predatory animal over all its operations.

These then are the factors that compound software complexity.

The original question in this section was: 'Is software inherently more complex than other human creations?' The 'penny in the slot' answer was affirmative, and perhaps the reader will now see why. Obviously, simple requirements lead to simple systems – as in the case of the type S software referred to earlier. In general, though, software is complex in its formulation, implementation and behavior. Creating it can be like com-

posing a musical symphony whose integrity is at issue; understanding software – even if you have made it yourself – can be like trying to comprehend all the features of several grandmaster chess games considered simultaneously.

Of all the worst pieces of news it is my fate to reveal, as in music and chess, there are no established and generally accepted metrics for measuring the complexity of a software system, although there is much research into this topic.

3.3 THEORETICAL APPROACHES, AND RESEARCH INTO COMPLEXITY METRICS

This is a daunting subject, highly conjectural and extremely mathematical in places, magnetically interesting in parts and implausible in places. It tends to frustrate and infuriate students on education courses because it merits attention but has arrived at few useful conclusions as yet. There is a general problem, in a work such as this, to determine the level of address where some subjects or topics are concerned, and the detail into which it is proper to go. Theoretical 'models' of software complexity is one such area. As this volume is intended as a primer for practitioners and an orientation for non-specialists, the matter resolves itself rather easily in this case.

Complexity theory is, in itself, of little potential use (whatever its achieved plausibility, or even truth) unless it, in turn, yields metrics and methods for assessing and dealing with real-life problems in software engineering. For instance, it tells me nothing to learn that the XYZ software has a complexity factor of 387.9 on some scale of values. It may help a little if I know that XYZ is a payroll system developed by Joe Soap and his amateur programmers from East Orange; that it was developed on a notched stick and is to be run on a CRETIN-I computer of specified attributes, that it is 49,821 source statements of code in Mumble, the wonder language, and so on. When I meet a similar system in future I *may* (stress the qualification) have some grounds for assessing its possible complexity if it is implemented in exactly the same way; or conversely, hearing that some unspecified system has a corresponding complexity (387.9 on this hypothetical scale), I may infer its characteristics by analogy and react accordingly – run for the high hills in this case.

Complexity metrics are, however, virtuous in their own right, of use only if they correlate with factors in software engineering such as estimating issues (effort, time-scale required), and with reliability and its cognate, the modifiability of software. There is, at the present time, no such metric that has been indisputably correlated with these rather pressing matters in software engineering and, consequently, has been widely adopted for the purposes concerned. So much is fact. As Conte *et al.* (1986) put it:

> There has been significant progress in the development of metrics and models in recent years. However a great deal of research is still required to validate existing models, and to develop new and existing ones.

This is certainly true in complexity theory as applied to software, and that is not to demean the work of researchers in this field. The results are not available yet, and that is all there is to it; that is not to say they will never be forthcoming.

To give an introduction into this field of research, on these terms, is not difficult. We will consider briefly the models of Halstead (*c.* 1977), McCabe (*c.* 1976), Thayer *et al.* (*c.* 1978), Davis (*c.* 1984) in Agrawal and Zunde (1984) and Belady and Lehman (*c.* 1976–9). Before undertaking this strenuous regime (for it will seem so to many), it is worthwhile to revisit the reason for doing so, and to review the purposes attempted here.

The intention is to warn practitioners of the existence of research in this area, in the hope that this will, in turn, alert them to monitor this (and similar) research in the literature of the profession. As already said, a dependable mensuration system for software complexity – or possibly several for different classes of software – may emerge some day, with correlations to problematic properties of software engineering such as effort and time-scale estimating, and the modifiability of a software system. In fact, the likelihood is that software systems will be seen to have a topography over which complexity varies, and with it the effort/time-scale requirements (so-called productivity) and the modifiability.

This view has some similarity with the ideas of Parnas on listing the likely difficult and volatile areas of a software design. Thus we will have areas of high complexity with low productivity and modifiability, median areas, low complexity regions (high productivity/ high modifiability) and so on. It behoves the embattled software engineer to track this subject assiduously, but also to discriminate stringently between research and developed method.

As for non-practitioners, our aim here is to introduce a flavor of the subject so that they too can hold out hope that their worst problems (usually in estimating, and the stability/reliability of software) can be alleviated. Also, our intention again is to council caution, at the present time, against any inflated or premature claims for these methods. The field of complexity metrics and models is one of research and should be treated with respect, optimism and caution as a result.

We now proceed with a short exposition of the five approaches listed above, according them an extended paragraph in each case. They are not the only approaches, merely some of the best known, by and large, and representative of the subject as well as its problems. There is one further warning due, however. Much of this work is what its researchers call 'phenomenological'. This rather grand title seems to suggest something credible concerning 'phenomena'. In fact, it means – even if the hypothesis it attaches to seems otherwise plausible – that there is no established causation involved. We cannot say 'it is like this because of such and such'; we can only say 'it is like this because it is like this'. Furthermore, much of the work to be quoted will seem quite alarmingly abstruse. Of this we can truly say 'it is like this because it is like this'.

With that apology we will begin our synoptic accounts of the five approaches listed as 'paradigms of form', rather than content, in this abstruse subject.

3.3.1 The work of the late Professor Maurice Halstead: software science and the 'information volume' model of computer program complexity

Halstead's work owes much to precursor research by Zipf in the field of philology and Shannon in the area of information theory. In the first, Zipf (1935) investigated the fre-

quency with which certain words occurred in natural language, and their rank number in a scheme of ranking this frequency. The later work of Shannon (e.g. Shannon and Weaver 1975) defines an information volume (or 'entropy') of a message, in which the units are 'bits' of information. The work of Zipf and Shannon is abstruse, and the reader wishing to find a description of it may refer to Shooman (1983).

Halstead defined a formula to measure program length as a function of operators and operands; simply stated it is:

$$N = n_1 \log_2 n_2 + n_2 \log_2 n_2$$

where N = program length, n_1 = number of operator types and n_2 = number of operand types. Now in philology, Zipf had derived a similar relationship for 'token length' in a natural language text and the number of token types in it:

$$n = t\,(0.5722 + \ln t)$$

When one substitutes $t = n_1 + n_2$, and $n = N$ from Halstead's formula, this becomes:

$$N = (n_1 + n_2)(0.5772 + \ln (n_1 + n_2))$$

Shooman shows how closely the Halstead and Zipf formulae correspond for measuring program length. This much is consoling if not convincing; if one accepts the plausibility of Zipf's work in general philology, then one might be prepared to accept the analogous work of Halstead as having merit in a restricted field of linguistics – programming.

Shooman defines the 'entropy' (H) of a message as:

$$H = \sum_{j=1}^{i} P_j \log_2 P_j$$

where P_j is the probability of message j occurring in a set of i messages and, using the previous symbols for tokens in a program (operators, operands), this can be re-expressed as:

$$H + N \log_2 (n_1 + n_2)$$

Again, the derivation is detailed elsewhere (Shooman 1983).

Halstead (1977) suggested that an 'information volume' V of a program, analogous to Shannon's general information 'entropy' H in a message, is given by:

$$V = (N_1 + N_2) \log_2 (n_1 + n_2)$$

where n_1 = the number of unique operators in a program
n_2 = the number of unique operands in a program
N_1 = the total occurrence of all operators in a program
N_2 = the total occurrence of all operands in a program

Once again, this is consoling if not convincing, this time on the basis that if we recognize (as in the general case) the importance of Shannon's work in information theory, then, by analogy, the 'information volume' may seem plausible.

In the matter of program length, and the analogy with Zipf's conjectures, Shooman shows a fairly good fit (average error +2.8 percent; variance −12 to +51 percent) be-

tween real and Halstead formula values for program length over a sample of seventeen small programs.

The situation is less convincing when it comes to an analysis of fit between Halstead's information volume and the number of errors discovered in software systems during development. A part of the trouble is that, of course, this factor – discovered errors during development – is susceptible to various interpretations and inaccuracies. However, taking the evidence at face value, the comparison produced the following results. Three hypotheses were used:

1. That error incidence is proportional to program length measured as the number of machine language statements (i.e. after compilation or interpretation in the case of a level 2 language).
2. That error incidence is proportional to information volume (Halstead).
3. That error incidence is proportional to incidence of the number of decisions in a program, and subroutine calls made from it (Akiyama's hypothesis; Akiyama 1971).

In the sample taken, known as Akiyama's data from the original experiment, nine software systems were studied with program size (machine code statements) in the range 699–5,453. Of the three hypotheses tested, Akiyama's produced the closest fit. Of the other two, Halstead's information volume showed no significant difference over simple program length.

None of this is really surprising. Akiyama's hypothesis is based on a crude count of factors that might plausibly be thought to affect complexity.

Halstead's conjecture is based on an unproven analogy with a theory of information content; mere program length is likely to be correlated with the number of errors incident, even if these occurrences are random. The work of Halstead and collaborators has not yet succeeded in providing indisputable evidence of its worth. For example Ottestein (1979) suggested that the total number of defects in a program may be measured by V (the information volume) divided by 3,000, as this denominator represents 'the mean number of mental discriminations between potential errors in programming' – although how such a quantity was, or could be, determined is unclear. As said in Conte *et al.* (1986): 'The model was shown to work well for data published by Akiyama and others, but was disputed by other studies . . .'. The same fate has befallen attempts to correlate Halstead's information volume with effort to develop software systems. There have, in fact, been several serious criticisms of Halstead's approach, e.g. Malénge (1980), and its worth is seen as dubious (if not actually refuted) at the level of its claimed conclusions. Its presentation here is for completeness, and because Halstead's conjectures absorbed a considerable amount of research effort, and received considerable reference and recommendation in the period 1975–85.

3.3.2 The work of McCabe (and others): the use of simple directed graph theory to obtain a metric for the logic structure of a program

This is (in this author's view at least) a more plausible approach than that of Halstead's software science, or software physics as it has been dubbed, although McCabe's work,

too, has been subject to considerable criticism. In general, a directed graph may be represented as a set of nodes N_i and a set of connecting edges between some (or all) nodes, E_j. Figure 3.3 depicts a simple directed graph of no particular context. It has seven nodes and eight edges.

A special case of directed graphs is that of a logic structure – whatever the context to which it pertains. A typical logic structure is that of a flowchart; nodes may be seen as the elements in the flowcharts, and edges as their connections.

McCabe (1976) has defined a factor which he calls 'the cyclomatic complexity number $V(G)$' as being:

$$V(G) = e - n + p$$

where e is the number of edges, n the number of nodes and p the number of connected components in a directed graph. In its application to a flowgraph of logic structure for some integrand this, by definition of the term 'connected components', becomes a special case:

$$V(G) = e - a + 2$$

as it is taken that there are two external connections to the flowgraph, the entry and exit points. In Figure 3.3, the 'McCabe number' $V(G)$ is 3.

Conte *et al.* (1986) show that, for a multi-component software system design (comprised, as is generally the case, of integrands a, b, c, d ... say, themselves comprising programs A, B, C ... in some form), then the cyclomatic complexity number of the system $V(G)_s$ is simply:

$$V(G)_s = V(G)_a + V(G)_b + \cdots$$

The use to which this work has been put, to date, is far from conclusive of its worth,

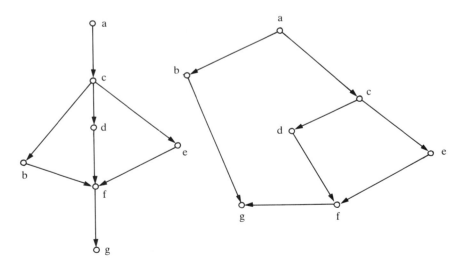

FIGURE 3.3 Two control flowgraphs (after Davis, in Agrawal and Zunde 1984).

although it may well have suffered some neglect compared with Halstead's software science, which attracted more attention in the period 1977–82. McCabe's own work seems to have shown, to his satisfaction, that $V(G)$ correlates well (at least at a judgmental level) with programs of particular complexity. He has also indicated a rough rule of thumb that might serve for integrand design and implementation – namely that a $V(G)$ value of less than 10 should be aspired to.

Others have proposed variants of the cyclomatic complexity measure, or composites of it and other approaches. To take one example, Oviedo (1980) proposes a composite complexity factor C comprising control-flow complexity and data-flow complexity, the first being based on a control flowgraph similar to that depicted, say, in a flowchart, and the second being based on a count of variable definitions and data references.

All this, to be frank, seems implausible. McCabe's work has the prima facie virtue of straightforwardness, and the suggestion of a simple, empirical formula which will succeed or fail according to its measured virtues. The composite models seem like rather arbitrary compositions and, not surprisingly, add little to the investigation for reliable complexity metrics. Even so, notwithstanding its virtues of relative clarity, McCabe's cyclomatic complexity measure has itself – like Halstead's work – attracted critical comment. One author (Shepperd 1988) sees cyclomatic complexity as no more than a substitute for, and often worse than, a 'lines of code' count at the program level, and attributes this to a lack of some explicit model on which cyclomatic complexity is based. Another author (Prather 1984) formulates three axioms in an attempt to qualify complexity metrics:

1. The complexity of the whole must not be less than the complexities of the parts.
2. The complexity of a selection must be greater than the sum of all the branches (i.e. the predicate must contribute to complexity).
3. For the same reason as previously, the complexity of an iteration must be greater than the iterated part.

As Shepperd says, a metric may be intellectually very appealing (and derived in an exciting way it must be added), but the value must be established through its validation by the software engineering community. McCabe's metric falls somewhat short of that at this time.

3.3.3 The statistical work of Thayer et al.

In a monograph on software reliability (Thayer et al. 1978), several authors at the TRW company set out a model for software complexity. The source is interesting in itself. Whereas some other works in our compendium here are from academia, this is from the sharpest of 'sharp ends' in the IT product industry. TRW is a major aerospace system supplier to the US Department of Defense, and its staff know the exigencies of fixed-price contracts at first hand – as well as the perils of software estimating (Boehm 1981) and the reliability of systems whose consequences in failure may be catastrophic.

To argue that such a provenance must make them infallible in some matters would be to commit an ancient fallacy. The source does, however, command our interest, not least on the grounds that if this is the best that such a supplier can do it may well be

representative (in its epoch at least) of the state of affairs in this subject. For that reason, we will briefly consider two aspects of the work; complexity models and software errors. The authors define five categories of complexity in a program. This limitation must be stressed, without detracting from the work, as it locates the endeavor precisely within our earlier category 'complexity of implementation' as a *part* only of the overall hazards of software complexity. The five categories listed are as follows:

1. Logic complexity; primarily concerning logical statements, in source code, of the branching case statement and conditional transfer types (such as IF statements and DO loops). The work defines a logic complexity metric (in our slightly amended terminology here):

$$c(\log) = n(s)/n(x)(\text{loops}) + n(\text{IFS}) + n(\text{br})$$

where $n(s)$ = number of logic statements; $n(x)$ = number of executable statements; $n(\text{loops})$ = is a loop complexity factor; $n(\text{IFS})$ = a measure of IF statement complexity; and $n(\text{br})$ is the number of branches (all branch statements) divided by 1,000.

The factors $n(\text{loops})$ and $n(\text{IFS})$ are themselves complex functions and are further defined in the source work.

2. Interface complexity; primarily concerned with the number of other routines called by a program, and the number of systems (i.e. 'virtual' software) facilities invoked. Here, an interface complexity metric is defined as:

$$c(\text{int}) = n(\text{ap}) + 0.5 \,(\text{sys})$$

where $n(\text{ap})$ is the number of application program interfaces, and sys is 'a factor chosen to assign what was believed to be the relative importance of system program interfaces to application program interfaces' [sic].

3. Computation complexity; primarily concerning assignment statements containing arithmetic operators. A computation complexity metric is defined as:

$$c(\text{comp}) = n(\text{cs})^2 \times \text{sum: } c(\log)/n(\text{ex}) \times \text{SUM: } n(\text{cs})$$

where $n(\text{cs})$ = number of computation statements, the $c(\log)$ quantity is the sum of all logic complexity factors in the system; likewise the sum of all cs values over routines in the system.

4. Input/output complexity; primarily concerning the usual i/o functions in a routine. An input/output complexity metric is defined as:

$$c(\text{i/o}) = n(\text{i/o})^2 \times \text{sum: } c(\log)/n(\text{ex}) \times \text{sum: } n(\text{i/o})$$

where $n(\text{i/o})$ is the number of input/output statements in a routine and sum: $n(\text{i/o})$ is the sum of i/o statements over all routines.

5. Readability, or uncomplexity, metric; primarily concerned with the degree of self-explanation of a program ('routine' or integrand) due to, for example, comments in the code. An uncomplexity factor for readability is defined as:

$$uc(\text{read}) = n(\text{com})/n(\text{ts}) + n(\text{com})$$

where $n(\text{com})$ = number of comment statements, and $n(\text{ts})$ = the total number of all statements, executable or comments.

TABLE 3.3 Correlation of complexity with number of software 'problems' (Thayer *et al.* 1978)

c(tot)	0.7534–0.9065 (this last for the 'function')
c(log)	0.6335–0.9138 (this, too, for the 'function')
c(tot) − c(log)	0.4343–0.7686 (in this case the lower value was for the 'function')

TABLE 3.4 Average of correlation factors (Thayer *et al.* 1978)

c(tot)	0.7948 and 0.7725
c(log)	0.7826 and 0.7564
c(tot) − c(log)	0.6026 and 0.6363

TABLE 3.5 Error symptoms (Thayer *et al.* 1978)

Incorrect processing (i.e. something wrong in an algorithm or its coded version)	30.4%
Change control (i.e. error resulting in an introduced amendment somewhere)	16.4%
Database incompatibility (i.e. error resulting in an introduced amendment somewhere)	14.5%
Routine data incompatibility (i.e. something wrong with local variables or parameters)	9.0%
Routine lacking capability (i.e. underspecified in some way, or underimplemented)	4.9%
Routine incompatibility (i.e. troubles with access or output)	4.4%

The reader will, by now, have a slightly apprehensive feeling no doubt; as though something inevitable was about to occur; it is.

Thayer proceeds to define a total complexity metric as a composite of the five foregoing categories:

$$c(\text{tot}) = c(\text{log}) + 0.1c(\text{int}) + 0.2c(\text{comp}) + 0.4c(\text{i/o}) - 0.1uc(\text{read})$$

The authors go on, most fairly it must be said, to admit that the assignment of factors in this definition is judgmental – that is arbitrary values for what might be believed to be the relativities in importance between the factors.

Again, as in the work due to Halstead, an attempt was made to correlate complexity, thus measured, with the 'number of software problems'. Here, a modestly interesting finding emerged – namely that c(tot) only correlated at about the same level of statistical significance as c(log) on its own and, inevitably therefore, c(comp) − c(log) correlated at an even lower level of significance. The ranges of correlation coefficient in each case, over a sample of five software 'subsystems' and one 'function', are shown in Table 3.3. The averages of these correlation coefficients, with and without the seemingly anomolous 'function' whatever it was, are shown in Table 3.4.

Too much must not be made of such things, there being higher correlation factors on some matters not obviously connected in causation (such as weight-lifting ability and Roman Catholicism – in men only it should be said; a rich field for theological speculation). However, the interesting feature of all this is that 'logic complexity' in this form seems to do better than all the rest put together, i.e. c(tot) − c(log), and the simple

interpretation of this – assuming some merit in the whole approach – might reinforce McCabe's conjectures, which also relates to logic structure metrics, *pace* the reservations listed against McCabe's cyclomatic complexity metric.

In concluding this synoptic account of the work of Thayer *et al.* we visit briefly a part of their work concerning error causes and their symptoms in programming. It should be noted that, in this short account, no claim is made by the authors for generality in these findings. The object problem was a 'state of the art, real-time software system' produced using top down, structured programming methods, incremental development and testing. It comprised about 11,000 Fortran statements of code and 17,500 statements of assembler code in addition; its intended modes of operation were 'real-time and batch', probably meaning the same as in our own usage elsewhere. By analyzing 365 problem reports, presumably produced on a daily basis irrespective of need, it was found that 80 percent of problems reported had six out of twenty-five defined symptoms (a neat demonstration of the 80:20 rule), as shown in Table 3.5.

Within these symptoms, the discovered causes present an interesting picture. Over half (56 percent) of the 'incorrect processing' was due to false logic (30 percent), or error in computation statements (26 percent). Errors due to change control showed no particular pattern – as would be expected if the fault lay in the specification and program change mechanism, i.e. organization factors rather than technical reasons. About half (53 percent) of the 'database incompatibility' problems were due to errors in the database itself, and the rest in errors of access or declaration within a program. Once again, this confirms the importance – for this class of application at least – of logical (and computation) complexity in programming.

We should at this point take a short break from the strict regime of this recital. We have summarized some of the works of Halstead, McCabe and Thayer *et al.* As one student on a course said, after such a gruelling: 'Phew, I knew it would come to this; I always feared as much'. Well, the work we have reviewed has – as the acute reader will have realized – concentrated entirely on the *complexity of implementation*, as is very natural given the things we had to say about complexity of intention and that of interaction. Furthermore, as is often pointed out with great vigor by students of software engineering methods, the approaches are interesting (or not, according to taste), but they are all deeply unconvincing either because their hypotheses seem tenuously founded, or their measured results are less than categorically positive and useful, or both.

On the other hand, there is the feeling that complexity models and metrics of merit *should* be possible for programs at least, even if the wider context of software complexity (intention and interaction as well as implementation) may be a problem of a different magnitude. The trouble is that so many aspects even of a program are subjective. What (in Thayer's scheme) is a 'software problem'? On the one hand, one may have instances of trivial errors – such as the ADD TEMPSTO for SUB TEMPSTO in our Chapter 1 example. Or one may have radically different classes of 'problem', ranking higher on any reasonable scale of values in severity. For instance, the intermittent failure of a real-time system, the synchrony of whose processes with external events may determine the life or death of an orbiting satellite crew.

A recent example, quoted in *ACM Sigsoft Notes* (July 1987), describes how lightning struck a rocket launched at NASA on 26 March 1987. The physical damage to the $160

million system was considerable – a hole punched through the fiberglass nose-cone. But 51 seconds into the launch of the Atlas-Centaur, ground controllers had to abort it because one instruction in its on-board control software had been changed by the electrical pulse. A striking instance (no pun intended) of the properties of software complexity and the behavior space difficulty.

Anyway, those are inherent problems in this field, and we have had our little intermezzo in this daunting recital; let us play on.

3.3.4 Davis's measurement of syntactic complexity in programming

A relatively recent paper (in Agrawal and Zunde 1984) outlines an approach which is similar again to the general work in philology of Zipf (1935, and thereafter) and, in information theory, due to Shannon. Instead of defining an information volume in a program, this new approach (by Davis) suggests as an element of programmer comprehension 'the chunk' i.e. a clump of generically associated statements of code, where the genus is some functionality. It is understood that 'the chunk' is an imprecise amount, somewhat less than an integrand (which, although imprecise in size itself, is at least precise in intention if Parnas's principle is followed). A chunk is said to be 'that clump of generically associated statements that can be held as a mental concept'.

Davis defines the entropy, H, of a system as:

$$H = \sum_{i=1}^{n} P(A_i) \log_2 P(A_i)$$

where the $P(A)$ values are the probabilities of occurrence of a set of elementary events A_1, A_2 ... in a set of such. Davis applies this to two simple control flow-graphs (see Figure 3.3).

The derived entropy in the first case is given as:

$$H_1 = \sum_{i=1}^{5} P(A_i) \log_2 P(A_i)$$

$$= (1/7) \log_2 (1/7) - (3/7) \log_2 (3/7)$$

given the classification of nodes in the schemes as (a), (b, d, e), (c), (f), (g).

The calculation proceeds to its destined outcome:

$$H_1 = 2.128 \text{ bits}$$

Davis then proceeds to classify the nodes between the two control flowgraphs in a different way, e.g. (a), (b), (d, e), (c), (f), (g) and calculates as before:

$$H_2 = 2.521 \text{ bits}$$

He concludes, plausibly in the given circumstances, that this demonstrates an increasing value of H with the degree of nesting in the control flowgraphs.

The work, as presented by its author, is extremely synoptic, but its aim seems clear and, on the face of it, the metric seems to work at a judgmental level. Davis writes:

> Application of the entropy measure to the prediction of debugging time and construction time has shown that . . . there is a significant variation in prediction as the equivalence relation is changed so as to refine its partition. (Davis, in Agrawal *et al.* 1984)

This rather obscure statement may be read to mean that the syntactic clarity of a program increases if its refinement into related 'chunks' is accompanied by a simplicity of structure (e.g. as in the case of nesting in the earlier example). This is intuitively clear anyway; having a metric to show it is helpful; correlating it with development time (if this has been done) indicates that it is harder to write bad programs than 'good' ones in the sense of syntactic clarity; and last, it indicates (if correlations are done) that debugging nasty code is harder than debugging nice code.

All that may seem to be much fluster about the obvious, but a metric should be seen to work in obvious cases – otherwise it fails its most trivial tests.

Davis's work is relatively new and of highly questionable value at this stage – which is not really to detract from it; it is research after all. It represents a skeleton of an approach only, and its defects are scrupulously listed by its author in the paper quoted.

3.3.5 The work of Belady and Lehman

These authors have defined three 'laws' of software evolution dynamics (Belady and Lehman 1976, 1979):

1. *The law of continuing change.* A large program that is in frequent use undergoes continuing change until it becomes more cost-effective to rewrite it.
2. *The law of increasing entropy.* The entropy of a software system (here used with its precise meaning in physics: the degree of disorganization of a system) increases with time, unless specific work is done to maintain or reduce it. This will be a consequence of two factors. First, it can be seen as the progressive degree of misfit with real requirements unless changes are made. Here the 'system' is seen as the totality of software and its real requirements, and entropy applies to the total. Second, it can be seen as the natural consequences of changes to software that deplete its structure and increase its complexity.
3. *The law of statistically smooth change.* However different software systems are in intent, style and internal construction, there will be immanent properties that display degrees of self-regulation and statistical invariance. One such might be a 'law' concerning when to change parts of a software system, and when to undertake a complete redevelopment of the whole.

Belady and Lehman predicated their work, at the time, on detailed studies of three large software systems; IBM's OS-360 and DOS-360, and OMEGA – a banking system. As remarked by others (Conte *et al.* 1986), 'law' 1 is almost self-evident; 'law' 2 is intuitively plausible; and 'law' 3 is hypothesis until more clearly established. Conte *et al.* go on to suggest that 'law' 3 is counter-intuitive. In fact it is rather the converse. Evidence that every new software system is a different system in every respect of its

structural properties is not strongly established, and might itself be thought counter-intuitive. The lack of statistical evidence for Belady and Lehman's invariant properties is probably no more than that; but absence of evidence is not, necessarily, evidence of absence.

Where software complexity is concerned, lemma 2 ('entropy') is the important one, and Belady and Lehman enunciate the definition of system complexity thus:

$$C_r = MH_r/M_r$$

where C_r is the complexity of the system at release r; MH_r is the number of modules handled (changed) during release r; and M_r is the total system size in number of modules at release r.

It is immediately clear that Belady and Lehman are defining totally different things here than those we have considered earlier, and that they are seeking a metric for *software version* complexity as distinct from the aims of others (Halstead, McCabe, Thayer *et al.*, Davis) which are, clearly, about *program* complexity. If confirmed, the work of Belady and Lehman would be significant, for it would hold out hope of rational decision-making in software maintenance and emendation. This point is taken in Chapter 10. Lemma 3, an invariance, would be a particularly significant adjunct to the entropy concept, and it may be that the invariance effects will turn out to be long term – as Belady and Lehman suggest.

Some evidence has emerged (Lawrence 1982) against the entropy concept. This suggests that, of five software systems studied, only two (OS-360 and OMEGA) showed statistically significant 'entropic properties', i.e. increasing number of modules handled (changed) with age. However, once more we are on spongy terrain. For Lawrence's refutation to be valid, it would have to be established that change policy was unconstrained for the other three systems under consideration in Lawrence's sample. Some software remains unchanged because its entropy (disorganization) is so high that no one dares to change it – as many would say should have been the case with OS-360!

3.4 A CODA ON SOFTWARE COMPLEXITY

Metrics and models for software complexity are lacking in the practical world of software engineering, and this impoverishes the approaches of researchers seeking software estimating methods and metrics for assessing software reliability.

The problems for software are, as we have seen, threefold – being conflations of complexity in intention, implementation and interaction. The simple truth is that little can help at the first and last of these levels other than orderly and rational approaches, as will be described elsewhere, in the face of the known facts of life at these stages. There is more 'good practice' known in design and programming than at other life cycle stages, but no reliable models and metrics for the complexity of its outcome – not even for static programs, let alone dynamic software. The 'good practices' have come about largely as a result of computer science endeavors, and the subjects of models and metrics for design and program complexity are still at the research stage within that subject.

The best that can be offered are guidelines for specification, design and programming, and for software validation. In summary, and to revise our previous advice, these are as follows:

1. Prototyping during specification may reveal hidden complexities in the system-to-be; one should embody the information 'bought' in this way in the feasibility assessment and then label the prototype clearly for what it is, or dispose of it lest it becomes incorporated in a release version. A detailed functional specification of requirements will draw attention to many areas of concealed complexity.

2. Good decomposition of requirements' features, and their transformation into solution details, based on notions of strong cohesion and simple coupling, will assist in containing complexity in design. Parnas's approach to difficult and volatile parts of a system should be used, along with the 'information hiding' principles of a single design feature in (and restricted access to) an integrand. At the programming level, the constructs of structured coding should be employed.

   These means will, between them, tend to clarify and simplify program designs and code. It should be noted, however, that some systems are inherently difficult to design and implement even in these ways. Systems for real 'real-time' requirements are generally difficult – particularly with respect to their properties (when present) of concurrency, synchrony of processes, priorities and interrupts, and parallel data updating and access.

3. A rational scheme for testing software is imperative for its convergence to operational status within the theoretical behavior space. Whatever rational approach is adopted (of several to be discussed later), it will be based on the notion of 'build a bit, test a bit; build a bit more, test a bit more' – with progressive and controlled integration of the system as it comes into being. Then, in the operational stage, the second 'law' of Belady and Lehman must be respected; work will need to be done to preserve whatever 'good structure' exists as the software becomes changed over time.

   Last, and not least even though unmentioned so far, the system and software documentation must be of high quality if complexity of interaction is to be a manageable item.

These, then, are the rudimentary guidelines for containing the threefold complexity of software systems. The most scrupulous care in all these matters will not avoid inherent complexity in the outcome, but they should avoid gratuitous complexity. All programs are complex, and some are more complex then others. All non-trivial software systems are very complex however well implemented, and some are – frankly – gratuituously too complex by design and implementation to be used with confidence.

In conclusion, it may be thought that I have dealt roughly with the research field of software complexity models and metrics. This is far from the intention, although both practitioners and their less subject-specialist colleagues need to be warned of what is and is not established method, and what is properly seen as research. Sections 3.3.1–3.3.5 are to convey the flavor of this work, through five paradigms of form – not to act as a survey of it in any detail.

There are several good reference works on this subject, and the reader wishing to study to a greater depth of detail might gain great benefit from them. With no offence

intended to any omitted from this list, we submit the following as warmly recommended to supply a clear and comprehensive review of ongoing work – in all cases presented in the greatest detail.

> *Software Engineering Economics*, Boehm (1981): This book is valuable for its general theses on modeling the software engineering process. It also serves as an advertisement for, and detailed description of, the COCOMO estimating model.
>
> *Software Engineering*, Shooman (1983): This work is particularly valuable for its review of research into models and metrics in software reliability.
>
> *Software Engineering Metrics and Models*, Conte *et al.* (1986): This sets out most, if not all, of the ongoing research work in this field.

We may now ask, as we asserted at the end of Section 3.2, do we after all know where we are with this tricky stuff, software? I am rather afraid that we do. One generally has the keenest view of the writing on the wall when one's back is up against it. The 'tiger' that had to be tamed at the start may not be the fully grown Bengal variety, but it is not the least tractable of felines.

I recall, most vividly, getting to the end of this part of my material in a course for (as luck would have it) hardware engineers, as commonsensical a body of people as one could find in a lecture room, with the healthiest attitude to pretension, hypocrisy and cant that I have ever met. It was as though each one had a built-in 'tripe-ometer', a device to detect deception and foolishness with the greatest sensitivity. Glazed, dazed and amazed, they sat a full minute after the lecture before one said, his tripe-ometer registering an off-scale reading, I fear:

'Is that it?'

'Is that what?' replied the tutor, depending on the lecturer's despicable trick of reposting to a question with another question, at whatever cost to grammar.

'It! You know. Is that it? Software engineering? Is there any more where that came from? Surely that's it! There can't possibly be any more – at least not like that lot. Logarithms to base two, and all that. I knew it would come to logarithms to base two, I had a feeling at breakfast that something like this would happen. Come on, tell us. That's it isn't it? There isn't any more surely?'

And, radiant with hypocrisy, the lecturer smiled. – 'Why', he said, 'of course that's it! What more could there be? And to prove it, take my hand dear student (or reader), whilst I lead you gently up the garden path into Chapter 4, without a logarithm to base two in sight to spoil the Arcadian prospect'.

The students knew their tormentor by then, and their pitiful cries would have melted a heart of tungsten steel with which, happily, nature had omitted to equip him.

PART TWO

THE MODALITIES OF SOFTWARE DEVELOPMENT

Bottom: I have a reasonable good ear in music,
let us have the tongs and bones
(Shakespeare, *A Midsummer Night's Dream*)

Part Two, comprising Chapter 4–10, presents an overview of the software development process. It is structured, from Chapter 5 onwards, in the sequence of main generic activities in a 'life cycle' of such, that is itself defined in Chapter 4.

The treatment of the six major issues (specification, feasibility, design, implementation, quality and change) is at an orientation level only, such as might be suitable for an introduction course in the subject, for managers or exponents new to it; or a 'refresher' course for others – to consolidate their empirically gained experience, as programmers, into a cohesive framework of practice.

Again, a balance is attempted between presenting competing arguments and approaches about how things should be done, and the description of known ways and means.

CHAPTER FOUR

THE LIFE CYCLE ISSUE BRIEFLY REVISITED

A software life cycle model is suggested as a framework for the further development of themes in this text. It is shown in its relationship to fundamental issues such as overall management practice, quality determination and the documentation of software systems. This short chapter acts as an introduction to the material in Part Two, and locates the value of prototype development within the software management life cycle concept.

At the start, I advertised my method as being somewhat anecdotal, and based on a lecture series given for people who were finding themselves at odds with an odd subject.

The last chapter ended on a note of incredulity, even despair. Some of the material in this subject, software engineering, *is* daunting on first (and even subsequent) acquaintance, and some of it may get even more intimidating before we are through with it. For instance, the adoption of formal methods relatively high in the life cycle of activities may confront users, whose own skills may be in entirely different subjects – with some baffling array of abstract symbols purportedly defining their requirements.

There is little to be done about this state of affairs at the level of education, other than to present such material in its necessary (but minimal) form, and to locate it clearly within some conceptual model of the process, so that people do not end up swamped by a deluge of alien stuff and the simultaneous problem of classifying it. Software engineering is a difficult enough subject as it is.

However, software engineering is also a practical subject, and one essential ingredient in any scheme aimed at its comprehension must be some practical medium for illustrating the essence of a topic, and its role in the scheme of things. On education courses at all levels, the timing of practical exercises is crucial; too early, and the audience may complain, legitimately, that it serves only to increase confusion; too late, and the class will either sit glumly through a recital of lectures, or may take to classroom terrorism and wage unsubtle guerrilla warfare on the errant teacher.

We have reached that nexus, in the parade of subject definitions and discussion of concepts, at which we must turn to the practicalities of software development, and the state of software engineering to provide for them. The grumbling and recriminating that tends to break out at the time when software complexity is mooted, turns into a pleasurable relief. To clear the decks for this, we will need to revisit, briefly, the issue of conceptual models of the software engineering process since – we contend – this helps to

locate material under discussion and, thereby, reduces the problems of classification in this difficult subject.

As we have seen, the main stages in software development are: requirements' specification; feasibility of solution (i.e. a system to do what is required); design and implementation of the solution; and maintenance/emendation of the solution when it is in operation. To avoid the charge of vacuity, all these stages may (and must) be represented in greater detail, not least because two essential factors are omitted from the list as it stands:

1. Quality.
2. The management of the whole process, including quality.

The relationships are simply depicted in Figure 4.1.

In the following chapters we will detail all three life cycles; management, quality and software engineering itself. For this last, we take a model that is an adaptation of Figure 2.4: very much a project-oriented life cycle. Its adoption will, as explained elsewhere, require adaptation for product development with prototyping, and for informal project development, such as for some internal supply or a 'time and materials' contract – particularly if these, too, require prototypes. Our model, with these caveats, is on view in Figure 4.2.

Before leaving the subject, at this stage of definition on our part, the reader might be interested to see how an alternative scheme might look – based on prototyping and interaction between non-contiguous stages. Figure 4.3 shows such a scheme for the software engineering process alone. It is when the essential matters of quality and management are considered that the scheme shown in Figure 4.3 is problematical. Figure 4.4 shows this effect; how the centralizing of prototype implementation makes quality determination difficult, and management of the whole even more so. In the event, we recommend that for software developments requiring intensive prototyping – for either of the two purposes, investigation of specification or technical means – a combination of Boehm's 'spiral' and Figure 4.2 is adopted.

Meanwhile, we will adopt Figure 4.2, albeit with its caveats of being a special case of software engineering for project/fixed price supply. The following sections summarize the main activities in software engineering without going deeply into any arguments or issues, as these will be the substance for extensive treatment in other volumes. A practical exercise will emerge in the course of Chapter 5.

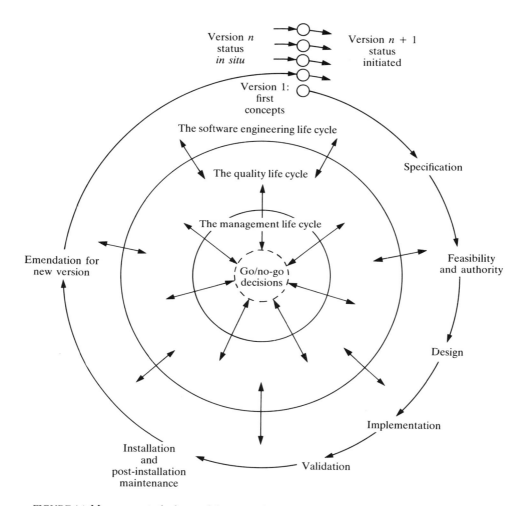

FIGURE 4.1 Management: the heart of the matter in software engineering.

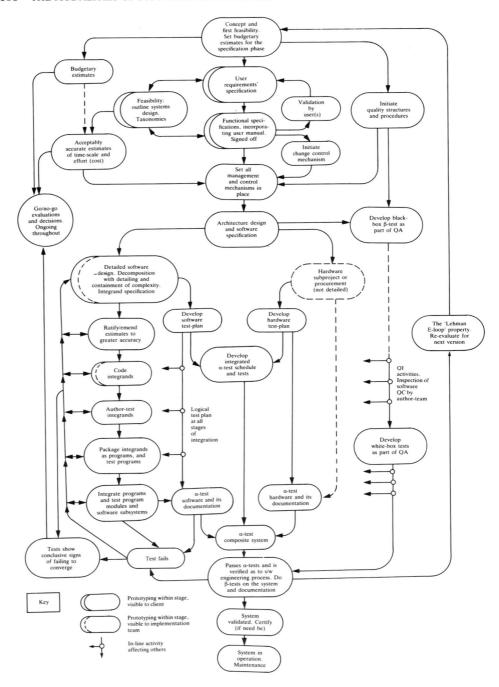

FIGURE 4.2 A software life cycle model. State of knowledge 1987–

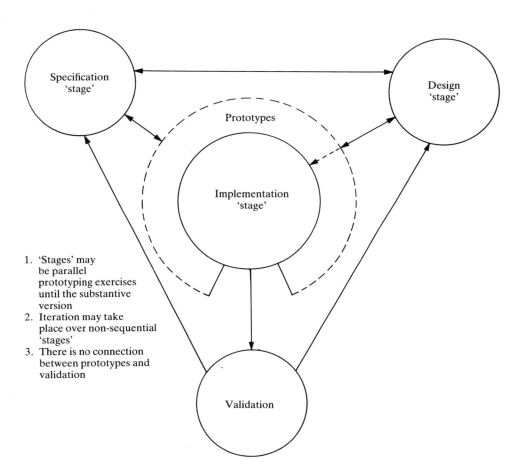

FIGURE 4.3 Software engineering seen as a prototype-based process.

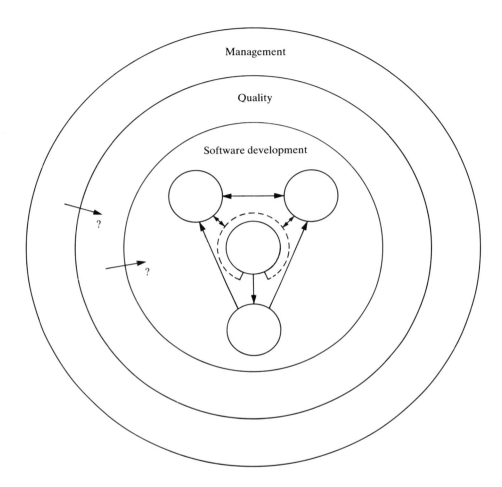

FIGURE 4.4 Management and quality–relegated to the periphery in a prototype-dominated philosophy.

CHAPTER FIVE

REQUIREMENTS' SPECIFICATION

Specification of requirements is a *sine qua non* for any purposive act of construction just as, for a journey of some definite intent it is generally advisable to have an apprehension of one's destination.

In this chapter, two approaches to specification are described – namely the use of 'formal' specification means, and that of 'informal' definition of requirements. Both terms are defined in the text.

The wide scale and inevitable practice of specification by informal means, within the limits of definition of this term and given the current state of knowledge of possible alternatives, is explained.

Preliminary ('user requirement') specifications are described, and an example given. The necessary definitions are then given for a substantive ('functional') specification, and guidelines are offered for producing such an article that is: (a) isomorphic in essential content with the users' specification of requirement, and (b) in a fit form to be authorized, by both users and suppliers, as the base-line document for a software development, and for validating the outcome of that process.

As with the user requirement specification, an example of this definitive, functional specification is given.

Everybody thinks they know what requirements are, what they are for and how they are best articulated and recorded. Specification is one of those subjects, seemingly, that lie in common knowledge, as easy as eating a pork-pie with a pint of ale at the Cat and Fiddle on Friday night. In the circumstances, then, it is a little surprising that we do such specifications so badly. Yet, I have never met a person in the software business who did not have views on the subject, and much variagated philosophy to surround it with.

Specification as a concept is self-evidently easy, and requires almost no definition other than that it is the articulation and, usually, the permanent recording of a set of requirements – making them explicit in fact. The difficulties arise when one comes to put this lambently clear understanding to practical use in some non-trivial application.

That is the purpose of what follows in this chapter. But rather than start in an apparently logical fashion, with a definition of purpose for specifications in general, we will assume that this is, indeed, a matter of common knowledge, and address first the two basic means whereby specifications may be extracted and recorded – those known as 'formal'

and 'informal' approaches. Then, as an entr'acte in this recital, we will visit the basic question of purpose, although the superficial answer will have been hovering over the work for some time: 'If you don't know what you want, you aren't likely to get it.'

First, then the approach of specification by formal means. As the reader will recall from an earlier chapter, this is a subject for much research in the modern epoch, with some question attaching to its general usefulness in software development.

5.1 REQUIREMENTS' SPECIFICATION BY FORMAL MEANS

A very brief encounter with this subject occurred in Chapter 2, in order to define and dispose of some of its myths.

The objectives of requirements' specification by formal means are (a) to provide an unambiguous definition of the features and functions needed, that can (b) be demonstrated to be coherent and complete.

Current research is directed to finding viable languages for these purposes, and one such that has been suggested is Z. This language is the basis for a research project in the United Kingdom ('Forsite') to develop a tool-set. We will use a recently published paper (Stepney and Lord 1987), on one of its practical applications to date, as an illustration of requirements' specification by formal means.

5.1.1 An example of specification by formal means

A symbolic language of Z notation is defined in the first place – see Figure 5.1. As the use of the example is as a paradigm of form rather than for rigorous instruction in the techniques employed, this definition of Z is held to be sufficient for our purposes here. In the application concerned, a network access control system is first defined in an informal overview [sic]. The features of the network ('Admiral') are suficiently described (autonomously administered nodes rather than a centralized administration and network control scheme), and its purposes are generally understood – it is a mutual linkage between the five academic and industrial partners in an Alvey Directorate research program, each of which has its own, autonomous network of which Admiral is the common interlinkage.

The common access control 'model' (as its authors call it) deals with four basic modes:

1. Where autonomous administrations work with each other but still retain control over their own facilities.
2. Where users' access to services are controlled, even when users and services fall under different administration, by an invisible (to users) regulation.
3. Where an administrator can make use of another's facilities, if they both agree.
4. Where multiple levels of security are available, on request, the level to be specified by users.

The access control model defines classes of users and services. Thus, 'principals' make requests for services; 'servers' provide services; 'clients' handle a request for a principal

$x : T$	declaration of x as type T
$x : seq\ T$	x is a sequence of elements of type T
LHS $\hat{=}$ RHS	LHS is syntactically equivalent to RHS
$P \wedge Q$	P and Q
$P \vee Q$	P or Q
$\forall\ x : T \cdot P$	for all x of type T, P holds
$\exists\ x : T \cdot P$	there exists an x of type T such that P
$e \in S$	set membership
$e \notin S$	e is not a member of S
$S \subseteq T$	S is a subset of T
$A \times B$	Cartesian product
$\mathbf{P}\ S$	power set; set of all subsets of S
$A \cup B$	set union
$\cup\ S$	distributed set union
$A - B$	set difference
$A \leftrightarrow B$	set of relations from A to B; $\hat{=} \mathscr{P}\ (A \times B)$
$A \nrightarrow B$	set of partial functions from A to B
$A \rightarrow B$	set of total functions from A to B
$x \mapsto y$	maplet; $\hat{=} (x, y)$
dom R	domain of relation R
ran R	range of relation R
$A \lhd R$	domain subtraction: dom $(A \lhd R) = $ dom $R - A$
$R \oplus S$	function overriding: $\hat{=}$ (dom $S \lhd R$) $\cup\ S$
N	$= \{0, 1, 2, 3, \ldots\}$
$\#s$	length of sequence s
$h \vdash P$	P is a theorem, given hypothesis h
$S - x$	the schema S with variable x hidden: x is removed from the signature and existentially quantified in the predicate

FIGURE 5.1 The 'Z' notation as used in formal specification.

and pass it to a server. Clients and servers are communicating parties in requests; principals have access rights and permissions to make certain requests of certain servers and so on. At this stage, all overviews of the network and the access model are in natural language, and we use an incomplete summary here to give the flavor of this approach only. The definitions go on to incorporate authorities and their relationship with principals, clients and servers, and to define 'trust' (a state of the access control scheme) and transactions. Finally, a diagram embellishes the text; see Figure 5.2.

The access control features and functions are then defined in Z. First a set of building blocks is set out, such as for requests, authorities, quality of service, statements of access rights, trust, etc. These are explained in paragraphs of natural language before formal definition (Figure 5.3), e.g.

Quality of service (QOS) describes a level of security provided; for example, none, confidential, secret. (No particular meaning is attached to these levels in this paper.)

QOS:
QOS is the set of all qualities of service. It is a set that can be ordered by the relation.

The specification is then built up from the basic, formal definitions and further statements in Z but with, in each case, an explanatory envelope in natural language. An impression of this is given in Figure 5.4.

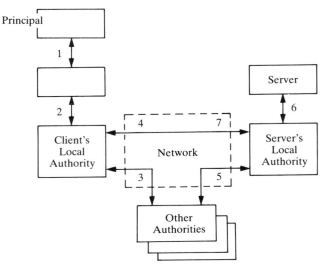

FIGURE 5.2 Network access control example (Stepney and Lord 1987). Communicating paths in a transaction.

$$\forall\ q_1, q_2, q_3\ :\ QOS$$
$$q_1 \leq q_2 \lor q_2 \leq q_1$$
$$(q_1 \leq q_2 \land q_2 \leq q_1) \Rightarrow q_1 = q_2$$
$$(q_1 \leq q_2 \land q_2 \leq q_3) \Rightarrow q_1 \leq q_3$$

FIGURE 5.3 A formal definition (Stepney and Lord 1987) as may be found in a requirements' specification.

Successful_login

$\triangle$ DCS
p? : ENTY $\cup$ UNKNOWN_ENTY
s? : ENTY
q? : QOS
sid! : SID

p? $\in$ ENTY   ... 1

sid! $\neq$ NullSid   ... 2
sid! $\notin$ dom owner

owner' = owner $\cup$ (sid! $\mapsto$ p?)   ... 3
members' — members $\cup$ (sid! $\mapsto$ (s?))
cache' = cache $\cup$ (sid! $\mapsto$ ( ))
qos' = qos $\cup$ (sid! $\mapsto$ q?)

FIGURE 5.4 Formal specification of a feature in the requirements' specification (Stepney and Lord 1987).

The diagram in Figure 5.2 depicts the communication paths in the network, and numbers them for further reference, at a very high generic level of definition and in no particular graphical notation. This schema is a simple addition to the textual definition and could have occurred, in this form, in any 'informal' statement of requirements. As for the abstract definition in Figure 5.3, placed next it for purposes of contrast, this means – when translated from Z symbols back into natural language:

(For) q, less than or equal to q_2 *or* q_2 less than or equal to q_1

(It follows that if): q_1 is less than or equal to q_2 *and* q_2 is less than or equal to q_1, *implies* $q_1 = q_2$

(Or) q, is less than or equal to q_2 and q_2 is less than or equal to q_3, *implies* q_1 is less than or equal to q_3

These relationships are true for all q within the category QOS

From the textual description, it is clear that any q represents a quality, type and level supplied by the network on explicit request. So far as the transliteration between the formal notations and natural language is concerned, it is quite straightforward, being little more than high-school algebra.

It is often useful for non-specialists to realize that mathematical expressions, such as the trigonometric equivalent of Pythagoras's theorem $\sin^2\beta + \cos^2\beta = 1$, can quite adequately be expressed in natural language, albeit at the expense of brevity and with an increase in potential unclarity and error; still, as Marcotty says in Volume 4 of this series, people concerned with specifying and implementing computer systems often seem to feel a need for complex notations where none exists.

The definition in Figure 5.4 is considerably more difficult to interpret for someone not involved with the development of the specification and familiar with the Z language. True, it is offered here out of context, but several features are immediately evident.

First, a list of type declarations is given: p?, S?, q?, sid!

Then a list of definitions by inclusion, exclusion or partial mapping is given, such as: 'p? is a member of set S; and "ownes" is a new set formed by adding the ordered pair sid! and p? to the set "owner".' It is easy to see that the definitional material, and its interrelationships in the specification, are becoming matters of some difficulty to read and interpret. The issue is not whether a natural language specification can be expressed in formal notation, or vice versa, but does the exercise have merit for software development in general?

Furthermore, it is clear from Figure 5.4 that the form of its definitional material is already close to that of a program, with a declaration of types and set relationships.

It is difficult to contain the question: does not specification by formal means tend to prescribe or otherwise limit software design activity, by taking matters at a premature stage, into a form analogous to a program? That is a legitimate question bearing on this work, and it is profoundly hoped that the reader will not take these remarks as demeaning the work of the quoted authors, nor anyone else associated with research into formal means for stages of software development.

In conclusion, the authors of the paper describe a relatively simple transformation of the Z specifications into a Prolog 'animation', i.e. executable version of the model. The

experience here was, apparently, that the basic transformation was relatively easy and that the 'animation' in Prolog (akin to a prototype) showed up an error in the formulation. The Prolog version is not yet a full implementation, and was not, at the time, revealed further.

This example is an interesting and quite typical representation of this field of research into formal means for requirement specifications. Of it (and others), the following can be conjectured with reasonable certainty at this time.

Firstly, the application itself is not extensive. It will probably be at the small end of medium sized systems on the rough scale of values set up in Section 3.1. Specifying requirements for large and very large scale systems is not yet attempted and, when it is, it will undoubtedly be accompanied by formidable problems to demonstrate (prima facie) the absence of incoherence, incorrectness and incompleteness of such a specification.

Secondly, the application is of a rather special type in which the features to be defined and described tend to be of the kind defined by mathematicians, computer scientists, researchers in network and information theory or whatever. This inclines the whole endeavor to one in which the designers or implementation features take on the role of user – a very 'special case' state of affairs, compared with the generality of software systems of the four types defined in Section 3.1, where users are bankers, engineers, process control operatives, and a thousand and one other types of human agency.

Thirdly, similar to but distinct from the second point, the formal specification language is tractable only to those with a training (and aptitude) in its use. It is difficult to envisage the average user having or getting this competence.

What will be the use of formal means for requirements' specification in the future? The answer would seem to be for a set of applications where the features can be seen as defining usage, and where the specialist users are mathematicians or computer scientists. Furthermore, there is possibly a limitation in sheer difficulty (even for experts) above a level of small and medium sized systems on our rough metric of software size. On the other hand, known areas in which these means will prove of benefit are likely to be in the definition and implementation of 'virtual computer' software features, and some other aspects of PSEs and Ipses – see Section 8.5.

These views are judgmental, that is they are this author's opinions – but there seems to be some degree of support for them, except from mathematicians and computer scientists, in business and the IT product industries. Nevertheless, the reader should form his or her own judgment and – in strictest equity – I must say that my reservations about the use of formal approaches will be viewed by disfavor in some research quarters. Such is life.

However, before we leave the subject, it is worth mentioning one other major endeavor to create software by integrated formal methods. The Federal Systems Division of IBM has, over the past few years, evolved an approach called the 'Cleanroom' software development method.

5.1.2 The 'Cleanroom' experiment

This 'is intended to produce highly reliable software by integrating formal methods for specification [sic] and design, non-execution based program development, and statistically based independent testing' (Selby *et al.* 1987). The approach eschews a life cycle-

based development viewed as a sequence of stages, in favor of producing 'a sequence of executable product increments'. In this respect, Cleanroom may be seen to resemble the spirals in Boehm's iterative prototyping scheme.

Of particular interest here is that Cleanroom utilizes an approach of 'structured specifications' to divide functionality into 'deeply nested subsets that can be developed incrementally', and the design procedures incorporate both this concept of structured specification (naturally so, one would interpolate, since that is how the development is to be ordered) and state machine models – for a description of which see Chapter 7. Further than this, program development and testing are done off-line, i.e. making particular use of design review, code reading and static (non-execution) tests on code.

Cleanroom must be seen as an experiment conducted in a very real environment, one that, unfortunately, does not make it easy to assess the results. Much of Federal Systems Division's work is probably classified, and even were it not, few software suppliers like to reveal the vicissitudes of their work to public view.

However, one independent, empirical evaluation has been done by Selby *et al.* (1987). In this, ten teams, each of three people, used the Cleanroom approach, and five teams of the same size used 'good software engineering practices' – as they might be found in this book for instance – including sequential life cycle stages and on-line program development and testing. A small problem was specified to the teams, expected to result in 1–2K source statements of code. Specification was done in 'Simpl-T', which is a structured language supporting string and file-handling primitives, and control-flow constructs as, for instance, in Pascal. All non-Cleanroom teams had access to sufficient development tools and computer resources for their purposes, including on-line testing; similarly. Cleanroom teams had adequate facilities for filing and execution, after off-line testing, of increments.

This and other studies, including one concerning the development of a '600–2,200' source statement compiler, do not – to this author – seem to indicate any strong conclusions in favor of the Cleanroom experiment. For example, of members of Cleanroom teams replying to the questions: 'Would you use Cleanroom again (a) as software manager?, and (b) as programmer?', only 30 percent answered with an unqualified 'Yes at all times' to (a), whilst 52 percent answered: 'Yes, but only for certain projects', and 18 percent replied 'No, not at all'.

To question (b), 15 percent answered with an unqualified 'Yes, for all projects'; 67 percent replied with an important qualification on their enthusiasm: 'Yes, but not all the time'; and 18 percent held the intransigent view: 'Only if I had to'. Similarly, other questions failed to reveal a developed predilection for the Cleanroom approach after its use. For example, 85 percent of people missed being able to execute programs during their development either categorically, or 'somewhat', whilst only 8 percent thought that this has 'substantially revised' their style of validating programs.

As a coda to this recital on the use of formal specification, and other methods within Cleanroom, the authors of the paper already quoted cite other studies that reveal some interesting conclusions:

1. In an experiment contrasting a prototyping approach to software development with one of specifying and revising specifications, and designing and revising designs, the systems

developed by prototyping were smaller and easier to use – this last being an expected outcome, of course, from specification prototyping for users. They also required less development efforts, but this should be seen in the light of the other findings. Further, the impression was gained that the specification/adaptation paradigm had more coherent designs and more complete functionality and the software was easier to integrate!

2. Selby *et al.* (1987) indicate that the development of software by formal methods, in an incremental way as in the case of Cleanroom, may involve a higher development effort, but a lower validation effort. However, the Cleanroom experiment and studies have said nothing, to date, about other aspects of software quality concerning reliability and ease of modification.

   A current study has, as its object, the assessment of Cleanroom on a development of about thirty thousand source statements of code and it is difficult to see how this can proceed without some inkling of quality control as a manageable activity.

These are some of the intermediate findings on one of the initiatives involving formal specification methods. With the caveats already given, and those arising from this quoted work, we offer the following synopsis of specification by formal means.

1. It invariably involves abstract, quasi-mathematical notations that are difficult for non-specialists to understand.
2. Such specifications seem, in form, to be close to program structures; this may lead to the error of design, as an explicit activity, being omitted.
3. Where life cycle based management is attenuated, questions of quality – technical and economic – may result.

5.2 USER REQUIREMENT SPECIFICATION BY INFORMAL MEANS

Before proceeding, we have to admit, and clear up, a problem with the term 'informal'. In this context, 'informal' relates to two different aspects of a requirements' specification, namely the method and the outcome.

Applied to *method*, informal stands in contradistinction to 'formal' as used previously, i.e. an informal method for expressing requirements will not be in some special (that is abstract) language whose competent use will (a) avoid ambiguity, and (b) help in the demonstration of coherency and completion. The most obvious language for informal specification is natural language: English, French, German, Spanish and so on.

Applied to *outcome*, 'informal' (and its converse 'formal') take us into the contractual domain again. Here, we speak particularly about certain levels of specification, done by informal means, being informal also at the commitment level because they are (as yet) insufficient as a basis for a software development. Conversely, we speak of one level (the 'functional' specification – even if done by informal means) as being formal, if it acts as the basis for a contracted (or pseudo-contracted) supply.

It is all a bit confusing, but we will adopt a simple convention by referring to informality of means, and formality (or converse) of outcome. Before leaving the topic, however, we

must draw the reader's attention to another drawback in specification by formal means. There is very little experience to date of specifications in formal language being used as the basis for a legal contract of supply, whereas there are many examples of functional specifications in natural language being the criterion for compliant supply. The fact that many of these contracts have not been satisfied is not the point – yet. We enter a very hazy area here. How valid would a contract be if neither the client party, nor a court, could understand the requirement, because it was expressed in Z say? One answer to all this, that may in the future be generally achieved, is the fulfillment of the following:

1. All contracting parties, including user organizations of all sorts, will have departments capable of formal specification.
2. Contention between clients' and suppliers' departments for formal specification will be settled by the use of expert witnesses before the court.

The second of these has been a growing business for some years now, although so much concerning software quality is judgmental that dispute between opposing 'expert' witnesses is not uncommon, and may not clarify a result. Notwithstanding this, the use of 'expert' witnesses will become a formidable industry in future, as more legislation of tort is introduced to make software suppliers legally accountable. Then, specifications will become, like Granny's glasses, 'all the better to see you with, my dear!'

So far as the first numbered point is concerned, major software procurement agencies have not yet moved far in the direction of emitting formal specifications against which supplies can be validated. Perhaps they see an advantage in the prevailing practice – specification by informal means – as it helps to keep specification within their own field of control. One exception is the defense sector, in which procurement agencies are increasingly requiring suppliers to use formal specification means. In the United Kingdom, for example, the MoD has emitted a policy statement to this effect, and a 'standard' (00–55) whereby to enforce it. Given the situation as it is described in Chapter 2 and Section 5.1, it is by no means certain how software suppliers will be able to respond.

Specification by informal means is, in general, a tripartite process.

In some instances, the specification of requirements may be done in one or two steps but, in the general case, it is better seen as a process comprising the following three steps:

1. Concepts.
2. User-articulated specification of requirements.
3. Functional specifications.

Although this is a summary account only, we will define and describe each of these, as we would in an orientation course for new practitioners, people who are unacquainted with the 'do's and don'ts' of software engineering. Functional specification, as befits its importance, gets a section (5.3) to itself.

5.2.1 Development of concepts

This is the first activity in our adopted life cycle. Concepts are the early ideas of requirements, generally a list of needs and wants, often including some details of the system

to be made. They are, for the most part, expressed at a generically high level of description. For instance, one may ruminate to colleagues or acquaintances on the virtues of having a computer-based chess-playing system.

'Can we program a computer to play chess?' is a question at the concepts' level of the life cycle, and much, at the same high level, will flow from it.

'Why not?'

'Do you mean intelligent play by the computer, or just a system to display human-user's moves on a monitor screen?'

'Can we get a VDU with symbols on it that can be used as chess-pieces, like a bishop or a knight?'

'How much is all this going to cost?'

'I can't play chess, it's too intellectual. My games are "Snap" and "Fish"'.

'Tough!'

'We'll need the thing to detect false moves...'

'...and false positions....'

'Why false positions? A chess-board always starts out in the same way doesn't it?'

'What if we want to start in the middle of a game?'

'How much is all this going to cost?'

'Oh, you mean if we save discontinued games?'

'Yes, or to solve problems like a "mate in four" puzzle.'

'Hello, hello. Testing, testing. How much is this going to cost?'

'Why don't we make a nice system to play something simple – like "Fish"?'

These are examples of the traffic at an early stage of the life cycle, when high level generic ideas are discussed. There is a tendency (that can be noted from the dialog) to admix the issues of requirement with questions of implementation (e.g. the characters on the screen) and resources (the aspiring financial controller, with this special interest in cost). There is no harm whatever in this conflation of ideas and questions at this stage, but there will come a time – not long delayed in life cycle terms – when matters will have to be better ordered, and material in certain categories kept apart.

The initiation of a 'concepts' stage is A Bright Idea. Who has it is neither here nor there, and how it occurs is equally unimportant. It may be that your friendly computer salesperson has sidled up to you again, much as the serpent did to Eve – and convinced you of the joys of some new and overpriced heap of junk. Alternatively, it may be that some innovator in your own firm wants to ruin you by putting the company light-years ahead of the competition. Whatever the engine of change might be, concepts and feasibility questions begin to flow and, before they have flowed too far, one had better ensure three basic things:

1. That there is some clear way, even at this high generic level, of stopping matters if need be (the 'go/no-go' bubble on the life cycle).
2. That even these early ideas are archived.
3. That, even if we proceed past 'go', we rather quickly stop this high level fandango and get down to detailing real, 'hard' requirements. This will be called the exercise of 'user requirement specification' and the same term, or its abbrevation 'URS' will be used for its outcome.

A brief word on each of these three will suffice here. The first, 'go/no-go', is not a difficult matter at this level. Either the interest and resources likely to be needed are there, or they are not. If one is unsure of either, or both, then one can allocate a notional budget (i.e. amount of effort/money without much precise attribution against specific targets), to fund the exercise further and, thereby, hopefully to arrive at some clarity of mind. In our rather simple case, a notional budget may be the cost of a few more hours or days of effort. But in other cases, of vastly wider scope, we may be contemplating a clarification/ feasibility exercise at the top of the life cycle, that involves building prototypes to assess (for example) solution means. We may be building new hardware and writing experimental software, and doing all sorts of fascinating and expensive things. Then our concepts' phase may need a notional 'budget-to-complete' of years of effort and millions (or more) units of currency. In these cases, the 'go/no-go' decision depends on one's means to take the high level question further. The finest, and most immediately available, instance of a real-life 'concepts' exercise' requiring some substantial funding is the SDI 'Starwars' enterprise, where the notional budget (a few billions merely) seems to have been within the means of its authority.

As for the second point – that of archiving – much more will be said in Section 11.2 where the visibility of the software development process, for management purposes, is discussed. Here, we will merely remark that archiving is a life cycle activity, going on througout a software development, to preserve an accurate record (or 'audit trail') of the work. One should start this good practice at the beginning – hence the point of starting an archive in the concepts' stage. The comparison of the archive with an audit trail in financial accounting is a useful metaphor in software management as it clarifies the need to be able to say not only where we are in its development process, but why we are where we are, and it performs this clarification in a way immediately understandable to managers and (other) non-specialists in software engineering. At the concepts' level, one is saying that we are starting out with ideas about (in this case) a requirement for some chess-playing features to be computer-based and displayed on a screen or screens. If we end up by making an inventory control system for a major automobile manufacturer, or doing a guidance system for sending a rocket to Pluto, then this interesting evolution of intentions should be traceable in the history of events; it might account for a slight over-spend on budget, for instance.

Finally, the point is made that, where circumstances permit, the concepts' activities should be transformed into a proper articulation and compilation of specifications for the real requirements. The reasons are almost self-evident. The sooner we start detailing the 'hard' requirements and discriminating desiderata (or 'soft' requirements), the better; and the sooner we begin segregating questions of implementation and resource the better, otherwise the result will be an increasingly detailed, tangled and confused morass of information, speculation and (ultimately) frustration. Naturally, though, the move to a user requirement specification stage must be seen in the light of remarks made earlier about 'go/no-go' decisions from the concepts' stage itself, the appropriation of any budgets needed for prototyping at that stage, and so forth.

In leaving this section on early ideas, concepts and feasibility, we must indicate its likely outcome. We said earlier that a useful management notion is that of 'deliverables' at different life cycle stages, and we hold to this view here. The 'deliverable' from an exercise

in concepts is an informal record (in both senses of 'informal'), in the archive, of the issues raised and the degree to which they have been explored. This will be true whether the result has been 'go', 'no-go' or a qualified 'go a bit further' at the decision level. In the case of 'no-go' the concepts form the entirety of a proto-archive for the aborted development.

In the case of extensive conceptualization activities (with prototyping, for instance), the archive entries may themselves be extensive and may refer to developed algorithms, new hardware designs or whatever. In cases of lesser scope, the archive entries for 'concepts' generally include checklist items detailing features as well as questions for future reference, block diagrams of quasi-solution details, and memorandum traffic between people jotting down new thoughts, asking for agreements and budgets and so forth. If arguments go on after office hours, at the pub for instance, ideas sketched on beer mats ('coasters') are filed in the archive. I have a collection of these informal documents, from all parts of the world and for all kinds of applications, each advertising a different beer and a novel concept of some sort.

5.2.2 User ('customer') articulated specification of requirements

Here we must make it clear that we will present a general case where there are identifiable people who will specify their own or others' requirements of the system-to-be, or will define the purposes of a computer-based implementation that will not necessarily present input and output interfaces with human users. This distinction is important to make, for not all computer systems have 'user interfaces' in the same sense; in some cases, e.g. an embedded microcomputer as a component in an electronic system of some sort, the 'user' might be another component merely. This puts a new complexion on the cliché 'user friendly'.

Anyway, we will proceed, as described, by taking the word 'user' to mean a person who defines usage in whatever context. An alternative term for 'user' might be 'customer requirements', and this should be understood to be a synonym. With that understanding, we proceed to describe the process of user specification of requirements, and the form this usually takes when compiled into a written record – as must be the case if we are to keep some semblance of control at this stage. The word 'informal', applied to a method of specification, *might* mean 'unwritten', 'oral', 'understood' and so on in general – but in this case it must not. Requirements, as they are identified, *must* be recorded – even for small and seemingly trivial applications – otherwise an unfathomable chaos may ensue.

This compilation may produce a volatile and somewhat disordered compendium, as contradictions occur, second thoughts become third and fourth thoughts, bits get forgotten and then defectively recalled, and so on. No one pretends that this is an orderly stage. It may, probably will, be a fearsomely messy business, and its intermediate and final outcomes may be lamentably messy documents.

Let them be so! So long as we get the needs and desiderata clarified and sufficiently detailed, then it is not very important that a user requirement specification is a messy document – because it will not, and must not, be the basis for an implementation in this form!

The URS even if sufficiently complete as a statement of real requirement, may still only be the basis for a better level of specification: the functional specification. This is the one to be used as the base-line for a development, to the extent that it becomes a contractual document in project/fixed price and time-scale supply. The final version of a URS is not destined to be the annex to a formal (i.e. legal) contract, nor equivalent for less exacting supplies, but will be archived as part of the audit trail within software management practice. Note, we need not archive all versions and evolutions of a URS, for there may be much redundancy and volatility of material before the document becomes stable; we need only archive the best (usually the last) version of the URS, on which the 'better, base-line specification' is predicated.

The methods of doing requirements' specification at this level are frequently known by the generic name 'system analysis', and any technique within this genus, known to the reader, may be legitimately seen as a URS technique. The better known ones in general, not specifically within software engineering but useful for any kind of systems analysis and depiction, are as follows:

1. Hierarchical input, process, and output analysis – HIPO.
2. Entity relationship analysis – ERA.
3. Structured analysis and design technique – SADT (a registered trade-mark of SofTech Inc.).
4. Abstract process characterization – an approach from the Charles Stark Draper Laboratory (De Wolf 1977).
5. Jackson's system development technique – JSD.

These five will do to go on with, although the assiduous reader may list many more approaches without much effort, that are deemed – or simply alleged – to be of use in determining requirements and for recording them. For instance, one work on software development practice lists Petrinets and finite-state machines as viable techniques, high in the life cycle, for 'definition' – i.e. specification in our terms (Birrell and Ould 1985). We have no strong quarrel with this, but would remark that their use tends to be rather specific. Petrinet notation is described in Chapter 7, and is useful for modeling and investigating properties of both the solution and the requirement, for systems containing concurrency with possible synchrony problems – in other words for 'real-time' requirements as we define them; the state machine notation, also described in the present section, is particularly useful for the functional specification of a certain class of requirement – namely for applications such as telephony, and those with menu-driven user features.

In fact, a strict mapping of analysis, specification and graphical design techniques, over life cycle stages, is not possible for the generality of application types. In some cases, for example, SADT may be useful from user requirements' specification 'down' to detailed software design in life cycle terms. In other cases, to assume this to be the case would be to overlook more appropriate technique at a certain stage and, thereby, incur unnecessary difficulty (or impoverishment) at a stage. Towards the end of Chapter 7, we will list a set of techniques and attempt a loose and judgmental mapping over both life cycle stages and application types. In the meantime, we give a brief description of the five 'systems analysis' techniques listed above.

HIERARCHICAL INPUT, PROCESS AND OUTPUT ANALYSIS: HIPO

This is now a dated approach to specification and program design for, basically, batch systems in the data processing category of requirements. It emanated originally from the dominant equipment manufacturer in this field, IBM, and was much in vogue with large scale users of data processing oriented systems in the 1970s – banks, airlines, administrations of all kinds. It is so dated as a method, and so type-restricted, that its use has almost died out at the program specification level. However, it still has a use in systems analysis (at the URS stage) for small and medium scale applications with high order data transformation, storage and retrieval, where there is little or no time-criticality within the process; i.e. batch and on-line systems in relatively simple and straightforward data processing.

The technique depends on the definition of hierarchies in a system, and the progressive detailing of data transactions between them by means of 'input, process, output' charts. Figure 5.5 depicts some abstract hierarchy (it may be elements in an organigram) and part of the decomposition and detailing. The fact that an approach is dated does not necessarily make it less useful, merely that – as in this case – a lot of new application types have arisen for which it is not suitable. Within its restricted sphere of relevance, HIPO is as good as most other approaches. It provides a structured way of detailing the functions and features in a real-life environment that are to be emulated by a computer system, and of defining their input and output properties. However, its main virtue is often than it is the *only* systems analysis done on the firm's organization structure. Then, whether a computer system eventuates or not, HIPO will have played a serendipitous role of considerable merit.

ENTITY RELATIONSHIP ANALYSIS: ERA

This is an exceedingly simple method, in vogue since the late 1970s, for systems analysis in (again) the small and medium sized data processing side of applications. The technique is intended to help in plotting structures within requirements, and the whole approach is redolent of the database management part of the software business. For example, data-structure approaches to software design follow rather easily from the definition of entities and their relationships in this high level approach. The technique depends on a simple, almost trivial, box and connecting line method of representing entities (generally nouns, or noun constructions) in the application, and the relationships between them. The symbols are shown in Figure 5.6.

As in HIPO, hierarchies are defined using the ERA convention, and then progressively, decomposed and detailed. The entity relationship diagrams are built up to depict this detail, with some additional legend attaching if clarification is needed, and relationships (lines) carrying text alongside – verb constructions usually – to define the type of relationship. The sort of diagram one ends up with is shown in Figure 5.7.

The reader may well wonder whether or not to be thrilled by all this, as an exposure to the white-heat of technology say, and the answer is 'hardly'! Like HIPO, ERA is a very simple, even trivial, notation. But if it helps, then fine. Both, it will be realized, convert what would otherwise be (more or less structured) text into simple diagrams; that is, what would be structured text in a well ordered URS – which is seldom the case. From this point of view, even simple diagrams like these may help to structure the classification of requirements at this level.

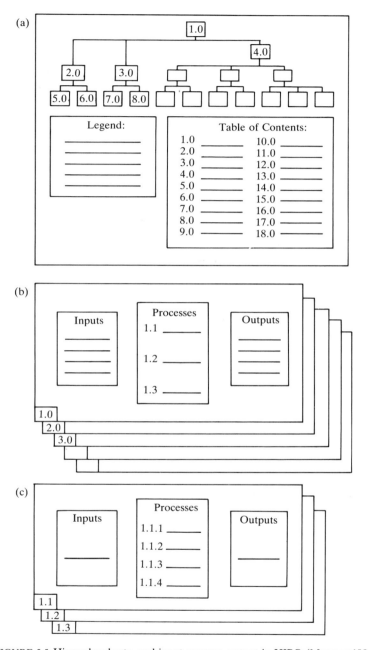

FIGURE 5.5 Hierarchy charts, and input–process–output in HIPO (Metzger 1981).

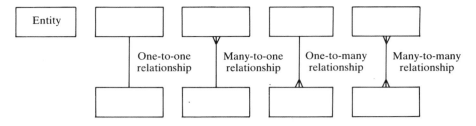

FIGURE 5.6 Conventions in entity relationship analysis.

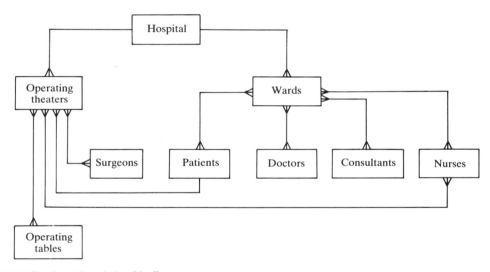

FIGURE 5.7 Simple entity relationship diagram.

The next approach, due to Ross (about 1975/77) takes this structuring via diagrams even further and with greater (though still limited) effect.

STRUCTURED ANALYSIS AND DESIGN TECHNIQUE: SADT*

Ross's approach is an altogether weightier affair than HIPO or ERA and provides a stronger tool, for many applications, in the control of functional decomposition of requirements and the depiction of their control relationships and data flows. Already, with that single sentence, the matter is taken beyond the reach of HIPO or ERA – which are rather weak notations, with even weaker procedures for their use, suitable only for application in the small/medium sized data processing field.

---

*SADT is a trademark of SofTech Inc.

SADT begins with several advantages, amongst which is one conspicuous virtue. It was intended and defined as 'a language for communicating ideas' (Ross 1977), and this is the essence of a good user requirement specification exercise, rather than a static recital of some known properties of the real-life situation. Specification is about communicating ideas – such as from an expert in the user domain (banker, gunnery officer on board a ship, production engineer, doctor, chess player or whatever), often to specialists in the implementation domain. Communication in the reverse direction should be encouraged and enabled also.

Discussing SADT enables us for the first time to distinguish properly between the notation and the procedure within a method, rather than loosely as before. Let this be the place at which we define these terms.

A *method*, or technique, is a defined way of doing something; we turn soil in the garden to invigorate it – that is a method; we use a spade, hoe or trowel and that is the instrument of the method. In software engineering a developed and defined way of doing something may be variously called an approach, a technique or a method, depending on the degree to which it is explicit, and established by practice. Thus an approach may be a matter of personal style, loosely based on some rationale, whereas a 'technique' or a 'method' carries with it connotations of definition, and asserted (if not demonstrated) fitness for a purpose.

If the method contains a set of rules, or even guidelines by which it is to be enacted, this may be known as its *procedure*; if, within the procedure, there is a special way for depicting things, this will be called a 'notation' or 'language' depending rather on its visible form; e.g. diagram conventions are often called *notations*, whereas special texts or symbols might be called a language. Strictly, notations and 'languages' in this context are really all languages in the formal sense, having a grammar and syntax as well as a vocabulary – however rudimentary.

Increasingly in this subject, procedures and notations become conflated and called 'methodology'; this should be avoided since comflation diminishes understanding of their separate worth in a particular case, and the term 'methodology' means a science of, or dissertation on, methods (OED).

In software engineering, although the same could be true in any field of endeavor, we speak of a method as being strong or weak in its procedures and notation. Thus, in general, we say that HIPO and ERA are weak procedures and weak notations – though in some, limited, applications, strong enough.

SADT has an extremely strong procedure and a not very strong notation – although far more so than HIPO and ERA. We will describe the procedure first and then show the notation graphically.

Done properly, SADT is a strenuous discipline. We have known it require several weeks of intensive indoctrination before students become adept in it. To attempt a description in a few lines is clearly a travesty, but the following summary will give the reader enough idea for our purposes here.

The procedure is strongly formalized in the sense that its rules for correct use are explicit, and set out – in writing – at length. To say that a method's procedure is 'formalized' does not mean that the method is a formal one, as that term and its connotations have already been discussed. In SADT, the procedure incorporates specific

role assignment for people involved in systems analysis. 'Experts' are the users in our terms, and possess the detailed knowledge of requirements that is to be extracted and ordered; 'authors' perform this task of extraction, and record it as a set of diagrammatic models in the SADT notation; 'readers' (or 'reviewers') comment on the written output of authors; and 'archivists' (or 'librarians') compile the definitive version of the document produced, plus any 'audit trail' history needed.

The regime is a strict one, and its objective is to control the analysis process. Staff roles can be interchanged for different parts of an analysis, so minimizing team size during this stage. Thus, 'Fred' can be author in this part of a requirement analysis, and reader in another; on some occasions, he may be the 'expert' in a third, and so on within obvious limits of capacity.

As for all notation-based methods, the volume of diagram output may be very large; we have seen examples of multi-volume, SADT diagram-based specifications, and the same tends to be true of HIPO, ERA and some others at this level of 'systems analysis'. This can be a drawback, as the accretion-level of some people to the information contained in large numbers of diagrams can be markedly lower than that for written text in natural language – given its reasonable clarity of expression.

The vocabulary and grammar of the SADT notation is exceedingly simple; in fact it exists in two not widely dissimilar forms, one of which (actigrams) is shown in Figure 5.8. Basically, the data-flow structure of a system can be depicted by datagrams, or the logical structure of relationship can be represented by actigrams. The latter is the more prevalent use of SADT notation.

The legends in boxes fit recognizable features or functions in the requirement, which are then related to each other as befits their role in supplying data, control or support for other features or functions (suitably 'boxed'). By convention, SADT diagrams tend to start at the top left of a page, and descend in a steplike fashion to the bottom right; normal A4/A5 sized pages can accommodate about five to seven boxes comfortably. An additional level of information, on data or logical coupling, can be incorporated by written legends along arrows. Figure 5.9 shows an example of an SADT 'page'. It refers to the example of concepts already coined, that for a computer-based chess playing system.

Here a simple extension of the systems analysis is depicted in actigram form. In fact, at this level the diagram is more a stylized logic flowgraph than an actigram in the real sense. This is almost always the effect of using a graphical notation at the systems analysis level. Elements of design creep in, also, and the result is – for a purist – an uneasy admixture of detailing in systems analysis, logic-flow design and definition of solution means – such as the VDU inputs and format checking, in this example.

Two further points must be made about SADT, before leaving it and passing on to other methods. First, it is said to be 'dated', and second it is alleged (in some places) to have had particular virtues (now superseded) as an implementation design language. These points are strongly related to each other. In fact, SADT has particular use as a stylized data-flow notation, and a strong procedure for systems analysis (which is why we are dealing with it here), and is of much more restricted use as a software design method. There, its limitations in dealing with time-dependency – let alone criticality – are decisive in excluding its use from a whole class of applications in the 'process' and 'rule-based' sectors. However, the datedness of SADT at that level has no bearing on its general

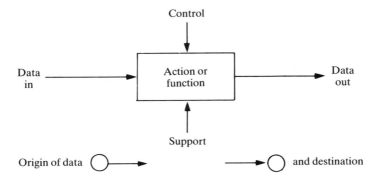

FIGURE 5.8 Actigram notation in SADT.

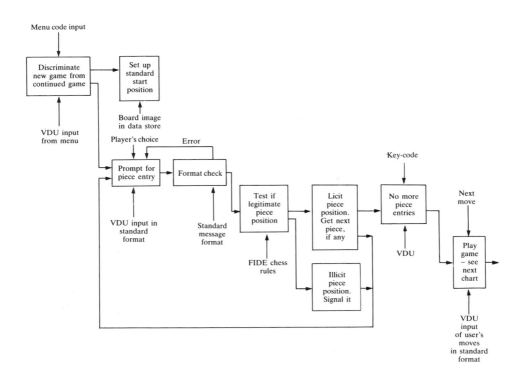

FIGURE 5.9 Example of SADT in use; CAISSA specification.

usefulness higher in the life cycle, and its specific usefulness for high level design of small and medium sized software systems in the data processing field.

Like HIPO in its epoch, and JSD as described below, SADT has suffered from being oversold by its enthusiasts as a nostrum for all stages of life cycle activity above programming, and by some naïve expectations of users looking for a single method for specification and design in any and all application areas. This does the method a disservice, and any disenchanted former enthusiasts should have listened to its author; it is a language for communicating ideas. Like JSD, it is useful (and justifiably popular) as a systems analysis method for data processing oriented requirements. Unlike some other approaches, SADT is popular with engineers – particularly electrical/electronic ones – probably because of the similarity of diagrams in the notation with circuit diagrams.

ABSTRACT PROCESS CHARACTERIZATION: THE DRAPER LABORATORIES
APPROACH DUE TO DE WOLF AND OTHERS

A distinct problem is encountered when analyzing requirements for, and designing, systems incorporating features in which the duration and sequencing of subprocesses is a dominant property. The element of time enters into things in two particular ways: the duration of a subprocess as a principal feature of the subprocess, and the time at which an event must occur. Both may reflect on the temporal relationship between subprocesses. A simple example will suffice to demonstrate the point.

In some abstract process P, a subprocess P_i takes t_i seconds after initiation, on average, to complete, and the completion is signified by an instantaneous event E_i. A subprocess P_j may be independently initiated and required to complete within t_j seconds; it may be initiated and operate concurrently with P_i. At some stage in its execution, P_j requires that E_i has occurred before it can proceed. Figure 5.10 shows several states of the world that might occur. Clearly, cases 2 and 3 are equivalent from the viewpoint of possible violation of t_j.

Many requirements outside the 'classical' areas of batch and on-line systems have problems analogous to that depicted by cases 2 and 3 in Figure 5.10. De Wolf and colleagues at the Draper Laboratories devised a method to assist with requirements' specification and development of solutions, for systems such as on-board navigation of space vehicles. As before, the method comprises a procedure (considerably weaker than SADT in its stipulations and regulations, but noticeably stronger than, say, entity relationship analysis), and a notation that epitomizes the kind of problems it is suitable to depict.

First, though, the procedures attaching to the method. All orderly classification depends on abstraction, and abstraction is the process of discarding inessentials whilst retaining meaningful content of some sort. De Wolf identifies 'abstract processes' within a requirement, and here a 'process' may be any feature of required functionality as well as those that may be time-dependent in the fashion shown in Figure 5.10. In its procedures, De Wolf's approach is completely general and is seen as attaching to orderly classification in any context.

As a result of 'abstract process' classification, a stylized, tabular statement of requirements is built up. An example is shown in Figure 5.11, of the sort of thing that may arise in the specification of the computer-based chess-playing system of earlier reference.

Figure 5.12 shows a relationship between abstract processes. This simple bubble and

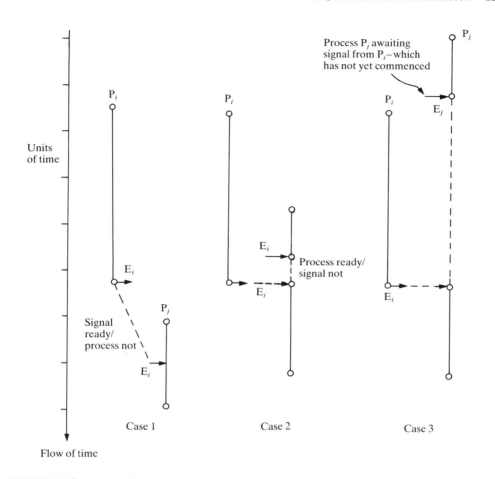

FIGURE 5.10 Process duration and synchronization.

line diagram used here is less a notation than a very simple extension of the classification procedure, and is basically that used to represent designs as 'finite-state machines' – see Chapter 7.

The method is said to be a 'weak' one, not because it lacks applications but because it lacks the strong, almost intense, bureaucracy of the SADT procedure. Many will find this relative laxity in De Wolf's approach a distinct advantage; it was developed in a laboratory after all, and one may reasonably expect its procedures to be enacted by highly trained staff. The generality of SADT within data processing, and some areas of engineering application, requires it to have far stronger, explicit procedures.

De Wolf's notation is based on pseudo-code and a simple predicate logic approach to making statements of meaning. It is here, in the notation rather than in the procedures,

Requirement	Description
1	A computer-based chess-playing system is required, incorporating all features described below, but expressly excluding 'intelligent play' by the system, in this version.
2	Starting configurations can be either:
2.1	Normal piece position at game start.
2.2	User (player) prescription of piece positions, by manual data input.
3	In 2.2 the validity of piece placement will be checked against the rules set out by the FIDE organization for legal chess, and what positions may not derive therefrom, specifically:
3.1	Less than, or more than, one king of each color.
3.2	More than eight pawns of one color.
3.3	More major pieces than can have occurred by pawn promotion.
3.4	Both kings in check simultaneously.
etc.	(enumerating a set of such disallowed configurations).
4	All syntax error in user (player) input will be detected, and diagnosed by a helpful screen message. For example, syntax errors arising from 2.2 and 5.
5	During play, arising from either 2.1 or 2.2 starts, the legality of piece move will be checked against the rules set out by the FIDE organization, specifically:
5.1	The geometry of a move must be correct for a piece of that type, e.g. (2 + 1) dog-leg for the knight, diagonal for the bishop and so on.
5.2	The path must be unimpeded, except for a piece of the opposite color on the destination square (capture), or any piece on an intervening square in the case of a knight's move.
5.3	A move must not exceed the playing area.
etc.	(Enumerating a list of such disallowed moves.)
6	Check, checkmate and stalemate will be diagnosed and signified by a clear screen message.
And so on	

FIGURE 5.11 'Abstract processes' – De Wolf tabular depiction.

that the time element within applications becomes the dominant feature of the method. Abstract processes defined within the procedure are successively restated with detailing, until one can identify elements within a 'process' that are capable of description as data inputs and outputs, and algorithms. Note, this is not necessarily solution detail; it will only be that if there is a one-for-one mapping between this detailed requirement statement and the solution design at its lowest level. In De Wolf's scheme, data-flow analysis is crucially dependent upon identification of temporal relationships, within the algorithms, that are hidden in high level, generic statements of requirement and which, consequently, need to be revealed.

Hierarchies of algorithms are constructed, using four 'primitives' to describe them; these primitives are called 'sequencer', 'selector', 'co-ordinator' and 'iterative sequencer', and are shown in Figure 5.13. Each of the primitives can be extended to incorporate constructions in structured coding (see Section 3.2), but this is a feature of the method more appropriate to its use at the solution-design stage.

We now have one particularly suitable method (SADT) for systems analysis and stylized data flow in small to medium sized data processing applications, and for many classes of engineering requirement such as computer-aided design. We also have a suitable method (De Wolf) for systems analysis and sequenced data flow for applications, in any category, that have marked temporal properties, i.e. need for rapid output from a process, or complex temporal arrangements within them. Of course, De Wolf's method can be used

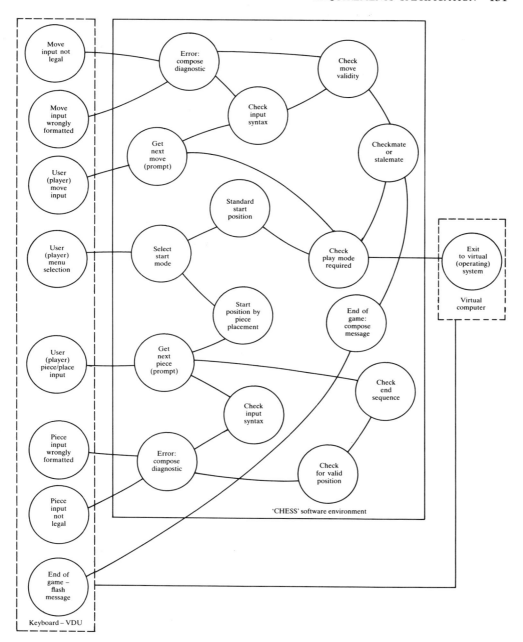

FIGURE 5.12 'Abstract processes' – finite-state representation; CAISSA specification.

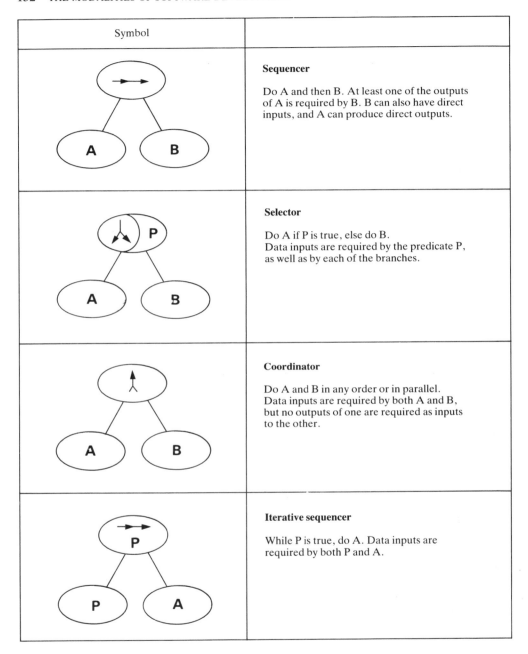

Symbol	
	Sequencer Do A and then B. At least one of the outputs of A is required by B. B can also have direct inputs, and A can produce direct outputs.
	Selector Do A if P is true, else do B. Data inputs are required by the predicate P, as well as by each of the branches.
	Coordinator Do A and B in any order or in parallel. Data inputs are required by both A and B, but no outputs of one are required as inputs to the other.
	Iterative sequencer While P is true, do A. Data inputs are required by both P and A.

FIGURE 5.13 Data-flow primitives in De Wolf's notation (Weizman 1980).

in a subset mode as an alternative to SADT. Its slightly more textual basis at the notation level – tabular presentation of 'abstract processes' (or features/functions) – makes it more applicable for the systems analysis of large scale applications, in this author's view. However, it does not lack for competition.

JACKSON'S SYSTEM DEVELOPMENT TECHNIQUES: JSD

JSD is a method which, for small and medium-sized data processing or computation problems (but predominantly the former, in practice) can be used at the stages of systems analysis (requirements) and software design. At its lower levels of usage within this context, JSD 'fits' with a sibling technique, called Jackson structured programming (JSP), to take development into implementation. However, we will summarize here its use in systems analysis.

The method comprises a strong procedure, between SADT and De Wolf in the force of its prescription, and a rather weak notation – weak, that is, in the amount of logical relationships, data relationships and temporal properties it can depict alongside the statements of functionality it incorporates. In this respect, it is rather like ERA.

The method has been extensively described by its author (Jackson 1983) and we offer here a summary only. In its procedures, JSD prescribes a six step process over definition (i.e. of requirements), design and implementation (i.e. of a system to fit requirements):

1. The entities making up the real-world systems, and the actions by which they are affected or that they affect are listed.
2. For each entity, an activity structure is modeled.
3. Processes in the real world are built up as aggregates of activity structures, and any temporal relationships are accommodated by time-ordering the activity structures within and across processes.
4. Functions and systems' outputs are introduced into the model.
5. Timing constraints (as distinct from sequencing) are recorded in the model.
6. The model is then 'implemented', i.e. programmed, sometimes by an 'automatic' conversion from the higher level symbols, into some lower level language such as Cobol.

A striking aspect of this list, of which the last does not concern us here, is that it is more a 'bottom-up' than 'top down' method in the sense that, for example, main generic functions are built up (step 4) rather than defined and decomposed 'top down hierarchically', as in HIPO, ERA and SADT. In this respect, step (1) has some correspondence with the identification of 'abstract processes' in De Wolf's approach. Jackson regards hierarchical 'top down' analysis of functionality as limiting, and he has a point. Done properly, his approach should make a system's evolution (in the Lehman sense of new version adaptation) more easy for the class of applications for which JSD is suitable, since the definition of functions is a dependent – even contingent – activity (4), rather than an *a priori* step. Thus there will likely be a close correspondence between the statement of requirements and the structure of an implementation. So, changing requirements may be mapped relatively easily into the code.

As a method, JSD has much to commend it although it is limited by the restraints placed on it by the notation – particularly where complex temporal relationships are concerned.

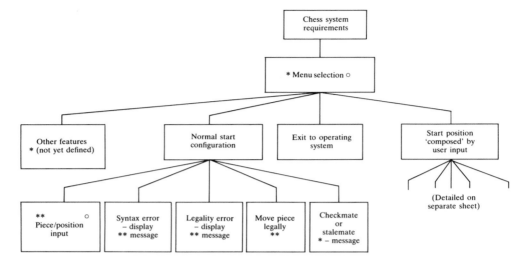

FIGURE 5.14 Concatenations in entity/diagram, JSD convention in CAISSA.

The JSD notation is an exceedingly simple box and line scheme, with an asterisk (*) in a box to indicate related actions, a circle in a box to indicate selective usage and a rather over-simple convention of left to right sequencing of actions at peer-levels in the hierarchy. The convention is, in fact, over-simple, being appropriate only for activities that can be scheduled sequentially; it is generally inadequate for response-critical applications whose implementation requires concurrency at the software level.

JSD diagrams end up looking like the concatenation of boxes depicted in Figure 5.14.

JSD, like SADT and – in an earlier epoch – HIPO, represents a rather typical class of methods whose procedures are stronger than their notations. Their fields of application have been over-prescribed by their enthusiasts and yet simultaneously limited by features such as the notation, and, in all three cases, the tendency to generate large volumes of diagrammatic descriptions. And yet, knowing their possible limitations, SADT and JSD are extremely useful when their procedures provide a discipline to help extract and order information on requirements. The use of De Wolf's method of 'abstract' process characterization, at this level of the life cycle, is probably restricted to specialist applications whose requirements are likely to be formulated by professional staff (engineers, physicists) who are comfortable with tabular specification, finite-state machine depiction of 'process' relationships, and the slightly mathematical (predicate logic) form of its sequenced data-flow notation.

Before moving on from the user requirement stage, and the process of systems analysis, it should be made clear to readers that – in this author's view – an inescapable part of requirements' specification is the *use of natural languages*. It is all very well doing entity or process analysis, or whatever else, and drawing pretty diagrams as a result. If these take on voluminous proportions, then they may not be read by the one set of people who, assuredly, must read them – the users; that is, the people whose competence and responsibility it is to stipulate the requirements.

As we have already said, the word 'user' covers a multitude of sins if not sinners. There will be actual users of the system-to-be, the people who prescribe input, and for whom output is intended. Equally, there will be people who will define features (i/o and algorithms) for software that is to act as a system component, where there will be no human interface with the software-to-be. Also, for products, as distinct from projects, 'users' will have to be co-opted from departments – marketing and technical support typically – within the IT product company. To prescribe a single method for systems analysis would be counter-productive; literally, *any* method that can help in extracting information, ordering it and recording it, is worth adopting.

In some of the methods with exceptionally strong prescriptions (e.g. for organization and procedures during systems analysis), the use of their rules and standard ways for extracting and ordering functions may inhibit users from defining their needs, by restricting the free flow of their ideas. Strong procedures tend to be of especial use in the logical ordering of a status quo, but of less use in recording innovative notions that may still be 'half-baked'. When this happens it is a distinct problem – as one tends to end up with a well ordered and recorded *subset* of the requirements.

There are, in fact, two purposes to be served when undertaking requirements' specification, and this crucial issue of information extraction and ordering should be seen in the light of these considerations. All this is dealt with in greater detail in Volume 2 of this series, but a summary here may be helpful to the reader.

5.2.3 The purpose of requirements' specification

The purpose of requirements' specification is to produce a definition that can be used as the basis on which to implement (i.e. design and program) a computer-based software system to 'deliver' the features and functions required. This definition must be sufficient for the system produced to be validated against it.

The fundamental purpose, sufficiency for implementation and validation, which bears on the software development process and its outcome, may be materially enabled, inhibited or disabled entirely by the information extraction and ordering process. To end up with an exquisitely ordered subset of real requirements will, eventually in the development process, lead to a strong tendency to change the specifications. If budgets have been set for costs and time-scale, this can lead to consequential problems of authority for changes, and – wrongly – tend to informal changes being adopted. The attendant risks are set out elsewhere in this volume, but the reader will have had that familiar sinking feeling already, no doubt, as when some unhappy experience is revised.

The alternative effect is equally traumatic. One may end up with a cubic meter of 'specification' that is a mess in every sense, and all through an imbalance between information extraction imperatives, and the need to abstract and order the 'data pile' as it is sometimes called. When this eventuates, neither the purpose of specification for implementation, nor that for validation of the outcome (if there is one), is served. Information extraction, and its ordering, are the Scylla and Charybdis between which the specification activity must be steered.

In practice, the best way to operate in the user requirement stage is to record

requirements as a semi-ordered 'stream of consciousness' in natural language. In fact, it will be a very application-oriented version of natural language. Some authors advocate 'structured natural language' (or SNL), and this too has its uses at the user requirement specification stage. Most structured natural languages tend to resemble the simplest constructs in a high level computer language; imperatives such as 'Do this', 'Get that', 'If this, then that, else the other', 'Case (X, Y, Z)' and so on.

Once again, there is nothing against this state of affairs if it helps, but it cannot be prescribed as a panacea. One distinct danger is that software engineers and computer scientists, who work at the URS as well as functional specification and design stages, may see specifications in structured natural language as pseudo-code specifications of integrands, programs, etc., and slip into premature implementation activities. We will revisit this danger during the sections on functional specification and solution design. It is sufficient to say, for now, that a thorough-going system analysis exercise, possibly involving prototype developments, should be done in all cases; its outcome should most likely be a user requirement specification document in natural language, plus SADT charts, or De Wolf tables and diagrams, or JSD entity structure pictures.

However, the most important properties of the user requirement specification are as follows:

1. It must be *complete*, in that all aspects of requirement are identified. Clearly, that may not be possible to achieve at the first pass, so any particular specimen of a URS may be a temporary version of it only. In the wider sense, it will be temporary too, as described by the 'E systems' properly defined after Lehman. Also, the level of detail may vary in the URS, with some required features being elaborated, perhaps, whilst others are merely defined as genera.

   The process of completion will be one of iteration. Unless convergence to completion occurs, it may be inferred that a process of apparently perpetual iteration means that real requirements are either non-existent or that they cannot be coherently formulated.
2. It must be *sufficiently intelligible*. A problem with the 'semi-ordered, stream of consciousness' approach to defining requirements is that it almost always produces problems of interpretation, if (as we contend should not be the case) it is used as the starting point for implementation, or the determinant in validation. The sufficiency of a specification's intelligibility is that its completeness must be determinable by users.

In the limiting case, it does not matter so much what other defects of substance the user requirement specification presents, so long as it is complete, albeit only at the time it formulated, and intelligible. It may even be contradictory, redundant and plainly wrong in places. Clearly these defects should be avoided if possible, but incompleteness and unintelligibility are the worst. For, to repeat an earlier stricture, the URS must not be taken as the 'base-line' for an implementation, but must serve as the basis for that – in other words, it must be the foundation from which a competent level of specification is derived.

We are now fast approaching the point at which an example can be usefully introduced, and our earlier promise to do so can be kept. There is a general problem in concocting such things for texts, as they are either (a) too trivial to be useful but small enough to incorporate, or (b) sufficiently representative of enough instances likely to be met in real life, but well beyond the scale possible to include in a text. However, a few

non-trivial examples have been evolved as vehicles for good software engineering practice on short education courses in the subject. The following is one such, invented by the author and put to many teams of software engineers to implement in full. It is useful here for practicing techniques in specification, and will be used at other life cycle stages to illustrate matters at that point, *and* as the basis for a consolidated example showing management methods, in Appendix 1.

What follows is an example of a URS that may show the deficiencies already noted, for purposes of implementation and validation. In fact though, to let the cat out of the bag a little, this is by no means the worst URS with which to be confronted.

EXAMPLE 1

USER REQUIREMENT SPECIFICATION FOR 'CAISSA', A CHESS SYSTEM

The Simpleton Corporation Inc. invites offers for a computer-based chess-playing system. Bidders must reply with a full, written offer on or before 1 January 1990. Your offer must incorporate the following system features.

The requirement is for a screen-based chess system that allows two players to key-in moves, in turn. There may be one of two starting positions, i.e. disposition of the pieces:

1. The normal layout of pieces in squares at the start of a game (mode 1).
2. A manual input of pieces to squares to enable play to continue from a game in which some moves have already been made and perhaps pieces captured, and so forth (mode 2).

It is recommended that bidders study the rules of chess closely, for only official (FIDE) rules are allowed. An example of this need to be clear on the rules is quite easy to give. Consider the manual input of pieces to the board – mode 2. For the rules concerning castling to be obeyed, there will need to be an indication given whether or not either the king or castle(s) have been previously moved. If, that is, they are placed on their normal squares of origin as at the beginning (e.g. as in mode 1). Another example, again in mode 2, concerns the *en passant* capture of pawns by pawns; if a white pawn stands on rank 5 with a black pawn next to it (rank 5 also) then, if it is white's next move, an indication will have to be given whether the last black move was by the adjacent pawn making a double square advance from the seventh rank; the mirror image of this situation occurs if it is black to move and a black pawn stands adjacent to a white one on rank 4. Other complexities in mode 2 abound; for instance a pawn in a promotion position (if white, on rank 8; if black, on rank 1) cannot be allowed to stay in

that condition, i.e. the other side has to move next, before the promotion has been done.

As well as for these instances, the system must check for all illicit positions in mode 2 input, such as kings adjacent, or both otherwise in check, simultaneously, from other pieces; king in check from more than two pieces simultaneously; too many of a piece-type on the board (e.g. more than eight pawns of a color; more then one king of a color); too few kings (i.e. none of one or both colors); an impossible number of major pieces of a type – such as queen, knight, bishop, castle – given the promotion possibilities from missing pawns; and so on.

Bidders must specify the full list of such infeasible input positions in mode 2 that their system will check for, and will refuse to accept (i.e. will not allow continuation of any sort in the position concerned). *Note*, impossible positions in a mode 2 input are all we seek to exclude; there is a set of *improbable* positions which it might be difficult to prove can arise from a game played under legal (FIDE) rules of chess; we do not require your system to test for these in mode 2.

Moves will be entered by players via normal operation of a keyboard at the VDU screen. The normal, algebraic (or 'continental') system of coordinate references for board positions will be used. Thus, ranks are labeled 1–8 inclusive from the front of the board (white's starting position in mode 1) and files are labeled a–h inclusive from the left-hand edge of the board. Thus, at the beginning of a game in mode 1, white's castles are on a1 and h1, black's bishops are on c8 and f8, and so on. The input convention will be lower-case alphabetic in all instances of location or piece-type. Thus, a6 is correct but A6 is not.

Piece-types are depicted on the screen, and for input at the keyboard, by upper-case letters:

K = King; Q = Queen; B = Bishop; N = Knight [sic]; R = Castle ('rook'); P = Pawn.

Furthermore, when need be, W = white and B = black.

Thus, at mode 2 manual input of a starting position, one might specify BR–f4, to put a black castle on f4. Note again, all violations of the lower-case, upper-case rule for input must be checked, as must other types of error (e.g. inversion, such as BR–4f, or 6R–4F, and so forth). All input syntax errors must lead to a helpful message displayed on the screen. Bidders must list these error messages in their responses, and show screen layout of these and other features of the system proposed.

It is not expected that your proposed system should incorporate 'intelligent' play by the computer itself. All that the computer system is intended to do is as follows:

1. Check input syntax for positioning pieces on the board, either in normal play or for mode 2 input positions, and in choosing the system features for use.

2. Check for legitimacy of piece position within FIDE rules either in normal play or for mode 2 input position.
3. Perform certain other features as listed below.

The second of these requirements (checking legitimacy of piece positioning) for normal play will require that your system performs a set of checks at each move made. For example, a check must be made that there is a piece on the square of origin concerned; that it is of the color corresponding to whoever side's move it is; that there is not a piece of the same color on the target square; that moving the piece does not leave the mover's king in check or reveal it to check; that the route of the proposed move is unimpeded (except for knights' moves) or – if castling – is otherwise legal and so on.

The 'certain features' referred to as being necessary components of the system are as follows:

1. The system must test for check, checkmate and stalemate, and must display a message on the screen accordingly, and take appropriate action in allowing/disallowing continuation.
2. At any stage of a game, one may revert to the position after a specified move. Thus, awaiting (say) black's 18th move, the system might be given a command to revert to the position after (say) white's 3rd move and allow play to continue from that point. The move counter will be adjusted, and the board position amended accordingly.
3. At any stage of play, a game may be saved. This will lead to all moves to that point being saved under a 'game identifier'. You may provide for this feature requesting the game identifier either at the start of play, or at the time saving is requested. You should allow up to ten alphanumeric characters in the identifier.
4. At any time, a game may be retrieved via its identifier. This feature must be available at the start, i.e. when choosing modes of play (it is a special case of mode 2), or during play itself. When this last happens, the user must be asked, via a screen message, if the game in progress is to be saved first. If not, then it is lost.
5. A retrieved game may be resaved, even before any moves are made. The archive of saved games may then have two entries under the same name; the system will – in these cases – add a numerical subscript which will increase by one at each subsequent saving; thus we may have FRED, FRED 1, FRED 2, . . . as a family of saved games. There must be an index of saved games showing all such, listed in sequence, under their game identifier. The index does not show the moves in a saved game – just the sequenced list of names.

A game can be retrieved in one of two modes:

1. To play on – in which case the board position at the last move is depicted on the screen.

2. As a list on the screen of all saved moves.

In this last case, the screen format will include a move number, and a white/black indicator; also conventions for castling (0–0/0–0–0) and *en passant* capture (e.p.); also check, checkmate and stalemate (ch, ch-mate, stl-mate); also promotion (e.g. P–a8 = N) and so on. Thus, if we retrieve FRED 3 in this way, we might see:

White	*Black*	*Game i/d*: FRED 3
1. e2–e4	e7–e5	
2. g1–f3	b8–c6	
3. f1–c4	f8–c5	
4. 0–0	g8–f6	
5. d2–d4	e5 × d4	
6. e4–e5	d7–d5	
7. e5 × f6	d5 × c4	
8. f1–e1ch	c8–e6	

and so on. Screen overflow can occur in this mode, and also for displaying the index of saved games. In these cases, a clear 'continuation' sign must be shown, plus a prompt as to how the user may display further elements.

Additional notes on requirements are as follows. A mode (c) of game retrieval is required. In it a game may be played automatically, one move at a time, by pressing the return key to get each new move. This feature requires the move at which to start to be specified, i.e. 1(W) or 10(B), or whatever, signifying white's first, black's tenth and so on. Clearly, error must be detected and diagnosed by a screen message. In the above example, if we had saved FRED 3 at 8(B), then later retrieved it for stepwise play from 17(W), that would have been impossible. Within this mode (c) of the retrieval feature, a reverse feature must be possible whereby the play proceeds backwards (one move at a time, effected by pressing the return key). Once more, a starting move must be prescribed, e.g. 13(W), 6(B) or whatever – and again, errors must be detected/diagnosed.

The backward play feature of retrieval mode (c) may be entered from retrieval mode (a), or from (a) after further play has taken place. Thus we may retrieve FRED 3 and either replay it (backwards) by 'back-tracking' 8(B) = e6–c8 then 8(W) = e1–f1, etc.; or we may play on:

9. e1 × e6 ch	f7 × e6	
10. f3–g5	g7 × f6	
11. d1–h5 ch	e8–d7	

and we may resave (as FRED 4) at this point, exit without saving, play on, or play back moves from either 11(B) onwards, or any other possible point. If, for instance we have reached 11(B) and want to replay from 8(W) then the board position, as depicted on

the screen, is adjusted accordingly. Having retraced a game, the play forwards feature may be invoked from either this point, or any other legally nominated point.

All screen features must be, at all times, 'user friendly', with clear features, lack of clutter, etc., and generally esthetically pleasing. A screen monitor with reverse-video features, to emphasize specific characters, should be used.

Examples of screen formats must be shown in the offer. A screen depiction of the board must show the 1–8 and a–h rank and file ascriptions alongside two orthogonal sides of the board. Pieces will be depicted on the board by initials within the agreed convention, e.g. WP, BK, WB, WN, BP and so on.

5.2.4 Comment on the URS

It is, perhaps, wise to remind the reader that this protracted subsection is still dealing with the user requirement specification, and how to elicit needs and desiderata from 'users' – putting the widest possible connotation on that word. The chess system described in our example is a serviceable vehicle for demonstrating all sorts of features in software engineering; it is in fact the smallest kind of 'medium sized' system, some of whose features are decidedly 'S' in type, according to Lehman's classification.

However, the whole software system-to-be is an E system as formulated, and can be implemented in about five thousand source statements of some suitable high level language. A development team of four would do the job in 2½ months or so – given all sorts of caveats about their ability, access to client, access to development computers, languages and – most important – their undistracted work.

The example itself is fairly typical of the sort of quality found in a URS. We will restrict our comments on it here as the subject will again crop up when we discuss functional specifications. However, the reader will have noticed that there is some fairly impenetrable argument around saving, retrieving and step-by-step playing (forwards/backwards) of games. Not to mention the 'mode (c)' as a quite clear afterthought! As for the 'reverse video' screen monitor, that is a blatant example of solution design in the wrong document; emphatic display is a legitimate requirement (specifics would need to be detailed about the characters to be emphasized), but means and methods to achieve it are not. Still, it is now time to move on, with the enjoinder that the URS is *not* to be seen as a basis for implementation, but as a stage in the process towards that basis.

And that basis is, or should be, the functional specification.

5.3 FUNCTIONAL SPECIFICATION: THE BASE-LINE DOCUMENT

For some reason, there are things that defy adequate expression. Some subject that proves elusive to the visual artist; some aim that remains beyond the reach of questing science. Fermat's last theorem is an instance; so is the famous tenor aria from Carmen, the 'flower song', which – it is said – has never been entirely satisfactorily recorded.

5.3.1 The problems of definition and description

In software development, this elusive role is played by the functional specification, which can be a subject as vivid yet baffling as the Cheshire Cat's smile. It is not that it defies definition or description entirely, so much as that both its importance, and the difficulties of doing a functional specification competently, tend to elude conceptual grasp. The reasons for this are not hard to find.

Apart from a few guidelines on how to compile a functional specification, plus a rather high level generic description of the aims, there is little or nothing to say about functional specifications in general. Inevitably, every instance of a functional specification will be a special case, through the particularities of the application; it will also tend to be unlike other functional specifications because of its author's style – which will, itself, change from instance to instance.

All this sounds very disappointing, particularly as we have stressed the importance of this document as a 'base-line' and a contractual (or pseudo-contractual) document of great significance. Naturally some abstain from this disappointment, in particular any clients, managers and software developers who are unaware of the perils of premature implementation; also, it must be said with reluctance, some advocates of formal methods, who may tend to understate the importance of specification as an expository act between parties to a development. The fact remains that it is disquieting to find so significant an instrument as the functional specification so difficult to explain adequately.

Audiences chafe at the limitation and, in despair and aggravation, turn to simile. It is not like this; is it not akin to that, or analogous to such and such? But one can lay all the similes in the world end to end, and still not reach a clarification for this particular matter.

So, devoid of these or other palliatives, one is reduced to the only available alternative; to set out, and to detail, such guidelines as we have for this crucially important document, and leave it at that. It may turn out to be more, and better, than we thought we could do.

5.3.2 Getting to the point of functional specification

We have arrived at this stage after a concepts' and user requirement specification, as described in earlier sections. We have a growing archive, possibly containing the essential results obtained through prototypes. The 'deliverable' to this stage from its predecessor is a URS that might be, probably will be, contradictory, redundant, disordered, ambiguous (through use of natural language – however 'structured', however impregnated with application terminology), possibly incorrect and perhaps (but hopefully not) incomplete. It may comprise reams of systems analysis diagrams in SADT, ERA, HIPO, De Wolf's notation or JSD – embellished, or not, by text.

Most probably, this user requirement specification will be a mess. As ex-President Nixon is reported to have said, in a deeply self-revealing comment on his predecessor Eisenhower, 'He was complex and devious – in the best sense of those words!' These are properties that almost perfectly describe the user requirement specification in most cases,

and ones that we must aim to avoid in the functional specification (FS), although I must admit to having seen some wonderfully devious FS documents – in the best sense of that word.

Even whilst the URS is being compiled, we will begin the processes of classification, clarification and ordering that constitute the functional specification activity. This will lead us into a highly iterative and hopefully convergent process with 'users', that 'expository act between parties' already referred to, which is shown in our adopted life cycle schematic (Figure 4.2) as a validation loop. One iterates around this validation loop until the URS is complete and intelligible, and until the functional specification is adequately compiled.

What then can we say about this process of compiling a functional specification? First of all, its aims are clear and simple to state. We need a baseline specification that is:

> The necessary and sufficient information from an adequate user requirement specification, unambiguously expressed. (Macro and Buxton 1987).

The caveat 'an adequate URS', concerns the completeness and intelligibility of that document. The definition also implies that the process of functional specification itself will identify and expunge any incorrectness and inexactitude from the earlier, imperfect URS – probably via the validation cycle with users.

That said, this fine, succinct definition of aims in fact demonstrates two sides in a potential conflict. Taking its second particle (unambiguity) we realize that our functional specification exercise concerns the adequacy of expression of information that is poorly represented; whereas the first part presages a continuation of the specification process to ensure that the functional specification, whilst isomorphic with the correct and complete parts of a URS, is also sufficiently detailed for its two basic purposes of enabling implementation and validation.

5.3.3 Language of discourse and representation; problems of ambiguity

It is clear that a functional specification that is deemed 'valid' for its purposes, should be authorized by both the demand ('client user') and supply ('developer') sides of the transaction – leaving aside, for the moment, the cases where these are the same agency. This may be expressed as another lemma for the subject:

> That, unless it is 'signed off' by authorities in both user and supplier domains, the functional specification will lack the status to act as the basis for implementation, and validation, of the implemented artefact.

This is true of both formal and informal arrangements for supply, and just who does the signing-off, and with what consequences, are topics for later consideration. The question here is, how can one ensure that the functional specification is in a state justifying its authorization? For, it will be recalled, it must be correct, complete and unambiguous – to which we must now add that it must be *comprehensible*.

In cases where the users are not themselves 'computer literate' to any great degree, this may prescribe the language of representation. Particularly tricky circumstances arise

then if specifications are detailed and ordered by people who are 'computer literate', such as software engineers or computer scientists, who may use 'technician friendly' languages of discourse between themselves. One such, in widespread vogue, is pseudo-code – the elementary syntax of some high level language. That is not too bad, unless it becomes 'pseudo-integrand' and 'pseudo-program' in which case it will not only prove incomprehensible to many users, but may well increase the danger of premature implementation, by tempting software developers to see the specification as a design. This point is elaborated further in Section 5.3.4.

Another danger, already discussed, occurs when even more abstract representations are used, as in formal specification. Then it is difficult for many users to cope with the result, and to authenticate it as the 'necessary and sufficient' representation of their needs. I have known cases where a user, threatened with a meter of predicate calculus, has set off purposefully in the direction of its perpetrators with a poker in his fist.

How then does one arrive at a consensus about the document, prior to signing if off? The key to this resides in two factors:

1. The validation loop, as shown in the life cycle schematic, Figure 4.2.
2. The communication abilities of parties to the transaction – users and software developers, where these are different.

The first of these must be understood exactly as to limitation of scope. What is verified is the status of an expository document (functional specification) as an adequate (true/complete) statement of needs or desiderata; what is not being verified is that its implementation will be possible – although in most cases that will be reasonably presumed, or self-evidently so. As explained in Chapter 3, some implementations are indeterminate at this stage, and a fraction of these may turn out, later in the life cycle, not to be implementable at all, through infeasibility of specification: however 'correct' and 'complete' this has been, it may lie beyond technical means.

The validation process should establish, judgmentally by the parties, the following:

1. Is the specification true and complete, and are the requirements expressed in it demonstrable? This is for the users, or user-surrogates, to decide during the 'validation loop'.
2. Is the specification clear enough, and sufficiently detailed, to allow software development to proceed from its definitions? This is the province of the supplier (development technicians).

The premium placed on 'communication abilities' is dazzlingly clear. And here, before proceeding, a further note of caution is needed.

The incessant use of technical notations and languages can deplete the ordinary educational skills of software staff, reading and writing, as these are required for written and oral discourse with users. This is not a continuation of the points made earlier, about the use of pseudo-code and formal methods so high (early) in the life cycle, nor is it unsubtle polemic by other means against these practices. The point concerns general literacy in technical staff, and we shall return to it in Section 13.4 when dealing with the topics of aptitude, performance-appraisal and subject-education.

The inability to communicate competently may not reside on one side only, for users

may be no better. However, the responsibility often lies disproportionately on technicians operating 'high' (early) in the life cycle, since the relationship between source and recipient of requirements takes on the form: 'You tell me what you want; I'll order and record it. Then you can tell me if it's right'. All this, of course, implies that – for the most part – the functional specification language is, basically, natural language.

There are two riders to this guideline. First, the use of natural language at this level of specification will be to express the requirements *unambiguously* rather than – as in the URS – to record a 'stream of consciousness' with minimal impedence. Thus, some structure will be desirable, rather than an essay style. This may be brought about by such things as tabular and numbered lists of requirements, as in De Wolf's scheme, or the use of structured natural language, with the caveats already given about the use of pseudo-code.

Second, the use of natural language can be enhanced by pictures, diagrams, etc. of the logical relationships and data-flow properties of the requirements. Note 'of the requirements', and not of the system or solution-to-be. This caveat is an important one to make, as the use of some diagrammatic means becomes easily conflated with and mistaken for solution design, and signifies a no less fundamental property of a functional specification:

> That it must exclude design information, properly pertaining to the solution or system-to-be.

5.3.4 Design and the functional specification

The reason for excluding design is obvious when one stops to think about it. If the user-fraternity is to 'sign off' the functional specification, as representing their real requirements adequately expressed, then they cannot be expected to do so if the article is corrupted (in this sense) by design ideas that are probably beyond their competence to judge, and which they can hardly be expected to approve prior to their successful implementation.

There is a corollary to this. The functional specification must assuredly exclude solution design. But there is a distinct danger that a clearly formatted, structured functional specification might be taken – on its appearances – as an indication of, or paradigm for, a design. A simple instance will suffice to demonstrate this danger.

Let us say that, in compiling the functional specification we identify a set of input functions, a set of internal processes and a set of outputs. The danger is that each element of each class will be seen as the specification of a discrete element in the implementation, i.e. an integrand, or a program.

In relatively straightforward applications, this one-for-one relationship between structure in the functional specification of *requirements* and structure in the *implementation* is possible without undue trouble. In fact, it can be said to have merit, as it enhances the ease with which the implemented software can be modified. Changes to functional specifications are easily prescribed at that level, and can then be relatively easily traced into the code, and vice versa. Some specification methods, whose procedures continue

into design and code – such as HIPO and JSD/JSP – seek to achieve such 'mapping' between the functional specification and code, for the applications in which their use is suitable.

However, most complex applications – particularly those with 'real-time' properties – will require features of the implementation that make it far more difficult to map the code on to the functional specification, and vice versa. To labor the virtues of a simple derivation of design from the structure of the functional specification is, in those cases, to risk violating good design principles (see Section 3.2 and Chapter 7).

Simply stated, the guideline is this;

> Where it is possible, without loss of good design, to derive implementation structure from specification structure, then it may be done to enhance one aspect of software quality – its modifiability. When it cannot done without presuming (and therefore precluding) a proper design stage, then it should not be done.

Unfortunately, it is not always clear when the structure of the functional specification can and cannot be taken, with safety, as an indication of the best code structure for the software. I have seen the most fearful morass ensue from simplistic derivation of low level design from the structure of the requirements. In one case, a team attempting the chess problem flashed through the FS stage, producing a pseudo-code-based document that, as role-player for the client, I flinched to see – and only signed off to see what would ensue. I was not detained long in my expectations. The team whizzed into implementation and, in half the time others were taking, had their 4,742 statements of Pascal ready to syphon into the VAX, bless them. Then the fun started.

Testing software is a highly dynamic process with changes and corrections pouring on top of corrections and changes. And something seemed subtly amiss. Days lengthened into weeks and, horror!, the testing would not converge. Due dates for alpha-tests came and went, as did those for beta-tests and delivery of the accepted system; documentation went down round the S-bend and down the drain. All all because of premature implementation – the amateur's urge to leap from some form of specification into code, without bothering with all the boring rigmarole of design – as they probably saw it.

So, in general, one should not incorporate design in the functional specification, nor should one presume a design, on the basis of the structure of functional specification material, either.

In fact, there are *two* moderations of this stricture about design in the functional specification. First, although the functional specification should be done without assumptions concerning the outcome of a solution – in order that it may remain a true specification of requirements – it is often done in the knowledge of existing facilities, or policies to provide them. For example, some format standards to be used for information definition; or an encoding algorithm for a 'secure' part of some system; or knowledge of some hardware and software already *in situ*, or to be procured in any case. As an example of this last, the URS given in the example might have read, at some suitable stage, '. . . and do the job on that 256K RAM Motorola 68000 standing under the dust-sheet in the corner, and write the programs in GRUNT.'

In all such cases, the solution information acts as a potential *constraint* on the functional specification, not onerous if adequate, but potentially very onerous if inadequu-

ate. The FS must then be done with this in mind, otherwise gross over-specification may result. The constraints must be detailed in the functional specification – typically as an appendix – with clear pointers from the text, indicating that its scope is held within the limits of the constraints.

Other than that, the functional specification must be free of the detail of hardware/ virtual software ancillaries that are properly the remit of supply rather than requirement. That is not to say that the *feasibility* of supply should remain unexplored, or that this exploration should continue in isolation from the revealed requirements, as posted in the functional specification. It is to say that the two exercises, though connected, must be kept apart.

The second exception to the rule for excluding solution design from the functional specification concerns the outcome of building prototypes. Here we face two possibilities, and the reader will recall them from a previous chapter; prototypes may be: (a) for helping to reveal the detail of requirements, or (b) for helping to develop means of solution.

Typical of the first is the question of human–user interfaces, and typical of the second is the exploration and invention of algorithms. Either or both will lead to prototype software being made, and the prototyping to clarify technical means may result in experimental hardware – one example of which might be the so-called 'bit-slice processor' for image processing in weather forecasting, geological modeling and tomography.

To repeat earlier advice, when the prototype has revealed the information required, it should be disposed of, i.e. clearly labeled and left for future use as a prototype, or thrown away. Its revealed information should, however, be incorporated in the software development process. That, for user requirements, will go into the functional specification – either directly, or through the URS. The information on technical means will probably be incorporated in a different category altogether, that of outline systems design, described in Chapter 6. Of the user requirements' material derived from prototyping, there is one topic that is properly seen as design – and yet it should, indeed must, get into the functional specification despite our 'rule'. That is the so-called 'user interface', and it is appropriate that we deal with this topic here.

The user interface issue in computer applications has spawned a special interest subject, within the wide-ranging genre of 'computing' in general, known as 'human factors'. Its protagonists would argue that 'human factors' is a lot more than just the user interface, but that was its principal topic and that is our interest here; the wider issues of 'human factors' will be dealt with in Volume 2 of this series, alongside a far more detailed exposition of all the issues in specification.

However, it is clear that a computer system for human usage should have a tractable means of input for its users, and an amenable form of output for them. The fact that so few computer systems in the past have furnished these needs emphasizes the case rather than refutes it. It is not uncommon, in all fields of application, to find a disenchanted user prodding glumly at a keyboard, and staring vacantly until some gnomic message appears as a congested clump of phosphorescent symbols.

One aim of requirements' prototyping should be to prevent that unhappy tableau. Early in the life cycle of activities, suppliers of the system to be (or users themselves if

adept enough) should fashion prototype programs for this purpose; nothing elaborate, just a set of high level language drivers for the input and output media, on which the users can experiment with different formats. In the case of product development, one may simulate users from within one's own company – commercial staff say – or invite a few good customers, or latent customers to help.

In this way, the justifiably feared injunction to make the inputs and outputs 'user friendly' will be forestalled. The outcome will be some definite views from users (or their representatives) on what is, to them, 'friendly'. These views will be in the form of input and output formats – design in fact – and they must be incorporated in the functional specification in order that the user's signature on that document authenticates them specifically.

5.3.5 Consolidated guidelines for functional specification

We may now return to our compilation of guidelines for the functional specification, and even add to it. In fact, so far we have the following precepts:

1. The functional specification is the necessary and sufficient information from the URS, unambiguously expressed.
2. The functional specification generally has contractual, or pseudo-contractual, connotations, and is therefore a 'formal' document; this means that it must be signed off, when complete, by authorized representatives from both the requirements' (user) domain, and that of the solution (supply). In the first case this says: 'The functional specification describes my requirements properly, and in a way that will make validation of an implemented system possible to do'. The second says: 'The functional specification is an adequate base-line for my supply'. For these statements to be possible, it means that, in most cases, the functional specification will be presented in natural language, plus diagrams to clarify meaning.
3. Solution design must be excluded from the functional specification, otherwise users will be unable to sign it off. Two exceptions to this rule are for any known constraints on requirements due to 'inherited' equipment as a given factor, and the design of input and output formats for human usage of the system.

I have frequently had questions of the kind: 'What about data formats between devices (e.g. in an embedded system); things like binary bit-patterns; should these go in the functional specification?' If they are the given properties of known devices, then they should be appended as part of the given (inherited) characteristics that might constitute constraints. Otherwise, in the case where they are invented at the time the FS is done, by its authors say, then they are properly seen as solution details (not necessarily 'given constraints' on requirements) and have no place in the functional specification at all. Their place then is – with a lot of other solution detail that emerges during requirements' specification – in the outline system design; see Chapter 6.

Although there is no cookery book for doing a functional specification, guidelines for good practice in the matter can, and should, include a checklist of the generic types of information that might need to be accessed, detailed and ordered in a particular application. The elements of such a checklist are (continuing the previous numbering system):

4. The application-specific features and functions of the requirement will be the dominant information to detail in the first place, but other features may occur or should perhaps, be considered. The full list of such genera is as follows:

(a) Application-specific features and functions, progressively detailed, to an adequate level of definition, in the URS.

(b) Input to and output from the system-to-be – these will, in both cases, comprise sources (e.g. human, sensor, other computer), devices (e.g. keyboard, screen, DMA link, buffered data communication, transducer device), specific formats (e.g. keyboard/screen formats as required by other devices), input–output profiles (e.g. arrival profiles, peaks, output response requirements), error checking and diagnostic features (on inputs particularly).

(c) Security and integrity features required – security is the prevention (or diagnosis) of unauthorized access to programs or data, whether purposefully done or otherwise; integrity is the prevention (or diagnosis) of accidental corruption to programs or data, where the definition of 'accidental' includes malfunction by the system itself.

(d) System performance requirements, including any limits on down-time, response delay and so forth (see also b) – these are defined for the parts of requirements whose needs would be critically violated by these limits being exceeded.

(e) Any backup or standby facilities required, e.g. for c or d, and the functional requirements pertaining, insofar as these will require specific implementation.

(f) Portability of software, or other general or specific purpose it must serve – such utilitarian needs must be specific, for example: 'The software for the chess system must operate also on a 512K RAM VAX 11/780, operating version 32A (iii) of VMS, and having DEC standard peripherals'.

It will be immediately clear that most of these can be extensive in their own right. For non-trivial requirements, the functional specification can become a voluminous and complex document. I have known one that eventually resulted in a software system of only about 7K source statements of program code, but amounted to 150 pages of closely written text and some elaborate diagrams.

This is not a datum point on some metric for the size of functional specifications (for none such exists, and there is no pro-rata law to help out either), but it is a cautionary note to the reader. The URS may be several volumes of canonical material in a fine state of disorder, as though actually having been discharged *from* a canon. But there is no inevitable reduction that will occur as a result of cleaning it up. For, in the process, more detailing will be done, and more factors may be considered, such as those in b–e above.

One more general guideline for the functional specification may be advanced. It follows from the users' authentication of the document and is (preserving the numbering to date):

5. Avoid the incorporation of any elements in a functional specification that are not capable of demonstration. The FS will be the yardstick against which a major consideration in quality (and, therefore, contract compliance) will be judged. Only trouble at this later stage will ensue from any vagaries of this sort.

Let us turn then from the problem of content of the functional specification, to the question of its form. How does one order the work in a functional specification, and

render the volume and complexity of it intelligible? For if the FS is unduly convoluted, or unclear for whatever reason, then it will violate the need for unambiguity, and may disable its authorization or, later, the acceptance of a system to meet the requirements.

5.3.6 Graphical notations as the way to clarify natural language

As we have repeated several times now, functional specifications are generally best done in natural language, with the limited use of notations to depict logical relations and data-flow properties within the requirement. Structured natural language may be used, but with care that it does not supply satisfy computer technicians (as in the case of pseudo-code usually) while confusing the community of users or their representatives.

The notations of most frequent use to enhance the clarity of text in functional specifications are (again) SADT, De Wolf's system and JSD, of those already described. Others include: (a) the 'activity-channel-pool' notation of Mascot, (b) timing diagrams, (c) data-flow diagrams and (d) finite-state machine diagrams. In each case, as in the section on URSs, these are described briefly below.

However, in doing so, the reader should note that we are speaking here only of the use of the *notations*, and not any other aspects of developed method that may attach. For example, Mascot is a developed method for both defining some types of requirements and designing systems to meet them. (In fact, one critic has attacked me fiercely for saying anything at all about Mascot in a chapter on specification). The same may be said of data-flow analysis and its associate, data structure-based depiction. In all cases, at this functional specification stage, we speak of the notation only, and repeat the advice not to confuse the diagrams that are for logical/data relationships in the requirement with similar schemes in the design of a solution.

As well as the following brief summaries, these notations and their procedures (where appropriate) are referred to elsewhere; e.g. in Chapter 7, and in Volumes 2 and 4 on specification and design respectively.

THE METHOD FOR MODULAR APPROACH TO SOFTWARE CONSTRUCTION,
OPERATION AND TEST: MASCOT
This method is due originally to the British Ministry of Defence – Royal Signals and Radar Establishment. The notation is essentially very simple in its symbols and rules of applying them. Figure 5.15 shows the basic symbols. The terminology is as follows. Two data types are identified:

1. Reference data, which are depicted by 'pools'.
2. Communicating data, which are depicted by 'channels'.

'Activities' process data to and from both pools, and other activities, via channels.

Data sources and sinks are depicted by subsystems of intercommunicating data areas (SIDA), and subsystems are bounded by the dotted line rectangle shown in Figure 5.16. Undetailed subsystems (e.g. in a cataloging scheme for Mascot diagrams) are depicted by the simple rectangle convention shown. The initials 'ACP' mean 'activity/channel/pool'.

An example of Mascot-ACP usage is shown in Figure 5.16. This example is again

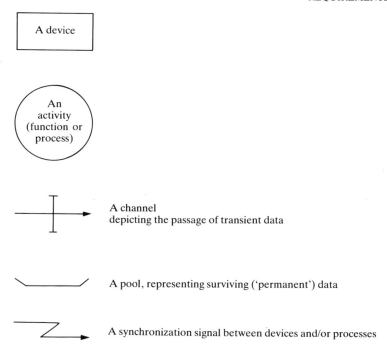

A device

An
activity
(function or
process)

A channel
depicting the passage of transient data

A pool, representing surviving ('permanent') data

A synchronization signal between devices and/or processes

FIGURE 5.15 Mascot symbols.

derived from the very high level, generic specification for a screen-based chess system. The 'fierce critic's' point, previously mentioned, that Mascot is a design method, for process oriented applications, is rather borne out here. The diagram presented may, in fact, fail two criteria for use in a functional specification – namely that it tends to be a representation of a solution, rather than the depiction of a requirement, and that it may not be easy for some users to understand.

Why include it then, or rather why include it here instead of in the chapter on design? The answer is that diagrams of this sort occur very frequently when trying to enhance the natural language specification of requirements by means of a graphical notation. If they are not quite suitable for the functional specification, then they should be incorporated in the archive documentation for an outline system design – part of the feasibility exercise done in parallel with the functional specification.

I remain unrepentant about revealing Mascot here. It *is* a design method and, as such, is represented in Chapter 7 of this book. On the other hand, its ACP notation is remarkably suitable for depicting certain types of process-oriented requirements, as well as their design as solutions. The fact is that the chess example is not particularly suited as a vehicle to display Mascot's notation. This helps to make an important point. Use an *appropriate* tool; I may have appeared to end up here driving screws with a hacksaw, and the result is a slightly perverse use of the Mascot notation – some way between a data-flow depiction and a flowchart for system design. Don't let that deter the use of Mascot, at the functional specification level, for process-oriented applications.

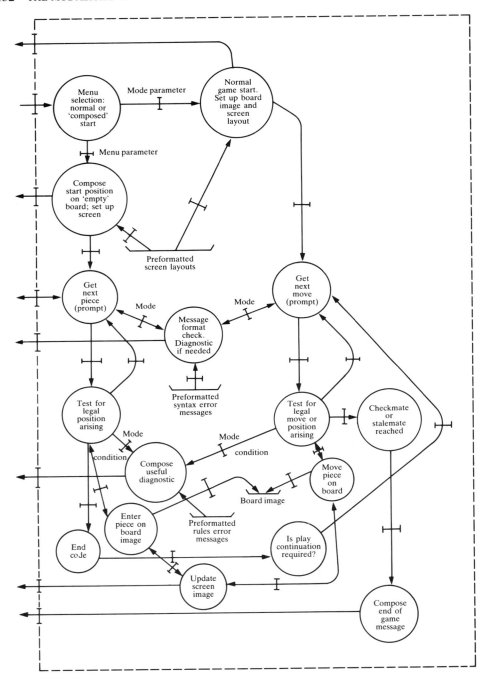

FIGURE 5.16 Example of Mascot notation in use; CAISSA design.

TIMING DIAGRAMS

In requirements such as those frequently met in the 'process' category of applications, the sequencing of subprocesses is often a dominant factor for one reason or another. Figure 5.10 shows an instance in the abstract. These subprocesses may concern either hardware or software, or both ultimately. As this is the functional specification phase we may not yet know which, unless the devices whose synchronization is at issue are 'defined' in the environment of requirements.

The notation for depicting temporal relationships is taken from the hardware field: it is called a timing diagram and is commonplace in electronics, appearing in one of several forms. Figure 5.17 shows such a timing diagram, with interprocess synchronization.

An interesting notion (attributed to Dijkstra) is that of the *granularity of time*, the fine or coarse resolution needed – in specification of a requirement, or implementation of a solution to it – to represent duration and synchrony. In strongly time-dependent, 'process' type applications, it is fundamentally important to determine the granularity of time within the requirement, and mis-stating this can cause trouble in the subsequent development. For instance, the state change of a device, in some electronic system, may require recognition within a defined time period. The rate of change, and timing aspects of 'recognition', may be crucial for the design of a compliant system – in the case, say, of one in which the state of the device is established by polling, that is inspecting it as distinct from having it assert its status on a system-interrupt basis. Here, the 'granularity of time' in the objective world will represent a hard, functional requirement that, although the design will not be a consideration at that time, will be crucial to the subsequent stages of software development. Timing diagrams for those aspects of requirements, play a useful part in determining a maximum allowable granularity of time.

DATA-FLOW DIAGRAMS

Data-flow diagrams can come in all sorts of shapes, sizes, notations – and probably flavors. Stylized data-flow can be done in SADT, JSD and Mascot. The simple vocabulary and syntax of another data-flow notation is shown in Figure 5.18, and Figure 5.19 gives an example of it in action, again based upon the chess example. In some ways this depiction is the most satisfactory of all those shown to date, allowing for the fact that it shows one more feature (retrieval of a saved game) than in the other cases. This observation is not to be taken as a general statement of preference. It merely means that the notation is particularly suitable to represent *this* application. As the gambling fraternity say 'Horses for courses', no more, no less.

In fact, data-flow (along with Mascot) often becomes an early favorite of programmers involved, for the first time, in functional specification. Sometimes it gets used in contexts for which it is entirely unsuitable, those with strong temporal features for instance, when it may fail to add anything at all to text. Then data-flow depictions can act as a great irritant at this level, as could anything else used inappropriately.

Clearly data-flow depictions will be useful at the software design stage also, as are others, depending on the application – SADT, De Wolf, JSD and Mascot. The important thing to remember here is that the notation of choice is being used to enhance structured text, and (in this functional specification phase) the notation may be used in isolation to the full procedures of the method. Advocates of fully blown methods as top-to-toe life

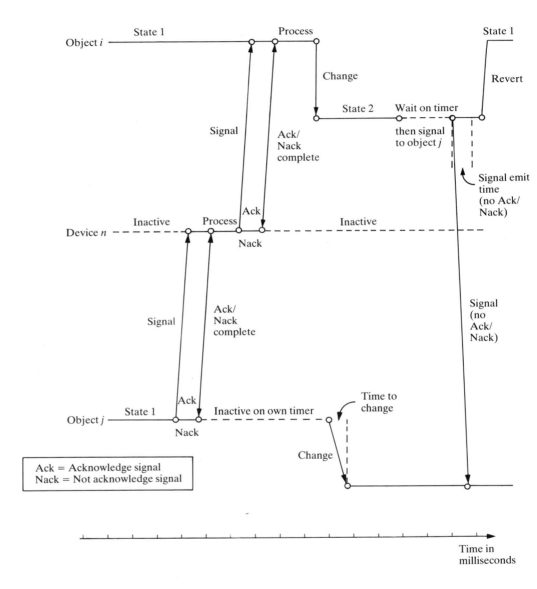

FIGURE 5.17 A simple timing diagram.

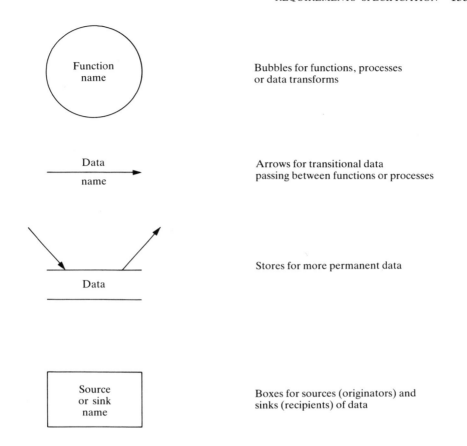

FIGURE 5.18 Data-flow notation.

cycle tools, such as Jackson's JSD/JSP may flinch a little at the idea of using a notation out of context, but there it is.

Of all notations, the primitive data-flow grammar of Figure 5.18 is by far the most popular amongst non-software engineers specifying functional requirements, once they know the various alternatives and given that they are left reasonably free to choose, i.e. they lack the prescription of some 'standard' method of the SADT, JSD type.

One of the slight drawbacks to this is that users tend to slip design features of a solution into the requirement specification, by using this notation. It is an easy thing to do at the FS stage, using any notation; to strike out bravely and determinedly at the requirements, start depicting their logical relationships and data interchanges and then, without a break in stride, blink or twinge of conscience, find oneself designing away like clockwork, all within the poor old functional specification.

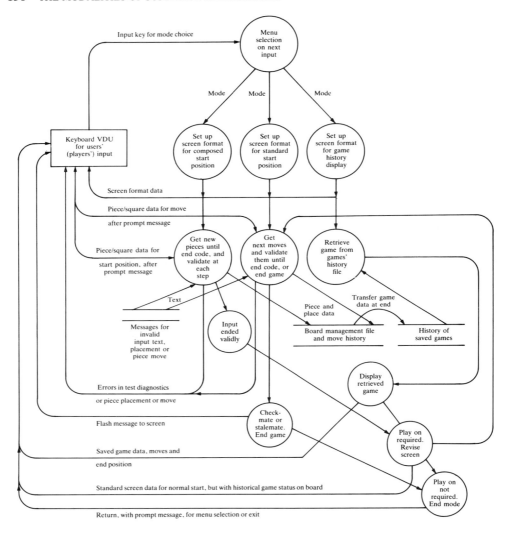

FIGURE 5.19 Data-flow example; CAISSA design.

FINITE-STATE MACHINES AND THEIR NOTATION – STATE DIAGRAMS

The elementary definitions and axioms of finite-state automation, within computer science, need not detain us for long here. Basically, what is being said is that a system comprising a set of subsystems will have a set of states S_i in which it will be operating in any epoch E_i; its global inputs will be I_i to put it in that state; its global outputs will be O_i from which it emerges from that state.

This can be seen as a simple black-box system, within which subsystems will be in

states $S_i(1)$, $S_i(2)$, and so on, with local inputs $I_i(1)$, $I_i(2)$, ... provoking those states, and out of which states they emerge with local output $O_i(1)$, $O_i(2)$, ..., etc. Within each subsystem (1), (2), ..., etc. there is a next-state function $F_i(1)$, $F_i(2)$, ... which, given an input and a state, produces a next state, and an output function $G_i(1)$, $G_i(2)$, ... which, given an input, a state and a next-state function, produces the output from that state.

Overall, the system may be said to have a general next-state function F_i and a general output function G_i for its state S_i. The issue for systems of this type is not time, so much as the epoch during which a certain system state or subsystem state applies.

Clearly, many types of computer system can be described in this way so long as their behavior represents actions occurring in an orderly way in the world, or their subsystem processes can be represented in the manner of connected states. Typical of this are all kinds of menu-driven systems, those computer-based applications in which users are prompted to their next action by choice-messages on a screen. The chess example, given earlier, will be seen as one such. Telephony is another application in which 'states' are the natural thing to speak about.

The notation of finite-state automation is the 'state diagram', a simple directed graph of the connection between defined states in a system or subsystem. A state diagram depiction of the requirements in the URS for a chess system is given in Figure 5.20 below. It is useful to note that such state diagrams are an ancillary notation to that of De Wolf, described in Section 5.2.2.

State diagrams are usually quite elementary depictions of the state relationships – as the reader will have realized – but they are no less useful for that. By a trivial incorporation, state diagrams can be made to carry data-flow information, and the next-state function/output function detail immanent to that state of that subsystem. One author (Salter 1976) has suggested an elementary procedure for using state diagrams in this way. The outcome is an alternative to other data-flow schemes we have described.

Here, for the functional specification, a hint to readers is pretty obvious; seeing a requirement in 'state machine' terms may be a most useful way of looking at it, and of representing it within the FS. This is particularly the case in many data processing and computation applications of both batch and on-line types. Seeing a *requirement* as 'states' does not necessarily say anything about its implementation.

These four notations (Mascot, timing diagrams, data-flow and state diagrams) added to the previous three (SADT, De Wolf, JSD) make up a choice of seven or so useful ways of embellishing text in the functional specification. It is not a fixed list, an algorithm or a miracle cure for problems with the specification. The notations in it (and other, better ones if you know of them) are the 'plus' in the 'natural language plus' as the means of writing the functional specification. As a demonstration of the freedom of choice available here, there is nothing against a state of affairs where one notation is used to depict logical relationship, or states, and another one is used for the data-flows in a requirement.

None of the notations is difficult to grasp. We have found that it takes somewhat less than an hour for even the most technology-dyslexic attendee, on an education course, to get into the swing of things in any of the notations listed. Where greater difficulty arises it is usually due to conceptual problems with an application, or the urge to use the procedures attaching to a method as well as its notation. Some methods have non-trivial

procedures (SADT and JSD, for instance), and some have hardly any procedure at all, e.g. Mascot and data-flow.

5.3.7 Abstraction and abstracting

Another non-trivial problem is that of amplifying a statement of requirements with pertinent information about it, as must be done to a sufficient level in the functional, 'base-line' document. This is generally achieved by a twofold process, enacted simultaneously, of detailing and abstracting.

The detailing part will cause little trouble to the reader, for it is obvious what is meant. In the chess example we say: 'a save-game feature must be implemented' or some such fairly high generic level imperative. Clearly we will need to know much more about this, and we can list a set of questions accordingly:

'From where can we enter this feature; i.e. from which other states can it arise?'

'To where can we go from this feature; i.e. which other states can arise from it?'

'What shall we save?' (i.e. the game identifier, the moves, what else?)

'Will any input to other features arise?' (clearly, yes; to the index)

'How will we save the game? Presumably in an internal (RAM) store; what happens when we overflow this? Do we then transfer the file store to disk store?'

Clearly some of these questions are getting near to design ('RAM; disk') and we can no doubt answer them more neutrally – e.g. 'store', 'overflow-store'. But on the whole the process is clear; we are *detailing* a feature.

Abstraction is a different matter. It is the selection of information, often done during detailing, on the basis of its pertinence. Abstraction is the process of discarding inessentials. Thus, to the question: 'What shall we save?' we may reply: 'Game i/d, moves to date, don't forget if it's a re-save of FRED (N) to call it FRED ($N + 1$), and save girlfriend's name, date, time, position of the planet Neptune, . . . ' and so on. Clearly some of this is good stuff, whilst some of it may not have an obvious purpose. Discarding Neptune's position will be an act of abstraction in this case, and the date/time might well be scrutinized closely for relevance too, not to mention more personal matters.

5.3.8 Formatting the document

It now remains for us to discuss the format of functional specifications. As the reader will have realized, there is almost no way of generalizing about this; it would not be plausible, for instance, to offer a 'standard' or 'usual' table of contents. In fact the checklist of genera in a–f of Section 5.3.5 is about as far as one can go toward that.

However, a few general guidelines can be given for formatting information in the functional specification:

1. The document should be clearly set out in chapters (or sections, or whatever), page numbered and summarized in a contents list.
2. An introduction should summarize the URS, to set the context. Note, this should be a

strict summary, and said to be such, comprising the main intentions or purposes in the requirement, and its main features. It is often helpful to put this in the form of a table of 'abstract processes', as shown in the description of De Wolf's approach in Section 5.2.2, Figure 5.11.

3. It is also generally helpful to format the detail in a functional specification, as follows. Either identify features first, or inputs to them, or outputs from them, and list the components of information (with detailing and abstracting) in those categories. Thus there may be a section defining and detailing features and functions, then one on all inputs, and one on outputs. Or, alternatively, inputs and outputs relating to features may be defined with the appropriate feature.

   Clearly, these inputs and outputs, however arranged, are the best place to define whatever has emerged from the specification prototyping exercises; keyboard and screen formats, and so on.

4. A clear numbering system for features and functions, inputs and outputs will help in cross referencing between them, and in the diagrammatic depiction of relationships in, for example, SADT, data-flow, state diagram or whatever.

5. Append any details of 'given' equipment that acts as a potential or actual constraint on the functional specification.

6. During the functional specification stage, be particularly sure to get the users involved. To repeat the point made earlier, this will ensure that the functional specification is done in the right way. Ultimately, when the definitive specification is finished (or confidently supposed to be), then have it validated by users, and 'signed off' by both users and suppliers as representing the requirements, and acting as a base-line for an implementation.

7. One may have to make assumptions about meaning in a functional specification, or one may wish to make 'systems engineering' improvements to the way things are done in the real world. That may be seen as a virtue by users, so it should not be shunned. But these assumptions/suggestions must be identified clearly for what they are. Have a section early in the FS, dealing with this – after the summary of user's requirements for example.

It now only remains to give an example of a functional specification, as we did in the earlier section on URS. First of all, though, a caveat. One example cannot serve as a vehicle for all the points made, and approaches identified in this section; nor can one part of a volume such as this go extensively into many examples.

Thus, we submit the following, derived from the previous (URS) example for a chess system – CAISSA. The reader may care to revisit that unordered, 'stream of consciousness' representation of requirements before proceeding further.

EXAMPLE 2

FUNCTIONAL SPECIFICATION FOR 'CAISSA', A CHESS SYSTEM

Contents

1. Introduction; summary of requirements

1.1 The requirement is for a computer-based system to assist players to engage in games of chess against each other (note, not against 'intelligent play' by the computer) with moves entered at a keyboard VDU, and shown as occurring on a representation of a chess-board on the screen. The features of the requirement are as follows:

1.2 In general, features will be offered as a menu of such to the players. A summary of the order in which features can be accessed is shown in Figure 5.20.

1.3 There will be a 'play game' feature which will permit chess moves to be entered, in algebraic chess notation (a–h files; 1–8 ranks; a1 square in bottom left). Check, checkmate and stalemate will be detected and shown by a message on the screen. The conditions for piece promotion will be similarly identified and an entry at the keyboard required before play can be resumed.

1.4 There will be a feature to allow choice between two states at the start of a game; that of normal piece/position with all thirty-two pieces in their given positions at the start of a game of chess; the alternative is for the players to insert pieces, by keyboard entry, to an initially empty board.

1.5 There will be a feature to save a game in progress, by user (player) command entered at the keyboard. Each saved game will be given a game identifier prior to it being saved.

1.6 There will be a feature to retrieve a game using a game identifier to search in the file of saved games.

1.7 An index of saved games will be displayed on the screen on receipt of a user (player) command entered at the keyboard.

1.8 Saved games may, on retrieval 1.6, be automatically played through – either forward or backward – from a particular stage in the game to be specified by the user (player) by input at the keyboard. The position at that move will be depicted on the 'board' representation on the VDU screen, and each move (forward or backward as specified) will be enacted on it a step at a time. A game from normal play 1.3 may be treated

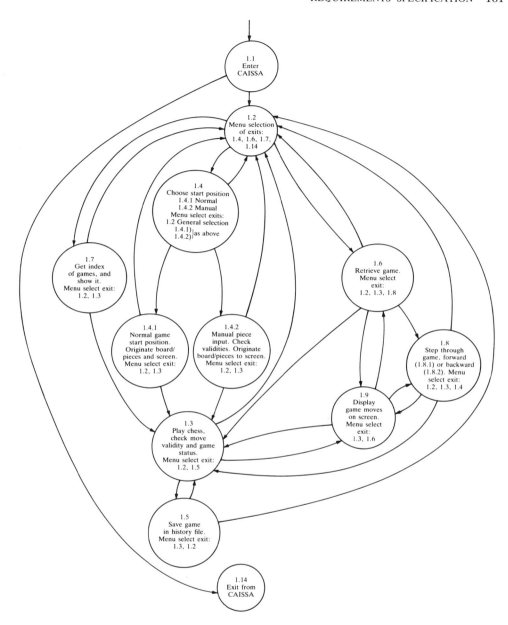

FIGURE 5.20 State diagram of CAISSA requirements.

TABLE 5.1 Tabular depiction of state relationships in CAISSA

a calls → b ↓	OS	1.1	1.2	1.3	1.4	1.5	1.6	1.7	1.8	1.9	1.10	1.11	1.12	1.13	1.14
OS	o														*
1.1	*	o													
1.2		*	o	*	*	*	*	*	*						
1.3				o	*	*	*	*	*	*					
1.4			*		o										
1.5				*		o									
1.6			*				o			*					
1.7			*					o							
1.8							*		o						
1.9									*	o					
1.10											o				
1.11												o			
1.12													o		
1.13														o	
1.14			*												o

Note: Table to be read vertically downwards i.e. 1.6 may call 1.2, 1.3 or 1.8.
OS = operating system

similarly, after which normal play may be resumed from the original position reached before the feature 1.8 was invoked.

1.9 A game in progress from 1.3 or a retrieved game from 1.6 may be displayed as a set of static moves (in the algebraic notation) on the screen, following a user (player) command.

1.10 Screen overflow from features 1.7 and 1.9 will result in a clear message to that effect, and will provide access to an available feature to display overflow games, and to repeat this overflow display until overflows have been completely shown.

1.11 User (player) input syntax errors will be detected, and diagnosed by helpful messages on the screen.

1.12 Violations of chess rules, via 1.3 or 1.4 manual input, will be detected and diagnosed by helpful messages on the screen.

1.13 All play (in 1.3) and manual input (in 1.4) will only be deemed licit if consistent with the FIDE rules governing chess play.

1.14 There will be a feature to exit from the CAISSA system altogether.

2. States of the CAISSA system, as required

The state relationships are also represented in Table 5.1. The use of these alternative means is to clarify exactly the workings and behavior between states within the requirement. The assumptions incorporated in this scheme are now listed:

2.1 The user features of menu selection are set out in the diagram and table above. It should be confirmed, before proceeding, that an exit from 1.2 alone is acceptable.

2.2 It must be confirmed that it is acceptable for 1.9 – display game – to return to 1.3 and 1.8 only, i.e. the feature to return to 1.2 is missing.

2.3 An adequate development system (computer, PSE software, ancillaries such as standard terminals) is assumed to be available. A Digital Equipment Corp. VAX 11/780; minimally 512K RAM; VMS operating systems with UCSD Pascal; 10 megabyte disk archival storage (minimal); a number of VT 100 keyboard VDUs; hardcopy printer.

3. Functions, inputs and outputs in the requirement

Functions 1.1–1.9 inclusive are detailed further, and their inputs and outputs shown. The features of 1.10–1.13 inclusive are incorporated, where relevant, in 1.2–1.9.

1.1/1.14 System entry and exit for CAISSA
It is assumed that CAISSA will be filed as a normal library routine (or 'executable image') under the VMS operating system. The user will invoke the chess system by an input command typed at the keyboard.

(ENTER CAISSA)

Entry to CAISSA will be signaled by a message on the screen:

(WELCOME TO CAISSA)
(ENTER "MENU" TO PROCEED)

On typing in this command, feature 1.2 – menu selection – is invoked. Errors in the input commands will result in an error message at the bottom of the screen:

(YOU HAVE JUST ENTERED "... (Message) ...")
(THIS COMMAND IS UNKNOWN AND YOU MAY HAVE MADE AN INPUT ERROR)
(PRESS RETURN KEY TO CLEAR, THEN RE-ENTER COMMAND – SEE SECTION/PAGE ... OF MANUAL)

Continuation after an input error cannot be effected until the error is cleared. The alternative is to exit the system via 1.2.
Exit from the CAISSA system (see 1.2 below) returns to the VMS operating system monitor.

1.2 Main menu selection
This is entered from 1.1 and, thereafter, from 1.3 to 1.8 inclusive until exit 1.14 takes place. When the input command:

(MENU)

is correctly entered from 1.1 or 1.3–1.8, then the following message is displayed to users (players) on the screen:

OPTION 1 – PLAY CHESS
OPTION 2 – RETRIEVE GAME
OPTION 3 – DISPLAY INDEX OF SAVED GAMES
OPTION 4 – EXIT FROM CAISSA

Users may choose by entering the following command at the keyboard:

(SELECT OPTION ...)

User's input error in presenting this command is diagnosed as before (see error message in 1.1 above). Continuation after input error cannot be effected until the error is cleared. The alternative is to exit the system.

1.3(a) Play game (start)

This is entered from 1.2 and may be returned to from 1.5, if that state has been entered from 1.5 (save game). When this feature is invoked, the user is presented with a choice expressed by a message on the screen:

(YOU MAY CHOOSE A NORMAL STARTING
CONFIGURATION OF PIECES, OR YOU MAY CHOOSE
TO ENTER PIECES ONTO AN EMPTY BOARD)
(CHOOSE BY ENTERING EITHER "NORMAL START"
OR "MANUAL INPUT")

User's input error in presenting this command is diagnosed as before (see error message in 1.1 above). Continuation after input error cannot be effected until error is cleared. The alternative is to exit the system via 1.2. This can be done by pressing the return key and entering:

(MENU)

1.4 Normal start and manual input

This is entered from 1.3. In the event of the option 'normal start' being chosen, 'pieces' will be 'placed' on the 'board' in the standard fashion, as shown in Figure 5.21. In the event of the option 'manual input' being invoked, the screen will show exactly the same format as in Figure 5.21, but the 'board' will then be empty of pieces. A message in the 'Prompt field' will read:

(PLEASE ENTER PIECE – UPPER CASE FOR PIECE TYPE,
LOWER CASE FOR SQUARE)

The user may then enter pieces to squares by typing in an input of the type (AB–yz) and then pressing the return key. AB is the piece type as shown in Figure 5.21 (e.g. BB, WN, WP, etc.) and yz is the square coordinate, file/rank, as in al, c7, h4, etc.

When all the pieces have been entered, this must be signified by an input command:

(END)

Then, if the position is licit, return from this mode to 1.3 occurs.

All piece inputs are checked for syntax validity. In the case of user's input error, the 'standard' error message is shown (see 1.1).

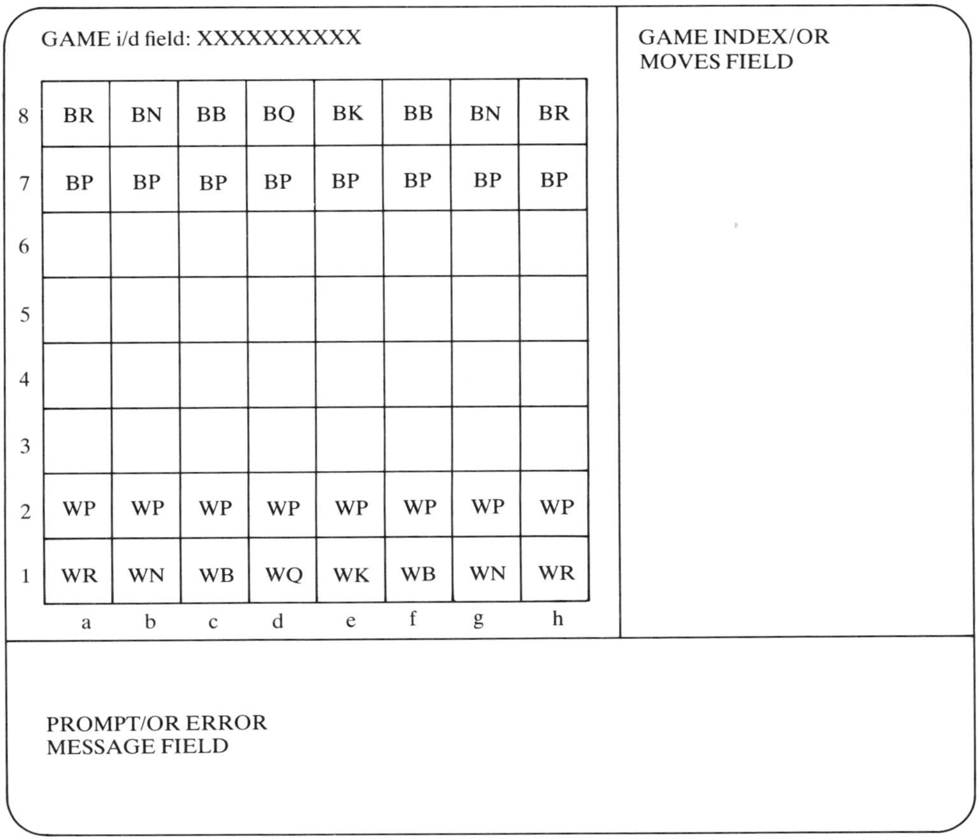

8	BR	BN	BB	BQ	BK	BB	BN	BR
7	BP	BP	BP	BP	BP	BP	BP	BP
6								
5								
4								
3								
2	WP	WP	WP	WP	WP	WP	WP	WP
1	WR	WN	WB	WQ	WK	WB	WN	WR
	a	b	c	d	e	f	g	h

GAME i/d field: XXXXXXXXXX

GAME INDEX/OR
MOVES FIELD

PROMPT/OR ERROR
MESSAGE FIELD

FIGURE 5.21 Screen layout – normal input at game start.

Continuation after error of this type cannot proceed before the error is cleared. The only alternative is to invoke 1.2 by entering the command:

(MENU)

All piece inputs are checked for legitimacy within FIDE rules for chess. In the event of an input being illicit, a special message is shown in the message field of the screen, and the attempted piece placement is not made. Thus continuation after such an attempt is possible.

The following illicit configurations are tested for:

1. More than one king of a color. The error message is:

(TOO MANY ... KINGS)

indicating BLACK or WHITE.

2. No king of a color. This is diagnosed when (END) is entered, and the exit to 1.3 is then disallowed. The error message is:

(NO . . . KING)

If both kings are missing then two error messages are shown.

3. Too many pawns of a color. The error message is:

(TOO MANY . . . PAWNS)

and the message occurs when the excessive entry is attempted.

4. Too many major pieces. The total number of major pieces (Q, R, B, N) of a color may not exceed seven plus the number of missing pawns of that color. In the event of no missing pawns the error message is:

(TOO MANY MAJOR PIECES FOR . . ., OF THE TYPE . . .)

White square and black square bishops are regarded as distinctive types for this purpose. Note, this check is only made when the (END) command is given, and continuation is disallowed, other than via (MENU) to 1.2. Note also that there is no conclusive test for too many major types in the event of there being missing pawns.

5. King in check by more than two pieces simultaneously. This situation cannot occur in real play, and is tested for when (END) is given. Earlier it might be a transitory effect, e.g. awaiting other pieces blocking a path. The error message is:

(. . . KING IN RECEIPT OF TOO MANY CHECKS)

If both kings suffer this condition, then two error messages are given. No continuation (other than via 1.2) is possible until the condition is corrected.

6. More than one back-rank pawn. This is detected when an insertion is attempted, and the error message is:

(MORE THAN ONE PROMOTION PAWN FOR . . .; THIS IS ILLEGAL)

7. Both kings in check simultaneously. This is checked when (END) is given, as earlier may be premature. Error message is:

(BOTH KINGS IN CHECK)

8. Pawn on the first rank of its color. The error message is:

(MISPLACED PAWN, NOT ALLOWED ON THAT RANK)

In addition to inserting pieces in the manner specified, the user will be required, under some circumstances, to indicate properties of kings and rooks (for castling), and of pawns (for *en passant* capture). The tests made and the end messages shown are as follows:

1. If a king is placed on its square of origin (e1 or e8) the question:

   (HAS THIS KING EVER BEEN MOVED? INPUT "YES" OR "NO")

   is shown. The user must answer this question before any progress other then exit to 1.2 via (MENU) can be effected. User error on this input command is followed by the standard error message (see 1.1) and a repeat of the previous error message.

2. If a rook is placed on a square of origin (a1/h1 or a8/h8) then a message is shown:

   (HAS THIS CASTLE BEEN MOVED PREVIOUSLY? INPUT "YES" OR "NO")

   The error messages for user input error are as before.

3. If a white pawn stands adjacent to a black pawn on rank 5, and the 6th rank square behind the black pawn is empty, then the question is posed by a screen-based message:

   (WAS BLACK'S LAST MOVE A DOUBLE PAWN MOVE? INPUT "YES" OR "NO")

   The error message for user input is as before.

   A symmetrical test is made for black pawns on rank 4 adjacent to white pawns, with an empty square on the third rank behind the white pawn.

4. At (END), when any error messages have been responded to (or not, if none) the user (player) will be prompted to indicate whose next move it is to be. The screen message is:

   (INDICATE WHOSE NEXT MOVE – INPUT "WHITE" OR "BLACK")

   User's input errors are diagnosed – as before – and the message format shown in 1.1 used to prompt correction.

   Several errors may appear as a result of the next move indication. Move cannot be allocated to a side if the other color (a) has a back-rank pawn unpromoted, or (b) has king in check. The error messages on these cases are:

   (... MOVE NOT POSSIBLE, OTHER COLOR PAWN UNPROMOTED)

   and:

   (... MOVE NOT POSSIBLE, OTHER KING IN CHECK)

   In each case, the additional message is shown saying:

   (RE-ENTER WHOSE NEXT MOVE IT IS – INPUT "WHITE" OR "BLACK")

5. Whenever a pawn is inserted onto the opposition's back rank, a question is displayed on the screen:

(PROMOTION DUE – INSERT PIECE TYPE BY
INPUT . . . P = Q (or R, N or B))

No continuation, other than exit via 1.2, is possible until this condition is cleared. A user's input errors are diagnosed and displayed as before.

6. If a piece is inserted on top of another (whatever color) it is diagnosed by:

(PIECE ON THAT SQUARE – TRY AGAIN)

and the attempted insertion does not take place.

7. Pieces may be subtracted from squares by pressing the return key at any stage, and then inserting:

(DELETE PIECE ON yz)

where yz represents the board coordinates. User errors (including trying to delete from an unoccupied square) are diagnosed as before (1.1 format).

Exit from 1.4, in either normal or manual input mode is either to 1.2 (by (MENU) command) to 1.3 (by (END) command) when all actions are properly completed, as described above.

1.3(b) Play chess
Player(s) input moves via the keyboard. A start to this procedure is shown, on return from 1.4, by the message:

(YOU MAY NOW COMMENCE – INPUT MOVES IN TURN)

This is achieved by pressing the return key and inserting:

(AB–yz)

where AB is the piece type as before, in upper case, and yz is the board square. Castling is 0–0 (short) or 0–0–0 (longside). All syntax errors are diagnosed as before, types are diagnosed and error messages displayed:

1. Trying to move from an empty square:

(NO PIECE ON . . . , TRY AGAIN)

2. Trying to move to a square already occupied by a piece of that color: (yz–yz is a case of this)

(TREADING ON YOUR OWN . . .?! TRY AGAIN)

3. Trying to move on a blocked path (except for N), including castling:

(PATH BLOCKED TO THIS MOVE, TRY AGAIN)

4. Trying to move in a manner alien to this type (e.g. straight line move for N; a variety of pawn moves, e.g. backwards, sideways, diagonal forward unless capturing):

(... DOES NOT MOVE LIKE THIS. TRY AGAIN)

5. Moving and leaving king still in check:

(KING STILL IN CHECK. NICE TRY, BUT TRY AGAIN)

6. Illegal castling (i.e. pieces previously moved, king moves through check, king in check):

(ILLEGAL CASTLING. TRY AGAIN)

7. Moving and leaving an unpromoted pawn:

(OH NO YOU DON'T, WHAT ABOUT THE BACK-RANK PAWN?)

8. Revealing check to own king or moving it into check:

(OOPS! KING IN CHECK NOW; TRY AGAIN)

Check, checkmate and stalemate are tested for at each legal move. Legal moves producing those conditions result in messages as follows:

(*** ... IN CHECK***)
(***CHECKMATE! ... WINS***; ENTER (MENU) TO PROCEED)

A pawn advanced to the back rank produces the following message requiring action before the opponent can reply:

(PAWN PROMOTION; INDICATE BY INPUT; P= ...)

Input error is detected and diagnosed as before (1.1 format). This includes anything but P = Q, N, B or R.

The promotion may produce check, with the diagnostic message shown above. Exit from 1.3 (1.4) is via 1.5 (with return after game is saved), or 1.2 (menu).

1.5 Save game

During 'play game' (1.3) the user (player) may, at any step, invoke the 'save game' feature by entering the command:

(SAVE GAME)

Immediately, a request for an identifier appears in the message field of the screen:

(IDENTIFIER NEEDED – PRESS RELEASE, TYPE IN ANY CHARACTER STRING OF YOUR CHOICE, UP TO TEN IN LENGTH, AND PRESS 'ENTER' WHEN COMPLETE)

Any input error is not detected, as it cannot be: all i/ds are legal. The whole game is then stored, and the game i/d is entered into the index. If the game i/d entered already exists, then a message is shown:

(GAME I/D ALREADY EXISTS – GAME SAVED UNDER THE I/D SUBSCRIPT +1; NEW GAME I/D IS . . .)

This is an automatic feature and requires no user input.
Exit from 1.5 is back to 1.3.

1.6 Retrieve game
A game may be retrieved by user input command during 1.2 (menu selection) or 1.3 (play game) or 1.8 (stepwise play through a saved game). In each case, the invoking command must be as follows: press release key then enter:

(RETRIEVE GAME)

A message is immediately shown in the messages field:

(ENTER I/D – PRESS RELEASE, TYPE IN I/D CHARACTERS, THEN PRESS 'ENTER')

User's input error is not detected. If an unrecognized i/d is given, a message is displayed:

(NO SUCH I/D – TRY AGAIN, OR ENTER (RETURN) TO PROCEED)

In the event that (RETURN) is entered, the exit from RETRIEVE GAME is to the feature/status from which it was entered.
Otherwise the game is then retrieved, and a message prompts continuation:

(YOU MAY PLAY ON FROM HERE: ENTER (PLAY GAME))
(YOU MAY INVOKE AUTOPLAY: ENTER (AUTOPLAY))
(YOU MAY EXIT BACK TO WHERE YOU WERE: ENTER (RETURN))
(YOU MAY LEAVE THE FEATURES: ENTER (MENU))

The appropriate input errors are detected and diagnosed as before (1.1 format). No continuation is possible until an error is corrected, or the correct invocation by (MENU) exits to 1.2.
Exit from retrieve game is to 1.2 (menu), 1.3 (play game), 1.8 (autoplay) or 1.9 (display moves).

1.7 Show index
At any stage of 1.2 (menu selection) or 1.6 (retrieve game), a display of the index of saved games may be achieved by the user (player) entering:

(SHOW INDEX)

The list appears in the right-hand field of the screen as shown in the format of Figure 5.21. User input error is detected and diagnosed as

before (1.1 format). No continuation (other than to 1.2 via (MENU)) is possible until an error is corrected.

Overflow is indicated by the message:

(MORE GAMES)

at the bottom right of the screen. The user invokes this overlow by entering the command (first press return key):

(SHOW MORE GAMES)

User input error is detected as before, and must be cleared (or exit via (MENU) to continue. Exit to 'retrieve game' feature is effected by the command:

(RETRIEVE . . . (i/d) . . .)

User input errors on the first parts of this message are detected, but not on the i/d. Giving an illicit i/d invokes the appropriate message from 1.6.

1.8 Step through game

This feature is entered from 1.6 (retrieve game) by the command prompted in 1.6:

(YOU MAY INVOKE AUTOPLAY: ENTER (AUTOPLAY))

A message is then displayed:

(STATE MODE – INPUT 'FORE' OR 'BACK')

followed by another, when that has been legally entered:

(STATE START OF . . . PLAY)

with 'FORE' or 'BACK' appearing before 'PLAY'. The user (player) then enters (MOVE . . . FOR . . .) specifying a move number and a side, e.g. 13 for black. Checks take place as follows on this input:

1. Is it a move within the game? The input might have said move 13 (say) in a 10 move saved game. (Note, moves are numbered as dyads in chess, e.g. 1. e2–e4; e7–e5). If the move number is out of range for the game, an error message is shown:

   (NO SUCH MOVE, TRY AGAIN)

2. Do the move and direction specified conflict? For example, play backward from move 1 for white; play forward from last move in game. These lead to error message of the form:

   (IMPOSSIBLE. YOU CAN'T PLAY . . . FROM
   MOVE . . . . . .)

No progress can be made until this error is cleared, other than exit via 1.2 (MENU).

When all is in order, a message is shown:

(PRESS RETURN FOR MOVE-STEP, OR EXIT VIA
(MENU) COMMAND, OR TO (PLAY GAME) IF YOU
WISH TO MAKE NEW MOVES FROM THIS POSITION)

After legal versions of these inputs, the game is stepped through
and moves are shown on the screen board, which begins with the
position at the specified start move. An alternative is, at any stage
of 1.8 and whichever mode (FORE or BACK) applies, for the
user/player to change mode, or skip forward/backward by some
moves. This is achieved by entering the command:

(MOVE ... FOR ...)

and the same viability checks are done, along with user input errors
(diagnosed by usual format, 1.1).

1.9 Display game
During play (1.3), retrieving (1.6) and autoplay of a retrieved game
(1.8), a feature may be invoked to show all the moves in the game
concerned. This is done, at any stage of the feature, by entering the
command:

(DISPLAY GAME)

All the moves in the game are then displayed, in normal chess
notation, i.e.

1. e2–e4   e7–e5

etc., appearing in the right-hand field of the screen. Overflow is
indicated as before (1.7):

(MORE MOVES)

and these can be shown by entering:

(SHOW MORE MOVES)

User input error is detected/diagnosed as before, (1.1) format, and
continuation other than by (MENU) exit is impossible until it is
cleared. Legal completion of this feature leads to exit back to the
feature from which it was invoked, or to general menu selection.
Input commands of either:

(RETURN)
or:

(MENU)

are required.

5.3.9 Comment on the specimen functional specification

The example is submitted to show several points, not as an example of a complete/
correct functional specification. In fact, several errors have been deliberately incorporated for use, later, in exercises. The points to be made are as follows:

1. The format is not bad; the whole thing is readable – although a bit disheveled in appearance – which is a distinct advantage. The fact that it may be more difficult to read than the URS often follows, in functional derivates from them; the 'easy-read' URS is a deception for the unwary. On the other hand the FS must not be prohibitively difficult to read, as we have already stressed.

2. The use of 'state' terminology, and a state diagram, is clear in this menu-driven requirement. However, it is not certain that the tabular method of depicting state relationships adds anything and, if it is incorrect in any way, it may subtract value. The message here is, if the matter can be expressed clearly enough one way, don't run the risk of doing it several ways unless you have software tool support that does consistency checking on different forms of the same thing.

3. This functional specification is virtually a user manual! For many applications (notably with computation and data processing paradigms – see Section (3.1) this is a possible outcome – and the opportunity should not be missed. It saves an inordinate amount of difficulty, often, in getting the user's cooperation with the process, and agreement with the outcome of functional specification.

   However, in many other cases of hybrid requirement-types, process applications and so forth, it may be by no means so straightforward.

4. Although relatively well formatted, this functional specification could be improved. One way would be to assign data flow (commands and outputs) to the state diagram, perhaps at the end as a recapitulation of Figure 5.21, with this embellishment.

5. The functional specification includes assumptions – which is good – although all the assumptions made are not detailed, being left to an interpretation of the state diagram. That is hardly the best way to clarify matters.

6. In this functional specification, all the features are expressed quite clearly by means of imperative clauses and intentionals ('will', 'does'); they are said to be 'hard' requirements. Where weaker, or qualified, clauses exist in a functional specification ('should', 'possibly'), these are 'soft' requirements. It is best, where possible, to express the FS in clear terms with a minimum of 'soft' items in it.

7. One major drawback, that would (or should) prevent its authorization, is that this functional specification lacks any reference to one specific feature in the URS. There, it is specifically required that, during play, one may jump back to some previous move and play forward from it. How will this be done? Will the original game, up to the point at which the 'jump back' is effected, be saved or lost?

8. Close students of the human factors aspect of software development will have noticed the use of upper-case text in the format of both keyboard input and screen messages. This is generally held to be bad practice. Having to type upper-case text leads to greater frequency of input errors; having to read unrelieved upper-case text is found to be more tiring than lower or mixed-case text.

   Another little quirk might have come to the notice of both puritanical and prurient readers; the abbreviated input for forward play might prove too exciting, and should – perhaps – be reconsidered.

We have dilated on specification, and with reason. From the management viewpoint of software development, it is important to emphasize the establishment of requirements.

Also, it is one of the life cycle stages at which management and non-technical specialists can (and should) make a strong contribution, not only in content but in quality assurance of that document. As for the base-line functional specification, it has proved possible to say a surprising amount – given the earlier fears that defining and describing this essential document might be difficult to achieve.

It is now, however, high time that we proceeded into the areas of feasibility and technical implementation, to give summary descriptions of these stages of software development. The approach adopted to date is preserved; the detail of these stages will be the subject of another volume in the series, and our treatment of it here is that level found suitable for management orientation courses in software engineering.

CHAPTER SIX

FEASIBILITY AND THE OUTLINE SYSTEMS DESIGN

During the functional specification stage it is both possible and necessary to evaluate the feasibility of implementing the system that is required, within some limits of determinacy. Earlier, any feasibility exercises will have arrived at substantially less confident conclusions, and will probably have proceeded on the basis of rough analogy, of the sort: 'This is a requirement to automate x, y and z features; well, we've seen x and z done before, and y is surely feasible. So, it is all possible.'

The limits of analogy are obvious. What if the features contain hidden perils in this case? What if the requirements change? Then, as well as technical feasibility, there is the question of its economic counterpart. Can we afford the development, even if it can be attempted with confidence about its technical outcome? This question, concerning the estimating of effort and time-scale for software development, is dealt with, in detail, in Chapter 12.

However, the key to it, and to its cognate question of technical feasibility, is the outline systems design (OSD) exercise described in this chapter. The functional specification stage is the earliest (in life cycle terms) at which the OSD can be done and, consequently, at which feasibility questions – technical and economic – can be answered with any degree of confidence, in general.

6.1 THE NEED TO SEPARATE 'HOW' FROM 'WHAT'

The essay on specification, in Chapter 5, has proceeded on the unreal assumption that a specification of requirements for a computer-based sofware system can possibly proceed in the absence of some simultaneous consideration of the means to achieve it. This is unreal because it is basically against nature; we almost always think 'how' when we say 'what'. In the specification stage, the 'what' may be articulated by users to suppliers of the system-to-be, that is to software or other computer specialists. However, to these people, the 'how' will be the dominant issue.

Conversely, on the relatively rare occasions that entirely non-technical people produce their own specification of requirements, one may run the risk of achieving the functional specification without ever considering technical means; steps must then be taken to avoid

this, otherwise one may end up specifying the infeasible – that is in either technical, logistical or economic terms.

A major problem is to separate the outcome of the two processes, specification and feasibility. For, as the reader will recall, the functional specification of requirements must remain free of solution information if it is to be signed-off by users. This separation of content is easily achieved by correct classification of information, and the existence of two archive categories as their respective repositories. The one, functional specification, has already been discussed at some length. The other, outline systems design – or OSD as we shall call it – is the topic of this section.

Before proceeding, the reader's attention should be drawn to the care with which we have stated our aims; that the objects of classification are the outcome from two, simultaneous and connected processes, and the aim is to separate the contents arising from those processes. The processes themselves must remain connected if the feasibility (OSD) exercise is the reflect the requirements (FS), as these emerge. This connection is very often achieved by the same staff doing the compilation of functional specification, and the outline systems design. When this occurs, it is a major task for them, and for management, to ensure the separation of contents in the outcome. The archive 'pigeon-hole', OSD, is invaluable for provoking this classification as well as enabling it.

Where different people do the functional specification and the outline systems design, the management task will be to ensure the connection of the processes to make sure that the outcome is coherent. It is little use specifying a weather-forecasting requirement, and predicating policy for it, on some feasibility exercise for a payroll.

6.2 WHAT IS AN 'OUTLINE SYSTEM DESIGN'?

In discussing the outline system design, we shall consider its contents and form, and show an example, based on the chess system, to demonstrate the precepts. First of all, though, we need one definition: 'taxonomy'. A taxonomy is a classification, by some means including hierarchies of type, deploying some specialized vocabulary for the purpose. Its particular meaning here will become obvious as we proceed.

The contents of an outline system-design, in the general case, will be sets of taxonomies of which – for a system incorporating a computer and software (both those features already part of the virtual machine, and those to be made) – the following are likely to be the most often found:

1. *A hardware taxonomy*. This is basically a list of computer and ancillary components – peripheral devices, communications subsystems, and the virtual machine software needed in the target computer; i.e. the one on which the run-time software system will operate. In many cases, this will just be a high level statement-set of equipment types; in other cases it will descend into detail of components where acquisition will be by purchase or construction – and this information too must be carried by this taxonomy. The hardware taxonomy is, therefore, a catalog in the special terminology of computer hardware, ancillaries and virtual software. It is usually accompanied by a simple

box and line diagram that adds little to the information, but satisfies a need in the cataloger.

2. *A tools taxonomy*. This is often a most important item, and generally the one most frequently forgotten. In it a catalog is made of the 'host', or whatever other development environment is needed to develop the software-to-be, and on which its subsequent configuration ('version') management will be done. Configuration management is a subject dealt with in Chapters 10 and 13, and environments in general are a subject in Chapter 8.

   Once more, this is a list of major components in hardware and software representing the programming support environment (PSE), or integrated project support environment (Ipse) needed for the development. Once more, some of the facilities might be *in situ*, some may have to be bought, and some may have to be made; this information must be carried in the tools taxonomy also, as it can crucially affect the procurement policy of a company for PSE/Ipse facilities.

3. *A software taxonomy*. This is, in fact, a slightly misleading name, as the cataglog concerned is not one of software items in the categorical sense, but of requirements expressed in the functional specification that *might* (even probably will) be done in software. The important thing to realize is that, at the FS/OSD stage, the final design decisions may not yet have been made. There is a simple precept in the design of any system: delay the hard decisions until they can be made in terms of stable requirements and clear design issues. The first will be true when the functional specification has been 'signed off' (although 'stable' does not mean immutable), but the second (clarity of design issues) may not be achieved until some design work has been done.

The outline system design is not, then, a design in the proper sense of that word, so much as a catalog of requirements, at this stage, that might be a software development task. In some cases, the OSD may be closely related structually to the actual design, in other cases not. It must not be assumed that the OSD will, automatically, show the best form of design decomposition although, in some special cases, it may do. Its purpose – the basis for feasibility and estimating – must be kept firmly in mind.

The outline system design may require prototype developments to establish technical feasibility. This point is taken further in Section 6.4.1. However it points to a fundamentally important precept: that the OSD (including prototypes, or not) is *not* a contractual item in itself, although a supply may be contracted, or pseudo-contracted if internal to a company, on its basis. Generally, the OSD is a working document of the development team; it is archived, of course; but it is not usually a 'deliverable document'.

6.3 THE SOFTWARE TAXONOMY

Perhaps the most significant thing about a software taxonomy is that it must, mandatorily, be done by software engineers, as the most crucial aspects of the subsequent development of the software depend upon it, i.e. estimates of effort and time-scale to develop the software.

Many times have I been asked the 'hard question' on orientation courses for managers and others – particularly by electronic engineers: 'Are you saying that I cannot estimate software, nor will be able to – even after this course?' And on just the same number of occasions have I found myself answering: 'Yes, that is exactly what I am saying – and if this course has no greater effect that to bring you to that realization, then it will have repaid your investment in it handsomely'.

This is sometimes not a well received view until, after a little exercise in the practicalities, the difficulties of estimating software without a taxonomy, and of doing the taxonomy and estimating from it, have brought home the realities. This is a specialist's job, as are those for hardware and tools taxonomies.

6.3.1 The form of a software taxonomy

The software taxonomy in the OSD is conveniently seen as a simple box diagram of the form shown in Figure 6.1. When such diagrams become large and profuse in the number of boxes and their connections, then decomposition over several pages may ensue, and a

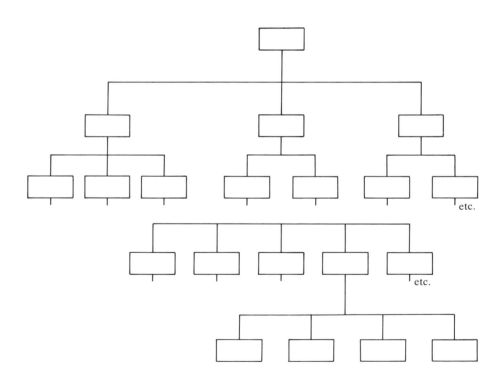

FIGURE 6.1 General case of a box diagram, hierarchical format for the outline systems design.

referencing system will have to be adopted to keep track of which boxes affix to which others over different pages of the taxonomy.

Another way of depicting the OSD is by an orthogonal form of connected, indented statements – such as is shown in Figure 6.2.

In both cases of OSD format, each 'level' of the taxonomy says everything to be said – at that level of detail – about the requirements possibly due to be implemented in software; subsequent 'levels' say more in detail but not (unless the taxonomy is wrongly done) in scope.

There is a superficial resemblance between the box diagram format shown in Figure 6.1 and the Jackson notation for specification and design, but this is hardly important so long as it is clearly remembered in this case that our outline design is speaking about the requirements for the particular purposes of feasibility: technical and economic. A slightly more sinister problem attaches to the so-called orthogonal format. Here, the software engineers often slip into pseudo-code to express the requirements to be done (possibly) in software, and then see this indented pseudo-code as a low level design of the artefact. As in the case against which we inveighed in the section on functional specifications, this leads to proper design being bypassed – often to the detriment of the software quality.

6.3.2 A worked example

An overall software taxonomy for CAISSA will be found in Figure 12.6, whilst examples of lower level taxonomies are given in Figures 6.3, 6.4, 6.5 and 6.6.

EXAMPLE 3

EXTRACTS FROM AN OUTLINE SYSTEMS DESIGN FOR CAISSA

6.3.3 Comment on the outline systems design example

1. The combination of 'straight' and orthogonal formats is shown clearly. There is no virtue in this, necessarily, nor in any alternative. One should use what is useful – with the caveats already noted. The orthogonal form allows depth of information on a page, but leads to clutter as well as the danger of premature implementation.
2. Figures 6.3–6.6 show labeling of a decomposed software taxonomy. This might seem a trivial, bureaucratic point – until one tries to read a densely nested, decomposed taxonomy over several pages.
3. The example fails to show, as should be done, indications of possible source code (i.e. high or low level), and size, for taxons – the elements of the taxonomy. Now the OSD is not the design proper, so why should these detailed considerations intrude here? Particularly as taxons refer to functionality in the requirements rather than features of

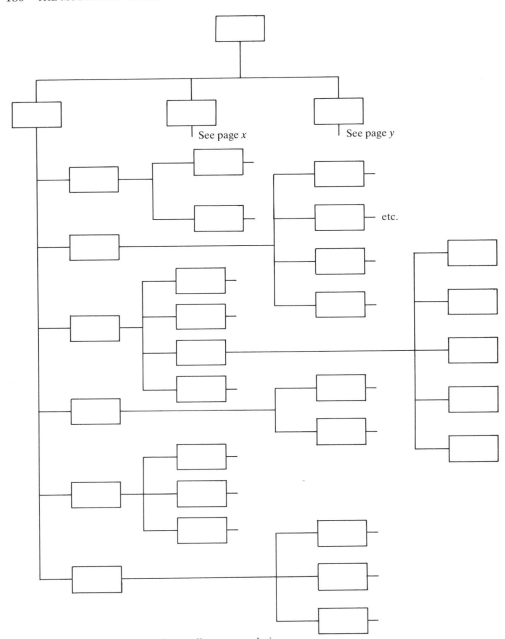

FIGURE 6.2 Orthogonal form of an outline systems design.

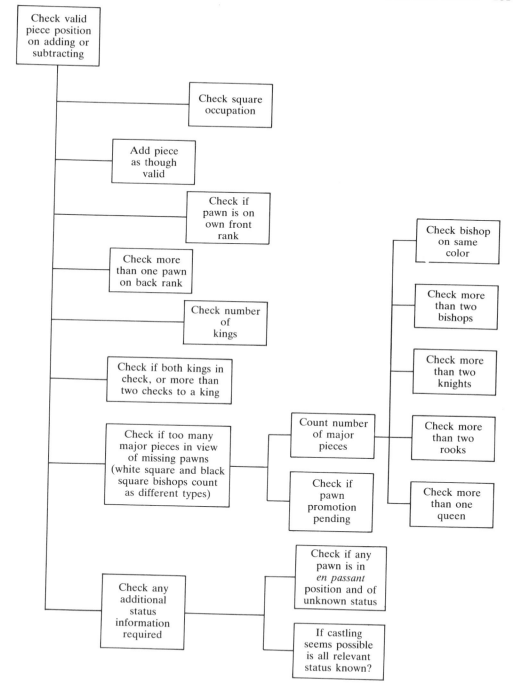

FIGURE 6.3 Taxonomy for CAISSA: check validity of piece addition/subtraction.

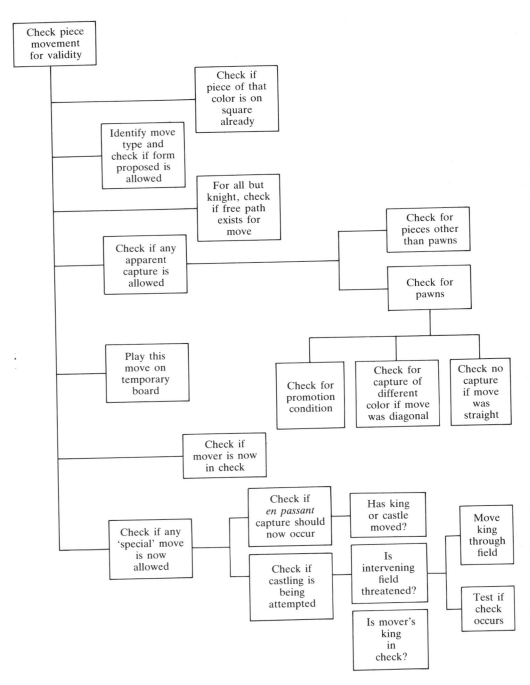

FIGURE 6.4 CAISSA taxonomy: validity of piece movement.

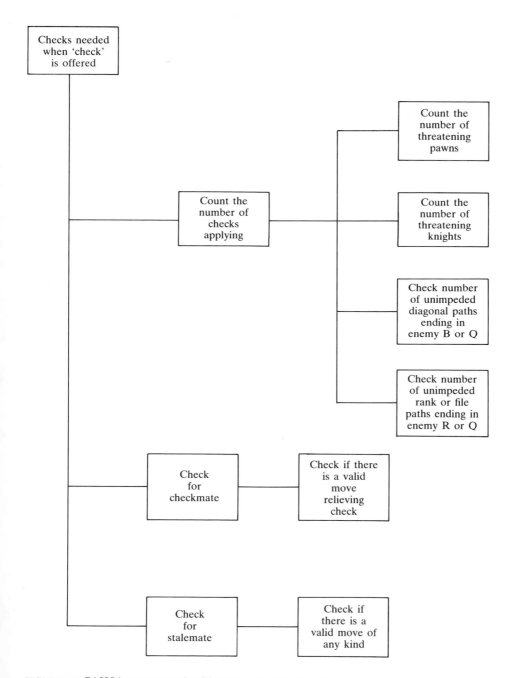

FIGURE 6.5 CAISSA taxonomy: algorithm to text for 'check' status.

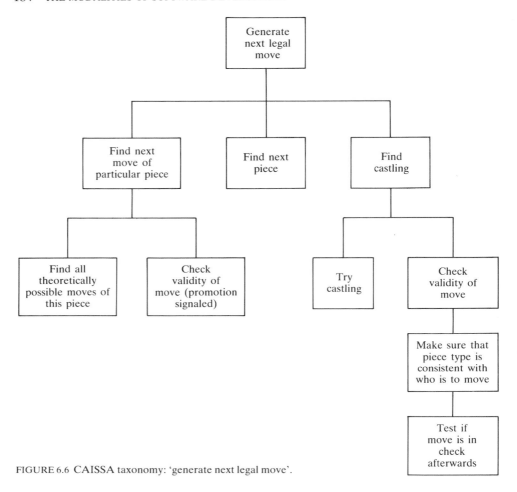

FIGURE 6.6 CAISSA taxonomy: 'generate next legal move'.

a software system designed to provide them. The simple answers are, again, technical and economic feasibility, and are dealt with below and in Chapter 12 – where the complete 'overview' taxonomy for CAISSA is presented, as it serves a specific purpose there (see Figure 12.6).

6.4 SOME PRACTICAL GUIDELINES

The OSD must be taken to a level of definition, in the case of each taxonomy, for the main purposes of feasibility assessment to be possible. There are no general rules that

determine this level of sufficiency in each case, and the matter will, perforce, remain judgmental, and one for case-by-case decision on the part of the subject-specialists compiling the taxonomies. However, certain guidelines can be offered, and some cautionary notes appended for practical use.

6.4.1 Technical prototyping

We distinguish here, as in Chapter 3, between prototype development at the specification stage, to assess factors bearing on utility of a system, and that done within the OSD to assess technical feasibility, including, perhaps, the economics of production for hardware parts of a system.

'Prototyping' is, in fact, a gross misnomer at any level of activity, as there is no such verb in the language from which it could be derived. The prototypes form an experimental development activity, and it is that which concerns us here.

Prototypes may be needed to assess the feasibility of any, or all, of the categories whose detail is to be incorporated in one of the three taxonomies. Obviously, the technical feasibility of a prototype cannot be assessed, before the event, if that is the *a priori* purpose of the exercise itself. And here we must be a little careful with the use to which we put the expression 'feasibility', for this encapsulates several possible questions, for a system or component:

1. Can it be made at all, in either hardware or software?
2. What medium is it best to use, of the two?
3. Should one buy or make?
4. What will a properly engineered version cost to develop, and what will production cost be for a 'customer-quality' article (e.g. in the case of a hardware component)?
5. How will it perform in terms of efficiency, reliability, security and integrity?

However, the matter of major concern, at the OSD level, is seldom the *technical* feasibility or options within a prototype development, since those may be, by definition, the matters at question; it is the *economic* feasibility, and the management imponderables that often surround it. The fact is that prototypes may be easy to define generically, and exciting and innovative things to attempt for enthusiastic technicians; but their development must be a managed activity if economic feasibility is not to be prejudiced. This is a legitimate concern at the OSD stage, although the techniques for estimating and controlling software developments are considered elsewhere – specifically in Chapters 12 and 13 respectively.

However, it is necessary to raise certain matters of concern here. The basic points about prototype development within the OSD are as follows:

1. It is often possible, within some limits of accuracy, to estimate the cost (effort) for a prototype development whose definition is largely 'high level'. If it can be done, it should be done, and managers should resist the engineer's refrain (software or hardware): 'How can we tell the cost of an experiment?' The *outcome* may be imponderable, but the route to it is often clearer than prototype developers admit.

2. Planning and control of activities for a prototype development are *not* necessarily two of the 'management imponderables' high in the life cycle, or should not be. The trajectory of an experimental development may change direction abruptly, so that plans may be frequently invalidated. But, with that caveat only, planning *is* possible as, at every step, something explicit is being attempted that can often be subdivided into activities. The same may not be the case in the specification part of early life cycle stages, where tasks are more amorphous. The two should not be confused or conflated.

3. Technical prototypes are often unlike their counterparts for elucidating requirements, in sheer scale. Requirements' prototypes are generally to determine human factor issues, such as what may be acceptable as input/output formats, and this is often a relatively trivial exercise, and its result a 'cheap and cheerless' artefact that is easily parted from by its progenitors.

   Technical prototypes often take years to do, and cost millions – in any currency – before they demonstrate their virtues. Consequently, they are often invested with virtuous properties they do not possess: 'If it cost all that, then it must be good enough to sell as it is'. We have inveighed against this elsewhere, but repetition in the face of so serious an error is no fault. The *result* of prototypes must be used to make the real thing, not the assumption made that they *are* the real thing.

4. The destination of results from technical prototype developments is one, or more, of the OSD taxonomies, if those results are positive concerning technical and economic feasibility. Otherwise, if the indications are negative for whatever reason, the result may be a moderation of, and modification to, the functional specification – for it must not be forgotten that the OSD exercise is both contemporary and cognate with the development of a functional specification.

These guidelines on prototype development, which have more the force of strictures in some places, have particular force in product development where a high degree of innovation is being attempted. In contracted project supply, however innovative, it is rare to find extensive development of technical prototypes, for the simple reason that the vagaries of estimating them (*pace* 1 above) stands in conflict to the aims of the contract, to do defined work for defined cost in defined time.

However, we now turn to one of the principal uses to which the OSD will be put. In general, there are two rather urgent considerations at this stage of the life cycle:

1. How much will it all cost? For software development, this is the subject of Chapter 12, in which the fundamental importance of the software taxonomy becomes apparent for this question.

2. Will the hardware be big enough? Here 'big' connotes a variety of capacities and performance, such as:
   (a) available random access, programmable memory;
   (b) archival store;
   (c) processing speed of the central unit; and
   (d) input/output transfer rates amongst devices in the configuration.

We will consider a simple example of the first of these issues of capacity.

6.4.2 Code size and the software taxonomy

The detailing of functional requirements within a software taxonomy proceeds level by level of that taxonomy. Reference to Figure 6.1 shows that one may speak with reason of 'levels' rather as one speaks of generations in a genealogy. As the functional detailing proceeds, an increasing amount of software implementation thoughts intrude, such as: 'Hey! This is a real-time bit! We'd better do this in C, or assembler or something'. Or: 'This feature has a common bit with that one, and with one over there. Let's make a general purpose facility of it'. Gradually, the software engineers realize that the OSD is turning into a quasi-design of the software, and they stop at that level, or the one before.

It is difficult to say more about this, as it is very much a judgmental matter for the software engineers. In general, the larger the requirement, the larger the taxons on the bottom line of the taxonomy – large, that is, in terms of source code to implement the features in a taxon *if that was to be done*. Thus, for large and very large systems we find taxons that are likely to be in the range of 250–750 source code statements in size. For small and medium systems, the taxonomies often descend to a level of 50–200 statement of source code.

Marking taxons, in the software taxonomy, for likely high or low level implementation, helps in feasibility assessment, as well as indicating requirement such as compilers for the tools taxonomy. Also, experienced software engineers can attribute notional source code sizes to the taxons. This is a useful thing to do, with the greatest care needed at the time, for estimating the time-scale and effort to develop the software. Code size estimates are also required for a cross-check on the hardware taxonomy, particularly in cases where there is a prescribed computer of given capacities. Here what happens – stated simply – is that competent software engineers do the software taxonomy, flag bottom line taxons for notional high or low level code implementation, and assign notional source code size – as shown in Figure 6.7. Estimates tend to be in units of 50, e.g. 150, 250, 300 and so forth. Finer resolution is neither possible nor necessary at this level.

A software size is then estimated by summing high and low level language taxons along the bottom line of the taxonomy, arriving at answers, say, of 2,150 source code

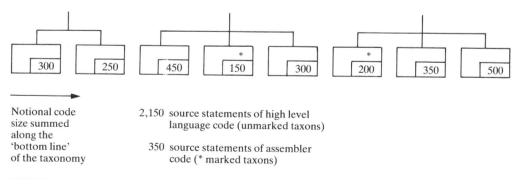

Notional code size summed along the 'bottom line' of the taxonomy

2,150 source statements of high level language code (unmarked taxons)

350 source statements of assembler code (* marked taxons)

FIGURE 6.7 Marked taxons, and notional code size estimating.

statements of Modula-2, and 350 source code statements of assembler. This is clearly a fairly small application on our crude metric in Section 3.1.

We then convert this source code into object code, by applying an average expansion factor to the high level code, e.g. × 4.7 for Fortran, 5.2 for Pascal or whatever is appropriate. The expansion factor between high and low level codes occurs during translation (compilation or interpretation) from the one to the other, as explained in Chapter 1. There is, in general, an $n:1$ relationship between an expression in a high level language and its equivalent assembler (low level) instructions. The 'expansion factor' of a language, produced by a particular compiler, is the average of n taken over a wide application set.

To return to our simple instance, the calculation might result in an object code size of

$$2,150 \times 5 + 350 = 11,100$$

This, in turn might require more programmable memory of the computer concerned, depending on the architecture of that machine, and so we must convert the 11,100 into equivalent units of programmable store – usually expressed in bytes. This is done by applying a second average factor, that for the expansion between assembler statements and machine storage, brought about by the lowest level of translation – assembly into binary bit patterns.

In a 16-bit machine architecture (typical PC, small minicomputer, etc.), this expansion factor will be about ×2. Thus we would say that the programmable storage requirement in this case would be about 22 kilobytes.

The virtue of these quick calculations is seen when one has some inherited constraint, or has estimated wrongly in the hardware taxonomy. For example, we may find ourselves cobbling away to get 22 kilobytes (plus) of program onto a 16 kilobyte microprocessor chip. We say 'plus' here, because our back-of-envelope calculation has excluded any provision for local data areas, variables and fixed parameters. A notional estimate of this requirement should be added to the previous result. Generally, a value in the range 10–25 percent of program size is added for program data-space; adopting 25 percent would increase the required program-space in our example to 27.5 kilobytes. It must be remembered, in all of this, that these 'estimates' are judgmental, and have no significance, other than for helping to assess the capacity of hardware required and, with extreme care which cannot be overstressed, to estimate the effort and time-scale to design and implement the programs required.

So, we have seen, in this hypothetical case, that we cannot fit the specified requirements to be done in software with the capacity of the equipment envisaged. It is better to know this early in the life cycle of development activities, rather than late in it, when little good may ensue from the knowledge. Now we can do one of two things, or a combination of them:

1. Increase the capacity of the hardware configuration, to fit the defined functionality.
2. Decrease the defined functionality, and revise the base-line specification accordingly.

When no preconception of equipment exists, then these points do not apply, and the hardware configuration needed is derived from the OSD calculations of this sort. Then, the two listed points may arise if the development is seen to be economically infeasible.

Analogously, the other issues of capacity can be considered on the basis of the OSD taxonomies.

6.5 OTHER ASPECTS OF TECHNICAL FEASIBILITY

Other feasibility questions that may occur early in the development life cycle include those concerning system throughput and response time, and the security and integrity of programs and data. As was noted in the previous chapter, such requirements must be made in an explicit and demonstrable form in the functional specification.

That being the case, what of the feasibility of these requirements? It is one thing to assert a requirement, and no less hard a task to enquire after the feasibility of achieving it; but can the question be answered? And, if so, when – in life cycle terms – and how?

First, a little in the way of definition is in order:

1. *Loading and throughput*: this is a concept attaching to a rather specialized type of application, in which data are received, at some variable rate, then processed and emitted. The considerations of input rates and volumes, taken together with the processing and output capacities of hardware and software, will determine if the system proposed is adequate, or if it must be augmented – for example, to provide buffered input – or if there will be data loss through overloading. Throughput, in these terms, may be seen as analogous to the diameter of a pipe allowing the passage of a liquid; in this case, we are concerned with the capacity of a computer system in terms of its hardware and software.
2. *Response time*: this is a concept in all on-line and real-time applications of widely differing types. In one kind, typically, a human user will enter an enquiry or transaction of some sort, via a keyboard terminal, into a computer system, and await a response – such as answer, or some message – to appear on a screen. In another kind of system, a device will send a signal to the computer an await a recognizable signal ('response') in return.

   In the one case, that of an on-line system as described in Chapter 2, the response requirement will probably be in the range 5–15 seconds; much less than the lower limit not being necessary, and much more than the upper limit not being acceptable. In the other case, the response time required may be fractions of a second, and some physically critical (and perhaps even life-depending) action may be concerned.

   Clearly, response time and system loading may interact, i.e. how many transactions can be processed, or real-time functions performed, in a given time, *under peak loading conditions*?
3. *Security and integrity*: these concepts concern programs and data, and lead to more general considerations of system reliability.

   Security is the prevention or detection of unauthorized access to programs or data; integrity is the prevention or diagnosis of accidental corruption of both or either. The concepts are not necessarily strongly related. A system of questionable security, in these terms, may be one in which protection against accidental failure is beyond

reproach, whereas a system with vulnerable integrity may have the most sedulous protections that encryption can achieve to protect against purposive, unauthorized access. In general, security is far easier to achieve than integrity since, in the latter case, one is trying to design software to deal with the caprices that can take one (and it) into obscure parts of the behavior space.

Questions must be asked, to provoke strong definition in the functional specification, about what programs and data are to be protected against unauthorized access and accidental corruption. In the case of integrity, these definitions, along with the consideration of consequences, may lead to the question of system performance – how much degradation of the system, through failure, can be tolerated.

This, in turn, may lead to the high level specification of requirements for *protection* against failure and this, in turn, may lead to OSD considerations such as the multiplication of systems or subsystems, and the state of readiness of standby systems – depending on how 'connected' they are for the purpose. A totally connected standby system, to ensure no loss of operation if the substantive system fails, is said to be in 'hot' standby state; a totally disconnected system, having to be plugged in at least, and perhaps transported to site first, is said to be a 'cold' standby – and one can expect considerable loss of operation after failure of the substantive system; a 'warm' standby is one whose connection can be achieved readily, but is not automatic. Loss of data is the most typical loss of operation, but in computer-based control systems that might be the least of concerns.

What, then, can be said of these matters when doing outline systems design? The rather disturbing fact is that some of the issues are so contingent upon the skill of design and implementation that very little can be said of them, other than judgmentally and in expectation, before the event of their implementation.

This is a disturbing state of affairs, as the authorization ('signing-off') of the functional specification is often part of a contractual process, and all the hard requirements (for throughput, response, security, integrity, limiting consequences of failure) will be contractual obligations thereafter in many cases.

Does this mean that contracts are entered into or, even if no stringent contract, that development proceeds in relative ignorance of whether or not the outcome will be compliant with requirements? In some cases the answer must be affirmative, as we have said before in the treatment on 'indeterminacy'.

6.5.1 Feasibility of throughput and response performance

So far as considerations of load, throughput and response performances are concerned one may *believe*, to the point of certainty, that the requirements, stated in the functional specification, will be achievable – given competent design and implementation – by the 'system' defined in outline by the OSD taxonomies for hardware and software. Further, if the foreseeable exigencies warrant it, one may flag critical parts of the software-to-be for especial attention, such as low level coding and 'tuning' to ensure required throughput or response.

Beyond that, for complex systems with exacting response criteria, operating under

extremes of input-loading, matters may be so contingent on the skill of designers and the competence of the implementation, that the judgmental opinion of competent software engineers as to feasibility, in these respects, must stand on its own merit. Nor, when one thinks about it, will prototype software help much in determining feasibility for throughput and response characteristics of the system-to-be. To serve any use, such a prototype would have to *be*, effectively, the end implementation itself – a contradiction in terms.

In some such complex, composite systems, where computer hardware and software is a system component merely – and not the totality – system simulation may help to delineate throughput or response *requirements* of the software, or critical parts of it. And this may, in turn, lead to a clarification of feasibility – if, say, the software taxonomy indicates an order of magnitude code size for a part of the software-to-be, and this can be seen to be comfortably within the limits of execution time clarified by the simulation, or not as the case may be.

However, the rather grim fact stands that, at the FS/OSD level of the development, throughput and response times are too contingent on designs and implementation to be anything other than determined, for their feasibility, by judgmental means. Firms contracting for exacting 'hard' requirements in these respects should take note! Any such firms that do so before a competent OSD, done by software engineers, are courting trouble, and may have that outcome most vigorously consumated.

6.5.2 Feasibility of security and integrity considerations

As for security, integrity and reliability in general, these can always be achieved to a high degree – but at a price. Hardware and software keys for security, fault-tolerant systems, and multiple standby systems and subsystems for integrity, can be defined as part of the OSD exercise, and costed accordingly. Where some provision may be unclear, such as a means of encryption/decryption for implementation, then prototypes can be developed. Likewise for the complexities of duplex, triplex and higher order 'hot' standby facilities – although again, it must be said, the costs may become very high.

In a later chapter, it is pointed out that the manuals for usage and operation of systems containing such features may not be possible to develop much before the detail level of the design stage, and this is true despite the fact that their feasibility and overall design may have been possible to assess, judgmentally, at the OSD stage. The difference lay in the fact that, at one level we ask: 'What may be done?' and at the next level, design proper, we ask: 'How may it be done?'

The relatively good news in this case, for security and integrity requirements, is that estimates and plans can be established, on the basis of an outline system design, so early in the life cycle.

6.6 SUMMARY COMMENTS

This, then, is the outline system design stage, at which a variety of feasibility questions can be raised, and most of them answered:

1. What equipment (hardware) capacity is needed, in each of several categories – such as processor, peripherals, communications, and so on?
2. What order of magnitude in size will the software be, expressed as statements of source code in appropriate languages?
3. What effort and time-scale attributes are required for the remaining development activities? (See Chapter 12 for detail).
4. What can we say about the feasibility of throughput and response requirements, and what may need particular attention during implementation?
5. How are any security, integrity and general reliability requirements to be achieved, and are they economically feasible?

Above all, one must constantly bear in mind the stricture that *outline design is not design proper*; one does not plough straight into an implementation on its basis, either for hardware or software development. The two elementary purposes of outline systems design must be paramount – it is for technical feasibility of a possible implementation, and to provide information for planning and costing it.

The further virtues of the OSD phase are subtle; it provides a pigeon-hole for design information during the functional specification activity; it defines the need for early ('high in the life cycle') involvement of appropriate technical staff, such as software engineers, and this, in turn, has strong motivational effect on those staff-members involved; and last but by no means least, it provides a *conceptual* starting point for the next stage in a software development – design.

This last, as the reader may well already know or, if not, will discover immediately, is a major problem area in software development. We are 'crossing the line' between activities that are generally comprehensible – within some limits of application knowledge – and those that are comprehensible only to specialist software engineers. How do we get started in design? What is this step 'across the line'?

CHAPTER SEVEN

SOFTWARE DESIGN

> The white knight is sliding down the poker. He balances very badly.
> (L. Carroll: Through the Looking Glass)

As specification is to the whole process of software development, so design is to be the subprocess of conceptualizing and implementing an artefact to supply that requirement.

Specification, as defined in previous chapters, provides the destination of the task; design should define the best way of getting there.

In this chapter, three basic issues are presented. In the first of these, the question of objectives is addressed; in the second, a survey is given of known approaches to design; in the third, the means and methods for detailing and recording designs are discussed.

All of this material is presented in summary form, for this is a Big Subject. As with other isues in Part Two, design is the subject of a volume in this series, in which its author, Wayne Stevens, expands on the summaries given here, and introduces a variety of other material salient to this topic.

Design is a subject fraught with difficulties and beset by easy misconceptions in software engineering. Unlike specification, where everyone and their uncles seem to have a 'theory' of best behavior, designers tend to be inarticulate about how they do what they do, best. As a result, design, as a subject, is a bit like the interior of a jungle containing head-hunters, and venomous reptiles: everybody knows where it is, but only the intrepid (or foolhardy) will go.

This is the only chapter to warrant an epigraph of its own, and most software engineers – having too slid down the poker – will recognize its aptness.

Software design is a part of software development that is more often defectively undertaken than otherwise, through sheer lack of means and methods, not to mention a set of closely associated misconceptions. For example, there is a widely prevailing misapprehension that design is either done as a part of programming – that it is an immanent property of writing program statements – or that, in some unexplained

fashion, it is derived directly out the form of the specifications into the substance of the code. For example of this, if the functional specification defines x unique features, y inputs and z outputs, then (the specious argument goes) the code must comprise x, y, and z discrete 'modules' – whether this is justified or not on other criteria of design.

In such cases, design may not be a stage in development that is done badly, it may be a stage that is not explicitly undertaken at all – and a crucial stage at that.

In other engineering subjects, this would be an intolerable state of affairs, and there would be an outcry from the 'big public' about the hazards of badly (or un-) designed aircraft, ships, nuclear power plants, and so forth, and associations of householders would petition parliament about high-rise dwellings thrown up at the whim of mad, de-frocked architects with a penchant for standing on heaps of rubble.

Omitting design, as an explicit exercise for definable purposes, generally precludes several aspects of quality in the artefact produced. In particular, the reliability and modifiability of software systems are issues that go by default if design is underdone in any material way; the tendency may be to emphasize the 'correctness' of programs with respect to requirements' specification – an essential criterion in its own right – but to ignore the other vital matter of quality, modifiability. Or, some aspects of compliance, such as run-time efficiency, throughput or response, or integrity considerations, may dominate the minds of designers.

Properly experienced software engineers, undertaking good software engineering practices, generally avoid these pitfalls, if allowed to do so by circumstances and by their managers.

It is possible to generalize about the significance of life cycle phases, in terms of percentage of software engineer's effort over one pass of the life cycle (i.e. excluding in-service maintenance and new version developments), averaged over a large sample of application types. The commonly accepted view is that software engineer's efforts are generally in about the following proportions for main life cycle stages: note though, these are averages only, and very approximate ones at that:

> 15 percent: specification phase – functional specification and outline systems design complete, and the former 'signed off'.
> 30 percent: software design.
> 15 percent: implementation – coding and limited testing by authors ('debugging').
> 40 percent: software quality – software integration and testing.

If that is a general-case representation of what happens in good software engineering practice, the following shows what happens when design is omitted to all intents and purposes.

A certain product development was done in an environment where, luckily, strict time-records were kept, from which the *a posteriori* analysis could be done to find out who had done what, and when. The development got into trouble, and duly failed to materialize in a form suitable for the market. Our *a posteriori* analysis found the following effort attribution during software development:

> 10.4 percent specification phase, *but no proper authorization of the FS*.
> 8.3 percent software design, basically a rudimentary program-structure plan based on the format in which the FS document had been written.

23.9 percent implementation, there being some admixture with the next category.

57.4 percent software quality assurance, up to the point that a guillotine was applied.

In fact, the guillotine was applied because software testing was non-convergent. Had the development been allowed to continue unlimited, 'software quality' effort would have approached 100 percent of the total, asymptotically.

Design is clearly a fundamentally important phase in software development, and its omission – by accident or intent – in all likelihood prejudices the quality of outcome. And not only does this occur through ignorance of the issues concerned, as might be the case with managers who are themselves inexperienced. Some practitioners (let us call them 'amateur' programmers) skimp or omit design as an explicit step; we have already pointed out the dangers of 'technician friendly' specification in this respect, where pseudo-code and abstract notations can incline the unwary to acts of premature implementation. In our sad little story above, that is exactly what had happened, and it is a happy circumstance to relate that the guillotine was applied only to the job, and that nothing (or no one) else got the chop.

What, then, is meant by 'design', that we may ensure its inclusion in the processes of software development, and undertake the evolution of its means and methods within software engineering? What is the software designer trying to do in the first place, let alone how is he or she tackling the task, and with what tools? These questions provide an essential means of classification, for in this, as in many other matters concerning software, there is an acute danger of confusing and conflating issues, and creating a veritable pudding of the subject as a consequence.

Therefore, in this chapter, we shall address the following main issues:

1. The objectives in software design.
2. The approaches to software design.
3. The means and methods for software design.

Each of these is accorded a section in this chapter, and a final section acts as a coda to it all. However, as elsewhere, this subject is too large a one, and too fundamentally important, to be properly treated in such a synoptic fashion. Thus Volume 3 of this series takes the matter of software design to its necessary level of detail. The account given here is such as might be found on an orientation course (to some non-trivial depth of treatment) in software engineering in general.

7.1 THE OBJECTIVES IN SOFTWARE DESIGN

One attempts, in software design, to plan an artefact that can be made (software) to serve – or 'deliver' – a set of specified features (the functional specification). The result should be – in some form or other – a blueprint of what can be made.

At the same time, and of equal importance in most cases, other aspects of quality than this correspondence with requirements must be held as design objectives. In particular, the design of software must ensure that, given its competent implementation, it can be

made acceptably reliable by a rational process of error detection and correction, and that it can be modified, with reasonable confidence, for maintenance and new version purposes.

Furthermore, it must be borne in mind that – from whatever basis it is done, and however it is progressed – software design will proceed against a background of features and facilities provided by the virtual machine on which the software is to be implemented and, perhaps, the nature of the target machine on which its operating performance is contingent, if this is different from the 'host'.

Seen in this way, software design is an intellectual activity in three dimensions simultaneously:

1. To transform information, from the specification domain, into implementation 'blueprints' that will, if competently undertaken, provide the features required.
2. To facilitate the achievement and demonstration of quality criteria in the outcome – compliance and modifiability in particular.
3. To achieve the first two of these within the bounds of the virtual computer facilities to develop and operate the software – either a host/target environment, or a self-hosted system.

Not surprisingly, software design is known to be a subject that is far from easy to grasp conceptually, is intellectually difficult to do, and in which the notions of 'good design' and 'detailing, with enrichment' are more implicitly understood than explicitly demonstrable. It is an aspect of software development that calls for a rare combination of both intuitive and analytic abilities in its exponents.

Software design can be seen as comprising three stages within this phase of the life cycle itself:

1. *Architecture* – the highest level specification of the software to be developed, to meet the specifications. The definition of these genera, to be detailed, represents a basic architecture.
2. *Decomposition with detailing*, proceeding from the architectural definition.
3. Lowest level detail of design – the *specification of integrands* or programs to be implemented.

They may be seen as step 1, step 2 to $n - 1$ and step n respectively, in a process of stepwise design with enrichment, as depicted in Figure 2.7. The first of these – architecture – being a rather special issue, is best treated separately from the others, and a discussion of it follows. The other two are the subjects of Section 7.2.

7.1.1 Architecture definition and design at high level

The software architecture stage of design is a step across a line between what is generally comprehensible in the specification phase, and what becomes progressively more comprehensible to the limited number of software engineers involved, as specifications are redefined as properties of a conceptual solution, and transformed into the abstract

languages of program implementation and software execution. This outcome, and the means of arriving at it, are said to be 'specialist-comprehensible'.

And yet, even on education courses for aspiring software engineers, this step can be a troublesome one. 'How do we get started in design?', people enquire.

Let us begin by defining what we have in hand, or should have, as we 'cross the line' into design. The first step is to ensure that a definition is done of the features and functions that will be implemented, ultimately, as software. In many cases, typically those of contracted project supply, this might have been done at an earlier stage – during the detailing of functional specifications and OSD taxonomies. On other occasions, such as product development in many cases, both hardware and software components may not have been fixed so early in the life cycle, as it is generally best to keep design decisions of this sort open until all ramifications of requirements are known. Then, if design is to proceed, a software taxonomy and feasibility assessment should be done anyway, however notional the outcome may be, and this case becomes identical with that of project-based software development.

Generally, then, we have a software taxonomy, that subset of functional requirements to be 'delivered' by software, that can be taken as a task definition for the design stage. However, one commonly met practice, another trap to the unwary, should be recognized and avoided.

This particular fallacy is that concerning premature definition of a hardware/software interface at an early stage of requirement specification, as Figure 7.1 portrays. This practice is common in IT product development companies, where electronics engineers may co-exist in unhappy symbiosis with their counterparts in software.

Then, as often happens, an entirely spurious and arbitrary definition is made of the hardware to be developed or procured and all 'the rest' – whatever that may comprise – is defined, by default, as the software. In this way, software becomes that part of the system not done in hardware – hardly a rational basis for decision – or the glue that sticks all the fine electronics together.

Needless to say, this is a design decision wrongly addressed, and its outcome can be catastrophic. Design should not begin by inheriting, from the specification stage, a sedulously detailed description of the hardware-to-be plus an arbitrary 'hardware/software interface', and some ragbag, default definition of software as whatever else is needed.

In the general case, therefore, we begin design proper with a rationally based definition of those parts of specified functionality that are best done in software, or in hardware as the case might be. This is seen as the first step in design, when the specification stage is complete – or declared to be sufficiently so for the functional specification to be 'signed off'.

This definition into hardware and software 'partitions' may correspond either 'somewhat', 'very' or 'entirely' with the OSD taxonomies already in existence – although, in fact, it would be rather worrying if the level of correspondence was low, as this may pose a dichotomy between the technical and economic feasibility of the system-to-be, and that as originally assessed in the OSD feasibility exercise.

The form of the architectural software definition may be identical to that for the outline design taxonomy – i.e. a box and line hierarchy – or may be a tabular list of

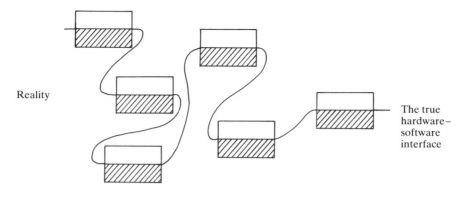

Reality

The true
hardware–
software
interface

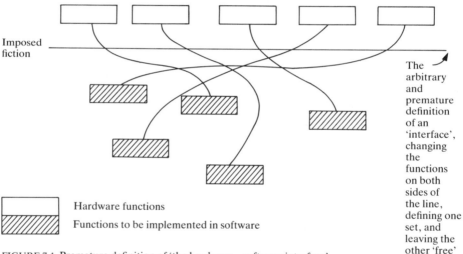

Imposed
fiction

The
arbitrary
and
premature
definition
of an
'interface',
changing
the
functions
on both
sides of
the line,
defining one
set, and
leaving the
other 'free'

Hardware functions

Functions to be implemented in software

FIGURE 7.1 Premature definition of 'the hardware – software interface'.

functions, a set of high level Mascot diagrams or one done in De Wolf's notation for example, or a composite of all these approaches.

Like the outline system design, the software definition is almost never a formal document, in the sense in which the functional specification may well be in a stringent contract for fixed price supply, or its approximate counterpart in a pseudo-contract. In such cases, the contract will have been 'signed off' at the FS stage – leaving the implementation detail up to the supplier.

The user/client will be likely to disclaim interest in (and therefore avoid responsibility for) solution detail. In other cases, such as less stringent contracts of supply, such as a loose 'time and materials' arrangement for staff, the software specification may be used as

a task definition – but can hardly be said to be 'formal', as the type of contract will hardly bear such a description.

It is rather a good job that the software specification is usually not required, early in the life cycle, for formal purposes. For software architecture-design can present severe problems.

For some systems, features that can be generically specified with some ease cannot be meaningfully addressed until the design stage. The two most obvious examples already quoted are security and integrity. It is one thing to state such a requirement and to evaluate its feasibility judgmentally, but it is quite another matter to say how it will be done, a question that may take a lot of time and specialist effort to answer.

Again, the most obvious example is a requirement for *total* integrity to be preserved in the case of system failure, for whatever reason, i.e. that no programs or data are lost or corrupted, and that operations continue uninterrupted. This would require at least one level of 'hot standby' (duplicated) system, with the components operating in parallel, and a highly elaborate fault detection system such as may be achieved by an odd number of 'hot standby' systems, a state comparison 'watchdog' and a majority-based election system between them.

Investigating the ramifications of such a complex system, before offering fixed price terms for its supply, may require a substantial amount of prototyping and design work to be done first. Then, the notional 15 percent of effort to specify requirements may be a very questionable figure indeed, and one may be forced to proceed in faith and hope, on the basis of a judgmentally determined feasibility. When this happens, it is an acute requirement, at the first step of design, to define (not yet design) the software required.

Other stringent requirements, whose detailed ramifications may have been beyond the means of an OSD exercise to define, may concern the need to meet real-time requirements. Here, as well as the problems of performance, such as throughput and response under severe load conditions, there are four potential problems of design, the threat of which pervades the process:

1. Unproductive looping ('deadly embrace').
2. Mutual exclusion between parallel processes ('deadlock').
3. Inaccessible topology in a software network seen as a set of asynchronous processes.
4. Asynchronous updates to, and retrievals from, data in 'real-time'.

These are potentially very severe problems in designing software systems incorporating parallel, concurrent operations. At the architecture level, it may be possible to model the abstract processes in the requirement as though each one was implemented in a separate microprocessor within a complex network of such. Simulation by Petrinet graphs and rapid prototyping by SDL design models are ways of investigating these properties during the architecture design stage. Both of these techniques are described below.

The results of such prototypes or simulations may determine changes to earlier notions of architecture, and affect the task-definition of what will be implemented in hardware and what in software. In any event, one ends up with an architectural definition of the system development task, perhaps still largely in the language of the requirement specification, with considerable detailing of some features such as for the throughput

requirements, security, integrity and real-time performance, if these are specified. With this material in hand, one must proceed into design proper.

7.2 THE APPROACHES TO SOFTWARE DESIGN

Moving away from architecture considerations, investigations and specifications one immediately confronts the problems of how to proceed towards that 'blueprint' of an implementable software system that is the end objective of design – presuming all other issues of quality, and the constraints under which the design is to be done.

Conscious by now of the need for 'good' design, in the sense that we are not aiming to define and implement a monolithic program, we recognize a need to see the design as comprising a holistic system that is defined, in the first place, by its statement of functional requirements. We admit a need to see (or split) the requirements into parts in some way, and to define these parts in terms of greater solution detail, such as algorithms and data. This has loosely been called 'decomposition' into 'design modules', and the whole process has been named 'modular design'. We may, in fact, attempt it in one of two ways, 'top down' or 'bottom up'.

7.2.1 'Top down' and 'bottom up' approaches

In the first of these, we proceed from the architectural task definition of functional requirements, into a top level of modular design, and from this to a next level, and so on – hoping to end up with a low enough level of decomposition that we can see as program or integrand specifications. In 'bottom up' design, we try to define a low level set of program specifications that will provide features and functions in the requirement, and general purpose service routines to link these in one way or another; then, a 'design' may be derived by defining the structure relationships between programs seen as individual units, then by sets of programs 'packaged' to produce a feature or facility, and so on up a hierarchy of structures.

In fact, the terms 'top down' and 'bottom up' are not very useful ones, nor are the philosophical concepts in design to which they refer. For a start, few non-trivial exercises in software design are either truly 'top down' or 'bottom up'. Presupposing, for a moment, some clear way forward to detail solution means, one may start a 'top down' design with an intent to proceed no other way, but at some stage one will see commonality emerging – often between quite disparate parts of the requirements – and, quite naturally, one will then slip into 'bottom up' design for a while, until expediency (or guilt) causes a reversion to the original approach. Or, one may start 'bottom up' and reach a stage where it is not certain that the programs being defined fulfill all the requirements. Then one has to do a 'top down' mapping to ensure that what is coming into being in the other direction is not redundant, or only partially a fit, or both.

Thus, in practice, it is generally incorrect to speak of a design as having been done entirely 'top down' (Figure 7.2) or 'bottom up' in terms of its decomposition and

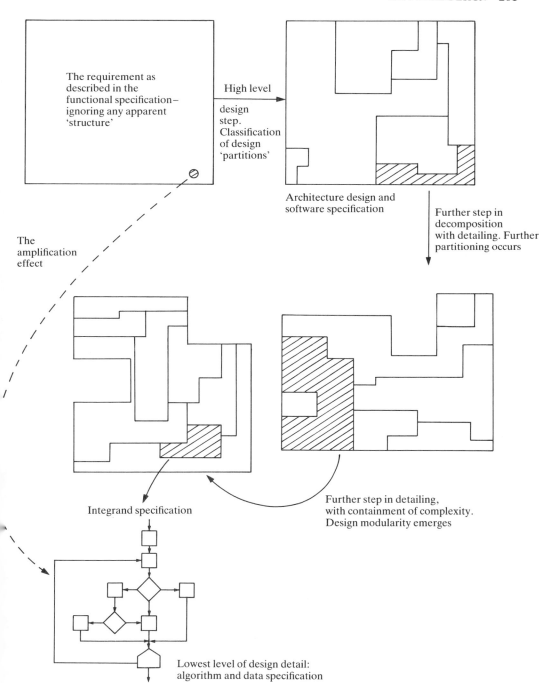

The requirement as described in the functional specification – ignoring any apparent 'structure'

High level design step. Classification of design 'partitions'

Architecture design and software specification

Further step in decomposition with detailing. Further partitioning occurs

The amplification effect

Integrand specification

Further step in detailing, with containment of complexity. Design modularity emerges

Lowest level of design detail: algorithm and data specification

FIGURE 7.2 Depiction of the process of 'top down' decomposition, seen as a magnification effect.

detailing. However, it is a mildly useful way to see the process of decomposition with detailing as analogous to magnification.

It is useful to remind the reader that, at each 'step' in this magnification process, a representational language will be required that suits the purposes and, as one proceeds away from the top level specifications – in their 'natural language plus' – these representational languages will become more and more solution specific, ending up with the programming language of choice.

7.2.2 Questions of decomposition

The thought persists that 'top down' and 'bottom up' are not very useful concepts as they stand. For they concern how the process of decomposition is to be undertaken, but they say nothing about one fundamental question: 'With respect to what do we decompose?' (Bergland 1981). Over the past two and a half decades, three general answers have been furnished to Bergland's question (but look at the date it was posed!) They are that we may decompose designs with respect to functions, or data or processes – deciding which way to proceed by identifying which is the dominant type amongst archetypes in the statement of requirements. In this context, the term 'archetype' refers to an element, or aggregates of elements, in the functional specification, that are clearly identifiable by a predominant property, such as logico-computational, data transformational or process-temporal. Further, the term 'dominant' refers to difficulty, as well as occurrence.

In fact these three objects of decomposition contain both 'classical' notions, such as functional decomposition and data transform driven design, and more modern suggestions – such as object oriented and data structure-based designs. Consequently, we can now amplify the answers to Bergland's awful little question. We probably try, or ought to try, to decompose designs and to detail features within them, with respect to the following:

1. Functions, or objects.
2. Data, in terms of transformations, or data structures.
3. Processes whose interrelationships are complex in time, not simply sequential.

These are the basic approaches to the problems of decomposition with detailing – the 'steps 2 to $n - 1$' referred to earlier. They are described forthwith. A description of the detail level of design ('step n') follows.

7.2.3 Decomposition with respect to functions or objects

Functional decomposition proceeds, and continues thereafter, on the basis of the main features outlined in the requirements. For example, in the CAISSA chess system, the first level of functional decomposition may be seen as comprising the elements of the state diagram in the functional specification (Figure 5.20). Within each function, subfunctions are identified – this is the process of magnification, or detailing – until a low enough level of substructure exists to be seen as the programmable definitions.

These function components of software are then finally 'designed' as algorithms and data structures, and coded. At some stage in the process, the 'bottom up' considerations of commonality of purpose, general utility and subroutine will have emerged, but, by and large, there will be a strong correspondence (or 'mapping') between the structure of coded integrands, and the functions in the specification of requirement to which they refer. This will assist (all else being equal) in the preservation of structure when new versions of the software are essayed, as a change to functionality will be relatively easily traced into the code.

For all the apparent virtues of this approach, its use is limited to a class of applications in which neither data nor temporal considerations are dominant issues in the software system. In fact top down, functional decomposition de-emphasizes data consideration, rendering such things as data structures and relationships a penultimate consideration before implementation, entirely derivative at that stage from the functional structure.

Thus, although code may be easily changed for functional variation in new versions, the derivative problems in the data domain may be extreme. Conversely, changes in the data domain may be very difficult to effect without wide-scale change being needed to the functional 'structure' of implemented code. For some systems these problems will pose great difficulty for software maintenance in general, and new version change in particular. Nor does this approach offer anything for systems containing concurrency in software subprocesses, such as for real-time requirements, with all their potential problems of synchrony.

In fact, the class of applications it is found most suitable for is the one described as the 'computation paradigm' of high order arithmetic transformations on low order aggregates of data. In such cases, the basic formulae are defined, elaborated into their numerical methods equivalent as need be, partitioned into a structure of logically dependent elements, and progressively substructured until the elements represent the low level structure of algorithms to be programmed, with the essential data (numbers) to be processed playing little part in the design considerations. Needless to say, the approach of functional decomposition – although entirely adequate for systems, or parts of systems, that are computation-intensive – can be extremely limiting for other application types.

At the same time as top down, functional decomposition became the vogue for software design – the period around 1965–75 – the methods of data transform and data structure driven design evolved also. These are described in Section 7.2.4. Later, partly in an attempt to avoid the limitations of both function and data oriented decomposition, and partly associated with other interests such as programming language development, the approach of object oriented specification and design was evolved. This, mainly because of its close association with language and artificial intelligence research, is still unestablished as an approach to the problem of decomposition in design, and program structure. Consequently, we offer only a brief account of it, and include it here as it is generally seen as an alternative to 'top down functional' design – an inaccurate view as it happens, as the reader will see.

The object oriented paradigm, as it is known, owes much to the field of simulation. As in that subject, one initially defines 'objects' in the real world as simple and unadorned noun constructions. Thus we may, for a multi-type transportation system, define

'vehicles'. One then defines classes within these objects – in this case 'land-going', 'sea-going', 'air-going' and this process is continued until one has the lowest level of relevant attributes, i.e. those that, if changed in any way, may cause relevant change in the real world.

One strategy to achieve this (Sommerville 1985) recommends that a very high level specification is defined in natural language, and that objects are identified by the noun occurrences within it – and that these are, in turn, regarded as the abstract data types in the system to be. The verb and adverb structure is then used to define the operators on objects and the attributes of operators respectively; the adjective structure is used to define the attributes of objects down to their lowest relevant level. When all this is done, a structure can be drawn, using a bubble and arrow convention simply, such as that for entity relationship analysis, to show the relationships between objects, and between them and operators – which are seen as performing message passing within the system.

An aim of object oriented specification is to offer an alternative to the 'either/or' of functional or data decomposition design. As in simulation methods, 'objects' are defined by their attributes as defined in data types, and operators are defined by the functions they perform (algorithms). Again, as in simulation, it is difficult to inject an element of 'real-time' into such a scheme, and our old friends – the problems of concurrency and synchrony – are not well provided for.

At the present time, research work on the object-oriented paradigm is directed toward the invention of quasi-intelligent tools to help in transforming an object-oriented specification, by means of intermediate executable prototypes, into a version that can be generated in code. The admixture of the approach with high level specification languages (such as Z), and the development of tools (see McDermid 1985), places the approach in the domain of research into alternative means for software development.

7.2.4 Decomposition with respect to data: transformations or structures

The problem of what happens to the data structure if one alters the functionality in a specification, for a new version of software, say, has caused considerable trouble and effort in the area of software maintenance and emendation. There are innumerable instances of functional change being quite straightforwardly reflected in changes to code – remove integrands I_m, I_{m+1}, etc., and add new ones I_n, I_{n+1} and so on – but where the co-lateral consequences to the data structures are fiendishly difficult to locate. To circumvent this, two approaches have been put forward:

1. Design oriented towards data transforms, due mainly to Constantine, Stevens *et al.*
2. Design oriented towards data structures, an approach due mainly to Warnier and Jackson.

These approaches to decomposition and detailing are now described.

DATA TRANSFORM

In data transform driven design, a data-flow map is constructed based on an analysis of requirements into data types and their flow within a network of transformations. A

simple instance of this is to take all of the external inputs and trace them in this way until they become outputs to the external world again. Each entity in the data-flow map comprises a triad of an *afferent* (or input) part that is depicted by an arrow with text, a *transform* that is text with a bubble, and an *efferent* (or output) part that is again depicted as an arrow with text. The result is a loosely related set of chains of these data-flows, and the question becomes one of how to derive a program structure from such a map.

The so-called central transform of the data-flow map can be identified by determining the points at which the afferent and efferent data are in their least recognizable form compared with their external manifestations as input or output. These 'central transforms' then comprise the highest level in a program structure hierarchy, acting like pegs from which the rest of the data-flow map hangs, each transform representing a program, or group of programs if further detailing of a transformation is required.

Once again the limits of this approach determine its usage. It has been closely associated with approaches to structured design at the program level (Stevens 1980), and its use seems to be particularly appropriate for small and medium sized data processing applications, where it combines the virtues of functional decomposition (changes in function/transformation easily traced into code) with a reasonably clear mapping of data elements. However, for large and complex applications, and certainly any containing stringent temporal properties, data transform driven design is inadequate.

DATA STRUCTURE BASED DESIGN

In another approach aimed at dealing with the effects on data structures of changes in requirements leading to changes in code, Warnier and Jackson, amongst others, have proposed that entities in the real world, and their data structures, are modeled in such a way that the program structure is determined by the data structure and not, as in other approaches, the other way round. The method of one of these authors (JSD) has already been outlined in Chapter 5, where it was seen that 'functions' are introduced relatively late in the sequence of steps comprising the method's procedure.

The intension in this data structure driven design is to provide a close mapping between the problem structure in the real world – entities and their relationships – and the data structures in the programs that operate on these data. Thus, sequences, repeats and alternatives in the data structure will have an evident meaning in the real world from which they derive, and will correspond directly with sequences, loops and choices in the program structure, and in the algorithms within programs. Also, the structure of databases for software to operate upon will bear a logical relationship with entities and their attributes in the outside world. Thus, if one changes an entity or its properties, the contingent changes in the data structure will be evident. This is the opposite of what normally transpires when data structures are determined to serve programs defined by top down, functional decomposition.

Software structures created this way, by data structure driven design, are not quite so easy to map with requirements as those done by top down, functional decomposition – there being a definite effort needed to see features and functions in a requirement as data structures. However, this effort is more than amply rewarded by the relative ease with which data structure designed software systems are changed.

Once again, the limitation of this approach is in its inability to enrich design decomposition and detailing when 'real-time' requirements exist, and elaborate structures with concurrency, synchronization and asynchronous operation may be needed.

On the whole though, for any other type of application in computation or intensive data processing, the data structure method of decomposition and detailing is probably the strongest contender on offer at the present time, and JSD/JSP (or close derivatives) are consequently widespread in use, and represents the basis for some PSE tools coming into being – see Chapter 8.

However, over all this looms the specter of 'real-time' requirements; with respect to what do we decompose in these cases?

7.2.5 Decomposition with respect to processes in a 'real-time' requirement

In Section 7.1, a set of objectives was outlined for software design comprising, in essence, three domains, or 'dimensions', of intellectual activity going on simultaneously within the overall design process, and between which, and within domains, there may be a mass of compromises to be made. These domains are as follows:

1. Transformation; between the languages of specification and computer operation.
2. Quality; the achievement of compliance and modifiability through good structure.
3. Constraints; the production of low level designs that can be implemented in the host, and will achieve defined objectives on the target equipment (if 'host' and 'target' are different).

In complex 'real-time' requirements, one aspect tends to dominate all others; how to fulfill the stringent temporal requirements within the bounds of the equipment provided. So severe may this problem be that other considerations will tend to become subordinated to it. Gone will be the decorous notions of 'top down' or 'bottom up', and gone too will be the structured approaches derived from functions or objects, data transformations and data structures. Spatial hierarchies, to represent logical connections and sequencing in a decomposition, will have little bearing on a design in which the representation and regulation of temporal relationships are the dominant issues.

This is the area of applications within the process paradigm, defined earlier in this work. It is an area that is not well served by developed approaches or methods at this time.

The problems of process-oriented applications have been discussed in the section on architecture design (Section 7.1). They are the nightmare occurrences of deadlock, deadly embrace, inaccessible topology and asynchronous data accesses that haunt the world of concurrent software systems. Here, the best approach on offer at this time is one based on decomposition with respect to process archetypes in the requirement.

The abstract process characterization of De Wolf, and its state representation and stylized data-flow connotations, may provide a useful start at the level of functional specification; alternatively, an identification of basic process activities, and their relationships and data – as in the Mascot/ACP scheme – may provide the archetypes from which further decomposition can be done.

At the architecture design stage, simulations may be done in Petrinet notation (described below), and executed as a program to detect the critical regions within the architecture. Or, alternatively, prototypes may be built using rapid prototyping languages – where these exist – and again used to detect problematical properties in an architecture, as in the case given by Zave (1982) and quoted in Chapter 3. These 'rapid prototyping' languages tend to be application-specific, and closely tied to design notations and programming languages. One such – the so-called S^3A system for executable specifications in telemetry/telegraphy – is strongly dependent on the design procedure and notation of CCITT/SDL, and the special language of Chill for that application area. SDL is described below.

Decomposition with respect to processes seldom proceeds in a decorous 'top down' fashion unless some very strenuous attempts are undertaken to keep it so. One such is to partition the architecture of 'real-time' systems very early in design – seeing the process archetypes as comprising a set of distributed microprocessors in a communicating network of such, whether this has any objective reality in the actual designation of computers within the system to be, or not. No attempts are then made to achieve either 'good' program structure or 'good' data structure across this scheme, although these notions may have bearing within each conceptual part; the dominant consideration remains compliance in the first place, and the particular avoidance of that nightmare quartet of problems already referred to.

All this is heresy of course to the schools of rational structure, and one can easily see why. Maintenance and evolution of process-oriented software systems is, more often than not, exceedingly difficult – often to a limiting degree. There may be little, or no, evident mapping between program structure and structure in the requirements; program sequence structures may be impossible to define, as they may be determined by asynchronous external events; and the consequential changes to data structures for changing archetypal processes in the requirement may be extremely severe.

This is the world of real-time requirements, process-oriented software and embedded computer systems arranged as distributed networks of microcomputers, or the parallel execution processes within a monolithic machine. There are no miracle solutions on offer, nor are any likely to emerge – although improved notations for design in this area are an urgently awaited need.

Above all, in this area more than any other, adopting a wrong approach to decomposition at the outset will quite quickly lead to an impasse. 'Classical' methods, as described in Sections 7.2.1 and 7.2.2, are basically 'wrong' for this type of application, and pursuing them will lead to clearly evident 'design impoverishment'. It is rather like the business of donning one's shirt; if you get the first button in the wrong hole then, however carefully you continue . . . .

Attempts have been made, recently, to upgrade some of the earlier methods and then to fit them for 'real-time' purposes. JSD purports to deal with concurrent systems wherein a design is done on the basis of communicating entities, and the notion of hierarchy is achieved by a process called 'inversion', in which pairs of communicating entities are made into master–slave dyads progressively, until one concludes with a hierarchy of time-dependencies. This, and other attempts to augment 'classical' methods – SADT is another – seem to be moving toward that paradigm of design mentioned

earlier, for concurrent systems, in which processes are seen as being communicating microprocessors of adequate properties. This does not mean that the system-to-be will be implemented thus, but is how the design is seen. This approach was presaged in Allworth (1981). In this respect, some of the 'classical' methods are moving toward a position that the Mascot method and notation were devised to fill.

Although the problems of synchrony – that fearful quartet – tend to dominate the design of process-oriented software systems, one other issue in real-time requirements can, and should, be held in its proper context at the time of design and implementation. That is the issue of response requirements that are, in some fashion, determined by the needs of 'real-time' events in the system itself, or in the objective world. It is best to provide for these as best as possible in design and implementation, by reasonably efficient program structures, but not to attempt optimization of code *ab initio*. For example, the precepts of cohesion, coupling, information hiding, single entry/single decision/single exit and structured coding concepts in general should be preserved. However, the result, particularly if implemented in a high level language, might give performance properties outside the range of requirements.

Then, during the testing and demonstration of the software, any timing faults may be attended to by 'tuning' the code, i.e. rewriting parts of it, such as the most frequently used parts like inner loops of routines, in low level languages, or even compromising 'good structure' to achieve run-time efficiency. The point is that one compromises from strength.

However, the main issue remains. The principal concerns in design of this sort are ones of synchrony between concurrent processes and data; response time requirements, which might give rise to concurrency in design, should not otherwise dominate the design of a solution, the 'optimization' of execution time of the resulting software being better done at the programming stage when a good design has been implemented.

7.2.6 The detail level of design

In Section 7.1 we commented on the first level of design proper, the architecture design, and in Sections 7.2.1–5 we described the basic approaches to decomposition and detailing for what might be called steps 2 to $n - 1$ in design. The last step in design is the definition (or specification) of integrands, and their structure into programs, program packages and load modules for the software-to-be.

These lowest levels of design are crucial to the 'good structure' of the programs, and all the recommended practices – as summarized in Chapter 3 – of cohesion, coupling, single entry/single decision/single exit, information hiding, and the use of structured coding constructs, will have force at this level. We may indeed have arrived at this point with a set of designs done in any one of a number of forms, and admixing design infomation on algorithms and the data they are to operate on rather indiscriminately.

It is the explicit role of detail design to produce the specification of integrands and their structure into programs, and the detailed design of data structures on which they are to operate, according to the precepts of 'good programming practice', so that the errors of monolithic programming are avoided along with those of inordinate (and

gratuitous) complexity. This is the same role exactly, whether the requirement is for a computation, data or process intensive system, and whether or not the object of decomposition has been functions, objects, data or the temporal properties of processes. The detail level of design ensures that both program and data structures to be implemented lack any *gratuitous* complexity, and that their implementation may proceed in a simple and straightforward fashion – however complicated might be the sum total of their collective features.

7.3 THE MEANS AND METHODS FOR SOFTWARE DESIGN

Given that we have some apprehension of what design is to achieve (Section 7.1), and some, hopefully useful, approach to the question of decomposition with detailing (Section 7.2), what is generally needed is a *method* for ordering and depicting the design information produced. We speak here in the singular – 'a method' – as we refer to a particular instance, such as the progressive definition in design of the CAISSA system.

In fact, as has been made clear elsewhere, there are many such 'methods', comprising more or less 'strong' procedures and notations. They are all members of a family whose use starts at high levels of specification, and which includes, as members, such 'low level' items as programming languages for adoption during implementation.

This continuum of methods, some inappropriate for particular purposes although suitable for others, causes great dismay to audiences outside software engineering. Why so many? Why so unclear in purpose and suitability?

In fact, although there are dozens of methods and notations for specification and design, and many more languages for coding, it is seldom necessary to be familiar with more than just a few. We will, in fact, consider only a representative fraction of those intended to help with requirements' specification and software design.

7.3.1 Classification of design methods by their principal level of suitability

In the first place, we define three possible main purposes, and, therefore, areas of suitability, for a method and its attached procedure and notation. They are: descriptive, architecture and detail.

A method may have a main purpose in one of these, and some subsidiary purposes (e.g. for particular applications) in another. For example, essay-form use of natural language will have a widespread use as a descriptive notation for specifications, and a more limited use in design architectures and details. On the other hand, structured natural language (as is the case of pseudo-code) may have a main purpose at low levels of detail design, and only a subsidiary purpose in architecture design and (if any at all) for the descriptive purposes of requirement specification.

We have, in Chapter 5, already listed seven useful methods, and briefly described their notations amongst others: SADT, De Wolf's abstract process', state diagrams, Mascot, JSD, data-flow and timing charts. To this list, we now add six others: CCITT-

SDL, Petrinets, structured flowcharts, BS 6224 design structure diagrams, pseudo-code and program structure charts.

Each member in this coven of useful methods may now be signified by its main purpose according to our scheme.

1. *Descriptive*: SADT, De Wolf, state diagrams, Mascot,* JSD and data-flow. All of these are potentially useful at the requirements' specification stages. Some (such as SADT and JSD) have procedures that may help in the process of specification; others such as De Wolf, Mascot and data-flow have notations that may help in recording the specification.

2. *Architecture*: timing charts, Mascot,* CCITT-SDL, Petrinets, These are particularly useful in the outline systems design (e.g. timing charts) and architecture design stages, for 'process' applications with stringent timing requirements.

   The architecture of other types of application may best be depicted in function, data-flow or data structure related hierarchies, such as in any one of the descriptive notations.

3. *Detail*: structured flowcharts, BS 6224 DSD, pseudo-code and program structure charts. These are useful, lower down in the design process, for depicting program definitions and the iteration, sequence and choice of integrand specification – at which stage, data dictionaries will be of use also, and explicit data structures will be defined.

Clearly, these are rather loose and judgmental assignments of main purpose. We have seen Mascot in use well down into detailed design, and BS 6224 DSD used relatively early in the process; likewise with SADT, Jackson's methods and data-flow.

There is no strict prescription; whatever is useful may be used. Nor is there any need for undue loyalty to one method. If what has been useful ceases to be so, then switch to another method. It bears repeating that one may set out, at the specification stage, using (say) SADT, do some architecture/feasibility work for the outline design in SDL and timing charts, switch firmly to SDL in the architecture proper and detailing stages, back-track several steps to adopt Mascot as being better in this case, switch again to BS 6224 DSD for program definition, and finally do the integrand specifications in pseudo-code. There is nothing wrong with this state of affairs, although four things should be said about it:

1. It causes some non-experts to become slightly phobic about what they see as a proliferation of 'high tech' means and methods. Engineers from other disciplines regard the prospect with incredulity and disdain; in their world they could build a house in Peru from architect's plans done in Poland, and do its electrical wiring from diagrams made in the Punjab – for there are standard notations for these things are there not? Where are our standards, they ask?

---

*Clearly Mascot is highlighted in this list, as it is an example of a method whose main purpose was, and is, at architecture stage of design and below, but whose use as a notation for recording requirements is, for a certain class of application, undoubted. We have seen it used vigorously and well as the '+' in 'natural language +' for clarifying the text of functional specifications for 'process'-oriented applications, whose operations are dominated in some way by temporal considerations. For that reason, Mascot is described in this volume as spanning both descriptive and architecture purposes.

Managers, and others, tend to doubt the software engineer's ability to be 'literate' in several methods. In fact none of the *notations* are particularly exacting, as we have already seen in Chapter 5. A *procedure* might be a fairly elaborate affair – SADT is perhaps the best example of that – but most notations are usually variants on the bubble, box, lozenge and line convention, perhaps seven or so symbols in total, with a simple set of syntactic rules of usage. An exception is BS 6224 DSD, as will be shown, as the scope of this is rather more ambitious (and lower level) than most others.

2. There may be a question of support, at the PSE level, for a multiplicity of methods and their notations. This will be undoubtedly true if rather rare methods are favored. However, most of the major methods listed here are becoming supported ('implemented') with adequate tools for them on PC-based, workstation equipment for software development.

   However, this is not, as yet, a particularly convincing state of affairs, and many 'cheap and cheerful' PC-based packages purporting to give you data-flow, Mascot, BS 6224 DSD, JSD and so forth merely provide a few tools for drawing and storing diagrams. In Chapter 8, as the subject of Ipse/PSE technology is taken further, it will be realized that an essential feature of a 'good' environment is that its tools are properly interfaced with each other, and can be used in whole or part as an integrated set. That prospect is a distant one for methods in general, and is only slowly arriving for a particular method or small set of such.

3. Allied to this problem of integration, at the support level, is the question of whether a change of method can really help design, if the methods do not provide continuity, being of such a radical difference in approach perhaps.

   In fact one seldom makes an abrupt switch, such as from SDL at step x to Mascot at step $x + 1$; more frequently, one back-tracks to, say, step $x - 1$, or $x - 2$, does that in the new method, and proceeds forward. This can have such startling and positive effects on a design team that it is almost worth advocating design by more than one means as a method in itself! Cost and, particularly, time usually militate against such a civilized accommodation.

4. Another question concerns quality assurance, Does this not require hard and fast standards, and the rigorous adherence to quality procedures? And does this not require more fixity of choice in design methods (as well as other things such as programming languages)? As will be seen in Chapter 9 on quality, a fixed standard may, if violated, disqualify a software system on two counts:

   (a) the process of software development cannot be verified according to the prescription;

   (b) the deliverable documentation is not compliant with the standard for it.

   In both cases it will be seen that these disqualifications say nothing about the software as such, whether it is compliant and modifiable.

   In short, in this author's view, it is seldom wise to put so creative a matter as program design and implementation into too tight a straightjacket of 'standards'. Obviously, considerations such as portability of code, familiarity of implementation staff and many others, have to be taken into account, but for particularly difficult applications the overriding concern is usually more to be able to do a 'good' design at all, and to follow it with a 'good' implementation.

This is not a polemic against standards, which will be dealt with at greater length in Chapter 9, and elsewhere – there being references in Chapters 11 and 13 as well.

As already said and repeated, the choice of a design method/notation will be a judgmental one. There is no algorithm or formula whose use will indicate 'best', or even 'good enough'. Even so, there may be a company 'standard' in force for some reason – either through internal edict or external force (such as a client's contract terms). Often such 'standards' are to ensure that some orderly, and generally useful, method – such as JSD/JSP typically – is used across a set of software developments, so that staff migration to different tasks is possible, and software maintenance work simplified.

There is nothing against this state of affairs, except when the dreaded exception crops up. I recall being asked interminably, amongst many others similarly importuned in the period 1980–85, why such and such an old favorite in the data processing sector seemed to make the software engineers so unhappy. On inspection, it was usually the case that the application types under consideration had moved on, and now incorporated problems of the 'process' type, for 'real-time' requirements.

Then there were furrowed brows about the answers, for there was no earthly way of proving the degree of misfit, nor of demonstrating it by objective means. The main argument against a standard design method is, in fact, the same as against a standard language – that none such exists that is suitable for *all* eventualities; if your applications set is well understood and pretty invariant, then all right – standards at design and implementation levels may be both desirable and possible: otherwise not.

7.3.2 Notations for architecture level and design detailing

Why notations? Why diagrams of any sort? Again, styles vary, and some people – notably computer scientists – try to avoid diagrams altogether, in favor of abstract notations, or language of special purpose (Z is an example). However, we will adopt the view that 'a diagram can say more than a thousand words' – given of course, that it is adequately done, for, if not, its utterances may easily speak more than a thousand words of meaningless or misleading trash. In general, diagrams – being relatively free in two dimensions – tend to depict complex relationships more succinctly than text. Nor does structured text help particularly in this respect.

Certainly, pseudo-code based designs are not fully two dimensional, even with indented structures within them; and subscripting to represent multidimensional properties is efficient but not always clear.

Diagrams, in reasonably strong notations, are vastly preferable in software design to text on its own, a fact recorded by the innumerable, almost instinctive, uses of a variety of logic and data-flow diagrams throughout the history of software development.

The same cliché, that a diagram can say more than a thousand words, can be used for formal specification means as well, but here we would say that an arrangement of symbols can say more than a thousand words, or something of the sort. This is undoubtedly true, as our earlier example said of the trigonometric form of Pythogoras's equation: $\sin^2\beta + \cos^2\beta = 1$. However, what is gained by efficiency of expression will be more than lost in clarity of design objectives, such as relative ease to test a structure

to determine its compliance, or to change it in the event of error or improvement.

In the following we shall deal, therefore, with the methods whose notations ('languages') are diagrammatic ones. In the first two subsections, we will describe the architecture notations of CCITT-SDL and Petrinet graphs. Then we will describe the notations of particular use at lower detail-levels of design.

THE CCITT STRUCTURED DESIGN LANGUAGE – SDL

SDL, not unlike De Wolf's scheme described earlier, is a notation and procedure based on the ideas of finite-state machines. It is particularly designed for process-oriented applications of the store and forware message transmission type in telephony and telegraphy, as the SDL symbols show in Figure 7.3.

It is difficult to see a use for this notation in the definition or design of our CAISSA chess system, used elsewhere as our running example, and specified in Chapter 5. The notions of states in suspension, awaiting signals and transitions, are alien to this application. However, if one added the requirement for 'intelligent' play by the computer, and the possibility to interrupt this if a deliberation is taking too long, that might alter the specification in favor of this notation. Even so, the experience of using CCITT-SDL on a problem for which it is inappropriate is an uncomfortable one. I once saw a woman, who believed in traditional ways, trying to beat a carpet with the new vacuum cleaner. Using an inappropriate tool in software development is the same thing entirely; a difficult and aggravating task that causes derision in onlookers, as anyone who

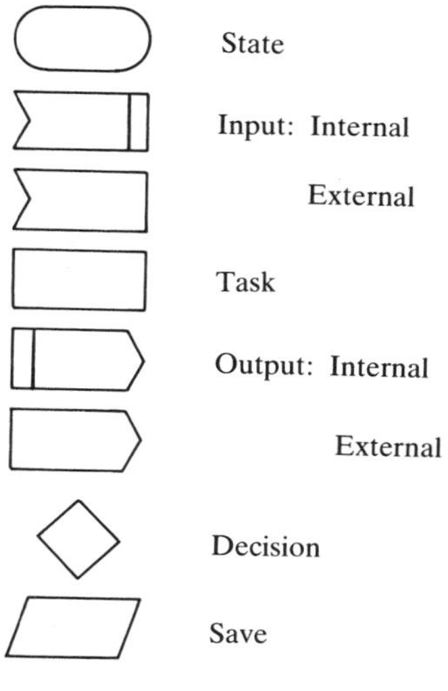

Symbol		Definition	
State	Process	A serial logic function; either in a status awaiting input or in a transition.
Input: Internal	Signal	A data flow between processes, input to one output from another (internal if processes with the same 'function block' or module).
External			
Task	State	A condition of a process suspended awaiting an input signal.
Output: Internal	Save	Postpone recognition of a signal unacceptable in current state.
External	Transition	A sequence of actions between states.
	Output	An action within a transition which generates a signal.
Decision	Task	Any action which is neither input nor decision.
Save	Decision	Selection of a criterion from a choice of continuation transition paths.

CCITT-SDL Symbols   CCITT-SDL Definitions

FIGURE 7.3 CCITT-SDL symbols and definitions.

has tried to write a matrix inversion program in Cobol, or design a real-time application using HIPO notation, will attest. In Figure 7.4, a CAISSA system is depicted in which users' input is – by a special dispensation in hardware – entered into an 'internal' buffer, whatever is going on in the main processor. This buffer can then be polled by an operating program, as is happening in the high-level SDL depiction of a routine ('state') for 'intelligent' play.

The CCITT-SDL notation is particularly important as it is integrated within some programming support environments – or it is 'implemented' as we say. This means that high, medium and low level designs of systems can be graphically supported, and code can actually be generated from the low level design. This is particularly important for rapid testing of design ideas, but the resulting code may lack several essential aspects of quality, and a proper implementation cycle is recommended.

Some other notations are similarly 'implemented', Mascot and JSD/JSP being two such. In the case of JSD/JSP, there may be little fault in taking code that is automatically generated from low level JSP designs as the implemented version of programs, and subjecting it to rigorous quality assurance procedures. Mascot and CCITT-SDL are slightly different, as the application set for which they are usually used is one in which there are often complexities of process concurrency and synchrony; these require a far more stringent implementation, generally speaking, than relatively straightforward data processing applications.

CCITT-SDL is not a very widely known notation outside Europe and the field of telephony applications. Nonetheless, it is a useful one as an adjunct to Mascot, timing charts and Petrinets for 'process'-type applications.

PETRINETS

We have described, elsewhere, the concept of the finite-state machine, its simple notation ('state diagrams') and the procedures such as that of De Wolf and the CCITT method that are based primarily on it. A finite-state machine is basically a single process whose states change in a prescribable (and describable) manner. Some applications, however, concern multiple processes that can occur concurrently, and whose 'states' may be independent of other processes, synchronous, linked with asynchronous features – and all kinds of complexity for which the finite-state approach and its notation are not particularly suitable.

The design and implementation problems arising, in these cases, include the list of four referred to earlier, i.e. unproductive looping ('deadly embrace'), mutual exclusion ('deadlock'), inaccessible topology and synchronization of data updating and access. These are the typical problems faced in designing 'process' applications with 'real-time' features – both of which terms have been defined earlier in this text.

A Petrinet, or Petrinet graph (PNG), is a useful device for simulating features of a requirement, or a systems design, to investigate its behavior in unproductive looping, deadlock and inaccessible topology. The basic notation of Petrinets is exceedingly simple, comprising the elements shown in Figure 7.5. Each transition bar has a set of input places and an associated set of output places. Directed edges connect the transition bars to these places. Places are seen as the output nexus for one or more transition bars, and the input nexus from one or more transition bars. Places may contain tokens (a dot at the

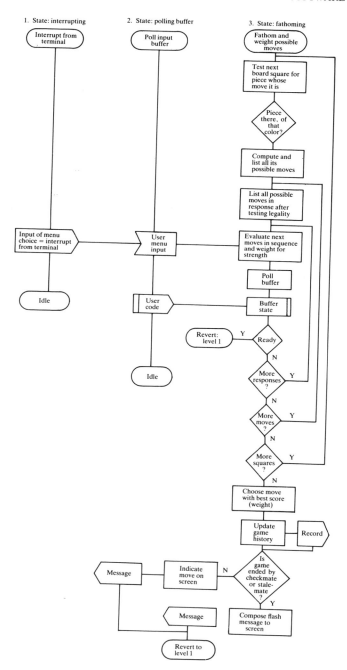

FIGURE 7.4 Example of CCITT-SDL in CAISSA design.

◯   A place

| A transition bar

←————   A directed edge between places and transitions, representing inputs and outputs

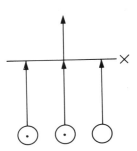

Marked places–incomplete state. Transition bar cannot 'fire' a token

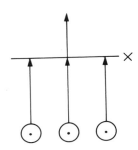

Marked places–complete state. Transition bar can 'fire' a token

FIGURE 7.5 Petrinet graph notation and convention.

center of the circle, in the Petrinet notation), and the functions represented by a transition bar associated with an input place can only commence when all its associated input places contain tokens – see Figure 7.6.

In the simple scheme shown in Figure 7.6, the transition bar X is said to be unable to 'fire' in the incomplete state. When all its input places contain tokens, X may change state. This is known as 'firing', there being performed whatever functionality in X is associated with the local change of state concerned, and the possibility thereby of adding tokens to its output places.

The rather nasty example in Figure 7.6 shows, on a very limited scale, the complexity that can arise. Magnify this a thousandfold for a large scale 'process' operating in 'real time'! The situation becomes even more complicated when one adds the notions of parallelism in the subprocess, synchronization and so forth. The scheme in Figure 7.6 depicts no element of time at all.

Parallel subprocesses are generally shown as boxes containing some naming or textual description to identify them, and each box will represent a subset of the Petrinets that can be expressed in the symbols shown in Figure 7.5. As a further ramification of this, one may be able to nominate precedence between parallel subprocesses, in the event that only one may be active in performing a certain task at a time. Such tasks, when

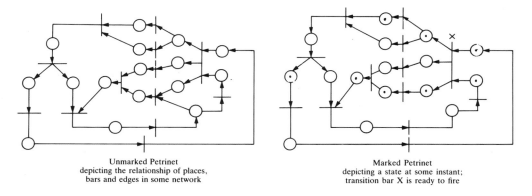

Unmarked Petrinet
depicting the relationship of places,
bars and edges in some network

Marked Petrinet
depicting a state at some instant;
transition bar X is ready to fire

FIGURE 7.6 Marked and unmarked regions in a Petrinet.

identified, are called the 'critical regions' of a Petrinet, and Figure 7.7 shows both the identification of parallel processes and the description of a critical region between two of them.

We can now use Petrinets as 'flat' descriptions of the subprocesses within a system, where 'flat' refers to the absence of either structural hierarchy or time consideration. We may merely – as in Figure 7.6 – show the elements and their dependencies. Then, by extending the picture to incorporate parallelism and the notions of precedence and critical regions, we can introduce the factors of time and synchrony as these are true in a particular case in the real world.

Petrinets are remarkably useful as a tool for two purposes, early in systems design, i.e. at the 'architecture' stage. Firstly elements in the requirement may be modeled, and the veracity of one's understanding of requirements can be checked in that way. In this usage, Petrinet models assist in the decomposition and detailing that are essential early in design. Then, when software architecture design has progressed somewhat, Petrinets may be used to reveal potential problematical areas in parts of the software-to-be. In these respects, Petrinets are prototype simulations, and the notation is for that purpose.

Analysis of Petrinets is generally by computer-based simulation, and some work has been done (e.g. Nelson *et al.* 1983) to generate programs from the Petrinet itself - although this should be seen strictly as research at this time. Other authors (notably Birrell and Ould 1985) point out that the original invention, by Carl Petri, c. 1962, has undergone much evolution in recent years. Of these, the ones we have found in major use are as follows:

1. Modification of the logical AND rule for firing, to incorporate a rule allowing firing of transition bars due to EXCLUSIVE OR conditions in input places.
2. Imposition of time constraints on firing.
3. Priorities in firing attached to transitions, to determine the rules for dealing with simultaneity.
4. Time-out tokens, to ensure that marking does not persist inappropriately.

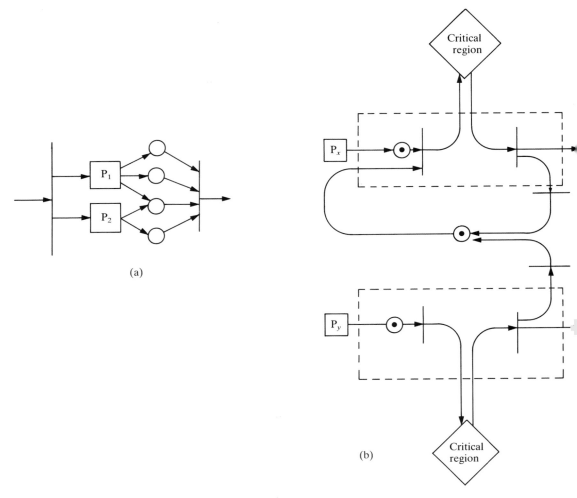

FIGURE 7.7 (a) Parallel processes in a Petrinet. (b) Regions and critical regions in a Petrinet.

The use of Petrinet graph simulation helps – at the stage of architecture design – to identify some of what, elsewhere, we have called the terrible quartet of problems often besetting software for real-time requirements. However, a Petrinet graph in no way represents a detailed software design. Nor does it help much with some of the problems for this kind of software system – in particular, the achievement of 'real-time' responses, and the problem of asynchronous data accesses for update or retrieval.

In the first case, as already advised, one does the best one can, within good design practice, to achieve appropriate response times, and later one 'tunes' the system – hopefully without violating its good structure in the process. For data accesses, one is again more often than not left, at low levels of design, with the need to define and design

data areas whose modes of access are through carefully arranged processes, with signal-ing and protection devices (e.g. as in the 'two phase commit strategy' recommended by Ullman 1982).

The notations suitable for more detailed design are now described. These are BS 6224, flow charts, pseudo-code and program structure charts.

DESIGN STRUCTURE DIAGRAMS – BSI 6224

We begin with the most powerful of the four we intend to discuss – although it is not yet the most widely adopted – the British Standards Institution BSI 6224 DSD. The full definition of this extremely fine notation is found in the document UCD 681.3.06.003.63 (British Standards Institution 1982/7), and we give here the briefest synopsis. Design structure diagrams are intended to: (a) express the logical sequence of actions in a structured system; and (b) achieve this in a form that can be easily transformed into well known programming languages.

Some of the basic symbols and conventions in BSI 6224 notation are set out in Figures 7.8–7.11.

The use of symbols in BSI 6224, and the whole convention of the notation, is exceedingly strong for the purposes of low level design, and is simple to use. To give two trivial examples, nodes are defined as branching points for the flow of logical control; and 'fall back' is defined as the return of control to a previously visited node from a simple activity, or function, having single input and no output.

Each node consists of one input path and two output paths, and the direction of flow is seen as from top to bottom of its depiction on a page. Branching occurs to the left, seen from the control flow point of view (right from the reader's perspective), and left-hand branches are investigated first, after which control flows back along the path and continues along the (then) right-hand path (Figure 7.8). In the case of fall-back, Figure 7.9 shows that A is executed before B, which is executed before C simply.

It is beyond our scope here to dwell on any notation. In fact, it might be thought that I have dwelt on this one inordinately, but, if pressed to nominate one whose increased use should be seriously considered for software design during the decomposition with detailing stage, it would be BSI 6224. I have even noticed software engineers tending to use it higher than might have been thought appropriate in the life cycle, for example in the outline system design, to show schematically how the functions notionally assigned to be done in software might be related as a notional software architecture.

BSI 6224 is an example of a 'strong' notation with a 'strong enough' procedure attaching to it in the sense of conventions for using the notation. It is not, however, a particularly strong 'method' in the overall sense, as SADT and JSD/JSP are intended as fully fledged methods with strong procedures and notations for full life cycle use where appropriate. BS 6224 is basically for use toward the lower end of the design steps.

The example of BSI 6224 shown in Figure 7.12 is taken from a low level design in the implementation of the CAISSA chess system. In fact, the example is slightly perverse, as the *general* structure of piece-move validation is shown, incorporating one instance of its detail, the queen's move. Such a scheme is unlikely to be found in real life, where all six exits from the case-statement tests would be referred to off-page element definitions. Also, it will be clear that the example does not carry many of the features of BSI 6224

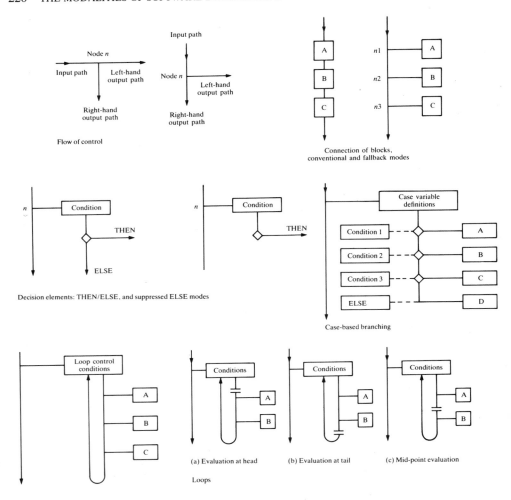

FIGURE 7.8 BSI 6224 DSD conventions (1).

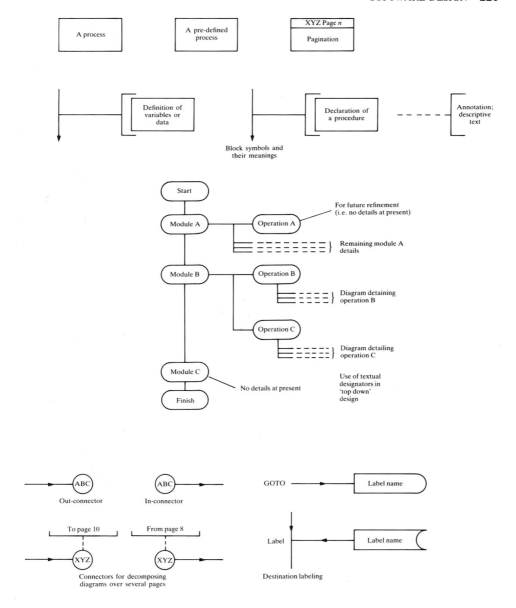

FIGURE 7.9 BSI 6224 DSD conventions (2).

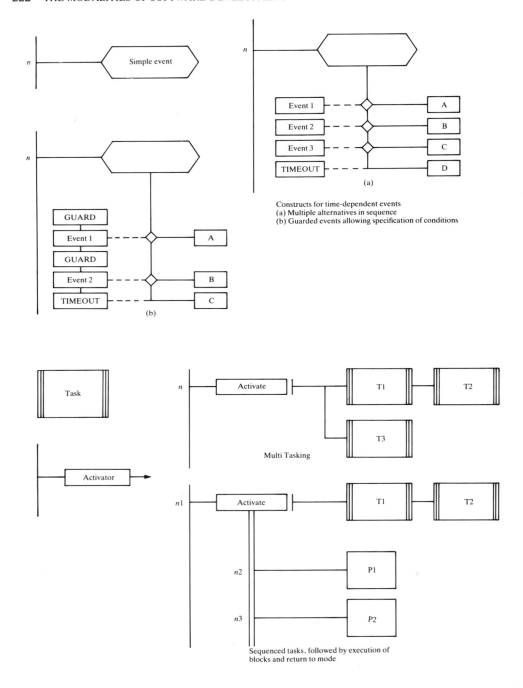

Constructs for time-dependent events
(a) Multiple alternatives in sequence
(b) Guarded events allowing specification of conditions

FIGURE 7.10 BSI 6224 DSD conventions (3).

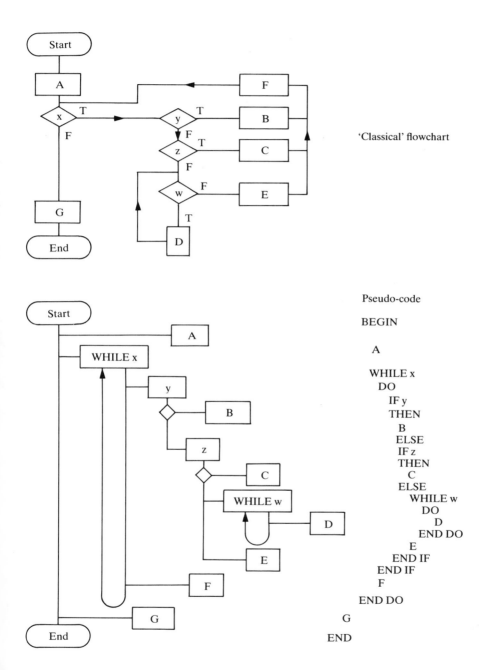

'Classical' flowchart

Pseudo-code

BEGIN

A

WHILE x
 DO
  IF y
  THEN
   B
   ELSE
   IF z
   THEN
    C
    ELSE
     WHILE w
      DO
       D
      END DO
     E
    END IF
   END IF
  F
 END DO

G
END

FIGURE 7.11 Example of the use of BS 6224 compared with a classical flowchart and a pseudo-code depiction (BSI 1982).

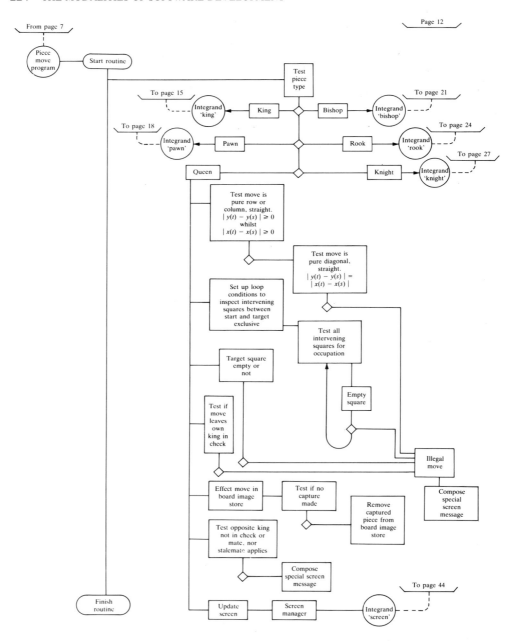

FIGURE 7.12 Example of BSI 6224 DSD in CAISSA design.

defined in earlier figures. In fact, the result is a stylized flowchart – but none the worse for that, of course.

STRUCTURED FLOWCHARTS

The simple, basic elements of structured code are shown in Section 3.2. Figure 3.2 sets out these elements, and the reader is advised to refer to that schematic at this point. These rules, for good structures of code, are also used when drawing flowcharts for the integrands and programs concerned. A set of typical flowchart symbols is shown in Figure 7.13.

Flowcharts have a bad name in some quarters, notably in academic (computer science) circles, where they are seen (or alleged) to be associated with poor implementation practice, known often as 'spaghetti coding'. In this, the control flow of programs becomes unnecessarily confused and confusing – mainly due to a lack of decomposition in the first place. In such cases the flowchart is trying to carry too much information, possibly about a whole module of software rather than just an integrand. Another cause of confusion may arise through the extensive use of unconditional transfers.

When these faults and failings occur, then grumblings are well founded. Otherwise, it must be said that flowcharting is a neutral activity, based on a simple and rather weak notation; where it falls down is where it also lacks a procedure to guide programmers (in particular) in its use, and here we turn to the equally simple precepts of design decomposition and structured coding to help out.

The admixture of flowchart symbols and the rules of structured coding (see Figures 7.13 and 3.2) provides software engineers with a convenient way of depicting the design and specifications for integrands and their composition into programs. Bad flowcharts are a fright, and lead ineluctably to frightful code. In fact, the process is often the opposite way round entirely; deplorable code is cobbled together prematurely (little specification, no design). Then, as *ex post facto* (or even *post mortem*) documentation, a hideous mess of flowcharting is derived from the code. However, none of this need be the case, for the fault lies not so much in the tool as in its user.

A detail of low level CAISSA design is shown in Figure 7.14. As will become clear in the next section, this could easily have been written in pseudo-code. In fact, flowcharting and pseudo-code are very much interchangeable options for integrand specification with the warning, given here for the umpteenth time, that pseudo-code loses this value earlier in the design process, and takes on some negative values too at those levels, such as inordinate complexity when complex design matters are being expressed.

In the Figure 7.14 example, some interesting little foibles appear, such as parameter passing across integrands. Perhaps 'information hiding' is not strongly in use in this design.

PSEUDO-CODE

The meaning usually ascribed to this hybrid of adjective and noun is that of some subset of a formal programming language such as Fortran, Algol, Pascal, Ada and Modula – some basic syntax of one's favorite high level language in fact – that serves one of two basic purposes, or both: (a) bridges between natural language and programming language;

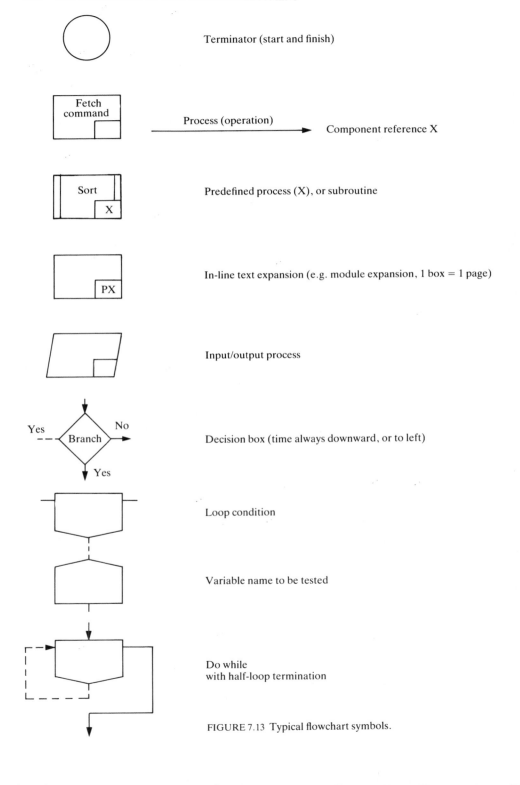

FIGURE 7.13 Typical flowchart symbols.

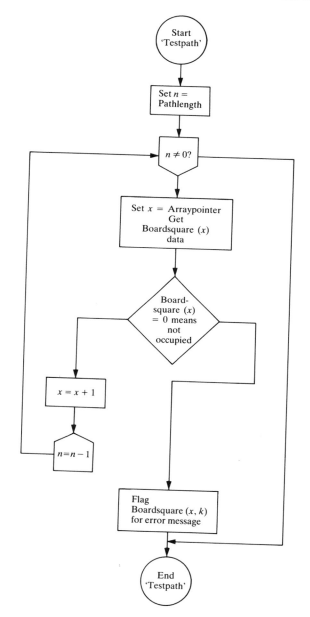

FIGURE 7.14 Flowchart detail from CAISSA.

and (b) acts as a 'programmer friendly' means of expressing thoughts about design, and the definition of integrands and programs.

At a superficial, visual level, pseudo-code resembles a program written in a high level language. For example, the design of part of the algorithm to test the legitimacy of piece-moves in a chess game may be expressed, in part, as in Figure 7.15. It is derived from the schematic Figure 7.14, to which it is an alternative. The point here is that no

Integrand: 'Testpath'   Page 42
Purpose: To test occupation of squares on move path, for all pieces except king, knight and any other
            piece making only one square move
Entry/exit: From 'Piecemove' integrand (page 12); exit returns to 'Piecemove'
Data: Array 'Boardsquare' (i, j, k) where i, j are board coordinates and k is a special indicator
State: Integrand is entered with 'Pathlength' parameter set to pathlength $-2 > 0$, and 'Arraypointer'
            parameter set for initial i, j values

```
enter:
     begin: "Testpath"
          let n = Pathlength
               while n ≠ 0 continue; else:
                                        end
               let x = Arraypointer
                  if Boardsquare (x) = 0 continue; else:
                                                  Boardsquare (x) = −Boardsquare (x)
                                                  end
                  let x = x + 1
                  let n = n − 1
               return while
     end
exit
```

FIGURE 7.15 Pseudo-code detail from CAISSA.

one would expect such a thing to work as it is, as there are probably many violations of the language's rules.

Pseudo-code is of great use at the level of design immediately 'above' (i.e. before) implementation proper. However, as has been made clear throughout, software engineers and others should be warned against its use early in the life cycle:

1. It may bemuse users; thus it should not be allowed into a functional specification for that reason alone.
2. Software engineers may think that enough design has been done before this is really the case, as the appearance of pseudo-code is so close to real code. For that reason also it should not be used in the functional specification, and should only be employed as a design 'notation' by software engineers who are properly knowledgeable about graphical design notations and their potential usefulness.

For these reasons we expect to see pseudo-code at, or not much above, the lowest step in a design process that is 'stepwise with enrichment' – i.e. for integrand specification. As exactly the same drawbacks afflict other 'formal' or 'semi-formal' methods of expression, the use of these in design should be similarly restricted to the level at, or about, implementation specification.

PROGRAM STRUCTURE CHARTS

At the lowest levels of design, when integrands are being specified along with their composition into programs, and the intended interrelationship between programs is

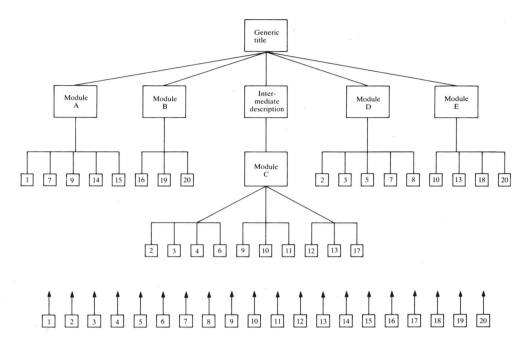

FIGURE 7.16 Program structure charts.

defined, it is useful to depict the structure – where one can do so (an exception will be for concurrent, asynchronous processes) – in terms of a program structure chart that refers by name to the programs and the element they contain.

A simple convention, shown in Figure 7.16, will usually suffice to show the calling structure relationship of programs in reasonably straightforward applications. The convention in Figure 7.16 owes something to Jackson's JSP notation for low level design of data and program structures in the area of 'classical' data processing applications. There is also a similarity between pictures in this notation and the convention we have suggested for the outline system design software taxonomy. The principal visual difference – there being a substantive one of purpose – is that in the case of OSD box diagrams we can speak of a 'bottom line' (e.g. 'sum the code size along the bottom line of the taxonomy'), whereas there is no such thing in a calling sequence diagram. There, the apparent 'bottom line' has no significance at all of this sort.

The JSP notation used, with adaptation, in Figure 7.16 is generally inadequate for software systems whose structures are complicated by such things as interruption of control. Many companies evolve their own simple conventions for program structure charts. Figure 7.17 shows a simple set of symbols for program calling sequence networks, including one for the interrupt purpose.

In each of the cases, Figure 7.16 and 7.17, the boxes may be represented in greater detail by schematics in either BS 6224 or structured flowcharts. Sometimes the design of integrands and programs comes about first, and the calling sequence that is determined rationally as a part of the process is then schematized in some way, e.g. as in Figure 7.16 or 7.17. On other occasions, the calling structure can be prescribed before the program and integrands are designed in detail. So long as the designs are 'good' in all the senses defined earlier (cohesion, coupling, information hiding, structure), and so long as the design stage is properly documented, then this minor detail of sequencing is not important.

7.4 SUMMARY

These, then, are the main elements of software design, and (in synoptic form) some representative means and methods available. Much greater detail will be found, for the reader primarily concerned with software design, in Volume 3 of this series.

7.4.1 Recapitulation of main points

For our purposes here, we recapitulate the following:

1. Design is a highly judgmental and intuitive matter. Good software designers are probably born, not made, Education and experience can improve but not create such people.
2. The design process is a non-trivial part of software engineering, and should not be overlooked, underdone, presumed from the structure of the application as evident in its functional specification, nor should it be avoided by amateur programmers mistaking pseudo-code, at too high a level of design (or even in specification), for near-implementation.
3. There are no standard methods for design, and no standard notations for representing design. This state of affairs is unlikely to change in the foreseeable future. There are, however, guidelines for good design practice, such as those concerning cohesion, coupling and single entry/single decision/single exit. There are guidelines too for choosing suitable notations for expressing designs, and it is possible to compile a shortlist for descriptive, architecture and detail purposes.
4. Design is probably the nearest that software engineering gets to being an art-form, as the authors of software systems struggle with a mass of conflicting objectives simultaneously, of which the main one are:
   (a) detailing a solution to requirements that can be implemented;
   (b) transforming between the languages of specification and implementation;
   (c) enabling the essential issues of quality – compliance and modifiability – to be achieved through good structure at the program level (minimum gratuitous complexity);

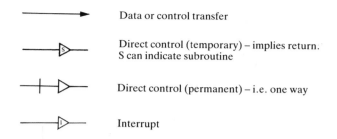

Data or control transfer

Direct control (temporary) – implies return.
S can indicate subroutine

Direct control (permanent) – i.e. one way

Interrupt

Conventions for network diagrams to show program structure – n.b. not flow. For example, in:

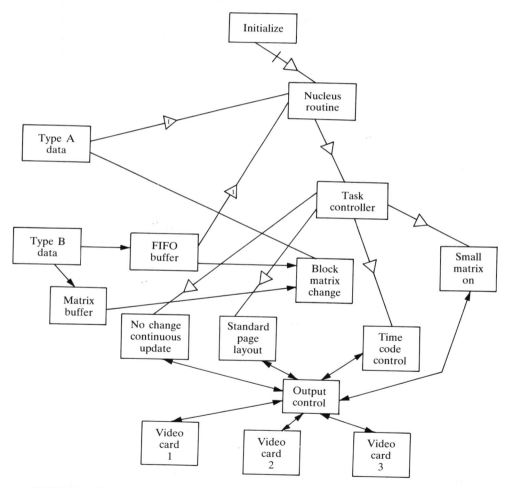

FIGURE 7.17 Program network convention and example of a complex program structure.

(d) working within the limits of a virtual computer, either for self-hosted or host/ target development.

7.4.2 Mapping methods and application-types; fitness of form

One group of authors has suggested a notation for describing notations (Sommerville *et al.* 1987). They define their Graph Description Language (GDL) as comprising fundamental types (nodes, links and gateways), basic to all diagrammatic design notations. They clearly and correctly distinguish between notations and their semantics as incorporated in an associated method, and classify the general case of design representation as comprising symbols and annotations.

These various definitions, based on the common properties of the plethora of graphical notations already remarked upon, and the fact the they are all forms of a directed graph, lead Sommerville *et al.* to identify three 'fundamental constructs' of GDL:

1. Type declarations, which allow object types to be named.
2. Use declarations, which define object representation.
3. Assertions which express rules on types.

The use of GDL will become evident when an associated method for classifying objectives as design types exists. Then, the question of 'fitness of form' concerning design methods and the purpose to which they may be put, may be tractable to other than judgmental means.

Something like GDL is desirable in the world of software design, and we hope that this research (part of a funded research project to develop a PSE, 'Eclipse'), or other research done elsewhere, will provide some way of evaluating the procedures and notations of design methods against particular needs. At the moment, the 'plethora problem' is extreme; Sommerville *et al.* (1987) refer to another source where it was revealed that at least twenty-four different design techniques were in use, c. 1982, in Holland alone (Blank and Krijger 1983). The Dutch are well known for their tolerance and famous for their grasp of foreign languages – but this is ridiculous.

Worldwide, the problem is several orders of magnitude greater than even this. A fair and informed guess at the number of distinct design notations in use would be likely to put the number between 75 and 100. There should be no wonder that other engineers scoff at their colleagues on the software side of things.

So, lacking as yet an algorithm for 'fitness of form', to map design procedures and their notations to (a) life cycle stages and (b) application types, we are reduced to a judgmental assessment. This is set out in Figure 7.18. These are approximations, as the diagram clearly indicates by the somewhat vague arrangement of titles within the sets, and the arrows indicating them for life cycle stages. Managers (and others involved) and software engineers should sustain themselves with the thought that one is not trying to fix on a single method for all life cycle purposes and all application types. Rather, one is best off using what is suitable, even if – as is very possible – this means changing out of one notation into another. These notations are so simple that little effort is needed to become literate in several.

'Classical' applications such as computational and data-processing paradigms: * small, medium and large * batch and on-line	Life cycle stage	'Embedded' and process-oriented systems for real-time requirements: * most probably in the range small to medium size. Large systems of this type require careful, prior decomposition of the networked microprocessor type in the system's architecture stage * possible problems of deadlock, deadly embrace, etc.
Natural language	Concepts ↓	Natural language and equipment specifications (e.g. telemetry devices, relays, etc. *in situ*)
Structured natural language, and high level method, e.g. HIPO, ERA	System analysis for URS ↓	Abstract process decomposition between URS and FS stages. Natural language, structured natural language. State diagrams, De Wolf's notation, Mascot definition of process archetypes. Timing charts
Structured methods such as SADT, JSD, data flow	FS in natural language 'plus' OSD taxonomies ↓	
Continued use of structured methods (SADT, JSD, data flow) in some decomposition approach, e.g. 'top down functional', data transform driven, or data structure design	Architecture design Design decomposition and ⌐detail⌐ ↓	Continued use of De Wolf's notation and Mascot, CCITT-SDL and Petrinet modes BS 6224, structured flowcharts (if appropriate), structure charts (if possible to do), pseudo-code
Low level structure and logic diagrams in (e.g.) Nassi-Schneiderman charts, BS 6224 DSD, structured flowcharts, pseudo-code, calling structure charts, detailed database design	Integrand specification ↓	
Suitable language, e.g. Fortran, Pascal, Basic, Cobol, PL1, Ada	Code and code testing ↓	Suitable combination of languages, e.g. Modula-2, Ada (?), RTL-2 as high level languages; assembler and C where need be

FIGURE 7.18 Mapping of methods and their notations, with application types and life cycle stages.

The urge to standardize has been commented on already. It can lead into a cul-de-sac, unless a very limited application set is at issue. In innovative environments, such as the IT-product companies, that is a limitation to be avoided at almost any cost. There software engineers are best off using whatever design approaches and notations are suitable, plus guidelines for 'good' design and its documentation, so long as they use something of the sort. The danger is when design is both slipshod and informal in the sense of being assumed to be done, as distinct from being seen to be done.

In other cases, such as administration applications of many types, and in scientific and engineering environments, it may be possible to prescribe a single method and its notation. Typical, in this respect, are SADT and JSD/JSP, both of which – within their limits – are very suitable for general adoption and use over both specification and design.

The reader, by referring to Figure 7.18, will see the qualifications we place on their general suitability.

7.4.3 Design methods and the electronic development environment

In the following section on implementation, we discuss programming support environments (PSE) briefly. These are part of the 'virtual machine' software described earlier in this work and depicted in Figure 1.1.

Some PSEs support the use of design notations, and it is obviously a trend for the future that the stronger and most widely used tools are supported in this way. It is much less common that the full method, in terms of its procedures as well as notation, is implemented. When a notation is incorporated in a PSE, we say that it is 'implemented'.

As things are at present, very few methods are strongly implemented in PSEs. By 'strongly', in this respect, we mean that both procedure and notation are incorporated, and supported, in the PSE part of a virtual machine's software. Thus, a PSE with a 'strong' implementation of (say) SADT would help to regulate the author/reader/reviewer cycle, as well as supporting it with easy word processing and text editing features, and enabling the graphical notation to be entered at screens, edited, stored, retrieved, etc.

At the present time, SADT, Mascot, CCITT-SDL, JSD/JSP, data-flow, state diagrams, BS 6224 and structured flowcharts have been implemented in some PSE systems, up to a point. These implementations tend to be localized by either (a) user, (b) geography, (c) equipment type or (d) a combination of some or all of these. Thus we may find (say) BS 6224 implemented on Intel equipment in the British Telecom company, with limited exploitation of this fact outside the company or the country.

On the other hand, JSD/JSP is used as the paradigm for one major research effort in PSE development ('Eclipse' – see next chapter), and in five years' time or thereabouts there may be widespread implementation of this procedure and its notation; or not. Mascot was originally implemented in a manner strongly associated with high level languages (Coral and RTL-2) which themselves had more local (UK) then general adoption. More recently, however, Mascot has been implemented with Pascal, and there is evidence that interest in it is growing in the USA and Europe, possibly as a result of the need to harmonize approaches to languages and development environments between Nato countries. CCITT-SDL is implemented within the community for which it was devised – European telephone and telecommunication technology.

This state of affairs, which tends to limit the usefulness of design methods in this epoch, when software engineers work mainly in an electronic environment, is unsatisfactory. Its likely rate of change is probably unsatisfactory too. The main problem here is that the manufacturers and suppliers of computer equipment are not necessarily the best sources of PSEs, as indeed they are not necessarily the best inventors of computer languages. Much in both of these areas is 'user driven' and the users who invent things, for their purposes, often place quite reasonable restrictions on their dissemination – as this might adversely affect their competitive position.

In Table 7.1, we offer a tentative and judgmental view of the relative strengths of

TABLE 7.1 Relative strength of methods and their notations, within their sphere of particular suitability

Method	Procedure	Notation	Implementation
HIPO	**	*	
ERA	*	*	
SADT	*****	***	*
De Wolf	**	****	
State diagrams	*	**	*
JSD /JSP	****	***	**
Mascot	***	****	***
Data flow	*	**	**
Timing charts	*	***	
CCITT-SDL	***	****	**
Petrinets	**	**	**
BS 6224 DSD	***	*****	**
Structured flowcharts	**	***	**
Pseudo-code	*	***	*****
Structure charts	*	*	*

various procedures and notations described in this and the previous section. The reader should treat this with great care, seeing it as related most strongly to Figure 7.18. Thus, one would hardly compare the De Wolf notation (****) with the SADT procedure (*****), particularly for an application more favorable to the one than the other. The two schemes set out in Figure 7.18 and Table 7.1 should help to find some bearings in what may otherwise seem to be a featureless landscape – but no more than that.

Before leaving the topic of design, let us see what some hypothetical team on our apocryphal course might have made of a part of the CAISSA design. Here, we have taken a real-life instance to use as our example – with some suitable and fitting emendation for our purposes here. On that occasion, a team achieved so high a standard as software engineers that grading them on the course was a privilege, and I happily acknowledge them at this distance. Readers will note a rather ideosyncratic 'structure' chart – none the worse for that – in Figure 7.21, being a parochial 'standard' in application.

EXAMPLE 4

EXTRACTS FROM DESIGN OF CAISSA SOFTWARE

1. Overall approach, and architecture design of software

1.1 An overall software architecture is determined; this comprised a main scheduler – known as CAISMAIN – and four subsidiary units dealing with input, output, specific (chess) algorithms and file management. These last four are designated CAISIN, CAISOUT, CAISALG and CAISFILE respectively.

1.2 The four subsidiary units have each a single generic purpose, and no cross connectivity below the level of CAISMAIN.

1.3 In general, the five architectural components of CAISSA are described as follows.

CAISMAIN: regulates all the behavior of the CAISSA software system. It invokes, but otherwise passes no information of its own to, and has no knowledge of, the four subsidiary units.

CAISIN: this passes all input commands and performs syntax checks on input. It passes coded commands back to CAISMAIN, which acts as a router only.

CAISOUT: controls all displays, such as chess-board, message areas and messages to go there, and the reserved area for index and moves. It performs screen management, including overflow management for Display Index and Show Moves features. In general, this is the screen management module of the CAISSA software system.

CAISALG: this embodies all the knowledge of chess such as legal moves; special situations (castling, *en passant* capture, promotion, check, checkmate, stalemate); specifically illegal positions for manual play, and the legal positions in manual start including the legitimacy of all piece addition and subtraction in this mode.

CAISFILE: this embodies all file management and manipulation in the CAISSA software system. It deals with save and retrieve games, and the stepwise playing of games if required; it maintains (and regulates if need be) the index of saved games.

1.4 The overall architecture of the CAISSA software can be simply depicted as in Figure 7.19.

2. Data-flow considerations in the CAISSA software

2.1 Keyboard input is either a menu choice or an input required by a chosen item from the menu. Both types are checked for syntax errors, and suitable diagnostics are displayed, as a result, on the screen.

2.2 All inputs are converted into an internal command format.

2.3 Any input concerning the chess game itself, i.e. concerning move or board status, is checked for that legality, and suitable diagnostics are displayed on the screen.

2.4 Some internal commands generate state change (see Figure 5.21), and some – such as move, piece placement, game i/d – are for use in a state.

2.5 Save Game leads to all moves to date being saved, plus the last board position. The command invokes the request to enter game i/d.

2.6 Display Index and Display Moves options lead to stored information being displayed on the screen.
A data-flow schematic is indicated in Figure 7.20.

3. Module interface description (top level only shown)

3.1 A notation is adopted in which an information set is defined as (a) exogenous information entering from outside the systems boundaries, i.e. user (player) keyboard input, and (b) endogenous information flowing inside the software system,

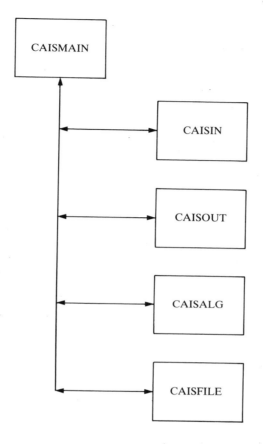

FIGURE 7.19 Architecture of CAISSA software.

e.g. internal commands, files of game or index information. The symbol for an information set is a lozenge (or parallelogram).

A function or process operating on information, or transforming it, is depicted as a circle.

A work-station is shown as a rectangle with a double upper edge.

Information sets and functions (processes) are tied to work stations by lines.

3.2 A referencing system is used that ties Figure 7.20 to software modules in design and implementation. Information sets are named with a prefix 'I' or 'O' to indicate input to or output from a process. Processes are numbered simply, and subscript numbers refer to submodules within the process, defined elsewhere, e.g. 1.7.

A schematic for the module interface is shown in Figure 7.21.

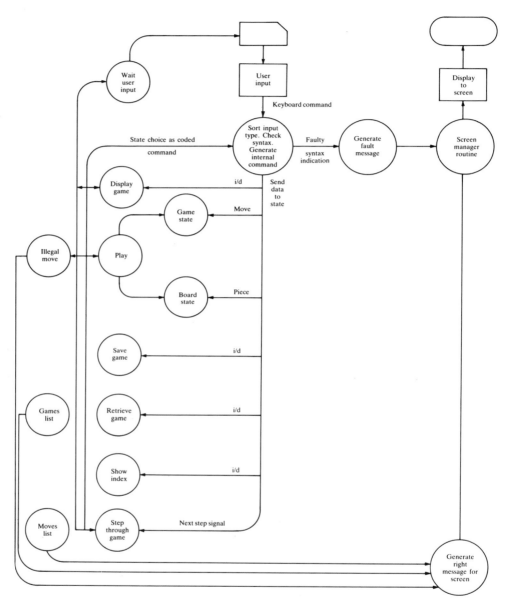

FIGURE 7.20 Data flow in the CAISSA software.

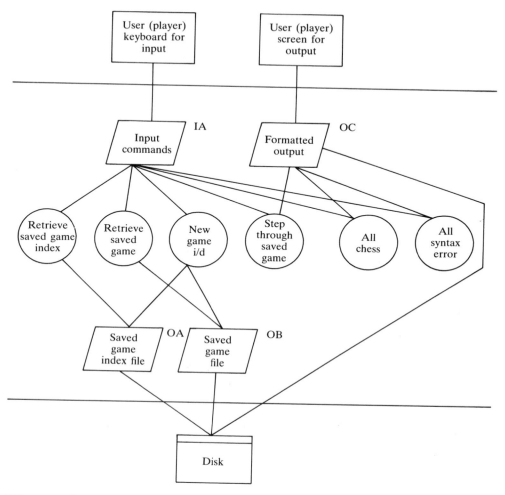

FIGURE 7.21 CAISSA software module interface description.

4. Program designs (one example only shown)

4.1 The user input module is described.

4.2 This module, IA, is called from CAISMAN which initiates the input device. Once input is expected, the only exit from this module is RETURN.

4.3 Characters making up an input message are read to an input buffer and flagged with a message type flag.

4.4 If no end message by RETURN is received within 15 seconds of the previous (last?) keystroke, a message is displayed asking if this message has ended. Two such tests, unanswered, cause a message to be displayed asking if anyone is at the terminal. If

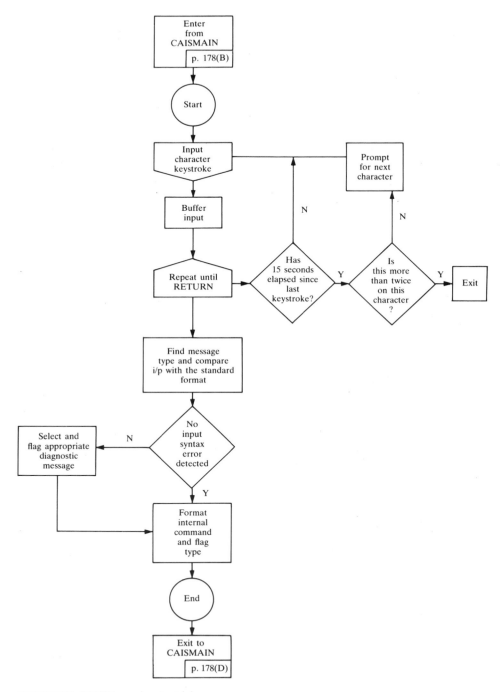

FIGURE 7.22 CAISSA user input module.

no answer is received (a RETURN) then control passes to the operating system, i.e. CAISSA exits.

4.5 After end message, the command is checked against a pre-stored message for that type. Errors of syntax produce preformatted diagnostics on the screen.

4.6 The input message is converted to an internal command format depending on if it is: (a) a chess input (move or piece placement); (b) a menu selection; or (c) an i/d.

4.7 The coded internal command format is passed back to CAISMAN, along with control.

The functions of this user input module (IA) are set out graphically in Figure 7.22.

7.4.4 Comment on design example

This brief example, sufficient for purposes of demonstration here, comprises about one-sixth of the design document for the CAISSA software system – so the reader will get an impression of both how extensive such matters can be and how truncated a selection we have had to make for space reasons.

Of several points of passing interest, there is (or seems to be on superficial inspection) a good 'top-down' approach, with architecture-level decomposition, a software module interface specification, and the sort of magnification effect down to program (or integrand) level of detail. The use of a structured flowchart notation is generally clear as to its meaning – which is all that is important. Figure 7.22 could as easily have been represented in pseudo-code, but that is a detail of this particular application.

In fact, for the reader's interest, implementation proceeded with few problems, so well was the design done. Implementation and testing were done within estimated schedules of effort and time, and the resulting (software around 5,000 source statements of Pascal code) proved of high enough quality to permit major changes to it for new versions. These were done by the implementation team itself, but quality assurance attempted a controlled disturbance of the code – and this too showed the system to be well constructed.

All these factors derived from the clear functional specification for CAISSA in the first place, and a thorough and competent design of it thereafter, of which a small sample is shown.

Another view of design, for the same application, is given in the composite, 'worked example' in Appendix 1.

It is impossible to overstress the need for clear, stable specifications. It is also impossible to exaggerate the value of thorough and competent design – from highest 'architecture' level down to the lowest level of detailed specification for an integrand. On that note we may proceed to consider the implementation stage of the software life cycle.

The white knight has slid down the poker, balancing precariously – but not necessarily badly.

CHAPTER EIGHT

IMPLEMENTATION

We continue with the presentation of technical issues in software development, the substance of this Part Two. There is, in fact, no fixed 'stage' at which implementation suddenly begins, in the sense that a previous activity ceases absolutely (in this case, design) and code starts to be written for the first and only time. In this repect, the life cycle schematic in use is an oversimplification, intended merely to indicate the order in which substantive activities can be viewed in an ideal world.

Implementation is programming. That means that it incorporates activities in low level design and program testing, as well as coding merely. We call it 'implementation' to convey the message that something substantive is being made – the artefact for ultimate use in fact, rather than any preludal prototypes that may have been developed.

The coding part of a programmer's task is a familiar topic, and it is beyond the purposes of this book, and this series, to provide a beginner's primer in it. An early misconception, that coding and debugging is the whole of the matter in programming, is challenged here. The view (Marcotty 1990) of programming as an expository act between peers, underlies the substance of this chapter, in which the following issues are presented: language choice, coding and programming concepts, good practices at this level, code generators and reuse, environments and testing.

On its own, the word 'implementation' is vague, and stands in need of substantiation; what implementation, or implementation of what? If we speak of program implementation, we naturally infer the coding of low level software designs to produce integrands – small, single-decision 'clumps' of code, the smallest quantity of such code addressable by name – or the composition of integrands into program units, or the further packaging of programs into modules with some loose generic or purposive association. In its limiting case, this definition leaves us with static and only partly tested programs, and abdicates all the issues of software as a dynamic entity. These – the definition tacitly assumes – will be taken up in some other stage, that of software quality for instance.

In fact, it is essential to see implementation in the wider context of the software-to-be, and in particular of its dynamic behavior. This, in turn, calls into question the notional allocation of quantities of effort to different life cycle stages. Earlier, we indicated that, on

average over different applications and software types, about 15 percent of a software engineer's total effort over one pass of the life cycle is spent on implementation. In fact, this most notional of numbers (not necessarily wrong, nor misleading) concerns the creation – coding in fact – of integrands, this limited testing in each of two ways by their author, and their composition into programs and program modules. The testing is at two levels only, within this definition:

1. Static testing; that is the inspection of code listings to detect errors without attempting to execute the code on a computer.
2. Dynamic testing; that is the attempted execution of integrands, programs and program-modules within the limited context of author-devised tested to demonstrate that the code works.

It is this limited testing only that is included in the notional '15 percent', and the result is only partly tested programs, and not (yet) software that is tested in any meaningful sense of the word. To find a quantity more nearly approximating to the proportional effort needed to create programs and have their authors test them as software, one would allocate some notional amount from the '40 percent allocated to software quality – taking us up to, say, alpha-test in life cycle terms – and this might well double the 'magic 15 percent' originally seen as due to program implementation. 'Alpha-test', it should be noted, is the final integration test of all system components by the implementation team.

Figure 8.1 is probably a better representation of relative efforts over one pass of the life cycle, with the following annotation referring:

1. The specification phase may be very 'front-loaded' if extensive requirements' proto-typing is done.
2. The design phase may be very 'mid-loaded' if extensive prototyping is done to establish technical means.
3. This stage, the barest of coding and debugging activities used to be viewed as the whole of the software matter – and sometimes still is, e.g. 'amateur programmers'.
4. Author level integration tests, up to alpha-test stage. with 'coding', this may make up a 30 percent implementation stage.
5. The quality activities are not sequential. Taking the elements of 'QI' (quality inspection by independent agents) from previous stages, and some elements of 'QC' (quality control) such as code reading and design review, these will, added to independent beta-testing, bring the quality activities amount to about 25 percent of total activity. How-ever, if extensive 'black-box' simulators are required, this might 'back-load' the amount considerably.

Our subject here concerns the 'notional 30 percent' represented in the software imple-mentation segments 3 and 4 of Figure 8.1, and not merely programming in its narrow sense. Software implementation is the subject of Volume 4 of this series, in which a rigorous treatment is offered that is suitable for the basic education of aspiring software engineers in what is – to adopt an available metaphor – the 'nuts and bolts' of software engineering.

Before continuing, it is worthwhile to revisit our own objectives. The treatment of

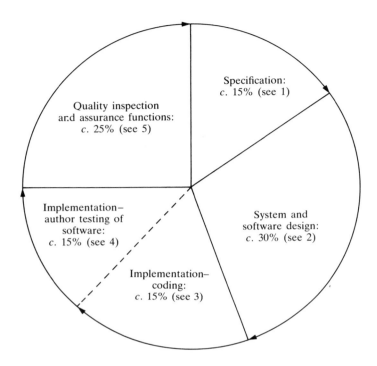

FIGURE 8.1 Average effort over main life cycle stages.

topics in this volume is to establish concepts and definitions, to achieve an overview of software engineering and a sufficiency of understanding of its modalities in the interests of management (and other associated 'added value' services), as well as software engineers; to furnish shared frameworks of reference, guidelines for practice, and a serviceable vocabulary with which to express all these things. With these clarifications and revisions of our aims now fresh in our minds, we proceed to define and discuss the elements of software implementation at greater length.

In this section we intend to deal with the following topics, in the order indicated:

1. Choice of programming languages.
2. Coding and programming.
3. Good programming practice in general.
4. Automatic program generation, and the question of reusable code.
5. Support environments.
6. Program and software testing.

A substantial amount could be written on all of these topics; in some cases a whole book. However space, and our restricted purpose here, precludes such an extensive treatment, and we proceed in summary mode.

8.1 CHOICE OF PROGRAMMING LANGUAGE

There is often a generally felt emotion, not unlike dismay, experienced by managers and others not too knowledgeable about programming, when the issue of programming languages crops up – as it has a nasty habit of doing from time to time. These occasions arise either because a particular application appears to require special consideration in the matter, or because some new language has appeared like an object in the firmament – strange and exciting, but remote. Then, an amazing amount of vitality may suffuse even the most torpid software engineer, and whole groups of them wander around interminably, discussing the merits and demerits of this new language, and wearing their most solemn expressions.

For that reason, if no other, the essential elements determining the choice should be defined and understood.

8.1.1 Issues of significance in the choice of a programming language

In fact, the issues involved are usually very straightforward and can be resolved quickly, cheaply and reasonably objectively if the will exists to do so. The following questions are usually sufficient, if answered properly:

1. Are there common properties between the application(s) and the language? For example, the arithmetic and array addressing features of Fortran make it suitable for a wide variety of computation problems for which data are stored in multidimensional arrays. On the other hand, the file processing and general character handling features of Cobol orient it toward information intensive problems of the administration type, for which data are stored as sequential or logically related files; and so on.
2. Is the language competently designed and implemented? Some basic criteria for language design (after Smedema *et al.* 1985) are defined below. However, we can say here that one essential property in this overall 'competence' of implementation is that programs written in the language should be easily readable!
3. Is the language in reasonably widespread use in (a) the world at large (b) your particular country, or (c) your particular industry/business sector? The best case is if all three answers are affirmative (b might not follow from a); the worst case is if none of them is; a minimally acceptable case is if the answer to (c) is affirmative.

    Yet, how are any of these conditions to be realized, without someone being the 'guinea pig'? Are your enthusiatic technicians voting your company into this role?
4. Is the language supported? This is a most important criterion in any procurement, and particularly so in the case of software. 'Supported' means maintained and improved.

    Not all computer languages are invented or produced in the first place by computer manufacturers; an example is Pascal, a language invented by Professor Nicholas Wirth and produced, in one of its best forms, as a result of development work at the University of California, San Diego. However, no one would mistake these innovators as sources of worldwide 'support', and it was only when major users and suppliers brought out versions of UCSD Pascal that the language could be said to be adequately sup-

ported. Similarly, Ada was not invented by equipment manufacturers, nor did the major initiative for it originate there, nor has its subsequent development been mainly by them.

5. Is the language relatively easy to learn and to use, and are there adequate facilities available for training in it? Most languages in reasonably widespread use are adequately documented, and the importance of this is realized when a software fault is seen to occur – i.e. a defect of the system as a whole that cannot be attributed to manifestly faulty usage or hardware error. Then, the question of specification may arise; which is correct, what the software documentation says that the software will do, or what the software actually does? As must obviously be the case, 'software' includes its accurate documentation, as well as the programs that comprise it.

Whoever sells and supports the language – often a computer manufacturer – generally offers its user and operator level documentation, and training courses in it. That does not mean to say that a 'good' language will, necessarily, be easy to learn or use, nor that if it is easy to learn and use can it be taken as suitable or 'good' in other senses. One major prohibition on the use of Ada, for example, is that it is a large language in terms of its basic vocabulary and syntactic rules for use; most languages just have a few dozen allowable statements and a similar number of syntactic rules; Ada has hundreds. At the other end of the scale of complexity, Basic is a 'cheap and cheerful' language (some would say 'cheerless') that is so easily learned that little Johnnie hammers out rubbish in it on the PC that you unwisely bought him for Christmas.

6. Is the language part of a strong environment, i.e. a good PSE?

These six quite straightforward questions are usually equally simply and objectively answered, although managers of software engineers must be particularly on the look-out for hobbyism where the first two of them are concerned – the issues of fit and competent implementation. At the time when Pascal was little more than a gleam in Professor Wirth's eye, software engineers were becoming febrile with excitement at its prospects. A language is usually acceptable – all other factors being sufficiently positive – if its 'environment' (i.e. PSE features) are accepted, and this takes at least ten years in many cases. One author (Riddle 1984) has advanced the view – and substantiated it – that new technology systems require at least fifteen years to become accepted on a reasonably widescale basis – if they are ever to do so; we are currently somewhat over the ten years' mark with Ada!

The elements of 'fit' between a language and the application set for which it may be deemed suitable and outlined in Section 3.1 where the four paradigms for computer applications are defined; computation intensive; data handling/data transformation intensive; process oriented (and possibly time critical); and rule based/adaptive.

Table 3.1 shows some judgmental assignment of languages to application types, and we stand by those rough and ready guidelines with the reservation that, of course, it is not impossible to use a language in an application for which it is not suited – it is just bad engineering practice, like any other arbitrary use of a tool. We have seen respectable (but small) data processing systems done in Fortran, and simple computation programs written in Cobol. They worked, and little harm was done until someone thought that the medium sized and elaborate computation system (to design a nuclear reactor, say) could be done

in Cobol too. There is an acute danger in extrapolating the use of defective methods – however successful they have been on a limited basis!

Any and all existing programming languages can be 'mapped' on to Table 3.1 or some similar scheme, some appearing in more than one place in the matrix. On education courses, for example, colleagues and I ask for other languages to be nominated – and ask for their assignment to be indicated also. It is a revelation. Many practicing programmers make the strangest suggestions, whilst a surprisingly large number of managers and other non-practitioners of the programming 'art' show a good working knowledge of life at this 'nuts and bolts' level of software engineering.

8.1.2 General requirements of a computer language

So far as the design and implementation of a programming language are concerned, the following checklist of points are indicative (adapted from Smedema *et al.* 1985):

1. *Clarity and orthogonality*. A language must have facilities that are simple to use in the situation where they can be used; this is the property of clarity. The facilities must not interact unexpectedly, or otherwise unfavorably, when used in combination; this is the property or orthogonality.
2. *Ease of use*. The notation of a language, its vocabulary and rules of syntax must be easy to understand and use.
3. *Ease of understanding*. The notation of a language must enable its programs to be read with ease, and understood.
4. *Orthodoxy*. It should be extremely difficult to misuse the language intentionally – i.e. to indulge in 'clever' programmer's tricks, which are often merely the stupid use of high intelligence on a programmer's part.
5. *Construction/deconstruction*. The facilities of a language must enable structured coding techniques to be used in implementation, and should facilitate the composition of programs from integrands, and the packaging of programs into software modules.
6. *Security*. The language must disallow illicit usage of facilities (by accident or design) and this property must be evident from the behavior of its compiler(s). In other words, the language definition will contain specification of security measures, and no compiler or assembler will be a licit implementation of it unless these features are competently embodied.

There are many ways to add to the detail of this list, but it is generally beyond our scope here to do so. A simple example, though, might be in the category 'construction/deconstruction' where, for a high level language, we could add to 'structured coding' a list of the following (after Birrell and Ould 1985):

> Abstract data types; information hiding features; concurrency; complex data structures; strings; bit manipulations; pointers; in-line assembly code; integrands in other high level languages; macros; recursion; dynamic storage allocation; dynamic data dimensioning.

These are details now generally incorporated in high level languages. They may occupy

the language hobbyists (and commensurately dismay the manager), and should certainly be held in balance when evaluating a language for its suitability.

The six questions in Section 8.1.1 are the substantive ones for language choice. The six 'good language' attributes above is a detail of the second question in that set. The list of specific language features is a detail of that detail.

As a final cautionary word on language choice, be careful to evaluate languages 'top down' and not 'bottom up' with respect to the hierarchy of questions and attributes listed. And when doing so, do not forget that at the very top – the issue of 'fit' with an application – there may be an efficiency consideration in use of the language, and some benchmarking may have to be done. This is particularly true for high level languages to be used in time-critical applications; it is also useful to determine expansion factors for a language in different types of usage – such as i/o functions, computation and logical manipulations. But remember; no one question of the first six should be used as the *solitary* determinant, and no one issue, or property, within the scope of its answers should prescribe the outcome. In Chapter 13, a technique known as 'weighted evaluation' is discussed for software procurement in general. The set of questions, issues and properties of languages listed in this section should be seen as the basis for use of this 'weighted evaluation' technique, when a choice of languages must be made.

On some education courses, the question is posed: 'Which set of criteria were used in your firm for the last language choice made, and who did the evaluation? Was it some specific language feature, appealing to technicians, that dominated the issue?' The sheepish expressions around the room give the answer more eloquently than words.

8.2 CODING AND PROGRAMMING

As we have said already, coding and programming are often assumed to be synonymous – a slightly fallacious assumption as coding is merely ordering statements to achieve some desired effect via the computer or its ancillaries; whilst programming involves coding, as well as an element of low level design and some validation activity.

8.2.1 The relative triviality called 'coding'

Furnished with an intention that is clearly formulated, and a programming language that is well chosen for the purpose in the various respects set out in Section 8.1 above, almost anyone of average intelligence can code integrands or programs. Take the simple example in which we want to sum to first 100 integers (i.e. 1–100 inclusive) and have at our disposal a computer, a printer attached to it, a keyboard to enter program statements, and a translator that allows the following instructions:

EXC   starts executing the program.
SXR   sets a nominated index register (address modifier) with a specified value e.g.
      SXR X = N; X must be an integer between 1 and 10 inclusive; N may be
      any integer value.

SSR   sets a nominated store (name up to ten alphanumeric characters) with a prescribed numerical value; e.g. SSR ABC123XYZ = 94.7.

CLA   clears the contents of a nominated store to the accumulator, e.g. CLA ABC 123XYZ.

ADD   adds the contents of a nominated store to the accumulator, e.g. ADD PQR7LM2.

STO   stores the value in the accumulator in a nominated store, e.g. STO TEMPSTO.

TXD   transfers program control to a nominated (relative) address, and decrements a nominated index register by 1; when this produces a value of zero in that register, the next instruction in sequence is obeyed and no other transfer of control occurs.

SFM   sets a format string in a nominated file. $n \times$ / will space n characters from the left in a line; comma denotes text format begins; brackets ( ) denotes value in named store to be printed.

CPR   calls (readies) printer.

SPL   spaces a nominated number of blank lines from top of page; e.g. SPL 50 will space 50 blank lines from top of page.

PNT   prints a nominated format.

EPT   ends a printing sequence.

END   ends program.

With these instructions (and some assumptions about how storage areas are declared for working storage and parameter values), we can proceed to code the required function. Note, this is very much a 'low level language' example.

```
ROUTINE SUMINT
    EXC
    SXR 1 = 99
    SSR INT = 1
    SSR ONE = 1
    SSR TOTAL = 0
    CLA TOTAL
    ADD INT
    STO TOTAL
    CLA INT
    ADD ONE
    STO INT
    TXD * − 6, 1,1
    SFM LINE 1 = 10 × /, "RESULTS OF CALCULATION NOW READY"
    SFM LINE 2 = 17 × /, "TOTAL = (TOTAL)"
    CPR
    SPL 20
    PTN LINE
    SPL 2
    PNT LINE 2
```

```
EPT
END SUMINT
```

We have needed thirteen unique instruction types, and have (hopefully) summed the integers 1–100 inclusive, and printed the answer (nicely page-centered) – in twenty-one statements of code. The whole exercise, inventing the machine in effect and then using it as shown, will probably have the programming purists puce with rage – but the excuse is that the exercise was merely to show how easy it is to code, given a clearly formulated objective a functional language and some familiarity with the language – which is usually easily acquired.

In fact coding is so easy that it takes some degree of self-discipline and rigor to avoid doing it very badly indeed. Coding is what hobbyists do – like little Johnnie bashing away at his PC, when any healthy minded kid of his age would have gone off to football hours before. At this level, coding bears the same relationship to the programming part of software engineering, as whittling a piece of firewood does to carpentry.

8.2.2 The proper matter of programming

Programming is a craft in itself, and part of the wider craft of software engineering. It is most often undertaken by people who have been involved actively in (i.e. done) the system specification and software design, and it incorporates all of the author's testing of programs, their integration and testing as software. The design of algorithms and data structures for integrands is properly seen as programming, and is discussed further here, whilst the testing of coded integrands, the programs composed of them and the software composed of the programs, is dealt with in Section 8.6.

Programming can be seen as the prevention, by several means, of the worst results of facile coding – that is quick and dirty coding done without that discipline and rigor mentioned earlier. The ways and means of programming include the choice of a suitable programming language in all the respects outlined in Section 8.1 above. They also include some guidelines – developed mainly in the period 1965–75 – to assist in structuring code (the 'discipline and rigor') in order to avoid gratuitous complexity at this life cycle level.

These guidelines are generally grouped under two headings: (a) structured design and (b) structured programming. Both of these have been dealt with elsewhere in this work. Basic principles in structured design are summarized in Chapters 3 and 7 and there is a synoptic account of structured programming in Section 3.2. However, we will revise and extend these treatments below.

STRUCTURED DESIGN
Simply restated, structured design ensures the logical decomposition of a system being designed in order to improve its quality in two fundamental respects:

1. That the demonstration of the system is able to show that it works as required, and that it is likely to go on doing so ('compliance' and its associated reliability).
2. That the system is relatively easy to change for maintenance or new versions' purposes ('modifiability' and its associated effect on overall reliability).

Wirth (1971) stated that the creative act of programming involved a general mass of design decisions containing real, apparent and spurious structures and dependencies. The following make up the aim in design and implementation of a software system:

1. To *decompose* (i.e. detail and clarify) these decisions to as great a degree as possible and, in later stages of the process, to identify (or invent) algorithms to deal with them, and data structures on which they must depend.
2. In doing the decompostion, to *disentangle* the real structure of the system from its apparent and spurious characteristics; a method for achieving this clarity will be the deferment of any decision (i.e. its unique identification and detail) until it is necessary to deal with it. Data structures are a conspicuous case of this.

Gradually, a modularization of the system-to-be is conceived, and the guidelines on cohesion, coupling and information hiding – as summarized earlier – can be applied. Each step in the process is one of refinement with detailing and, hopefully, enrichment – in the sense that the detail is material at that stage, and both overall (system) complexity and local (implementation) complexity are contained.

In this last paragraph, the terms modular/modularization are fairly clear, although it is often neither useful, nor grammatically pleasing to have gerundives cobbled together by the easy attachment of the particle 'ization'.

As we have remarked earlier and not infrequently, the use of 'module' in software engineering is very confusing; it almost always means 'a part of', of 'some generic or logically determined unit of', but its use crops up all over the place. Consequently, to speak of a module without some qualification is extremely confusing. In design, we mean a chunk of the design, with no particular precision attaching to the word 'chunk', and we may be 'modularizing' at architecture, intermediate or detail levels. In programming, some people think of a module as a chunk of code (usually not more than a couple of pages, or about 100 source statements in total), identifiable by name; it may also be a collection of programs, generically or otherwise related, that is seen as a 'package' or software module. It is all very confusing. For these good reasons, we recommend that one speaks of *design* modules (architecture, intermediate or detail) at that stage, and reserves the term 'integrand' for the smallest part of a program (lowest level of design) invokable by name. Then, at the implementation level above this, one may speak of programs (collections of integrands) and program modules (packages of programs).

STRUCTURED PROGRAMMING AND CODE

Structured programming and structured coding are fundamental to the 'discipline and rigor' needed to prevent bad coding practices. In both cases we are referring, hereafter, to the implementation of integrands in the first place – so called because we shall be integrating them (into programs) subsequently.

Structured programming, described earlier in the Chapter 3 treatise on complexity, is rather a theoretical approach. Yet it has a fundamentally important application at the practical level. 'Abstract' machines are defined to deal with the issue (integrands or combinations of them) at hand, and an abstract machine on which to implement the first abstract machine is defined, and so on until the abstract machine deined can be implemented in the language of choice on the real machine of choice. Clearly, the abstract

machine concept (mainly due to Dijkstra) is conceptually similar to the decomposition notions due to Wirth. The other level of importance derives from the idea that the implemented software system is an extension of the highest level machine in the sequence of definitions of abstract machines, i.e. the actual computer of use, in fact the 'virtual' computer as defined elsewhere.

This distinction is fundamental to programming in the current epoch. Figure 8.2 shows two schemes. In (a), program integrands are coded as an extension of top down design using a knowledge of the language and other (virtual computer) facilities available, and the software sits on top of the virtual machine in effect. In (b) the lowest level designs are built out from the available facilities and, if these are insufficient, a first task will be to amplify them by building more software facilities before the application itself is implemented.

In previous epochs, programmers required only a knowledge of the programming language, and what the operating system would or would not permit. Now, a team of software engineers needs a high degree of expertise not only in the language of choice for implementation, but also in all the facilities of a programming support environment. In a section to come on organization (13.4) the point will be restressed that, in many cases, software teams should have a 'tools and facilities' specialist nominated within it, or assigned to it.

Structured coding is the 'discipline and rigor' of using a limited set of constructs (three) for all purposes in a single entry/single decision/single exit integrand. The three basic constructs are shown in Figure 3.2. In fact, only the first two are both necessary and sufficient and the third can be derived from them.

An original purpose of these constructs was, in part, to aid in the proving of programs, but this purpose has only been achieved on extremely limited program sets. In fact, the preponderant virtue of structured coding has been to avoid the hilarious mess of so-called spaghetti coding in which, frequently, two fundamental errors of approach occur:

1. The system to be coded is not decomposed far enough in design, and 'integrands' are left at too high a level of definition, i.e. containing too much to be done by the program element; this leads to monolithic structure in the code, 'integrands' comprising hundreds of source statements of code, or higher numbers still.
2. The coding of a bewildering forest of program control transfers, conditional and uncoditional. Structured coding practices, and associated guidelines for structured data, are intended to minimize this effect.

Many people, coming new to computers and their possibilities, when programmed, still believe that a quick grasp of some language, and a bit of practice at the keyboard and VDU are enough. Away we go into the dazzling 'high technology' excitements of information processing. Managers particularly must be careful not to fall into this trap themselves, nor to let hobbyists on their staff do a sort of 'lover's leap' with them into the gaping pit of what we call 'amateur programming'.

Programming is not an intrinsically difficult task, even when undertaken with self-discipline and rigor. Nor does this necessarily slow things down (another phobia of managers). As anyone knows, by simile from a variety of other activities in life, quick is not necessarily good.

(a)

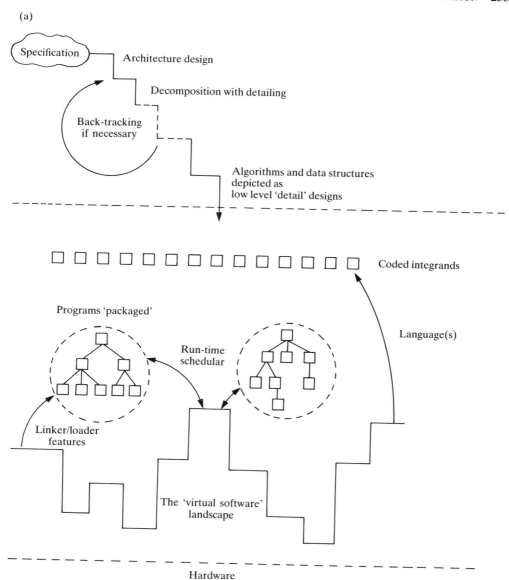

FIGURE 8.2 (a) Top down software design and implementation.

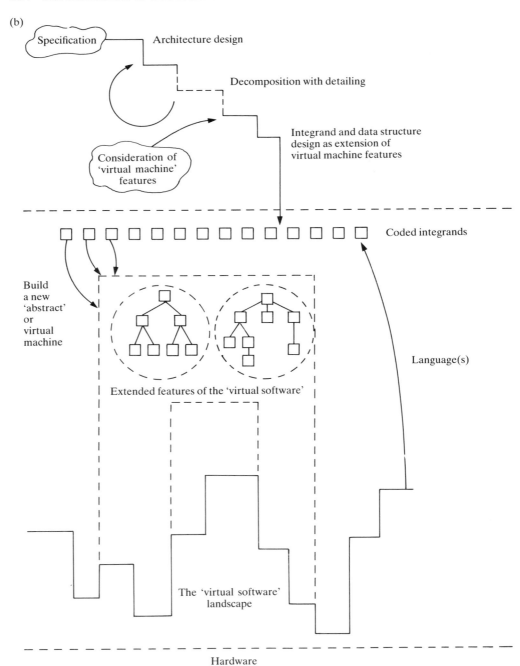

FIGURE 8.2 (b) Top down design with bottom up implementation.

As George Bernard Shaw writing to a friend said, quoting a Chinese source: 'Please excuse long letter; did not have time to write a shorter one.'

8.3 GOOD PROGRAMMING PRACTICE IN GENERAL

Everyone who writes code has his or her own style, just as every author does. George Orwell set out to write a book without using a single semicolon (an example of self-denial not followed by this author), and his book, *Coming up for Air*, was none the worse for it. Every program shows the ideosyncratic style of the person who wrote it, even though the programmer's universe of discourse is limited by application, programming language and other features of the 'virtual computer', plus whatever force the precepts of 'good' design and 'good' programming might have. Weinberg (1971) found that different programming teams produced systems differing in code size by a factor of about four, for exactly the same requirement. Someone might write the current book in twice the space (and to twice the quality), whilst someone else might write it in 100 pages and put us all to shame.

Style is all – well, nearly all; content too matters, of course. But in software engineering, programming style has a fundamental importance all of its own. The point here is that the ease with which a program can be read and understood has direct bearing on both the fundamental aspects of software quality – that it is compliant, and seen to be so by demonstration, and that it is modifiable and is tested as appropriate for that purpose.

Large scale programs may be fiendishly difficult to validate, and similarly difficult to modify; in fact, beyond a certain point, degradation of a factor such as reliability means that real modification of software as distinct from its mere change, is effectively impossible. These difficulties increase steeply if the programs are unstructured (or badly structured) in the design and implementation senses. They also may increase to prohibitive levels, where testing is concerned, if the programs are difficult to read and understand.

Many software engineers regard this point as 'mere cosmetics', so subjective a matter of style that no one can make a meaningful statement about it. Some theoreticians take an even more extreme view, due mainly to their predilection for proof as distinct from demonstration.

Such views are wrong; not just mildly misguided, nor a bit erronous, but categorically wrong. When we come to the issue of software quality, the point will be made that the code is often the first level of access, the visible instrument closest to hand, in software maintenance or emendation. Equally often, the parties accessing it (the code) are not its authors but some unfortunates roped in to fix what has gone wrong, or is in other need of improvement. It is as easy for us to imagine their feelings as it is difficult for them to dissimulate their emotions. Poor programming practice causes heart attacks – in others!

In the most stringent summary of the main issues that contribute to the 'readability' of a program or programs, the following will be discussed here:

1. Syntax clarity.
2. Size and limitations of purpose.
3. Use of global versus local variables.
4. Naming.

5. In-line comments.

6. Layout.

If intelligent policies are adopted in each case, and given a well chosen language in which to write them, programs should be readable and understandable – whether correct or incorrect.

8.3.1 Syntax clarity

Choice of programming language, size of program units (integrands) and the limitation of their purpose have all been dealt with earlier in this text. As well as being suitable in all the respects defined there, a programming language should have a vocabulary and syntax that is, in itself, an *a priori* source of clarity. Thus, a language with highly abstract symbols for its operators is worse in this respect than one that has mnemonic abbreviations of some sort. Thus in:

    X TEMPSTO

as distinct from

    ADD TEMPSTO

the first is bad and the second is good, since the latter is far more evident in its meaning. Most high level languages have adequate vocabulary and syntax features from this viewpoint, but many require an inordinate amount of clutter of the colon, semicolon, comma and stop variety. Low level languages tend to be staccato in their use of mnemonics; that tends to make high level languages far easier to read – and increases their usefulness proportionately. This matter should not be underestimated. The readableness of a program will be due to both the language of use, and the way in which the programmer goes about matters. But the features allowing program clarity are of fundamental importance as their absence will tend to deplete the testing of programs, and anyone's ability to change them once they are in operation. This is the most urgent of all arguments against unnecessary use of low level languages, assembler and – it must be said – the C language.

'Size' and 'limitation of purpose' concern those issues, already dealt with, for decomposing designs, and for reducing complexity in both design and implementation. The result, done competently, is an infrastructure of integrands within programs where the separately invokable units/integrands are a few dozen source statements of code at most. In a particularly dense presentation, e.g. on a code print-out formatted with a statement (or continuation of a statement) on each line of the page, most integrands would be one or, at most, two 'pages' long.

The limitation of purpose helps as much as the limitation of size in the matter of program clarity. Logically dense code can be villainously difficult to understand. This can be true even of small amounts of code, and even by its own author after a surprisingly short absence from it. The programmer's retention time, in this respect, is about two to three weeks, in my experience. 'What the devil's going on here?' is a frequently heard outburst at the programmer's terminal, along with: 'What cretin ... ?', followed by an uneasy silence of some duration.

The so-called structured coding constructs are very useful in containing logical density, as is the composite notion of single entry/single decision/single exit for integrands.

8.3.2 Local versus global definitions

The use of global variables, or their prohibition in favor of local declaration of storage areas and parameters, is a topic of some dispute. The principles of localization of purpose and information-hiding are violated by the definition of storage areas, parameters and variables for general access; this is called the global definition of these items. On the other hand, it has been pointed out that localization of 'live' variables increases their number and leads (in some cases) to unacceptable problems of performance in the run-time software system (Dunsmore and Gannon 1979). From the comprehension point of view, there is no doubt that the strong use of local (or 'own') variables is preferable, if they are competently named – which is a whole topic in itself, dealt with in the following section.

The principal author in this field writes:

> programs should not contain any global variables (except for globally defined variables needed to implement the concept of 'own'). The global variable problem is a general one. It is one of the volatile factors that can influence the quality and maintainability of a computer program.
>
> The global variable issue is a logical not a syntactic issue. Avoiding global variables has two great benefits. For the programmer, poor solutions are exposed, and, implicitly, better solutions present themselves more readily. For the program reader, full specification of interfaces is guaranteed and, implicitly, so is easier reading. Avoiding global variables requires a rigorous application of discipline. But the rewards of quality and maintainability in the final product are well worth it. (Ledgard 1987)

So there! Ledgard's is the purist's line, offered with a zealot's clarity.

He is undoubtedly right that the quality of software is likely to be higher, and this more easily achieved, if programs are well ordered in this way. Dunsmore and Gannon's point will undoubtedly have force where some stringent efficiencies are required, such as program space or run-time. It is the old argument of the depletion of quality when optimality supervenes. One cannot have the penny *and* the bun, so to speak. The nearest one can get, usually, is by relaxing a good design – proceeding from a position of strength in other words – to achieve efficiencies by 'tuning' critical parts of code.

Ledgard's propositions stand on their merits. In my experience they are usually treated with incredulity and disdain by 'amateur' programmers, until some quality audit has to be done, or a change made to someone else's code. Then, somewhere in the rat's nest of code, the aggregation of global variables and excessive parameter passing amongst integrands will appear as a major disablement.

Conversion can be a pleasant experience it is said, and converts often take to fanaticism to distance themselves from past failings. The reader should be clear; the admonition here, on the subject of global and local definitions, is a *guideline* for good practice, not a hard and fast formula. The ducking-stool and pyre are not needed for transgressors.

One equally important topic is how referents are used in definitions, and how the parameters and variables in use are named.

8.3.3 Names and 'magic numbers'

Naming routines, programs, integrands, data areas, parameters, constants and variables presents another area where sin stalks the world of the simple programmer. Once again, the issue is one of imparted meaning. The statement:

C = D * 3.14159

is no doubt a fine way (and a licit one within the language) to represent a function. But what is C? What is D? What is the magic number?

The restatement:

$$PI = 3.14159$$
$$CIRCUM = DIAM * PI$$

tells all, at least to anyone with a grasp of simple mensuration and the circle. The moral of this story is, name things meaningfully. Either spell out names in full, such as:

CIRCUMFERENCE = DIAMETER * PI

or use a clearly recognizable abbreviation – in so far as abbreviation permits. At all costs, avoid the use of unexplained 'magic numbers'. The value of PI is pretty obvious, but how about 1/137 or some bug based on it; 1/136, or 1/138 say? Or some *lapsus manu* such as 1/37 or 1/13! Better to declare a local (or 'own') constant:

FINESTRUCTURE = 1/137

and put a useful, comment adjacent to it, such as (from physics)

A FINE STRUCTURE CONSTANT IS DEFINED, AND ITS VALUE = 1/137 IS EMPLOYED IN COMPUTING THE BINDING ENERGY WITHIN THE NUCLEUS

As with the issue of global declarations, this matter of naming things is taken as a 'cosmetic' point by many programmers. Until, that is, they are faced with a cubic meter of code listing containing a large number of abstract, or otherwise ill-name definitions. Keeping track of what 'AA12X' means, or something like it, is not easy – even if a dictionary of definitions exists in the code listing itself, or in the archive.

When debugging or changing code, one wants to be able to concentrate on the creative issues at hand, without distractions to search for yet another mysterious definition.

8.3.4 Superscriptions and in-line comments

Many compilers and assemblers permit the use of in-line comments, basically textual statements in and amongst code statements, that will not be compiled/executed because

they are not statements in the vocabulary of the language. Their use is to explain on the code listing, as printed out or displayed on a screen, features of the code or whatever else one desires to say. Generally, a comment of this sort has to be flagged in some way, so that the compiler will not try to translate it, but will merely pass it into the output file for program listings.

Comments are both useful things to use, and a trap for the unwary. Let us deal with the bad news first. There is a common misapprehension that peppering a code listing with in-line comments constitutes a sufficiency of software documentation for all purposes. For trivial applications, that may well be the case. For non-trivial applications it is a dangerous over-simplification of an issue. What is the necessary and sufficient 'deliverable' documentation for a particular software system? This question should be determined high (early) in the life cycle – and often is done, particularly for strongly contracted supplies of the fixed price and time-scale sort. This specification of deliverable documentation seldom (in fact never in my experience) stipulates that a commented code listing is both necessary and sufficient. Necessary – may be, with some reservation; sufficient – no. The issue of deliverable documentation is dealt with, in full, in Section 13.1; it includes, but does not consist of, the commented code listing.

Comments can be seen in one of two categories: (a) superscription comments prior to the code; in this case they are not really 'in-line', as are (b) in-line comments between statements. The superscription comments tend to be essay-type style and, as Ledgard points out (1987) they tend to stagger and dribble all over the place in the sense of meaning – showing all the severe problems that lack of planning often brings to text (including books!). Superscription comments are best restricted to a short statement of purpose of the integrands; a brisk definition of inputs, algorithms and outputs, and a description of names used – for example as in the 'fine structure constant', as even an abbreviation such as FINSTR may be a bit baffling if one just trips over it as an operand in some program statement.

As for the real in-line comments, I state a personal preference here, they are best omitted entirely as they tend to add no value whatsoever – certainly if a 'good' high level language is being used, along with 'good programming practice'. In assembler coding, the features of the language often fail to help comprehension and readability, and here the attached comment field to a statement is often to explain what is going on. Even here, though, there is a dangerous tendency to state the already obvious. Such comments actual detract from readability through clutter, and detract from comprehension through redundancy.

The precepts about 'in-line' comments are simple: keep superscription comments to the point, and imagine that you are providing for an unknown colleague who will have to maintain the code in five years' time; if the superscription comments are good enough, if the naming of variables is done well enough and if a language is in use whose own grammar is clear, real 'in-line' comments should be redundant, and therefore may be omitted.

8.3.5 Program layout

The points to make about the layout of program texts are exceedingly simple, even trivial. Nonetheless they have substantial bearing on readability. There are three simple precepts

to assist in clarity of a program text: (a) use blank line spaces to separate lines of a text; (b) use character spaces in a line to demarcate phrases; (c) use indents to depicit logic within the code.

Figure 8.3 (from Ledgard 1987) shows all these guidelines in good use. The reader may like to contrast the readability of this with the rectangular, dense morass of text and symbols usually produced, under extreme time-pressure it must be said, by 'amateur' programmers either using development systems with inadequate text formatting facilities, or not using the ones available.

Over all these strictures lies the shadow of literacy, and the necessity for clarity and unambiguity of expression. The guidelines given may be operated in the most assiduous fashion by exponents, but will be a vain pursuit for them, and a vainer one for those who follow, if the 'clear' and 'unambiguous' program texts are, at the natural language level, illiterate.

Marcotty's point, that programming is an expository business, can hardly be over-stressed. Exposition with the computer, via the language, is not enough: exposition of intention and detailed meaning in programming and design, with one's peers, is the essence of programming too. That will manifestly be beyond any person of questionable literacy and this, in turn, reflects upon education and recruiting matters in the manage-ment aspects of software development. The point is take further, under the appropriate headings, in Chapter 13.

8.3.6 Auto-documentation

This almost completes our brief recital about programming style. But there are two questions still to be answered: What is 'self-documenting' code? And, more pertinently, whatever the claims made for it are, is it generally adequate as documentation?

The answer to the first is that self-documenting code is rather a grandiose name given to code that is liberally (and hopefully 'well') commented. Thus, the inference runs, the code listing *is* the documentation. This, in turn, infers that it contains a self-evident purpose for the code (specification), and that, through its naming, layout and comments, the code listing reveals the design in some clearly apparent way. These are very large claims to make for most systems above a trivial level of size and complexity, and assuming it to be the case that this level of documentation is sufficient can leave a software system danger-ously unprovided with its necessary means for maintenace and other changes.

When, in Section 13.1, we come to discuss software documentation in full, we will see that a code listing – however well-commented, laid-out, readable or whatever – is seldom an adequately clear description of all the features of a software system.

When, as sometimes happens, 'self-documenting code' becomes conflated with auto-matic documentation devices such as flowchart generators, the question of adequacy may arise in an amended form; the answer to it is still best assumed to be 'no'. Only in the simplest cases, such as small data-processing systems are 'self-documentation code' and flowchart generators useful.

```
procedure LINE_TEST (LINE NUM: INTEGER),
{ — Read a line from each of two files. If the lines are identical, set a
  — flag to indicate the result. If the lines are not identical, the lines
  — are printed with a marker under the first pair of differing characters}

  var
      END1, END2,
      POSITION, LAST POSITION: INTEGER;
      LINE1, LINE2; LINE IMAGE:
      CONTINUE TEST. BOOLEAN;

begin
  GET_LINE (FILE1, LINE1);
  GET_LINE (FILE2, LINE2);
  END1 : = LENGTH(LINE1);
  END2 : = LENGTH(LINE2);
  if END1 < END2 then
    LAST_POSITION = END1
  else
    LAST_POSITION = END2;

  POSITION : = 1;
  CONTINUE TEST : = TRUE;
  while CONTINUE TEST do begin
    if POSITION > LAST POSITION then
      begin
        LINE_FLAG : = SAME;
        CONTINUE TEST : = FALSE
      end
        else if LINE1 [POSITION] < > LINE2 [POSITION] then
      begin
        LINE_FLAG : = DIFFERENT;
        CONTINUE TEST : = FALSE
      end
    else
      POSITION : = POSITION + 1
    end;
    if END1 < > END2 then
      LINE_FLAG : = DIFFERENT;
    if LINE_FLAG = DIFFERENT then
        PRINT PAIR(LINE NUM, POSITION, LINE1, LINE2)
end;
```

FIGURE 8.3 Code with line and character spacing and indenting.

8.4 AUTOMATIC CODE GENERATION, AND THE QUESTION OF REUSABLE CODE

These are two distinct issues and any connection between them would constitute a third issue.

8.4.1 Automatic code generation

Automatic code generation means the production of coded programs from an input of some kind; the generator is a program that creates computer code from this input. There

are three distinct types of code generation in practice, distinguished by their purpose, input-type and the life cycle stage at which they are used:

1. Rapid prototype code generators based on systems' features in the requirement.
2. Code generators as part of an implemented design method.
3. Code generators from output specifications in the requirement.

As there is considerable potential overlap between these categories, we will take their definitions one stage further in each case.

Rapid prototyping in general is a technique, already discussed in Chapter 2, in which requirements can be clarified by making a model of the system-to-be, and a model of the environment in which it will operate, and interacting the one with the other. Rapid prototyping requires a specification language for the purpose, and these languages are generally based on some familiar high language, adapted for a particular application set. The models are defined in the rapid prototyping language, and code is produced by simple compilation.

The generated code is seen as a prototype model of the system-to-be (and its environment), and cannot with safety be regarded as the finished system since no aspects of quality in its production have been observed. One example, *Paisley*, is given by Zave (1982) and quoted in Chapter 2. There are many others, all strongly application-oriented and language-dependent.

Implemented design methods (such as Mascot, JDS/JSP, CCITT-SDL) frequently contain a provision for casting the design done in the notation of that method, into code in the language of the implementation. Thus, Mascot designs may generate RTL-2 code in one implementation. In another instance, a hypothetical case at the present time, perhaps, but one likely to eventuate in the Ministry of Defense, Mascot diagrams may generate Ada code, JSD/JSP is implemented, in some cases, to produce Cobol or PL/1 code, and in large scale user organizations such as a petroleum company, a special design notation for geophysical modeling may be linked to a generator of their in-house dialect of Fortran.

In these cases, the intention is not so much to produce prototypes so much as the system-to-be itself. In this respect, automatic code generation as a part of an implemented method differs from that due to rapid prototyping, and a simple consideration of life cycle stages shows the difference most clearly. Rapid prototyping is generally taken to be an activity undergone during requirements' specification; code generation via an implemented design method is generally seen as occurring deep within the software design stage itself or, in some cases, in lieu of design altogether. Rapid prototyping is intended to produce code for a prototype purpose. An implemented specification and design notation is intended to facilitate those steps, and then to produce the object system automatically.

Code generation direct from output characteristics in a problem (or requirements') specification may *sound* like rapid prototyping, but it is fundamentally different in purpose. In this case, the code generator operates on clearly identified output formats in a well understood application. A simple example might be the use of a report program generator, and the whole field of code generation from 'spread-sheet' specification – much a topic for research at the present time – falls within this category. In fact such systems exist in great numbers in the world of '4GLs' (fourth generation languages, so-called).

On such, of some antiquity, has a well known very high level language report program generator (or RPG) affiliated with it. In effect, such code generation steps straight from specification to implementation, and its limitations are clear as a consequence. The approach can only be utilized for applications which are simple enough, and well enough understood, to generate suites of programs for their various transactions, whose quality of compliance is easily established, and whose modifiability is not at issue due to the ease of regenerating the suite.

All three types of 'automatic' code generation suffer from the same deficiency – that they tend to produce code that is not quality controlled or assured in some way. For rapid prototypes this does not matter so long as they are properly classified as prototype models, and not confused with substantive, release versions of the software system-to-be. For output-driven generators the matter is less one of generating code than configuring existing routines into a suite.

In the case of implemented methods the generated code frequently has some unacceptable performance property, i.e. its 'real-time' properties may be inadequate, it may have deadlock, unproductive looping and so forth. The safest course of action for an implemented method, that goes down to code generation level, is to see it as a rapid prototyping language (notation plus source code generator) for *design*, rather than for specifications. Once again, the stricture on correct classification of prototypes *as* prototypes holds for implemented methods, when the outcomes is transliterated to the level of executable code.

At the present time, except for JDS/JSP in the realm of fairly straightforward data processing applications, code generation from implemented specification and design methods is uncommon, for reasons that may now be clear. In the case of application code generators using output formats in simple data processing, there is little more to say. They are useful within their limited context, and many users of small scale business data processing equipment of the IBM-PC type, Nixdorf, Philips, Olivetti, Datasaab and so forth, operate such things perfectly happily. Outside their area of suitability, they serve no useful purpose as yet. Ongoing research, in some places, into a 'spreadsheet' paradigm for code reuse may in future extend the field of application for code generators, via the so-called 4GL, ultra high level means.

The spreadsheet technique, taking advantage of developments in the available features of VDUs, aims to offer a paradigm in application definition based on the formulation of states of an output screen format. Defined, variable screen areas (windows) and variable cursor features (mouse) offer attractive options for output formats. The processing of available data, following spreadsheet definition, transpires from program suite generators of the 4GL type, by linking existing 'standard' features, via some declarative very high level syntax. Much of this is research at this time, and is of limited application anyway, most likely in the areas of data processing and computation.

8.4.2 Reusable code

Making reusable code is a widely shared objective, yet, in this author's view, relatively little is achieved in practice. New versions of software systems may cause an older version

to be ransacked for software that can be transferred to the innovation, and used there unaltered – but frequently the research in half-hearted, and quickly abandoned in favor of a complete rewrite. Given the high cost of software development, this is a most undesirable state of affairs. It accounts for code reuse being 'a widely shared objective' as one author puts it.

Hardware cost-effectiveness has increased dramatically over the past three decades, but that for software has, if anything, traveled in the opposite direction. It has been estimated that simple hardware processing capability has increased a millionfold since 1955 (measured in MIPS, millions of executed instructions per second); on the other hand, software engineers' productivity has increased by a factor of only three or four in that time, and that mainly as a one-off effect due to the introduction of high level languages in the period 1960–70 (Dolotta 1976). Discount, from this improvement in productivity, an inflationary effect on the cost of software engineering where its exponents are 'scarce resources', and the overall cost-effectiveness of software, compared with hardware, shows no similarity in trend at all.

With this perspective, it is no wonder that reusable code is a widely shared objective. 'Why can't we make a software library, have software components that are standard over our application?', one is asked. And 'Why didn't the fools do that last job with this in mind? We have another 200 man-years of effort to put in on this new software – why didn't we think?'

As we shall see, there is some mitigation of this rather bleak picture; some companies have application sets that do not vary much from one decade to another – or, as in the case of a dominant computer manufacturer, they can determine the rate at which their systems evolve. In these cases, software libraries do exist, and code reuse is a living issue.

However, in the world at large, IT product and project applications are a more dynamic affair entirely. It is there that we find both an urgent need for, and a conspicuous difficulty in achieving, reusable code. It is for this community above all that the subject is one for research at the present time. This view is substantiated by a major researcher into software productivity means, Boehm. This author has estimated that, in the decade 1984–93, the average productivity of software engineers could quadruple, a consummation devoutly to be desired. He goes on to list ten sources for this possible improvement (Boehm 1983). Figure 8.4 and Table 8.1 show the factors with informed, notional values attached; these are taken from a US Department of Defense database of sixty-three projects. Numbers such as these do not constitute an exact science, nor do they derive from one. They must, therefore, be viewed with caution. Their significance here is the weight placed on the role of reuse in improving productivity. The author concerned expects that half the expected improvement will come about by these means. Is he justified in this expectation; is there yet any evidence of it?

In the cold light of experience, one has to say that there is not much to base one's optimism on at this halfway stage towards 1993. Reusable code is still an urgent necessity for many firms; likewise, it is still mainly a research topic, except in cases where applications are fairly stable variants from version to version – or can be arranged to be, as in the case of a major computer manufacturer's operating and application programs. However, in the areas of application where program reuse has proved possible, there is some evidence, quoted below, that the productivity savings made are in the order of those

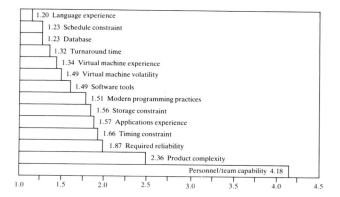

FIGURE 8.4 Factors affecting software development. The relative significance of factors is measured as the ratio of 'productivity' (delivered source lines of code per person-day) with all factors at 'normal' levels except the one concerned (applying maximally) to the productivity level when all factors apply 'normally' (after Boehm – © IEEE 1983).

expected by Boehm. Still, it is in the qualification of this statement that the problem lies. Literally, the amount of program reuse is too low, at the present time, to justify Boehm's expectations in software development, in general.

To find out why this is the case, one must begin with a quite careful inspection of what might be meant by the term 'reusable code'. There are, in fact, two distinct meanings possible:

1. Where commonality in requirements is seen, at that stage of the life cycle, between otherwise independent systems.
2. Where commonality of purposes is seen, in design, that may be served by a utility program.

These two might seem to be different forms of the same thing, but considering them further leads to somewhat different views. As we have defined matters, code reuse does

TABLE 8.1 Factors affecting software development: estimated D.o.D. software initiative impact on software productivity (after Boehm – © IEEE 1983)

Cost driver	DoD average-effort multipliers		
	1976	1983	1993
Use of software tools	1.05	1.02	0.85
Use of modern programming practices	0.98	0.95	0.85
Programming language experience	1.03	1.02	0.98
Software environment experience	1.05	1.03	0.95
Computer execution time constraint	1.25	1.18	1.11
Computer storage constraint	1.22	1.15	1.06
Computer turnaround time	1.03	1.01	0.90
Reduced requirements' volatility	1.17	1.15	1.00
Re-tool avoidance	1.06	1.06	1.00
Software reuse	0.93	0.90	0.50
Relative effort	2.01	1.54	0.36
Productivity gain		1.30	4.34

not include several possible interpretations of the term. For example, it does not mean one using programs repeatedly, as in the case of a payroll program run every month; nor does it mean the communal use of a product, such as the virtual computer software on your PC. Nor does it really mean the fraction of a system retained when a new version is made, as the basic considerations then concern what is not common between requirements for the two.

As our dual definition shows, code reuse results from a prior, purposive determination, and its future utility is defined, and not supposed.

There is a question of perception involved. In 'seeing commonality', who does the seeing? In the first case listed above, it is usually the managers in a user or supplier organization, aware of the similarity of features over applications, and frustrated out of all mind that software takes so long and is so difficult to develop. They tend to ask why the programmers cannot think ahead from one job to the next, why they cannot make components to use, as other species of engineers have done? The etymological question about software 'engineers' hovers in the air. That is the demand side of the matter, vigorous and thriving, clamoring in some cases: but what of the supply?

Here one faces a problem of some complexity and subtlety, which gets a full airing later in this section but can be adverted here under the caption: 'Reuse is not a technical problem, merely'. The point is that perceived commonality at the requirements' level does not necessarily infer a simple one-for-one correspondence at the level of implemented code; there *might* be such a possible inference in the case of relatively straightforward applications, where mapping between functionality in the functional specification, and structure in the code, has been both possible and effected; otherwise, the inference might be unjustified.

A feature f in requirement R_1 might be 'delivered' by elements f_1, f_2, etc. across the code structure, for excellent reasons concerning the design of R, as a whole. To assume that the occurrence of f in a different requirement R_2 will, or should, produce the same elements, in terms of the design of the whole of R_2, is not necessarily justified.

Of course, it will be pointed out that many 'standard functions' across a lot of applications *do* exists as library routines – things such as mathematical functions and the basic elements for administrative systems of a wide variety of types. Nevertheless, the fact remains that a considerable gap exists in software development in general, between users' and suppliers' expectations; and the amount of reusable software actually being developed as such remains relatively small for use as components in new systems.

Part of the problem lies in the argument that design decisions should not be constrained; another part, it must be admitted, lies in the instinctive beliefs of software developers that they can code things better themselves, and it will prove no more difficult to do so than (say) to use an old 'log' or 'sine' routine from a library. Another disablement undoubtedly lies in the different scope of perceptions involved. The manager (or user) will tend to see 'f', in the earlier example, as a fairly wide-ranging generic feature, seemingly or supposedly common to requirements R_1 and R_2; it might comprise elements (f_1, f_2, etc. in A), amounting to hundreds, or even thousands of source statements of code.

Software development staff, on the other hand, tend to think of detailed level utilities, of undoubtedly common use across low levels of design and implementation, in the applications' sector with which they have to deal. These tend to be far smaller in scale than

the common feature 'f'. Herein lies the genesis of miscommunication between parties. The expectations outweigh the actuality by a large amount, and the demand side's frustration grows.

Yet another obstacles is the E property of software systems, and the fact that it may be far better recognized by software developers than managers and users, by and large. Identifying f as a common feature over A and B is less than convincing in the knowledge that A will tend to become requirement A' over time, and B will evolve into B'.

These are *not* arguments against reuse, either as aspiration or actuality. It is an attempt to account for the fact that not more reusable software is made. 'Why isn't the situation like that in electronics', we are asked, 'with standard components and known ways of assembling them?' It is possible in some places and cases to achieve reuse of code. Major suppliers of long-life software systems, such as computer equipment manufacturers, are conspicuous examples. An evidence of this may be seen in claims made that a relationship exists, in some locality, between the effort to make a software system and the cube root of software size! (Walston and Felix, 1977).

It is very difficult to account for this surfeit of productivity other than by code reuse. For it says that it requires only twice the effort to make a software system of 8,000 source code statements as it does to make one of 1,000, all else being equal. And for three times the basic effort, one can develop a software system of 27,000 statements. This sort of thing is rare, and can really only be accounted for by code reuse. For we can hardly believe that if it takes Fred four months to make a respectable system of 1 kilostatement of some tricky code, this hero will be able to do a software task of 27 kilostatements (of similar difficulty, and to similar quality) in one year.

The cold fact remains. Despite the *réclame* of its enthusiasts, Boehm as already quoted, and others (*inter alia*, Balzer *et al.* 1983 and Mathis 1986), code reuse has not yet arrived as a prevalent or even a reasonably common practice. And, given the fundamental requirements for it listed earlier, this is unsurprising. Moreover, other, deeper understandings are beginning to emerge about the difficulties of making reusable code, as researchers reveal their work in progress and, with it, some of their frustrations.

One author puts the stark picture with a minimum of embellishment:

> Unfortunately, software reuse has not evolved beyond its most primitive forms of subroutine libraries and brute force program modification. (Tracz 1988)

Others make similar points:

> there needs to be a concerted effort by customers, suppliers and educational establishments in order to encourage software reuse to take off. (Geary 1988)

And:

> formidable obstacles remain which make it unlikely that [software reuse] will become commonplace without detailed planning. . . . This need for extreme care, and hence high initial cost in the development of re-usable components is only one of the managerial factors that militate against the widespread adoption of software re-use. In fact it is hardly an exaggeration to say that the main obstacles to the widespread adoption of reuse . . . are managerial rather than technical. . . . (Bott and Wallis 1988)

The non-technical aspects of the problem of software reusability need to be stressed. Tracz, in his articles, goes on to identify no less than nine commonly encountered myths surrounding the subject. With due acknowledgment, we take these headings as the basis for further discussion, with the passing observation that this list of myths accounts, in part only, for the imbalance between demand and supply for reusable code. The fundamental problems, listed earlier, have especial and supervening force in the matter.

THE MYTH THAT SOFTWARE REUSE IS A TECHNICAL PROBLEM
This is not to say that all the technical problems have been solved, or never existed, but that they are part of a far wider panoply of concerns. To repeat an earlier point, this must be the case given that *the* major impediment to developing reusable components is that of identifying commonality of purpose.

Making a library of software functions in computation intensive, and data processing applications, is one thing; sine, cosine and logarithm routines are obvious if the need exists; also, extending the virtual computer environment by adding database management and filing systems, and a small universe of other facilities, is not difficult. But that leaves the main part of the issue untouched.

One technical initiative has been to see the Ada language as a vehicle for some future software components industry (Barnes 1982), and not surprisingly this led to Ada being 'taken up the life cycle' – that is, seen as a *notation* suitable for design, and a language appropriate for specification (of a 'formal' nature, it must be said).

The arguments against the use of abstract notations for these purposes have already been given in Chapters 5 and 7. Further, as one source reveals:

> How best to use Ada to produce re-usable software components has proved a surprisingly difficult problem and has revealed significant weaknesses in the language. (Bott and Wallis 1988)

The main problem, however, derives from the supervening fallacy that any language, or other technical means, can do more than enable the development of software components, given that a set of other consideration (a) require, and (b) do not, themselves, disable such development. The development of Ada, and its environments and their use, must be seen in the context of these caveats, lest the unfulfillment of exaggerated expectations leads to a proportionate disillusion. The virtues of Ada in providing *low level* (implementation) facilities for making software components, are excellently set out in Booch (1988; which also gives a useful introduction to object-oriented design, but that is only a small part of the issue.

THE MYTH THAT SPECIAL TOOLS ARE NEEDED FOR SOFTWARE REUSE
This is, in fact, analogous to – if not a subset of – the previous point. But here we see the technical impetus concerning not so much a language as the environment around it, PSE, Ipse or whatever. As the features of a language may help or hinder the development of reusable software components, so many those of the PSE.

Unix, for example, allows commands to be composed, and new commands built, as part of 'standard sets' of such. Another example is the availability of a growing number of real-time executive (RTE) facilities, as virtual software, providing such features as low level

scheduling, process switching and interrupt handling. As in the case of languages, these are useful tools. But tools do not use themselves, and their utility is always contingent on need, and on the factors modifying or standing in opposition to this need. The reader interested in Unix features for these purposes is referred to Kernighan (1984).

THE MYTH THAT REUSING CODE RESULTS IN HUGE INCREASES IN PRODUCTIVITY

Tracz quotes 'studies' (Horowitz and Munson 1984) that purport to show the following economics of software reusability:

1. Software created with its reuse in mind costs 20–25 percent more in effort to develop and learn to use.
2. A software development in which 40 percent of design and 75 percent of code is achieved by reusable components, shows a net reduction in development effort of only 40 percent overall for the development stage of the life cycle – i.e. 'concepts' to beta-testing.
3. The previous case might well show far higher effort reductions for the in-service maintenance of a software system, as the use of reusable code, code templates and application generators has shown 'up to 90 percent' saving in these costs.

As pointed out, application generators tend to be evolved and used in relatively straightforward and well understood sectors of application, such as small and medium sized data processing systems, and the suspicion exists that the 'maintenance statistics' quoted are related more to that than anything else.

Generalizing from such a base is a dangerous exercise, and one might think that, for example, the 20–25 percent cost might, in many other cases, be a very underestimated amount. However, just taking the figures at their face value, some interesting things may be extracted from them. It has been pointed out, by Boehm (1975) and Putnam (1982) that, of the total effort to develop and maintain software, about 40 percent resides in the former task, and 60 percent in the latter. Putnam's work is described in Chapter 12. The effort reduction figures quoted by Tracz show a threefold (3.33) increase in productivity over the whole life cycle of development and maintenance (but not major new version) activities. This should be compared with the cubic increase seemingly implied earlier (Walston and Felix 1977) for software development alone.

Also, it must be said that the inference, from Tracz's figures, of a threefold productivity increase through reuse is in line with Boehm's predictions, but is hardly 'huge', particularly if, as seems the case, it is restricted to a subset of application types. Some managers, particularly, would expect software reuse to produce much more dramatic savings. As one product development engineer said to me: 'If it takes a workman an hour to mix and pour concrete to make a paving tile, I cannot believe it should take him twenty minutes to get one from a pile of prefabricated articles – unless it's a mile away.'

THE MYTH THAT ARTIFICIAL INTELLIGENCE WILL SOLVE THE REUSE PROBLEM

Here we must make a distinction between artifical intelligence and expert systems. Properly, what is meant by the first of these is *simulated* rather than immanent intelligence, where this last term bears a connotation of conscious purpose. One would, for example,

expect an 'intelligence', simulated or otherwise, to have a learning, or 'heuristic', capacity.

Expert systems, on the other hand, are rule-based information retrieval systems, in the main. It is fairly easy to see that, across a class of applications, the search for commonality at the specification level may be helped by an 'expert' system incorporating 'knowledge' (i.e. rules of recognition) for that type. In this limited sense, expert systems may – in future – help with one of the problems of reuse. As for 'AI' itself, this is a much more distant prospect in its own right, and its use in this context is not less distant consequently.

THE MYTH THAT THE JAPANESE HAVE SOLVED THE REUSE PROBLEM

Much misleading *réclame* was given, early in this decade, to Japan's foray into things like 'fifth generation' computer architecture, logic programming and the so-called 'software factory' for software development and reuse. The Japanese research and development effort stands on its own merits, but it has not yet revolutionized the world of computing and its applications. In fact, on reusability, Tracz points out that some of the simplest technology is in use:

> The Japanese software factories use a simple key word in context (KWIC) index to locate a desired function.

Other instances involve the use of proprietary relational databases and other information retrieval systems, but, as yet, no revealed cure for the basic problems of software reuse.

THE MYTH THAT ADA HAS SOLVED THE REUSE PROBLEM

This has been commented as under the first subsection above; it is a subset of the general point that the issues of software components and reuse are not merely technical problems awaiting solution by these means. Whilst that myth remains, software reuse will remain as a relatively low order effect in software development.

THE MYTH THAT DESIGNING SOFTWARE FROM REUSABLE PARTS IS LIKE
DESIGNING HARDWARE USING INTEGRATED CIRCUITS

Two things are at work to produce this misleading conclusion. First, the deeply and sincerely held view of many engineers – from disparate disciplines – that making software should be analogous to hardware circuit development; second, that because some well understood and relatively straightforward applications can lead to program generators, 4GLs and the development of 'standard parts', therefore any and all applications should be tractable to the same means. Misconstructed simile is a fallacy in logic, as is the un-justified inference of a general rule from a special case. This myth commits both fallacies. The arguments are set out in the early chapters of this book, where some myths surrounding the basic etymology of 'software engineering' are discussed.

THE MYTH THAT REUSED SOFTWARE IS 'REUSABLE' SOFTWARE

Tracz distinguishes between properly planned development of software components for anticipated purposes of reuse, and 'software salvaging'. This last-named is a dreadful practice of amateur programmers under acute time pressure, when old code is lifted out its context and 'patched' to make it fit a new one.

Clearly, in such cases – which are not even analogous to stripping an old machine for

spare parts – criteria for good design play no part in the process. As with patching code, as distinct from effecting a carefully designed and executed change to it, salvaging code *can* be done. But the prices for doing it are paid at the design level of the new system, and in its sharply diminished reliability, maintainability and general modifiability.

THE MYTH THAT SOFTWARE REUSE WILL 'JUST HAPPEN'

A corollary of the argument that software reuse is not just an issue awaiting the advent of a technical solution, is that the alleviation of problems in other domains affecting software development will have to be addressed.

These concern a whole range of management issues which must be directed to solving the problems of identification of commonality across requirements' specifications, and the adoption and execution of policies to take the results of this identification into a carefully planned design, implementation and configuration management of software components – for which the best technical means will then be required. In other words, managed, 'top down' policies are required, not the converse – based on the fond hope that such and such a language or environment will, ineluctably, lead people at low levels of program implementation to effect the reuse revolution 'bottom up'.

Not that there is likely to be a miracle cure to the problem by management means either, in my view. The Utopian view, quite common over the past few years, that the 'software crisis' will go away when the problems of reuse are cracked, faces many impediments, of which the major ones are as follows:

1. The E property of most software systems, the tendency of requirements to change over time. This is compounded, as an effect, by the widespread view that the 'flexibility' of a system can be made to reside in its software, because software is easily changed – another myth of course.
2. If this world was one of a small set of relatively stable requirements we would have no problem. What we actually have is a relatively small set of problems that are so comparatively stable in their requirements that *some* degree of commonality over types can be assessed. But this is to be seen against a backdrop of the immense range of highly mutable applications throughout the whole range of 'IT'.

    The contractual and pseudo-contractual requirements under which much software is developed, impose effort and time-scale limits that militate against the development of software components in the first place. Of course, everyone would use software components if they were available, accessible and appropriate, but how many software teams have the explicit remit, and resources to consider reusability during the exigencies of a project or product development? How many managers would bite their false-teeth in two if told that 'the software would cost 25 percent more to make' as a consequence, or be completed n months outside its window of opportunity, and so on?

    This problem is endemic to many other fields of endeavor too, no doubt. But it is only in software engineering that a 'miracle cure' has been expected, through reuse and the evolution of components. Arguing for a change of behavior in, or new paradigm for, software development – such as more informal supply contracts – is defying both market requirements and management imperatives. It may be true that I can get my next-but-four system quicker and cheaper if I invest in reuse now, but this current

system has to be done for $x and in y months, otherwise it is not worth doing; so the argument goes, and so the argument will continue to go in many places.

3. The problem of recognizing true commonality across a requirements' set, particularly a future and undefined requirements' set may be, and may remain, beyond organizations to achieve. The cost of wastage through mistaken policy may deter many from even attempting the task. A library of undisturbed software components, having consumed scarce resource to make, is not a happy prospect for management to contemplate.

That, then, is a summary of the current situation on software reuse. It will come as a let-down to many; managers hoping for some simile with electronic component assembly; researchers engaged in the search for a cure to the 'software crises' afflicting economic and technical quality.

About seventy years ago, there arose a school of chess-players known as 'the hyper-moderns', who claimed virtues for their novel insights into opening and middle game play. Software engineering is a bit like that today. To its hyper-modernists, these comments on software components and reuse many appear disappointing in the extreme, a meager compendium of fogey views, and a prolongation of a not-so-golden past and present in the subject. We shall see.

8.5 SUPPORT ENVIRONMENTS

As must be obvious by now, the essence of good software engineering practice is competent management of resources – a fact that places the subject in common with a very broad spectrum of other human activities in construction and creation. In our case, 'resources' fall neatly into two categories: people and material. Both subsume a variety of properties and other associated commodities. For instance, 'people' infers 'suitable for the purpose', 'available for sufficient time' and so forth. These aspects of resource are dealt with in Chapter 12.

Material resources for software engineering, apart, that is, from usual office supplies, come in one of two categories between which there is substantial overlap. Both are known as 'support environments'. One concerns the support of all software engineering activities – such as management methods and technical facilities for designing, programming and testing software; such things are generally known as Ipses or integrated project support environments. Another type of environment, a subset of the Ipse concept, is the programming support environment – or PSE – which comprises the technical facilities for software development, and little in the way of support for management methods.

It may be thought that the distinct features of an Ipse, the provisions it makes for managing software development, should properly be dealt with apart from the strictly technical facilities of a PSE. Yet the matter is better still viewed as one of 'environment' in general for software development, and treated as a whole rather than as two separable parts. In this way, the Ipse is seen as the *set* of support facilities for management and technical purposes, and the specific features for both management and for technical support are consequently seen as its subsets. Attempts to establish a 'superset' category – called 'the software factory' in some places, and intended to incorporate development in artificial

intelligence and knowledge-based ('expert') systems – is at too early a stage of suggestion to be considered in detail here.

That, then, will inform our approach. First, though, we need to review a little of the history of Ipse/PSE development so that the current status of facilities on offer in these categories will become clear.

8.5.1 Ipse and PSE technology in general, seen as a historical development

Logically, one should begin with the Ipse, as this is the set of tools and facilities of which the PSE is a part; that is to approach the issue 'top down' so to speak. The chronology, however, shows a different kind of evolutionary process, with something of a discontinuity in it. In this subsection, we shall look at three aspects of the historical development of environments:

1. The evolution of PSE facilities.
2. The cost component.
3. The appearance of Ipse features.

THE EVOLUTION OF PSE FEATURES
Strictly speaking, PSE technology has been with us from the advent of computing in the modern epoch, since the definition of a support environment includes the most primitive tools such as existed then, a bootstrap (or independent program) loader and a very low level language translator. Developments from this rudimentary state of affairs can be seen as comprising four main epochs, overlapping with each other in time, and far from distinctly demarcated anyway:

1. Primitive tools, as already described, for 'self-hosted' program development, i.e. on the equipment which will subsequently be their basis for execution.
2. More advanced 'virtual computer' systems, incorporating a variety of high level languages, and some simple development tools such as linkers, loaders, editors and debug facilities. By and large, in the period around 1965–75, these 'environments' were mainframe (rather than mini- or microcomputer) based, still basically for 'self-hosted' rather than 'host/target use, and emphasized the operational features of mainframe applications, rather than development purposes for self-hosted software development.
3. A main impetus towards PSE development occurred in the period 1975–80, having two principal stimulants. First, software development for mini- and microcomputers found those devices underprovided with even the basic tools for these purposes – a situation analogous to that in the early 1950s; further, it was clear that to provide adequate development features, for self-hosted practice on these devices, would substantially utilize their available capacity as required for execution of the developed applications; thus the concept of host-target development grew, with a consequent emphasis on the PSE features of hosts – usually mainframes or large minicomputers.
   Second, the initiative, by the US Department of Defense, to define and develop a common language (Ada) for use across its departments, and across the totality of

its applications, resulted in a colateral definition of its ancillary requirements, the Ada programming support environment, or Apse ('Stoneman': Buxton 1980). By the early part of the present decade, the concepts of host-target development, and of PSE features in a defined sense, were established – even if satisfactory environments had not yet materialized. The notions of a kernal Apse (Kapse), comprising a set of basic tools, and a minimal Apse (Mapse) constituted great progress over a previous state of affairs in which PSE features were, by definition, what lot or little the hardware suppliers thought to provide with their equipment, and were usually subordinate to the virtual computer facilities for operation – such as task schedulers, device drivers and information filing and updating features. Not least, the definition of kernal and minimal features led to a realization that technical tools for software development should be sufficiently *integrated*, so that movement between them is possible within the electronic environment.

4. Although the enhanced interest, even emphasis, on PSE facilities represented a great step in the period 1975–85, it represented (or rather presaged) an improvement at the technical level of software development. Dealing with the management and administrative aspects of software development had been defined as necessary within computer-based development environments, but disproportionate emphasis continued to be placed on the technical tool-set and its integration. About 1985, the idea of an integrated project support environment (Ipse) became established in some quarters, and work on Ipses included the technical (PSE) features as a subset.

Details of the features comprising an Ipse, and those for kernal and minimal PSEs, are listed later in this chapter.

At the present time, software development is being done, in different places in all the ways listed above. For example much use is made, for administrative applications, of the self-hosted mainframe, with elaborate 'virtual computer' features that provide mainly for task scheduling and logistic regulation of computer and peripheral resources. In these cases, the PSE features are often not very advanced from their state in the early 1970s, Cobol language and some simple loader/linker operating system, and this is generally sufficient for the applications concerned. In fact, the most onerous task for the software developer may be to learn the job control language (JCL) of the 'virtual' system – an essential task for using a 'virtual' system, even though its facilities for software development may be a small component of its volume.

At the other end of the scale, considerable use is still made of the self-hosted microcomputer, with almost no PSE or 'virtual' features at all. This was the state of affairs in the mid 1970s, when the invention of the programmable microprocessor opened up a universe of applications for using these devices as components, 'embedded' in electronic systems. A further complexity, here, arises from the fact that many such 'embedded' systems have 'real-time' response requirements. As we have seen elsewhere, languages, design tools and other PSE features were, and can be argued still are, not well developed for this sector of applications.

Another difficulty, if one was needed, is that the capacity of microprocessors (programmable store, archive store that can be attached, and computing power) largely ruled out the incorporation of large 'virtual' software systems for them. Consequently, the

practice of host-target software development arose, where the 'host' was some mainframe, minicomputer or large capacity microcomputer that was better equipped with PSE features than the 'target', and included a facility for down-line loading of the developed and validated software to the 'target' equipment. However, this strategy requires a host configuration which, as we will see, tended to cost some orders of magnitude more than a 'cheap and cheerless' near-naked micro – and not all software developers had or have access to one. Thus the self-hosted practice remains in some places most often involving almost 'naked' target equipment with little more than a bootstrap loader and a low level language translator, or, at best, a compiler for some rather insufficient high level language for embedded, 'real-time' purpose.

THE COST COMPONENT

The development of advanced Ipse and PSE facilities for host–target based software development has come about, in some places, through the considerable impetus at the PSE level of Ada and the Apse. However, apart from the very largest organizations doing software development as a major (or *the* major) part of business, the use of large scale Ipse or PSE facilities is still quite rare, owing to the most ancient of all impediments – cost. That is not to say that an advanced 'environment' may not be *cost-effective*, for that is another argument altogether. If one cannot afford the *a priori* investment cost, then one is excluded from any benefits of cost effectiveness by cruel economics alone.

Ipses and PSEs are prohibitively expensive in two respects:

1. An elaborate PSE (or Ipse) will be a large or even very large software system on our rough scale of values set up in Chapter 3. Their development, like all product developments, can and frequently does involve innovation, prototypes and the like. They can, therefore, be exceedingly expensive to develop. One authority on the subject estimates the development cost of a very extensive PSE (incorporating some Ipse features) as *circa* $20 million at 1980 values – for the software development of the PSE alone! (Boehm 1981). Which brings us to the next component of cost.
2. Extensive PSEs provide features for simultaneous access by a multiplicity of users of the system and, as a corollory of this, they are generally subject to economic justification on this basis; such-and-such a PSE will be said to 'support' (say) three hundred concurrent-access users without, for normal software development activities, degradation of performance on the part of the 'virtual machine'. Another will comfortably support ten to fifteen, and so on. A 'naked micro', as self-hosted 'target' machine, may support one user at a time, and that not very well.

   The higher the level of support required, the larger the PSE or Ipse is needed; the larger the PSE or Ipse the more expensive it is as software – rental or purchase. Also, the more ambitious the requirements and extensive the support software are, the larger the hardware complex (and therefore more expensive in terms of processing, peripheral and communication hardware) on which it must be operated. The necessary hardware for a medium scale PSE only may cost several hundred thousand dollars; for an elaborate PSE one may need a hardware complex costing millions of dollars – as well as the software costs. And that is only for the shared technical tools facilities that are a subset of the Ipse concept.

THE APPEARANCE OF IPSE FEATURES

Attention in the computer industry, hardware and software suppliers and users, turned to the development of PSEs – as distinct from the mere aggregations of languages and operating system features that had occurred up to that point – around 1980. The main impetus was to provide an environment for software to be developed in the newly defined language, for the US Department of Defense principally – Ada. Since that time, PSE technology has been a major development.

The Ipse, on the other hand, is an idea that sprung, partly grown already, out of the PSE technology, as that increasingly incorporated management tools as well as strictly technical software development facilities. Also, whereas most of the work on PSEs in the period 1978–85 was done in the USA – as an outcome mainly of the Ada development activities in and for the Department of Defense – the Ipse concept for overall software development support was much more internationally based, and language-independent. It was almost as though, around 1985 or thereabouts, the accretive growth of PSE technology – rather 'bottom up' it must be said, at least until Ada and Stoneman (Buxton 1980) – suddenly became transformed into a major area of development in its own right, with the associated 'top down' concept of the Ipse lagging behind somewhat.

At the present time, and here is a reason for our rather lengthy exposition on the historical evolution in PSE and Ipse technologies, there is a fairly wide choice of PSE systems available, ranging – as we have said – from primitive features on hardware systems of limited capacity, up to very extensive environments on large scale computer hardware complexes, possibly involving elaborate communication networks as well.

Ipses, on the other hand, are just beginning to appear on the market – and rather expensive items they are, in most cases.

We will, of course, come to the point of defining the main features of both PSEs and Ipses, but one further topic may first be clarified. That is concerning the sources of software development and management environments.

Historically, albeit recent history inevitably, virtual software features and facilities were made by computer hardware manufacturers – or commissioned by them to be made by 'third party' software suppliers. This was (and is) a simple extension of commercial policy to sell computer equipment.

More recently, it has become clear that such PSEs – however elaborate they are, and some are very extensive in their incorporated features – are not sufficient for some major users. These users tend to develop their own PSE or Ipse systems, or commission them to be made by others. The US Department of Defense is a perfect case in point with Ada, the Stoneman project and associated Apse developments since 1980. Another outstanding example is the Bell Laboratories of AT&T and the Unix/C language environments emanating from that source, with the added interest in this case that, unlike the intentional deliberation of Ada and Stoneman, the widespread success of Unix has rather not been intentional at all, so much as circumstantial.

The diversification of these sources is a very positive element in PSE and Ipse evolution, but it does contain a drawback. Many large electronic and IT product development firms correctly see their management and software environments as being a matter of competitive advantage over other firms operating in the same commercial sector. This

may, understandably, retard propagation of environments. There is little to be done about this state of affairs; propagation and acceptance of new technology is – even in such an apparently whirlwind business as computing – a slow affair (Riddle 1984). The purpose of this recital here is to complete a certain part of the picture concerning Ipses and their subsets – PSEs. In summary one can say of this major issue for management that an advanced electronic environment is, basically, a *sine qua non* for good software development, along with technical and management practice. However the following must be kept in mind:

1. Environments of any real worth are expensive in two ways: the software itself is costly to make and, therefore, expensive to buy or rent; secondly, the hardware facilities for an advanced PSE (or Ipse) can also be extremely expensive.
2. Good Ipse/PSE facilities cannot be expected from equipment manufacturers so much as from major users; this will delay the good effects, on a wide scale, of inventions in this area.
3. Taking all into account, managers (like software engineers themselves) should prepare for a degree of frustration through the possibility of wide gaps between need and supply, and between the price of available systems and the sustainable economics of procurement.

We shall return, briefly, to the issue of Ipse/PSE economics before leaving the topic of support environments. Now we must progress to a somewhat overdue definition of what might, or might not, be found as part of an Ipse and/or PSE. We leave this part of the discussion with a quotation:

> Tools and toolsets for the software builder are receiving increased attention. Research into new concept tools is progressing. However, use of tools in the software workplace is not. (Glass 1982)

By now we understand some of the factors militating against the acquisition of support environments half a decade on from Glass's well considered comments, which should now be extended to include Ipse facilities as well as the more limited field of his criticism – PSE tools and tool-sets.

Having now reviewed the history concerning Ipse-PSE development, we turn to a more explicit treatment, in Sections 8.5.2 and 8.5.3, of the state of affairs at this time in PSE and Ipse technologies, before returning (in Section 8.5.4) to the issues of cost and how to choose an environment.

8.5.2 PSE technology

The software engineer works mainly in an electronic environment in the present epoch. In former times we may have occupied offices at a distance from the computer complex, and either walked to it with our programs, or employed a courier/operator service for access. It was rather as though all telephone calls had to be made from the central post office, or a local branch of it, and no one had a telephone in their home, or office at their work-place.

Evolutions of computer hardware and software have altered all that, largely since 1980.

Now, multiple concurrent use of computer facilities – by software development teams and other users – is the norm, and only in relatively rare instances (such as occur in the use of self-hosted micros) does one find sequential access facilities. Moreover, software engineers, from graduate entrant level upwards, *expect* to work in an advanced, electronic environment, and can become a little volatile (in the employment sense) if denied one.

All this is very much a recent phenomenon in software engineering. Previously, in the period from 1950 to 1980 say, software was developed in primitive ways, and consequently its exponents were widely regarded as primitives. Some of these attitudes persist, but 'times', that we were told were 'a-changing', have changed. Software need no longer be something that everybody confidently expects to be developed to inadequate specifications, with inadequate facilities, during an inadequate time – although any and all of these hazards might still be present, and might produce their historic effect – lamentably low software quality.

TABLE 8.2 Levels and features of a PSE (after Boehm 1981)

Rating	Typical tools
Very low (basic microprocessor tools)	Assembler Basic linker Basic monitor Batch debug aids
Low (basic mini)	HOL compiler Macro assembler Simple overlay linker Language-independent monitor Batch source editor Basic library aids Basic database aids
Nominal (strong mini, basic maxi)	Real-time or timesharing operating system Database management system Extended overlay linker Interactive debug aids Simple programming support library Interactive source editor
High (strong maxi, Stoneman Mapse)	Virtual memory operating system Database design aid Simple program design language Performance measurement and analysis aids Programming support library with basic CM aids Set-use analyzer Program flow and test case analyzer Basic text editor and manager
Very high (Advanced maxi, Stoneman Apse)	Full programming support library with CM aids Full, integrated documentation system Project control system Requirements' specification language and analyzer Extended design tools Automated verification system Special purpose tools: crosscompilers, instruction set simulators, display formatters, communications processing tools, data entry control tools, conversion aids, etc.

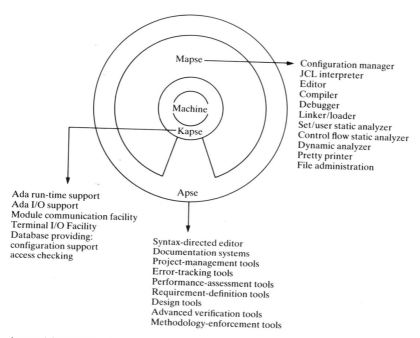

Configuration manager
JCL interpreter
Editor
Compiler
Debugger
Linker/loader
Set/user static analyzer
Control flow static analyzer
Dynamic analyzer
Pretty printer
File administration

Ada run-time support
Ada I/O support
Module communication facility
Terminal I/O Facility
Database providing:
configuration support
access checking

Syntax-directed editor
Documentation systems
Project-management tools
Error-tracking tools
Performance-assessment tools
Requirement-definition tools
Design tools
Advanced verification tools
Methodology-enforcement tools

Apse = Ada support environment
Kapse = kernal apse
Mapse = minimal apse

FIGURE 8.5 PSE as a part of the virtual machine — Ada support (after Reiffer 1982)

There is no commonly accepted PSE tool-set that all computer suppliers (or others) retail, all software engineers presume, and (*ergo*) all managers of software development enthusiastically provide. However, it is a strange environment that lacks at least the following: a language translator (or several) such as a compiler or assembler; a linker-loader for relating integrands into programs, and into software (run-time) modules; a source code 'debug' feature, and a control flow analyzer; listing and dumping features to display programs and parts of memory; a text editor; and a program filing and document emendation feature for configuration management. These 'primitives' in a PSE are, of course, in addition to operating system features that regulate access to the equipment – such as program libraries to manage input/output.

To give some idea of the state of the art in this decade, we will cite three main sources each of whom set out to define (in the early 1980s) the scope of PSEs.

The first (Boehm 1981) defined five notional levels of PSE – from very low, at the facilities' level, to very high in a full implementation of the Ada programming support environment (Apse) on a mainframe compex. This classification is set out in Table 8.2. Another specialist in this area (Reiffer 1982) depicted the features in terms of their virtual machine properties – Apse, Mapse (minimal Apse) and Kapse (kernal Apse). This scheme is set out in Figure 8.5. A third source, from the same period, is Glass (1982). He provides a matrix representation of the features of certain environments in development (Table 8.3).

TABLE 8.3 A mapping of some environments with tool-set features (after Glass 1982)

Category	Function	DoD Mapse	DoD Apse	AF SDVS	NASA HAL/S	Softool 80	Navy MTASS	Army Ada	BITS	Navy SDL	AF CSDP	TI ISS	GTE Phoenix	Boeing SS	FASP	KERN	Unix
Requirements	Requirements' tracing		X									X					
Requirements	Requirements' language									X							
Design	Design support		X							X	X				X		
Implementation	Compiler/assembler	X	X	X	X	X	X	X	X	X	X	X	X	X	X	X	X
Implementation	Linker/loader	X	X		X	X	X	X	X	X	X	X	X	X			X
Implementation	Conditional compilation							X					X	X			X
Implementation	Control flow analyzer					X					?	?					
Implementation	Report generator										X			X			
Implementation	Preprocessor generator					X										X	X
Checkout	Statement execution monitor	X	X	X		X					X				X		X
Checkout	Interface simulator	X	X														
Checkout	Source debug	X	X			X	?			X	X	X					X
Checkout	Formal verification system		X														
Checkout	Test case generator									X	X	X					
Checkout	Symbolic executor																
Checkout	Instruction level simulator				X		X							X	X		
Checkout	Environment simulator				X	X											
Maintenance	Global cross-reference	X	X		X	X	?				X			X			X
Maintenance	Disassembler										X						
Maintenance	Call structure analyzer					X				X				X			
Maintenance	Timing/performance	X	X				X				X			X			X
Management	Configuration management	X	X	X	X	X		X			X	X		X			
Management	Project control		X								X	X	X		X		
Management	Fault report		X						?	X	X						
Management	Standards' auditor					X											
Management	Graphics generator										X						
Documentation	MIL/SPEC generator	X	X								X						
Documentation	Word processing		?					X		X	X					X	X
Documentation	Typesetter										X						X
Documentation	Documentation templates					X											
Documentation	Interface documenter					X											
Documentation	Text Primitives															X	X
Documentation	Speller																X
Multipurpose	Database file manager	X	X					X	X	X	X			X	X	X	X
Multipurpose	Text editor	X	X					X		X	X			X	X	X	X
Multipurpose	Pretty printer	X	X								X			X			X
Multipurpose	File compare	X	X		X						X			X			X
Multipurpose	Mailbox									X	X						X

Some extremely interesting things emerge from a comparison of these schemes. Since about 1985–8 the situation has begun to clarify. Some software developers have remained at the 'very low' level of PSE acquisition, basically that of the self-hosted micro, for one of two (or both) reasons: (a) management unawareness, or (b) economics.

Of these two, the most virulent is the second, and we shall come to address the matter imminently. The problem of unawareness is a transient and curable one, and the persistent expectations of software engineeers will reveal (if not remedy) it, 'bottom up' so to speak. Dating from an even earlier time, *circa* 1982 onwards, some large scale developers of software systems have enjoyed 'high' to 'very high' levels of PSE, using Boehm's scale of values. These companies are the large aerospace companies, departments/ministries of defence, telephony and telegraphy equipment suppliers, automobile manufacturers, large systems and software houses, and some computer equipment suppliers.

For the most part, software development is done at the present time with 'nominal' facilities (Boehm). This of itself would not cause adverse comment but for the fact that, half a decade or more after the definition of reasonable requisites for software development, they are only now becoming fairly widely adopted.

One should not forget the inhibitors in operation on this process – cost and property. Also, as already pointed out, contrary to the generally accepted view of this whirlwind industry, new technology in computing has a long gestation, development and probation period during which it may become established, or be superseded, or merely fall into desuetude. According to one author this can be up to 'eighteen, plus or minus three, years' (Riddle 1984) The PSE initiatives of 1978–87 are unlikely, on this basis, to provide systems that become the norm in software development much before 1995.

Many users of computer systems and software have large complexes of mainframe equipment for both self-hosted development and subsequent operation of software, with extensive archival storage. Banks, airlines and public administrations are in this category, for instance; others such as petrochemical companies have similar complexes for an admixture of usages including both data processing and computing applications. Electronics and IT product firms in general may have similar facilities (e.g. for their internal administration, stock control and so forth), but basically these companies tend to do their software development on medium or large minicomputers, or large microcomputers – although some, as indicated above, depend on the features of a target machine (usually with 'low' or 'very low' level PSEs).

By and large, the 'virtual machine' software of large mainframes for data processing applications is suitable for software development only within that sector of endeavor, and lacks many of the language features, support of design methods, and cross compilation/ cross assembly tools needed for IT product development in the round. On the other hand, such 'admin.' configurations (as they are often seen to be) contain facilities that can be very useful in the Ipse area – such as the sort of database management system and text editing/word processing required for storing, retrieving and updating software documentation in configuration management.

Conversely, many mini- and microcomputer-based PSEs lack just these facilities, and may be adequate to support software development, at the levels of language and programming tools, whilst being inadequate to support the management of the process, or the policies for version release of the developed software. Both of these cases, the large

mainframe complex for administration applications and the dedicated PSE on a mini-computer, will be referred to in the note on economic justification below.

The current state of affairs in PSE usage can be summarized as comprising the following:

1. Self-hosted practice, i.e. use of the target machine facilities for software development. Facilities tend to fall into two vividly different types; very large operational mainframe systems whose PSE features may be specifically adequate for their application type; and nearly-naked micros corresponding to Boehm's 'low' or 'very low' categories. The first type of self-hosted system will serve a plurality of concurrent users; the second type will most likely be a one-on-one facility.
2. Independently hosted development systems, i.e. the use of minicomputer or mainframe facilities for software development; these are usually at the 'nominal' level on Boehm's scale of values, plus cross-tools and downline loaders if the PSE environment is to be used in software development for a variety of (for example) microcomputer target systems. Generically, because of this type of usage, such systems have become known as 'MDS' facilities – or microprocessor/microcomputer development systems. Originally (c. 1980–85) they were single user systems for small scale software development, using desk-top PC equipment. More recently, larger scale 'host' systems – fit for concurrent access by software teams – have appeared, and these are far more suitable for software development in general.

8.5.3 Ipse technology

Ipse development is a relatively recent subject involving, in principle at least, full management support, as well as sufficient PSE features for technical purposes, during software development. As recently as 1987 the need to distinguish Ipse features and properties from those of PSEs was noted:

> In particular, a clear distinction must be made between Ipse and, to coin a term Icse, where 'c' stands for coding. (Lehman and Turski 1987)

Those authors proceed to define an Ipse as:

> An embodiment of software technology in a collection of tools for capture, representation, transformation, control, refinement, and other manipulation of project [sic] related representation.

'Icse' means PSE in our terms, and the word 'project' here does not have our special meaning assigned in Chapter 3, to distinguish the specification and validation characteristics of product development from other types of software supply. In the quoted text 'project' is synonymous with software development.

In fact, the essentials in any approach to the problem of an electronic environment for managing software development are as follows:

1. Retention of information; we have already introduced the notion of an archive (to be discussed again in Section 11.2) and it is this, essentially, that serves as the information basis for an Ipse.

2. A software development paradigm (or model) that represents the process in some manageable form, electronic environment or not. A life cycle model such as that in Figure 4.2 – or as adapted between Figures 2.11 and 4.2 – is an instance of such a serviceable basis.
3. PSE features for software design, implementation and validation; configuration management facilities for maintenance and new release versions of software ('deliverable') documentation; see Section 13.1.
4. A management paradigm that incorporates;
   (a) activities' planning and control, including structured walkthrough techniques;
   (b) cost budgeting, and control;
   (c) quality procedures' management.

It is perfectly possible to envisage an electronic environment to support the management of a software development. We have already defined (or shortly will have completed definition of), items 1–3 on the list; item 4 is similarly furnished with some ease. The soundest 'management paradigm' is one based on a contract of supply. In this case, the 'deliverables' at identified stages of a life cycle model are taken as contractual supplies, whose authorization within the electronic development environment enables (or, if absent, disables) further software development within the Ipse. Thus, the practitioners of software development are regulated by the 'contract paradigm' and life cycle-based management features in the development environment.

In their paper, Lehman and Turski (1987) identify several properties of an Ipse which, amended here, comprise the following:

1. Models of software development and management paradigms (effectively 2 and 4 above).
2. A sufficiency of tools in respect of both models, e.g. for both purposes in 3 and 4 above.
3. The coherence and consistency of tools; in other words that they make up a system for use and not a disaggregated collection of units. For instance, that their inputs/outputs and linkages are formal and harmonized.
4. Conservation of information; in effect that all archives and/or deliverable documentation (both described elsewhere, in full, in this text) are preserved, unless specifically 'purged' by an accredited authority. This implies security of information as the means to its intended conservation and a process for evacuating unwanted information from the system.
5. It follows, from 3 particularly and 4 in part, that Ipse data must be structured – even (as Lehman et al. point out) multistructured; that is, interrelated in several ways.
6. An Ipse should be seen as an E software system, and its likely evolution should be a considerable factor in its design and implementation.
7. Ipse tools should be configurable so that they may be used in subset forms by exponents having different specific requirements. An Ipse, or its tools, should be distributable and portable – the former meaning 'over geographically separate computer installations', and the latter meaning 'over different virtual computer types'.

Not surprisingly, the main author of this paper has been closely associated with a major, successful Ipse development – Istar – and has described it (Lehman 1986). At the time of

writing, Istar is one of the few genuine Ipse developments, as distinct from 'upwardly' extended PSEs. By now, it is hoped, that distinction is clear to the reader. Istar incorporates a software life cycle and contract-based paradigm for software management, and its tools require the authorized completion of life cycle stages. The software development paradigm itself is based on Lehman's notions of a canonical design step, and stepwise transformation as a 'disciplined development process'.

The result is an impressive but costly system – or, better, a collection of system components. Istar is one of several promising developments in the Ipse field that incorporate (at least a 'normative') PSE. Other developments in Ipse technology include Eclipse and Aspect, two multi-source developments owing much to the initiative and funding of the British 'Alvey directorate', Smalltalk and Cedar in the USA, and important work in Europe and Japan. A synoptic account of these research and development endeavors follows.

ASPECT AND ECLIPSE

Aspect seems to be more of an architecture for Ipse developments than as Ipse in itself. For instance, its principal property is provided by an 'open tools interface' (OTI) to enable its host system tools to be invoked (Hall *et al.*, in McDermid 1985). Its host is Unix – so its effective tool-set is extended accordingly – and it aims to support all activities in software life cycle stages.

As well as an OTI, Aspect incorporates a 'public tools interface' (PTI) to enable other Ipse facilities, or those of a PSE, to be interfaced. In this respect, Aspect is a 'meta-Ipse' rather than a true one. Aspect's database approach is founded on work by Codd (1970) on relational databases, and its interfaces are specified in Z, although that language is not, as yet, supported.

Eclipse is a different approach again. Here, there is a strong emphasis on the definition of requirements as entities and relationships, and the use of a proprietary database system itself based on ERA (SD52) from one of the development partners – Software Sciences Ltd. The aim is to provide a 'permissive Ipse' that, rather like Aspect's open and public tools interfaces, is intended to allow large teams of distributed users, using disparate software development methods, to work within the same framework. Work-stations are developed to use Eclipse and, in what we have earlier identified as the PSE part, methods such as Mascot and JSD/JSP are supported. However, with all its generality of purpose, it is not so clear with Eclipse (nor with Aspect) quite how the 'management paradigm' aspect of an Ipse will be implemented.

CEDAR AND SMALLTALK-80

Lest this account seem too parochial to the UK, some comment is due on developments elsewhere. In the USA, much work (in fact most of the ongoing work worldwide, it must be said) has gone into Ada-related developments, such as the invention of Apses. The management features of software development are extensions of the PSE technology in effect. This not-too-healthy approach seems inevitable given the view of Glass, set out in Table 8.3. Under 'Management' we find slightly over 50 percent of listed systems have configuration management features for updating documentation sets relating to releases and versions of a software system. This is a surprisingly low proportion for so crucial a

feature – something close to 100 percent would have been expected, even at the beginning of this decade. If that is thought surprising, even worse is to follow; 'Project control' finds incorporation in only 25 percent of tool-sets listed.

A further evolution originating in Ada programming language development, and the emphasis placed on environments and tool-sets suitable for it, is the attempt to produce a common Apse interface set (CAIS). This, plus attempts to find ways of dealing with the problems of requirements' specification, e.g. via new paradigms such as 'object orientation', has occupied much development effort over the past half decade. An indication of the fundamental difference of emphasis between work going on in the USA and that undertaken elsewhere, such as that of Lehman, and others, as described, may be found in a paper by Deutsch (in McDermid 1985), under the general collection of papers at a conference on Ipses at the University of York, UK. The two papers in question describe different species of experimental work proceeding at the Xerox Corporation in Palo Alto. They may be generically named as Cedar and Smalltalk-80. Both highly interesting papers go on to discuss what can only be described as PSE or extended PSE systems, rather than Ipses in the discriminated sense of that term given here. Lest this comment be thought too censorious (after all, it mirrors one made earlier about the inclusion of Zave's (1984) paper in Gehani and McGettrich 1986), a short account of Cedar and Smalltalk-80 is given here for its relevance to the issue of support environments in general.

Cedar is an environment to facilitate experimental programming, that is programming with a higher incidence of quick changes to code than normal, and a need to re-establish a former status if need be. From that point of view its claim to Ipse properties is rather shallow, and is based on the fact that Cedar assists in making large numbers of small, incremental changes 'safely'. In that respect its features (including a 'safe language', the concept of 'interfacing' rather than 'implementing' and the notion of the use of the programming language as the sole source of truth about a program) are extremely interesting and useful extensions to the ideas of a PSE.

Much of the work centers on the use, from networked work-stations, of the Mesa language and tools to reduce error; compilation allows inspection of, but hopefully not ad lib interference with, the object-code file. For the rest, the 'management of incremental changes' comprises an extension of configuration management notions including the use of highly protected 'description files' of the contents of all files needed to compose a package.

Smalltalk-80 (a trademark of Xerox Corporation) is described in Deutsch's paper (in McDermid 1985). Here the environment is based on two main approaches. The first is an exploitation of current technology in the area of visual display – such as bit-mapping on a screen, and the use of interactive screen management via manual control ('mouse'); the second concerns the creation of tools to use at these work-stations, based on an object-oriented paradigm deriving originally from Simula-67.

Object-oriented programming, which is conceptually associated with object-oriented specification as described earlier, is a research topic, and is seen as an alternative to conventional programming methods in which features and functions in design are achieved by defining algorithms and data structures, and using the statement vocabulary of a given language to make the computer perform the algorithms on the data. In object-oriented programming, requirements are expressed in a textual from and a solution statement

derived from this, still in textual form. As summarized in Chapter 7, from this very high level design, abstract data types are defined using the noun occurrences in the specification as the means of classification. Verb and adverb structures are then used to define operators and data. The structure may then be depicted as a bubble and arrow diagram, very much akin to an entity relationship diagram, relating operators to operands and showing data flow and message passing in the system.

Smalltalk-80, as a system, is based on a formally specifiable, portable and virtual machine similar to the Pascal-P system. There is a Smalltalk-80 language, and implementations of its exist in APL, Lisp and Basic. There are 'version' (configuration) management features but, it would seem, little or nothing in the way of wider project costing, control and quality management for the full software engineering process, although there is a full archiving facility ('historical record').

From this point of view, Smalltalk-80 looks like a wonderfully interesting hobbyist programmer's toy – with splendid screen management, some useful tools including what is known as a 'browser', a window presenting a four level tree structure (being the only mechanism whereby a programmer normally writes code), debugger and so on.

Although dating from 1969 in some of its concepts, and commercially available since about 1983 and therefore well established in its technology maturation path, Smalltalk-80 has not yet revolutionized the world of software engineering as some of its enthusiasts predicted. The bit-mapped work-stations and open system nature of Smalltalk-80 make it a wonderfully attractive looking system. But the object-oriented paradigm for software development is not yet widely accepted for software development – and rather unlikely to become so in this author's view. This and the fact that Smalltalk seems suitable more for individual use than as the basis for team activity in software development stand against its general use as a tool.

OTHER WORK ON INTEGRATED ENVIRONMENTS

Other work merits mention, but space and the main purpose of this book militate against a complete review. One endeavor – the portable common tools environment (PCTE), an ECC initiative between computer manufacturers in Western Europe – is approaching fruition. It is also generating some concern between Nato allies to ensure that it may be successfully interfaced with Apse/CAIS developments in the USA. As with the babel of languages referred to earlier, we face a kaleidoscope of environments and the different tools and methods they support.

Of other possible sources of evolution, principally Japan and its central research endeavor to produce a 'fifth generation computer architecture', with new programming paradigms, and the development of 'intelligent' tools, little is heard as yet – apart from the sort of rumors of travail that make professional pessimists chuckle. Initiatives such as the British 'transputer' and the language Occam have had some local success, without ever coming near, as yet, to the original *réclame* which seemed, for the transputer architecture, to suggest far more than just the cleverly networked minicomputers that make it up.

Evolutions are best proclaimed after their results. Some endeavors ascend like a rocket, and come down like the stick.

In the background of all this there looms the economic question. When all the Apses and PCTEs are up and flying, and all the Istars are twinkling in the firmament and Small-

talking is breaking out all over the place, will they be within the financial means of most employers of software engineers? That is, as they say, the 64 thousand dollar question – or perhaps twenty times that amount if one is not careful.

8.5.4 Deciding on an environment

In my travels I have found that the acquisition of support environments comes about as a result of two countervailing forces, the initiative in the first place usually being found in one specifically. These forces may be roughly described as the following:

1. Practitioner's discontent with a status quo environment (or lack of one) for software development.
2. Manager's innocence of the need (a euphemism) and their innate caution (another euphemism).

The original initiative for, say, an improved PSE, or a multi-user concurrent access MDS, or whatever the issue is, generally originates in 1. That is in cases where software engineers have been struggling away with inadequate tools for long enough to become frustrated, and say so. Elsewhere – amongst amateur programmers say, electronic engineers perhaps, who only program intermittently – there is a tendency to demean software environments, tools and even some high level languages, as though they were symptoms of weakness or moral decay. Then, generally very late in the day, management bestirs itself and the issue of a support environment is promulgated 'top down' in organization terms.

We have seen (Table 8.2) how PSE facilities can be viewed on a scale of values from 'very low' to 'very high'. The two sides in a process of determining PSE requirements tend, not unnaturally, to take rather different stances to each other on the matter of need. The malcontents on the shopfloor tend to see their irreducible PSE requirements toward the higher end of the scale, whilst managers (with that natural gift for spotting impending cost) incline to the lower end of Boehm's scale. Often the two viewpoints are not too far apart; but sometimes they are light-years distant from each other. A typical instance is when the community of software engineers fixes its interest on a particular system and its alluring features, whilst 'management' draws an arbitrary finanical limit at some level which – by accident and in retrospect – turns out to be less than 25 percent of the cost of the miraculous system. Compromise, in these circumstances, is far from easy to achieve. Both 'sides' end up disgruntled.

Of course, in a well regulated world, there would be no 'sides' or 'factions'. But this is life; in fact – worse from the viewpoint of human behavior – it is Business Life.

The problem is exacerbated by there being very few analytical means to deploy in its solution. The usual rationalization is to appoint a study group to, well, study the problem – to analyze the requirements (for a PSE), review the options in supply, evaluate the benefits to accrue from the various options, and then to do a cost/benefit analysis and draw from it a recommended course of action.

All this sounds splendid! The drawbacks are that 'requirements' are very difficult to formulate at the level of real need – above the most obvious elements of a 'very low' level of PSE, the sort of rudimentary features without which the equipment is unprogrammable

and – therefore – useless. It is always possible to get a 'wish-list' of desiderata, in fact it may be difficult to contain the flow of wants, likes and dislikes once it starts; half a dozen different design procedures (all implemented), eight programming languages, a full Apse with a CAIS 'open gateway' for all new tools from everywhere, and of course Smalltalk work-stations with mice running all over the place. . . .

A more reasonable approach to this technologist's bonanza would be based on a close perusal of all the 'tools' taxonomies', from outline systems design exercises done over previous years, for products and projects that were developed, or perhaps not done due to a lack of means. This always assumes that OSD exercises have taken place in the past. Is that the case in your company?

Then, as if all this was not enough, when it comes to an evaluation of benefits the same problem occurs from another angle. How do we quantify the benefits? The only answer would seem to be 'judgmentally', by assertions such as 'using the Maniac system will increase programmer productivity/improve quality/allow us to do version (configuration) management'. Of these, only the last is reasonably provable, although all of them may well be true. Even proving the effects *ex post facto* is fraught with the greatest difficulty. Everyone may be deleriously happy with Maniac, five years after installing it, but it may well be that nobody knows exactly why. Finding out that, say, productivity (measured in source statements of code per programmer-day for working systems) may have gone up by 100, 200, . . . 1,000 percent is one thing; but saying, categorically, that this is due to Maniac is to overlook a variety of other possible causes, let alone the fact that ten times an abysmal number may still be a lamentable one.

Acquiring improved support environments is usually an act of faith brought about by some urgencies that can be articulated (and usually are) but cannot be proved. The elements already identified are usually conclusive, if pressed properly as argument:

1. Improvements in *real* productivity, i.e. the ratio of statements of high quality code in a working system to the effort to make it. It is asserted (Boehm 1983) that the effect of a 'very high' level PSE over a 'normative' one is about 50 percent additional productivity – although it is far from clear how any such isolated effect could be evaluated in practice.
2. Improvements in the quality of software systems. As will be seen, this too is easy to assert and – short of some metrics for software quality – difficult to demonstrate. It usually comes down to an evaluation of fault incidence of particular frequency and severity – the latter being 'measured' by the effort to fix an error, factored in some way by the familiarity of the maintenance staff with the software.
3. Improvements in post-installation service through the configuration control and management system in a PSE, if any (see Table 8.3).

A phase is then gone through in which, basically, the features of available systems are matched against the software engineers' wish-lists, with the latter subjected to stringent enquiry to determine reasonableness and economic justification. Then the competing products are investigated for performance with questions of the following type: 'How many concurrent users *for software development* will the Maniac hardware plus software support – on average and approximately?' If the answer is fifty and your company has only half a man, a boy and a dog doing software development then one might suspect that

Maniac is a bit over-configured for the purpose – whilst always reserving against the productivity of the dog. If the answer is, say, twelve to fifteen and you have a department of seventeen due to grow to twenty-seven over the next two years, then Maniac may still not be the right answer (or at least one Maniac might not be – you may end up with a veritable asylum of them if the software activities in the firm grow like Topsy).

A major mistake to avoid when trying to justify a PSE configuration is that of admixture of usage without regard for the possible interactive effects. Such a dramatic example concerned the justification of a Digital VAX-780 system operating VMS for a software development group of about thirty people. Problem 2 of earlier reference occurred, and management first of all adopted the unpleasing posture of a fetal crouch – possibly sucking its thumb at the same time. Eventually, though, the position was established, and the system procured. But it was for software development *plus* CAD usage, the latter for a large department of people doing design of mechanical and electrical systems.

Woe and calamity! CAD systems are very greedy when it comes to processing and, lo, twice a day every day the system performance degraded in a most noticeable way. Software development staff could be seen, puce in the face with rage, waiting at terminals for responses to commands that were taking five, ten and even up to twenty minutes to return. Staff from the two departments would not even sit together in the lunchroom, and one promising love-affair foundered on rather different matters of respone-time than usual.

Beware the effects of different types of usage for which a software development support environment may be required. Our example concerned CAD; it could easily have been a hundred and one other applications whose effects brought ruin (twice a day) to the software department.

The perceptive reader will have noticed, throughout this section on choice of an environment, that we have labored the question from one viewpoint only – namely that of the *subset* PSE facilities, of what might be thought to make up an environment. What of the management features? What of the 'strong paradigm' for development, such as contract form based on life cycle-stage 'deliverables'? It is an eloquent comment on the state of affairs in this world of Ipse/PSE technology, that PSEs are at their stage of the acceptance/adoption gestation period where it is very possible to pose the question of choice meaningfully. The same will, no doubt, be the case for Ipses in the period 1995–2000.

In the meantime, the embattled manager will have to struggle on, somewhat disenfranchized from the 'total electronic' world of software development. Most seriously, this will lead to a preservation of that gap between managers and managed that formed the basis of our earlier strictures, and which will form the backdrop for Part III – software management. Meanwhile, it is time to go on with our main topic here – implementation; in particular how the authors of programs test their programs.

8.6 PROGRAM AND SOFTWARE TESTING

Here we refer to the testing of programs and software by their authors, as distinct from the testing done by others, as may be the case for different parts of quality determination.

Author and author-team based testing are collectively known as 'author testing', and are part of quality compliance and modifiability.

Both program proving and testing techniques by authors of code concern the compliance of the programs. Do they 'fit' with specifications of purpose? Neither says much about modifiability. In the case of testing, this is because the modifiability must be assessed from the viewpoint of people less familiar with it than its authors. However, establishing compliance is important enough for us as a first step. At the implementation stage, we proceed with that as our main imperative.

8.6.1 Proving versus testing as approaches to software compliance

It is beyond the scope of this work to go deeply into the argument of testing versus proving, and the following points are offered as a synoptic review of the present (and likely future) situation. Anyway, we have already touched on the subject peripherally at several stages already, particularly concerning the use of abstract 'formal' methods, and the notions of stepwise computations of 'correctness' in a process of transformations. However, here is the place for a review of the topic, as it stands in contradistinction to testing:

> Testing can show the presence, but never the absence of errors in software

This famous aphorism (Dijkstra, in Buxton *et al.* 1969) appears to denigrate testing. However, in the absence of any real, viable, alternative it will take on another significance entirely. Proving anything (that is in subjects such as mathematics, physics, accounting, law and a very wide variety of others) concerns the formal derivation of a post-condition from a pre-condition. The pre-condition may contain conventions (axioms, lemmas, etc.) that must be stated; the derivation method may contain rules (such as those of logical inference) that must also be stated; all will be circumscribed by language, which may be natural language or some functional notation (an algebra, predicate calculus notation, etc.). In this context, 'proving' concerns programs or their component parts – integrands as we have called them. For semantic simplicity we will refer to both as 'programs' here.

The pre-conditions of a program or part of a program may be seen as its first state, and may be expressed in terms of input and parameter values, the condition of logical operators and so on. The post-condition may be said to be its final state and may be expressed in terms of its output and final parameter values, the condition of logical operators, etc., in the same fashion as before. The precondition must itself be true, and the demonstration of the post-condition's truth is with respect to its asserted values. A proof of total correctness concerns its demonstration by formal means.

In practice, two aspects of total correctness are generally considered. First there is the proof of partial correctness, whereby the state of a program, given that it terminates, is demonstrated by formal means to be inevitably that of the post-condition; and the proof of termination, which demonstrates by formal means whether or not a program will terminate.

Proof of partial correctness is generally based on sets of intermediate assertions within a program, for each of which a pre- and post-condition can be stated. These assertions are

the particles within a program – statements or clumps of statements – in which some particular operation is taking place. Often, the formal demonstration of a particle of some program involves the question of termination of an internal loop and the consistency of its internal functioning. This latter concerns, in turn, a further level of intermediate assertions within the loop, and these are called the loop invariants in a particular case.

The formal demonstration that a program commencing from a true pre-condition arrives ('terminates') at a true post-condition involves the rules of formal logic. These, and their immediate application in a case, must be 'true' also, i.e. valid in their own right, and used consistently on the program statements. This formal demonstration of method is called verification, and automatic (i.e. programmed) verifiers for proof methods exist.

Several questions immediately suggest themselves. The first, and most obvious, is the question 'what relationship is there between the status of a program (i.e. 'proved') and its status as software, given our earlier definition of the distinction?' The answer is – virtually none. Program proving produces, at most, proven programs. It does not say anything about their status or behavior as software that is not heavily contingent on a set of extraneous but associated factors, such as the behavior of the 'virtual' equipment, and the behavior of other programs in the suite.

Of course, we may believe with good reason that a proven program (in the formal sense) will be likely to contain few, very few or even no programming errors with respect to its specifications – and that would be a distinctly helpful and confidence-enhancing thing to know. However, it may not be inferred that – as software – the programs will always execute successfully, will not corrupt each other, will be defensive in the face of random and accidental extraneous effects, and so on. The dynamic behavior of software may be vastly different from its apparent static properties as programs.

Another question that arises is, who verifies the verifier, and verifies the verifier–verifier, and so on? Like the famous rhyme: 'Dogs have little fleas, upon their backs to bite 'em; the little fleas have lesser fleas, and so *ad infinitum*'. The answer is, of course, that proof is essentially a social (peer-group) process in any subject (Perlis *et al.* 1979). This is no great surprise, as it has become well known in physics (after Einstein and Heisenberg) and in mathematics (after Gödel) that categorical statements, and their unqualified proofs in the areas concerned, may not be possible. Program proving programs are, indisputably, programs, and as such will require proving. It is not easy to see a way out of this problem for the subject of formal correctness proofs in computer programming. That limits certainty in our subject. However, it is reasonable to say that program proving, where it can be done, is an alternative to testing as a means of validation by demonstration, for increasing one's *confidence*, albeit in a highly contingent and therefore qualified fashion.

However, another little problem is deeply hidden in an earlier sentence; the precondition of a program (or particle of it for proof of intermediate assertions) must be 'true'. Now in this case 'truth' concerns a set of identifiable properties of the first state that can be extracted from the *program* specification. Thus, any proving of a program or particle of it will be an entirely local matter within implementation – and may or may not, therefore, have bearing on the requirement. For what happens if the transformation from requirement to program, via design, has deviated from the specification of requirements? Or what, for that matter, if the requirements themselves were wrong ('untrue')?

In the light of all this, an earlier, and very alliterative sentence can now be extended;

program proving produces proven programs ... that may or may not fit real (and themselves 'true') requirements. To get round this, formal specification languages have been proposed that – via 'canonical steps' in transformation – will produce programs which, when the transformation process has been computably verified, will be said to be *a fortiori* correct with respect to requirements.

On any meaningful scale of usefulness in software engineering, this prospect is a distant one – for reasons set out in Section 3.3. The entirely local program-proving at implementation level is of more likely and immediate use, in my view – particularly as a discipline in static testing of software by inspection (see below) – for purposes such as investigating loop invariants in code.

8.6.2 Software testing by its authors as a part of implementation

That leaves us with the alternative – program and software testing. And here we must revive the aphorism quoted earlier: 'Testing can show the presence, but never the absence of errors in software' to which one would add? '... and it jolly well better had do!'

Testing, with some small additions from the field of program proving (but seen within testing nonetheless) is the 'classical' method of determining the positive virtues of software – such as, does it work, and will it be likely to go on doing so? There have been times, up to quite recently in fact, when software testing was a very makeshift affair – and it still may be in many places. Where that happens it is a severe weakness, potentially catastrophic to the outcome, and should be corrected.

There are three prerequisites for good testing, seldom found in ideal combination:

1. Adequate staff – i.e. quantitatively and qualitatively, with the latter subsuming knowledge and use of good testing practices.
2. Adequate support facilities – i.e. as in PSE tools.
3. Adequate time.

'Ah!', I can her the embittered software engineer say, 'when did we ever have adequate time?'

Before proceeding, there are many matters of definition that we must resolve. First and foremost is the issue of documentation. It is already clear that a code listing is a necessary level of definition and description of a program, but it is not sufficient, in itself, to be the software documentation. This, the necessary and sufficient level, is called the deliverable documentation of a software system, as it may be a contractual requisite. It is described in Section 13.1. Clearly, this software documentation cannot be excepted from testing.

As to testing practices, these fall into six categories: (a) author; (b) adversary; (c) static; (d) dynamic; (e) top down; and (f) bottom up. Either of both of (a) or (b) may perform either or both of (c) or (d). The practices (e) and (f) concern software integration and its testing.

AUTHOR AND ADVERSARY TESTING

Author-level testing means, literally, if you wrote the code, you test it. If you have written several elements (e.g. programs or integrands, or both) then you still test it, by static and

dynamic means, in its disaggregated units. You then proceed by progressive integration of elements (if they are intended to fit), up to a required level of aggregation. If there is more than one author, the integration process will involve multi-author testing (again static and dynamic).

Adversary testing means that someone, other than the author of the code, tests it. Members of the same author-team doing static, adversarial tests on each other's code are performing a quality control function known as 'code reading'.

When adversarial testing is done (at static or dynamic levels), by non-author-team persons, hopefully software specialists themselves, then this is part of quality assurance; it is dealt with in Chapter 9. It is unusual for author-team's adversarial testing of each other's code to include dynamic tests, excepting cases of software integration (X integrating the programs of self and Y), or contingencies such as arise when staff are unavailable.

STATIC AND DYNAMIC TESTING

Static testing is the inspection of program code, including the use of approaches from program proving, such as establishing loop termination and loop invariant properties. This should take place by authors, and author-team adversaries, as part of quality control; it should also be undertaken by 'independent' agents in software quality assurance. Static testing should not be confused with simple checking of the program language syntax – most adequate compilers and assemblers will do that. Static testing, when done properly, owes much to the notions from formal methods of pre- and post-conditions, and the intermediate proof assertions for program statements or particles. In this case, the posited pre-conditions are traced, by inspection, though the particle, and the plausibility of the outcome (post-condition) is judged.

Dynamic testing is attempting to execute ('operate' or 'run') the program code on its target computer. It is undertaken by authors, author-teams during integration, and 'adversaries' during quality assurance. Two main aspects require mention: (a) a test plan is required, so that dynamic testing does not proceed illogically or in a haphazard, unpurposeful way; and (b) a test strategy is required, concerning how test environments and data will be arranged for the dynamic testing. The first of these, a test plan, can be determined (and should be) from late stages of design onwards – perhaps earlier in some cases – when the software modularity is known with certainty. If should take the form of an activities' netplan with resource allocation.

INTEGRATION TESTING 'TOP DOWN' OR 'BOTTOM UP'

Test strategies for integration may be viewed as 'top down' or 'bottom up', or some mixture of the two. In the first, a test-frame is made early in the design stage of the life cycle to be ready at the time implementation begins. It may be seen as a framework to discharge two purposes in top down testing:

1. To allow (or even generate) plausible input as from the outside, or 'exogenous', world, and to route it to appropriate parts of the framework.
2. To provide dummy (or 'stub') routines within the framework, that will be a simple reflection of, or will reply in some form to, stimuli.

As real programs come into existence, they will be author-tested in relative isolation to

other programs (the disaggregated testing), by static and dynamic means. Then they will be entered into the framework to replace 'stubs'. As more and more stubs are replaced, the test framework takes on the appearance of the system-to-be, and its exogenous inputs must be made to mirror the real-world operating environment. Figure 8.6 depicts a top down testing scheme.

Bottom up testing proceeds, via the author's testing of units – programs or integrands – in their disaggregated form, through progressive stage of planned integration. At each stage, a parochial test environment is created until, in the later stages of integration, this becomes a highly complex and comprehensive environment as in the top down method. Figure 8.7 shows this build-up.

The art of making software systems that really work, and can be seen to do so, is the art of modularity. One must design for a modular construction, implement a modular contruc-

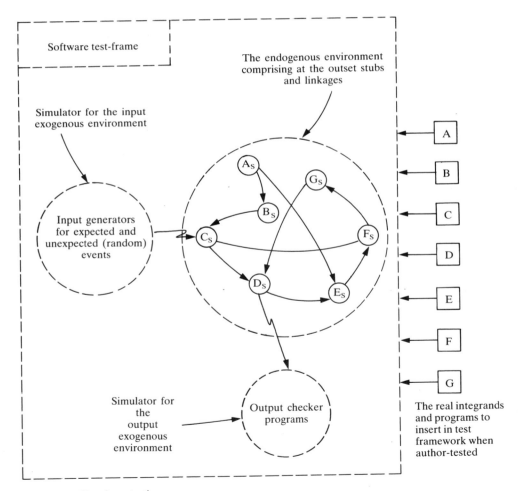

FIGURE 8.6 Top down testing.

tion, and test it in a modular fashion. The aphorism 'build a bit, test a bit; build a bit more, test a bit more' applies equally to top down and bottom up strategies.

The perils of monolithic construction (e.g. one huge program) are obvious. A less obvious problem is if tests of modular software components are undertaken in a monolithic fashion. This can be envisaged by omitting intermediate steps in the bottom up process, and trying to test all software modules together without any prior stepwise integration; a bit of author-based program testing and then – wham! Bung it all together, fire it all into the computer and have one glorious test. And have one glorious shambles too, for this nefarious practice – popularly known as 'big bang' testing – propels the untested software into a truly gigantic behavior space. As in cosmology, 'big bangs' cause 'black holes' – in this case

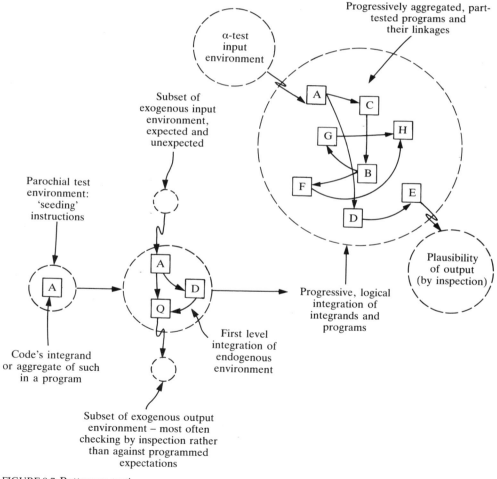

FIGURE 8.7 Bottom up testing.

down which large amounts of effort and money disappear, as though past a Schwartzchild radius, beyond view, beyond recall.

Dynamic testing starts at a small scale level then, with authors testing their own integrands and programs piecemeal. These tests involve the seeding of integrands or programs with trace instructions and test data. In effect this sets the pre-condition for a particle of a program or integrand, and the trace approximates to the means of demonstrating a very local 'correctness'.

When this level of dynamic testing is complete, that is, when the author thinks the thing works so far as can be seen in isolation, then the seeding instructions are removed, and the program (or integrand) proceeds to the next level of test. This will be a rational process of integration and accretion into larger assemblies with, at each stage, the same sort of testing techniques deployed by authors as in the case of testing individual integrands.

ALPHA-TEST AND THE STATUS OF 'BENEVOLENTLY' TESTED SOFTWARE

At the culmination of integration, either within a 'top down' framework or a 'bottom up' test environment in its final stage of evolution, a comprehensive test is made on the complete system – incorporating all hardware units as well. This is known as the alpha-test, and is a very significant feature in quality control. At this time, also, the software documentation must be complete; it must also be incorporated in the alpha-test – done by the authors (or some subset of authors) of the software. Any variation between software behavior and the documentation must be seen as a software error in general, even if the resulting change is made to the documentation and not the software; remember – the documentation is an inseparable part of the software, not merely of the programs. That this slightly contradicts the earlier definition of software as the dynamic state of programs is unfortunate but inescapable. Software *is* the dynamic state of programs, plus this extremely static depiction – documentation – of the software's most static state – programs!

Author, and author-team, based testing is said to be 'benevolent'. This is for a very simple reason in what may loosely be termed 'behavioral psychology'. It does not infer that independent or adversarial tests in quality assurance are 'malevolent' – although I have known some unlovely examples of that lack of human charity enter into affairs.

The point is that testing one's own creation is beset by two intrinsic difficulties – or, better, immanent disabilities in the author/tester:

1. The instinct or urge to show that one's own creation works.
2. The tendency to incorporate in the testing process exactly the same defect as one committed in the construction in the first place.

The word for this is 'subjectivity'. It is not a crime or a sin. People who have letters typed miss 'typos' for these reasons; people who write books make poor reviewers of them.

In life cycle terms, from the time in implementation when code starts to exist until the alpha-tests on software including its documentation are complete, the process being undertaken by the authors is 'benevolent'. We shall progress, in the next part, to the other forms of testing. But here it is enough to say that benevolent testing is necessary but not, on its own, sufficient.

Necessity and sufficiency are what we are to aim for. Benevolent, or subjective, testing is

generally a substantial part of implementation. As we said earlier, the notional 15 percent of total life cycle effort attributable (on average) to implementation – meaning coding and author-based testing of program units – becomes 25–30 percent when all the essential elements of author-team testing up to alpha-test level are incorporated.

This is a part, but only a part, of *quality control*.

CHAPTER NINE

SOFTWARE QUALITY

Apart from some programs written as the object of research of one form or another, software quality is the whole of the issue in software engineering.

It is already clear, from the earlier text, that quality is a complex issue in any subject, with two mutually interacting components – those concerning economic factors such as: 'Is the development within cost and time limits that make it worthwhile?', and the technical issues like: 'Does it work as required; will it go on doing so; will it be clear if it does not go on working properly; can one change it with confidence?'

The modalities of managing economic aspects of software development are detailed in Chapters 12 and 13.

The current chapter deals with issues of technical quality, specifically the following:

1. Quality criteria, and associated definitions for quality control, inspection and acceptance and for verification, validation and certification.
2. Measurement and metrics in software quality. We are found to be in an unenviable state in which our artefacts, that often are components in systems whose failure would be catastrophic in some way, can be subject to no agreed rules of mensuration to assess crucial aspects of quality, such as: the real degree of 'fit' with requirements; intrinsic 'strength', or reliability, in operating circumstances outside the bounds of expectation; and relative ease to repair or improve.

How, then, for this most important topic of all, are we to proceed?

Many of the management issues of software quality, for its achievement in the first place and preservation thereafter, will be dealt with in Chapter 13. We are concerned here with the definition of concepts and the description of technical means in the subject.

Software quality is another of software engineering's Cinderella subjects. As one reviewer said 'it is nobody's favorite'. Too often it is seen as an activity at the very bottom end of the life cycle, just before delivery of a software system under whatever terms, an

afterthought as though to say: 'Wait a bit, we'd better make sure this rubbish really does work'. I have known this called 'end control', and have seen departments whose sole job it was (is!) to take delivery of a system that has been tested by its authors, so far as possible, and in some palpably insufficient time before a contract deadline – sometimes, even, a negative time in those terms. 'End control's' job was then to authenticate the software, and authorize its release to a client. The results were predictable in several respects.

First of all the task, to be done at all, needed so much preparatory work in the quality department itself that either: (a) it was done inadequately but in time, (b) it was done more or less adequately but outside the allowable duration for it, or (c) it was done inadequately and outside the time-scale.

There are no prizes for guessing which of these sad options occurred most frequently. Then the managers sat up! And when they did so, they tended to regard the quality group doing the 'end control' with disfavor, as though their efforts were so much time wasted in trying to fault their colleagues. The quality group growled at the implementation department, where software engineers (to whom this was all a way of life – and that is the saddest part) whistled insouciently and filled in another job application form. The commercial department, that had sold the job over a weight of the most virulent commercial competition (and, perhaps, over a considerable weight of luncheon at the same time) said rather little; the 'quality of sale' aspect had not really occurred to them.

This simple anecdote, not apocryphal by any means but being enacted a thousand and one times as you read this, has hinted at a rich variety of problems. We will let it lapse now, in favor of a treatment of the Cinderella subject itself.

Software quality depends on the criteria by which it is judged. Set those incorrectly, and the outcome will be meaningless. To take a trivial example, if we deludedly think that the only acme of virtue for a CAISSA chess-playing system is its size, then a team that writes 10,000 source statements of code for it will have done a better job than one that made it in 5,000 – exactly twice as good a job in fact. That is total nonsense of course, but it indicates a point; it unintentionally exposes another one too. In the case given, we can at least *measure* the property of CAISSA against the metric. What happens if we have a criterion for software quality and no objective means of determining the property of the system in that respect. 'Ah, my friends', says Mr Chadband in the Dickens story, 'consider the birds of the air and how they soar. Why can we not soar?' To which Mr Jellaby replies, 'No wings' – thereby demonstrating the point perfectly.

In the following treatment of this subject, we will discuss – in summary of course, as this is but a presentation of concepts and definitions – the following, three issues in software quality:

Criteria
Metrics
Methods.

A section is devoted to each of these, and the reader is again reminded that the economic issues of quality are dealt with in Chapter 12, whereas management considerations, such as a quality plan and manual, are to be found in Chapter 13. The briefest survey of the three topics is given here, such as the definitions of quality control, inspection and assurance as

software engineering procedures, and verification, validation and certification as software quality states.

9.1 CRITERIA FOR SOFTWARE QUALITY, AND OTHER DEFINITIONS

Not so long ago, I polled an audience on a software managers' course with the simple question, loaded as it was with furtive cunning: 'What properties of a software system, if present, would – in your view – add to its quality? You may list as many as you wish, rank them in decreasing order of importance, and assign any weight you want to each one, in the range 1–10 (1 being least, and 10 being most important). You may give the same weight to several, or all, if you wish'. The winner, by a convincing margin was 'reliability', expressed in different ways by different people but indisputably reliability nonetheless.

I have played this game elsewhere and amongst different audiences, such as hardware engineers, software purchasing officers, and software engineers themselves. Sometimes there is no 'winner', but a group of roughly equally weighted desiderata. On other occasions there has been a sectorial interest expressed – such as 'cost-effective' (guess which group), 'works' (software engineers usually), or 'really works' (the hardware engineers, this). On all occasions, 'reliability' has featured high on the list, as of course it must do when one thinks about it.

What has also been the case, and this is true of the subject literature also, is that the listed factors tend to become confused, with admixture of the primary quality criteria, optional issues, means and methods, and even some items that have little relevance to software. The following is a list of just some of the entries and, lest it be thought unfair to quote the innocent, let it be remembered that some of the subject literature is little better. Software, we are told, should be: Modular; according to specification; portable; cost effective; flexible; well documented; maintainable; reliable; readable; reusable; on time; efficient; strong; usable; .... Even more interesting was the debate that followed my poll of opinions, with a ranked and (average) weighted list written on an overhead transparency. I have presided over some very good-natured and wonderfully useful discussions in the education sense – my own not least.

What invariably emerges is the perceived need to categorize desiderata and, closely following this realization, a differentiation of the mandatory from the optional, and a discrimination of ends from the means by which they are achieved. Take, for example, the list given above. Modularity is a means to an end, good design, and good design is a means to two ends in itself. First, the demonstration by testing that the software does what it is supposed to do (for badly designed software may tend to show divergence in a process of diagnostic testing and correcting); and second, the relative ease by which the software may be changed for whatever reason.

Then, also, the realization dawns that there are two aspects of quality, as we have already pointed out elsewhere; technical quality, of which we are speaking here, and economic quality which we shall discuss in Chapter 12. They tend to be mutually interfering, in the sense that too great an occupation with the one might adversely affect the

other. Also, a conflation of the two does not imply 'cost-effectiveness' since that concerns consideration of need in the application domain as well.

9.1.1 The mandatory criteria for technical quality

There are, in fact, two mandatory criteria for technical quality of a software system – and these two subsume a third one between them:

1. Compliance, and its continuation.
2. Modifiability, and the minimal potential depletion of both (or either) 1 and 2, as a result of modifications.

These are rather extensive and complicated issues. Clearly they are related in some way. For instance, in low quality software we might have a high degree of compliance by the time we have finished the subjective, author-based stage, but the software may be very difficult to modify without drastically reducing complicance, and reducing (or destroying entirely) our confidence in its future modifiability as well. The converse case, in which a software system has a low compliance for some reason but is so well made that it is relatively safe and easy to modify it, at least holds out the hope that one can – by successive modifications most carefully effected – improve the compliance without depleting the modifiability.

This is, in most cases, the state of affairs during integration, and integration testing. Where the modifiability is low, and compliance too is low through the existence of categorical error in the software, integration testing can become a highly divergent affair, with corrected errors apparently generating rather than revealing other errors. Compliance and modifiability, and their interrelationship and subsumed properties, are the mandatory criteria. We discuss each one further below. First though, we need to understand the 'interrelationship and subsumed properties' in a little more detail.

By compliance we mean that the software works according to its functional specification, and that if left unaltered it will go on doing so. As we have already seen, this will be a matter of confidence rather than categorical proof, but we can take this definition of compliance as being reasonably clear. The property of continuation in compliance may be said to be its reliability of performance, or 'static' reliability. Modifiability is the property of a software system to allow its change, give adequate technical facilities and people, with relative ease and safety (both of these words needing amplification), and without depleting either its compliance or future modifiability. The latter may be said to be its reliability in change, or its 'dynamic' reliability.

Thus, we have two components of reliability each one of which is subsumed in a mandatory criterion; furthermore, they overlap and interact. This interaction is depicted in Figure 9.1. A and B are points on an imaginary scale of values for composite reliability. A is a datum point for reliability of performance, and B is a similar 'value' for reliability in change. The potential effects of each component of reliability on the mandatory criteria are shown by arrows. In some cases, the 'uncompliant' performance of a software system may progressively deplete its own structure and, thereby, its current and future modifiability. Moreover, the notion of a 'first state' for software, which can always be resumed by

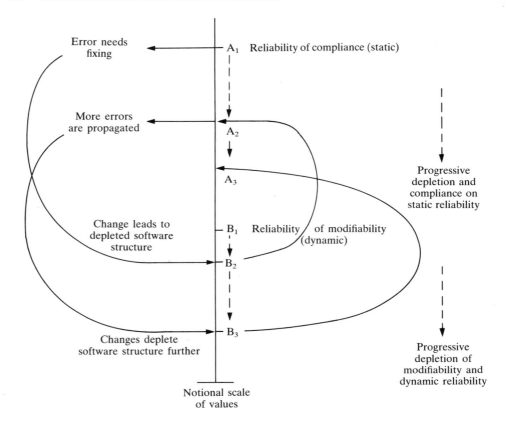

FIGURE 9.1 Reliability relationships in software.

just reloading programs and repeating their execution is not the whole of the case. Some software systems – particularly in the 'real-time' sector of applications – operate in so dynamic an environment that a particular 'state' may not be recreated by simply reloading programs in their 'first state'. This accounts for the connection between A and B entries in Figure 9.1.

The whole topic of technical quality of software is a slippery subject, as we have seen. Classification with clarification will take us some of the way toward grasping it – but it will still, for some people, be a subject that tends to shoot from one's firm grip like a piece of wet soap.

Knowing what the mandatory criteria are will help. Of the two of these, it is far easier to speak with certainty about compliance than it is about modifiability. Compliance refers to the 'hard' requirements embodied in a functional specification – and it behoves us to ensure the quality of that document accordingly. It bears repeating here how unwise it is to incorporate vague (or 'soft') statements in that document. If a desired property is not

demonstratable it should not be written into the functional specification. Typical instances are 'portable', 'efficient' and both 'modifiable' and 'reliable'. This point will be revisited below.

Many people begin to have great difficulty grasping the piece of wet soap at this point, not least electronic engineers, whose views on software in general – and on this aspect of software engineering in particular – are derived from a seductive premise that is, sadly, wrong. They tend to think that software is like hardware. We will not repeat all the arguments here, there having been much said on the subject in earlier chapters. But one fundamental respect in which the two are different is in the matter of reliability.

Hardware components, mechanical and electrical can be evaluated, even rated on numerical scales, for their reliability. Engineers do component testing to determine the failure rate and average lifespan of components, and the results will be true (on average) for all components of that type. There is no real analogy for this in software. The nearest one gets to it is in wide-scale system usage (note, of *systems* and not of individual components). Examples are popular language translators, operating systems and other 'parts' of the virtual machine software. In these cases, there may be a thousand, ten thousand or one hundred thousand users, all exercising the software in possibly dissimilar ways and to varying degrees.

On these occasions we observe another intrinsic difference with hardware. Mechanical and electronic components tend to wear out with use or, in some cases, just through the passage of time and the slow effects of chemical change perhaps. Software cannot wear out, although the hardware on which it works or is stored may do so. In the sense in which its errors are detected and corrected, good quality software 'wears in'. That is, it becomes more dependable over time – or should do so if (a) it is being exercised strenuously over the period concerned, (b) it is well made in the first place, and (c) its errors are detected and corrected competently. This intrinsic difference between hardware and software behavior is depicted in Figure 9.2. Once again it must be stressed that time, as in Figure 9.2, must be qualified. For software at least, 'time', in this sense, is a duration during which the system, including its software, is being extensively used in its most exacting circumstances.

The compliance component of software quality arises from, and is demonstrated in the first place by, testing it rigorously against its specifications. As we have seen, in Chapter 8, this begins at a very parochial (and subjective) level when authors test the integrands and programs they have made. This subjective level of testing by the authors of the software, culminates in what is called an alpha-test of the system – hardware and software in many cases.

Clearly, a *sine qua non* for this and other levels of demonstration is that the specifications are adequate for this purpose. This should direct the reader's attention, yet again, to the extended section on specification in this volume and, for further detail and demonstration, to Volume 2 of this series. The functional specification should contain all 'hard' requirements, i.e. mandatory ones, stated in terms that can be demonstrated. A requirement stated in non-demonstrable terms becomes a 'soft' requirement whether that is the intention or not. Thus, all generalities and normative expressions of the following type become 'soft' requirements: 'The software must be portable, efficient, extensible, modifiable [*sic*], flexible, reliable [*sic*], well made, maintainable'; and a whole variety of such.

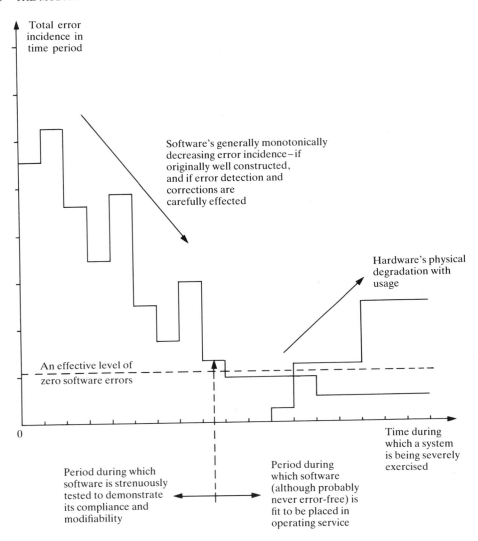

FIGURE 9.2 Hardware and software incidence with usage.

They are meaningless when it comes to determining compliance. Specific utterances –
where these can be made – such as: 'Portable to an XYZ computer, operating ABC system
and language, and having PQR capacities and ancillaries' is a hard requirement.

The modifiability criterion of software quality arises from good design in the first place,
and is demonstrated up to a point by the author-team's subjective, static tests of the design
and implemented code. The first of these, done in the design stage itself, is called design
review; the second, done in the implementation stage, is known as code reading.

The object of both design review and code reading is the internal quality control of the software during its development, and performs two functions:

1. Increased early detection/correction of errors.
2. Improved program structure.

However, it is undoubtedly the case that, in the integration and alpha-testing stages, the demonstration of modifiability most often takes a very subsidiary position to that of compliance – more is the pity!

9.1.2 Definitions of quality processes and states

There are several ways to look at quality control, inspection and assurance – and more than a few ways of referring to them. We define the terms as follows:

1. Quality control (QC) is the subjective attempt by the author/author-team, and by whatever means available during software development, to enhance the quality of software in terms of both of its mandatory quality criteria. This means that, throughout the life cycle – from prior to functional specification up to, and including, alpha-testing – the author(s) are concerned with, and undertake, specific actions to improve software quality. The actions include good specification, design, and implementation practice in the first place, and design review, code reading and stringent testing within a competent plan for such thereafter. Design review and code reading are discussed in Chapter 13, along with strategies and plans for software testing at both benevolent and adversary (independent) levels.
2. Quality inspection (QI) is the objective determination that quality control has been properly undertaken, and also that all life cycle activities up to and including alpha-tests have been properly undertaken and achieved. QI is undertaken by an independent agency (i.e. non-author team) and, given its scope, it spans the pre-functional specification stage of the life cycle, down to alpha-test. When this, and all else prior to it, has been properly completed, then QI has finished – and the software engineering process is said, in this case, to be 'verified'. QI methods are those of inspection and review, and it is the author-team's software practices and quality control procedures that are the objects of this inspection.
3. Quality assurance (QA) is the objective determination of mandatory criteria of compliance and modifiability – again by an independent ('objective') agency, usually identical to that for QI. QA commences when alpha-testing has been satisfactorily done as the last part of QC, and the whole life cycle process to that point is declared 'verified' as the outcome of QI. Thus unlike QC and QI, QA is an 'end control' type of function.

Methods for QI are known as 'black-box' and 'white-box' testing, both of which are described in Section 9.3. These two types of objective tests, taken together, are known as the 'beta-tests', to distinguish them from the subjective, author-based alpha-tests done (as a part of implementation) at the completion of integration testing. It must not be forgotten that software documentation, as well on the behavior of the software in terms of its

mandatory criteria, is an object of QA. When the software and its documentation have been quality-assured, the software is said to be have been 'validated'.

It is useful here to see that the terms 'verified' and 'validated' fit the meanings for them defined as long ago as Chapter 2. The process is verified and its outcome is validated. Thus:

Verified: Have we made the software right? This is the basic question for QI.

Valid: Have we made the right software? This is one of the questions (compliance) for QA.

This set of definitions gives us an outline for managing software quality in all its variform senses. The matter is taken further in Section 13.6. Basically, though, it should be stressed that quality is a total life cycle concern, not just a 'bolt-on' afterthought of the simple 'end control' type. For that reason, it is useful to see quality functions (QC, I and A) as processes, having duration during the life cycle or its stages. In this way it will be seen that the quality *states* – verified, validated and certified (or V, V and C as they are called) – attach to achievements of the quality functions.

Thus, it is the good software engineering practices that are independently *verified*, including the author-team's QC practices up to and including alpha-tests. Similarly, the software itself should be independently *validated* through beta-tests within the QA function and, on some occasions, *certified* by its end user or client.

Before proceeding, reference must be made to a slight oversimplification through generalization made, up to now in this text, in the matter of QA. The 'independent agency' for QA is, sometimes, two agencies – and two, or even three, levels of testing is done beyond the alpha-test stage of QC. For example, in the case of a contracted project supply on a fixed price and time-scale basis, there may be the following levels of testing – all parts of QA, in essence:

1. Supplier's independent beta-tests.
2. Client's acceptance trials.
3. Client's certification period.

The first two of these are done before the software is released for use. The supplier's own independent beta-tests should comprise black-box and white-box testing although most acceptance trials concentrate on a black-box testing technique that throws light on compliance, but little or none at all on likely modifiability and reliability.

That is unfortunate, to say the least, when it happens. Often, the reason for this omission is the client's inability to do adequate investigations and tests, and in those cases it may be correctly supposed that the software will be more thoroughly tested in its real environment. So, after a full sequence of QC and QA test (alpha- and beta-level as described), the software may be placed under warranty (free maintenance) for a period of time. After satisfactory performance over this duration – say not more than x software faults taking more than y units of time each to fix – the software is said to be certified (the 'C' in V, V & C).

Both acceptance and certification may be formal, contractual steps.

9.2 MEASUREMENT AND METRICS

We have three cases to consider. What measurement means and metrics exist for: compliance, modifiability, and the reliability components of either (i.e. 'static' and 'dynamic' reliability), or the composite 'reliability' of both? We will take each of these questions in turn.

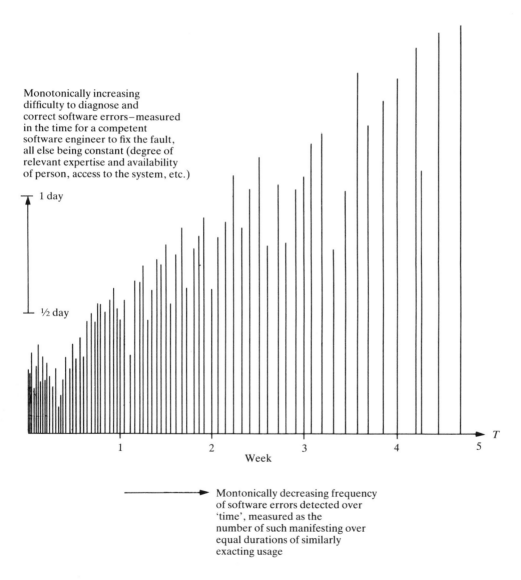

Monotonically increasing
difficulty to diagnose and
correct software errors – measured
in the time for a competent
software engineer to fix the fault,
all else being constant (degree of
relevant expertise and availability
of person, access to the system, etc.)

1 day

½ day

Week

T

Montonically decreasing frequency
of software errors detected over
'time', measured as the
number of such manifesting over
equal durations of similarly
exacting usage

FIGURE 9.3 Extract from a software testing record.

9.2.1 On what scale do we judge compliance?

Short of categorical proof of correctness by objective means, the demonstration of compliance by QC and QA testing is an exercise in confidence accretion. In the integration stage we may say 'Phew, this software seems to be particularly verminous'; then, during alpha-tests, we may have cheered up somewhat: 'Things look good, I'm sure this is the last bug'.

It is always 'the last bug' isn't it? In fact it may be the *latest* bug, but can never be assumed to be the last. 'Testing demonstrates the presence but never the absence of error', we are told, for absence of proof may never be taken as proof of absence. Thus, in the beta-test stage we may say (with glee if we are the QA agency): 'Whoops! Here's another one'. And even later – years after delivery – the client may be rubbing the back of his head, like Gogol's peasant, and grumbling: 'Who would have thought it would come to this?' as the software falls in a grinning heap on the floor.

Either confidence increases, or it decreases (or stays low) about compliance. We may co-opt statistics to help, but this is not usually necesary. In case it is, Figure 9.3 shows an extract from a software testing record. 'Time' is once again that duration during which the software is being used, rather than that when the disk on which it is stored sits on a shelf. The amplitude or 'difficulty' of a bug may be measured reasonably fairly as the time it takes to fix it – given a mass of caveats about who does the fixing, and also about when the clock starts and stops to determine the quantity of time taken. Basically, though, one is looking for decreases in both amplitude and frequency (the rate of error incidence over 'time'), so that both effects are seen to be perceptibly and monotonically decreasing trends.

For the rest, the software either does what it is required to do by specification or, if it has been clearly enough specified to tell the difference, it does not. Measurement and metrics for compliance do not really enter into the affair. I (the author) will demonstrate that my software works; you (the QA agency) will try to demonstrate that it does not; he or she (the client/manager) will have an access of confidence in the matter – or not, as the case may be.

On closer inspection, it will be realized that Figure 9.3 is also an indication of the 'static' reliability component of software compliance. It is not a particularly strong method in its mensuration though. For all its caveats in definition, confidence accretion is usually a more intuitive matter.

9.2.2 On what scale do we judge modifiability?

For modifiability, we are a little better off for metrics and methods of mensuration. One weak method may be derived from the work of Belady and Lehman (1976), already cited in Section 3.3. Here a ratio is defined:

$$M_i = C(I)_i / I_i$$

where M_i is the modifiability index at a release i, $C(I)_i$ is the total number of integrands that had to be changed for a set of changes I_i to known integrands to be achieved. Thus, if

at release three we have had to change sixteen integrands as a consequence of substantively modifying seven of them, we have an index of modifiability of 2.3. If then, at release four, we have to change thirty-two integrands to effect changes to twenty of them, we have an index of 1.6. By a simple 'moving average' technique, one may see – over a long enough sequence of changes – whether or not the modifiability index seems to be increasing or decreasing.

We make no claims for this approach, other than that it might be indicative if, say, a definite upward trend is shown, and there is no significant difference in the type of changes commissioned. As it is, it is just about all that is on offer – except, that is, for complexity metrics. These have been discussed in Section 3.3, and the reader will recall that they are at present held to be in the research domain. Thus, even an assertion that modifiability is proportional to complexity does not get us very far if complexity metrics are lacking. Apart from this weak approach, the method of determining the modifiability of a software system is essentially judgmental. Someone has to emit an opinion on the issue, of the form: 'Could I, or you, or he/she, *dare* to change this software, for whatever purposes (correction or improvement), and even if competent to do so – all other factors being conducive to it?' This concerns change, and the management of change, and is discussed under that heading in Section 13.2.

However, our question is answered sufficiently. We have no scale on which to judge modifiability of a software system. The *programs* may, and probably will, be trivially easy to *change*, just as one could put a square wheel on a car, or a rubber steering-column in it. But what then, one may ask?

Software modification concerns its whole behavior, and an objective metric for this is lacking. There is no scale, and our answer must rest on subjective (although hopefully expert) human judgment.

9.2.3 On what scale do we judge reliability?

On the subject of reliability we are little better served in the matter of metrics – hardly surprising, since reliability is so closely associated with the mandatory criterion of modifiability and its connotations concerning the structure of a software system.

The analysis of error frequency and amplitude (severity), as shown in Figure 9.3, plays a role in evaluating reliability. Again, what one is looking for is an increase in the time between errors surfacing. We really do have to look at life that way in software – the errors are probably there, we just have not seen this particular one before.

Ideally, as well as a decreasing frequency of failure, we would also like to see a decreasing severity of failure. However, whereas in well conditioned software there is quite likely to be a monotonically increasing time-span between error detections, there is almost nothing to say about error severity – except that, as one would expect, the errors tend to get more obscure. One would, after all, expect to find the more obvious defects most quickly. And in all of this, these 'errors' that we have been so glibly talking about are the categorical and self-evident failures of 'fit' between the software and its specification; the compliance in fact, and its 'static' reliability. There is no such notion as an 'error of modifiability'. Software is more, or less, modifiable – and there it is.

Another 'method' for trying to quantify reliability is that of induction, or 'seeding' as it is sometimes called. In this, a known number of categorical errors are planted in the software, which is then executed and the emerging defects are used to infer its condition. For example, if x known errors are introduced and y of them are found, plus z hitherto unknown bugs, then it is inferred that some quantity of errors, indicated by the values of x, y and z remain undetected in the software. The problems with this approach are obvious, and mainly concern the justification for any inference at all being drawn from so dubious a practice as 'seeding'. However, it is by no means easy to see how any formula could fail to be counter-intuitive, in some circumstances quite well known to software engineers.

What are we to infer, other than that something is clearly wrong, if we add one known error that then fails to appear? Or, on the other hand, what about the added error producing a crop of derivative errors that then appear as the 'hitherto unknown errors of the type z'? There is an obvious formula for residual errors:

$$r = z(x/y - 1)$$

with a convention to round up fractional values of x/y. This seems to work quite nicely for simple values such as $x = 10$; $y = 5$; $z = 1$; therefore $r = 1$. But it is deeply counter-intuitive nevertheless, for the reasons given.

A third approach is to try to use analogies with hardware, so as to derive mean time between failure (MTBF) and mean time to repair (MTTR) figures. This, too, is unlikely to succeed in providing a metric for software reliability, certainly not one that could be used (as is often the case for hardware) in a contract of supply. Again, the nearest one may get to saying anything about MTBF for software is if the frequency of error emergence permits some prediction to be made with reasonable confidence. An obvious example is if an error occurs in a software system in January, another in February, another in April, one in July and a further one in November. One may predict that the next one will crop up in the following April or thereabouts, although it is in the nature of software that thirteen will crop up on 7th December, or none at all for the next ten years.

Of course, in speaking of things 'cropping up', I have tended to make it all sound grimly inevitable, as though software 'behaves' in some fashion independent of human agencies. The antithesis of quality, in whatever sense it is present, will probably arise from complex and highly dynamic interactions between software components, software and hardware, and the whole systems' behavior in the operational environment. The defects of a software system, relative to its requirements and to other quality criteria, and although contingent on lots of other factors, will have been 'engineered in' by 'human agencies' who have been unable to foresee the complexities of its behavior sufficiently, or have been incapable of 'engineering in' a higher degree of quality.

The real difficulty lies in exposing these defects, and correcting them. Even after the most meticulous testing and demonstration, and perhaps after years of successful use, errors in a software system may appear, particularly in relatively unused features of it. It is then that non-software engineers look askance, as though the stuff has suddenly come to life and is behaving malignantly. 'Heaven help us', they cry, 'we had fallen into the habit of assuming its reliability'. And this opens up the next part of Pandora's Box.

Software reliability is best regarded as an exercise in confidence accretion under a supervening axiom. That is that software is probably never entirely error-free, and the best

thing one can say about it is that the conditions under which the next defect will materialize have not yet occurred. Furthermore, the *apparent* reliability of software is its 'static' reliability – that is its tendency to go on working apparently compliantly if unchanged. The 'dynamic' reliability of a software system tends to remain unexplored and unassessed until the need to change the software is faced. This need may arise for corrective maintenance reasons, or if major improvements are planned. Then the modifiability of the software must be appraised if the changes are to be commissioned with confidence. The only approach really on offer is one already referred to for the modifiability aspect, competent judgment.

All this is not a counsel of gloom, doom and despair – although some researchers and theoreticians tend to see it as a standing self-condemnation of software engineering practice, and electronic engineers frequently refuse to credit it at all. The nearest one can get to explaining why software is as it is, in this respect, is to appeal to a metaphor of chess. Sometimes, the analysis required to fathom a chess position is quite beyond human means. The best example I know of is a 'standard' grandmaster draw in an end game of king and rook versus king and knight ('KRKN' as it is called). Several grandmasters in the game have exhaustively analyzed this position (Reuben Fine and Paul Keres, *inter alia*), and given it as an inevitable draw. Many games were declared to be draws, when the position was reached, on this authority; KRKN became a 'standard grandmaster draw', and one did not continue in futile play.

However, workers in the field of artificial intelligence (Michie and Bratko 1980) have shown the possibility of a forced win for the color having the rook, which can take up to eighteen moves from the time some KRKN position arises, and requires an amount of combinatorial analysis apparently beyond human means to do unaided. This is all very redolent of life in software engineering, where one rapidly learns never to say 'never' about the dynamic behavior of programs.

More important still is never to *contract* for 'never' in the matter of software reliability. Having confidence in a software system is light-years distant from guaranteeing its performance. Even the most carefully constructed, sedulously tested and widely used software system will have this caveat attached to it, which is the main reason why computer manufacturers will contract to support their software in the sense of its maintenance, but will seldom contract for it to be error-free.

All of this may be deeply disturbing to purchasers of software systems, and the electronic engineers who work with software engineers on composite systems. The hardware may have component failure statistics that allow a calculation of likely mean time between failure and mean time to repair for the electronics, and these may be contractual points. They are almost always selling points of the form: 'Our hardware has 99.9 years' MTBF, and a 1 day guaranteed MTTR given that the following components are stocked locally.' MTBF/MTTR may even be contracted points for hardware, by a client: 'Your mickey-mouse gadget had better not fail for 99.9 years – or we'll sue until you're cross-eyed.' There is no equivalent statement possible for software – which does not, incidentally, mean that all software is intrinsically less reliable than hardware. I have known exactly the converse on many occasions, the only difficulty being to express one's confidence in software other than by some generalization. Unlike geophysics, where there is a logarithmic scale, due to Richter, for measuring the 'strength' (energy release) of earth-

quakes, we have no 'Smith scale' for compliance, 'Bloggs index' for modifiability or 'Flange factor' for reliability.

Yet, I have, on my travels, seen reports on software containing the most startling nonsense. One such, from a supplier to its client – the latter about to sue the former for failure to deliver error-free software – read: 'At the present time, the software contains only eight errors'. To which the calamitous answer came, with an awful inevitability: 'Why?'

9.3 METHODS FOR ENHANCING CONFIDENCE IN SOFTWARE QUALITY

Confidence accretion depends on the quality methods involved in the software development process. The accretive testing and integration of code during implementation has been dealt with up to a point in Chapter 8, and strategies for achieving it are discussed further in Chapter 13. What remains to be done here is to expand on the three quality functions defined earlier – quality control, inspection and assurance – as being the means whereby confidence in the quality of a software system may be enhanced.

9.3.1 Quality control and inspection

Quality control is the internal activity at all life cycle stages, up to and including alpha-test, to ensure a quality of achievement in the outcome of that stage. Thus we think of 'deliverables' from life cycle stages – although the recipient of a 'deliverable' may be the author-team itself. Typical 'deliverables' requiring quality control are functional specification/outline systems design, estimate and plans [sic], management constructions and practices in general for the development, software design, software implementation and testing, and software documentation. Adherence to good software engineering practice, as described herein, is essential – as is the provision of adequate technical facilities (PSE) and staff resources to exploit them. Design review and code reading practice are the internal quality control methods at the appropriate stages, and are described further in Chapter 13.

As already pointed out, the subjective testing of software by its authors during its implementation tends to confirm, or to lead to its compliance, and says little about the criterion of modifiability. In fact, the cycle of testing and correcting may even deplete modifiability if carelessly undertaken. On the other hand, the objectives of design review and code reading are dual:

1. To detect and correct errors early and, therefore, relatively cheaply.
2. To improve the structure of programs and, thereby, to improve the testability and modifiability of the software system.

The importance of the first of these should not be overlooked. It has been estimated (Boehm 1981) that the relative costs of correcting specification errors are in the following ratios dependent on the stage at which they are detected and corrected:

1. Specification (i.e. in the functional specification): 1.
2. Design (i.e. during decomposition): 3.
3. Implementation (i.e. alpha-test): 30.
4. In service (i.e. after certification): 140.

Quality inspection is the independent auditing of all the software development practices including quality control, at all life cycle stages up to and including alpha-testing; it culminates in the development process being declared 'verified', or otherwise. Its methods are ones of periodic involvement as observers – particularly at management structured walk-throughs (see Section 11.2) and at author-teams' design reviews and code reading sessions. One important aspect of quality inspection is the determination, by the QI agency, that the functional specification is adequate both for a software development to proceed on the basis of it, and as the yardstick for assessing compliance during quality assurance.

Another important function of QI is to ensure that a competent test-plan exists at the right time, and that it is enacted competently as a part of QC. Generally, the earliest stage at which it is possible to make this plan is late in the design of the software – when the likely design modularity is known, and may even be named. It is particularly important to plan the software integration and its testing, even if the detailed plans have to be changed in the light of altered circumstance later.

9.3.2 Quality assurance and the role of black-box and white-box testing

Quality assurance concerns the independent testing of the software in two senses: black-box and white-box tests.

Black-box testing is the determination of compliance in all respects as detailed in the functional specification of requirements. It is so called because it treats the software as a single, responsive entity, whose behavior will be initiated by stimuli, and will be evident and therefore assessable for compliance.

The final alpha-test, the authors' last step in quality control, will be a form of black-box test, mainly to demonstrate that the software works as required. For this, and for beta-tests using this method, an actual or a simulated test environment may be required, which will test the features of the system under real or realistic conditions. Thus, for example, a system that is to operate in high load/high required throughput conditions can only be realistically tested if realistic 'loads' – such as volumes of input and high rates of arrival – are available.

There are often problems associated with black-box testing, not least the definition of tests that are adequate for the system to be deemed compliant with its requirements. In some cases, a system is small enough and simple enough for users (or their surrogates) to establish a degree of confidence in it by trial – that is 'hands on' usage – over a period of time and in a realistic way. Makers of small scale audio/video equipment let employees take early versions home for the children to play with. Larger scale software systems may require a whole 'black-box' test environment, with automatic test data generators and output checkers. In these cases, one meets the behavior space problem again. I have known even a relatively small software system (less than 1K source statements of code)

have a behavior space comprising several million plausible circumstances and their possible outcomes – let alone any and all of the random and accidental ones that could have occurred. In fact the total possible behavior space for this small system was an almost unbelievable 10^{23} possible permutations of usage, accidents that might change states in the system significantly, and outcomes of all events. There is no law that says what one should do in these circumstances; common sense dictates what reasonable reductions in the behavior space can be made, whilst still achieving a plausible level of these tests, likely to enhance confidence if the outcome from them is positive.

Not surprisingly, black-box test generators can be very expensive. Furthermore they may engender loss of confidence in the software they are supposed to exercise if they, themselves, are wrong. In fact great care must be taken with this method of establishing software compliance.

White-box testing is, in Einstein's phrase (and another context), 'opening the watch'. It can take the following forms:

1. Disassembling the software and re-testing its components in a different way from that done by its authors.
2. Making controlled changes to the software, including 'seeding' it with errors.

The object of each is different. The first kind of test, disassembly and re-testing of parts, is to try to falsify the software – the converse of its authors having tried to justify it by similar means. Stringently undertaken, by competent software engineers, this method is extremely useful for confidence accretion. For medium sized and large software systems, and clearly those even superior in size to these, disassembly testing can be done on a sampling basis. At its best, it may say little about compliance (unless an actual error is found); but it may enable eloquent comment on the structure and likely modifiability of the code.

This is taken further by tests involving controlled changes to, and even error-seeding of, the software. In these, the modifiability and reliability of the software are being investigated – not, the reader will recall, to provide a numerical foundation to confidence, so much as to enhance it (hopefully) by judgmental means.

Both forms of white-box testing depend, for their viability as tests but not their outcome, on the software documentation. Whereas black-box testing requires the quality assurance team to have a proper knowledge of the functional specification and instructions to users, white-box testing needs it to have access to the software documentation in full; this, then, is quality-assured as a part of white-box, QA testing.

9.3.3 The various contributions to confidence accretion

In the synopsis to this chapter, I wrote that quality was the whole of the issue in software development, excepting the rare cases of programs written for some specific research purposes. As quality is so fundamentally important, and as its status is a matter of confidence rather than objective determination, it is wise to try to encapsulate all the points made to date in a coherent and concise manner.

Certain matters comprise, in combination, an irreducible code of practice for technical quality to stand a chance of being achieved:

1. A proper functional specification, properly authorized, must exist.
2. Adequate technical facilities must be available for the purpose, such as PSE tools and Ipse features of the electronic environment.
3. The proper quality and quantity of development staff must be assured, with an 'arrival profile' of staff to the task determined by its state and needs, and not by their availability alone.
4. There must be minimal interference between technical and economic aspects of quality. This implies good management practice in general, and specifically requires it for estimating, activity control and cost reporting.

    'Good management practice' is the subject of Part III, and affects all items in this list, of course, as well as the points made here; for example, in 1 above, the signed-off functional specification must be put under change-control for the duration of the development, and the management of change effected accordingly.
5. Good design and implementation practices must be maintained, to ensure the relative ease (and therefore likely success) of testing, and of modification during testing or after the system becomes operational.
6. There must be quality control, practiced by the author-team. Specifically, the practices of design reviews and code reading; and accretive testing, of the static and dynamic types, up to and including the subjective, final integration test, the alpha-test. This will be a black-box test of the software, usually including its 'deliverable' documentation.
7. There must be quality inspection, from an independent source, of the quality control aspects of the development, and all other aspects of 1–5 above. This should 'add value' to the quality process, and enhance overall confidence in the outcome of the development by 'validating' the process.
8. There must be quality assurance of the software and its documentation, by independent 'adversarial' beta-testing practice comprising black-box tests.

    For products, beta-testing will be done by an internal product group or some externally contracted surrogate for one. On relatively rare occasions, this will be the case also for projects.

    In the main, projects are black-box tested by clients as part of client acceptance procedures and, if required, further black-box tested through a certification stage in operation. Consequently, projects tend to lack white-box demonstration of modifiability, and this should be provided by explicit QA means in all cases. Quality assurance validates the compliance and modifiability aspects of the software, including its documentation, to a high level of confidence – though inevitably short of certitude.
9. Above all, the confidence of all parties to the process – users, clients, managers, sales persons, quality officers and software engineers is amplified beyond measure, by quality being an explicit issue all down the life cycle, and not just a 'bolt-on-goodie' at the end.
10. A frequently forgotten matter is that quality is a continuing requirement, beyond acceptance and the software becoming operational. Both compliance and modifiability can be eroded, as can reliability consequently, as a software system becomes changed over time, either for correction or improvement. Then confidence will be withdrawn in a flash for, as we know, converts to any cause can be more zealous in its pursuit than they had been for its converse.

Changing software and its documentation is software engineering too, and must be done competently.

This little catechism, comprising ten precepts, if not actual commandments, would repay being cut out from this text and pinned to the wall of the offices of everyone purporting to be on the supplying or receiving end of software development. It would have saved my skin a dozen times, as a software manager, if I had known it then.

The requirements for software quality are not hard to state, but they may be less easy to achieve. How does *your* current software development task rate against the ten precepts? And would a software engineer's valuation accord, even within an order of magnitude, with that of a product manager? On one occasion, I was brought in to a firm to assess the quality of a product about to be entered in the catalog as a salable item. There was an atmosphere of vigorous dissent between various parties. The marketing group had orders for fifty, and were panic-stricken about the competition; they wanted to release the product and had been taking clients' money rather like a chap with weak nerves may take a double brandy. Some software engineers, either with stronger nerves or access to better brandy, when asked for a quality assessment, declared the system unfit. Managers had called for the sanitary inspector (me), and retired to the rest room to have their breakdowns in peace and quiet.

Skimming quickly down my list, I found the following:

1. A so-called functional specification, unauthorized, that bore a stronger resemblance to a user's wish-list, plus some very poor design work.
2. That the development had been done on a grossly inadequate, nearly 'naked' micro.
3. That the author was an enthusiast for writing ultra-clever, compressed code, in assembler. Worse, he had proceeded from the inadequate specification straight into code, without the vestige of a design.
4. That the job had been contracted to a supplier, chosen on a least-price basis (the reader will notice the avoidance of the term 'least-*cost*'; there is a profound distinction between 'price' and 'cost' in software supply).
5. There was no documentation, save for a congested code listing that committed all the sins outlined in Chapter 8, plus a few more.
6. There had been no QC practice, and no QI to detect it.

That took me to about half-way down my checklist. No category had scored much on my admittedly judgmental scale of reckoning. Need I have gone further? Need I now? All the quality practices on earth could not compensate for the errors of omission and commission.

Beyond a certain point, defects in a software development become mutually interfering, and act to amplify each other. One may get away with a less than ideal situation, applying with respect to one precept or another. But one's confidence in quality, economic and technical issues included, is likely to shrink to vanishing point if several of the precepts are simultaneously unfulfilled. And what can one say when they are *all* missing?

There was not much point in going further, although we did – laboring through blackbox tests in an unmeasurable behavior space, and trying to deduce some design, 'bottom up' from the code listing and primitive flowcharts that had been done as an afterthought.

Our unconfidence was registering an off-scale value. All our fears were realized by the black-box tests. As for white-box tests, no one could be bribed or threatened to touch the programs to assess their tractability to changes. It was as though they were highly radio active, and required disposal in a block of high density ferro-concrete.

One set of confidence levels remained high, however; the product appeared in the company's sales catalog, and good money duly changed hands for it. Later a lot more equally good money changed hands too, but in other directions, when the field-main-tenance reports began to come in.

Is that example the exception or the rule in software development? Is there a vector of improvement in our work? Sadly, it is more representative of grim reality than should be the case, four decades into the development and use of computers. Electronic engineers, and others, may be incredulous at this. We share their concern.

CHAPTER TEN

MAINTENANCE, NEW VERSIONS AND THE PRESERVATION OF SOFTWARE QUALITY

When a physical artefact goes into use, a bridge or a production-quality car, or your telephone, television or personal computer, one will expect it to need only intermittent change, hopefully very intermittent indeed, and this to replace any broken or worn-out parts. For reasons already revealed in the last chapter, the status of software quality is never established to the same level as that of a physical artefact, and Ralph Nader's designation 'unsafe at any price' may be modified for software quality in general: 'unsure at any price'. From the moment a software system is validated it tends to change. Corrective maintenance requires the implementation of emendations to either code, or data, or both. Then, also, the agreed fiction of an invariant specification gets relaxed, and the institution of improvements may be freely considered.

Policies are required whereby the decisions to effect these changes can be decided. Frequently, these are commercial decisions, and concern commercial imperatives to emit new versions of a software system that are either (a) less wrong, or (b) of improved features and functionality for users.

Change is potentially a major source of loss of original quality, in software engineering as in any other construction business. We have all seen examples; physical objects so patched that it is a wonder they serve any useful purpose. Many long-life software systems are the same. The loss of quality, and confidence in quality, can be extreme.

When a software development exercise has successfully reached its ordained conclusion, a validated software system of some sort will exist, presuming that there has been a thorough process of quality assurance and (perhaps) acceptance and certification, and given that the development process has been fully verified by an independent inspection process. The software is now ready to go into service since it, and its documentation, are as fit as can be judged possible in a reasonable allowed-time for such excogitations.

If our software has been developed as a contracted project of supply, then the end client receives it into service, and either undertakes the maintenance or enters into a software maintenance contract with a competent agency – usually the original supplier. Depending on who maintains it, the documentation set corresponding to the delivered software goes to either the client or the contracting party for maintenance, in which case it may stay at

home (so to speak) if that party is the original supplier. In any event, only the party maintaining the software will have its documentation and, *ergo*, only they will be able to make authorized changes to software and its documentation.

If a product is involved, then the party maintaining the software will be the product supplier's own field support and maintenance group, and if there is no such group in existence then one will very quickly have to be put in place. In any event, the documentation set goes to the agency maintaining the software – and precisely the same principles regulating change to it, or to the software, hold.

10.1 SOFTWARE CHANGES FOR CORRECTIVE MAINTENANCE OR EVOLUTION OF PURPOSE

Changes may occur for one of the following reasons:

1. Circumstances in which categorical error in compliance needs correcting, such as if the software is wrong, or (if otherwise seemingly right) if it fails to go on working; this is known as the 'corrective maintenance' of a software system.
2. Improvements may be called for by clients, users, managers or whoever, so long as they are in a position to commission them – and this process is known as 'evolution' of a software system, and corresponds to Lehman's P and E system properties.

The type of software change may, therefore, be said to be *corrective*, *perfective* or *adaptive*. In the first of these, one is trying to detect and correct errors prior to the software being defined as 'valid'; in the second, one is detecting and correcting errors in operational software; in the third, one is emending a software system, by addition, subtraction or both, to improve it in some defined way.

10.1.1 Corrective maintenance

Not all corrective maintenance requirements may need commensurate action to correct them at the same level of urgency. A minor nonsense in a screen format can be corrected at leisure. A serious flaw in a closed-loop control system for manned satellite navigation is another thing again. Basically, though, error reports can be divided into two categories; 'do it for a future release' or 'do it now!' The 'do it now' changes get done now, because delay is – for some reason – unacceptable, whilst the less urgent ones are first clustered, then effected over some tolerable period of time and – according to whatever policy prevails in the matter – are the subject of a 'next maintenance version' release of the software. This may be determined on an elapsed-time basis, e.g. a new maintenance version release every two years – if there has been anything to correct in that period. Or it may be determined on the basis of changes made – i.e. a new maintenance release every *n* corrective changes made. The usual policy is based on elapsed time qualified by number. For instance, every two years if more than a minimum number of changes have been made, or earlier if more than a maximum have been required.

In passing it may be noted that, unlike some aspects of hardware engineering, 'preventive maintenance' is not appropriate in software engineering. There is basically no such thing, because there can be no such thing. As software does not wear out, nor otherwise deplete over time or with usage, all the 'preventive maintenance' is done at the start, prior to the software going into service. Fault diagnosis is often confused with ongoing preventive maintenance, when, after a failure of some kind, some software tests are run to see if the condition can be clarified.

10.1.2 Evolution

Evolutions of software are things like new features, or improvements to existing ones for whatever reason. In fact, the call for software to be changed for these purposes may come long before the completion of a first, substantive version of it. When this deferment occurs, it is usually due to explicit action of a change control construction – between user/client on the one hand and supplier on the other – to regulate the changes made to scope and detail of a specification. A dossier of deferred features and changes can be kept from before completion of the functional specification, and this can represent a sizable task by the time the first version is on the point of acceptance, certification, release into service or whatever.

Over the months and years of its service, more evolutionary changes will be seen to be desirable if not necessary – that is in the nature of things. Perhaps the user environment changes; perhaps new technology or methods become available; perhaps competitors bring out products of greater allure than one's own. Whatever the reasons, evolutionary as distinct from maintenance changes will occur. And the two must be discriminated. It has been said (of the US Department of Defense) that adding a new wing to the Pentagon would be called maintenance! In fact it should be seen as the new 'hexagon' version of that building.

10.1.3 Version release policies

The reason why the two types of changes should be distinguished is that there may be two quite distinct release policies in operation – one for the aggregation of maintenance changes of the non-imperative type, and the other for evolutionary improvement to the software. These two policies will probably have vastly different economic assumptions as their predicates. For instance, maintenance changes – concerning as they do the fault of software – may have to be free or very low cost to clients, whilst evolutionary improvements can be advertised as the virtues they no doubt are, and clients can be charged what the market will bear. The administrative nightmares that accrue from even one release policy, let alone two, are dealt with in Section 13.2.

Suffice it to say here that for all but prototypes of software – that is for projects and products – there will be issues of maintenance and evolutionary change to software, and (for products particularly) this will result in a need for release policies for both. Thus we may envisage a maintenance version release policy, and an evolutionary version release

policy. The first may be on a relatively short time-scale – months or years; the second may concern longer durations – probably years rather than months.

The important issue is that, for either reason or both, change is to be introduced into the software.

10.2 WHETHER TO CHANGE A SOFTWARE SYSTEM, OR REDO IT

Entry 27 in Hymns, Ancient and Modern has the famous lament: 'Change and decay in all around I see'. That sums up the matter in software engineering exactly. Change and decay – with this last, sad process applying to the structure of the software, unless one is especially careful. Even a 'good' or 'strong' original structure, as judgmentally determined, slides progressively into a patchwork affair unless a definite effort is expended – in addition to that for a change itself – to forestall it.

10.2.1 Lehman's laws of software evolution

Five 'laws' have been enunciated to account for this, and associated properties of software systems (Lehman 1980). They have been referred to earlier, in Section 3.3, and are, paraphrased somewhat here, as follows:

1. *The law of continuing change.* Programs concerning real-world requirements either undergo continual change, or become progressively less useful. This continues until it is judged more economic to replace the system than to change it.
2. *The law of increasing complexity.* Changes to software systems increase the complexity of their construction and, commensurately, reduce their degree of good-structuredness with detriment to quality. That is unless explicit work is done to maintain the degree of good structure, or improve it and, thereby, preserve or reduce the level of complexity – and thereby enhance quality.
3. *The law of program evolution.* Program evolution is subject to a dynamic which makes it, and measures of its development and system properties, self-regulating with statistically determinable trends and invariance.
4. *The law of invariant work-rate.* During the active life of a program, the overall activity rate in associated programming tasks is statistically invariant.
5. *The law of perceived complexity.* During the active life of a program, the change content (changes, additions, deletions) of successive releases of the evolving program is statistically invariant.

The word 'law' is used rather loosely in this list; the items are informed, judgmental views and can be seen as more or less plausible hypotheses. Most software engineers would agree intuitively with 2, and would know of 1 as an apparently infallible fact of life; many managers do not recognize 1 and know nothing of 2. Hypotheses 3, 4 and 5 are highly interesting conjectures – but currently lack substantiating evidence.

10.2.2 Guidelines for changing software with safety

Everyone, or almost everyone, knows how software should not be changed. The example, given earlier, of a quick patch to the object code of a system, is engraved on the folk-memory of all who program. Even the brashest amateur or hobbyist will have the simple decency to blush if caught in the act, whilst real software engineers tend to take a high moral tone towards such practices.

Non-specialists are easily deceived by the lure of facile change, but they too see reason, once it is convincingly pointed out. Sales personnel and product managers have the hardest task, as the imperatives bearing on them provide an overwhelming excuse for instant remedies at times. Yet even in the face of outraged clients and implacable higher management, the arguments of specious economics can be deployed with force; short-cuts often take longest; cheap fixes to software almost always end up costing far more. It is a surprise, therefore, to find that software maintenance and improvement are not very well undertaken, in the main, in IT product supply. In the world of contracted software project supply it is often different, when the original supplier remains contracted for the purpose.

The main problem might be that people do not like doing maintenance and improvement work in software engineering. It is certainly the case, in many places, that it is difficult to get people to do such work permanently. They, the software engineers, tend to see it as a task devoid of real interest to them, because it is lacking in scope for their creativity as they see it.

Software engineers, at whatever level of their calling, tend to become very fractious if job interest, in their terms, is lacking. Novelty acts as a narcotic, and is strongly habit-forming. What to do with recusant software engineers is a question of personnel management 'culture' within a company, and the fact that it is a seller's market for their services. All one can do is belabor the issues of false economy through casually done change, suggest guidelines for proper practice, and leave the rest to the professional probity of software developers, and to good management to encourage it.

Managers and software staff alike should be aware of the simple principles involved, and clients would do well to note them too, for their software supplies and their ongoing quality. To all, the following aphorism applies with force: 'There is no such thing as a free change to a software system'. The reasons are clear:

1. Any, and all, changes to software must be done with extreme care, and due regard to good software engineering practice – specification, design, implementation and testing – with respect to the change itself.
2. Any, and all, changes to software must lead to a review of the overall structure of software after the change, and after any commissioned actions as a result to reduce complexity/improve structure. These actions must themselves be undertaken with due regard to good software engineering practice – specification, design, implementation and testing – with respect to any of these consequential changes.
3. Any, and all, changes to software must be fully documented, at all relevant levels of deliverable documentation, for the substantive and any consequential changes.

The relationship between these precepts and Lehman's 'laws' – the second in particular – is clear. Point 2 accounts for the 'explicit work' referred to in that item.

There is no way of telling how much consequential change (and associated work to do it) will arise from a substantive maintenance or evolutionary change; the result will depend on the original structure – how well it can stand up to change, and on the competence with which changes are made.

10.2.3 Change, or redo?

Another perfectly legitimate and widely occurring question concerning software change, has no explicit answer; at what point is it generally held to be uneconomic to go on changing software – as distinct from replacing it? ('Law' 1, part two.)

This question can take may forms other than that of the original. One variant concerns the percentage of change that it is 'safe' to make – above which one would (whatever the economic considerations, presumably) replace the system rather than 'dare' to change it. In fact this is not a very meaningful question, as the following is intended to show. If, to make substantive changes to x percent of integrands, one has to change a further amount, y percent (the consequential changes to preserve structure), then one may – in some extreme cases – draw a conclusion from that fact. For example, 1 percent of changes causing a consequential 99 percent tells us something about the structure! It is probably best discarded entirely. But, in other cases, nothing clear may be seen from review of past cases for the software (see Table 10.1).

TABLE 10.1 Real and consequential changes to software for new versions

	Change (%)			
	17	18	19	20
x	7	19	13	42
y	4	26	17	?

There is little way of formulating an answer to $y = ?$ short of getting on and performing the $x = 42$ percent of known changes to be made. Judgmentally, software engineers, mainly by inspection, will 'dare', or not, to attempt the changes. They may also have the judgment rendered superfluous by edict: 'Yours not to reason why: yours but to code and die' (Tennyson, or nearly).

In other cases, there may be a clear and monotonic upward trend in the ratio $y:x$ and this should raise doubts about the efficacy of work done to preserve 'good' structure and also – perhaps – about how 'good' the structure was in the first place. Then $x = 42$ percent may look a very daunting task indeed; in fact $x + y$ may be tending to 100 percent – and a new development of the system may then be by far the best option.

In any case, the cost of change – if being held against the cost of new development – most always contain a provision for y, the cost of consequential change. Otherwise the calculations and comparisons will be specious, and ancient and 'decayed' software will be preserved in service for far too long. 'Oh thou who changest not, abide with me' becomes a lament of greater force than the first part of the verse. Bad software deters change; if its total replacement bears with it a prohibitive cost, then it 'abides'.

10.2.4 Coda to Part Two

Chapters 5–10 have taken us from the genesis of a software development, its concepts, to the limits of its useful life, when the merits of throwing it away and starting all over again become real considerations. We have been, in effect, at least once and possibly several times round the life cycle as depicted in Chapter 4.

We have suggested an approach to specification that *includes*, not disenfranchises, the user. We have described the complex and highly intuitive talent of designing software systems of worth, and offered guidelines through the maze of means, methods and mere approaches to software design. Then we entered the *sanctum sanctorum* of the programmer, where time stands suspended at All-Hallows Eve, and who knows what arcane rites are due. There we addressed six fundamental matters having bearing on the quality of outcome. Finally, we arrived at the issue that stands at the beginning of all software engineering endeavors – technical quality and its preservation.

At many points on this pilgrimage we have come close to questions whose answers take us to the outer circle in the bull's-eye diagram of Figure 4.1. These, and many others like them, are 'people things', matters of management practice as applied to software development.

We now, therefore, move on from the modalities of software development within software engineering, to address these management issues within the subject.

PART THREE

SOFTWARE MANAGEMENT

FAUSTUS. How comes it then that thou art out of Hell?
MEPHOSTOPHOLIS. Why this is Hell, nor am I out of it.
(Marlowe, *Dr Faustus*, Act 1, Scene 3)

This book is, like Gaul of old, divided into three parts. In the first, some general issues of understanding and definition were addressed, to light a pathway through the undergrowth of claim and counter-claim, fact and fantasy about software engineering.

Then, in the second part, we buckled down to the task of understanding how software systems come into being, how they are made, what tools are available and what limits to perfection result in the outcome.

Now we address the supervening question; how to manage software tasks – for this, too, is an integral component of the subject 'software engineering'. First, we deal with the perceived or supposed problems of comprehension and visibility of what, to many people, is a deeply hermetic practice. Then we address the 'other' component of quality – economics of development – and, in particular, how to set realistic cost and time targets. The crucial question of an effort : time-scale relationship is addressed.

Last of all, we present a redactional chapter, in which the various strands are brought together into a coherent set of guidelines for managing software development tasks. Techniques such as structured walkthrough and archiving, having been discussed earlier, are the underlying fabric for activities and cost planning, managing for change, managing for quality, organization and personnel factors, and software services procurement.

CHAPTER ELEVEN

COMPREHENSION AND VISIBILITY IN SOFTWARE DEVELOPMENT

Software management is a central issue in software engineering, and de-emphasizing or ignoring this fact reduces the subject to a collection of technologies, merely, and impoverishes the outcome of software development accordingly. The chapter deals principally with the problems of comprehension that tend to arise amongst non-specialists in the subject, how to make the process visible so that it may be comprehended, and how to keep it so. Archiving and structured walkthrough are dealt with as the means to visibility and, within limits, to comprehensibility.

This is where we began, all those many pages ago. 'Once upon a time, there was an orientation course for managers and others. Protected by little other than their God-given innocence they sat in glum discomfort as the lecturer seemingly berated them, in what sounded like a foreign language....' There is no need to repeat the dose here. Earlier parts of this work have dealt, adequately we hope, with the definitions and descriptions required. The treatment there of some subjects – notably specification, design, implementation, testing and software quality – has been synoptic, and these subjects are each dealt with, in greater detail for those with particular interest, in a separate volume of this series. The aim here is to tidy up the issue of comprehension, to complete our notes (so to speak) on this side of the difficulty experienced by non-specialists in the subject 'software engineering'. For it is an underlying truth in any practical subject that what cannot be comprehended cannot be managed.

Later we deal with visibility of the software process, and here the proposition is that what is not visible to non-specialists is unlikely to be understood, and therefore equally unlikely to be managed.

11.1 COMPREHENSION

Software engineering, however, contentiously named, seems more congenial to some types of people than to others. In the course of orienting many different audiences in

several countries, some fairly safe generalizations have become clear. In the main, the populations have comprised people from one of five backgrounds:

1. People with an education background from business schools, and in 'the professions' such as accountancy and law, whose subsequent experience has been in general business administration, commercial and legal departments of firms, personnel management and so on. We will refer to this category as *administration and management*.
2. Those with an education in 'natural sciences', in particular, physics and mathematics (subsuming computer science here), whose vocation had led them into technical product management, including commercial activities and many general management functions. We will refer to these people as being in the *science and management category*.
3. People with a basic education in physical engineering subjects, and applied sciences, such as the engineering specializations for chemical, marine, building, aerospace and production industries. Here we find plant and project managers for large scale engineering constructions, and we refer to this category as *engineering and management*.
4. Those whose education was in electrical or electronic engineering, and who have acceded to positions in technical product management. These are referred to as *electronics and management*.
5. Clearly there are others in management functions, from a wide spectrum of disparate educational backgrounds – such as philosophy, natural languages, history and so on – or with no higher (vocational) education at all, but having an abundance of 'what it takes'. We will refer to this broad category as *general and management*.

11.1.1 Subject-compatibility

It is a self-evident proposition that ability and inclination can be countervailing forces in any field of endeavor. Where inclination is lacking, it may be impossible to discriminate ability from inability, and this, in turn, highlights questions of mutual compatibility between individual and subject. These issues of compatibility occur with everyone, and with every subject, from theoretical physics to slicing a cabbage for soup. And closely associated with this congeniality is aptitude.

The conspicuous differences in comprehension of software engineering, and its topics, across the five defined groups are summarized below. It must, in all fairness, be stressed that these are the judgmental views of this author and carry no other weight of authority; nor are they absolute statements of any sort, so much as perceived trends and tendencies. There are five particularly noteworthy observations:

1. People in the 'administration and management' group, despite their worst fears, are by no means unable (or unwilling) to tackle the problems of comprehending software engineering and its topics. They are probably not quite so facile at the implementation stage and thereabouts as, say, someone with a background in natural sciences of electronics, but at other life cycle stages there is little to choose in the matter of aptitude for, or achievement in, subject orientation. In fact, it is a great pleasure to see people – previously quite phobic, and for good reason, about 'the tiger' – happily doing functional specifications, drawing Mascot diagrams, making up taxonomies (code sizing

tends to be a bit beyond many of them of course) and even designing parts of a software system in, for example, BS 6224 DSD.

Between late design stages and author testing of code, there tends to be an area of dyslexia for this group, for which lack of interest and time only partly accounts. But this is a relatively minor matter, as there are management means to cope with this – as detailed below.

2. The 'science and management' category is generally held to be that most congenial with the subject of software engineering. Increasingly, people with degrees in natural science subjects and mathematics have some non-trivial exposure to programming within their course, as indeed is the same in engineering subjects. The relative ease with which physicists and mathematicians treat abstraction as a process, and the use of abstract notations, provide a basic congeniality with some of the means in specification, design and implementation of software systems.

This is by no means a guarantee that people with these advantages will exploit them well, or wish to do so; however, in recruiting software engineers it is a good guess that people from this sector, if they have the inclination, will possess aptitude for the subject. In the special case of computer science within applied mathematics, there is a danger that exponents will assume or assert that their subject *subsumes* software engineering, or renders it redundant, when that is not the case. This point is taken forward in Chapter 13, when the topic of subject-education is addressed.

3. Some 'engineering and management' people often have surprising difficulty in comprehending what software really is, and what the potential exigencies are in its creation. The principal obstacles appear to be: (a) the tangible/intangible question about software, and (b) the abstraction processes and the abstract notations involved in programming. There may be two possible consequences flowing from this tendency to incomprehension, and its frequent partner – lack of sympathy with the issues. First, companies may find it more difficult to train staff, from these backgrounds, in software engineering, than might be the case with others – conspicously, physicists and mathematicians/computer scientists. Second, some applications may be disadvantaged if their 'clients' or 'pseudo-clients' come from this sector; for example computer-aided manufacturing systems, at the process (production engineering) more than product design level. We have seen both of these consequences occur, with force, in practice. It must be stressed, however, that they are tendencies and not inevitabilities.

The cause, when it occurs, is not difficult to find. There are insufficient common features of aptitude, in the two areas of study and endeavor, to make them congenial.

4. The 'electronics and management' sector is the main source of amateur programming in the world. These are the skilled electronic engineers who, as an intermittent activity alone or with a few others, create a few thousand source statements of code (assembler usually), and then siphon it into the microprocessor component of an IT product. Next time, it might be several orders of magnitude more code, larger teams, more money, far higher risk, three years late, 600 percent over budget, sets the place on fire when you try to use it, and so on. There is no basic incompatibility of aptitude here, rather the opposite. Many electronic engineers pass happily into software engineering via amateur programming, and the reverse journey is by no means beyond a roughly equivalent fraction of software engineers – although one that is rather rarely embarked

upon. What is noticeable is an impatience on the part of some electronic engineers, particularly when they have succeeded to management positions without having had much real experience of software development themselves, with the essential differences between electronic 'hardware' and software. This impatience may change into outright hostility, disdain or indifference. Nowhere is it more evident than in the subjects of software design and quality. The paucity of real means in software engineering and the plethora of seemingly weak methods are incomprehensible to many senior electronic engineers; the more junior ones just tend to shrug and swear a bit, before getting on with the job as best possible.

5. The class of 'general and management' may be seen as roughly equivalent to that of 'business and management' in the matter of compatibility with software engineering. Sometimes people have an added difficulty, needing to orient with management practices in general, as well as the software engineering-specific matters (as is not the case with graduates from business schools); but in the main the orientation is not a major exercise, and their needs in this matter are no greater than are others', such as scientists and engineers.

These comments are offered, with some trepidation it must be said, to help in the anticipation, understanding and (hopefully) resolution of 'cultural' problems that may arise when software development or procurement is attempted. Generalization of this kind of a perilous game, and any aggrieved readers who feel like hammering the author into a happier frame of mind, or jolting a bit of sense into him across a high voltage circuit, can console themselves with the news that I have many instances of excellent software engineers with backgrounds in unlikely subjects for the purpose – such as modern languages, psychology (perhaps not so strange) and even theology – perhaps even less strange given some of the invocations from monastic figures, hunched over terminals.

11.1.2 Facing phobia

The aptitude for, or congeniality with, software engineering as a subject is a most important part in software development and procurement, and this does not only operate at the level of specialists. Perhaps the most debilitating condition to find in a company, that has some need to develop or procure software, is that occurring when managers, and others who should be actively involved, fear to become so. This alienation often derives from a mixture of actual or supposed inaptitude and a concern not to be made to look inadequate in an aspect of technology that one might think should be within the scope of a person in such a position.

Many aspects of this phobia can be remedied. Genuine inaptitude cannot, nor can management of software development (or procurement for that matter) proceed with confidence in its presence. We must not minimize the problem of comprehension for people to whom it all seems like a bewildering and arcane art, undertaken by a hermetic order of initiates. I sincerely hope that anyone reading this, who has that impression, will take heart from the basic message of this book. Software and software engineering *can* be understood to a sufficient level by most people, and certainly if they have the will and

interest to do so. Even the subject's most captions critic should not frighten the people with tales of wild animals to be tamed. Non-specialists in the subject should heed the words of a great president of the USA: 'We have nothing to fear but fear itself'.

Software can be managed, not always easily it is true, but it can be done. Comprehension of the process and its modalities is a perquisite; after that, it is a matter of applied common sense.

The best way to conquer fright is to face the source of it. People with phobia about software engineering and yet some palpable need to know about it, to some level, should take a short orientation course in the subject – preferably one that will demonstrate just how much of a software process they can 'add value' to, and manage, as well as some elementary practice in coding and the use of 'virtual' computer facilities.

A preludal question on such a course should be: 'Would you dare or be able to do a structured walkthrough of a software development task?' This question should be put at the end of the course too. If the answer has not changed for the better, then the orientation course will have failed, as will its presenters – not the attendees.

11.2 VISIBILITY OF THE PROCESS

Associated with the question of whether software is tangible, is a similar conundrum about why the process of developing software is so miasmic. Now the same answer to both – *viz.* that software is intangible – will not serve, because software development produces many tangible items (which can be viewed as the part-finished products of software), such as specifications, designs and programs. Nor does it necessarily follow that an intangible outcome, such as software as distinct from programs, requires an intangible process to produce it.

In fact there is nothing particularly invisible about the software development process, unless it is the thought-processes of people engaged in it, before they are fixed in some form. Just because we cannot stub our toes on pieces of cast-iron or festoon ourselves with wires does not make software development less visible. One must know what to look for, and be able to recognize it when it is on view.

Management is not a singular affair. As S. J. Perleman wrote 'It takes two to tango, but only one to squirm'. There is the manager and the managed – that is one way of looking at life. Another, better, way to see the issue, is that it is a combination of parties towards a mutually achievable end; any disablement of this joint process may be through the inadequacies of either partner to it, or both.

The major fault with most software management is that it becomes disabled at the outset by either or both of the following:

1. The manger's lack of comprehension and, therefore, lack of confidence.
2. The exponents' omission to make their work visibly understandable.

In such circumstances, a progress report can become something that passes from the mouth of the technician through the ears of the manager, without going anywhere near the minds of either.

In fact, there are two perquisites for software management; a visible record of what is going on, and a procedure for both parties to review it periodically. The first of these is the archive. This was mentioned briefly, in passing, in Chapter 5. The second is a technique called 'structured walkthrough'. Both of these are dealt with forthwith.

11.2.1 The software development archive

This is no more, or less, than a necessary and sufficient historical record of all the steps and stages in a software development exercise. If we see this process in life cycle terms, the archive is a living entity throughout it. That means that not only is the archive affected and emended by all the activities in each stage of its first development, but also that subsequent evolutions too – such as maintenance and new, evolutionary versions – lead to changes in the archive: additions, perhaps deletions and so forth.

In general, there are four questions attaching to the software development archive:

1. *Content*; what should be put in it?
2. *Format*; how should the material be arranged?
3. *Volume*; what should be discarded, and what kept?
4. *Medium*; how are software developments archived?

Each of these is accorded a few descriptive paragraphs below, the first two being conflated for convience.

CONTENT AND FORMAT

There are, in fact, two quite clearly separable classes of archive content – technical and management information – which should, in the interest of clarity, be demarcated by format. This, then, is the first guideline here:

1. Have separate sections, or even volumes, for technical and management information; for convenience, we shall allude to these as the technical and management archives respectively.

The technical archive can, and should, be arranged on the basis of a life cycle model, such as that in Figure 4.2. This both categorizes the content and indicates the form of the archive. Each major stage constitutes a chapter, and the ordering of chapters fits the life cycle sequence. The ordered contents of a typical technical archive are as given in Table 11.1.

The issue of discarding ('purging') from the technical archive, to achieve a reasonable volume whilst preserving the concept of necessity and sufficiency for its purposes, is dealt with below. As for further detail of the contents of each category ('chapter') in the technical archive, these issues – with one exception – should all be clear enough from the earlier parts of this work.

So-called 'Chapter 14: technical correspondence' requires a little further elaboration. Often, in large and multi-source supplies, considerable traffic occurs across suppliers, and between them and the client, to clarify technical details, and even aspects of requirement, during the design, implementation and testing stages. In such cases, it is

TABLE 11.1 The technical archive

Volume 1	Contents list of *both* archive volumes
Chapter 1	Initiatives for the development; concepts and early feasibility
Chapter 2	User requirements' specification
Chapter 3	Functional specification
Chapter 4	Outline systems design
Chapter 5	Systems' architecture, and software specification
Chapter 6	Software design; architecture (decomposition) and detail
Chapter 7	Implementation; integrand specifications, data and program structure definition
Chapter 8	Code listings
Chapter 9	Test plan; author and first level integration tests and results
Chapter 10	Integration and alpha-tests and results
Chapter 11	Deliverable documentation; definition of deliverables and their actuality
Chapter 12	Validation and certification; beta-test and results (black/white box)
Chapter 13	Client (or pseudo-client) and other suppliers' technical correspondence
Chapter 14	Maintenance record; reports and consequential actions

TABLE 11.2 The management archive

Volume 2	Contents of both archive volumes
Chapter 1	Management structure (all parties in supply) up to highest accountable levels.
Chapter 2	Task definitions; computer or pseudo-contract
Chapter 3	Activities' plans; original (rudimentary and OSD notional); all updates
Chapter 4	Overall time-scale and effort estimates, and all updates
Chapter 5	Cost control documents and status matrices
Chapter 6	Change control traffic
Chapter 7	Record of management structured walkthrough
Chapter 8	Internal (supplier) memoranda and correspondence general
Chapter 9	External (client/pseudo-client) correspondence – contract and commercial

advisable to institute a formal process for enquiry and answers at the start of a functional specification stage, for use throughout the life cycle. Simple forms may be devised, making sure that the originating agency, date and addressee are clearly provided. It is these, along with any letters, specification manuals or other documents from Chapter 6 of the management archive, that delineate parts of the basis on which implementation is done. The management archive is set out, schematically, in Table 11.2.

VOLUME

Volume and volatility of archive materials are distinct problems for all but the smallest software development. Unless care is taken, several cubic meters of 'history' on a 'save all' basis are the result; if one discards carelessly, one ends up with a document that is useless for any practical purpose – whatever its virtues of brevity. The volume problem is dealt with simply. 'Chapters' of the technical archive concern either formal or informal stages of specification or development. The formal stages concern Chapters 3, 9, 10, 11, 12 and 13. It is advisable to keep all versions of all documents in these categories, carefully dated and designated with some version code invented for the purpose. Documents in the functional specification may contain unauthorized drafts, but most contain all signed-off versions – such as the first base-line functional specification – and all subsequent amend-

ments (duly authorized) that have passed change control evaluation and management approval.

Other 'chapters' of the technical archive may be seen as informal, and the current document plus only a limited number (e.g. one or two at most) of previous versions need be kept. Older versions may be purged from the archive. Two levels of the technical volume may prove particularly volatile, the user requirement specification and the code listings. Either or both may lead to an explosive growth in the volume of material, so discarding is particularly important; it must be carefully regulated though, as chaos may otherwise ensue.

In the case of the management archive, the matters of volume and volatility are much simpler. In general, volumes are small and of intermittent generation, and they are not volatile in the same sense as technical topics. In the case of management archives, it is the mutation of content that is of major importance and, consequently, all versions of all documents must be retained as though the whole affair was one of the most stringent formality – as indeed it often is, for example in legal contracts of supply on fixed time-scale and cost bases.

MEDIUM

In the present epoch, much of the former difficulty of keeping archives, and maintaining them in a properly updated form, is ameliorated by the use of the software engineer's electronic working environment – PSE or Ipse – the better ones of which have a sufficiency of features such as text-editing/word-processing, implemented methods and their notations, high level languages and data management systems for configuration or versions' control. In previous epochs, archiving activities were based on a ream of paper and a well bitten stub of pencil, and one may speak with justification of a cubic meter of archive material. Nowadays it may be a kilobyte, megabyte or gigabyte – or anything in between. Nor, it must be recalled, are archives required only for that pass of the software life cycle that concerns a substantive release version of software. Prototypes need archiving too, and there may be many passes of prototype activity, as Boehm's 'spiral' scheme depicts in Figure 2.10. Finally though, the prototype archives will give way to the archive for definitive development and this will, in turn, give way to the deliverable documentation and its variants for new versions. To demarcate these documents, one may have an archive management system for prototypes and substantive development distinct from the version configuration management for deliverable documentation. Given the importance of the latter for systems' maintenance service, and the public interest that may be involved in it, such a separation is generally desirable.

In one life cycle area, archiving is still not too well served by the PSE or Ipse; that is software design. Graphical notations are neither easy nor cheap to implement (in fact they may not be possible to implement at all on insufficient VDU hardware, lacking essential features for the purpose). However, increasingly more work-stations and stand-alone PC equipment are being brought out, incorporating notations such as Mascot, SADT, BS 6224, data-flow and so forth. The cheaper systems tend to have insufficient features at this level, and also lack management or other life cycle support tools; still, what can one expect for less than $10,000? They may also be single concurrent user facilities, so one may be speaking of 'less than (but not so much so) $n \times \$10,000$', and the economics of worth may look unattractive.

What is more serious is that we have seen this deficiency quite seriously deter software engineers from using graphical notations in design, preferring to go into pseudo-code very early after specification. On small and small-to-medium tasks, say for systems up to 10K of source code, this might not be too great a hazard to good design, although it may still leave a comprehension problem for people modifying the system later. To repeat an aphorism of earlier reference; 'A diagram says more than a thousand words'. As a last word on the subject of archives, it is worthwhile stating the obvious for, however obvious it may be, it is surprising how often this trap is sprung; archives of any sort are useless if they are not kept up to date.

11.2.2 Management and technical 'structured walkthroughs'

Structured walkthrough is a planned and purposive review of a software development, for one of two clear purposes. A technical walkthrough relates to the status and technical issues of a stage in development, or a deliverable from that stage (such as a design), and generally is limited to the technical considerations and includes few of the management ones. In contradistinction to this, a management walkthrough will review technical status only in the general sense, for example as emanating from a technical walkthrough ('the software design is not good enough, because . . . '), and will concentrate more sedulously on activities' and resource planning, contract milestones, cost control and so on. The two types of walkthrough are defined further forthwith.

The technical (structured) walkthrough is part of software quality control procedure, which has been dealt with, in part, in Chapter 9, and will be returned to in some detail in a later section; it is mentioned here only for purposes of distinction between two topics that are often conflated, to the detriment of both. It is the periodic (i.e. scheduled), or contingent review of an ongoing life cycle stage, and its work in progress.

Typical examples of such stages might be: specification, design, implementation and testing. The 'work in progress' under review would, therefore, be either functional specifications and outline system design, software specification and designs down to integrand specification, code and author testing of code, integrand test plans and the progress thereof. The 'contingency' that may bring about a technical walkthrough, may be anything from a palpable crisis to the imminence of a deliverable outcome at a stage. Technical walkthrough is usually undertaken by some agency outside the implementation (or specification) team, such as an internal quality assurance group or an external, contracted consultant.

Generally, 'structured walkthrough' is understood to mean a management review technique, with a greater degree of explicit purpose and formality than the rather vague term 'review' may connote, and it is with this in mind that we proceed.

Now management styles differ from place to place, and epoch to epoch, but five basic questions suffice to bound the space in which the question 'What is a structured walkthrough?' can be answered:

1. Who initiates a management structured walkthrough?
2. When is one held?
3. What are the objects of assessment?

4. Who attends?
5. What procedures apply?

As has been our method to date, we accord each one a descriptive subsection.

INITIATION OF STRUCTURED WALKTHROUGH

To answer this question, we need to consider the organization in which the walkthrough is taking place. This might seem out of place, or digressive, to some – but there is no way of speaking of levels in an organization, which we will be doing, without revealing within what type of structure the 'level' applies.

The four most commonly found organization forms, in business and industry in general, are: centralized, decentralized, adaptive and innovative. As pointed out by Ansoff and Brandenberg (1971), the first two have fixed hierarchies and a permanently established workforce within them; the centralized form tends to optimize profit margins but limit growth; the decentralized form may achieve some rational balance between margins and growth.

The centralized form will tend to disfavor invention and business diversity, in favor of centralized control and the maximization of profit; the decentralized form will favor geographical expansion and product diversity, at the cost of centralized control and profit margins, although gross sales will be easier to increase than in the case of a centralized firm. Innovation may tend to be easier to achieve in a decentralized organization not stressing the 'steady-state' efficiency of the centralized form, but questions of the dissemination and exploitation of its results – products – may limit its value to a decentralized group.

An 'adaptive' organization has a fixed management hierarchy in its topmost structures only, and otherwise a mutable organization form – often called a 'matrix' – in which management accountability may be episodic over time, and staff may migrate from 'pools' of resources of projects or produce developments, for their duration. The adaptive form tends to balance growth and margins with the need to achieve and fully exploit technical innovation.

The 'innovative' form has an almost entirely mutable management structure, below – perhaps – just one level of 'fixed' and uppermost management, and, ideally, an 'adaptive' workforce migrating from semi-permanent 'resource pools' to tasks where they are transitorily accountable. It is the archetypal research structure, and tends to be incapable of the 'steady state' efficiency of the centralized form, or even the qualified degrees of it achieved in decentralized and adaptive organizations.

Many large organizations are hybrids of these organization forms. It is usual to find that so-called multinational corporations that are in some manufacturing and distribution sector, such as petrochemicals or electronics, are decentralized/innovative, with an uneasy relationship between essential central functions and the decentralized autonomies, and between the finance generators (e.g. manufacturing/marketing) and research. The effect of organization form on the development of software engineering competence in a firm can be considerable, as the reader will appreciate. Little work seems to have been done on this aspect of the subject, and most firms are as they are as a result of short term considerations rather than long-term planning, and the influence of 'company-cultural' attitudes to organization issues – whether justified or not.

The matters bearing on software development that might be affected include such things as the following:

1. The 'user'/supplier interface, for product development and internal supplies.
2. Management of the software development process itself.
3. Accretion of a 'professionally competent' software development group or groups, and the environment in which that competence level can be maintained.
4. Technical facilities, such as Ipse/PSE justification and policy.
5. 'Independent' quality functions.
6. Competence in post-delivery support.

However, a full-scale treatment of the effects of organization form on software development is beyond our purpose here.

This short digression into organization studies will be revisited, up to a point, where management topics under discussion justify it. It is given here to prevent the assertion that different organization forms have special requirements for structured walkthrough. In fact, centralized, decentralized and adaptive structures have no such distinctions between them for these purposes and, as they account for the vast majority of organizations in which software development is done, we will take this set as our structural paradigm when dealing with management walkthrough of software development.

The exception, an adaptive form for research organizations, frequently gives rise to difficulty with managing software development in general, and there is no one clearly discernible cause in these cases. The organization form may provide little in the way of a permanent basis for strong and structured management approaches, but – in addition – the acquired attitudes of researchers to the 'tyranny' of life cycle-based development (as they see it) may be an equivalent contributory factor.

Most management structures in centralized, decentralized or adaptive organizations can be seen as hierarchies. Figure 11.1 depicts such a hierarchy, in this case for a hypothetical company in the IT product sector. The assiduous reader will realize that this scheme is deeply interesting in its own right. For instance, how task structures in the quality area are 'mapped' with those in product development, how this affects and is affected by new prototypes, and what relationship exists between the 'quality' functions and existing product support within a commercial department. On management-level orientation courses in software engineering, this diagram stops the dog and pony show with a vengeance, and precipitates the most wonderful response – rather like that famous Dutch beer that reaches otherwise inaccessible parts. Sadly, we cannot dwell here on all the questions that arise. Our original topic cries out to be treated.

In a structure such as that depicted in Figure 11.1, some elaboration may occur concerning the 'technical managers' – so that there occurs a bunching together of products in development, under the control of (say) 'product sector' managers. This bunching may go on, introducing a new level to the hierarchies each time, whenever there is too great a number or diversity of management tasks for one person. All this is strictly according to 'the book' of management theory; 'bananas (clusters) are good, sausages (linear linkages) are bad' in organization structures.

Now, the bearing this has on structured walkthroughs is that they are initiated by the highest level of *directly accountable* management in the structure. Going 'bottom up'

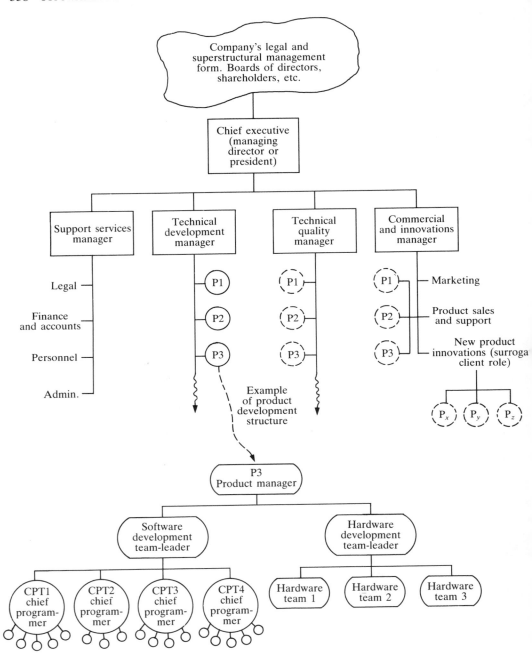

FIGURE 11.1 Company structure (hypothetical), seen as a hierarchy.

through the hierarchy in Figure 11.1, we have – successively – software engineers, chief programmers (software development task-leaders), software team-leaders, product managers, product sector managers and so on up to product division managers and managing director.

Now at each level, the question can be asked; 'Could you make a direct contribution to this job, e.g. "add value" to it in the technical development sense, if need be?' At some level the answer will change from 'Yes' into 'No', although it may not be so clear a transition. But, above that level, managers are generally accountable, within defined limits of a management task, whilst, below that level, managers are specifically accountable for all tasks within their sector.

In Figure 11.1, this highest level of directly accountable management – that can add value to the development process if need be – will probably be the 'Technical development manager' as the schematic stands at present. If the amount of developments, the P1, P2, etc., becomes unmanageable on this basis, then no doubt a 'P3' walkthrough (say) would be initiated by a 'product sector manager', although the correct course of action would be to devolve task management over more 'technical development managers'.

SCHEDULES FOR STRUCTURED WALKTHROUGH

There are two aspects bearing on the question of periodicity for structured walkthrough: (a) the ability (or otherwise) to plan and schedule these events some time in advance, and (b) the need to call for structured walkthrough in the event of contingencies arising. We will address the general case first.

Two related questions dominate the planning of management structured walkthrough. Should anything significant have occurred or been achieved since the last one, and will we be able to know if any statements or evidence on the subjects under review are plausible? Consider an example that highlights the negative possibilities that may flow from these questions.

In a specification exercise it may not be clear what event or status is to eventuate before – say – the one to draft the first version of a user requirement specification, as complete as it is at that time. The information collection, collation, ordering and recording activities are not always entirely explicit for a particular item or set of items in requirements. Users tend to reveal needs, wants, desires, wish-lists and so forth in a disordered fashion with a strong element of interleaving the details of different items.

They may say, in effect; 'I need A, and B, and oh! A is made up of A1, A2, A3, A4 and I need (where were we?) D, and E, and F, and ah (expletive) I've just remembered, A5 is a requirement strongly related to V7. Have I told you about V yet? Oh (double expletive), V comprises V1, V2, V3 and so on'. The chess example 'CAISSA' in Chapter 5 makes the point, up to a point; other examples in Volume 2 of this series will make it with more force.

A structured walkthrough in the middle of this may have difficulty with its own structure; what can be asked that is likely to produce a non-vacuous response?

Obviously, this extreme example – the URS stage – is not representative of all the stages comprising the life cycle. Moreover, each 'stage' will have its outcome – functional specification/outline systems design, software specifications, 'next level' architecture designs in Lehman's terms, decomposition and detailing in design (with respect to functions, data or processes), integrand specifications, coded integrands, programs packaged

from integrands, software load modules and so forth. All are explicit, that is visible, outcomes – or 'deliverables'.

Clearly, a minimal schedule of management walkthrough activities must be related to these 'deliverables'. They must be scheduled shortly before, or at, the time scheduled for the achievement concerned. Equally clearly there is a suggestion of 'marking' an activities' plan, and for this we must have such a plan. Section 13.1 deals with this aspect of management technique.

Sometimes, of course, there is too great an interregnum between successive structured walkthrough events done on this minimalist basis. Then, the intervening interval must be closely reviewed with respect to the original questions – can anything real be achieved, and will we be in a position to evaluate its plausibility? A dreadfully common occurrence at poorly scheduled reviews of this sort is that the only apparently strong statement of any kind to be made is something along the lines: 'Design (or functional specification, or whatever) is 38.432 percent complete!' That third decimal place is the killer. What does it mean? What can it possibly mean? The usual meaning is, in fact, generally quite useless. It may mean: 'We are 38.432 percent through the time allowance'; or: 'We've spent 38.432 percent of the money'; or 'We've defined 38.432 percent of integrands to be coded'; or almost anything of the sort. It *sounds* as though it *should* be telling us something. Usually, quantified 'progress' during a stage of development is so contingent for its meaning on other, imponderable, factors that it is meaningless.

In the absence of any expectation of use, or outcome from a walkthrough, one should not be held. Vacuous reviews do more harm than good. That means, in turn, that considerable time may elapse between *scheduled* structured walkthrough events. That is not to say that management is reporting lapses, but it may be a semi-active process in the sense that managers receive reports, emendations to plans and so forth, without a strong, face-to-face and formal interaction such as is the case in structured walkthrough.

There is nothing necessarily against this state of affairs; management styles differ, as has already been said, and some would leave matters as they are, given that no need becomes evident from the management reporting. Others would occasionally spring a structured walkthrough on the unwary development group, whether or not it seemed likely to be useful, and despite my warning against 'vacuous' processes, I incline to the latter myself. An unexpected walkthrough can have a galvanizing effect, and I have seen the most astounding progress made in the shadow of one.

All that concerns management structured walkthrough. What of its technical equivalent? In the main, of course, this is the province of QC and QI activity. But what happens when major technical problems arise? Any evident, or supposed, technical contingencies will cause a technical (as distinct from management) structured walkthrough – or should do so. But here, as elsewhere, the technical investigations should be distinguished from the management interest so that conflation of issues and resulting confusions can be avoided. A typical example might arise if, during implementation, some awful design problems arise.

Then the first thing to do, either at the implementation team-level or above, is to halt the development, put the red light on, about 'Whoa!', or whatever it takes to stop the software engineers from blasting away at their terminals. Next, a detailed design 'walkthrough' must be done. This might be a highly non-trivial activity, and management

approval must be given for it; however, the contingencies cannot be evaluated, at management level, until such a walkthrough has been done.

In walkthroughs caused by technical contingencies, the review is to determine technical quality at that stage. It might have come about through QI activities; it might involve an external agency contracted for the purpose; it might last for weeks or months – thereby stopping the whole show. There are no general guidelines for how to do a technical walkthrough, other than that a competently kept archive will be essential for it, and its outcome should be formal – i.e. written reports to management setting out both technical and non-technical aspects of the problem and its solution.

As well as contingency reviews, technical walkthroughs should be scheduled, within a quality control plan, for all major stages of software development. Thus there should be major design reviews and code reviews scheduled by the author team, as full technical structured walkthroughs of that status. Likewise for author testing, where the method and status of tests needs to be revealed.

WHAT ARE THE OBJECTS OF ASSESSMENT IN A MANAGEMENT WALKTHROUGH?

A management structured walkthrough of a software development task addresses the following issues:

1. The archive, its status and quality.
2. Quality inspection report: general and detailed stage-specific.
3. Status of any special activities, e.g. test planning, deliverable documentation.
4. Chief programmer's technical report on the current stage, any difficulties, changes, etc.
5. Review of activities' plans and status matrices (q.v.), time-scale and effort estimates and budget consequences.
6. Status of resources; staffing and technical facilities.
7. Relationships, e.g., with other development teams, suppliers, client or pseudo-client.

This list is, as the lawyers say, 'enumerating but not limiting'. A normal agenda at a standard walkthrough may include other items as appropriate, special reports and so on, and an agenda for 'other business'. The seven items on the list are reasonably obvious, along with the definitions already given and to be detailed in the sections of this chapter yet to come. What is not so obvious, perhaps, is the dependency of this agenda on the life cycle model of software development, with its identifiable 'stages', and on the archive providing the visibility of this process. Quite how other theories of software development, such as those involving non-stage-based 'iterative prototyping' approaches, deal with the clarity required for scheduling and defining management structured walkthrough is not entirely clear.

WHO ATTENDS?

Many exercises in management structured walkthrough resemble astrological conferences, but without their sense of rigor. A collection of personages gather, whose interest may be acute, but whose relevance may be minimal; an atmosphere of tobacco-impregnated disorder prevails, and the software chap is seen in a corner trying to reduce his normal displacement volume by one-third. Getting the practitioners right is a useful start.

Basically, the 'law' of small numbers is a helpful guide here. The highest level of directly accountable management must, particulary if initiating, attend; QI/QA must be represented; last, but not least, the chief programmer(s) must be present. This alone would be the ensemble necessary for a management walkthrough of a software development.

If a composite software/hardware walkthrough is attempted, then the equivalent representatives of hardware teams attend. Implementation team-leaders, i.e. the bottom level of Figure 11.1, may co-opt other technicians from teams as necessary – so long as the precepts of minimalism prevail. The highest level manager should chair the meeting, and a meeting secretary should take (and produce) minutes of major decisions, actions, actionees and due dates; a suitable person for this is usually the QI/QA representative. If the highest ranking manager feels incapable of running the walkthrough, it has probably been initiated at the wrong level, or he or she is operating at the wrong level.

Small developments tend to have small teams doing management walkthrough, say three or four people only. Large and very large tasks tend to have a fairly rare 'super walkthrough' procedure, and more frequent reviews of the decomposed tasks. I have seen a 'super walkthrough' fill a fair-sized room, and involved fifteen to twenty people, say.

The sum of a set of walkthrough events is not a detailed review of the whole. Quite how they cope on something like SDI ('Star Wars') makes me wonder; do they hire a football stadium, or have they arrived at that sublime level where complete overview is impossible? Or is SDI in the realm of the 'innovative' structure for its achievement – i.e. research – and thus beyond the demands of development management?

WHAT PROCEDURES APPLY?

A structured walkthrough, unlike semi-active management reporting or some of the quite casual species of review, must be formal or else it is of very little use. The elements of this formality are notice, agenda, competent chairmanship and secretary functions, and accurate minutes. These minutes must have the force of management decision and, to be effective, must be produced within a short time after the walkthrough. The draft minutes go from chairman to all parties at the meeting, and to a wider audience (if need be) on a 'need to know' basis.

Under normal circumstances, a planned walkthrough has a clear notice period flagged ('marked') on an activities' plan; minimally, a two days notice period for a contingency walkthrough should be sufficient; and even the scare-them-out-of-their-skins walkthrough should give the bottom level groups at least one day to get their acts together, to fish that anorexic archive out from under a few months' mildewed garbage behind the filing cabinet, and so on.

For the rest, agenda, chairmanship and secretary functions have been commented on already and, being matters of applied common sense, as well as individual style, need detain us no further.

11.2.3 How to treat 'invisibility'

Genuine invisibility as an immanent property is rare. Concealment might be going on, or no archiving and walkthrough activities as is more often the case; or a particular stage

might be work-in-progress involving a genuinely intangible activity – thought. But, usually, invisibility lies somewhere between a lack of confidence in the viewer, the confusion of issues where incomprehension is equivalent to invisibility, and the arcane and perhaps slipshod methods of people doing software development. The following checklist for managers, and other non-practitioners, may be helpful:

1. Become literate in software engineering, up to whatever limits of necessity, ability, inclination and time permit.
2. Cause the software development process to be visible in your environment, by archiving and structured walkthrough means.
3. Manage the software life cycle process *actively*, and not *reactively*.
4. Where genuine problems of comprehension occur, such as in the detailed design and implementation stages, delegate the visibility of the process to subject experts. This comes about, to some extent anyway, if proper QC/QI/QA procedures are adopted. In extreme cases, this may be supplemented by an added level of expert audit, possible contracted from an outside agency. Again, this is far better arranged as a planned activity than as a spasm of panic.
5. Make it explicitly clear to software developers that they are expected to subscribe to both visibility and comprehension of their activities and creations. This should become an instance of virtue in staff appraisals – see Chapter 13.
6. Never forget that there can be no failure to fulfill what has not been explicitly required, and for which the adequate means are lacking. In other words make sure that software engineers are themselves trained in management methods, and that your requirements are clearly known to them. As Gogol wrote: 'It is no use blaming the mirror if your own mug's awry'.

This last is a reprise of the reason, given right at the start, why managers and software staff should have a shared conceptual framework and vocabulary for the software development process.

CHAPTER TWELVE

ESTIMATING EFFORT AND TIME-SCALE

It was said earlier that quality of outcome is the whole of the matter in software development, and that is comprises two frequently interacting subjects – technical and economic components of quality. Here, we address the latter, on the understanding that the definition of economic quality concerns the competence of estimating only, i.e. the setting of achievable targets. Other issues, such as cost justification and control are either beyond the scope of this work, or are treated elsewhere – as in the case of the activities and cost management sections in Chapter 13.

Software estimating concerns both effort to do a software development task and the time over which this effort is to be expended. In the following we outline some of the fallacies in approach that surround the subject, and describe ongoing research. A recommended method for estimating software tasks is given, and especial attention is paid to the very sensitive relationship between effort and time in this process.

Viewed properly, this subject is a part of overall quality, as ineluctably linked to technical quality as the 'head' is to the 'tail' side of a coin. And, just as compliance and modifiability comprise the mandatory criteria for technical quality, so do the topics of effort and time-scale dominate in its economic counterpart.

That some software developments achieve a working system at all is little short of a miracle, and it is often a miracle sought at a pauper's price. Then it is not too fanciful to see software engineering as a kind of warfare, with software engineers fighting with objectives under malign circumstances, in harrowing and aimless battles, where something like heroism is in evidence.

Pressed to define 'malign circumstances', the following four factors would score high on most lists of the banes that afflict software development:

1. The use of inexperienced (or otherwise insufficient) staff, including managers and others whose activities are contiguous with software engineering.
2. Ill-conditioned, volatile or otherwise inadequate specifications.
3. Paucity of technical means, such as PSE/Ipse facilities, relevant to the purpose.
4. Insufficient time.

It is clear that the first and last on this list concern the sufficiency of relevant effort, and the time-scale over which it will be deployed for the task. Of these, the most subtly virulent in its effect is 'time'. Insufficiency of staff, in any one of several respects, may be obvious, or possible to make obvious. Not so with allowed time for the task – as we shall see.

For a given software development task, although one should not view life this way at all, one *may* be able to get away with a rudimentary statement of aims jotted down on an old tram-ticket, programs cobbled together on a venerable MORON-I machine, in octal-code, and the whole ramshackle affair done by a couple of old fellows who last wrote a program, and one in Cobol at that, in 1965. As remarked, one might 'get away' with such a thing – at a terrible price in technical quality, no doubt. But what can never be got away with is a radical insufficiency of time.

Nor is the matter as simple as having too little time to travel from A to C; in that case, B is reached in the given time, and that is that. In software engineering, a deadline is violated generally at some substantial cost. If a project is concerned, the 'single end client' might sue you until your teeth rattle; if a product slips out of its window of opportunity, it generally takes your shirt with it.

The consequences of this are that time terrorizes software development. Take, for example, the relative effects of development cost overspend, and those due to development time overrun, on the profit of an IT product. A major, international management consulting firm found that, for clients in the technical product sector, given a five years' product life, a 20 percent annual growth rate for its sale and a 12 percent annual price erosion on it, the picture was as follows:

1. A 50 percent development cost (effort) overrun erodes the profit margin on the product by 3.5 percent only.
2. A six months' delay in bringing a product to market erodes profit margins on the product by 33 percent.

As we proceed in this section, the specter hovering over all questions will have the face of a clock, and its hands will point at one minute to deadline.

12.1 SOME ESSENTIAL DEFINITIONS

First, though, we need to set out – with some care – the material that is to follow. For in few other subjects is it so possible to mislead unintentionally. And, although the material presented here is synoptic, it is essential to start with a clear set of definitions.

12.1.1 Phase definition for estimating

Estimates of effort and time-scale may pertain to one, or more, of three parts of the software life cycle:

1. The specification and feasibility phase; that is, the activities up to and including functional specification and OSD. These activities may include substantial exercises in pro-

totype development, for clarifying requirements or technical means. We call this *'phase 1'* of the life cycle.

2. The software development activities, from architecture design up to – and including – software validation and certification if called for. We call this *'phase 2'* of the life cycle.

3. The software maintenance phase, commencing when the system goes into service, and terminating when the software is taken out of service. This definition excludes major new versions, as each of these will involve a new triad of phases. We call this *'phase 3'* of the life cycle.

In the following, we identify and discuss three classes of approach to estimating (in some cases, it is overstating the case to speak of a 'method'). These are: the fallacies, research endeavors and recommended methods.

It is very easy to see how confusion can arise between the two lists. Are we (at some point) speaking of a fallacy, or research; and does it concern phase 1 or 2, or both, or neither? Is a method, for which positive experiences are claimed, common to (or concerning) all phases, or some of them and – if so – which?

First though, when we speak of estimating, to what quantities do we refer? As we said at the outset, the two issues that comprise economic quality in software development are the effort to make the system to acceptable criteria of technical quality, and the duration (or 'time-scale') over which the effort will be needed for this purpose. The usual units, or dimensions, of effort are people multiplied by time – as in man-hours, person-years and so on. The units of time-scale are the normal ones of time simply – hours, days, months, years. That one author debunked this unit of effort will be dealt with in Section 12.5 (Brooks 1976).

12.1.2 The general fallacy of premature estimating

We will take as our point of departure, one fallacy, above all others, which dominates this topic – and that is the error of prematurity. We have met prematurity elsewhere and in a different context – that of diving straight from some level of specification into coding. Here we refer to prematurity of estimating.

When it occurs, and it is horribly prevalent, it concerns a conflation of issues, namely the derivation of 'order of magnitude' (or budgetary) estimates for phase 1, and the need to know reasonably accurate values of effort and time-scale needed for phase 2. Of course, circumstances conspire to produce this fallacy, and it is simple-minded to plaster blame all over clients (or pseudo-clients), managers or commercial operatives. The elementary fact of the matter is that clients need to know the price for a 'bespoke' system to be contracted, just as much as managers in product companies have to know what development budgets to set aside. However, elementary as such facts are, other issues are inescapable; phase 1 activities can only be estimated (and that rather inaccurately) during that phase, and estimates for phase 2 cannot be said to be possible at all before a critical point late in phase 1. The matter has been trenchantly expressed, and vividly illustrated, in the literature of software estimating. One representation is shown in Figure 12.1 (after Boehm 1981). Most practicing software engineers would recognize this scheme with a narrowing

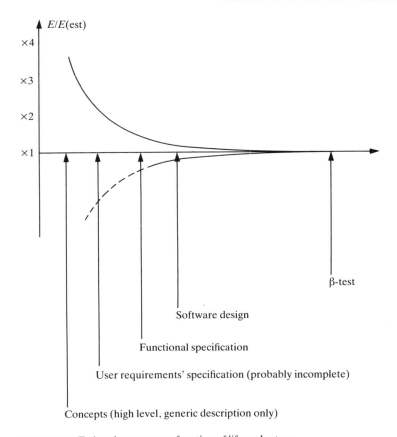

FIGURE 12.1 Estimating error as a function of life cycle stage.

of the eyes and a clenching of the jaw muscles. How many times have you been stranded up the left end of that horizontal axis, without a paddle?

However, without losing sight of our topic, there are two small quarrels to be had with the Boehm scheme, if we may dub it thus. First, it is unlikely that estimating errors as high even as 400 percent adequately represent the problem of premature attempts to determine phase 2 costs. On many occasions, a figure like 400 percent is the limit of managers' (or clients') patience, and a software development task is abandoned, rather than allowed to stagger on to 500, 600 . . . 1000 percent overrun on cost. If anything, then, the extreme left-hand part of the upper curve understates the case. Second, it is extremely unlikely that the left-hand part of the lower curve is representative at all. It purports to say that there is an equivalent chance of overestimating software as there is of underestimating it. This is counter-intuitive for two reasons: (a) specifications are much more likely to grow than to shrink during the phase of identifying requirements, and (b) complexity too is almost always underestimated. The consequences are obvious. There will be a high degree of

imported complexity in most software developments undertaken and, therefore, an inevitable tendency for the complexity of 'phase 2' to be radically underestimated.

Notwithstanding these defects, Figure 12.1 represents the fallacy of premature estimating well enough. Prematurity is a general-case term for a variety of misguided approaches to estimating 'phase 2' effort and time-scale and is – in fact – one of two basic fallacies that are now described.

12.2 SPECIFIC FALLACIES IN SOFTWARE ESTIMATING

The fallacies in software estimating may be summarized as follows:

1. Premature attempts to make hard-and-fast determinations of effort and time-scale needed for phase 1 specification activities, or those for phase 2 implementation, or both. More rarely, phase 3 estimates for the maintenance of a system are essayed prematurely too, but our main concern here is a more fundamental matter as stated.
2. The use of spurious 'average productivity factors' to compute effort 'estimates' from some evaluation of code-size.

We will consider each of these in turn.

As Figure 12.1 attests, premature estimates for phase 1 plus phase 2 are generally essayed before the functional specification is stable – in other words, whilst newly articulated requirements are being uncovered and incorporated, whatever the complexity of implementing them may turn out to be.

There are four specific fallacies of prematurity quite commonly encountered in practice, and one dreadful pseudo-method none the less frequently found:

1. Analogy (based on 'expert' assessment, or on inexpert opinion).
2. Parkinson's law.
3. Price-to-win.
4. Top down systems analysis.
5. Productivity factors.

We describe each of these, briefly, in the following subsections.

12.2.1 Estimates based on analogy: expert and inexpert

'Expert'-based analogy takes a high level, generic statement of purpose – such as 'a chess-playing system' or 'the controller for a car radio' – and has some software 'expert' say of it, in effect; 'I did one of these two years ago, and it took six of us two years to do', or something of the sort. The dangers of this approach are, of course, obvious. No high level generic statement of purpose can be sufficient for an adequate assement of complexity.

If that is bad, not least because it trades on Fred's so-called 'expertise' to legitimize what can only be a guess, inexpert-based analogy is worse. In this, not only is the insufficiency of requirements' specification in question, but also the dubious process of analogy

is even more suspect. Now Fred's cousin's girl-friend's uncle, the omnibus driver, is required to say (in effect): 'Oh! It's software is it? Well, it'll cost a million – bound to do. These things always cost a million'.

There is manifestly no merit in such an approach, but it is surprising how often things of this sort go on 'high' in the life cycle – either to fix product development budgets, or to set a limit for a project. The results are the sort of thing that afflict the leftmost part of Boehm's graph, and this fallacy is to be avoided like the plague although, as we shall see, some aspects of analogous estimating by 'experts' may be of use as a *part* of other approaches. But even the most 'expert' opinion on phase 2 costs, delivered early in phase 1, is of no value, whilst inexpert advice at any stage is no advice at all, and both must be avoided.

12.2.2 Pessimism and Parkinson

A close relative of this dire approach is known as 'Parkinson's law', after the famous author C. Northcote Parkinson, who expressed an axiom about bureaucracies in one, trenchant, aphorism: 'Work expands to fill the time available for it'.

Applied to software, this has anyone imaginable – expert or inexpert – say, or suppose: 'Give it x man-years, and they'll take that; give it y man-years and, as night follows day, that's what they'll require'. In other words, why bother to estimate? Set some arbitrary amount (time, money or both), light the touch-paper and retire to a safe distance. Again, the fallacies fall off the page in their urgency to be noticed. Whereas the analogies are little more than blind (or, at best, monocular) guesses, 'Parkinson' produces a definition of some kind. 'Give them a million and they'll take it' is substantially different from 'It'll cost a million', although neither is what one would call an estimate.

All these approahces should be avoided, and it is the managers in a company who should do the avoiding in the first place.

One conspicuously seductive aspect of 'analogy' true also of 'Parkinson', is that it is cheap and quick to achieve. We can express the 'cost' of an estimating approach as that proportion of total phases 1 plus 2 effort of software engineers, to arrive at the life cycle point when the approach can first be used. Likewise, we can express the relative rapidity of an approach on a rough scale of values according to the life cycle stage at which the approach can first be used.

On the basis of these crude metrics, all of the premature approaches described 'cost' next to nothing, and are almost instantly revealed once a high level, generic scope is defined. However, in no other instance is the expression 'cheap and nasty' more apposite, as Figure 12.1 graphically illustrates. Yet what are beleaguered managers to do? Budgets for product development must be set aside; clients will clamor for estimates, and at the most inopportune times. This brings us to the next of the fallacies listed.

12.2.3 'Price-to-win'

An instance of this occurs when the sales department bids for a software (or composite) development contract on a 'price-to-win' basis. Here, what happens in that a client's bud-

get (perhaps itself done prematurely, possibly involving the blindest of blind guesses) is taken as an inviolable guideline for an offer on which some binding contract may be made. The client wants to pay no more than x, so bid x. If a competitor does the same, then bid $x - 1$, and so on.

Again, the fallacy is not hard to spot. 'Price-to-win' is not necessarily related to *cost-to-do*. A job won, against trenchant competition, may have had some quite arbitrary amounts in terms of the task itself stipulated for its phase 1 and 2 estimates. Values of twenty person-years of effort, and two elapsed years of time may turn out, in reality, to be orders of magnitude too small. The task may require 57.8 person-years of effort, and 37 months of elapsed time. What then?

It is easy to dismiss 'price-to-win', along with Professor Parkinson and Fred's friendly bus driver and all his helpful epigrams. But the question persist: 'What is one to do?' It may be legitimate policy to loss-lead on a job, either to keep one's own staff in gainful employment over a slack period for work, or to exclude a competitor from the opportunity to gain a favored client's confidence. Then, bidding for jobs on a 'price-to-win' basis becomes something of a necessity.

The answer lies in a concept quite strange to most organizations, that of the *quality of a sale*, whether it be for services or for a developed system. In this respect, one would see the quality of a sale comprising the quality of its estimates relative to the quality of definition of the tasks, and the quality of the contract (or any other, less formal arrangement) defining the modalities of supply. Clearly, all three must be in balance with each other – qualities of estimates, of task definition and of contract. It may be exceedingly dangerous to have a very high quality contract, such as for a fixed-price and time-scale supply, if the task is defined by some chaotic 'concepts' document and estimated accordingly. Conversely, it is of little commercial use to have the most sedulous specification of scope, and an ambiguous contract defining how it will be achieved.

When embarkng on a price-to-win strategy, for whatever good reason, that fact should be clearly identified, within the company at least, and the likely 'cost-to-do' should be established as early as possible in life cycle terms. The methods appropriate for phase 1 and 2 estimating are set out in Sections 12.4.1 and 12.4.2.

Price-to-win is most often the cause of premature estimating, and the fallacies of expert and inexpert analogy, and Parkinson's law, have grown up over the years as the means to justify the results. 'Fred' becomes required to legitimize a limit that may have little or nothing to do with the task. These first three fallacies described have the properties of cheapness and speed to achieve, on our rough scale of values, and they are all likely to underestimate effort and time-scale by some large but unpredictable factors.

12.2.4 'Top down' estimating by systems analysis and 'expert analogy'

Fourth on the list of fallacies at the start of this section – that of 'top down systems analysis' is a little less cheap, a little less instantaneous to achieve and a little less inaccurate. In effect, the high level of definition concerning purposes, e.g. 'a chess-playing system', is taken a little further in terms of systems analysis detail, and this is then used as the basis for an informed guess as to its real scope and complexity. Typically, about 3–5 percent of

the total phase 1 plus 2 effort is expended to detail the generic requirement to that point – that is, somewhat less than half the amount normally required to extract a full user requirement specification.

As in the fallacy bearing its name, the method of analogy proceeds as before, but on the basis of more (but hardly enough) evidence: 'Ah-ha! This is like that chess system we did twenty years ago, except that they don't want this and that, but they do want such-and-such. Well, it cost a million then, and took five years, so we'll knock this little lot off in ...'; and so on, and so forth. Once more, the problems are ones of concealed complexity, and to hope that 'estimates' done in this way will always, or even often, err by about 200–300 percent is to overlook the possibility that a set of complexities, in some particular case, may take one well outside this range.

Again, the notion of quality is appropriate, and particularly the fit between estimate, task definition and purpose of the estimate. In cases where phase 2 costs and time-scales are required for 'hard' contracting purposes, 'top down' is an inadequate approach, although not so obviously pop-eyed in its lunacy as some others. Indeed, to gain a quick and cheap insight into costs and time-scales – rather than making a blind guess at them – it has a little merit, to which we will return in Section 12.4.1.

First, however, a warning repeated; 'top down', as defined here, is not an approach to use for substantive estimating and 'hard' contracting of phase 2 development.

12.2.5 The nonsense of productivity factors

Those, then, are the problems of premature estimating. The reader may well doubt their occurrence in nature, particularly in the cases of inexpert analogy and Parkinson's law. Sadly, however, the facts are unavoidable. For reasons of this sort, software development tasks are often grossly underestimated, because something little better than a guess is accorded a false status.

Managers do not only allow that unhappy state of affairs to arise – as might be defensible on grounds of innocence – but they actually commit and commission it, often in the full knowledge of error. Given what was said earlier about the severity of outcome (particularly from time-scale problems), this is astounding, getting on for forty years into the practical applications of computers.

Another great favorite amongst the fallacies is that of applying spurious productivity factors to code size estimates, to derive a value of effort required. We proceed to describe this non-method (for such it is), with some trepidation; it would be ironic if clarifying a fallacy helped to perpetrate it.

In the first place, a code size is determined for the system-to-be. Clearly, this too may give rise to concern, whatever might be to follow. A code size estimate based (again) on an early guess by the bus driver, will be a poor basis from which even a fallacy is to proceed.

Assume, though, that a code size estimate exists, perhaps even from such an unimpeachable source as a competently done outline systems design, and that it indicates that some 93.5K source statements of Ada code are to be written, plus 17.5 of assembler instructions; a 'medium sized' software system in other words.

Now the fallacy of productivity factors goes something like this. Assume that, on average (whatever that means), your software staff or colleagues have a productivity of twenty to thirty source statements per day, of debugged code, for Ada, and five to fifteen for assembler. Now if we divide these productivity values into their appropriate code size, for the system to be, we get an answer whose dimensions are those of effort:

Code/code per person-day = person-days

What could be more lucid? To every problem there is a solution: simple, elegant and wrong. But to take matters a fallacious step further along the road to perdition:

93.5K/25 = 3,740

and

17.5K/10 = 1,750

then finally

3,740 + 1,750 = 5,490 person-days

Clearly, some more averaging has been going on (the denominators 25 and 10); further, we can express our answer in person-years if we assume an average number of days in one working year, e.g. 220. Then, effort for the task = 5,490/220 = 24.9 person-years! Bingo! One is almost inclined to offer a prize of this splendid achievement, a coconut, say. Now, the fallacies here are chasing each other, lemming-like, off the page again. And of them, by far the most gross is that 'effort' has apparently been estimated in isolation. Let us demonstrate the problem.

Manager X asks Fred for an estimate of some task, and our friend duly returns and says, perhaps entirely plausibly: '24.9 person-years of effort, in 2 years of elapsed time; give me about a dozen people of the right caliber, and let me schedule them on and off the job at the right time, and you'll get your system'. Well, this is a bit simplistic, but we take the point. Fred is radiating confidence on all wavelengths.

Now; let manager X reply, in effect: 'Splendid news! Twenty-five person-years is just fine, and I've no doubt we can shake a decent team together. Good old Fred!'

Everything looks lovely, and, for the first time in their relationship, each thinks the better of the other. However, nemesis is at hand. As our hero turns to leave, the rosy glow in his little thought-bubble disappears rather abruptly when he hears the coda: 'Oh, and Fred, that business of two years will have to be changed you know. We need a bit of, ah, flexibility there. Say eighteen months? Is that all right? Twenty-five person-years in, what was it?, eighteen months? Why, what seems to be amiss?'

Fred's face has undergone a red-shift, that's what seems to be amiss, or evidence of it, as though he has begun to recede out of this galaxy at some considerable velocity. For 24.9 person-years of effort in 2 elapsed years is by no stretch of the imagination equal to 24.9 person-years of effort in 18 elapsed months.

'Grr', Fred says, with simple feeling, and manager X recognizes a lapse in the good relations so recently inaugurated.

'Ah-ha', he babbles rapidly, 'I see what you mean. Reduced time but not increased effort – just so! Now let's see; $24.9 \times 24/18 = 33.2$. That should do it. Take 34 person-

years of effort over 18 months . . . oh dear, you seem to be steaming. Do stop grinding your teeth, there's a good chap, and please put me down!'

The point, which should by now be lamentably clear, is that effort and time-scale are ineluctably linked – they comprise a dyad in fact – and the relationship does not seem to be a simple one of the pro rata type. Halving the one does not double the other. What the exact relationship is may not yet be clear; in fact we deal with this question progressively in this section. But if the state of Fred's visage is anything to go by, we may well have tripped over some quite fundamental property in software engineering.

The immediate lesson to learn is this: any 'method' that purports to estimate one element of the dyad in isolation is palpable nonsense. 'Productivity factors', applied as an estimating 'method', does just that.

If that was not enough, there are other, equally fundamental, objections to productivity factors, although it may strike the reader as unnecessary, and like persecuting a corpse, to enunciate them. Still, as the then Archbishop of Canterbury said when denouncing Edward VII over the abdication, what point is there in kicking a chap when he's up? There are, in fact, two main residual objections:

1. 'Productivity' says absolutely nothing about the quality of outcome. Boehm (1981), and others, use as a unit of measurement a quantity DSLC = delivered source lines of code. Well, I have known times when the only reasonable objective, on this basis, was the lowest level of productivity; who wants a prolific source of drivel?
2. There can be no such thing as an 'average' productivity, even assuming some connotation of quality, over all application types, the staff categories attempting them, adequacy of PSE facilities, and so forth.

These are serious objections, even to what is palpably a fallacy for another reason. The one about quality is, like the error of separating effort and time-scale, unanswerable. It need not detain us here, therefore.

12.2.6 Productivity as a contingent factor in estimating

Whatever we have to say, perjoratively, about 'productivity' it is instructive to consider its possible modifiers in some detail, and any representative method must discount these effects if it is to qualify for serious attention. As will become clear in Section 12.3, many attempts have been made to identify the modifiers of productivity – or their reciprocal, 'cost drivers', as one author describes them.

However, the main factors may be classified under four headings: staff, specification, facilities and time. The first three are detailed further below, but the fourth stands alone in more respects than one. Its effects will be investigated at great length in the rest of this chapter, particularly, as already said, with respect to its relationship with required effort.

'Staff' includes such potential problems as inexperience relative to the particular task type, too few suitably experienced staff, unmanaged (or otherwise badly managed) staff and demotivation.

'Specification' covers inadequacy and instability of requirements' definition and, for

adequately specified requirements, the vast differences in difficulty between application types.

'Facilities' means not only the existence of adequate technical means for the task, but adequate access to them.

As already pointed out, one or two of these things going wrong may place a software development task beyond any means to complete. The severity of the factors taken in isolation, even if one could dependably determine them, becomes extreme when they operate in combination. We must remember that fact in the sections to come because, having dealt with the fallacies, we must now proceed to the research currently in progress into estimating methods and, ultimately, to our recommended means.

12.3 RESEARCH; PARAMETRIC SOFTWARE COST MODELS

Over the past quarter of a century, many attempts have been made to develop models suitable for producing values of the required effort and time-scale for software development. It is well beyond our scope to treat this work in detail here, and a fuller account of it will be found in Volume 5 of this series.

However, for one reason in particular, the work will be outlined below. That reason concerns the insight into our question of an effort and time-scale relationship that derives from work on some of the parametric models. The following is, therefore, a highly synoptic account of work in this field.

The aim in cost modeling is to relate, within some mathematical formula, two fundamental parameters with each other, and both of these with two sets of properties that will vary from occasion to occasion. The four quantities are as follows:

E = effort for a software development.

T = time-scale over which the effort is to be expended.

P_t = properties of the task; a set of application-specific factors such as 'big', 'complex', 'database intensive', 'optimal response' and 'volatile specification'.

P_e = properties of the environment; a set of factors comprising the relative fit of resources to the task at hand, such as sufficient PSE, average level chief programmer team, need for on-task training and new language.

The general objective can be seen as an attempt to identify a formula of the type:

$$F(E, T, P_t, P_e) = 0$$

or a family of such, that gives a plausible account in terms of the fundamental parameters E and T of the behavior of all software development tasks within some substratum of application. Thus, for a particular task type we may identify:

$$F_a(E_a, T_a, P_{ta}, P_{ea}) = 0$$

The search for plausible models of this type has been a serious endeavor, in research, for many years. Norden and colleagues at IBM studied the histories of completed tasks (systems engineering composites of hardware and software) in the late 1950s, and the SDC

Corporation produced an exceedingly simple model by 1965. To give the reader a general flavor of things in this area, we can reveal that the SDC model was a linear relationship, of the form:

$$\text{Effort} = a_0 x_0 + a_1 x_1 + \ldots + a_n x_n$$

where x_0, x_1, etc. are numerical values for identified factors affecting Effort, and a_0, a_1, etc. are their coefficients of fit, determined empirically.

Not least of its defects is that 'time' was largely missing in the set of factors (x_n) identified. Not surprisingly, its results were both counter-intuitive and statistically poor. However, so were the early cosmologies of Ptolemy and others, so too censorious an attitude should be tempered.

Research has proceeded in two basic directions since the late 1950s. These may be summarized as follows:

1. Development of models whose formulae are basically derived by analytical methods in mathematics. The starting premise for this analysis is generally some empirical equations achieved in one of two ways; either by inspecting the statistical distribution properties of large scale data samples from completed tasks (after Norden); or from some *a priori* assumptions concerning the principal factors comprising a property of software such as complexity (e.g. Halstead; McCabe).
2. Development of models whose formulae are basically asserted to be of some form relating sets of postulated factors and their values. The SDC formula given above is a simple instance of this, in which factors (x_n) are related additively, and their coefficients of fit (a_n) are determined by factor analysis methods.

    More complex developments have applied factor analysis to mutiplicative models of the form:

    $$E = (a_0 x_0)(a_1 x_1) \ldots (a_n x_n)$$

    and formulae with non-linear components:

    $$F(E) = f_0(a_0 x_0) \cdot f_1(a_1 x_1) \ldots f_n(a_n x_n)$$
    $$F(T) = f_0(b_0 y_0) \cdot f_2(b_1 y_1) \ldots f_n(b_n y_n)$$

The first of these approaches is generally called 'analytic modeling', and the second 'factor fitting'. We shall proceed by giving a brief account here of some of the research work going on in each sector; as said before, a fuller treatment of this whole subject will be found in Volume 5 of this series.

12.3.1 Analytic models

In part, this work coincides with that done in complexity theory as applied to software systems, and a synoptic account of that can be found in Section 3.3. The attempts made to date, at correlating complexity formulae due to Halstead and McCable, with effort and (or) time to do software tasks, have not been convincing, although claims to the contrary have been made (DeMarco 1982). As the work on complexity models has been outlined earlier, we will not dwell on it here.

By far the most important contribution has been by Putnam, and is based on original work by Norden (1963). This is now described further. Norden, and others at IBM in the period circa 1960, investigated the staffing and effort statistics of completed tasks in systems engineering in general. In particular, a distribution of team size against time was plotted. Obviously, one would expect a small number of people to start a task, an accretion of more people up to a manageable maximum of required team strength, and then a decrease in team size as tasks were completed, and their results incorporated in the object system. And so it proved.

The incorporation of all task histories in this way, irrespective of type, size and other properties, produced a very 'noisy' distribution of team size with time, with little possibility or discerning any intrinsic shape to the distribution. However, decomposition of the data set into task type-specific subsets produced the familiar bell-shaped distributions beloved of statisticians. In this case, however, the shape of the distribution was not best described by the well known formulae or Poisson or Gauss, but was found to correspond closely to a formula asserted some years previously (and for other purposes) by Rayleigh. All of this, of course, concerned the team size against time behavior of systems engineering tasks in general.

In about 1970, Putnam applied the same approach to an exceptionally large sample of completed software tasks, and found strongly analogous results to those at IBM. Readers interested in details of this investigation, and the earlier work of Norden, will find an excellent account of it in Putnam (1982).

A 'clean' depiction of the distribution of team size over time, done by a least squares method of curve fitting, for different software life cycle stages, is shown in Figure 12.2.

The essential properties of the main Rayleigh distribution, discovered by Putnam's analysis, are as follows:

1. The basic distribution is described by:

$$y = 2kat \cdot \exp\left(-at^2\right)$$

   in which the linear component ($2kat$) dominates the early part of the distribution, and the negative exponential part supervenes for higher values of t.
2. The quantity a is a shape parameter for distributions generally described by the Rayleigh formula.
3. The quantity k is the area under the curve, and has the dimensions of effort (i.e. people × time).
4. The time t_d at which the average team-size is maximum, the 'peak' of the distribution curve, is approximately equal to the sum of phase 1 plus 2 durations for a software development task. Thus, the area under the curve to the left of t_d is – to a first order approximation – the effort for a software specification and development; the area to the right of t_d is the maintenance (and small improvements) effort required after delivery of the software.
5. Irrespective of task properties, approximately 40 percent of the area lies to the left of t_d, and about 60 percent to the right. This indicates the relative effort in software development, due to specification plus implementation, and that due to maintenance. These findings have been substantiated by other means (Boehm 1981).

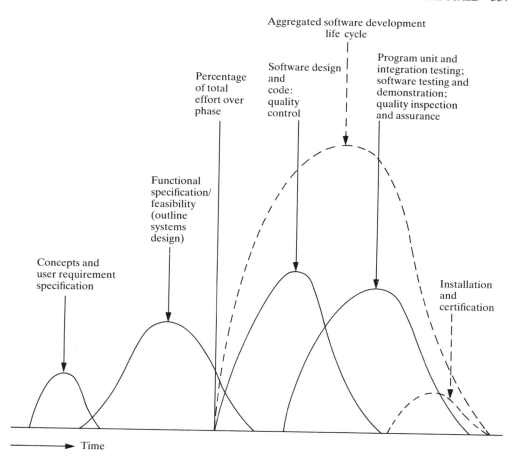

FIGURE 12.2 'Manpower loading' curves, with phase distribution.

There are some very interesting things on this list and, unlike the rather tense time on courses when work complexity theory is presented, people of all types on software courses revive noticeably at this point: '60 percent due to maintenance? Is that true? Is it the same for projects and products?' Gone are all the phobia about the higher mathematics, and logarithms to base two, and one finds lawyers trying to integrate the Rayleigh formula on the back of an old envelope, and dimly recalling the calculus of infinitesimals down forty years of carefully applied neglect. Even better is to come.

From this work, Putnam derived a 'software equation' by performing a set of mathematical transpositions on the Rayleigh formula, as adapted to describe the team-accretion properties of software tasks. This 'software equation' relates effort, time, task size and the properties of the technical environment, as follows:

$$S_s = c_k \cdot k^x \cdot t^y$$

where: S_s is the software size in source code statements;
c_k is a constant of proportionality that can be correlated with the degree of sufficiency of a technical environment for a task of the type concerned; i.e. PSE, staff competence, etc.;
k is the area under the Rayleigh curve, and therefore represents effort; its exponent here is $x = 1/3$;
t is time, and its exponent here is $y = 4/3$.

This equation is at the heart of Putnam's parametric cost estimating model, 'Slim', which also incorporates minimax techniques for deriving optimal values of E and T given ranges over which the constraints (such as those in c_k) might apply. Now there is no intention to dwell here on the details of this, or any other model, for the whole work belongs in the realm of research at the present time, and no one model is sufficiently accurate, or reliably so, to be recommended for general adoption. However, without generating a 'Slimmers' cult, the Putnam model deserves inspection for one other reason.

By a very elementary transposition of the 'software equation', we see that:

$$\text{Effort} \times \text{Time}^4 = (S_s/c_k)^3$$

Given that for a particular task and environment S_s and c_k can be regarded as properties of that task, and therefore (probably) constants, it follows that:

$$E \cdot T^4 = \text{constant}$$

expresses the underlying relationship between effort and time-scale, for software development, if the first premise is accepted. This, if true, is a terrifying little formula. I have known its announcement to cure incipient curvature of the spine in a software audience.

For what it says is that small incremental or decremental changes to time will result in rather large concommitants in effort. Consider the earlier example that threatened to launch our legendary friend into orbit; an apparently plausible estimate of about 25 person-years of effort, over 2 elapsed years of time, had its allowed duration reduced to 18 months. Now, the predicable effects of this, according to Putnam's derivation, can be assessed as follows:

Step 1: The intrinsic property of this estimate is given by $25 \times 2^4 = \text{constant} = 400$.
Step 2: In the new circumstances, effort $\times (1.5)^4 = \text{constant} = 400$.
Step 3: It follows then that a new value of effort is required, and this may be computed from $E = 400/(1.5)^4 = 79.6$ person-years.
    from $E = 400/(1.5)^4 = 79.6$ person-years.

In other words, a 25 percent decrease in time-scale has led to an increase of 216 percent in effort required.

Another way of looking at the relationship would be to consider increasing the time-scale. What would happen if we tried to do the job in 125 percent of the originally estimated time? In this case, we find that the new value of effort is given by $E = 400/(2.5)^4 = 10.2$ person-years. Think of it; an increase of only 25 percent in time-scale leads to an effort reduction of 59.2 percent. This, of course, causes the greatest excitement amongst

commercial staff, marketing and sales people, and so forth. They cannot wait for the session to end when, around the bar with a quart of gin and tonic, they can tell each other how that contract with the Simpleton Corporation need never have been lost. In another corner, the software engineers are wondering where to buy hemlock after ten o'clock at night, but one cannot make everyone happy.

There has, in fact, been much argument about this little formula, over the past decade or so. We will defer further comment on it until other sorts of parametric estimating model have been defined, when we will see that Mr Putnam is not short of competition.

12.3.2 Factor fitting models

We have already given the general expressions for additive and multiplicative formulae with linear components $(c_n x_n)$. In truth, neither the additive nor the product formulae with linear (first order) components of factors provided particularly convincing models, and research in factor identification and fitting switched – around 1965, or so – to formulae with more complex functions. One such was proposed by Herd *et al.* (1977) at the Doty Corporation, and comprised two formulae:

$$E = 5.288 \, (S_s)^a \qquad \text{for software systems up to 10K in size}$$
$$E = 2.020 \, (S_s)^a \cdot \text{Prod} \, (f_j) \qquad \text{for software systems over 10K in size}$$

where S_s is the software size in numbers of source code statements. The value of a is 1.047 in both cases. Prod (f_j) is the product of fifteen 'productivity modifiers' of the form:

'scientific application' = 1.67
'business application' = 1.43

There is a well known list of these, known as the 'Doty' factors after the company of their provenance; for a property not applying in a particular case, its Doty factor is taken as unity, to prevent the formula arriving at an unarguably nonsensical answer.

Another derivation, at IBM this time (Walson and Felix 1977), saw the definition of a 'productivity index':

$$I = \text{Sum} \, (W_i \cdot X_i)$$

where $X_i = 1, 0$ or $+1$ depending on whether the task rates 'low', 'medium' or high' with respect to a list of certain attributes called 'productivity variance values' (PV_i). Then;

$$W_i = 0.5 \log_{10} \, (PV_i)$$

These examples, due to Herd *et al.* and Walston and Felix, are on view here to give the reader a general flavor of this work. Perhaps the most interesting aspects of it, in both cases and some others of similar type, is that the tabular factors – f_j and (PV_i) respectively – give some insight into the relative importance of issues affecting software development. For the rest, the Doty model has not produced particularly impressive results, and the work of Walston and Felix is not quite clear enough for independent inspection to allow much comment either way.

Another model, of more recent vintage, is due to Boehm at the TWR Corporation.

Unlike some others, it has been widely described by its author – not least in a rather large book (Boehm 1981). The summary here may seem a travesty in comparison, but is not necessarily unrepresentative for that. Boehm's model, 'COCOMO', incorporates two basic formulae that can be viewed as his equivalents of Putnam's 'software equation'. They are:

$$E = C_1 S^a$$
$$T = C_2 E^b$$

Where C_1 comprises the product of a scaling factor, f_1, and the product of a set of 'cost drivers', analogs of the Doty factors referred to earlier. Boehm's cost drivers are set out in Table 12.1. The value of f_1 is 2.4, 3.0 or 3.6 depending on the type of application. These 'types' are rather loosely designated 'organic', 'semi-detached' and 'embedded'. C_2 is a simple value 2.5 in all cases. $a = 1.05, 1.12$ or 1.20 depending on application 'type' (as before), and, $b = 0.38, 0.35$ or 0.32 depending on application 'type'.

Thus, for a 'semi-detached' application of some sort, we have a duplex formula comprising:

$$E = 3.0 \ S^a \ \mathrm{Prod} \ (D_i)$$

and

$$T = 2.5 \ E^b$$

with a set of values for the 'cost drivers' D_i, and exponents $a = 1.12$; $b = 0.35$.

The author defines his terms as follows. 'Organic' refers to small software tasks, done 'in-house' by a competent team familiar with the application, and with each other's working style. 'Embedded' refers to any size of software system, in which the dominant considerations for development are less ones of task size, complexity or staff familiarity, than constraints such as hardware limitations, software engineering regulations of some sort, and operating procedures that affect the issue. 'Semi-detached' applications are defined

TABLE 12.1 COCOMO 'cost drivers' (Boehm 1981)

	Very low	Low	Nominal	High	Very high	Extra high
Required software reliability	0.75	0.88	1.00	1.15	1.40	
Database size		0.94	1.00	1.08	1.18	
Product complexity	0.70	0.85	1.00	1.15	1.30	1.85
Execution time constraints			1.00	1.11	1.30	1.66
Main storage constraints			1.00	1.06	1.21	1.56
Virtual machine volatility		0.87	1.00	1.15	1.30	
Computer turnaround time		0.87	1.00	1.07	1.15	
Analyst capability	1.46	1.19	1.00	0.86	0.71	
Application experience	1.29	1.13	1.00	0.91	0.82	
Programmer capability	1.42	1.17	1.00	0.86	0.70	
Virtual machine experience	1.21	1.10	1.00	0.90		
Prog. lang. experience	1.14	1.07	1.00	0.95		
Use of modern prog. practice	1.24	1.10	1.00	0.91	0.82	
Use of software tools	1.24	1.10	1.00	0.91	0.83	
Required development schedule	1.23	1.08	1.00	1.04	1.10	

as being somewhat between 'organic' and 'embedded' in type, with a considerable spread of experience and degree of mutual familiarity between team members. Needless to say, these very vague classifications are more unhelpful than otherwise in establishing the plausibility of this research, or its proclaimed outcome.

Before leaving this topic, it is worth noting that a hybrid model has been proposed within Hughes Aircraft (Jensen 1984). This compounds the notions due to Putnam, with the 'Doty factors' of Herd *et al.* (1977) to produce yet another 'software equation':

$$S_s = C_t \cdot E^a \cdot T^b$$

where the exponents a and b equal 0.5 and 1.0 respectively, as distinct from 0.33 and 1.33 in Putnam's derivation; and C_t is a technology factor comprising the ratio of a 'basic technology parameter' and the product of a set of adapted 'Doty' factors as the modifiers of productivity; thus:

$$C_t = C_{bt}/\text{Prod}\ (f_j)$$

Of immediate interest here is the very acute attenuation of Putnam's fierce little formula; Effort × Time^4 = constant. Here it would seem that, by the same species of derivation:

$$E \cdot T^2 = \text{constant}$$

This is a much milder affair altogether, of course, and much less likely to cause unseemly excitement in software audiences. In fact, we can take the whole process of pacification even further, and put the lot to sleep. For Boehm's duplex formula can be cast in the same form, by a very simple piece of algebra; we arrive then at:

$$E \cdot T^x = \text{constant}$$

where $x = 1/1-b$. Given the Boehm values for his exponents (a and b), this yields an exponent varying between 1.47 and 1.61 depending on application type.

The plot thickens, doesn't it? There is some explaining to be done, for they cannot all be right. Or can they? As we shall see, the better question might be: are any of them right?

12.3.3 The current status of cost modeling research

There are many more models in existence than those listed and described above. One survey listed thirteen: SDC (1965); TRW (1972); Putnam (1977); Doty Corp. (1977); RCA (1979); IBM (1977); Boeing (1977); GRC (1977); TWR (1980); Telecote; Sofcost; DSN; Hughes Aircraft (1982). It is not possible to evaluate some of these, as their detail is seen as having proprietary value to its inventors or the firms they represent. Thus, the IBM and RCA models are examples of 'black-box' systems, whose existence is known – but little more – outside the company concerned. This is in spite of the fact that the RCA 'Price' system can be leased for use by others.

The current status of cost-estimating models is not yet sufficient to claim that the research endeavor, in general, is likely to produce methods or systems sufficiently realistic in their results, and reliably so, to be used as the sole sources for effort and time-scale

estimates. That is the challenge still to be met by this species of research. Would you bet your company on the results? It is fine to use them for in-house developments, or products, where pseudo-contracting may have little force. But would you enter into a formal, fixed-price contract based on estimates given by a model? Well, I would think many times before doing so, and then probably deny myself the experience. I may well deny the liquidator a certain experience in the process.

The simple facts of the matter seem to be that the results from cost-estimating models do not correlate very well with each other, let alone actuality, when tried on a common problem. A recent trial of two models, Putnam's 'Slim' and Boehm's COCOMO, has shown variances in results of 500–600 percent compared with actuality for small and medium sized data processing and applications, and has stressed the need for especial care in calibrating models to an application type and development environment (Kemmerer 1987).

The current outstanding requirements in this species of research can be summarized as follows:

1. A major parameter for input to all models seems to be task size, as would seem to be justified on intuitive grounds if nothing else. However, source code size of the outcome from a software development is a notoriously unreliable metric for any purpose. As was pointed out two decades ago, software teams usually produce systems of widely varying size for the same requirement, with little other inference being derivable from this factor alone (Weinberg 1971).
2. It is extremely unclear how individual 'cost drivers', or 'productivity modifiers', can be isolated so as to measure their ranges of effect in different operating circumstances. What seems to be the case is that sets of factors are assigned values, and these are juggled until the combined result 'fits' some predetermined outcome. That is not a proper form of identifying factors nor a scientific means of measuring them.
3. The dynamic properties of software development, such as evolution of requirements, changes in implementation team, upgrading (or converse) of PSE, are not well incorporated in models. Yet these things concern reality, and the stark facts of life. The one thing that is unchanging is that just about everything in a software development is doing its level best to change – often dramatically for the worse.
4. Models say little about phase 3 matters (e.g. maintenance, see Weiner-Erlich *et al.* 1984). Nor do they help, in the sense of Lehman's second 'law' (q.v.) concerning new versions, nor with the 'chuck it all away, and start again' question that flows from Lehman's first 'law'.
5. Data set; there is no generally accepted way of classifying data from software development tasks, and therefore no 'standard' data sets for different application types. Thus, models tend to be developed on one sort of data or another, and this means that their validity (such as it may be) is most likely restricted entirely to those data, and any other emanating from the same source. No wonder different values appeared in the effort/time relationship.

This is a pretty formidable set of topics for further research. It is disappointing to note that the past ten years in this field have been somewhat disfigured by premature claims for cost-estimating models, and – worse – premature sales of them, as though the ques-

tions of research were foreclosed, and that 'GUESS', the wonder-model from Meretricious Enterprises Inc., was really a fully demonstrated means for determining effort and time-scale.

We have now investigated the fallacies and the research – which must not be conflated with each other. It remains to propose viable means for estimating software tasks, and then to return to the terrible excitement of the effort and time relationship in software development.

12.4 RECOMMENDED PRACTICES FOR ESTIMATING

At this point, it is worthwhile to recall that we need to cover three 'phases' of a software task:

1. Phase 1, so-called; covering specification and feasibility of requirements, up to the point of signing-off the functional specification.
2. Phase 2, so-called; covering the development from architecture design up to a point of delivery and operations.
3. Phase 3, so-called; covering the maintenance of the system in operation.

We will deal with each one, in turn.

12.4.1 Estimating the specification phase

This is an issue that frequently (and rather frightfully) gets conflated with the basic problems of prematurity in estimating. What we must hold in mind, throughout, is that here we are speaking only of estimates – of effort and time-scale – that concern phase 1 specification and feasibility, and not estimates done in this phase (1) concerning any other phase. Having said that, it is still obvious that fallacy may attach to estimates for phase 1 activities themselves. And, again, the most obvious fallacy is that concerning premature assertions that are either unqualified entirely, or are 'justified' on the basis of some supposed analogy.

It is, in fact, not possible to say anything meaningful about the likely cost or time to do a software requirements' specification before some 'top down systems analysis' has proceeded. This, then, is our *terminus post quem*, the point after which we can say something.

As before (see Section 12.2.4) what we tend to say then – perhaps after a 'cost' expenditure of 3–5 percent of total effort, and some commensurate time – is that the requirement will probably require x person-months and y elapsed years to define and assess for feasibility, up to functional specification level. This means, in effect, that the first work – the 3–5 percent of an unknown total – cannot be estimated at all; and that is indeed the case. We may call these the 'bootstrap' costs, for they concern the age-old problem of getting started.

The 'bootstrap' cost is not estimated, nor is its concommitant in time, they are defined. At the very topmost levels of the life cycle one says, in effect, 'we'll look into this pro-

spect further (i.e. do some systems analysis), and Fred and Bill can do it over the next six weeks'. We then have the first assertions of bootstrap costs, twelve person-weeks over an elapsed time-scale of six weeks. If that is inadequate, then we either continue (on the basis of another bootstrap cost) or not, as the case might be. Thus the boostrap costs may be the sum of a set of assertions up to the point when some statement can be made of the cost to complete phase 1. At that stage we will apply 'top down, expert analogy' for completion of phase 1 only.

The effort and time estimates, done 'top down' for phase 1 only, will be likely to have a fairly high probability of significant error attaching. After all, the specification stage is not guaranteed to converge quickly, and prototypes for this purpose (or to evaluate technical means) may have to be developed.

Now, the answer to all this uncertainty is to grasp the notion quite firmly that, whatever it is that can be said about phase 1 costs at this stage, any estimates will be of the 'budgetary amounts' type. In other words, one would not contract on the basis of such estimates, except in a fairly loose way, with a suitable caveat about uncertainty. This idea of budgetary estimating, along with the notion of asserting 'bootstrap' costs, is fundamental if the various errors due to prematurity at this stage are to be avoided.

At some stage, then, we will have values that are very likely to be substantial underestimates of effort and time-scale to complete phase 1, and these will have cost some amount of effort and time to do. It is then possible to 'factor up' the phase 1 estimates, on the basis of some known or supposed multiplier ($\times 2$ or $\times 3$, or values read from the Boehm graph, or whatever seems appropriate and plausible), to improve the likelihood of accuracy. This practice must not be confused with a widely prevalent one – another fallacy in fact – that allows premature estimating (in phase 1) of phase 2 values, and then merely multiplies them by the 'inaccuracy values' for expected error, as set out in Figure 12.1. This dreadful practice leads to the multiplication of one guess by another, and has nothing whatever to recommend it.

In the case of phase 1 values, we are factoring an inaccurate estimate of some small proportion of total cost, probably between 10 and 12 percent at most, that is based on some system analysis, and we are designating the outcome very clearly and cautiously as a better 'budgetary estimate'. At this stage, there is nothing particularly harmful in proceeding on the assumptions that n times an inevitably poor 'estimate' is likely to be a better one. One may even continue with this as the estimating basis (with an external client, say) under some relatively informal contract of supply, such as 'time and materials' or 'cost plus fixed fee'.

12.4.2 Estimating the development phase

There is one tried and trusted method for estimating effort and time-scale. Its abiding attractions are: (a) that it requires software engineers to do it – and is therefore motivating to the development teams if they are required to do the estimates; and (b) that it produces values of effort and time, from the same process, that are interdependent. It is the method of critical path analysis, or Pert planning as it is sometimes called. Predicated on the right

basis, and done in the right way by competent people for the purpose, it is an accurate way (*c.* ±25 percent) of estimating the values required.

The basic method is very well known outside software engineering, and not well enough known within it. CPM was developed as a tool for planning and controlling tasks comprising many mutually interrelated activities, and a variety of resources necessary for different activities. The fields of civil construction engineering and 'heavy' mechanical engineering use the technique extensively to achieve planned time-scales and efficiency in resource utilization.

In recent years, the method has been adopted in large scale electronic engineering applications too. Lamentably, the practice has not spread to the software counterparts, and in firms where the hardware technology is dominant it is not unusual to find a major software development task represented in the fashion of Figure 12.3.

This state of affairs is, needless to say, fatal to the prospects of both the task at hand, and that of inculcating good software engineering practices in the firm concerned. The main reason for it arising may be a distinct antipathy to the subject on the part of non-software staff and, it must be said here, few err so determinedly as electronic engineers who may themselves be amateur programmers.

The effects on software development staff are catastrophic in these cases, and will not be improved by the sight of their hardware colleagues leaning against some gleaming artefact, completed weeks before, and growling about the usual software delays, and generally making merry in the most lugubrious way.

Estimating is indivisibly linked to planning and control or most assuredly should be. For, there is little use in meticulous estimates if the most unspeakable chaos breaks out the moment they are done. In what follows, it is implicit throughout that the original estimates will only remain as originally valid if the activities to which they pertain remain properly planned and controlled. This trivial point is so often forgotten that one may be forgiven for supposing that its triviality stultifies the senses.

Software estimating is a by-product of CPM planning, and this technique is far from difficult to grasp. Its essence lies in three simple actions:

1. List all activities that will need to be undertaken and completed, to perform the whole task. This may, in the first place, be an unordered list.
2. List the activities in a logical order, i.e. A before B, B before C, E after A and D, and so on. This set of relationships is then depicted on a netplan of connected activities, indicating dependencies left to right across the diagram, i.e. B will be to the right of A. This, then is a logically ordered activities' plan.
3. Reconsider and if necessary reorder activities on the netplan in the light of resources (people, material) available for the purpose. An objective should be to achieve a balance between the tendency to minimize resources, and a need not to maximize the time for the whole activities-set. The netplan is then recast to show three things per activity; result to be achieved, e.g. 'Code A'; resource, e.g. 'Fred'; and duration, e.g. two weeks.

These percepts are the same, whether the issue is building a ship, planning a holiday or setting up a software task. The method is described in greater detail later in this section.

In software development, the earliest time at which such a netplan can be compiled is

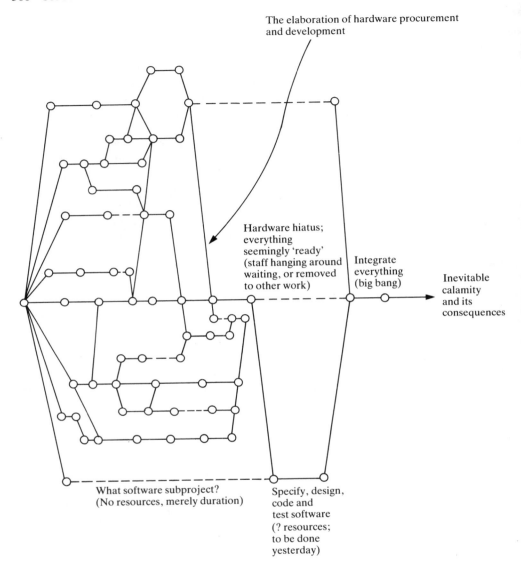

The elaboration of hardware procurement and development

Hardware hiatus; everything seemingly 'ready' (staff hanging around waiting, or removed to other work)

Integrate everything (big bang)

Inevitable calamity and its consequences

What software subproject? (No resources, merely duration)

Specify, design, code and test software (? resources; to be done yesterday)

FIGURE 12.3 Software development seen as 'the Cinderella' subject.

when the OSD has been done. That corresponds to the late stages of functional specification, and bears with it the important proviso that whatever activities we define will
apply to notional not actual tasks, as the software taxonomy is not a proper design. At a
later life cycle stage, sometime during software design proper, the activities' plan will concern actual tasks, as it will be based on the most likely modular structure of the software-
to-be. Equally, at this later stage, one will be assigning actual resources to tasks whereas,
at the functional specification stage, the team composition may not be fully known. We
return to this point later.

On average, the 'cost' of a CPM method, done in this way, will be about 10–12 percent
of total phase 1 plus 2 'costs', in terms of software engineers' effort, because that is the
proportion of total effort generally expended to get to the stage (OSD) at which this
method can be undertaken. In my experience its accuracy, if done competently by experienced software engineers, can be in the range ±25 percent. At the later stage, during
software design, the 'cost' may be 20–25 percent, and the accuracy as high as ±10 percent.
Clearly, one can seldom wait until a quarter of an unknown quantity has been spent, in
order to determine that quantity, and the software design stage is too late (and costly)
for first, substantive estimates of phase 2 quantities. On the other hand, it is a time at
which estimates, done earlier and to lesser accuracy, may be amended with precision.

In general, then, one does accurate enough estimates at the functional specification
stage (after some exercises, to get there, of 'budgetary estimating'), and one 'fine-tunes'
this at the software design stage.

There are four basic steps in a CPM approach using the software taxonomy from an
OSD. With a simple adjustment, these can be adapted for the same method as used on
real software design information. These steps are defined below, but first we define the
fourteen possible types of activity that might be required on a plan for some development
or other.

1. Overall software design: systems' architecture, and software specification.
2. Define beta-test (1): detail black-box tests to be done in QA.
3. Design decomposition: function, data or process analysis.
4. Software module design: software structure, algorithms and data.
5. Low-level definition: program design and integrand specifications.
6. Define beta-test (2): detail white-box tests to be done in QA.
7. Design reviews: define and do technical reviews for QC.
8. Test plan and alpha test: define QC test plan and design alpha-test.
9. Implementation: code integrands and unit test them.
10. Integration testing: integrate integrands and test them to a plan.
11. Documentation: consolidate and improve documentation.
12. Alpha-test: benevolent demonstration for QI verification.
13. Beta-test: adversary tests for QA validation.
14. Management: events for structured walkthrough and QI/QA.

With this list in mind, the following four basic steps are undertaken, using the OSD
software taxonomy:

Step 1: The taxons on the lowest level of the software taxonomy are aggregated into notional tasks for a person, or a small team of such.

Step 2: The essential activities for each 'task' are then listed, and a logically and resource-bounded scheme is drawn up for the result, showing the order and mutual dependence of activities. This is, possibly, a 'doubly notional' activities' plan – if activities are the properties of notional tasks, as in the case when outline design taxonomies are their basis, and if notional staff, not actual people, are assigned.*

Step 3: The 'doubly notional', logically ordered and resource-bounded activities' plan is now reviewed to see if the disposition of resources over 'tasks' is consistent with a reasonably efficient time-scale for the whole. Where necessary, and possible, the activities' plan is emended to achieve a 'comfortable' overall time-scale, and most effective utilization of resources.†

Step 4: Effort and time-scale are now derived from the activities' plan, the former by simple arithmetic across the scheme:

$$\text{Effort} = \text{Sum } (x_i t_i)$$

where x_i and t_i are the number of staff assigned to, and duration of each activity. The time-scale is derived equally easily as:

$$\text{Time} = \text{Sum } (t_{ci})$$

where t_{ci} is the duration of activity i on a critical path c of the netplan.‡

Ordering activities can be done by asking 'what must have been completed before this can commence?' and 'what can proceed now that this is complete?'

Activities' plans can be depicted in one of several, rather elementary, formats. The simplest one, and by no means worse for that, is a line and node convention shown in Figure 12.4. Other notations include the well-known 'precedence' convention, and one in which the three basic elements of information are carried in the node, and not along the connecting line; this is shown in Figure 12.5.

The earlier reference to 'slack' activities, on non-critical paths of a netplan, is explained

---

* When assigning 'notional' people, if the development team is not fully formed for example, some normative assumptions will be needed, such as 'that bit can be done by Fred and trainee, but we'll need a senior software engineer for this part; the bit to do with screen management is easy – an ordinary enough person, with a couple of years' experience could cope with it.' And so on. The matters are judgmental, and for that reason the whole process is best undertaken by the software team leader-to-be; no one likes to inherit other people's judgment.

† Balancing resources allocation with time-scale must not develop into, nor begin from, a view that such and such a time-scale is mandatory – even though something of the sort might well be the case ('The job must be done in eighteen months, because we sold it on that basis, and signed the contract last week'). At this stage, we must establish the 'comfortable' time-scale, and its associated effort, in isolation to any such constraints.

‡ A critical path on the activity plan is one which cannot be compressed. If adding resources to an activity means that it may be done in less time (usually a dubious assumption), then this represents a different case altogether. For the plan and its resource assignments, some paths will contain only incompressible activities, and some may contain 'slack' activities; the latter paths are not critical ones, the former are. A definition of 'slack' is given below.

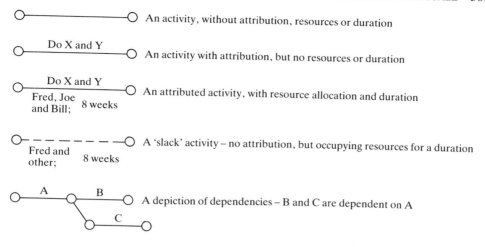

FIGURE 12.4 An activities' planning notation.

in Figure 12.4; the dotted line convention between nodes indicates a duration during which some resources (people in this case) are effectively unproductively awaiting some other event to complete. The slack activity has no task ascription, but should show resources and duration. Clearly, a plan with excessive 'slack' in it, of this type, is usually considered with disfavor – for obvious reasons; by the same token, a plan with several (or many) critical paths might be thought a wonderfully efficient construction – but it may well be rather dangerously efficient at that.

Sometimes one finds what looks like 'slack' activities in a netplan that are really nothing of the sort; they have no task, resource or duration. In this case, the convention is being used wrongly, to balance or align the graphical representation. This practice confuses, and should be avoided. Dependencies are left to right across the page, and any dependencies between activities on different paths are indicated by near-vertical lines, in which the slight left-to-right angle of slope indicates the dependency. Dependencies going backwards across the page (right to left) must be avoided as they cause the most hilarious mess to ensue.

Activities' plans carry a lot of information, and can become difficult to read and update in consequence. It is often advisable to have a code for both tasks (as in the case of the fourteen listed above) and resources.

The notional task assignment, an encoding scheme and a resulting activities' phase for the CAISSA development are shown in Figures 12.6, 12.7 and 12.8. Figure 12.6 gives a complete software taxonomy for CAISSA. The single most fundamentally important thing to hold in mind about this method, and estimating software development activities in general, is that software estimates should be done by competent people for that purpose – i.e. software engineers. As the method depends on software taxonomies (or, if used later, actual designs), and as these too must be done by software engineers if feasibility is to have any real meaning, the possibility or conflating the activities in OSD and estimating

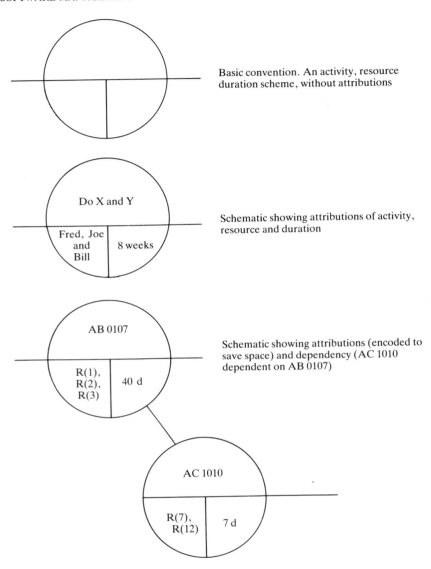

Basic convention. An activity, resource duration scheme, without attributions

Schematic showing attributions of activity, resource and duration

Schematic showing attributions (encoded to save space) and dependency (AC 1010 dependent on AB 0107)

FIGURE 12.5 An alternative netplan notation.

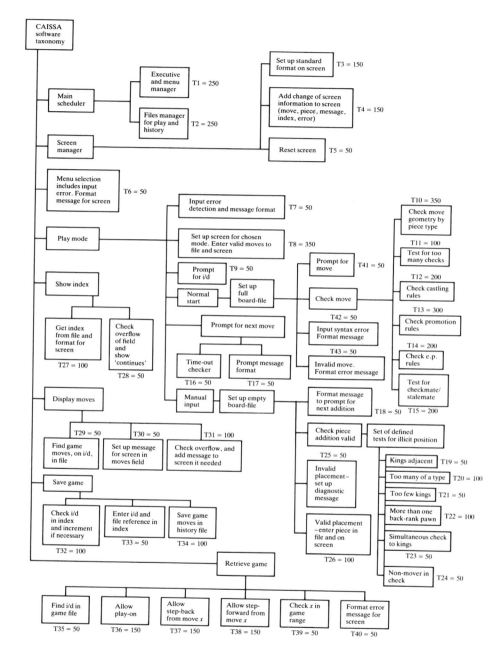

FIGURE 12.6 CAISSA software taxonomy with task codes and sizes.

(I)   Task attributions
      Chief programmer (CP): T1–8 inclusive; T25 and 26
      Senior software eng. (SSWE): T27–40 inclusive
      Software eng. (SWE): T9–17 inclusive
      Junior software eng. (JSWE): T18–24 inclusive; test plan and documentation coordination

(II)   Integration schedule

Level 0	Level 1	Level 2	Level 3	Level 4
All routines by their authors, plus scheduled design reviewers and code readers	Local integration of routines by authors – as in I. T25/26 = unit 1 T18/24 = unit 2 T10/15 = unit 3 T16/17 = unit 4 T1/6 = unit 5 T1/8 = unit 6 T27/28 = unit 7 T29/31 = unit 8 T32/34 = unit 9 T35/43 = unit 10	U1/2 = unit 11 T7/U3/U4 = unit 12 Authors as appropriate	U11/12 = unit 13 Authors: CP, SWE, JSWE	U9/U13 = unit 14 U10/U14 = unit 15 U8/U15 = unit 16 U7/U16 = unit 17 and alpha-test. All of units 14–17 done by entire team

(III)   Activities' duration (days)

Task	T1–6	7–8	9	10–15	16–17	18	19–24	25–26	27–28	29–31	32–34	35–40
Code size* (plus contingency)	1,080	480	60	1,620	120	60	480	180	180	240	300	720
Design (plus review)	5	5	1	10	1	1	10	2	2	2	2	15
Code (plus read)	10	10	1	25	2	1	25	5	5	5	5	15
Test	5	5	1	10	1	1	10	2	2	2	2	5
Netplan code	A	B	C	D	E	F	G	H	I	J	K	L

*All HLL statements (e.g. Pascal)

Integration	U11	12	13	14	15	16	17	β-test
Duration (days)	3	3	3	3	3	3	3	2
Code	M	N	O	P	Q	R	S	T

FIGURE 12.7 Encoded information for activities' planning.

is obvious. Get the same people to do both; and it will be all the better if both are done by the senior member(s) of the development team-to-be. In this respect, the OSD/CPM methods are highly motivating to software staff. This is particularly so if the estimators are allowed freedom to discount into the notional activities' plan all the hazards that they foresee.

Here we return to the notions of 'cost drivers' and 'productivity modifiers', as we found those potential properties of software development tasks represented in the parametric cost-model research. In this case, however, software engineers do not normally carry

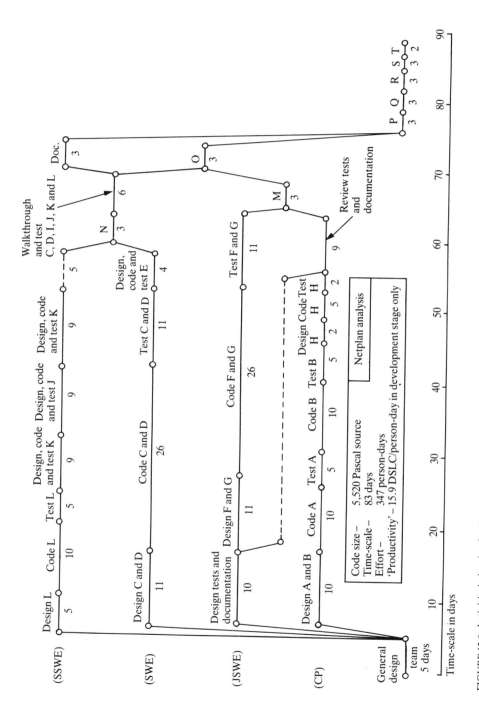

FIGURE 12.8 Activities' plan for CAISSA development.

around a list of factors to apply, in isolation or combination, to activities. What happens is less formal but no less effective. Known exigencies are allowed for in the plan, on the basis of arguments like: 'That will be a tough bit to do – we may have to code it in C' and 'We'll have trouble at this stage, because our PSE is being upgraded around that time', and so on.

At its best, the OSD/CPM method achieves sufficient accuracy quickly and cheaply enough for 'hard' contractual purposes in supply. And, not least of its virtues, it is motivating to its users – the software engineers – who inherit the consequences. Even when some 'price-to-win' process has apparently pre-empted the whole affair, the late stage of functional specification is the first time at which a reasonably accurate 'cost-to-do' can be determined – as it should be, along with an even more accurate determination at the software design stage.

And, lest the reader suspects that some little problem has been conveniently skated around, any imposed time-scale constraints in the development will have to be reviewed for their effect – beginning when the 'OSD/CPM' method has established the comfortable time-scale, and its associated effort, in which the software engineers think the task can best be done. Effort times time raised to the power – what?

Yes, time-scale imposition is a question of exactly that form, and we defer further comment on it until the whole issue is set out in Section 12.5.

12.4.3 Estimating the software maintenance phase

Here, rather as in the case of specifications in phase 1, the fundamental questions are: (a) can we estimate anything at all about software maintenance, and (b) if so, when is the earliest time – in life cycle terms – at which we can say whatever is to be said? The reader will quickly grasp that question (a) is dominant, and that it will take a fair bit of answering. Let us review the problems.

It is a fair bet, no doubt, that the effort needed for software maintenance will be a function of the intensity with which the software in question is being used, as well as its intrinsic reliability. Are programs sitting on the shelf in a shoebox most of the time, or is the software having the stuffing knocked out of it (metaphorically speaking) by a platoon of users, queueing up twenty-four hours a day to use it in a variety of ways – some correct and others incorrect? In the one case, the maintenance calls will be minimal, i.e. none; in the other, there may be howls of rage every five seconds, as the miserable stuff gets into the most wonderful knots.

Then again, one might suspect that the size of a software system would have some bearing on the likely failure-rate; lots of statements – more to go wrong; fewer statements – less to go wrong. This is a seductive argument, up to the point when one meets some evil little example, just a few hundred statements of code, that seems to contain more bugs than can possibly be contained in so meager a vessel. Size is a notoriously bad metric for anything, except – well – size.

On the other hand, surely complexity has something to do with it; the more convoluted the code, the less likely that all the bugs have been found and, in turn, the more probable that Fred (with his oil-can and spanner) is going to be called out at 4.30 a.m., on a wet Sunday morning, to fix it. True, but complexity, and its relationship with reliability, is an

unquantifiable matter – as we have seen – and it is quantity that we require in some form, such as effort likely to be required for maintenance.

Clearly, it will be very difficult to say anything at all about a maintenance phase before the scope of requirements is fully known. So, if called for before a functional specification has been completed, the best one can do is to estimate the possible frequency and severity of software failures on some basis of analogy – always assuming that the company, or persons, doing the assessment have precedents of some sort for the purpose. Thus one may say (in effect): 'It is a such and such system, not unlike the one we did three years ago. So its failure rate, and the severity of failures, may follow a similar pattern. It's the best we can say at this stage.'

In effect, one is doing a risk assessment before the artefact is attempted. The result is unlikely to be accurate, unless by accident, but there may be an inescapable reason to go through the process – such as a client insisting (misguidedly) on contractual arrangements covering all three phases of supply. Then one ends up assuming x person-days of effort for maintenance in aperiod t_x after delivery, and y person-days of effort for maintenance in a period t_y, following the period t_x, and so on over as many 'tranches' of time as seem reasonable. Frequently, the first tranche (t_x) is a warranty period; free maintenance for a project supply, often with supplier's staff on-site for the warranty period, and some analogous special provision for products. Thus, say, x may equal 120 person-days, over a period $t_x = 6$ months for a major supply.

Then, it would be expected that the error incidence rate would have dropped to a very low level, although error obscurity might have gone up considerably (see Chapter 9). In this case, one might be prepared (and have) to contract for a fixed price maintenance service over, say, the next $t_y = 2$ years. Now, our thinking may have gone as follows for the warranty period: 'two bugs a week, and a day each to diagnose and fix them, for six months; the rest of the time (60 percent of the total), will be on-site so as to minimize response time and cost.' That is how crude such computations have to be, if they are done too early. Mind you, the situation does not get much better later, as we shall see. Anyway, the analogous computation thunders on to its destined conclusion.

For period t_y (two years, say, after the initial six months on-site warranty), we may say something of the following sort: 'Assume an average of one bug per week for the six months ($t_x = 6$), then one every fortnight for six months, then one per three weeks for half a year and, finally, one per month for ever thereafter. Let the time to travel and fix each bug be two days; therefore we need 100 person-days of effort over the next two years, for software maintenance'. Needless to say, we are obviously not speaking of software maintenance here for a 5K Pascal program for CAISSA! Unless, that is, something has gone seriously wrong and we have one of those 'evil little programs' of earlier reference, and an even more evil little contract of supply for it.

That then is premature estimating for phase 3 costs. Note, no time-scale estimate is called for, as one merely slices the time between systems release (or delivery) and its withdrawal from use, into periods over which some confidence limit in the software will apply. This 'confidence' is usually taken to be a monotonically increasing feature over time in which the system is in use, as one assumes (often wrongly) that error-incidence will be a monotonically decreasing property of the software as its usage 'flushes' the bugs out of it. 'Ho-ho', as software engineers say, 'time will tell'.

If one wants to make the rather gross computation a little more refined, one may weight the later errors for obscurity; in our earlier example, this might appear as an increased time (first to three days, then four) to detect and correct errors in the period $t_y = t_x + 12$ to $t_x + 24$. Even so, if done at too early a stage the 'method' is – as we have already said – risk assessment for an artefact that has not yet been attempted. In other, and better, words – we are guessing again! Still, at that stage (pre-functional specification), analogy and rationalized guessing are all we have for phase 3 costs. Better than get into that sort of tangle, one should persuade clients (or managers) not to ask questions that cannot be answered.

There are two prerequisites for an informed estimate of maintenance costs, and one of them defines the *terminus post quem* for this – the life cycle time after which such estimates can be done, given that the other consideratons are met. The two prerequisites are as follows:

1. An assessment of reliability for software must be done by some competent source, independent of the authors of the system.
2. Some plausible scale of values must exist, by which 'reliability' is correlated (however roughly) with on-site/off-site costs to detect, and correct, software errors.

The first of these, comprising a competent and independent assessment of software reliability, clearly describes the white-box tests to be undergone, in beta-testing, as part of the validation of the software with its essential ('deliverable') documentation.

That then is the *terminus post quem* for which we have sought – in other words, it is not until the beta-testing stage of a software's life cycle that we can convincingly begin to assess its risks (and costs) in the maintenance stage. Equally, as before for other phases, that defines prematurity as being (in this case) any point before beta-testing.

Clearly, the assessment of maintenance requirements will be a judgmental one, although we have known instances when reliability was expressed on some locally invented scale of values. There is no harm in this practice, so long as its exponents and others do not endow it with virtues it cannot posses, or presume its universality.

The second requirement listed above needs a statistical base within the company, comprising data on error incidence and severity, from previous software developments – product and project as appropriate. Table 12.2 shows a simple example for one software system, as might have been derived from the sort of record shown in Figure 9.3.

Every company making software for its own, or other's, use should develop a statistical foundation of this sort, and risk assessment – as for warranty and fixed price contracted maintenance – should be the result of an independent view of the likely reliability of some particular software, as done during a proper evaluation of its validity. It is important to

TABLE 12.2 Software error frequency and severity

Year	Bugs per 1K source statements	Time to fix per bug (days)
0.0–0.5	5.0	0.25
0.5–2.0	0.5	1.0
2+	0.1	2.0

remember, when considering the severity of software failure in this respect (i.e. how long it will take to detect and correct errors, rather than will the failure put all the lights out, or set the place on fire), that Lehman's second 'law' is not forgotten – that work will be required, over and above mere detection and correction, to preserve software structure, lest it deteriorates over some maintenance period. Thus, 'find and fix' is fine, but it tends to understate the effort needed for *proper* maintenance of software.

12.4.4 Revision

We have now defined the following general precepts for estimating quantities, such as effort and time-scale, for software development:

1. At the 'top' of the life cycle, during the early concept and ideas stage, one cannot even guess at time-scales and costs for the work to come. Then, one asserts some values – effectively setting budgets – to do an amount, not necessarily the whole, of systems analysis concerning the requirement. This is the 'bootstrap cost' to get the show on the road, so to speak.
2. Having done 'an amount', whatever is deemed sufficient, of systems analysis on the requirement, one estimates the effort to complete phase 1 – the specification phase – to some degree of approximation, by analogy. As this phase may, probably will, involve prototypes for both functional specifications and outline design, the inaccuracy may be high. One can use the rough and ready precept that n times an underestimate is likely to be less bad than otherwise, so long as one realizes that the result is a budgetary estimate only, and for phase 1 only, and is not a basis for any 'hard' contractual arrangements of the fixed price and time-scale form – and certainly has no bearing on phases 2 or 3 estimates at all.
3. When a detailed and stable functional specification enables the compilation of a notional software taxonomy, phase 2 development costs and time-scales will be possible to estimate accurately (± 25 percent) by the OSD/CPM method described. If these values have already been fixed ('price-to-win'), then this is the point at which the real 'costs-to-do' are determined.

   These estimates, in all cases, should be redone during software design to achieve greater accuracy (± 10 percent, or so) on the residual development – which may still be 70–80 percent of the total phase 2 quantities.
4. If required, maintenance cost (effort), over prescribed durations for maintenance, can be done at beta-testing stage, by reliability assessment and corresponding risk evaluation on some statistically substantial basis.

By proceeding this way, and not losing sight of the need to recast plans and to control activities most sedulously, software development and its maintenance may be freed from the terrible tyranny of misestimating or, worse, not estimating at all its needs in effort and time. Then, the equally terrible and consequential tyranny that money, or time, has over technical quality, can be avoided, or – as is most often the case – the misconceived attempt to substitute money for time will not arise.

12.5 THE EFFORT AND TIME RELATIONSHIP REVISITED

Most software tasks that get into economic troubles of the form 'too little effort, too little time', do so in the development phase. We have just reviewed some of the reasons for this state of affairs, and they can make sad reading in their own right. Also they, for the most part, begin well outside the development phase. In software engineering one often starts out by shooting oneself in both feet!

Likewise, most software tasks that do get into such economic trouble get into the one concerning time far earlier than any similar thing concerning effort. There may be the odd twinge about team sizes during (say) the late design stage, but it is seldom on the same scale of panic as when a delivery time emerges over the planning horizon, moving briskly and purposefully toward one. The imminence of a scheduled alpha-test, let alone its adversarial counterpart, can be enough to act like a most stringent emetic on the software team.

As we have seen at the start of this chapter, the reason for this are rooted in the effect on company profits that overrun on development time-scales may have. If a 50 percent cost overrun only erodes product profit margins by 3 percent in some particular case, and delaying the product release by six months (usually in the range 25–50 percent of total development time) reduces the profit margin by 33 percent, then the options seem to be clear.

12.5.1 Brooks' 'law'

What often happens, given that the due-date is clearly going to be exceeded by some rather noticeable, possibly spectacular, amount, is that an attempt is made to 'buy time back' in some curious way, and the usual currency in this bizarre transaction is people. Now this is another of our seductive little myths, and deserves to be held up to view: 'Putting more people on a late job makes it later' (Brooks 1976). In fact, this famous aphorism is not quite adequate as it stands – although its power is in the economy with which it spotlights the sort of thing that managers get up to. Without being too pedantic about it, the issue is that putting more people on a late job is not a specific for saving its time-scale; in fact it *may* make matters worse. The reasons are not difficult to find either. Inducting new people into a team takes effort (and time!), and the mean relevant competence level of a software team is inevitably diluted when people unfamiliar with it are drafted in, for whatever reasons.

Earlier, in Section 12.3.1, we raised the question of an effort and time-scale relationship and, particularly, if Putnam's conjecture has merit:

$$E \cdot T^z = \text{constant}$$

and, if so, what values of z might apply. First, though, we may inspect the hypothesis to see if it has any bearing or sheds any light on Brook's aphorism.

First, we may reformulate the Putnam formula by substituting $(P \cdot T)$ for E, since effort is the product of numbers of people (P), and the time over which they are expending their efforts (T). Thus according to Putnam:

$$(P \cdot T) \cdot T^z = \text{constant}$$

where P is the average team size during T.

Now this is an even more fearsome relationship than before; it says, in effect, that the incremental (or decremental) effect of changes in time-scale, on average team size required, will be proportional to the reciprocal of the $(z + 1)$th power of that change. Conversely, it says that the effect on time-scale of changes in average team size, will be proportional to the $(z + 1)$th root of that change.

This is exactly the effect that Brooks is getting at. The beneficial effects of increasing team size, by adding numbers of competent software staff who are unfamiliar with the task, will be an extremely weak one. If Putnam's conjecture is correct, and $z + 1 = 5$, then the effect of doubling the average team size (+100 percent) will be time-scale reduction of about 13 percent only – always presuming that the added staff are up to the job in the first place.

When such extremely weak, potentially positive forces are accompanied by far stronger, negative forces – such as for task orientation and increased overhead for communications between larger groups of people – then the weaker effect is entirely submerged within a virulent attrition on productivity; Brooks' law, in fact.

Nor is this conclusion much mitigated if we reduce the stringency of Putnam's formulation. For a value of $z = 3$ in the effort and time formula, a doubling of average team size still only leads to a decrease of 16 percent in time-scale; for $z = 2$, an increase of 100 percent in average team size tends to decrease time required by 21 percent; and even a pro rata relationship between effort and time, in which $z = 1$, produces only a 29 percent decrease in required time. Surprising, isn't it?

This insight also explains why Brooks' aphorism seems to be counter-intuitive for small team size. Can it be true that putting an extra person on a one person team, facing an imminent overrun, can make that condition worse? Well, clearly, the marginal effect here will not be submerged by such strong, countervailing forces for induction or overhead for communication between two people. But if we have a job being done by five teams, each comprising six people, then drafting another thirty people on to it is another matter altogether. Again, the mind boggles, along with the bowels and a few other organs, about 'Star Wars'; putting more people on that job, if it becomes late, may alter the meaning of the word 'later' into 'never'.

12.5.2 The heart of the matter

Now, as a last excursion into this matter here, we consider the question of an effort and time-scale relationship. Should we believe that $E \cdot T^4 = \text{constant}$ or $E \cdot T^2 = \text{constant}$, or that something else altogether – such as some far more complex function of the two – describes the relationship? For it is certain that the two are intimately linked, as we have seen elsewhere.

A subsidiary question concerns the range of values, of whichever one is regarded as the degree of freedom, over which the relationship operates. For example, does a formula relating E and T operate for all values of T in the range $T = 0 \to \infty$, where T represents the

duration of a software development task over which values of suitably competent effort, E, will be required to complete it?

In offering the following answers, it must be stressed that any opinion is judgmental, as there are no definite outcomes regarding this issue from the research endeavors into such empirical matters. Not that falling back on informed judgment in this or any other matter is an admission of weakness; I should rather be told an engineer's opinion of a structure than depend on some theoretical view of its stability.

On that basis, the following synopsis can be offered with some confidence:

1. The relationship between effort and time for software development tasks (n.b. not phases 1 or 3) is well enough represented by:

$$E \cdot T^z = \text{constant}$$

although it may well be that this is a first order approximation to some far more complex function or set of such.

However, the empirical work of Norden *et al.* and particularly Putnam, bears about it a more convincing aura than that of some other research endeavors. Moreover, Putnam has made strenuous efforts to explain his discovered effects, in terms of software engineering realities (Putnam 1982) and has thus at least tried to avoid the catch-all explanation of 'phenomenology' to account for some rather odd relationships.

2. The simple, perhaps approximate formula:

$$E \cdot T^z = \text{constant}$$

undoubtedly represents a family of relationships, distinguished from each other by relative difficulty of an application type, and (in general) the relative 'fit', to this degree of difficulty, of the environment in which it is to be attempted. The composite of 'difficulty' and 'environment' (staff, PSE), will be represented within the constant of proportionality in:

$$E \propto 1/T^z$$

and, also, these task and environment factors will account for different values for z.

Thus $E \cdot T^2 = \text{constant}$ may be perfectly adequate to describe a class of fairly straightforward data processing applications, to be done in Cobol by a team of extremely experienced 'dp' and Cobol programmers, on an over-configured IBM mainframe with lots of appropriate tools.

On the other hand:

$$E \cdot T^4 = \text{constant}$$

may scarcely be stringent enough to describe a wicked little (or large) task, with lots of concurrent features in the implementation, to be written in a language that does not yet exist, on a machine that is a glint only in some mad inventor's eye, and to be done by the same team of Cobol programmers – who might not know what to do with concurrency if they found it swimming around (in real time) in their beer. We presume, therefore, that researchers – such as Putnam, Boehm, Jensen and others as quoted – have been looking at particular (and different) subsets of the total sample space in possible software applications.

We will now inspect the sensitivity of $E \cdot T^z$ = constant from two viewpoints; the range over which variations in E affect T, and the range over which variations in T affect E.

3. Whether incremental changes to effort affect time-scale over a limited or unlimited range of values, seems rather beside the point, given that the team size effect will be in force at the same time.

   If $z = 3$ in a certain case, I will have to *multiply* my average team size by 16 to get a 50 percent reduction in time, and the effect of increased team size is going to show up very quickly. So, basically, I neither know, nor much care, if $E \cdot T^z$ = constant applies in some critical range for value of E; depending on Brooks' 'law' will be good enough. I had better not try to 'buy time' at the expense of effort, because the weak positive effect of even competent additional resources will be swamped very quickly by the other effects of team size.

4. On the other hand, $E \cdot T^z$ = constant is far more sensitive to incremental or decremental changes in T. And here it behoves us to be more scrupulous than before. Not least because people get so excited in different ways by this prospect. For instance:

   Manager: 'Oh dear, oh dear,' (known as the manager's mantra), 'if we get T wrong, then we're in the septic tank with a vengeance, aren't we?'

   Salesperson: 'Hang on a bit! If we increase allowed time, we cheapen the job sensationally, is that it? This could be the marketing breakthrough we've been waiting for!'

   Engineer: 'Drivel. Special pleading. No such thing in electronics – $E \cdot T$ to the thingummyjig equals, what was it? Typical software engineers (engineers indeed!). Their trash is going to be late again isn't it, that's what you're trying to tell me, and it won't work properly when we get it.'

   Software: 'Sir, if you reduce the "comfortable time-scale", done by a scrupulous application of OSD/CPM, I may well try my hand at murder.'

   Clearly, the stakes are high. Over what range of values, for T, can we see the formula applying? Can the sales team sell a job for nothing given that a phantom team of no people take eternity to do it? We already know that we cannot do the job instantaneously by drafting an infinitely large army of chaps in, then shouting 'Go!', and the next second all is revealed and completed.

   In fact, judgmentally speaking, it is difficult to see a time-scale relaxation having much effect at all on effort. Up to a point, some force – likely to be far weaker than for the concomitant effect of time-scale compression – might apply, but the effort apparently 'saved' may be reabsorbed in better testing and better documentation. Then, beyond this point, Parkinson's 'law' may take over, and the (relatively unproductive) effort may stay constant over time.

   Equally, time-scale compression may only be valid up to a certain point when, as in the case of the 'gas laws', an empirical relationship breaks down.

   These points are taken forward in 5 and 6 below.

5. It is best to regard $E \cdot T^z$ = constant, for values of z in the range 2 and above, as describing the effect of time-scale compression, up to a limit of $T - 25$ percent of T. This should then be the absolute maximum of reduction to a 'comfortable' time-scale, as properly determined by some OSD/CPM method.

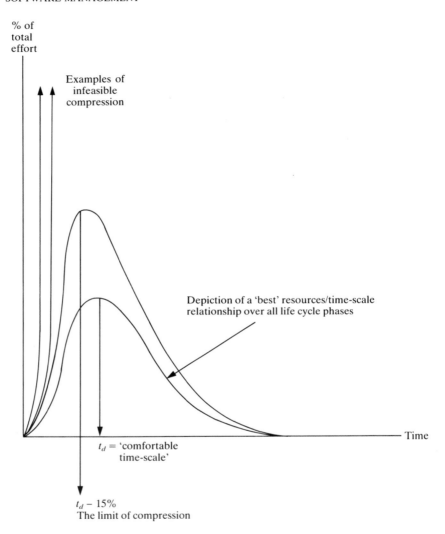

FIGURE 12.9 Resource loading curves with extreme compression.

It may well be that for low values of z, 25 percent is too stringent a limit, and for high values it may be too permissive; in general, however, it is a reasonable 'rule of thumb' that, up to 25 percent of a comfortable time-scale, compression can feasibly be done – with the full effect on required effort, whatever that is. Above that limit, one effectively 'breaks the equation', just as in the case of van der Waals' relationship for the behavior of gases; one can compress, up to a point, with concommitant heating. Above that point, we might have some entirely different behavior. Figure 12.9 represents this situation.

6. It is best to regard the value of z in $E \cdot T^z =$ constant as having half its effect for time-scale relaxation, with the rider that $z/2$ will not reduce to less than unity in value. Thus, for $z = 4$ in the case of time-scale compression for some difficult software task, $z = 2$ for its time-scale relaxation – and this only up to some defined amount; likewise, for $z \leqslant 2$ (an easier application, for whatever reason), the effect of allowing more time might be a simple, pro rata relationship $E \cdot T =$ constant and, then again, only up to a point.

In all cases, I should not trust this half-exponent rule beyond $T + 25$ percent. And, again, this 'rule of thumb' might be too accommodating for really difficult tasks – where no effort reduction may accrue – or not quite liberal enough for easy tasks where, instead of two people doing the job in nine months (say), one person could do it in twelve months. We all know of such cases.

Those, then, are the rough and judgmental 'rules of thumb' for viewing the effort and time-scale relationship for software development. Of all the effects of research into parametric cost models, this is by far the most revealing – if only for the fact that the question 'E times T to the whatever power?' has been raised. It is a hook on which one can hang much in the way of comment about, and insight into, the realities of software development.

How then does one relate $E \cdot T^z =$ constant to the very immediate realities of the OSD/CPM approach to estimating? Can the strongly non-linear effects, particularly in time-scale compression, be explained? The answer is, of course, affirmative. It would be surpassingly strange otherwise, and cause one to doubt either the empirical relationship or the CPM method, or both. For CPM provides a rational and evidential (not 'phenomenological'), basis for comfortable time-scale and a 'resources smoothed' effort that is indissolubly associated with it.

Any alteration to this derived time-scale must alter the assumptions on which the method of arriving at it was based. This alteration is to what was, in the first place (and however notional), a very sensitive act of balancing issues and 'trading-off' effects to achieve both reasonable time-scale and ultilization of resources. It is not that we are thundering about, like bulls in china-shops, where an optimum of some sort is concerned, but we are indisputably disturbing a complex construction (the rational activities' plan) if we take the pruning-shears to our 'comfortable' derived time-scale.

Equally, we can see the converse effect – or relative lack of it. If one floods the activities' plan with some superfluity of resource – a brigade of Freds, say – it may have a less than desired effect on the overall outcome, not least as regards time.

12.6 THE VIEW FROM THE COAL-FACE

As an undergraduate student in mathematics, so long ago that it is surprising how memory of it persists, I shared accommodation with members of a mining engineering faculty and, one day, they carried me off with them to see a coal-mine. At the mine-head, I was much impressed by their discourse on the depth of shaft, temperature at the seam, seepage from the local water-table, stress and strength of props, and all the paraphernalia and pantomime of their trade. I even joined in, with a bit of amateur mechanics and a dollop of fifth-grade organic chemistry. I seem to remember seeing a piece of coal.

Then, as we stood there, improving the atmospheric pressure, and increasing its ambient temperature with our views, the night-shift of miners came up, winched to the surface in ramshackle lifts, grimy with their labor, bowed from working in a half meter high gallery, the troglodytes of their trade, bearing its cruel detritus in their lungs.

Software engineering is not unlike coal-mining in some respects, not the least of which is that we often expect it to be done in poor conditions which we are content to assert that nature forces on that activity. Yet that assertion is untrue. In software development we dilligently create those 'poor conditions' for ourselves.

Those miners took a small bird, caged, to the coal-face with them, to detect fire-damp; if it keeled over, so might they. Would that managers, in software development environments, had a canary in a cage, to thrust it at the specification, at the PSE, at the qualitative and quantitative levels of resource on offer, and at the time-scale. Perhaps a cat would be better; they are supposed to have nine lives.

The following is a tale, anecdotal but far from apocryphal, from the real world of software engineering, from the coal-face so to speak. A certain software task, part of an oil pipeline, closed-loop control systems (telemetry equipment all over the place, special displays, real-time responses required for opening and closing valves) was contracted out, to be done in twenty-five person-years of effort, over a two year time-scale. The successful bidder was a company that had done part of a similar job before, and thought little of the risks as it wrote an offer, against a very dubious 'commercial specification' – the sort of thing that defines a requirement to model the universe on half of one A4-sized page.

The supplier's estimating method seemed to have as its leitmotif an unhappy conjunction of facile analogy and the client's financial limits, creating a 'price-to-win'. And, if one could have applied some objective metric to the vital factors (or had a canary in a cage, suitably calibrated for its rate and angle of fall), the picture to emerge would have resembled that in Table 12.3. Of course, there is no accurate and objective way to determine values for the factors included in Table 12.3. As an instance of this, it is difficult to calibrate PSE facilities relative to a given task. The old contraption, chugging away in the corner, may have cost $50,000 a mere twenty years ago, and the software staff may have been clamouring for a $5,000,000 model, but that does not mean that the MORON-I rates 1 percent on a normative scale.

Equally, one may ask how staff adequacy rates 70 percent merely. Some computations can be extremely misleading. For example, one may define adequacy in terms of a number, n, of software engineers each having an amount, x, years of relative experience. So, for this task, the normative 'adequacy' might be:

$$2 \times 8 + 6 \times 4 + 4 \times 2 + 2 \times 1 = 50 \text{ years of relevant experience}$$

But 70 percent of this would be 35 'years of relative experience'. Would it be equivalent if

TABLE 12.3 Vital factors in a software development task

	Staff	Spec	PSE	Difficulty	Time	Effort
Adequacy	1.0	1.0	1.0	1.0	1.0	1.0
Actuality	0.7	0.5	0.3	2.0	?	?

this was supplied by 14 people having 2.5 years of relevant experience each; or a team leader in the business for 22 years, plus 13 chaps with a year's programming each under their belts? It is not likely, is it?

In the event, an entirely objective, forensic determination of these values was not called for. The supplier blasted ahead, and Table 12.3 represents very much an *ex post facto* reconstruction of the various inadequacies.

Contract in haste, repent during development. After about twenty-one months, the software testing should have been in full swing, but was not. Five extra software engineers, of various skills and experience levels, were drafted on to a team – two subgroups really – already thirteen strong.

Time passed, as it will in the best regulated circumstances. Test schedules, and the delivery time, came and went. At twenty-nine months, the overall team strength – if that is the correct expression – was increased from eighteen to twenty-two. Prodigies of work were undertaken, and the company even paid for overtime, and created a precedent in the process that it later tried to deny. More time passed. Then at thirty-six months, a mere 50 percent overrun on the originally contracted time-scale, the client intervened. At their insistence an independent audit was commisioned by the supplier, on pain of certain legalities.

The auditing consultant, wisely, went back to first principles. On the basis of what passed for the functional specification, an OSD/CPM-based estimate was drawn up that showed how the orginal task should have been undertaken in something like about forty-three person-years of effort, expended over a duration of thirty-three months. The management in the supplier-company clenched its teeth, not for the first time it should be said. How had they managed to underestimate effort by 43 percent and time-scale by 27 percent? And hadn't even more effort and time been expended by now? In fact, about fifty-seven person-years, and thirty-six months, respectively?

The answers were predictable:

1. The original error had been to employ a species of guesswork, that inevitably failed to appreciate the defects illustrated in Table 12.3.
2. Then, piling more people on to the job, near to its deadline, had brought Brooks' 'law' into force – a weak, potentially beneficial effect being offset by a virulent negative one.

Well, reposted the supplier, what should we have done? They, the client, had wanted the system on the 1st September – two years from the start date. 'Ah' retorted the consultant, edging towards the door (which, unfortunately, provided access to a broom-cupboard), 'we'll need to redo the estimate'.

And, lo and behold, the answer to this new conundrum turned out to be: 'You should have finished the FS first; then, knowing your likely problems in staff and PSE facilities – which you should have discounted into the estimates on a realistic basis – you should have bid the job at something in the range of 100–150 person-years, probably nearer the latter than anything! Better, you should not have bid for it at all. With your quality of staff and development environment, and the state of their specification, the job was not achievable really.'

The client, who had been listening all along, turned sadly to the consultant-company. How much time and effort would it take *them* to complete the job, from the present

position? The answer broke everyone's hearts. By starting anew, with a just-about-usable functional specification from the previous shambles, the consultancy – with its own software engineers and PSE – could do the job, note, not 'complete' the work of others, in a time-scale of two elapsed years, at an effort expenditure of about fifty person-years.

They got the job, and did it – on time and to cost estimate – then took their profit, and went on their way. The original supplier had been contracted so poorly that they managed to shuffle clear of the wreckage with only a few unpaid invoices to write-off.

But the worst of it concerned the client. A few years later, a second system – with somewhat novel features – was to be developed, and then installed. Had they learned anything from the previous catastrophe? Did they leave their own budgeting until after the bidders round? Did they assiduously seek out a supplier that showed evidence of competence in their estimating? Did they contract competently?

No, no, no and no are the answers, respectively.

The results were predictable, if not predicted. 'Another cave-in at the coal-face. Dozens buried!'

CHAPTER THIRTEEN

MANAGING SOFTWARE DEVELOPMENT

We have taken the subject of software engineering out of its box, turned it this way and that, taken it apart, and examined it piece by piece. Now we must see how to make it work, how to apply all that has been learned, in order to manage a software development task.

In this chapter, we begin from the position of a manager who is neither phobic about the subject, nor deluded about the limits of visibility and comprehension – a person with a conceptual grasp of life cycle stages and the modalities of software development, and how reputable task estimation should be done.

The essentials of management are treated, *viz.*: activities and cost control; deliverable documentation; managing for quality/managing for change; organization and personnel issues, including subject-education; and procurement of software services and systems.

Finally, the question of standards or guidelines is revisited for, amongst the many threats, the delusion of universality must be avoided. The simile, struck earlier, should be remembered: software development is more like the evolution of a theory in science than anything.

For the development of software that is of high quality in both technical and economic senses there must be good management of the whole process, and disposition and effective regulation of resources – people and material – to those ends. There are many aspects to this 'good management', which we have aggregated under five headings in the following sections:

1. Activities and cost control; deliverable documentation.
2. Managing for change – to specifications and to programs.
3. Managing for quality.
4. Organization and personnel factors.
5. Software procurement – services and systems.

Taken with the issues and techniques of estimating (Chapter 12) and those of archiving and structured walkthrough (Chapter 11), these are the essentials for managing software development. Their competent adoption, and that of adequate technical facilities, ensure there is a chance – at least – to produce high quality software.

Of all the questions I have had put to me on education courses, or as a consultant, manager, chief programmer and so on over the various roles of a varied life in software engineering, perhaps the one that has come closest to unmanning me is the following: 'Is it not the case that software engineering is little more than competent management of the software development process?' I shall leave this question until the end of this chapter: I recall needing a little time to answer it on the previous occasion!

13.1 ACTIVITIES AND COST CONTROL;
DELIVERABLE DOCUMENTATION

Here we deal with three fundamental issues in software management although, on the face of it, the third item – deliverable documentation – may seem to be located here only through some personal idiosyncrasy, or as an afterthought, or for lack of better place to put it. In fact, it is included here for a better reason altogether, and that is that its particularities must be seen as *planned* activities (and costed ones too), if the deliverable documentation is not to be overlooked, or assumed to be coming into being. Of all the many and various things that can go wrong with software development, one of the most virulent is this assumption, that deliverable documentation is somehow coming into being or, worse, that it can be brought into being at the end of the development, e.g. sometime between the end of alpha-testing and the end of beta-testing. We shall defer the arguments about this fallacy until Section 13.1.3, when we will return to them with some vigor.

13.1.1 Activities' planning, resources' bar-charts and status matrices

Activities' planning can take many forms, but they all basically say the same things in different ways. Two schemes for depicting activities' plans were set out in Figures 12.4 and 12.5, and the basic method for casting these charts has been set out in Section 12.4.2. Although it is hardly important which scheme is adopted, the requirements for *control* as distinct from estimating may lead one to more elaborate methods. One such is the 'precedence/successor' form of netplan representation, and its subsequent portrayal in tabular form. This convention is indicated in Figure 13.1, and an example of the analysis from such a netplan is shown in Table 13.1.

For the estimating that takes place when functional specification and software taxonomies are available, the simple node and line schemes set out in Figure 12.4 are sufficient. That is not to say that these will be trivial netplans. For anything above a small sized software system, the 'doubly notional', resources-constrained activity plans may be formidably large in their own right, and may require substantial decomposition over many pages of their depiction.

The estimating netplans may be seen as the first-order approximation for activities' control at the functional specification level. Thus, a fixed price supply contract, entered into at that stage, may have such a netplan attached as evidence of this management planning and control method, as well as the justification of effort and time-scale.

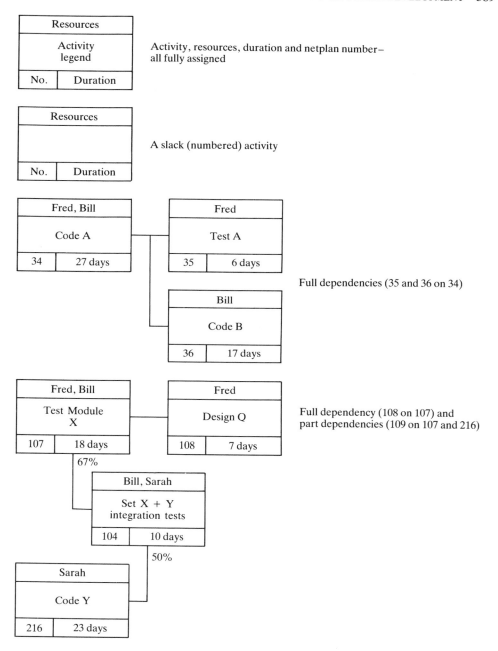

FIGURE 13.1 Precedence/successor netplan convention.

TABLE 13.1 Predecessor and successor activities' analysis

Precedence Analysis

Activity name	Number	Estimate (person-days)	Start date (project day)	Predecessors
Sched.–design	738	16	236	707, 719, 724
Sched.–det. design	759	8.5	252	738
Sched.–review	762	1.5	260.5	759
Sched.–code	764	19	262	762
Sched.–code read	770	1.5	281	769
Sched.–author test	839	6	282.5	770

Successor Analysis

Activity name	Number	Estimate (person-days)	Start date (day)	Successors
Integration tests	1078 =	14 =	492	1109, 1127, 1139,
T1–u4/13	1079	3	492	1264, 1300
T2–u10/14	1080	3	495	
T3–u8/15	1081	3	498	
T4–u7/16	1082	3	501	
T5–beta	1297	2	627	

However, beyond the functional specification stage, one rapidly proceeds to the point where actual software components or 'design modules' are being spoken of, rather than taxons in what is, after all, not a design so much as a catalog of the functionality that may possibly be done in software. Also, one is speaking about real resources at this level, and not presumed staff as may have been the case earlier. These actual, as distinct from notional, activities' plans for estimating will be done as described for the OSD/CPM method in Chapter 12 – but may involve more elaborate, and perhaps computer-based conventions, such as the precedence/successor method. These will first be undertaken during the software design stage, and must be updated regularly thereafter.

For small tasks, this update period may be some compromise between a feeling of what is reasonable on the one hand, and the brief time-scale involved on the other. Thus, we may have six weeks of software development during which it may only be reasonable to update activities' plans every week. In that case, the update frequency is easily determined.

For large sized development, the matter may be more complex, with activities of far longer duration within the plan. Whilst this might well call for status review, and even formal walkthrough to determine the intermediate status of activities, it will probably lead to a longer update frequency for the activities' plan. Thus, we may find a two, three and even four week period between updates of activities' plans for very large software development tasks. Four weeks should be the absolute maximum in these cases, and examples where netplan updating is allowed to slip into larger numbers of weeks and months cannot be said to be activities' control in any meaningful sense.

It is common practice in other engineering fields, such as construction and plant engineering, to develop activities' plans and to update them by using a computer-based CPM, Pert or precedence plan system. There is a minor danger in this. People rapidly fall

Date Staff	January												
	1	2	3	4	5	6	7	8	9	10	11	12	etc.

Aldridge   X   X ———— PQR test ———— —— Holidays ————

Bentham   X   X ————————— PQR test —————————

Bentley   X   X ————————— Pascal course ————— - ABC design

Burroughs   X   X —— Macro software course ——— — I11 —— — Dead

Carstairs   X   X ————————— ABC design —————————

Clegg (J)   X   X ————————— Holiday —————————

Clegg (M)   X   X ———————— Sales ———————— —— LMN test ——

Davies   X   X ————————— Pascal course ——— · LMN test —

Davis   X   X ————————— Code Prototype 101 —————————

Denholme   X   X —————————— Design Prototype 77A ———

Dudley (A)   X   X ——— Macro software course ——— – Resigned and left

Dudley (P)   X   X —— PQR test ————— —— Seconded to client

etc.

FIGURE 13.2 Resources barchart – example.

into the habit of thinking (and saying) such things as: 'The computer shows that the job will be finished next March', or some such, as though 'the computer' was actually in charge. Hand-done, and updated, netplans for software development are far more real to their authors, because the bottlenecks in them, and their other problematical features, are then more obvious.

Activities' plans, in whatever format, should not be confused with resources' bar-charts, as sometimes is the case, as I have found. These are simple schemes, often involving pre-formatted charts to hang on office walls, to show staff-to-project assignments in a division or department of many staff doing many different tasks. Figure 13.2 illustrates such a scheme. As will be clear from this example, a resources bar-chart is very specifically not an activities' plan, although it may be possible to erect the one from the other. For instance, it would be possible to do a time-ordered activities' plan of the PQR development, or for the LMN project, and so on. However, there is little virtue in holding activities' planning

information on a resources' bar-chart alone. The purpose of these bar-charts is simply to be able to see complex resource allocations over a large department of people; this purpose should not be conflated with that of activities' planning and control.

Sometimes the resource allocation and duration of activities are depicted in this tabular form too, analogous to a bar-chart, as distinct from one of the graphical forms suggested. Thus one may have activities as rows, and people as columns, and the ascriptions of the one to the other shown by 'bars' whose length indicates duration. There is nothing against this, except that it can be surpassingly difficult, although in theory never impossible, to detect critical paths.

A most useful device with which to take a snapshot of activities (as it were 'through' the netplans) is the *status matrix*. In this method, a status is defined for each activity in each part of the development. For example, this status may be as follows:

　− means activity not yet started
　0 means activity started but not completed
　+ means activity completed

At the software design stage, one reaches a point when the design modularity is evident, and one may name modules as A, B, C, D, E, . . . (in real life they would carry meaningful ascriptions, such as an abbreviated module, program or integrand name of some sort). The activities to be undertaken can then be listed, exactly like the specimen given in Section 12.4.2, and a matrix can be drawn up – see Figures 13.3 and 13.4.

The second of these schematics shows both progress (modules A, B, C, D, E, F, G, H, L, M, N) and back-tracking (modules B, I, J and K). This back-tracking clearly indicates that not all has proceeded according to plan. Either categorical errors in design or implementation have been found, or some substantial change has been effected.

	Gen	A	B	C	D	E	F	G	H	I	J	K	L	M	N
Overall design	+														
Module design		+	+	0	+	0	0	−	0	+	+	+	−	0	0
Design review		+	+	−	+	−	−	−	−	+	+	+	−	−	−
Code		+	+	−	+	−	−	−	−	+	+	+	−	−	−
Code read		0	+	−	+	−	−	−	−	+	+	+	−	−	−
Code test (author)		−	+	−	+	−	−	−	−	+	+	+	−	−	−
Integration															
Level 1 (A + B)		−	−												
2 (A + C)		−		−											
3 (C + D + E)				−	−	−									
4 (F + L + M + N)							−						−	−	−
5 (L3 + 4)				−	−	−	−						−	−	−
6 (G + H + I)								−	−	−					
7 (L5 + 6)											+	+			
8 (J + K)															
9 (L1 + 2 + 3 + 7 + 8)		−	−	−	−	−	−	−	−	−	−	−	−	−	−
Alpha-test design	+														
Alpha-test	−														
Beta-test design	0														

FIGURE 13.3 Status matrix − state X example.

It is important not to conceal back-tracking, and an important element in 'good software engineering practice' is the recognition by practitioners that falsification of real progress, in this and other ways, is self-deception in the first place. As has often been said; 'God bless the software engineer who admits difficulty and error in good time'. The ones who conceal it are more usually consigned to the infernal regions.

In general, the right update frequency for status matrices is determined by the frequency of updating activities' plans. If this is a short time-scale itself – one week, say – then status matrices may be kept and updated on the same frequency. If activities are updated (an extreme case) on a six weeks' basis, then one may have status matrix updating every week, fortnight or three weeks, depending on the expected rate of change of information carried by the device.

Perhaps the greatest virtue of status matrices, apart from the very clear depiction of back-tracking that they give, is that the information carried is essentially binary. Is X finished, or is it not? The progression and, at times, regression of a software development is easier to see in this way than from the activities' plans. On the other hand, one should not dispense with the activities' netplan and merely proceed with status matrices. What status matrices fail to show is the interactive schedule of necessary events toward a future end-date. The two devices, taken together, are an extremely powerful way of managing software development tasks from the design stage onwards.

13.1.2 Cost control

The essential prerequisite for cost control in this, and any other endeavor occupying people's time and the acquisition or usage of materials, is a cost accounting system

	Gen	A	B	C	D	E	F	G	H	I	J	K	L	M	N
Overall design	0														
Module design		+	−	+	+	+	+	0	0	0	0	0	+	+	+
Design review		+	−	+	+	+	+	−	−	−	−	−	+	+	+
Code		+	−	+	+	0	0	−	−	−	−	−	0	0	+
Code read		+	−	+	+	−	−	−	−	−	−	−	−	−	+
Code test (author)		+	−	+	+	−	−	−	−	−	−	−	−	−	0
Integration															
Level 1 (A + B)		−	−												
2 (A + C)		+		+											
3 (C + D + E)				−	−	−									
4 (F + L + M + N)							−						−	−	−
5 (L3 + 4)				−	−	−									
6 (G + H + I)								−	−	−					
7 (L5 + 6)				−	−	−	−	−	−	−			−	−	−
8 (J + K)											−	−			
9 (L1 + 2 + 3 + 7 + 8)		−	−	−	−	−	−	−	−	−	−	−	−	−	−
Alpha-test design	0														
Alpha-test	−														
Beta-test design	+														

FIGURE 13.4 Status matrix – state X + 1 example.

adequate for the purpose. This need not be an elaborate affair. A simple code system for tasks, and an elaboration of it for stages of the task, will suffice – always with the caveat that such things do not operate themselves, and the 'system' must be managed to ensure that its adoption does not fall into desuetude.

Thus, some abstract 'project' or 'product' classification such as ABC 000, or PQR 100 or whatever, may be assigned. Or, and more usefully, the classification for configuration control may be as is described in Section 13.2.2. Here a product designation – such as CAISSA for the chess system – may be invented.

For cost control, one may then attach designation for life cycle phases. For example: CAISSA (URS), or CAISSA (alpha-test) or whatever. These are, in effect, job numbers, and at any stage, they may have people accounting time and other costs to them. Clearly, the most sedulous review of all such claims must be made to prevent false accounting. It is on the assumption that such a system is in place that the following ways and means are suggested, with the aspect of time-accounting (as distinct from materials' costs) as the object.

On most of the occasions I have met in practice, the ability of a directly accountable manager to tell me anything really significant about the cost of an ongoing software development, has been extremely limited. After some struggle, and an amount of calculation by the manager concerned, one may extract a profile of the cumulative cost (of effort) to do the job, as a function of the allowed time. The sort of information concerned is on view in Figure 13.5.

This information is usually available in, or may be derived from, an original costing

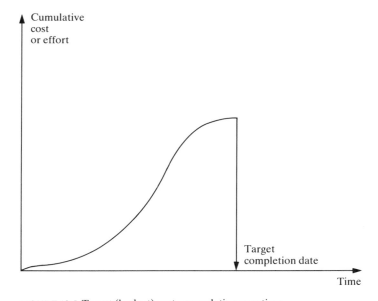

FIGURE 13.5 Target (budget) cost – cumulative over time.

exercise for the job concerned. What will be missing, unless a time-accounting system against the specific task is in place, is an idea of the actual cost to date and its derivate – the cost to complete – as depicted in Figure 13.6. Just to have the picture shown in Figure 13.6 would be priceless information for many software development managers, not to mention *their* managers.

On the relatively rare occasions when this has been available, one is inclined to let well alone, to quit whilst ahead. Yet the picture is not quite informative enough. Mere cumulative cost (or effort) says nothing of the value of its expenditure to the task at hand. One may accumulate cost by having a bunch of people sitting around like parrots on a perch, decorative and garrulous–but unproductive.

One way around this is to compile a cumulative cost histogram, to which increments of cost are only made when an activity is complete–such as 'design module X'; similarly, the histogram may be decremented when back-tracking occurs, by the amount of cost originally incorporated for that achievement, or set of achievements. Figure 13.7 shows such a system in practice.

In effect, this weighted cost histogram is related to the status matrix 'snapshot' through an activities' plan, in the following fashion:

−   no cost accretion during state (−), as an activity is not yet begun; cost weight = 0.

− **to 0**   no cost accretion during state (0), as an activity is not yet complete; cost weight = 0.

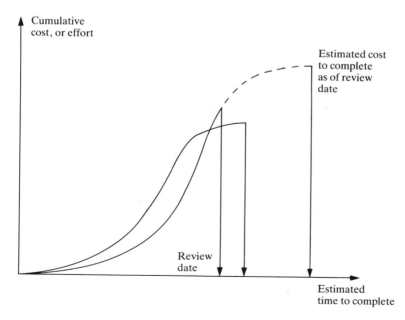

FIGURE 13.6 Target and actual cumulative cost graphs.

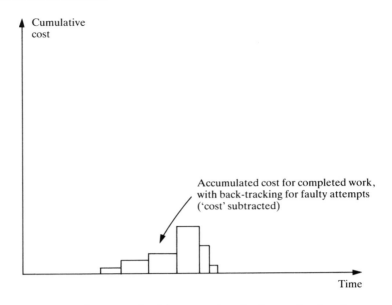

FIGURE 13.7 Incremental and decremental costing for completed work.

0 to +   incremental accretion by the cost of the completed activity; cost weight $= 1$.
+ to −   decremental accretion by the cost of completed activity; cost weight $= -1$.

The three factors–target, actual and weighted cost information–may now be represented on one diagram, Figure 13.8.

Refinements to this scheme can be made to fit whatever management style prevails. For example, adding back work to recomplete activities, when back-tracking has occurred, can be done according to one of two conventions. Either the new work to recomplete may be added, or that and the previously subtracted work in the first place may be added. In the second case, the final weighted cost histogram will coincide with the actual cost curve when the task is completed; in the former case, there will be a gap between the value of cumulative cost shown in the weighted cost histogram, and that at the final point of the actual cost curve. This difference is the cumulative cost of back-tracking during the development.

Is cost control of software development the prevailing practice in your company? Do software managers blame the accounts and administration departments for lack of the underlying means, or do these departments wring their collective hands at the lack of time-reporting in the technical sectors of the firm? Do both managers and accountants long to wring the collective neck of the hapless software engineers?

When the practices are not generally implemented as management method, software engineers often undertake time-accounting and cost (effort) control based on it, at a parochial level. That, certainly, is better than nothing. Moreover, managers observing the process should take the lesson to heart; if it can be done locally, it can be done globally.

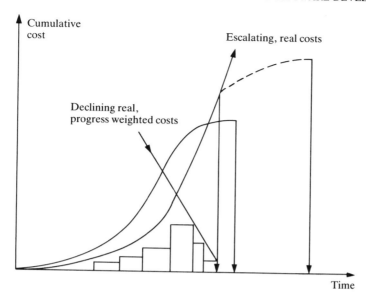

FIGURE 13.8 A portrait of trouble. Real and progress weighted cost histories.

On such occasions, good management practice is brought about 'bottom up', with technicians acting as the agents of change. It is staggering to have to admit it, but there are innumerable cases in which this has occurred, and one is left asking: 'What on earth has happened to management?' The simple fact is that much 'management' of software development is in no meaningful sense management at all; it is titular but not effective. In some cases this is due to unfamiliarity with the subject, and the phobia this may engender. In such cases, a manager may feel there is a choice to remain silent and be thought a fool, or to open one's mouth and remove all shadow of doubt on the subject. In other cases, particularly where the managers in a firm are very strongly hardware-oriented by personal background, the omission is often for other reasons – including, it must be said, simple prejudice. It is not unknown, for instance, to find groups of electronic engineers who are deeply and sincerely convinced that software 'engineering' (their qualification but one can sympathize with it now) is an intellectually inferior discipline – if it is a subject at all – that it is cocooned in an intolerable mystique and subject to the most abject special pleading for its defects.

As I write, and this is no isolated example, I have the rather arduous privilege of educating a group of aspiring software engineers who work in a company where the dominant technology is production engineering. My students nod away like clockwork when I deal with cost control – as they do, also, for other management means when these are discussed. And when I suggest the parochial adoption of these means, and their propagation 'bottom up' when all else fails, our sense of agreement is complete. The only shadow darkening this beautiful prospect, is that none of their managers, 'back home', has

the faintest interest in target costs, real costs, weighted cost histograms or anything of the sort. What they want is an unimprovable job done, under whatever circumstances, by yesterday. What is one to recommend in these cases? It beats me, as the schoolboy said of the headmaster's cane.

13.1.3 Deliverable documentation

The point has already been made, frequently, that any meaningful definition of 'software' includes the documentation of programs comprising its static state. For that reason, any assessment of software quality must include an assessment of its documentation, and any procurement of software must pay particular attention to this factor – either for ongoing maintenance purposes, or when a meaningful guarantee of ongoing support is required.

For such a fundamentally important topic, it is a little surprising to find that it is yet another in a, by now, impressive list of 'Cinderella subjects' in software engineering. The reasons are not hard to find. Software engineers dislike documenting their systems, as this is seen as a rather boring task compared to the excitements of creation in design and implementation. Added to this, in many cases, is the lack of management impetus in this as well as other matters, for whatever reason. Lack of strong requirements, plus lack of interest, equals lack of achievement. Lack of documentation, where 'lack' can mean defect just as much as omission, means lack of software quality. For these reasons, we speak of 'deliverable' documentation, as that term bears with it the ineluctable connotation of a *hard*, even contractual, requirement.

In this section, we will consider the following questions of deliverable documentation:

1. To whom is 'delivery' due?
2. What does it comprise?
3. When should its parts be done?
4. What electronic support may assist in it?

We treat the answers to each of these questions in the following subsections.

THE RECIPIENTS FOR DELIVERABLE DOCUMENTATION
Deliverable documentation is made for, and due to, whichever group is to maintain the software. In this matter, the cases of software projects and products are substantially different.

1. In the case of projects, we have two different circumstances to consider, depending on the terms of supply. In one, the supplier is contracted to supply ongoing maintenance. During this period, the repository for all documentation – except users' and operator's instructions – *must* be, and must remain, with the supplier. Why, and why so forcibly expressed? It is because no supplier can sustain a responsibility for software if the other party's amateur programmers have got programs disassembled, and are cobbling away at them with wild abandon – and it is no argument at all that they are not amateurs, and that it is not 'cobbling away', nor in 'wild abandon'. The best place for the documentation is with whoever has to maintain it.

In the other case, a supplier has contracted to deliver the software in the fullest sense – an operational system of programs and all the relevant documentation for use, operation *and* maintenance. In this case, the responsibility for maintenance *must* travel with the documentation – i.e. to their client.

2. In the case of products we have one case to consider only, and it is roughly analogous to the one for contractual maintenance in project supply. It is a contradiction in terms to have product software available to a client to change. If some most favored client wants that arrangement, then the matter becomes one of project supply with transfer of maintenance responsibility, and, no doubt, severe distrainers on wider exploitation.

Generally, software product firms, or those making IT systems in which products are a component, have product 'field maintenance' groups. These are the repositories for documentation pertaining to products. In fact, in a well ordered world, such a group will have been the QI/QA beta-test agency for the product and its documentation, and will be responsible for all change authority and configuration management – as described below.

Two factors bedevil the use of deliverable documentation by whichever group has received it. The first is the need to control changes to the software to which it relates. The moment that programs fail to correspond with their documentation, both may be said to be categorically wrong. To prevent this, a bureaucratically formal means of configuration management is required – see Section 13.2.2. This problem is more specific to products than projects.

The second problem, also more specific to projects than products, is less tractable to management means, but must be faced nonetheless. It concerns the depletion of familiarity with a software system over time, as this affects post-delivery maintenance and emendation of the system. Software suppliers who contract for ongoing maintenance tend to schedule the original development staff on to other development tasks.

Deliverable documentation must be written with this in mind; at some substantial time after the delivery of a software system, a group of strangers to it may (probably will) be asked to effect changes, or to correct or improve it. Poor brutes, to be confronted by an uncommented code listing, or less. At least let us deliver an adequate level of documentation to these heirs, assignees and successors, however distant in time they may be.

THE COMPONENTS OF DELIVERABLE DOCUMENTATION

The purposes to which deliverable documentation will be put determine its essential composition. These purposes are threefold in general, but often only twofold in practice:

1. The user's manual.
2. The software maintenance manual.
3. The operator's manual.

For non-batch software systems, the user/operator manuals are generally combined into one document whilst, for embedded systems, the concepts have no relevance at all.

A user's manual generally consists of the following:

1. A general statement of purpose, such as a précis of the user requirement specification.
2. A definition of input required, and the media and format for it.

3. A definition of error diagnostics and remedial actions for erroneous input.

4. A definition of output that may be expected, and its media and the format for it.

Any special usages, such as for security, integrity and portability as explicitly defined by hard requirements in the functional specification, will be detailed, with descriptions of the features available and how they must be invoked if required.

An operator's manual generally consists of instructions for starting the system in operation, and for stopping it. It also contains any and all systems error diagnostic messages for erroneous operation, and corrective actions required – even if these only say 'Call Fred on East Orange 999', or something equally desperate.

The security and integrity features may be trivial, exceedingly complex or somewhere in between. There is generally little to worry about if a computer game is involved, but there may be a very thick manual to deal with if the system is a fail-safe, fault-tolerant one, for putting a manned satellite into orbit, with 'hot, medium or cold standby' features. Neither a user's nor an operator's manual will contain much detail of how the system is made, algorithms, data structures and so forth. These are the proper subjects for the software maintenance manual.

Usually, the most problematical of all components of deliverable documentation is that for software maintenance. If others are defective, they may be reconstructed from the archive, given that an archive exists. But could a maintenance manual be reconstructed from the archive? One has only to place oneself in the plight of a person required to maintain or change an unfamiliar software system, several years after its creation by a team of now dispersed software engineers. In cases like this, the problems of comprehension are formidable. However, there is a question of higher priority even than that; it concerns whether the software is intrinsically maintainable or modifiable: it is the question of quality.

As we have seen in Chapter 9, a software system's property of modifiability is a judgmental one, as there is a lack of algorithms of metrics for determining this, and other aspects of software quality. The way this judgment is formed is depicted in Figure 13.9, in which an ideal process is contrasted with a very typical practice.

In 'typical practice', a software engineer will attempt comprehension by, first of all, trying to use the software and, second, by staring at the code listing. This usually produces little in the way of enlightenment, other than that the software exists, has a user interface of such and such characteristics, is written in BUZZ the wonder-language (its statements are, naturally, called Buzzwords); that it does or does not seem modular at the code level; does or does not have useful comments on the listing, which is – itself – either generally readable, or the converse; has intelligently chosen abbreviations or acronyms for local variables and data areas; lacks 'magic numbers', or is riddled with them, and so on.

This might seem substantial, given that we have said that it is only supposed to shed a little enlightenment, but the issue is one of comprehension first. Staring at a commented code listing is generally of little use in the first instance, although it will be an unimprovably good thing to do ultimately. As a first step it is little better than brooding over a hexadecimal dump.

The better way to proceed is depicted in Figure 13.9(a), and this reveals the nature of the maintenance documentation required. There are, in fact, four components:

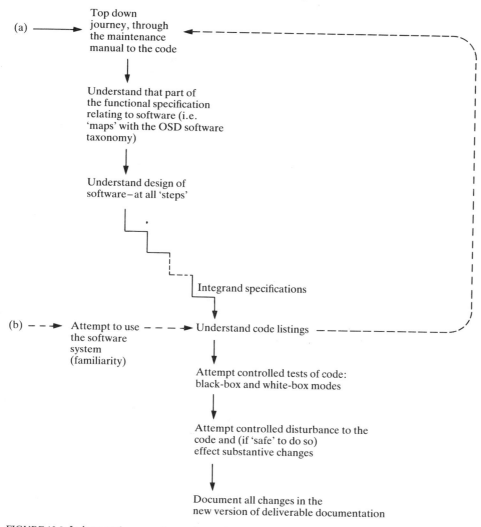

FIGURE 13.9 Judgmental approaches to determine software reliability and modifiability: (a) the right way – top down; (b) the usual way – via a bottom up false start.

1. A subset of the functional specification of requirements defining the features to be incorporated in software.
2. The software designs in their totality – i.e. all design steps.
3. A well commented and well set-out code listing, having good use of variable names, minimal 'magic numbers', local rather than global variables, useful superscription text, and so on.
4. The plans, data and results for and from the software tests, both benevolent and

adversarial, both black-box and white-box. This is to allow previous tests to be replicated, if need be.

The first of these items, a subset of the functional specification, defines the purpose of the software. It should be, in fact, the so-called 'software specification' that emerges from an architectural design – see Chapter 7. It should be accompanied by the general introduction to the functional specification – see Chapter 5.

It is important to restate here that (a) it is a perilous practice to tamper with software whose purpose is not understood (how, for instance, can one interpret the outcome?), and (b) the purpose may not be easy to deduce by 'bottom up' inspection of the code listing. Certainly, in most cases, there will be little evident 'mapping' between code and functional specification although, in relatively simple applications, such as have been designed by functional or data-oriented decomposition, a simple code structure may be derived directly from the functional specification.

The disturbing fact that mapping is so difficult is an inevitable outcome from the transformation and compromise processes undergone in design and implementation, which produce a dichotomy of structural forms, as well as their more obvious means of representation in language. Nor do in-line comments on a code listing help very much in this matter of understanding purpose. For however carefully they have been done, as remarked in Chapter 8, they will tend to refer to the particular purpose a particle has within an integrand within a program, and not to any higher level perspective in the matter. The superscription comments, as essay-style texts at the start of integrands, programs and program load-modules, may be more revealing than the in-line comments. They most certainly should aspire to be so. However, they cannot adequately represent overview of purpose, nor the reasons for design.

These are the arguments for incorporation of specification in the deliverable documentation.

Having assessed and understood the purpose of the software, the next step is to form a quite detailed grasp of its structure. Once again, this is unlikely to result from a mere inspection of the code. Certainly, at the level above the code-listing, some depiction of structure – such as a calling sequence diagram – is a necessity and, at the integrand level itself, some idea of design is highly desirable. This may be in the form of BS 6224 diagrams, structured flowcharts or whatever is suitable. Yet even these aspects of detail and low level design structure may not be enough. As a reader of maintenance documentation strives to understand the structure of the software, he or she will benefit by seeing the design decisions that were made at the time, as these are (or should be) represented by the activities in high level decomposition, 'bottom up' clustering of generically similar functions and utilities into possible 'subroutines' and so forth. All this should be available in its final (that is substantive) form, as graphical descriptions in the notation(s) of choice. One does not need to see all the abortive designs, or the ones that needed correction, and that is why they may be purged from the archive, as described.

An understanding of its purpose, and a grasp of the program structure, will enable a competent software engineer – however previously unfamiliar with the system – to approach the question of changing the code with some definitive views on the quality of the software to be changed, and the likely effects of change on that quality. These views might

be either: 'It looks good, let's go ahead', or 'I wouldn't touch this stuff with a barge-pole', or anything between. Moreover, such an opinion may be determined at any stage of the evaluation shown in Figure 13.9. For example, a software engineer doing the usual thing of calling up the system, trying to use it and so on, may get a most lamentable impression of its worth from the screen management features merely. On turning to the code listing, and finding a cubic meter of material in the form of a hexadecimal dump of the state of store at some instant, this impression may be substantially reinforced.

Thus, a disqualification of the software as something that a competent software engineer would be prepared to emend, may take place as a result of anything in the sequence of evaluation and comprehension activities undertaken, and for which the maintenance documentation is the basis. Sometimes, for example, the 'extracts from a functional specification' are missing, incomplete or otherwise useless; more often, the design documentation is defective, partial or (in a quite staggering number of cases) missing entirely.

So serious is this last named problem, and so prevalent, that consultants asked to pass opinion on a software system may well ask first for the deliverable documentation, and then immediately turn to where that for design should be found. The awful gap, revealed, will tell its simple story – above all of a lack of proper quality inspection and assurance, and a software system that was consequently born into a sea of troubles. Would you dare to mend or add improved features to this software? Would you bet your company's life on it, or your own?

WHEN SHOULD DELIVERABLE DOCUMENTATION BE DONE?
There is a simple precept underlying the answer to this question. It is that any documentation that is deferred beyond the time at which it can be done, will tend not to get done at all. The reasons are simple enough, and widely known nowadays.

Software development often becomes an unholy scramble to create and correct programs before some deadline such as a quality review, or a due date for delivery. In such circumstances 'mere' documentation – or even the upkeep of an archive – may lapse, unless strong management practice prevails. Also, it must be said (and not for the first time), software engineers tend to disdain administration of their activities as being 'non-creative' endeavor. This, too, is a curable condition, in which bleak experience proves an adequate medicine.

In fact, it is quite easy to summarize when elements of deliverable documentation may first be made and, therefore, should be done:

1. The user's manual should be done during the functional specification stage, as all the 'user interface' features must have been exhaustively defined by then – often through requirements' prototypes. In fact, as pointed out in Chapter 2, the user's manual should be appended to the functional specification and, thereby, 'signed off' along with all its other contents. Beyond this point, it falls under change-control practice within the software development; this is dealt with in the section below.

2. In most cases, an operator's manual depends, for its detailed content, on decisions and information that are clarified in the early stages of design proper. For instance, the detailed definition of security and integrity features can first be done at that point, along

with any remedial measures for system degradation, and so on. This manual may, therefore, be compiled during the early parts of architecture design, although its contents thereafter may well be volatile as implementation practicalities interact with first, and subsequent, design ideas.

3. The maintenance manual should have defined contents by early in the design stage, but the substance of these contents will be too volatile to be anything more than archive documents until late in the software testing stage.

Within the archive, one will maintain a currently valid version of designs and code listings, plus the previous version in all cases. At about alpha-test stage, this 'current version' set should be duplicated in both the archive and the deliverable documentation set. Both should be maintained and updated as necessary and, in addition, the version in deliverable documentation may go through some 'beauty-parlor' treatment to fit it for delivery.

Unless some stringent contract of supply stipulates otherwise, it is this late-in-the-life cycle activity to ensure a proper level (and appearance) of deliverable documentation, that most often fails. Moreover, the most sedulous management practice, and quality inspection activity, may be needed to ensure that even the basic material exists in the archive.

By the end of alpha-tests, all the deliverable documentation must be available. If it is not, then quality inspection should not declare the development process to have been verified, and validation (beta-testing by the independent QA group) should not proceed or, if it does, it should not occlude the fact that a previous quality status has not yet been achieved.

THE ARCHIVE AND DOCUMENTATION ENVIRONMENT

In previous epochs, the archives and documentation sets were compiled and maintained by hand. Software engineers or (more likely) amateur programmers, scribbled gnomic messages and notes on scraps of paper, almost always in pencil to ease the inevitable processes of elision and emendation, and stuck them in a bottom drawer where they may, or may not, survive the passage of time. Nowadays, they scribble their equally gnomic message, via keyboard VDUs, into a development computer's working store, and alter it at will (or whim) by using a PSE's facilities to edit, word process and otherwise maintain textual and numeric information.

None of the three manuals defined, with one small but important exception, would tax the resources of even small 'host' and limited PSE – such as a PC in the $5,000 range, say. However, the software engineers' archives and documentation sets should not be nugatory and, most assuredly, should not be scribbled down as if in intolerable haste or under unreasonable duress. When done properly, and for anything but small software development, the supporting facilities required become substantial, and an additional burden on them arises when multi-version configuration management of documentation sets is required. As has already been revealed, in Chapter 8, 'host' hardware and elaborate PSE or Ipse facilities tend to be expensive.

As was said in Chapter 11 for archives, and bears repeating here, one particular defect of most PSEs is that they either fail to support, or do so in an insufficient manner, a range

of useful graphical design notations and their procedures. Once more, the reasons are rooted in cost. It is an expensive job to implement Mascot, SADT, BS 6224 DSD, data flow, CCITT-SDL, JSD/JSP, De Wolf's scheme from the Draper Laboratories, Petrinets, timing charts, structured flowcharts and so on down to a not so short list of useful notations. Some of the attempts, to date, to do this in a 'cheap and cheerful' fashion, on desk-top PCs or workstations, has proved more expensive and even less useful than the well chewed stub of pencil and grubby scrap of paper of former epochs.

Where the means are lacking, within the electronic environments, to support graphical design approaches, the result must not be to abstain from them if they are appropriate, nor must it be to dive into some technician-friendly means such as pseudo-code, which will generally be more than adequately supported by the existence of an editor-adjunct to high level translators.

Reluctantly, or not, the right course of action will be to adopt the most expressive design notations on offer, and to document the results (if need be) by hand; not gnomically, nor nugatorily, but adequately and well. It is of no use whatsoever for software engineers, as they do, to groan aloud at the prospect; consider the alternative. Would *you* like to do a new version of some software system whose deliverable documentation lacks an adequate account of design?

13.2 MANAGING FOR CHANGE

We will consider two forms of change, the management of which requires particular care:

1. Changes to specification.
2. Changes to programs – version control and configuration management.

The first of these requires a change control construction, its operation and management. The second requires a policy for version release of software, administration and management means to ensure it, and electronic support facilities to facilitate it. These factors are considered in some detail here.

13.2.1 Specification change control

However carefully the specification has been done, and whatever the quantity of proto-types made for the purpose of buying information of different kinds, requirements for computer-based systems will tend to change – even *during* the first venture to develop a system to provide the features thought necessary. Typical causes of such changes are discovered errors or deficiencies in specification, and supposed improvements that may be revealed by a variety of means. These include technological improvements from outside sources, changes in the real world that require consideration (at least) for incorporation to specifications, perceived advantages in competitor's products, and so on.

These are the motive forces behind Lehman's first 'law' – quoted in Chapter 10. During the software development itself, specification changes may occur in one of two forms, and have one of two priorities. The forms in which they occur are as follows:

1. Self-evident changes in specification through some change in requirement.
2. Implied change in specification through features of the implementation.

The priorities attaching to changes are either imperative or optional.

The object of specification change control is also twofold; to regulate the implementation of changes, and to evaluate their consequences thoroughly before commissioning them. These motives apply to changes of either type described, and of either priority level defined.

Regulation of the implementation of changes is a paramount concern, as one of the principal failings in software engineering practice in the past has been the common occurrences of informal changes. Half-way through implementing the CAISSA system, Fred is approached by the user/client, usually in informal circumstances. 'What a pity it is', muses the user, 'that the splendid system you're making couldn't do our payroll as well'. Several drinks later, and Fred has sketched out a few patches to his code on the back of an old envelope. 'Payroll?' says our hero, smiling slightly into his beer, 'No problem – I know that software backwards. In fact I wrote it backwards.' An informal change is on the way.

The feasibility of a proposed change is extremely important, and so is the question of resources to achieve it. Many of the decisions to commission a change, or not, will revert to these considerations. This applies equally to 'imperative' as well as optional changes. It is surprising how relative a term 'imperative' can be when the fact that another million units of currency are involved, and a delay of five more years.

Software development should proceed, from functional specification stage onwards, under the aegis of a change control construction. The elements of this will be nominated people from the user (or surrogate user) community, and their counterparts from the domain of technical solution. A guiding principle for determining who to assign is that of their likelihood to understand the issues presented to a change control construction. This is not so obvious as it seems. The issues with which the construction will be confronted are likely to be a combination of three crucial questions:

1. Technical feasibility?
2. Economic consequence?
3. Degree of need?

In general, it is easier to find assignees from the supply domain than from the user community, and there is a tendency to overburden the construction accordingly. This must be resisted. The object of change control is to review countervailing forces, and imbalance in the construction cannot but prevent this.

Another guiding principle for change control constructions it to keep them small, but not too small. A rule of thumb might well be that, for small systems, one may expect that the change control construction will probably be two or three people; for medium sized systems, four to six; for large systems, six to twelve. As in most other matters, super-large systems tend to register off-scale values, and one can only hope to approach some rational state by some severe decomposition into sets of medium or large developments.

The appropriate organization form for change control is the committee, and this represents a rare instance of the suitability of this form for anything in software engineering. Committees are generally poor vehicles for making decisions, although they can be excel-

lent crucibles in which countervailing arguments can be assessed as a precursor to recommendation. That is precisely the role of change control; it evaluates and recommends to decision-making management. The change control committee should endure, and not lapse in usefulness during a software development task, but it should be inactive between events requiring its deliberation. The construction and its nominees should be evident in the management archive, and change to it should be noted there also.

Typically, the recommendations flow from a change control committee to the highest level of accountable management involved in the development, and instructions (decisions) flow from that point. Recommendations and their (hopefully) equivalent decisions may be to one of the following:

1. To implement the change, with its foreseen economic consequences in cost, and time.
2. To abandon the change entirely, due probably to considerations of technical or economic feasibility.
3. To defer the change as being desirable, but beyond the scope of the present development.

The proceedings of a change control committee should be formal, and its formal records (minutes and memoranda) must be archived.

It should go without saying (but I shall say it anyway) that specification changes put into effect without change control consideration and explicit management decision, should be seen as having been actions outside regulatory authority of management. Their achievements should have no status, whatever their virtues, and their authors should bear whatever consequences attach to such anarchic activities – i.e. 'the chop'. Clearly all this concerns changes to specification by direct or indirect means. Other changes, such as are required in the implementation and testing stages to rectify defects in the software, fall outside this definition. They will tend to be profuse, and great care must be taken amongst this tumult of activity, that real changes to purpose, i.e. specification, are not smuggled in.

13.2.2 Program change, version control and configuration management

Lehman's first 'law', quoted in Chapter 10, draws attention to a basic property of software systems – namely that they evolve or die. This is one reason why software must be changed over time. New requirements are thought up and old ones become obsolete but are seldom removed; circumstances in the real world tend to change, and technical means are invented whereby to mirror them.

Another reason why software has to be changed is that, as we have seen in Chapter 9, it probably contains errors – in whatever the state of testing, certification or operation it may be. These errors, when revealed through testing or usage, must be rectified, and this is the corrective maintenance of the software. (There is, incidentally, no such concept as preventive maintenance, as has been pointed out earlier.)

Furthermore, Lehman's second 'law' points to a fundamentally important precept that, when software is changed – either for evolutionary or maintenance purposes – work has to be done to preserve quality of structure, let alone improve it if need be. This work may be seen as additional change to software which, in fact, it frequently is.

A change for evolutionary purpose may be called an E change, and one for maintenance purpose an M change. An E change will always result, if successfully implemented, in a new version release of the software. That is the purpose of the evolution in the first place, to supersede the status quo, although previous E versions may be preserved in existence and continuingly supported in operation. On the other hand, maintenance changes may require a new version release if the corrected errors have been unduly severe, or if a reasonable number of them have been corrected since the last release. This assumes a release policy for M changes, and all IT product companies incorporating software in their artefacts should have such policies.

The version of a software system is a designation – quite arbitrary as to form – to distinguish prototypes from substantive, release-status developments, and to distinguish different variants of these from each other. For example, in the case of the CAISSA software, we may have undertaken an extensive prototype exercise for both requirements' clarification, and determination of technical means. A life cycle depiction of this might well be represented by Figure 13.10.

For software release purposes, a version may be said to be an M version if it supplies a maintenance need, such as correcting an error or errors, or an E version if it serves an evolutionary purpose. In Figure 13.10, CAISSA has a pre-substantive development existence (of a form) as prototypes A, B, C and D. Since the information 'bought' by prototyping is satisfactory at this stage, and incorporated in URS and OSD work, the development proper proceeds as the null version (0) for substantive, i.e. release, purposes. Assuming that all goes well, validation and certification will see the software released as E version 1, whereupon it must be placed under both M and E version control. This, in turn, presumes that such control constructions exist within the development organization.

Over some period of time, weeks or months perhaps, non-critical faults will be detected and corrected, but no M version release commissioned until enough of these M changes have been aggregated to make the release worthwhile; any critical faults appearing may trigger an M version release irrespective of this, when properly diagnosed and corrected.

Also, the software will begin its evolutionary life as described in Lehman's first 'law'. Indeed it may well have some considerable impetus in the matter if, as suggested might be the case in Section 13.2.1, changes contemplated in the 'version 0', development have been deferred.

Table 13.2 depicts a notional history of versions for CAISSA in its first years of life. It demonstrates several points. First of all, the initial system began, as shown in Figure 13.10, as a set of prototypes. These are retained as documentation sets with a special status, evidenced by the keyword for access being in parentheses and having a prototype version designated alphabetically; the substantive version for release is carried also – e.g. A.1.

It is clear from this list, as we would expect anyway, that maintenance versions are released more rapidly than evolution versions, although six in the same number of years may seem excessive for a system comprising only about 5,000 source statements of code. Perhaps that is why we see version 2 appear, although an equally feasible inference is that '64' being started as a development (also, like CAISSA.2, without prior prototypes) might infer that version 2 of CAISSA was a short-term palliative merely. It would be interesting to know the difference in scope and features between CAISSA.1, CAISSA.2, '64' and CHESS.

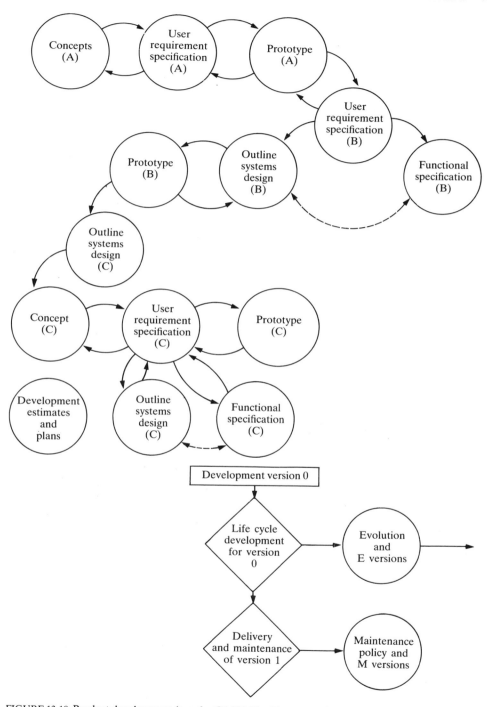

FIGURE 13.10 Product development (e.g. for CAISSA) with prototyping.

TABLE 13.2 Versions of CAISSA, and others

Release date	System	M version	E version	Documentation keyword
	CAISSA. 1		A.1	(CAISSA. A.1)
			B.1	(CAISSA. B.1)
			C.1	(CAISSA. C.1)
			D.1	(CAISSA. D.1)
			0.1	(CAISSA. 0.1)
3 July 85	CAISSA. 1	1	1	CAISSA. 1.1
4 Oct. 86	CAISSA. 1	2	1	CAISSA. 1.2
6 Oc . 87	CAISSA. 1	3	1	CAISSA. 1.3
17 Nov. 88	CAISSA. 1	4	1	CAISSA. 1.4
	CAISSA. 2		A.2	(CAISSA. A.2)
1 Jan. 89	CAISSA. 1	5		CAISSA. 1.5
	CAISSA. 2		0.2	(CAISSA. 0.2)
1 Feb. 89	CAISSA. 2	1	2	CAISSA. 2.1
	"64". 1		0.1	("64". 0.1)
1 June 91	CAISSA. 1	6		CAISSA. 1.6
10 Dec. 91	"64". 1	1	1	"64". 1.1
	CHESS. 1		A.1	(CHESS. A.1)

One would expect the access to documentation sets, depicted in Table 13.2 as a keyword, to lead to a greater level of definition – and this is generally the case. Each M and E version of a software system will comprise program modules, probably given generic names to ease linkage and access, and each program module will probably comprise aggregations of integrands, again named in some meaningful way to assist invocation and its understanding.

Table 13.3 shows this next level of definition, using neutral symbols in place of mean-

TABLE 13.3 Program version substructure within CAISSA versions

Release date	System/module version	Integrand	M version	E version	Documentation keyword
3 July 85	CAISSA 1.1 K	K(1)	1	1	CAISSA 1.1/K(1)1.1
		K(2)	1	1	CAISSA 1.1/K(2)1.1
		K(3)	1	1	CAISSA 1.1/K(3)1.1
		K(4)	1	1	CAISSA 1.1/K(4)1.1
	L	L(1)	1	1	CAISSA 1.1/L(1)1.1
		L(2)	1	1	CAISSA 1.1/L(2)1.1
		L(3)	1	1	CAISSA 1.1/L(3)1.1
	M	M(1)	1	1	CAISSA 1.1/M(1)1.1
		M(2)	1	1	CAISSA 1.1/M(2)1.1
		M(3)	1	1	CAISSA 1.1/M(3)1.1
1 Feb. 91	CAISSA 2.1 K	K(1)	1	1	CAISSA 2.1/K(1)1.2
		K(3)	4	1	CAISSA 2.1/K(3)1.4
		K(4)	1	2	CAISSA 2.1/K(4)2.1
	L	L(1)	5	1	CAISSA 2.1/L(1)1.5
		L(2)	3	1	CAISSA 2.1/L(2)1.3
	M	M(3)	1	2	CAISSA 2.1/M(3)2.1
	N	N(1)	1	1	CAISSA 2.1/N(1)1.1
		N(2)	1	1	CAISSA 2.1/N(2)1.1
		N(3)	1	1	CAISSA 2.1/N(3)1.1

ingful names, and indicates that the version status of integrands (and, therefore, program modules) may be at different levels for an overall status. It shows both the initial release version of the system, comprising three main modules and ten integrands within them, and version 2 of the system. From the latter it is clear that some maintenance versions of the original system have been retained, some replaced entirely, some (K4 and M3, whatever they are) have been 'evolved', and completely new versions of integrands in a new module (N) have been created.

Access to documentation sets is again by keyword. Thus, at some ungodly hour on a wet and windy Sunday morning, when a maintenance call of top priority arrives (for a mickey-mouse chess system?), and Fred is wrenched out of his warm bed to fix it, he can, at least, find the deliverable documentation in the documentation set, so long as a client/product/version list exists. Table 13.4 shows such a list.

In practice, a three-level access system is sufficient. The client/product/version matching file; the keyword expansion file shown (by example) in Table 13.4; and the documentation sets corresponding to each version, i.e. specification extracts, design, code-listings and test records in each case.

Setting up a configuration management system is not difficult. The simple example given outlines this logical classification of what any such system comprises, however voluminous or elaborate it becomes thereafter. Nor is it difficult or prohibitively expensive to support such a system by electronic means, as Section 8.5 on support environments attests (that is, the configuration management features should not be expensive, nor the hardware for them in isolation; the rest of a PSE or Ipse might well be).

However, maintaining a configuration management system in practice, and preventing its violation or its falling into progressive desuetude, are acute problems in many cases. There are two extreme cases that may be described here to illustrate the potential problems – albeit in an aggravated form – and their possible solution:

1. There may be a free-for-all, with unrestricted access to write to the deliverable documentation files, to emend source code, and (the ultimate peril) the object code. Divergence between code, source or object, and deliverable documentation may occur through change to one without a colateral updating of the other, and dichotomies may even arise between source and object code, with the documentation corresponding to neither.

TABLE 13.4 Client/product version list

Client	Product	Versions (E M)	Keyword To Doc. File
Alfagames Ltd	CHECK	3.1	CHECK. 3.1
M. Mouse Inc.	CAISSA	1.8	CAISSA. 1.8
	CAISSA	2.1	CAISSA. 2.2
	"64"	1.1	"64". 1.1
Fred Bloggs & Assoc.	CAISSA	1.2	CAISSA. 1.2
	CAISSA	2.2	CAISSA. 2.2
Mafia Health Products	CHESS	1.1	CHESS. 1.1
	CAISSA	2.6	CAISSA. 2.6
	"64"	1.3	"64". 1.3

2. There may be highly restrictly access, involving security checks and software or hardware keys for any attempt to write to the deliverable documentation files, or to emend the master copy of source code. Tampering with object code should be out of the question under a decent operating system but, if it is not, then this too must be secured.

There are both technical and management requirements to achieve the second of these states. Elaborate keys and codes, including hardware card-readers for identification, may be required if the consequences of violation could be particularly severe in some sense. Equally, nomination of authorized staff (first-line authority, second-line authority, and so on) will be necessary to complete the system of restricted access.

These fairly extreme requirements occur in a surprising number of instances, but the recognition of this state of affairs in a company might be slow. Managers unaware of the possible consequences – of which the more obvious financial ones may be the least onerous – may not initiate a configuration management 'culture' in the company, and it will be unlikely to come about by other means.

Having said that, in the absence of an adequate version and configuration management system, sales personnel may become disgruntled at the loss of reputation due to the ensuing chaos, field support groups for products may – in despair – set up their own, parochial, systems using card files if they cannot get electronic facilities, and software engineers who are called on to maintain or improve software may find themselves confronted with an impossible task. They, the software engineers, may be the agents of change if all else fails, and if they refuse with sufficient vigor to do the impossible.

13.3 MANAGING FOR QUALITY

Software quality is the whole of the matter, so far as the process and outcome of software engineering are concerned, other than for some research and prototype purposes. All of the modalities of the subject are (or should be) directed to that end. In fact, more properly, we should speak of 'those ends' since there are two aspects of quality at issue, as we have, by now, frequently pointed out:

1. Economic quality.
2. Technical quality.

This duality, and the interaction of its parts, is never more evident than in cases where both are imperative. The history of engineering in general is filled with instances, from the commissioning of coal-mines to the construction of nuclear reactors. As one astronaut is quoted to have said, to the question 'How did it feel at the moment just before launch?': 'How do you think it felt, sitting on top of a pile of stuff all supplied on a least cost basis?' One can only share John Glenn's concern.

Figure 4.1 depicts the importance of quality (by which we mean both economic and technical) and its continuance, through good practices, throughout the software life cycle. It also sets out to show that the precept of engineering technical quality into the artefact must be managed, otherwise it cannot – with confidence – be presumed to be present.

There are three widely occurring defects afflicting the management of software quality in the real world of practical software engineering.

The first defect occurs when the potential interaction of technical and economic quality issues is ignored. Most people take 'quality' to mean something about the performance properties of the software artefact. Does it work, is it reliable, is it easy to mend? This oversimplification leads to dire consequences in many cases. Technical quality costs money and, for that matter, so too does economic quality in the sense that proper cost estimating must be done, a thorough-going cost/benefit (or opportunity) justification undertaken, and competent cost and activities' control maintained.

Technical quality assuredly costs money, and this undoubtedly affects the economic equation. But lack of technical quality costs even more. Specious economies in the first place lead, ineluctably, to defects in technical quality and, thereby, to loss.

The second defect occurs through lack of understanding of *how* software quality must be engineered in, or a disinclination to face the costs of doing so, software quality practices being seen as some unnecessary 'rain-dance' done by software engineers for their own gnomic and perverse pleasures.

Design review and code-reading practices are the greatest casualties in this respect within software engineering practice, whilst staff education and PSE facilities are the equivalent casualties within technical means. Do your software engineers habitually do design reviews and code reading? Has your company got an 'enlightened self-interest' policy in continuing education in this subject? Has it acquired an adequate environment for software development and configuration management? Are you telling the truth?

The third defect concerns quality procedures and, as a defect, it may take one of two forms. There may be no guidelines whatsoever on software quality, its modalities, its management and its ongoing preservation. Alternatively, there may be standards that are of such consolation to managers by their mere existence that they are thought to operate themselves, whereas, in fact, these 'standards' rest in undisturbed tranquility on everybody's darkest bookshelf. To have no guidelines or standards for software quality is categorically bad; to have a cubic meter of mandatory practices that no one has ever read is not one whit better.

Managing software quality begins by avoiding these three defects. It begins by securing adequate guidelines in quality procedure; it proceeds by ensuring that practitioners have had adequate education or experience in the issue concerned, and that they have sufficient technical means for the job. Most importantly it ensures, by active management means and not passive or 'default' management, the good use of practices and appropriate facilities. The wherewithal for this activity on the part of managers has been set out and described elsewhere; it comprises archives, structured management and technical walk-through techniques, specification change and independent quality agencies, activities' and cost reporting systems, and so forth.

However, all the wherewithals in the world will not galvanize a recalcitrant manager if that person fears the issue. Then we see miracles of delegation and prodigies of default management, regulation by committee, adoption of panacea (such the Japanese notion of 'quality circles') and a variety of other stances which, it is hoped, will compensate for inability. 'Delegation' is frequently abdication, as the cliché says; committees, though fine for evaluation, are generally useless for decision, and a platoon of them usually could not

manage its way out of a wet paper bag. (In fact the collective noun for committees should be 'cocoon'.) And of what use is a quality circle, or any other geometrical arrangement, if its members have not got a clue about software, its 'engineering' and its quality methods? There is a distinct need to avoid management by gimmick.

Most of the issues have already been defined and described in previous chapters and sections of this book, and some merit whole books to themselves. Other issues, such as continuing education, are yet to be defined and described.

In the present section, it remains to deal with two aspects of software quality management:

1. The software quality guidelines or standards.
2. The software quality plan.

13.3.1 The basis for quality management: guidelines or standards?

Guidelines, as their name suggests, are far less stringent in their enforcement than standards. On the whole, software engineering and its practitioners incline to the use of guidelines – if these are well considered – and away from standards, except for the ways of proper access to a virtual computer, or its PSE facilities such as languages.

This inclination tends to be the case, whatever the supposed virtues of some 'standard' software engineering prescription. The history of software development down the years is a trail along which the detritus of abandoned standards is strewn, and most IT product companies that have been at it for any length of time have at least one cubic meter of software development 'standards' gathering dust.

The reason for this is not, as commonly supposed, the rate of change of technology that invalidates precepts from a bygone epoch. The 'eternal verities' of software engineering remain reasonably invariant. The main reason is that a single method, comprising a single procedural prescription, a single means of doing design, implementation, etc., is impossible to define for as wide a spectrum of applications and circumstances as exists. On the other hand, trying to define all the permutations of possibilities, and prescribing means and methods for dealing with them, leads, literally, to the 'cubic meter' of written regulations that software engineers so blithely disregard. We return to this subject in Section 13.6.2.

These strictures on standards in general, for software development, must not be extrapolated to include the management's regulatory and technicians' own procedural bases for software quality. In many cases external clients insist on quality standards, and may audit supplier-companies to ensure that the standards exist and are in practice. So, although one may inveigh with good reason against profuse and bureaucratic 'standard procedures' for software development in general, one must not undermine the wherewithal for managing the process. There is a fine balance to be struck.

The basis for good software management and technical practices is the software quality procedure handbook. This will best be created for a particular 'culture' in a company involved in software development, and is unlikely to be procured ready-made, from your local bookshop. Such an article should be drawn up to fit two requirements, namely: (a)

any national or international standards with which compliance is either mandatory or desirable, and (b) the particularities – structures and practices – within the company. There is little to say on the second of these, but the first merits comment.

Some dominant organizations in the IT sector require that their 'standards', almost exclusively concerning software quality practices, form the recognizable basis for suppliers' practice. To date there has been some, but not enough, harmony between these sources of quality standards of software development practice. Suppliers to main procurement agencies, such as departments of defense and telecommunication authorities, comply – or die. Other software companies turn to national standards agencies for help and advice, if the notion strikes them at all (in the United Kingdom, the rate at which companies have adopted BS 5750 seems disappointingly low). However, adherence to some standard practices for software development may well be imminent; the International Standards' Organization ISO has ratified QA standards, as ISO 9000, 9001, etc.

To give an idea of the variety of 'standards' on offer, a fact that surely calls the name itself into question, the following sources are: (a) for specification only, and (b) some of those in the English language only: IEE (1985), ANSI/IEEE (1984), British Standard, Naval Engineering Standard and JSP 188. There are equivalents for acceptance testing, quality assurance and a variety of other topics (e.g. ANSI/IEEE Standard Glossary of Software Engineering Terminology). A 'standard of standards' seems remote.

13.3.2 The quality manual

All organizations developing software should have a quality standards manual defining the main issues and practices to be followed for all software tasks. Of these practices, the first one to be undertaken at the commencement of any development task, other than at the prototype stages, is the creation of a quality *plan*.

Typical contents in a quality manual are set out in Table 13.5. The first three chapters will contain definitions and descriptive material about software engineering in general.

For example, a life cycle model (essential for strong management practice) may be defined from any one of the various examples on view in the subject literature, including Figure 4.2 of this work, or some local version if adequate. On the other hand, a variety of approved design methods, their procedures and notatons may be described in Section 3.3; such as Mascot, Petrinets, De Wolf's scheme, BS 6224 DSD, structured flowcharts, and so on.

To repeat an earlier stricture, one error to avoid, in 'standard' design methods within a company, is that of over-prescription. It should be possible for software engineers to adopt appropriate design tools, particularly if they are supported by PSE. It is important not to put software designers into a straightjacket; design is a difficult enough operation as it is. The same stricture is not the case for implementation. Here one would undoubtedly prescribe the exact versions of languages and, of course, the PSE would probably disable any attempts to violate the language. Thus, a standards manual would prescribe, say, Microsoft UCSD Pascal, Version 3.7, release data 1 Jan. 88 and so on.

An important feature of Chapter 3 in Table 13.5 is the definition of 'deliverables' from each life cycle stage. These will become major milestones on the activities' plan, and will

TABLE 13.5 Contents of a software quality manual

0. Contents

1. Authority and force

2. Definitions of:
   2.1 A life cycle model and glossary of terms attaching to its main stages; the archive(s).
   2.2 V, V and C as states of the software development process and outcome.
   2.3 Q(C), Q(I), Q(A) as subprocesses within software development.
   2.4 Terminology within testing.
        Author/author-team benevolent testing, and independent team adversarial testing.
        Integrand testing, multi-integrand testing, integration and alpha-testing.
        Beta-testing; black-box/white-box testing.
        Static and dynamic testing.
        Documentation as an object of testing. Contents' classification of deliverable documentation.

3. Modalities and methods
   3.1 To ensure the quality of specification. Definition of outcome from this stage.
   3.2 To ensure the quality of estimates and plans. Definition of outcome from this stage.
   3.3 To ensure the quality of software design. Definition of outcome from this stage.
   3.4 To ensure the quality of software implementation. Definition of outcome from this stage.
   3.5 To ensure the quality of software testing. Definition of outcome from this stage.
   3.6 To ensure the overall quality of software – compliance and modifiability – and its deliverable documentation.

4. The quality plan
   4.1   Nomination and updating of responsible individuals. How they will operate.
   4.2   Definition of QC milestones.
   4.3   Definition of QI activities.
   4.4   Definition of QA activities.
   4.5   Test plan for benevolent levels of correction and demonstration. Definition of alpha-test.
   4.6   Beta-test plan. Definitions of black-box and white-box tests.
   4.7   Specific contents required in deliverable documentation.
   4.8   Specific classifications, and technical means for configuration management.
   4.9   Minimal staffing and competence levels throughout the life cycle.
   4.10 Minimal PSE facilities.
   4.11 Purchaser's acceptance trials; procedure, certification, specific tests.
   4.12 Management activities in QI/QA; schedules of technical/management walkthrough sessions, progress and cost review points. Milestones and walkthroughs marked on activities' plan.

have principal walkthrough activities associated with them. It should be noted that there are two 'deliverables' from design, one at the start of the process – the software specification from architecture design – and one at the end, a set of integrand specifications and data designs.

The first act in software quality (it being presumed here that the quality manual has been thoroughly assimilated), is to set up a quality plan. The categories of this plan are set out in Table 13.5, and it will be immediately obvious that some will remain categorical only – i.e. empty of information – until later in the life cycle. A ready example of this is '4.5 Test plan ...'. This will only come into existence during the software design, when the structure of the software becomes evident. Until that time, this category in the plan exists only as a checklist item and an activity posted on a netplan.

Each category in the quality plan infers an action to be undertaken (such as 'develop the test plan'), and an action or set of ongoing actions to ensure it, and the quality of its outcome. To take an example other than that of the test plan, staffing the task will need to be defined and done; it will need to be checked for adequacy and the ongoing preservation

of adequacy. Poor quality staff produce poor quality software. One may start out with a plan to have the most sensationally competent software team. Put in place a fairly senior software engineer, a junior programmer and two trainees, and then find oneself at the implementation stage with only the junior programmer, a very recent electronic engineering graduate and a contracted-in 'body' from an external supply company of uncertain reputation. All this is a lapse of quality and its management, however much it may be excused as *force majeure*.

Analogous to quality in the development of software is the issue of quality in the procurement of software or software services. This should not be overlooked as it, in turn, may materially enhance or deplete quality in the software development process. Items 4.9 and 4.10 in Table 13.5 demonstrate this point, and the hypothetical example on staffing illustrates it. Staffing and procurement matters are treated in some detail below.

There are five fundamental principles for software managers to observe if software quality is to stand any chance of being achieved. They cannot be stated too often, and although simple to say are often fiendishly difficult to achieve:

1. Get the right people for the job, and preserve this competence level.
2. Get the right equipment for them to do the job, and make sure its sufficiency and the sufficiency of access to it are maintained.
3. Manage the whole software specification and development process for the quality of outcome at each stage. Make scrupulously sure that the base-line (the functional specification) is of high quality – and that it is signed off, and subject to change control.
4. Make sure that there is a 'comfortable' time-scale for software development, properly determined.
5. Make sure that a competent QI/QA agency – person or team – is in place and active as appropriate at different stages of the life cycle.

13.4 ORGANIZATION AND PERSONNEL FACTORS

In this section it is proposed to deal with the following issues, which are sufficiently common to companies making software to allow a detailed treatment:

1. Accountability and control structures for software development.
2. Software team structure and practices – the peer-group software development team.
3. Quality structures.
4. Personnel management; recruiting and retaining software engineers.
5. Continuing education and career development.

13.4.1 Accountability and control structures for software development

For companies in which software engineering is just a part of development activity, in an IT product company for instance, there is generally one single and substantive question to answer. Should, or should not, the software engineers be consolidated into one 'profes-

sional' group or department? Clearly, as said in an earlier section, the supervening organization form will influence the outcome – whether the company is strongly centralized, decentralized, 'adaptive' or 'innovative' in this respect. However, although there can be no general-case answer to the question of a single, consolidated department of software engineering, it is instructive to look at two basic options:

1. The 'homogeneous department'. This comprises a group of software engineers and administrative staff acting like a small 'software house'. Work may be transferred into this department and done on a pseudo-contract basis, and staff may be seconded out of it (pseudo-contract supply) to work under the jurisdiction of some other manager.
2. Software engineering competence may be dispersed to product groups requiring it on a more or less permanent basis. This is the 'heterogeneous department' approach.

Figure 13.11 shows these two options schematically.

The disadvantages of each structure are easy to enumerate, and their relative virtues are not too obscure either. A 'third case', composite of the two distinct options, can exist, and its virtues and vices are compounds of those for the alternative constructions listed, with a tendency to emphasize any tensions arising from the product manager's desire for option 2.

The strengths of a 'homogeneous software department' are that it can act as a single center of competence/excellence, and that the company's acquisition policies for specialist staff and technical facilities may be the more competent for it. Also, aspects of personnel management such as appraisal and remuneration can be better determined, and the motivation of software engineers should benefit as a result.

The disadvantages, when they accrue, are usually due to defects in a firm's abilities to pseudo-contract supplies and services in a meaningful way. That is, the firm cannot make pseudo-contracting sufficiently similar to the realities of outside contracting to provide its manifest advantages of clarity and responsibility in supply. Things become blurred. An attitude of 'its only Fred on the third floor, so what's all this contracting nonsense?' tends to prevail on both sides. It is possible to overcome this disadvantage, but only with continuing effort, and only if the will exists on all sides.

There will always be a tendency for a 'product group' to claim that it needs its own, permanently assigned, software engineers; that staff migration from a central software group (however sedulously 'contracted') is not enough; that the product group's competence is depleted when seconded software engineers return to their division; and that management of 'contracted' personnel is made obscure by them 'belonging' to one manager whilst working for another. Reporting to one part of an organization whilst working for another part tends to tear the hapless software engineers up the dotted line of loyalties. It can also lead to the total breakdown of quality practices, demotivation at review and appraisal time, people playing two managers off, one against each other, and all sorts of fun least helpful to the primary aim.

The strengths and weaknesses of a 'heterogeneous department' approach may be deduced by inverting the previous arguments. Dispersion of software resources over product groups leads to unambiguous management authorities and staff relationships, and the identification of software engineers with particular products. On the other hand acquisition of new staff and technical facilities such as Ipse/PSE equipment, and the

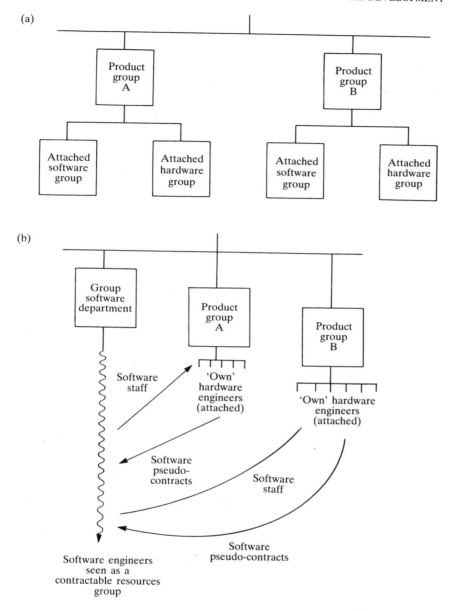

FIGURE 13.11 Alternative group structures for software product development, with hardware. (a) The decentral or heterogeneous divisions form of product development organization. (b) Central or homogeneous form of product development organization.

establishment of good software engineering practices, may be highly suboptimal. As a result there is extreme demotivation of software engineers and high attrition in this area.

Simply stated, the centralized/homogeneous group approach tends to have strength in software engineering, at some cost to specific product orientation, and the close management of composite product development. Software development departments are, and should be, professional software engineers and should represent those values in the performance of work to achieve high quality software.

The decentral/heterogeneous group approach tends to strength in product orientation and local management accountability, at a potential cost to software engineering practice. Software staff in such groups are often inadequate 'amateurs', and tend to stay so if their interest in, and adoption of, good software engineering practices and facilities are not developed, or are not properly recognized. Strongly centralized organizations find it easiest to adopt the centralized/homogeneous approach, and many such have first rate 'centers of excellence' in software engineering, acting as quasi-software houses for the company. Conversely, firms having decentral/adaptive organizations often find it surpassingly difficult to aggregate 'rare resources' into centers of excellence, against the competing pressures to employ them adjacent to requirement – where this diffusion concerns either geography or product, or both.

13.4.2 Software team structure and practices

Within either of the two schemes depicted, or any variant or hybrid, the question of infrastructure organization and methods for specific tasks will be raised. How does one order and regulate a number of software engineers doing software development?

Perhaps the best known method is that of the 'chief programmer team' (CPT), although there are reservations to this approach in some areas, and the concept has evolved from its original form as promulated by Mills and others, c. 1970. We will not go into the last twenty years' arguments and evolutions of the CPT concept, but summarize the main items and issues involved at the present time:

1. A chief programmer team is a small peer-group of software engineers of appropriate, but probably different, experience levels relative to the task.
2. For tasks whose size justifies it, a 'small' team will be between three and six people. Less than that lower limit, and anything above small task-size, results in unnecessary decomposition into team-based subtasks; greater than the upper limit, and the communication overhead within teams becomes prohibitive.
3. All team members are active (not ex-) software engineers; the 'chief programmer', as team-leader, might be unable to do much detailed technical work in a stage – but that should be through circumstance not choice. The 'peer-group' aspects are highly desirable over the alternatives, such as an 'administrated team of technicians' approach.
4. The chief programmer must have commensurate authority and responsibility for the performance of the team to discharge the task at hand. This is best achieved by having the chief programmer (and others of the team if need be) do estimates and plans for

the task. 'Inherited' estimates or schedules, such as 'price-to-win' contracts (q.v.) are disastrous in their impact on this balance between authority and responsbility.

5. Assignment of the CPT, and job allocation within it, must be on a team- (or person-) to-task basis, and not the other way round. It is wrong to say 'we have *n* people for that job'; it is right to say 'we have a job for *n* people'.

6. There may be several areas in which a team must contain specialization, such as application type, target equipment features, host equipment and its 'virtual' and PSE facilities, specific client requirement (e.g. quality standard/quality plan) and so on down what may be a quite extensive list.

    CPT members should have 'expertise assignments' requiring them to be (or become) its 'expert team member' in the first place. This is to prevent the disarray of everyone trying to do everything at the start. By the end of the task, most or all team members will be equivalently familiar with many (or all) aspects of required expertise. A most important assignment will be that of 'software tools' expert.

7. Archiving, and other administration tasks such as updating activities and status matrices, accruing effort or cost information, and so on, should be aggregated as 'librarian tasks' within the CPT. This task may be assigned to one person for the duration of the task or (better in my view), assigned sequentially to team members on, say, a monthly basis.

8. A deputy chief programmer should be appointed, usually the second most senior software engineer in the team. This person should be able to deputize for the chief programmer during that person's absences or distractions with other tasks. The most usual distractions are management reporting/walkthrough activities, and dialog with clients or pseudo-clients. The deputy must be extremely careful not to polarize the team. In a dozen instances of failed CPTs at my disposal, defective performance by the deputy is by far the most prevalent cause.

9. The basic means and methods for quality control within the CPT include major technical 'walkthroughs' scheduled by the chief programmer at key stages (such as when a 'deliverable' is pending), and design reviews and code readings. Archives, activities' plans, status matrices and cost control information should be maintained, as described elsewhere.

10. Depending on the test strategy to be adopted, a CPT may nominate a team member to be 'tester'. Usually this involves the scheduling and creation of integration tests, or the construction of a 'test-frame' for 'top down' testing if this is the adopted approach. The tester 'role-plays' for QA white-box testing.

Much of the foregoing will be recognized as applied common sense. In the circumstances, it is surprising how seldom it is applied, and for this one must identify managers' phobias as a major reason, phobias of the subject and even its exponents.

The team, or teams, are normally formed at about the time a functional specification is complete, although the senior members may have been active in requirements' analysis and estimating, and teams may have existed for feasibility exercises as part of outline design.

Precept 5 above is fundamental to the whole concept of peer-group chief programmer teams; teams must be fitted to tasks, and not vice versa. Properly effected, this provides

the CPT with its most conspicuous property – task orientation, and strong motivation to do high quality work. The small, highly motivated group exercising the best of available practices and tools is the epitome of software engineering practice.

Of course, all may not be sweetness and light, as various things can go wrong with a CPT. The following list covers the main possible exigencies:

1. The team may be highly motivated, but may be prevented from full effect by one or more of a variety of circumstances. There may be a significant shortfall in relevant competence amongst team members; or an insufficiency of technical means. Management control may be lacking, the quality of a sale defective, client relations poor, and so on. All such things can deprive the team of the performance it is designed to will and to achieve. The results on team motivation can be sudden, and extreme, in their effects.
2. When a peer-group CPT experiences motivational or internal management trouble of any sort, it may resemble a high-speed train being derailed in full progress.

    As well as those reasons already enumerated that might well bring about this unhappy state of affairs, the methods of design review and code reading can cause some trouble also. Not everyone is comfortable as either reviewer or reviewee, and acute problems of personality conflict can arise when reviews are undertaken. This is discussed further below.
3. The peer-group CPT is an élitist construction. In effect, it is challenged (and challenges itself) to do what a lesser group could not achieve. It takes its successes in its stride, and its failures to heart. None of this may be consistent with the overall 'culture' in the company concerned which, for other good reasons, may be more consensual in its processes and – as a result – tending to normative in its performances. This, too, is discussed further below.

The problems falling under category 1 are, or should be, tractable to direct means in containment or avoidance. The others are more subtle, and are treated in turn forthwith, under the following headings:

1. Sensibilities, and the techniques of reviewing.
2. 'Cultural' problems.
3. Other properties of the chief programmer team.

SENSIBILITIES, AND THE TECHNIQUES OF REVIEWING

Technical reviews, by one's peers, are ego-fraught. No schoolchild wants to have its homework marked, no composer relishes the criticism of a première, authors dread the flood of rejection slips, and parents will the world to want their darling prodigies. One's creative work is a subject of great emotional vulnerability.

Software engineers are not exempt from these feelings. A design review will comprise a critical assessment of your decisions, such as decomposition approaches, and algorithms and data definitions. To hear that this is all so much rubbish (however diplomatically expressed) may not be the happiest news on a wet Wednesday afternoon in November.

Design reviewing and code reading are indispensible parts of software quality control. In my experience, done properly and as habitual 'good practice', they double productivity – if this is properly viewed as delivered source statements of validated and documented

code of high quality, complaint and modifiable. I have known instances when software engineers themselves have claimed that the practices have saved the time-scale, with no loss of quality. That sort of evidence, alone, generally secures adoption for this aspect of 'good software engineering practices' in a commercial firm making software.

Design reviews and code reading sessions must be scheduled when authority and responsibility attributions have been made for different parts of the software-to-be. This is normally a chief programmer's task. I may have my design reviewed by Fred, and its code by Joe; Fred's designs for a part of some system may be reviewed by Sid, and so on.

It is not necesarily a cosy little exchange schedule. The apparent object, at both levels, is for the reviewer/reader to comprehend the creation in detail; the real object is, of course, to detect and correct errors early. For, as we have asserted elsewhere, the earlier (in life cycle terms) errors are corrected, the cheaper it is to do so. Author and reviewer sit down together with the object of review. Sometimes this is a design diagram on a piece of paper the size of a bed-sheet, or the diligent pair may huddle over a code listing called up on a monitor screen.

Generally, at the design level, improvements rather than categorical correction are offered, and there is usually little significance in whether they emanate from reviewer or reviewee. The element of joint purpose and joint achievement is the prevailing ethic at this level – if ego problems are absent.

At the code level, the situation is dramatically different and most errors are found by the author of the code, whilst explaining to an apparently stupid reviewer what the self-evidently perfect program is doing. The most commonly heard expressions are oaths or rhetorically phrased questions of self-motivation, and these may be heard floating from the pairs of programmers code reading at all times of day and night.

In the limiting case, ego problems through design review and code reading may be solvable by draconian means. Somebody has to go. Often, of course, reasonable people come to reasonable conclusions, or the chief programmer makes an acceptable decision. In some extreme cases, however, review or its results may be prevented by extreme outbursts of temperament – usually (but not always) by the reviewee.

Simply, some people are unsuited to this aspect of software engineering, and one is forced to a conclusion that places them beyond the definition 'software engineer'. If someone is incapable of participating properly in peer-group self-critical processes, the peer-group tends to exclude them. Fortunately, the profession of software engineering tends to attract people robust enough to face the possibility of their programs failing, and this is no great step from accepting colleagues' critical comments.

Over the past twenty years there has been a gradual but persistent decline in CPT failure through ego-based problems with design reviewing and code reading. Whereas, in earlier epochs, the failure rate of chief programmer teams for this reason may have been as high as three out of ten, it is now less than one out of ten, and the problems listed under 1 above have become the most common sources of 'the express train', that is the CPT, leaving the rails at high speed.

'CULTURAL' PROBLEMS

The 'cultural' problem, wherein the chief programmer team approach is antipathetic to the prevailing style in a company, is far less tractable than the parochial difficulties described

above. The issues are bound up with software engineering being a young industry, predominantly employing a young workforce; the average age of a software group within a firm is often in the 30–35 year range, compared to other professional sectors in which the average age may be 10 years higher. (The question of what happens to aging software engineers is a pertinent one. It is dealt with – up to a point – in a following section.)

Then there is the undoubted effect of imbalance between supply and demand for software engineers – a 'soft' market for jobs from the employees' viewpoint, perhaps. The peer-group chief programmer team is, as has been noted, an élitist construction and can only thrive in a meritocratic environment.

Perhaps wrongly, software engineers erect metrics in the mind for their own measurement of success in a firm, and these generally concern differentials in remuneration, and accelerated career progression for particularly virtuous performers. All this may sound very short term to a strategic planner within the company but if the software engineers feel that way about life, all the longer terms and broader visions on earth will be to no avail; the more competent will reach for the 'jobs' page of the computer trade-press, and you may find yourself back in a recruiting round.

The dominant culture in a company has an inertia, usually of considerable magnitude although impossible to measure by direct means. It is the way people think about the firm and their work; it is the way they order themselves and organize others to undertake the business of the firm. The culture resides, in part, in the formal (i.e. explicit) structures, procedures and norms of behavior and performance.

More importantly, perhaps, it also resides and is perpetuated through the *informal* structures and people's mutual understanding of how things should be done. All this cultural inertia takes time ('history') to accrue, and the unique characteristics – the 'flavor' of the culture – will have derived from that profession or business sector in which the company has been dominant for longest. In this respect the inertia is not only inevitable, but beneficial. If one could dispose of it, one should not do so. It is the ballast that stabilizes the ship, and the adhesive that keeps its spars in place.

The prevailing culture in a company will be polarized toward the ways and means of the historically dominant technology, profession or business environment of that company. The Royal Dutch Shell organization has a distinct 'culture' that is, in part at least, common to all companies in the petrochemical industry; it has its own structures and procedures, but many factors derive from the predominance in the firm of petrochemical engineers of different types. Similarly, Philips Electronics has a 'culture' based, in part, on decades of employing (and being managed by) electronic engineers. Likewise in every main industry sector.

To graft a new technology on to such an organization can cause the most radical upheavals and, in the limiting case, the 'body' may reject the transplant. For some historically well founded industries, the 'new' technology of software engineering is just such a case, particularly when sectoral 'meritocracy', élitism, and job rewards and career progression become emphasized. The chief programmer team structure, and its underlying mores, may well act as an irritant where this is so, and there are many cases of peer-group chief programmer teams being disabled as a consequence.

There are no patent remedies for this. If software is a crucial enough component of business opportunity and risk, then, in the final analysis, simple business acumen will

determine the cure – although, in some very large companies, detecting the business realities may not be a straightforward matter. They may be overlaid by many 'cultural' factors peculiar to the company, or particular to the country in which it is operating.

The simple facts for management to recognize are that: (a) the peer-group CPT is (in my humble view at least) just about the best construction known for attempting software development tasks; (b) its staff should be encouraged and challenged to be élitist in their profession; (c) they must have the wherewithal to be successful; and (d) they must be recognized properly – in all respects – within a meritocracy. However, to balance these views, managers should beware some insidious properties of the élitist, peer-group chief programmer team.

OTHER PROPERTIES OF THE CHIEF PROGRAMMER TEAM

The peer-group chief programmer team is a wonderfully conservative construction and, if successful in performing its daily miracles of creation, it may strike many unhelpful attitudes. Most of these can be accommodated reasonably easily, as they usually boil down to material matters such as better working conditions, a more up-to-date PSE, a better salary review or whatever. However, there is one rather subtle stance that it mght take some time to spot, and one that – if acceded to – puts the software engineers outside the domain of regulation in a crucial respect.

Successful chief programmer teams tend to try to pick themselves from job to job. It is as though people say 'I will work with her, and him, and him. But I wouldn't be found dead in a ditch with that chap Fred who caused the catastrophe on my last job'. Given the strong task-orientation of the CPT, and its tendency to meritocracy, this is understandable. However it pre-empts management and cannot, in the general case, be allowed. The answer is not to say 'Tough! You're the chief programmer, so shut up. And I'm allocating Fred, a couple of trainees, and a yo-yo who's otherwise unemployable. Get on with it!' The real remedy lies in the high quality of software engineers employed, and their critical career appraised by management, and in the realism of chief programmer staff.

One question that is contiguous with the issue of self-selection and recurs with startling regularity concerns how many, if any, trainees may be assimilated into a peer-group chief programmer team without noticeably depleting its real productivity. This can be a most depressing issue, as it often crops up *ex post facto*, after some catastrophic policy has been instituted, and has borne its bitter fruit.

The question is a fundamental one, as it affects both the quality of software engineering and its artefacts, and it sets limits on the ability of a company to grow through acquisition of trainees. For, if the answer is a limitation on assimilable trainees into CPTs, then this sets the limits on growth, in this sector, by these means.

In general, it is true to say that trainees (people with, say, less than one year's experience in software engineering) may be assimilated into software teams, within limits and with caution. And it is a relief to hear this news, for how else are trainees to be trained at all? However, the operative words are 'limits' and 'caution'. It is a frightful error (as I have seen it done) to stick clumps of trainees around an experienced chief programmer in the hope that his or her virtues will prove catching, like the common cold. What generally happens is that something more similar to galloping consumption attacks the whole endeavor, as will be shown.

The best rule of thumb, in answering this question, is based on a highly judgmental view of the marginal effect of trainees on the real productivity of the team. There are two factors at work here; (a) the productivity of the trainee, and (b) the supervision 'overhead' required from other team members to ensure that the productivity of the trainee is 'real' in quality terms. These two effects tend to cancel out for one trainee on a CPT of four or five people. It is a safe assumption, therefore, that one trainee may be incorporated with zero net effect on the team's productivity; if, in the event, this proves pessimistic, then it is fortuitous and there will be no repercussion for conservative budgeting – nor will the trainee have been overburdened by expectation.

More than one trainee per CPT tends to deplete the endeavors of other team members (not least the chief programmer) by steeply progressive marginal amounts. In my experience, the first trainee results in a 0 percent decrease in overall (team) productivity in real (i.e. quality) terms; two may result in about 10 percent depletion in real productivity; three causes 20 percent and four causes 40 percent; five trainees on a CPT, of presumably six people, effectively stops the show altogether.

This is all very dispiriting news for companies or departments with an insufficiency in software engineering staff – quantitative or qualitative, or both. It basically says that the organization can grow, with safety, by about 10–20 percent p.a. only, if one assumes that it takes, on average, two years for a trainee to become a fully competent software engineer. Now, from the demand side, the software part of the IT business sector is growing at a rate two to three times this number – even though constrained by a paucity of supply from education sources. And the usual staff-attrition rate may not be much below 10 percent either.

So what is happening? All of three things are probably happening simultaneously:

1. Software tasks are being attempted by quantitatively under-resourced teams.
2. Trainees are being assigned in too great numbers to software teams, and so deplete them qualitatively.
3. Software work is being contracted out to independent, third party suppliers who may pay above the market average for software engineers (thereby perpetuating their own market), but who will feel little compunction in overloading teams with trainees, as this represents 'revenue growth'. (What? Limit revenue growth by constraints on trainees per team? Never!)

The result contributes to the generally prevailing state of affairs in software engineering; deplorable quality of software, at frightful expense.

13.4.3 Quality structures, operations and staffing

So far in this section we have dealt in some detail with general and specific issues concerning organization of software groups and teams for the often onerous task of software development. What remains is the issue of an independent quality group, and its modalities.

For the purposes of this discussion, we define an independent quality group as an internal construction. Certain special cases will require consideration, such as those in

which no quality group exists or can be made for some reason, and that in which there is a very limited amount of software activity anyway; these cases are deferred to the end of this section.

Here, we will address the following issues, in turn:

1. Structural issues.
2. Ways and means.
3. Staffing.

ORGANIZATION AND STRUCTURE OF QUALITY GROUPS

In organization structure terms, there are two cases to consider; the first is that of a disaggregated quantity of people performing quality tasks, dispersed over a project (or product) group structure; the second concerns that of a consolidated group for QA purposes. The latter comes in one of two basic forms itself, and thus there are three possible structures at issue – as shown in Figure 13.12.

There is little to indicate which to adopt in preference to the others. The disadvantages of 'case (a)' are fairly obvious, although I have known such constructions that worked adequately. The drawbacks are as follows:

1. Fragmentation of resources leading to depletion of quality standards and practices. Local variants tend to flourish, and the total effect ends up as considerably less than the sum of the parts.
2. Relatively low-level significance of quality, without representation at any of the higher levels of management. This, and the previous point, tend to deplete the quality, by depressing both the status of the subject and its practitioners in consequence.
3. A question of objectivity in evaluating the reports and results of 'independent' quality assessments accruing from a source within the same department. The same criticism may be leveled, but less strenuously, at 'case (b)'.

In companies where the status and motivation of the independent software quality group is essential, 'case (c)' type constructions are required. Then, any contention that may arise over an independent quality assessment may escalate unimpeded in the organization, with an increasing chance of its objective resolution.

A typical case in point may arise if a deficiency report is due, as a result of quality inspection revealing that (say) the implementation is proceeding in the absence of a test plan. Now the appropriate procedure is for the quality officer(s) for this development to report the omission to the chief programmer concerned, via a 'deficiency report'. This may be nothing more formal than a scrap of paper saying 'Hey Fred, you've forgotten the test plan'. If, after a reasonable time for the omission to be rectified, the defect remains, then a repeat is required – with escalation. 'Hey Fred, what about the test plan I told you (date) is missing? You have no integration schedule, no nominated "tester", and no developed test coming into being. Incidentally, I've sent a copy to the product development leader.'

Now, both Fred and his immediate superior have the deficiency report. In 'case (a)' of Figure 13.12, something completely inadequate may result, and the 'independent' quality group may be powerless to proceed without violating a simple commandment: 'thou must report to thy boss, and not to thy boss's boss'.

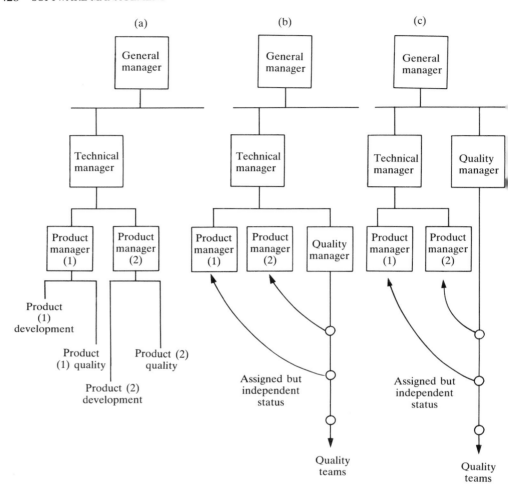

FIGURE 13.12 Alternative structures for the independent software quality group: (a) disaggregated resources, low organization status; (b) aggregated resources, medium organization status; (c) aggregated resources, high organization status.

The same problem may occur too, but at a higher level, in 'case (b)'. Here, the independent reporting lines (whose separation constitutes the real degree of independence) do not converge until the penultimate organization level. It is to be hoped that, in this case, the 'technical director' would solve the problem in a very crisp fashion, by a little invigorating intervention on the technical development side of his or her domain. These are not trivial matters. It has been pointed out already that quality costs money, and no amount of persuasive argument seems to convince some companies that a lack of it can cost an awful

lot more. In no case is this clearer than in how the independent software quality group is allowed to work.

MODUS OPERANDI: 'STOPPING THE FACTORY'

In the limiting case, some extreme instance of defective practice in the development of a system to whose failure the company is outstandingly vulnerable, the quality group should be able to 'stop the factory'. That is, in practice, it should be able to schedule a structured walkthrough at the current stage of development – during which no further development activities occur on the task in question. Presuming that it has the competence to arrive at its dire conclusions, and the means to do so (such as unimpeded QI access), does the software part of the independent quality group have the authority to 'stop the factory' in *your* firm?

On how many occasions is one *told* that the quality department can truly stop a software development in full flight so to speak? On all, or nearly all occasions, when the hard question is asked. That is not the problem, usually. But on how many occasions is it really *true* that the quality group has 'stopped the show' – even for the best possible reasons – amid the shot and shell of real developments that were to contracted deadlines and rapidly dwindling (or dwindled) budgets? On very, very few, when the evidence is examined. That, most categorically, is the problem when it occurs.

To be effective, the people doing independent quality inspection and assurance must be seen as more than just a harmless bunch that might throw in a bit of advice from time to time. Quality is more than just a few tips that may, or may not, be acted on.

COMPETENCE: WHERE TO FIND THE PEOPLE

If an independent quality group is to have teeth, other than the sort you can slip into a glass of water if they hurt your gums, then it had better have the competence to use them properly. This competence resides, in the first place, in people. Only on the basis of personal ability are quality standards and practices operable.

For the software competence in a quality group, one would be looking for two technical attributes – software engineering competence and application knowledge – and several personal qualities in the people concerned. In the technical attributes' category, by far the most important attribute to secure is that of software engineering competence.

I can hear the outraged howls from product engineers at this news, but the matter is perfectly clear cut. There is normally sufficient product orientation around to ensure that software engineers become oriented too – and rather quickly at that. The converse is often not the case. Furthermore, the early involvement of the independent quality group (at the functional specification stage), and their creation of black-box tests from the functional specification of requirements, generally ensures a sufficiency of application orientation.

This is not to say that software quality staff should have no product orientation at all; if both attributes can be supplied in the same person then they should be. There is often one splendid way to achieve this, and one other dire course of action to avoid.

To achieve both software engineering and product engineering (or application orientation) within the quality department, it is a good idea to transfer staff from the software product development group(s) to the independent quality department as a part of career

development. Let the poachers turn to gamekeeping. If this policy is adopted, there are several things to note:

1. The aspect of career development is crucial. Otherwise the quality group will be seen in a depleted light within the organization, a dumping ground for people whose careers are uncertain. This will be particularly true if 'failed' software engineers are transferred to it, for instance people who are temperamentally unsuited to the chief programmer team practices of design review and code reading. If a person is too fragile to be a reviewer or a reviewee, they will hardly cope with the vicissitudes of QI default reporting, and beta-testing!

2. If the transferee is inexperienced in software engineering, as may happen to people with however much 'amateur programming' experience, then an education program is called for. One will not get software quality assurance from amateur programmers.

3. The 'personal qualities', already referred to, will require at least as much attention, in selecting suitable people for quality tasks, as the technical attributes. Apart from the obvious need for acuity (after all, who wants a quality officer with the wool already pulled over his or her eyes?), quality staff will need to be persistent and personable. The need for persistence is obvious; the need for good personal relationships is none the less clear. Quality staff should be persuasive and diplomatic, but never so agreeable that their critical faculties are suspended. Neither should they be carpingly critical, nor fatuously pedantic.

A careful reading of these guidelines will lead to one clear conclusion at least; staff cannot be recruited into the quality group from outside without running several risks in the matter of their technical and personal attributes. A quality department is better recruited from within – as a part of career development. Any gaps left in development departments, as a result, may then be filled, at lesser risk, by outside recruiting.

The career development factor is crucial if a quality department is to be established by internal transfer. In software engineering particularly, this is no convenient fiction either. There is real insight to be gained into 'good software engineering practice' by doing QI and A, after several years of software development experience. One should not view this as other 'side' of life, because the adversary aspect should not be overstressed. However, it other view of life. White-box testing alone ensures that at least the demerits of bad are engineering are learned directly.

other strategy to adopt is to transfer software staff from development to quality ments on a limited-time basis. Minimally this would be for two years or so, as little development could be achieved in a lesser duration. After four to five years, such a might be offered the option to stay in quality, or to transfer back with an enhanced evelopment potential.

these notes and guidelines clearly refer to companies in which the magnitude of ctivities justifies a quality resource, however organized and staffed. This might case for companies with much smaller or intermittent software development en QI/QA functions may be assigned to one small development team in respect and vice versa. Or a third party, from outside the company, may be contracted roles and tasks required for independent quality inspection and assurance. endence factor, in this latter case, is clearly evident. But there may be

problems with application orientation and the personality factors alluded to. An outside contractor may be quickly (and unfairly) labeled 'incompetent' because it has not labored exclusively in such and such technology or application for the past fifty years. Also, it may be seen as the 'police force', ready to grasp an errant programmer's collar, pointing to a hexadecimal dump and growling ' 'Ere, 'ere, 'ere. What's all this about?'

If outside contractors are used for quality assurance purposes, their introduction and subsequent operations will have to be carefully managed by the contracting party. Given that this happens, much benefit might then accrue, particularly in the matter of technology transfer if the contractor is properly qualified and experienced in software engineering, and if they are contractually required to do technology transfer, e.g. by cooperative work schemes.

13.4.4 Personnel management; recruiting and retaining software engineers

Employment conditions vary so much over companies that it might be supposed that there is little to say about software personnel management in general. Equally, such wide variations exist in supply and demand, geographically and over different skill-sectors, that it might be assumed there is even less to say about getting and keeping good software staff. In fact, although few, some guidelines can be given, and some of the mythology of software personnel management exposed in the process. In the following section, we shall discuss the following:

1. Are software engineers a 'special case' in personnel management?
2. Guidelines for recruiting software engineers.
3. Guidelines for retaining software engineers.
4. Career progression.

'SPECIAL CASE'?

The folklore amongst managers and their non-software specialist colleagues can be extremely funny, but it may also be potentially harmful to the accretion and preservation of strong software groups.

One picture is of the manager, with a button-down hairstyle and sincere suit, regarding askance a motley and hairy mob with its peculiar and rather menacing ways, generally 'the young' who shamble about with the appearances of an unfastidious and impoverished refuse-collector. Unfair, certainly, but not the only source of inequity.

Another view, widely supported by engineers in electronics laboratories, is that the software engineer is a fragile creature, effete and unable to cope in a sweet little open-plan workshop, with wall-to-wall trash (called sub-assemblies), where Fred is for ever plunging the place into darkness when he plugs his hardware in, or setting his bench on fire.

It is easy enough to see the genesis of 'us and them' attitudes.

However, much of this passes as levity, being part of the banter due to and from colleagues of a different stripe. But one myth needs nailing, and that is the one about how different personnel management of software engineers is, because they are so captious and demanding – forever droning on about poor specifications, no time to do a decent job,

lousy PSEs, and a seemingly unending catalog of excuses prior to the inevitable catastrophe. In this author's experience, the opposite tends to be the case.

Software engineers are frequently too accommodating when faced with ill-conditioned tasks and a paucity of means. For the past three decades, software engineering has been regarded as a penny in the slot device for producing miracles. The reality – low quality programs that make unreliable software, done at exorbitant cost – is not necessarily because its exponents are bloody-minded, shiftless or incompetent. Some may be any or all of these things, but the supervening problems may lie elsewhere.

Required to list the prominent attributes of software engineers down these three and a half decades, one would be forced to highlight optimism and tenacity. Those are not simply desiderata, but actually characterize many practitioners. And, as only real patriots criticize their own country, software engineers' true optimism is often accompanied by signs of its converse, carping gloom or gallows-humor.

But the job gets tackled anyway and, in those circumstances, more is generally achieved than should be expected in the circumstances. However, no one would claim that software engineers are saints and martyrs, merely that their personnel management might require a few special insights, but in the main it will resemble that for any other group of employees.

First of all, let us clear about the distinctions to be made where people who program computers are concerned. There are three basic categories to consider:

1. *Hobbyists*. These are people whose programming is for fun or self-instruction, usually a few S programs done in Basic on a home (PC) computer. The endeavor is unlikely to be part of the person's everyday work, and the quality of its outcome would seldom merit its use for these purposes anyway.
2. *Amateur programmers*. These are people for whom programming is not a main vocation, but who – at some time or times – write programs as a part of their everyday work. The motivation and opportunity to establish 'good software engineering practice' will probably be missing, either through the factor of alternative vocation, or through the intermittency of their programming activities.
3. *Software engineers*. This designation spans a wide range of experience levels, from trainee to chief programmer, and beyond. Software engineers are people who work (at all life cycle stages) to produce software systems, as their exclusive vocation. They will have had some opportunity to consolidate a corpus of subject knowledge into some framework of good practice – although that is not to say that such will have happened.

Now, calling someone a hobbyist or an amateur is not necessarily a perjorative term. I am an amateur in many fields of endeavor, as I am sure are we all. I am a very amateur gardener, chess player, musician and a dozen and one other things including, some may think, an amateur author.

However, when one undertakes a task that requires a professional's skill in an inadequate fashion, and goes on doing so over several tasks with little hope or chance of improvement, then amateurism becomes a menace, and the term takes on its perjorative meaning. However, there are stages of amaterism that should and sometimes must be experienced.

For example, many managers, and others, should become 'hobbyists' in the sense of familiarizing themselves with programming on a PC. This will, at least, help to overcome a

natural inhibition towards the otherwise rather inaccessible-looking technology, and its hermetic literature. The great dangers are 'amateur programming' and the perpetuation of haphazard approaches to software development by 'software engineers' lacking a consolidated working practice in the subject. In this problem, some computer scientists may unwittingly play an unhelpful part unless their own experience in software development has been sufficient, as it may be presumed that they are the repositories of all knowledge in the subject.

There is an allied danger that computer scientists who are inexperienced in software engineering may act to amplify this presumption, in which case 'amateur programming' may become very difficult to eradicate, as managers are confronted by the vision of Santa Clauses fighting for territory again. Understandably, this is not a popular view with some computer scientists.

RECRUITING SOFTWARE ENGINEERS

The simple guidelines for recruiting software staff are easy to enumerate:

1. Evaluate, and face up to, the realities of supply and demand. Yours may be a company used to operating in a buyer's market. Your sector of requirement might constitute a seller's market. Can you adjust? This point is taken further below.
2. Offer competitive conditions (n.b. not only mere money, but including it). Unless you do so, you will either (a) not get staff, or (b) not get the ones you want, or (c) not keep the good ones you do get. If the 'going rate' is above prevailing norms for remuneration packages in your company, the fact will have to be faced.
3. Write good copy for advertising purposes. Most staff advertisements are too verbose, lead with disinteresting recitals about the company's history and have the wrong text-to-space ratio. Advertising is a specialism within public relations methods, as every modern president or prime minister will tell you. Good adverts are eye-catching, with what is called in the USA 'a grabber up front' – which sounds to be a painful proposition but is, in fact, something to rivet the attention of a job seeker. The obvious thing here is an announcement of some really challenging position, succinctly defined, and some pretty large salary set out in 5 cm high bold font. Then, a crisp description of the challenges and opportunities of the job and, last, a short statement as to what a good, stable employer you are – or not, as the case might be.
4. The period from an applicant responding to the advertisement, to receiving a letter of offer, should be minimal. Obviously, papers must be assessed, interviews held, references checked, colleagues consulted and internal formalities concluded. If all this has a nine months' gestation period, the continuing interest of your applicant is unlikely, to say the least. It may even be so if the delay is nine weeks.
   Software engineering is a fearsomely competitive business. Depending on the outcome of 1 above, you may have to be prepared to accelerate the normal recruiting procedures in the company. A response period of three to five weeks may be maximal for some categories of staff – such as chief programmers.
5. Interviewing, like advertising, is a specialism. Everyone has a unique interviewing style, but certain truths should be common to all. The applicant should do most of the talking, being guided by questions from the interviewer; also have a checklist of questions to insert. Clearly, a technical interview requires a technical interviewer.

It is surprising how often an elementary question from such a source exposes the most dreadful inadequacy. Explain, as to a layman, what is meant by the claim that the XYZ microcomputer is a 32-bit machine? (Collapse of stout party!) 'What is a block-structured, high level language?' (Applicant swallows false-teeth.)

6. Software engineers must be sufficiently literate, as well as numerate and a lot of other things beside. Set applicants a short, written essay to do at the interivew. Any topic will do; one of the technical check-list type, or something topical: 'Set out a case, whether you believe in it or not, why capital punishment should be restored for (a) working in the software industry, (b) stealing sheep'.

7. Avoid too many interviews per applicant. I once knew a situation in which the unfortunates called for interview faced seven sequential interviews in a day, each one of twenty to thirty minutes' duration. No one wants to play the role of baton in a relay

TABLE 13.6 Specimen of appraisal checklist, showing the effect of discussion

Appraisal of FRED BLOGGS by: SALOME SMITH on 1 January 1989

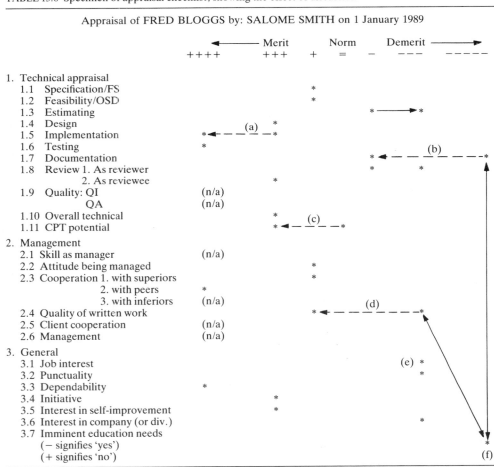

	Merit ←			Norm		Demerit →	
	++++	+++	+	=	−	−−−	−−−−−
1. Technical appraisal							
1.1 Specification/FS			*				
1.2 Feasibility/OSD			*				
1.3 Estimating						* —→ *	
1.4 Design		(a) *					
1.5 Implementation	* ◄ − − − − *						
1.6 Testing	*						
1.7 Documentation						* ◄ − − (b) − − *	
1.8 Review 1. As reviewer						* *	
2. As reviewee		*					
1.9 Quality: QI	(n/a)						
QA	(n/a)						
1.10 Overall technical		*					
1.11 CPT potential		* ◄ − (c) − *					
2. Management							
2.1 Skill as manager	(n/a)						
2.2 Attitude being managed				*			
2.3 Cooperation 1. with superiors				*			
2. with peers	*						
3. with inferiors	(n/a)						
2.4 Quality of written work			* ◄ − − (d) − − *				
2.5 Client cooperation	(n/a)						
2.6 Management	(n/a)						
3. General							
3.1 Job interest						(e) *	
3.2 Punctuality						*	
3.3 Dependability	*						
3.4 Initiative		*					
3.5 Interest in self-improvement		*					
3.6 Interest in company (or div.)						*	
3.7 Imminent education needs							*
(− signifies 'yes')							
(+ signifies 'no')							(f)

race. Two interviews should be enough or, better, two interviewers with different purposes at the same interview.

8. An attempt should be made to explain to applicants details of remuneration package, working conditions, the actual job and career development opportunities. The component usually omitted is the last one named – *career development*. The excuse is that it may be cited later as a promise. That need not be the case, as sufficient caveats can be given. Omitting to describe career development is a terrible weakness in recruiting practice; it may be inferred that the employment is static. Join as and die. In some cases, it probably does mean just that.

9. An adequate technical interview need not take longer than an hour and a half; an adequate interview with general/personnel management need not take more than half an hour. I have known most impressive cases where applicants have been presented with written offers at the interview, and asked to respond within, say, a two weeks' period. This avoids the problem of job offers becoming blocked in the entrails of an organization. Clearly, such offers were subject to satisfactory references.

The reader will have realized, some time ago, that none of this is particular to software staff. Only the modalities of 1, 2 and 5 are special cases; the rest is good general practice anyway.

There is always some purprise over point 6. 'Literate software engineers – why, for heavens sake? They have to think in, oh, Pascal and what-do-you-call-it, Ada? Don't they? The answer is, of course, that *programmers* need to be literate in design and coding languages, but that *software engineers* need – in addition – to communicate with things other than machines. The whole set of issues in specification depends on communication ability at the oral and written levels; much of the deliverable documentation will be text rather than programs.

It is a crippling disability if one's software engineers have a literacy level that barely enables them to cope with a 'Peanuts' cartoon on a good day. There is no need to go overboard and expect software engineers to spout chunks of Shakespeare, Goethe, Proust or Pushkin. But a good, basic ability to express oneself is essential. In this respect, some formal education systems fail the community conspicuously.

RETAINING THEM ONCE YOU HAVE GOT THEM: APPRAISAL TECHNIQUES
The guidelines for retaining staff are equally straightforward.

1. Maintain your competitive position with regard to job interest and remuneration. If these decline, or just one of them falls out of balance, staff attrition will increase.
2. Appraise staff regularly with respect to their technical and other performances. Notes on this are set out below, as it is *the* fundamental point in staff retention.

Maintaining a competitive position on job interest is sometimes far more easily said than done. The epitome of interest is variety, and this cannot always be arranged. Our version 6 product may be very much like the first five and not much can be done about It. On the other hand, if version 7 is radically new, and if we contract the software to an outside firm to do, then we may expect our best software engineers to wear a hurt expression for a while, at least.

Appraisal is a major issue, central to good personnel management. It is the process of technical peer-level assessment, and evaluation of behavioral attributes. That a 'peer'-level assessment is involved does not mean that an exact peer in the organization should do an appraisal. Usually, the immediate superior of a person does the appraisal; a chief programmer will appraise people who have worked on the same team; a product development manager, or software group manager, will appraise a chief programmer and so on. The general practice is to have the appraiser complete a checklist of attributes before the appraisal. Then, during the appraisal, the checklist may be annotated. Table 13.6 indicates such a 'before' and 'after' on a fairly typical checklist. As can be seen, these appraisals highlight much in a person's performance and potential.

What I should construe from the hypothetical case in Table 13.6 is that the appraisee is a rather junior staff member having had little opportunity to show management potential, either at CPT or other levels, no client contact, and so forth. The alternative explanation, that Fred is a worn out old programmer, is too distressing to contemplate.

Clearly, the appraisal has not been one-way traffic by any means. Taking the unbroken arrows to mean agreed changes in the meeting, and dotted arrows to mean unresolved differences of opinion, we see the following:

1. Rather curiously, the appraiser started with a higher opinion of estimating capability than was the case at the end; likewise, the appraisee's work as a reviewer. This can happen in appraisals. A rather mild criticism can become a much harder one during the discussion.

   Ideally, the appraiser would have ommitted her real opinion before the event, and Fred would hardly have striven to worsen it. (Or, if so, there should be off-scale readings for honesty – high; and common sense – low.)
2. On the other hand, the appraiser has resisted some pressure to upgrade scores for implementation, documentation, CPT potential and quality of written work. The appraisee is clearly ambitious (CPT), or at least thinks he could do as well or better than some chief programmer. If this is the one he is working for presently, it may not be a happy sign, and we might hold out some question on the quite high score under 2.3.
3. The overall picture in Table 13.6 is of a very good performance over the appraisal period, with a few worring areas (1.3/1.5), and two extremely debilitating attributes – presumably related – in 1.7 and 2.4. One presumes that 1.3/1.5 have been left to correct themselves over the next appraisal period, which, when its checklist is done, should highlight these points. 1.3/1.5 are clearly connected to 3.7, 'further education needs'. This, too, should make interesting reading next time.
4. Annotations (a), (b), etc. on the appraisal form will show appraiser's notes on the disagreements. It is not uncommon for both appraiser and appraisee to initial the final working document, to avoid the 'I said so-and-so'/'oh no,you didn't' type of arguments one year on, or more.

Before the next appraisal, a new checklist must be done. Often the same appraiser is involved; sometimes not, for obvious reasons such as reorganization or staff leaving. In any case, the appraiser should proceed in a simple but significant fashion.

First, before the appraisal, complete the new checklist *without* reference to the previous one. Then compare the new scores with the old ones to see if any of the new ones are

TABLE 13.7 Specimen of appraisal checklist, one year on

Appraisal of FRED BLOGGS by: SALOME SMITH on 1 January 1990

	← Merit	Norm	Demerit →
	++++ +++ +	= −	− − − − − − −
1. Technical appraisal			
1.1 Specification/FS		*	
1.2 Feasibility/OSD	*		
1.3 Estimating			*
1.4 Design	*		
1.5 Implementation	*		
1.6 Testing	*		
1.7 Documentation			*
1.8 Review 1. As reviewer		*− − − − − ⁄− *	(a)
2. As reviewee		*	
1.9 Quality: QI	*		
QA	*		
1.10 Overall technical	*		
1.11 CPT potential		* (b)	
2. Management			
2.1 Skill as manager	(n/a)		
2.2 Attitude being managed		* (c)	
2.3 Cooperation 1. with superiors		* (d)	
2. with peers		*◄ − − − − * (e)	
3. with inferiors	(n/a)		
2.4 Quality of written work		*◄ − −(f)− − *	
2.5 Client cooperation			
2.6 Management	(n/a)		
3. General			
3.1 Job interest		* (g)	
3.2 Punctuality		*	
3.3 Dependability		?◄ − −* (h)	
3.4 Initiative		*	
3.5 Interest in self-improvement		* (i)	
3.6 Interest in company (or div.)			* (j)
3.7 Imminent education needs			
(− signifies 'yes')	!!! *◄ − − − − − − − − − − − − − − − − − − * ???		
(+ signifies 'no')	(k)		

unjustified in any way. Finally, run the appraisal with both the new (undiscussed) scores and the old form in front of you.

An example of the one-year-on checklist, annotated in the appraisal, is shown in Table 13.7. What a change has occurred over just one appraisal period! Fresh-faced Fred of the previous year is now at odds with his peers (2.3.2) and, perhaps, not so well disposed to management (the change in 2.3.1, from very good to merely normal). Can it have anything to do with Fred's attitude as a reviewer (the change in 1.8.1 from poor to very poor)? The annotation (a) should make interesting reading. Perhaps it accounts for the motivation problems shown under 3.

There has been some improvement in documentation and written work, but some dispute about the latter. Otherwise, all the technical scores remain very high – although estimating still seems to be a minor problem.

This appraisee seems to be very much the specialist technician, with little interest in the world around him – company or division – and possibly little interest in self-improvement in those terms. The appraiser has tried to rivet Fred's attention on certain defects (the arrogance of a wizard technician towards his peers, perhaps), by stressing the detrimental effects they have on his team-leadership prospects. The rather emphatic score of 'definitely not' for further education (3.7) is, perhaps, the most significant thing on the form. What can annotation (k) be saying? Can it be that the matter is now one of attitude and motivation, and is therefore intractable to education means as such? The appraisal shows a sad picture. There may be no 'next time'. One of several things may occur in the succeeding period:

1. Fred may take the messages to heart, if they are fair and valid that is, brace himself up, and there is a happy continuation all round.
2. Fred may take the appraisal as indicating the writing on the wall, and that his back is up against it, and leave.
3. Fred's performance may be seen, or supposed, to remain defective – or even more defective – and the company 'exploys' him (a euphemism).
4. Fred's performance may remain as defective, or worse, and neither he leaves, nor his employer dismisses him.

As appraiser, I should feel considerable disquiet after such an event. The main concerns being: (a) if I have been entirely fair, after all much of this is judgmental; and (b) that another person's future is now at question. The best course of action would be to reschedule the appraisal, but this time in the presence of some higher management representative. Also, the appraisee should be entitled to bring along some independent counsellor from within the firm.

Appraising staff is a very serious and central affair in personnel management, as will now have become apparent from this sad little example. Appraisals are not just an annual chore, to be dashed through at the greatest velocity, a couple of quick pats on the back or a mild kick up the corridor, and it is all over for another year. Appraisal is a process that should aim at agreement, but not agreement at any price. Trying to reconcile the different views of a matter can be time-consuming. One appraisal consumed seven hours in my direct experience. A reasonable 'average' time for appraisal of software staff tends to increase with seniority. My companion over seven hours was a chief programmer, but that was an extreme case. It should not take more than four hours to appraise someone's performance, in the most sedulous detail, at that level. On the other hand, for trainees such as graduate entrants in the first two years of employment, less than two hours usually suffices.

Several further guidelines to appraisal may be given here, in summary:

1. A mini-appraisal should be done fairly shortly after employment begins, say at the four to six weeks' period. This should be to ensure that the new appraisee is settling down properly, knows where the coffee machine is, has been issued with a pencil to chew, and so on. All this has a serious side to it as well. Complaints are best dealt with early, and employees get an enhanced impression of the company as a result.
2. Another appraisal should be done before the end of the first twelve months of employ-

ment, whether this coincides with a normal appraisal point or not. The purpose of this should be quite openly to review whether the employment has been a mistake from either side. Errors are best rectified early, and no recruiting process is perfect. What is indefensible is to 'bake mistakes in', by retaining clearly unsuitable staff for some role. This imbalances the whole environment, for software engineering particularly, all the more so if a chief programmer team philosophy is in operation.

3. Appraisal should be kept distinct from salary reviews – although there are clear links between them. It would be odd, for example, if a swingeing appraisal was followed by a staggering pay increase. The main object is to keep financial bargaining out of a process – appraisal – that might be tricky enough in its own right. Typically, an appraisal cycle is undertaken in the months September/October, and a salary review procedure enacted in late November/early December. Then the connective is in the right direction; that review may depend on appraisal, not that appraisal may be disrupted by review.

4. Sometimes it is expedient to delay an appraisal. One example is when a software development task is due to end fairly shortly afterwards. The one thing to avoid is having too great a duration between appraisals; fifteen months may be justifiable, two years (or more) would not be.

5. It is worth repeating that the technical parts of review must be done by, or at least based on inputs from, technically qualified people. It is no use a member of upper management trying to do this part of appraisal, unless he or she has the technical basis for it, and the direct knowledge of the individual's performance to go on.

6. It is also worth pointing out the obvious, clearly lacking in the Tables 13.6/13.7 examples, that appraisals – like other aspects of personnel management and its records – should be a matter of confidentiality. Leaving a copy of the specimen 13.7 in the photocopying machine might cause Fred to express himself forcibly and well (even in writing!) on the subject.

7. One should never lose sight of the fact that a 'fair and critical assessment', as an appraisal must be, may have a terminal outcome from the employment viewpoint. Persistent actual, or even only supposed, insufficiency should lead to an individual and their employer parting company. Otherwise these mismatches become 'baked in' to the organization. It is not a kindness to people to avoid this issue. How does your company do it? Does it face facts clearly in this respect, or does it equivocate?

Perhaps I have stressed the negative possibilities flowing from appraisal at the expense of the positive ones. It must be said that in the vast majority of cases, properly done appraisals are the source of considerable motivation to employer and employed. The leitmotifs must be fairness and justice, the right to reply and have the reply properly considered, and – above all – the objective of improvement. This last named is the pivot on which the world of personnel management turns. Few people are uninterested in improving their performance in a chosen profession – if it can be shown that such possibilities exist. If and when you meet such a person, it is time for point 7 above to some into play.

PERFORMANCE IMPROVEMENT AND CAREER PROGRESSION
There are, in fact, two aspects to improvement. The first concerns the questions 'how?' and 'with respect to what?'. The second concerns any benefits that may be contingent on improvement.

'How?' should be an issue for planning between the parties when it has been established why some remedial or more fundamental education is required. Typically, if some specific defect – like Fred's literacy – can be detected, then, in a well ordered environment, a personnel department will be able to suggest a fit between some known remedy – such as a course – and the condition. This requires a degree of external view, in the personnel department, to hold up-to-date information on the sources of short courses in subjects likely to be called for. Most often, strong relationship with local colleges of further education are helpful for training in basic technologies, and specialisms such as programming languages. Issues of wider context and deeper significance – such as education in software engineering itself – may not be so easily come by. This question is taken further in Section 13.4.5.

It is important that training or education for improvement is decided as a consensual process with the 'trainee'. 'Why are you on this course Fred?' 'Because I was sent on it' is an indictment of a process and its exponents. Clearly essential is a view of career development, and this hovers above all aspects of performance appraisal and improvement. Now every firm has its own style in organization, management, career evaluation and progression. However, seen from the viewpoint of a profession in its own right, software engineering has certain characteristics. Figure 13.13 shows a typical progression from trainee onwards; at the upper end, a mapping is shown into the general regions of a firm, and all this is commented on below and elsewhere – notably Section 13.4.5.

The schematic, Figure 13.13, embodies a considerable amount of generalization, and some assumptions that should – at least – be revealed. The following annotation to it sets its contents in context:

1. The scheme shown is a specimen of how things go or might go in some abstract environment in which software development is a significant part of business activities. It is not, nor can any other scheme be, a general cliché for universal application.
2. The issues subsumed in 'preliminary and vocational training' are detailed further in Section 13.4.5. Briefly stated, they comprise aspects of applied mathematics, electronic engineering and programming, as may comprise the basics of a computer science course.
3. The techniques of software engineering can only be conferred by a form of 'craft apprenticeship'. This is shown as occurring within the first two years, but there is a large caveat attaching to it; the 'craft apprenticeship' should be within a peer-group chief programmer team construction, or something of the sort, that employs a strong and clear philosophy for software development. Empirically gained education is fearsomely expensive, in this subject, for someone or other – trainee, employer, client and sometimes all three.
4. Some continuing education will be required beyond the apprenticeship stage, and this is detailed in Section 13.4.5.
5. The bifurcation in career development, toward either chief programmer tasks or technical specialisms, is normal; not everyone has a potential for team-leadership, and many people would rather not have that sort of responsibility.
6. Beyond chief programmer status, one may go on doing the same sort of thing up to some naturally occurring maximum in experience accretion; or one may (given

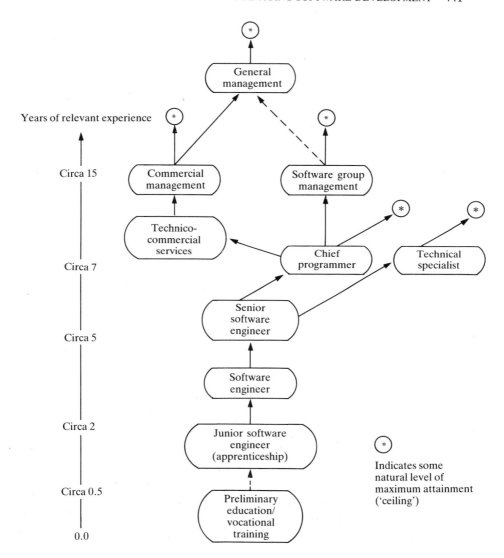

FIGURE 13.13 Progression in software engineering.

the opportunity) progress into software group management, with general recruiting policy and staff responsibilities as well as technical ones; or one may move into the technico-commercial area, such as marketing/sales of software products or services, acting pseudo-client for product development, and so on.

7. The strongest possibility for software engineers to accede to general management levels, in business and industry in general, would seem to be along the trajectory of apprenticeship, senior software engineer, chief programmer, technico-commercial services and commercial management. There are some adequate justifications for this, such as the possibility of narrow specialization in other career trajectories, such as those shown as ongoing 'chief programmer' and 'technical specialist' tasks. It is less clear why software management has such a weak connection with the general management career trajectory.

This sort of scheme, or similar notions to those underlying it, should be the basis for both recruiting and appraisal practices. In combination with appraisal, its natural outcome is a policy concerning subject education at several levels.

As this is a part of the wider issue of software engineering education, which is an extensive and contentious topic, it is treated in the following section.

13.4.5 Software engineering education

This most contentious of topics cannot be avoided, as it stands at the center of that most important question: 'How are we to reduce the ill-effects of "amateur programming"?' and, in doing so, to ameliorate the so-called software crisis by proper means.

There are a bewildering amount of factors and arguments, and people's opinions of them, to complicate or confuse the issue, as well as policies in education for this subject at national and company levels. Contention begins at the very start, with great difficulty being experienced to define what software education may comprise in a manner to suit all parties. And the dispute then spreads into the means and methods to achieve it, and curricula to be followed.

Part of the problem lies in the fact that 'software engineering' is difficult to define in a snappy catch-phrase that tells anyone who enquires enough for a clear understanding. The reader will, having got this far in the text, appreciate the reasons for this. Another part of the problem is that the 'all parties' referred to earlier, who tend to fall into contention over the subject of software engineering education, include a rich variety of sectoral interests – manager, practitioner, academic, politician. To this must be added 'amateur' because, like some other topics such as specification and documentation, everybody has an opinion on this subject's education modalities – and tends to express it; I have seen schemes for college curricula being drafted at the pub, between the third and fourth gin, by people who know little about software engineering and less about education means and methods.

However, nice as it would be to slip around it with nothing more than a goggle of fright, the issue stands before us as a bar to real progress in solving the 'software crisis', and must be faced.

In the following section, we will wrestle with the complex and contentious matters

involved, beginning by attempting to get some order into the subject. We will offer four major subsections:

1. Suitability of means for educating software practitioners.
2. Prerequisites for educating software practitioners.
3. Modalities of continuing education, for practitioners and others.
4. Some notable examples of misfit in software education.

But before we embark upon this schedule, some terms need to be defined:

1. *Formal education.* The accredited state system, operating at the levels or primary (middle) and secondary schools, and of further (or 'tertiary') education in polytechnics and universities.
2. *Continuing education.* The 'in employment' means to improve subject knowledge, at several levels of need: primary-skill; secondary-skill; and orientation.
3. *Primary skill.* Knowledge needed, in whatever combination of theory and practice, to undertake major tasks in software development, as practitioner.
4. *Secondary skill.* Knowledge needed to enable one to work with software practitioners on composite systems, and to avoid slipping into the errors of 'amateur programming' and assumed competence in the subject of software engineering.
5. *Orientation.* A sufficient exposure to the classifications and terminology in, and modalities of, good software engineering practice, for managers and others whose jobs require them to 'add value' to software development.

With these definitions in mind, we now proceed with the schedule of topics.

SUITABILITY OF MEANS FOR EDUCATING SOFTWARE PRACTITIONERS

Two great and forbidding problems beset this topic. Can software engineering be seen as a subject for some primary-skill curriculum, within formal education, such as might be found at secondary or tertiary levels of general and specialist teaching, i.e. in schools providing for education up to the age of about 18 and, thereafter, universities and polytechnics? And, what relation is there between a higher education in computer science and the education requirements in software engineering – whatever they are?

These are contentious questions. One body of opinion holds that software engineering can be taught, *a priori*, as a subject – like, say, physics or law. Another faction asserts that software engineering education of this sort is computer science theory, plus a dollop of software practice. Yet another school of thought holds to the view that software engineering is a skill that can be *learned* but not *taught*, rather like riding a bicycle, swimming or playing cricket, and that computer science – whatever *it* may seem to be – is an academic subject that counts for little at the practical level.

The arguments, and their conclusions, profoundly affect software engineering practice. In an earlier chapter, some of the issues received attention, if not detailed treatment – for instance, the definitional difficulties involved in both software engineering and computer science, was dealt with at some length in Chapter 1.

It is not useful to revisit those arguments here save to say, again, that it is an unhappy state of affairs to be forced to conclude that computer science should be re-named 'computology' as a better description of what actually the field of endeavor covers.

However, there is little cause for any 'side' or faction to celebrate such disarray; compared with software engineering, seen as a subject for education, computer science has an enviable degree of definition, the basis for a canonical literature and, most admirably, some apparent scope for research. None of these claims can be strongly made for software engineering.

On the other hand, the question persists – 'Does this have anything to do with software engineering education?' The fact that computer science research has, and should continue to have, an outcome in software engineering seems self-evident. If computer science is an applied science, or a part of applied mathematics – as its curricula would suggest it is – then its investigations should be intended to have practical application. As one philosopher has put it, truth lies at the extremes – not in the middle. Equally, 'truth is that view fated to become accepted by all who investigate' (C. S. Peirce in Russell 1946).

Between software engineering and computer science lies a wasteland of conjecture and opinion, to which – I am afraid – I may be about to add. The questions, as we have seen, are contentious; their conclusions tend to be matters of opinion. None of the contending views has, as yet, seemed likely to be fated for acceptance as 'truth'.

In this situation, one can only emit another opinion just as, in theological disputes, one may submit one's beliefs. It is with this caveat that the following remarks are offered:

1. Software engineering is not really a subject for secondary and tertiary education courses, for two basic reasons. First of all, the subject-matter to be taught is, although substantial, much less than a full two or three years' degree course warrants.

   Other engineering subjects have the same characteristics it is true, but require a grounding in other subjects such as mechanics and the physical properties of materials, chemistry and so forth as appropriate to the type of engineering concerned. Seeing software engineering in the same way is very difficult, and in places where the subject has been made an adjunct to the department of mathematics, engineering or computer science, the outcome seems to have been far less satisfactory for the needs of business and industry than in cases of other engineering subjects.

   Secondly, it is a practical 'craft' in which knowledge accretion is far more dependent on the progression 'doing – failing – doing – succeeding' than can be accommodated in an academic curriculum.

2. Units of software engineering topics within a computer science curriculum produce slightly better oriented computer scientists. The admixture does not, however, produce 'educated software engineers' in any sense. The reason for this is again that advanced in 1 above.

   Lectures and limited practical exercises about 'the realities' have little effect on people not yet fully exposed to the actualities of life in software engineering. The 'evidence' for this is that the time it generally takes for software engineers to become useful and dependable varies little, whether they have had a higher education in 'software engineering' (whatever that may comprise), computer science, computer science with software engineering, or software engineering with any other discipline for that matter. The period seems to be two years plus or minus six months or so, in most cases.

3. It follows from this that software engineering education either does not exist at all, in the sense of a canonical subject (one being left with the indelible impression of knowl-

edge accretion by empirical means as the only available possibility), or that some other way of viewing software engineering education is necessary. This theme is developed further below.

4. The associated questions of aptitude, and prior orientation and training, before a learning apprenticeship in software engineering, are as crucial as those of education in the subject itself.

If we are to embark young people on a career in software engineering by involving them in practical matters straight away, then how are we to judge their likely aptitude? And what necessary and sufficient equipment will they need before being introduced to the chief programmer and team they will be working with, and shoved in at the deep end so to speak? These too will be discussed at greater length imminently, but it is sufficient to say that the answer 'computer science' is not the whole of the case for either aptitude assessment or prior education.

We take up the matters raised under 4 above in the following section dealing with the prerequisites in people and precursor events necessary for educating software practitioners.

As we do not see that software engineering can, or need be, a full-time study of the academic type, and as we clearly need to avoid an entirely empirical method of acquiring subject knowledge, we shall be developing arguments towards continuing education as the logical route out of the impasse.

PREREQUISITES FOR EDUCATING SOFTWARE PRACTITIONERS

There are four prerequisites, some concerning target populations, and some defining precursor activities in which they should be engaged:

1. Personal attributes in the aspiring practitioners, including 'aptitude'.
2. Preparation.
3. Apprenticeship.
4. Continuing education.

We deal with the first three in this subsection, under three headings: 'aptitude', 'attributes' and 'preparation, apprenticeship and career development'. Continuing education, being a major topic in its own right, is dealt with in its own section following this.

Aptitude. It is effectively impossible to measure aptitude for a career in software engineering without doing a certain amount of software development to demonstrate it. Whereas we may say that a good baseball player should be able to play a reasonable game of tennis, having some athleticism and coordination, unhappily there is almost nothing we can say that is helpful to prior demonstration of possible aptitude in software engineering.

In the early 1960s we were treated to a deluge of so-called 'aptitude tests' about which large claims were made. The 'methods' were the sort of standard apperception tests given to determine 'IQ' (whatever that is), and comprised number, word and shape associations principally. The claims made for them, to ensure aptitude for software engineering, were largely specious.

However, some of its apologists do assert that a prior education in computer science infallibly demonstrates an aptitude for software engineering. In fact, at most, it will de-

monstrate an ability in one of the requisites – ability in abstraction at the levels of process and notation. But in this it is far from unique. As we have pointed out earlier (Chapter 11), pure mathematics and theoretical physics may provide an even more dramatic evidence of this ability. However, although it does not have an exclusive lien on this property, it is good to remember that computer science serves other purposes as well, as we shall show. In fact, a full computer science degree represents a substantial amount of over-kill for the numeracy/abstraction requirement in software engineering. Mathematics, incorporating algebra and the differential calculus, taken as a major subject up to the final years of secondary education, is usually sufficient evidence of numeracy. Of course, if one wants to specialize in some sector of applied mathematics – such as numerical methods, statistics, the applications of algebra in linear and non-linear methods, or in computer science itself seen as a subject of applied mathematics – one should read for an appropriate degree in mathematics or computer science.

Attributes. Some of the desirable attributes of software engineers can be listed and, if they are judged present in sufficient quantity, a person possessing them may be thought suitable to attempt the subject. And that is about the best we can do – guess, or (only slightly better) guess with reason and judgment.

I should list, but not rank, the following main attributes: as already discussed under 'aptitude', ability to deal with abstractions at two levels – abstractions of process and notation; a sufficient (fairly high) level of literacy; attention span, for loss of concentration causes error; attention to detail, for there is no such thing as an approximately compliant program outside research in artificial intelligence; patience and persistence; and qualities of personality that enable the person to work in teams (e.g. helpfulness, open-mindness, sense of humor, modesty, understanding). As if all this is not enough, the virtue of creativity must not be oveolooked. Whereas much else can be measured in some way, for example 'literacy', creativity cannot – for the simple reason that it may, probably will, be a sporadic attribute.

Now, as the reader will have realized, much of this is quite general, and may apply to a wide variety of vocations. Moreover, it will be equally quickly realized that this seems more like an attribute specification for the second coming, and that we are unlikely to get a high degree of 'fit' between all the qualities and real people – who may be numerate but not literate, or vice versa, a bit slipshod, have a tendency to be a little impatient, unforgiving or downright ratty, and so on.

The next attribute, literacy, is a difficult property to define in this context. In fact some would argue that a more general level of 'communication skills' is required for both oral and written discourse. The first of these (oral) is easy to determine; did he (she) sit in a fetal crouch at the interview sucking his (her) thumb; or did he (she) talk sense, or babble a torrent of the most staggering garbage?

However, a good oral communicator – whatever that means, and however it is displayed – is not necessarily good at the written level. A blank sheet of paper makes a paralyzed fool of us all, if we have the misfortune to find ourselves in front of it with a pen in our fist. Pushed to define literacy in this context, and how one might improve it, or determine it in an employee, I should fall back on the old and now largely defunct practice of writing an accurate and readable précis – a technique my readers might have wished me

to rediscover somewhat earlier than this. A typical examination question in former epochs required the miserable examinee to summarize some morass of irrelevance. Faced with that sort of thing, inability to read or write is not helpful, and might well be revealed – as might any shortfall with the bit in the middle, analysis and synthesis. If determining literacy is beyond these means, then one falls back on the essay method – as referred to earlier.

Preparation, apprenticeship and career development. The properties of aptitude and suitable attributes in aspiring software engineers are not hard to list, but are far from easy to establish with certainty. Yet, however the judgments are made, we must hypothesize a group of people, probably in the age group 18–25, poised on the brink of a career in software engineering, wide-eyed with expectation (or something; greed, fear, lust), and awaiting our further advice. What next, they may ask; some may be hobbyists already, or even amateur programmers; others may lack even a clue about the subject.

Given what we have already said about it being a practical craft, not suitable for treatment as a full academic level course, it follows rather naturally that software engineering education is seen, increasingly, as a suitable case for in-company, or pan-company, 'continued education'. The most suitable precursor for courses in such a program is an apprenticeship of one to two years, say, and the prerequisite for such an apprenticeship is a preparation course, or programming courses, well short of a full academic level education course in the formal state-education system of such, e.g. the typical computer science degree.

The purpose of the apprenticeship is to provide paradigms of experience in a knowledge accretion scheme based on the 'doing – failing – doing – succeeding' cycle. Without putting too fine a point on it, software engineering cannot be taught to people who have never seen, or experienced at first hand, its vicissitudes – and to try to embody this experience within a course, or program of such, places unachievable goals for its practical basis; the course has to become the real-life practice, or it fails by definition.

The most adroit way around this little puzzle is to equip the aspirant software engineer to begin an apprenticeship in software engineering – as an amateur programmer in a sense – and then, quite early in life (after a year, say), to begin the process of continuing education in the subject. A primary-skill course in continuing education, for use at the one to two year period, is set out under the 'specifics' heading below, along with cognate courses for secondary-skill education and orientation, as these terms are defined elsewhere.

Educating software engineers is a two year exercise, the most part being taken up by the productive apprenticeship. The painful aspects (to a company) of continuing education – release of *in situ* staff, to long courses – is mitigated by having a medium length 'preparation' course at the start of employment, and then a much shorter 'consolidation' course in the one to two year period.

By this time, practitioners are – or should be – suitably equipped, by both education and experience, to undertake software development work at all life cycle stages, without the direct and detailed supervision of other, more experienced, practitioners. Beyond this stage, the only education requirements in this subject should be for technical specialism, as these occur through need and opportunity. For instance, a Modula-2 course may be needed, or one in Ada or C, if these (or other languages) are to be used; similarly for PSE

facilities, design methods and so forth, if new systems have to be evaluated or procured. These are all in the realm of *ad hoc* technical topics.

As for the education requirements of software development staff already *in situ*, some mapping on to the 'preparation' and 'primary-skill consolidation' courses may be done, for remedial purposes, at whatever rate these practitioners can be liberated from tasks. Both courses are defined further, in (A) and (B) respectively, below.

Later in career development, a distinct switch in emphasis may be made away from day-to-day technical involvement, toward more commercial and general management tasks. Some special reorientation education is required in these cases, but it is beyond our scope to detail this, in either requirement or supply. The whole of this scheme may be depicted on the schematic for software engineering progression – see Figure 13.14.

Perhaps needless to say, this whole approach to software engineering education is only as good as the determination of firms to invest in it, the available means to achieve programs and the 'good personnel management' practice – such as appraisal – needed to map suitable employees on to appropriate components in a program.

We will now begin to define elements in such a program, beginning with the 'preparation' course.

(A) Primary-skill: preparatory course. A necessary and sufficient – and short – preparatory program, to establish basic competences, and to establish some of the fundamentals in the subject, should comprise the following elements, preferably in this order:

A1. An introduction to programming and the use of a PSE – however simple. A high level programming language should be introduced, and Pascal may be as suitable as any at this stage. Examples should be done in this, tested until apparently valid, and then submitted for independent scrutiny and comment. The same should then be done with a low level language such as assembler.

This part of the program may take in total about four weeks.

A2. Basic concepts in computer science. General introduction to computers and computing; algorithms, data structures and structured programming; computer architecture/logic circuitry/(V)LSI; programming and language translation; operating systems, and other features and facilities of the 'virtual' machine; the foundations of computation (Church, Turing); the foundations of structured methods (Dijkstra, Hoare, Naur and others); introduction to any elements of discrete mathematics not currently known to the audience – e.g. symbolic logic, statistical and numerical methods; formal methods in programming, and proof methods; the theory of information storage and retrieval, strings, pointers, relational structures; paradigms in programming – computation, data transform, process and rule-based; introduction to artificial intelligence.

This part of the program may take, in total, about four weeks – with one caveat; for groups having little or no background in mathematics, the element for discrete mathematics may have to be extended.

A3. Software engineering. Definitions, and a basic life cycle model; specification and practice in doing it; outline design and prototypes; software specification and design, introduction to – and practice in – design procedures and notations; the principles of 'good' design (Constantine and Myers, Parnas and others); implementation, in-

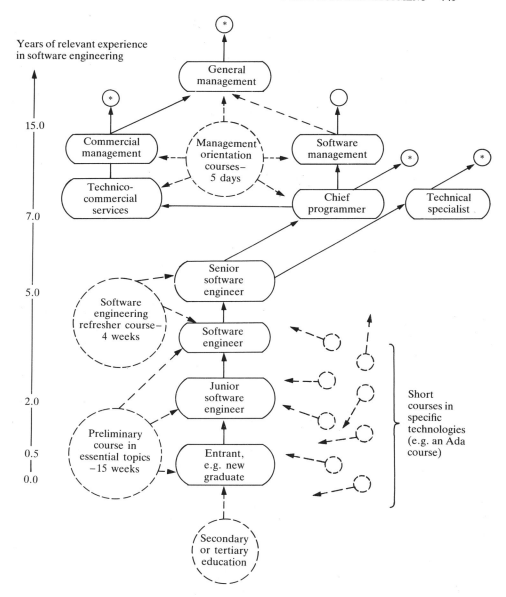

FIGURE 13.14 Educating software engineers and their managers.

cluding PSEs, 'good' programming practice and deliverable documentation; testing and demonstration.

A practical covering the complete life cycle should be done. A typical instance of such a practical is the chess example used as a vehicle in Part II. The user-level and functional specifications are set out in Chapter 5, and a consolidated 'worked example', comprising extracts from an archive, is given in Appendix 1. Another such practical may be found in a previous work by this author (Macro and Buxton 1987).

This part of the program may take, in total, about six weeks.

A4. Management. Archiving; structured walkthrough; change control; estimating; task planning and control; organization structures, teams, the CPT and its 'methods' (e.g. review/reading); quality definitions, VV&C, QC/QI/QA, quality plans and methods; contracting and purchasing issues; issues in 'literacy' and communication.

This part of the program takes little time (days) to explain, and can be practiced as part of the 'software engineering' module by interleaving the two.

This curriculum represents a short program – maximum fifteen weeks – for first time employees in software engineering. Most often, these will be people who are joining their first employer anyway.

It is advisable to put this sort of course on at the outset of the association – say as part of a several weeks' induction program – during which any technical or product specializations may be introduced as well. The first and third/fourth parts of such a course should each be continuous, but not necessarily contiguous with the next, in time; the second part may be modular lectures. The total course duration may be reduced therefore to about twelve weeks.

As can be seen, neither the computer science component, nor that for software engineering (together about 75 percent of the total), represent anything like the full curriculum for a degree course taking two to three years to complete.

It can be argued that entrants already having a degree-level qualification may be excused the initial course. For graduates having read for a degree in computer science with software engineering, or in software engineering itself (*pace* the earlier comment on such things), it may be the case that the short course is largely, or totally redundant. However, for normative purposes in staff orientation, and the teamwork aspects of much of the course (50–60 percent of total course hours being allocated for practical work), it is probably best to assign all new entrants for software engineering work to such a course – whether they are new to the subject, or not.

Equally, some existing 'amateur programmers' and software engineers may benefit from an education exercise of this sort. However, one major problem will intrude, and another may appear. As has been pointed out, it may be difficult to release software staff *in situ*, for courses of other than a few days' duration. Current work-schedules usually prevent it and, given the commonly prevailing problems of staffing in this sector, there is often little or no 'slack' between job assignments; in fact, in many cases, there is negative 'slack' – people are required on their next task before they complete the present one. This makes all forms of continuing education difficult once the real employment has begun. Releasing staff from assignments is by far the largest cost-component is software engineering education – far larger than costs of mounting and running courses.

The other potential problem for already active software development staff is that, whilst they undoubtedly need to consolidate their empirical experience into a useful and usable framework of practice – for which the defined course would be ideal in some respects – much of the mathematical material in the computer science module may well be beyond them.

This is by no means a disqualification for a career in software engineering; many of the best software engineers I have met have only a dim memory of a few aspects of discrete mathematics done at high-school level, such as simultaneous equations, differentiation and integration, and so forth. For that reason, as well as a judicious use of Occam's razor, the computer science component of the curriculum is kept to a minimum of necessary and sufficient material. Once again, it is prudent to warn that this view may find disfavor with some computer scientists.

However, the time has come for us to move on to the more pressing matters of continuing education in general for this subject.

SPECIFICS IN CONTINUING EDUCATION

Continuing education is essential in software engineering, with a rationally structured program and a personnel management 'culture' conducive to it. Otherwise one is, by default, left with the prospect of education by empirical means, which is haphazard, slow on some occasions, and potentially very costly to all parties.

Oscar Wilde wrote that 'experience is the name given to our mistakes', and that is nowhere more true than in software engineering. In this respect there is a value, up to a point, in empirically gained experience. One cannot learn to ride a bicycle, to swim, to play cricket and so on, by reading a book on the subject, or attending a course of lectures. The 'theory' is no substitute for the practice. So too in software engineering. That is not to say that 'theory' is unnecessary; for example, some grasp of the basic principles of computer science is highly *desirable* for a career in software engineering.

Alongside the questions of primary-skill education courses for software engineers, at an early stage of their career development, is the problem to consider of people in management positions and other vocational areas whose need to know about software engineering is acute. In the following part of this section we will discuss and define three courses in continuing education.

The first (B) concerns the *consolidation* of primary-skill education for software engineers, and is based on the premise that aspiring practitioners have had the short preparatory course in the subject-matter (c. twelve to fifteen weeks), then one to two years' 'apprenticeship' within a good 'chief programmer team' structure.

The other courses discussed and defined here (C and D) concern different levels of education, as required for manager's *orientation* and *secondary-skill* education for other technicians who need to deal with software engineering.

(B) Primary-skill: consolidation course. The contents of a consolidation course are really rather obvious for, in most cases, the apprenticeship period will have highlighted a set of problem areas for practitioners, with a surprisingly high degree of commonality. The most commonly occurring requirements at this stage are for methods (or further experience) in design, a chance to exercise quality practices and an opportunity to use

management planning and control methods. In fact, after the apprenticeship, practitioners are like amateur programmers who know far more about their defects and shortcomings in real software engineering – and wish to remedy them.

A consolidation course should comprise the following elements simply:

B1. Design as the central feature of software development. Detailed treatment of design criteria, approaches to 'good' design, and a selected set of design methods and notations – e.g. SADT, data flow and JSD; Mascot, CCITT-SDL and De Wolf's approach; Petrinets; BS 6224 DSD and pseudo-code. The use of prototypes in design should be practiced.

B2. Quality as the overriding objective. Determination of compliance and modifiability. Use of formal means and program proving, as useful methods in static testing at the coding stage. Quality plans, QC/QI/QA techniques. Deliverable documentation as the static representation of software.

B3. Management. Estimating and quality planning particularly. All aspects of team working and organization of independent quality activities.

B4. Team-based practical work to consolidate the previous three modules. This should take the form of a QA/new version exercise on a not-so-small system, about 5K source statements, say.

The whole of this should take about four weeks of full-time endeavor. Of the total course hours, some 70 percent will be spent on the practical exercise, if such a course is to achieve its aim – which is to provide an environment in which new or relatively unpracticed approaches may be worked out in a realistic fashion. As for the preliminary course, access to a good, present-day PSE is essential for this. Unlike the preliminary course, the duration of this course cannot be shortened, nor can it be made discontinuous without undermining the practical basis.

We have now defined the wherewithal for software engineers' ('practitioners') primary-skill education:

1. Aptitude and preferred attributes, as best determined.
2. A preparation course – defined in (A) above.
3. An apprenticeship, such as in a peer-group chief programmer team, for one to two years.
4. A consolidation course – defined in (B) above.

However, that is not the whole of the picture.

Especial care must be taken that the need for continuing education is not seen as confined to software engineers only. Many people may 'add value' – or, more likely perhaps, subtract it – from software development. The obvious examples are some managers who either refrain altogether from their calling, or could well be wished to have done so, any salespersons who contract not wisely yet too well, practitioners in quality departments who could not recognize lack of quality in software if it had set the room on fire, and technicians with other vocational expertise who develop contiguous parts of a composite system – and tend to sequestrate themselves to do so.

Any and all of these people, and others such as clients, personnel officers and people purchasing software systems, may adversely affect software development.

Merely educating (or retraining) software engineers may not be enough. The saddest thing of all to find is a company in deep and dire straits in its software developments, and with a mute incomprehension at all levels about what to do. Even when blames is not flying around like arrows in an old Western film, there is a spirit of uneasy reproach in the air – perhaps unassigned, but ready to affix itself to any suitable target.

The second saddest thing to find is a company in which the managers, aided and abetted by 'others' such as the personnel officer, see the problem in too simplistic terms: 'Put the programmers on that four weeks' course if we have to – although it's damned expensive I must say! Why can't we get them already educated from college?'

It is true that the ham in the sandwich might be the most likely source in a case of botulism, but it may not be the only tainted part, nor that most virulently infected.

The education needs of 'other' populations may be seen in terms of two curricula for courses that would supply the large part of requirements:

1. An orientation course for management level staff, and other non-specialists in software development.
2. A secondary-skill education course for technicians from other vocational sectors, who will be likely to participate with software engineers in the development of composite systems. In fact, this population produces a high degree of 'amateur programmers' if one is not careful.

We now describe each of these courses.

(C) An orientation course. An orientation course for managers must face several problems if it is to be effective. It must be very short in duration for, otherwise, it may be inferred that 'managers' attending it can be easily spared from their tasks – and that is not a happy inference. It must be practical, so far as possible, so that the accusation 'just theory' is avoided; there will be limits other than time on one's ability to make it practical – e.g. understandable limits amongst participants to comprehend some technical issues. A viable approach is to structure such a curriculum as follows:

C1. Definitions. Some rather fundamental material is needed to overcome terminological difficulties; elementary descriptions of computer systems – hardware and how it works, programs and programming, software and how (if) it works.

  The basic issues in software quality must be defined and explained.
C2. Limited practice in programming. Introduction should be made to a simple, high level language; coding and debugging simple examples (in, e.g., Basic) on a PC. This is more to overcome phobias and inhibitions than to teach anything, although some hobbyists may be made in the process.
C3. Software engineering definitions and a life cycle model of the process. There should be a stagewise description of software development based on this life cycle model, and an exercise in the early 'above the line' activities, such as functional specification (from an ill-conditioned user requirements' specification), outline systems design and task estimating. Examples of such 'ill-conditioned' requirements' specifications will be

found in Volume 2 of this series – but many IT product development companies will have an abundant source of their own.

C4. Key lectures in software management. Emphasis must be placed on the quality of specification and the quality of design, and on estimating technical quality of the solution, and management techniques for software development.

The duration of such a program is about eight days, and these should be as sequential working days if the proper benefit is to accrue.

Now, the stock attitude found in most business enterprises is: 'I could just about get away/be spared from my harrowing but immensely important management (or other) tasks for half a day/one day/two or three days at the absolute maximum. But eight days? You clearly can't be a manager/sales operative/quality officer/whatever else, to suggest such pop-eyed nonsense.'

Of course there is no real answer to that. If you go to the doctor, and he tells you a month in hospital is essential or you will die in two, you may elect to ignore the advice; then, whatever ailment is in you will follow its destined course.

This attitude to orientation in a crucial subject frequently pervades a whole company's mentality concerning continuing education and vocational training. The managers who cannot possibly spare more than a miniscule time to equip themselves for a fundamentally important part of their task, often also divide the necessary quantity of education for their software staff by a large and arbitrary amount. Thus, a twelve to fifteen weeks' preliminary education becomes a grudging one or two weeks – with no reference whatsoever to necessity.

There is a highly illustrative parallel to this from the world of opera. In the early 1930s, the management at the Metropolitan Opera House in New York offered the tenor Gigli a new contract for less money than before. Those were the recession years, and some belt-tightening was called for. Now Signor Gigli had neither the inclination nor physique for belt-tighening. His response was strictly operatic. 'You want-a cheapo?' he is reported to have cried, in A-flat. 'There is Mr Lauri-Volpi down the road [another tenor]. Go to him. They tell me he is cheap.'

Just so in software engineering; if one wants 'cheap', one gets 'cheap' – and often worse into the bargain. At least the incomparable Gigli recommended another tenor in the same genre; he did not nominate Signor Pinza, the bass, nor Madame Ponselle, a soprano. In software engineering education you cannot get x percent of a course in the subject just because that is the time available to your staff. Half a software engineering course is usually no software engineering course at all, but 100 percent of something else entirely.

(D) A secondary-skill course for other technicians. 'Contiguous' populations, such as electronic engineers, process engineers and so forth, have no such inhibitions. Time is not usually an excuse here, in fact many hardware practitioners who are, perforce, amateur programmers are only too glad of a chance to become 'intermittent software engineers'.

However, this good news is not often enough celebrated by actual attendance at courses of the right type. Once again, the pernicious attitude within the culture of some firms stands as the inhibiting factor, where software engineering is concerned. It is as though the office walls echo an attavistic refrain: 'Why can't people come already equipped in it?'

'Because the schools and universities cannot teach a subject that must be learned by experience, nor can they enable the acquisition of that experience to a sufficiently useful level' is the answer.

A course for 'contiguous populations' would comprise the following elements, preferably in this order:

D1. Introduction to modern programming languages (Ada, Modula-2, Pascal, C), and their advantages and drawbacks. Practice in two of these (say Modula-2 and C). Modern programming support environments, including the use of one such.
D2. Software engineering. Definitions and a life cycle model. Detailed exposition of key stages; specification; OSD/feasibility; design; implementation and testing. Deliverable documentation as a part of software (a representation of its static state). Practice in specification, outline systems design and estimating.
D3. Software management. Issues in estimating, visibility and control. Task planning and team management. Software quality; definitions, methods and practices.
D4. Design and implementation approaches put into practice. Short practical endeavors to exercise 'good' design and programming.

The duration of this course is about three weeks, the second and third elements being done in one week, and the first and fourth each requiring the same time. In this case, the whole course may be seen as three quite distinct modules, which may be presented with some interregnum between each – but this hiatus should not be too long in each case, four to six weeks being maximal.

We have now defined a set of education courses for primary-skill, secondary-skill and orientation purposes. Some of the material is clearly common between them all, and a 'core curriculum' could easily by established. It would basically include the software definitions; the life cycle model and detailed explanation of stages such as specification, feasibility, design and implementation; and software management approaches, particularly for estimating and technical quality.

It is appropriate that we see matters in this light. Not only is software development often inhibited by all the factors listed so extensively elsewhere in this work, but sometimes there is a lack of any possible communication between people merely because a serviceable and shared vocabulary is lacking. A 'core curriculum' of the sort suggested should reduce that tendency, if not obviate it entirely.

SOME NOTABLE EXAMPLES OF MISFIT IN SOFTWARE EDUCATION
If anyone doubts the disarray in which we find ourselves, a recent symposium ('workshop') on the whole question, and its contemporary answers, reveals a rich assortment of views (Gibbs and Fairly 1987). It would be tendentious to belabor the stark differences emerging from this work, but it is clear that two quite separate issues are at question which, with their mutual connection, make three questions in all:

1. Whither computer science education?
2. Whither software engineering education?
3. How should either one affect the other?

My opinions are already clear. To recapitulate them, computer science teaching is a

very useful preparation in part for a career in software engineering, and its research should produce means and methods for adoption – not prescription; if they are worthwhile they will be adopted. Furthermore, computer science equips its students to operate in the more mathematical areas of application; this fact should be seen clearly – the mathematics part of a computer science degree has far more relevance to an area of application, and to computer science research, than it does to software engineering.

Software engineering education is a matter for continuing education, of the short-course type, where 'continuing' has the rather special meaning that a first employment in the subject should begin by 'continuing', so to speak, through a preparatory course. In this sense, the term 'commencing, and continuing education' may be better employed. The 'commencing' education should include some computer science, on precisely the same grounds as an education in chemical engineering should include a grasp of thermo-dynamics – if only to stop pop-eyed enthusiasts from trying to invent perpetual motion, or periodically rediscovering steam.

The sources of computer science teaching and research are obvious – at least in most countries; they are schools, polytechnics and universities. This is fine so long as govern-ments do not conflate computer science with software engineering and say, in effect, 'If we need n times more software engineers, we will have to amplify the computer science sources by, er, n'. That is, as they say, a *non sequitur*.

Government attention can be a source of discomfort to the academic community. The temptation to compound a politician's innocence of the issue must be immense – parti-cularly when funding is involved. And what about the perplexity of the poor politician? Ask specimen X what the answer is – 'Computer science'; ask specimen Y the same ques-tion – 'Not computer science'. The matter becomes like a virulent theological argument going on in front of a visitor from Mars. Well may it scratch its heads in bemusement 'while words of learned length and thundering sound, amaze the gazing rustics gathered round.'

The sources of software engineering education present little cause for confusion, as they are virtually non-existent. Computer science plus a dollop of software development (done in an academic environment) is not software engineering education in this author's view. Neither are ultra-short programs of lectures – two or three days at most – in topics such as 'estimating', 'quality', 'software management' and so forth; nor are training courses in specific techniques such as design methods, or programming languages, etc.

In fact there is a distinct danger that these latter, usually short, courses, are substituted in managers' minds for the real thing. 'Better to give the chaps a few of these courses – only cost ten days or so – than all those weeks of commencing and continuing education'. The allure of this view is clear. The firm is investing in education, isn't it? Its seductive appeal is amplified by the fact that there are few, if any, external sources of continuing education is software engineering. Very large firms in the electronics and IT product sector may afford an internal program, and have the numbers of staff entrants and *in situ* practi-tioners to justify it. But what of the rest, the not so large enterprises? To whom or what do they turn?

The simple fact of the matter is that we are articulating past, present and future needs of a most acute nature and degree, and that the remedy lies not in the present but in the future also. And the remedy – provision and use of sources of continuing education in software engineering – is contingent on our overcoming the misconceptions detailed in this section. Simply stated, the conclusions are as follows:

1. Empirical 'education' for software engineering is, on its own, extremely costly, in direct and indirect terms.
2. Computer science teaching helps in a part, but not with the whole of software engineering education. However, it does equip one for work in a particular application area.
3. Software engineering is not really a suitable subject for academic courses because of the peculiarities of its highly practical nature. These peculiarities include that practicals must be significant, team-based enterprises. Otherwise they are worthless. Furthermore they must be the vehicles for a variety of management and technical approaches to be tried, not just the 'standard' engineering methods as in other subjects.

   Some endeavors, such as the 'software hut' approach in the USA, have recognized this fact, and provide 'project courses' usually less in length than a full academic degree course, and almost entirely based on practical work.
4. Effective software engineering education should be phased, and related to the experience-level of its participants. In other words there is not a single course.
5. Other levels of software engineering education than primary-skill education in the subject are needed for management and the 'continguous populations' referred to earlier.
6. Managers, particularly, must face the oldest of business realities. If you buy cheap, you get cheap. There is no such thing as a free lunch or a free education in software engineering.
7. Governments must stop throwing money at the wrong issue, and then abuse it when it fails.

That list probably sets a world record in feather-ruffling, so it is best to pass on to other – no less exciting – topics.

13.5 PROCUREMENT OF SOFTWARE SERVICES AND SYSTEMS

Two major management questions, in many firms, concern how best to secure competent software services and how competently to procure software systems. We will consider each of these in turn.

13.5.1 Contracting for software services

Most companies doing software development, for whatever reasons, need additional resources at some stage. In one case, a technical specialism may be missing in the firm, and yet urgently needed. Alternatively, a general shortfall in software engineering staff may be the case.

For whatever reason, the call goes out: 'Find a software house. Contract six senior programmers (or two data-base specialists, or whatever).' What results may be a competent service, competently contracted. Or it may not.

There are a few, simple guidelines to follow; the rest lies in the ability of the contracting party to apply them:

1. One should investigate the *real* need most carefully (as in the case of recruiting) before proceeding. Often a request for six senior programmers masks a real requirement for a couple of very experienced chief programmers – but the software manager may have his/her own capabilities exposed in the presence of such real experience.
2. One should decide, in advance, which of two contractual approaches is appropriate – that of the relatively informal 'time and materials' type, or the more formal 'fixed price and time-scale' supply. These are described further below.
3. One should have a list of approved suppliers. If you have never done this sort of thing before, there will have to be some preliminary research and evaluation of possible suppliers. This is usually fairly easily effected; there are lists of supplier companies available through local computer societies, in the trade-press, and so on. Also, there is much 'word of mouth' advice available from other user companies, banks and financial advisors. One must be careful, however, to seek 'horses for courses' in the sense of fit with any specialist requirements; it is useless to seek a database specialist from a source of computer-aided engineering services.
4. One should interview all staff on offer for time and materials supply, or to be contracted under fixed price terms. The form of these interviews is in no ways different from those in recruiting – except that employment terms are not (or should not) be at issue. It is bad practice to recruit a supplier's staff – and even worse vice versa.

The *time and materials* supply is quickly described. It is informal, in the sense that only a rudimentary job or staff-type specification is defined, the arrangement may be highly flexible in the sense of duration, and the contract form is exceedingly simple. A description of this is definitive of this type of supply:

1. A simple, letter contract from client to supplier is usually sufficient.
2. The 'contract' should begin by defining the task or people's attributes in outline at least. It should then contain:
   (a) a definition of duration of assignment for each assignee;
   (b) a definition of fee rates and any additional expenses or taxes, for each assignee;
   (c) a definition of working conditions, hours etc.;
   (d) a definition of notice to terminate; client's rights and, co-laterally, those of the supplier and supplier's staff on assignment;
   (e) a definition of notice to terminate; client's rights and obligations; supplier's right and obligations;
   (f) any special conditions; for example, details of secrecy, need to travel, need to represent client, etc.;
   (g) invoicing mechanism and payment terms.

The obviously missing components in this type of supply concern quality (in the economic and technical senses) and liability for failure in quality. It is impossible to incorporate such notions in a supply where assignees will be working in mixed teams and under client's management. For these reasons, and a general tendency to too much informality in the supply (easy come, easy go), the practice is known, detrimentally, as 'bodyshopping'. Indeed, it is a fact that contracting staff on a T & M basis can lead to a marked diminution

in quality control, and in the pre-eminence of quality as an objective, within the supplier company, and one can easily see why. Fred is on contract to the Lead Balloons Corporation; it's their job to make him run – isn't it? The best tip to give for choosing a T & M supplier is to select a company that has a strong track-record in fixed price supply. That, at least, should indicate something about their general approach to management and quality issues, and the caliber of their staff, although it is not a specific for selecting a T & M supplier – after all, the firm may be about to go into liquidation through one of its fixed price contracts.

Fixed price contracting is a far more formidable exercise altogether. In fact it is one in which a qualified lawyer is required by each side, to ensure the equity and feasibility of the contractual arrangements. Both of these are important as points of departure in this sort of supply. It is asking for trouble to have inequitable contracts in either direction – too much supplier interest, or too much of client's rights; equally, it is not only fatuous but perilous to enter into a mutual, formal arrangement whose terms are not licit under the law operating.

There are three mandatory prerequisites to contracting for fixed price supply:

1. Ensure a competent supplier, whose company is financially stable.
2. Ensure that a detailed task description exists, and detailed/plausible estimates of time-scale and effort for the supplier to complete the job.

   These are best achieved by the supplier-to-be completing a functional specification, outline systems design and estimating exercise, possibly all under the cover of a T & M contract of supply. Needless to say, the functional specification will have to be 'signed off' by the client company.
3. Ensure that a competent contract is drawn up – one that is equitable and feasible.

In this case, it is much more important to have a shortlist of approved suppliers than in the case of T & M arrangements. In fact, it is the practice to request tenders from several possible sources, and to select a supplier from them.

This procedure is described further in Section 13.5.2, for software system procurement. Even if potential supplier X produces the functional specification (under T & M supply perhaps), this multi-tendering approach may be used. 'Company X' may be prevented from bidding, by prior agreement, or may be permitted. Obviously, they hold the inside track, so to speak. But it is also surprising how often other company's offers are more impressive.

A useful device is, then, to contract 'company Y' for the supply and 'company X' as management and quality consultants.

The contractual headings for fixed price and time-scale supply, are usually of the types shown in Table 13.8. There is little need to comment further on this list, as most of the headings are reasonably self-explanatory. However, one further word of caution is in order. It concerns the appropriately numbered clause XIII – cancellation.

There are, in fact, four possible circumstances. The client may seek to cancel the contract and supply with, or without, asserting the supplier's fault; or the supplier might seek to cancel the contract and supply with, or without, asserting the client's fault. Clearly, the matters of recompense and damage attach only to two of these – the circumstances in which one party's fault is asserted. The stated consequences are usually a fine of some defined amount. This must be set out, equitably, in the contract. Also, it must be deter-

TABLE 13.8 Categories for a formal, fixed price contract or supply

I	Scope of agreement (legal statement of intent and definition of parties).
II	Statement of supply, e.g. an accurate, generic description plus reference to appended functional specification.
III	Definition of total fixed price, including expenses, fees and taxes; definition of entire time-scale to deliver.
IV	Definition of any other costs accruing to client, i.e. for other necessary purchases for this supply. Statement of property of such.
V	Detail of supplier's price under (III), and definition of client's payment schedule and method.
VI	Specific obligations of the client, e.g. to enable supplier's work and delivery.
VII	Specific obligations of the supplier, e.g. to enable client's overview of work in progress.
VIII	Definition of quality and acceptance procedures.
IX	Definitions of certification and warranty period; definition of maintenance responsibility.
X	Definitions of risks and liabilities – damage to system or other equipment during the supply, third party liability, infringement of third party's rights.
XI	Property; who owns what; further exploitation.
XII	Secrecy/confidentiality. Publicity.
XIII	Cancellation. Allowable causes of cancellation, and consequences thereof.
XIV	Non-competition.
XV	*Force majeure.*
XVI	Settlement of dispute, and arbitration means.
XVII	Procedures for varying contract terms covered under I–XVII inclusive. Detail for each heading.
XVIII	Law applying.
XIX	Entire agreement; inclusion of appendices as follows:
A	Functional specification and software definition.
B	Activities' plan showing main milestones and deliverables, review points and payment schedule.
C	Management structures and procedures definition, including change control.
D	Documentation standards.
E	Quality assurance procedures, and acceptance trial schedules and procedures.

mined sensibly. A client contracting for fixed price and time-scale supply of a crucial part of some product with a $100 million worldwide sales potential, may choose a company with a gross annual income of $10 million to do a task of contract value $1 million. Obviously, if it really is a crucial component then the contract is perilous from the outset but, if it has to be thus, there it is. What is nonsensical is to write a contract stipulating liquidated damages of $100 million, for failure, against the $10 million company. Damages of $1 million would probably wipe it out.

The object of the exercise is not to underwrite the contingent risks in this way, but to recover some reasonable recompense in the case of failure to supply; another aim is to provide the supplier with a clear incentive not to fail. In our example, there is no sense in nominating any amount above $1 million; the rest is over-kill.

13.5.2 Procurement of software systems

We take, as our starting point in this discussion, the purchase of non-trivial software systems already developed by product suppliers. Most of the remarks to follow will not apply to small scale purchases – such as a $50 software system from a catalog. We will consider the procurement of large and costly software systems, by purchase or rental. It is not sensible to quantify 'large', because such matters are relative to the puchaser's capacity

to some extent, but anything over $10,000 (outright cost, or annual rental price) might qualify in most cases.

There are several kinds of 'worst thing' to avoid in the practice of software procurement, and we will get some of them out of the way immediately.

1. Beware the hobbyist technicians' zeal, within your own company, for some new 'wonder package', and their impetuosity to get it. It may not fit any real requirement, nor be cost-effective, nor properly supported, nor properly contracted. Its creators may be a fly-by-night outfit, who have flown by night.
2. Beware the salesperson's zeal. Here the old axiom of *caveat emptor* – let the buyer beware – applies. The collision between a fast moving hobbyist and a salesperson with a quota to meet is usually a nasty sight.
3. Beware all other species of urgency. As in software development there should be concepts of quality in procurement, and a 'comfortable time-scale' in which to do it.

Clearly, the correct course of action for procuring a major software system is to condition the requirement definition and supply process, sufficiently. Some guidelines for this may be listed, as follows (always assuming that the purchaser is in a position, i.e. competent, to undertake them):

1. A company that may need software systems supplied, as developed packages, by contractors, should carry a list of approved suppliers in the likely areas of application. Once again, it is fruitless to expect (say) a CAD system from a supplier of computer languages, and vice versa.

   Thus, the commercial, purchasing or legal department should initiate the definition of application sectors, and the research necessary to find and evaluate suppliers of software packages as appropriate.
2. Companies should have a clear procurement procedure as the necessary condition for authority to proceed at any stage of a procurement action. This is described further, piecemeal, in the following text; it should be consolidated into a company's procurement procedure, to fit with 'cultural' aspects of behavior in these matters.
3. A procurement team should be constituted at the outset, comprising user representatives, software specialists and contracting specialists, which should then operate the procedures.
4. Before any procurement action commences toward potential suppliers, a statement of requirements must be drawn up. This is analogous to a functional specification in software development. It must involve users of the system-to-be, who may (or may not) be software specialists. In the case where users, e.g. for a CAD system, are not software specialists, then some software engineering competence must be ensured within the specification team.
5. When the requirement specification is ready, a price range should be set – based on several criteria. The cost–benefit exercises should be done on the basis of several possible price ranges. Furthermore, a 'fair price' may be roughly estimated by having competent software staff perform estimates to develop the system required. If this is, say, circa $1 million, and if a supplier is offering outright sale of a package for $2 million, we may construe that an unfair price is being levied – either to amortize development costs over one sale, or to make a robber's profit over several.

6. A procurement action can then commence, with potential suppliers being asked to offer their technical system, and for its support and enhancement, training, etc.; and to detail all commercial and legal factors pertaining from their side.

   The results should be evaluated by the procurement team (n.b. not just one part of the team such as users, or software specialists).
7. Technical evaluation should be done as for software quality in general; the compliance against requirements must be demonstrated, although less than 100 percent 'fit' may be acceptable (there may be too many features of some kind, and too few of another); the dynamic reliability (= modifiability) must also be assessed. this is dealt with further below, as it invariably causes trouble.
8. The questions of continuance in support and meaningful guarantees of this continuance, must be clarified. This, too, is dealt with below.

Two matters of procurement practice cause especial trouble in almost all cases. They are risk assessment by the purchaser concerning the reliability of the software; and determining a meaningful escrow for guarantee of ongoing software support, maintenance and (if required) software improvement. Incidentally an escrow is a valuable property (often, but not always, money), deposited as a guarantee of some performance or other.

Reliability and escrow are the terrible twins of the software package business. The reasons for this are clear. A part of the purchaser's obligation and entitlement to establish, through investigation and (perhaps) trial, the technical quality of a software package, involves the sort of white-box, quality assurance investigation described in Chapter 9. Yet, not only are suppliers understandably leery of letting anyone look into or dabble with their software, they are even chary of exposing its 'deliverable documentation' to view. The arguments are plausible and seemingly irrefutable; they concern commercial advantage, possible plagiarism and theft of software.

Behind this barricade of reason lurks the specter of incompetent software engineering within the product. It *looks* all right; it *seems* to work all right; but what if it is – in reality – a rat's nest construction, thrown together by Fred and his happy band of amateurs from East Orange?

Caveat emptor! But how? The law of supply seems built around a different precept altogether – *caveat vendor*, or something, 'let the seller beware'. Could you imagine a manufacturer of computer equipment letting you do white-box tests on its operating system software? No, neither could I.

The problem of escrow against ongoing support, maintenance and enhancement is another problem. Here, the question is what – other than money – might serve as an escrow object? Not that money is much use in many cases anyway. If your firm's operation depends upon the software, mere money is no substitute. You need the software.

Often, a code listing is offered as escrow, to be lodged with a third party to prevent copying. Is that any use? As we have seen elsewhere, a code listing on its own is not the slightest use and, in fact, has little or no value. What might have value is the full deliverable documentation set, all manuals of it, as defined in Section 13.1.3.

But here we meet the former problem again. Who is to assess the value of the escrowed object (documentation), and how are they to do it if the supplier hides behind the barricade of commercial confidentiality again?

Purchasing officers of the world unite! Every claim of commercial confidentiality may be, and probably is, hiding the most startling tripe, all of it on sale to you at the most exemplary price. There is no earthly reason, in logic, why the fear of plagiarism should have the force it does in this argument. Software reliability, and the quality of its documentation, can be established by sampling, and fairly brief inspections and trials on the supplier's premises; neither programs nor documentation need be placed in a position where plagiarism is a possibility.

I can take the back off my television set, and stare at its innards until mine ache with the effort, and my eyeballs are lying like boiled oysters on my upper cheeks. I can inspect in some detail the car I am about to buy, or read the descriptive manuals until the effort paralyzes me. But not for software products. Why? Because familiarity might put me off. Should we not be put off anyway?

With these limitations, which can be circumvented if a purchaser has enough 'muscle' in terms of potential future opportunities for sales to it, the evaluation of suppliers' offers should proceed in a well conditioned way by the procurement team. A useful technique in this is the 'weighted evaluation tree' approach. This is an orderly method to categorize suppliers' information, and to score it on a weighted basis to reflect the relative importance of a category. Figures 13.15 and 13.16 depict such an approach for a fixed-price software development, offers for which were solicited by an invitation to tender.

The procurement team should define such a scheme, for its own use, before the procurement action towards bidders begins. Then, different specialists in the group (technical, commercial, user, legal) can evaluate and score their part of submissions. However, simple though it is, such a scheme often comes as a revelation to many procurement officers in companies whose history in acquiring systems should have caused them to invent similar approaches but – for some reason – has not. Thus, a short explanatory note on Figures 13.15 and 13.16 might be helpful here.

One begins by drawing up a basic 'tree' – rather like a software taxonomy – in which evaluation categories are progressively detailed. Figure 13.15, bare of its weights, would be such a first step although – in practice – far greater elaboration of categories, and detailing of them, might be incorporated. Then one assigns the weights to each level in the tree, depending on the relative importance of the category. This is best done 'top down' (left to right in Figure 13.15), to set the major issues in context at the outset. Thus, in the example shown, there may be a major dispute within the procurement team concerning the relative importance of 'technical' fit and its commercial counterpart; such fundamental issues are best met, head-on, early rather than when a procurement action is in process.

Figure 13.16 shows how the possible maximum scores, in each category, are assigned. To assign possible maximum scores in each category one may proceed 'top down' or 'bottom up'. For example, one could begin by allocating a maximum of (say) 1,000 points to the total ('Choice' in Figure 13.15), and proceed from left to right applying the weight assigned at each level; e.g., using Figure 13.15 values for weights, commercial = 500 and technical = 500, and so forth. That would be an assignment of maximum scores done 'top down', and a small drawback to this method is when one finds that the first choice (1,000 points) has led to some very small values lower down the tree that do not, then, form the basis for a reasonable scoring system at that level. Then one may have to backtrack, and multiply all maximum scores by (say) ten, or fifty, or whatever is needed.

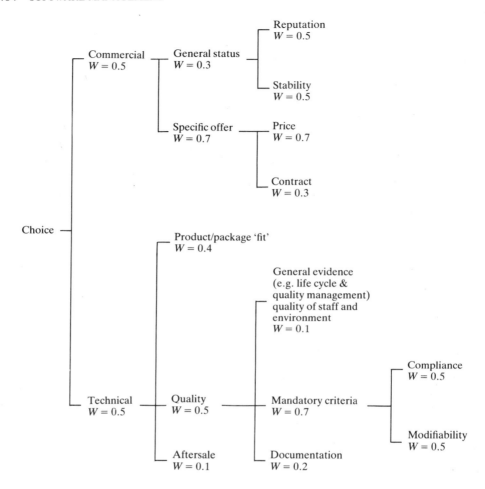

FIGURE 13.15 Example of a weighted 'evaluation tree' for use in software product procurement.

This is avoided when one starts 'bottom up', and assigns big enough maxima at the lowest levels – as depicted in Figure 13.16. In fact, as the figure shows, this approach is better described as bottom–top–bottom, for one starts at the lowest level of one limb of the tree, works to the top, and then descends the other limb. What may then occur (as is the case in the examples given) is that the total – i.e. at the level of 'Choice' in Figure 13.15 – may come out to be a rather strange number, in this case 1,140 points. However, this is easily overcome by expressing all real scores in a procurement as a percentage of the possible maximum score.

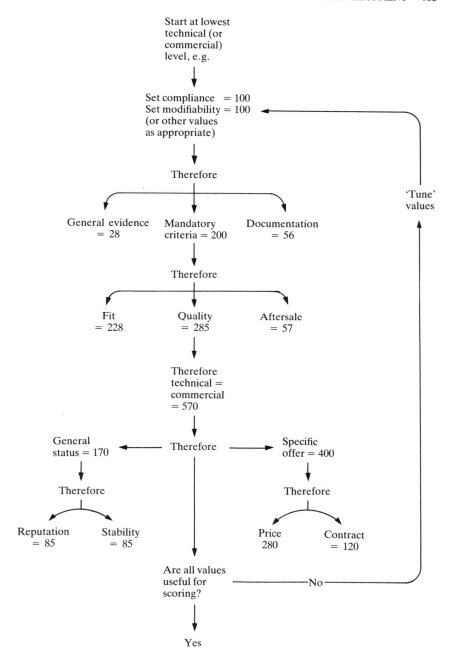

FIGURE 13.16 The process of assigning maximum possible scores to evaluation elements.

A third way is to work out the weights at each level, then allow scores out of 100 for any item at any level, before correcting it.

The sort of contention that may break out within a procurement team, comprising several different interest groups and sources of experties, is due to causes clearly depicted in Figure 13.16. Everything may proceed reasonably and equitably by progressing right to left along the lower branch of the Figure 13.15 'tree', and then left to right along the upper branch of it. However, at some stage, it will be noticed that the 'price' for the software package seems to be 1.4 times more important in the evaluation than the mandatory criteria of its quality!

When this kind of thing occurs, it may cause grave heart searching, head scratching, teeth clenching and even more robust pastimes such as head punching within the procurement team, until the relative weights attaching to categories and their maximum scores have been 'tuned' to everyone's satisfaction, or (the more likely case) to their minimal dissatisfaction. Then the procurement action, and the scoring of responses – each section scored by an 'expert' part of the procurement team – can proceed.

As to the final result, a simple rule should be set down and adhered to at all cost: if none of the suppliers reaches a critical score (which I would set at 85 percent of the possible maximum score), then there should be no winner, no procurement and no supply from any of these sources.

A second precept is that, given there are possible winners, always chose the one with the highest score, otherwise you are making a nonsense of the process. However obvious it sounds, I have seen it violated. On one occasion, a shortlist of six supplier companies were evaluated exhaustively and a clear winner emerged. Yet the contract was placed with the fourth in merit, who did not even pass the 75 percent let alone the 85 percent test. Why bother? Put the names in a hat and extract one at random, or contract your brother-in-law's aunt's boyfriend's company.

As to the legal issues of contracting for software systems as distinct from services, here again we enter the domain of contract law, with some niceties of the laws of tort, property and copyright thrown in.

It is beyond the scope of this, or any other, work to detail what must be different under all different legal systems. The subject is a rich field for lawyers (in more ways than one), and is best referred to them. We have inveighed against amateur programming, and amateur educationalists in software engineering; let us not fall into our own trap by becoming amateur (or, as they are often called, 'tap room') lawyers. Anyone seeking a wider definition of the issues is recommended to the several source works existing in this area, e.g. Wolk and Luddy (1986). As may be expected though, as is the case in many legal issues, law does not travel well between different countries, and most source books have national rather than general application. The quoted source is, for example, mainly American.

13.6 CODA

We know what Alice said about the dormouse's tale. This, too, has been a long one. It remains only, in this chapter, to answer a few outstanding questions, including the one we

began with at the start of this chapter. The question, all those pages ago, was: 'Is software engineering anything more, or less, than good management of software development?' The answer, of course, is that it is substantially more – the whole repertoire of technologies and techniques for specification, design, implementation and validation, that are the connectives to computer science teaching and (particularly) to computer science research. The point is (and this accounts for the potency of the question) that management is the heart, yet not the whole, of the matter, but defective management *might* easily become the whole of the *problem*.

The answer to whatever software crisis we perceive, or suppose, to exist will never come about through mere technology, whilst the subject underlying the process by which software is developed (software engineering) remains an unmanaged or badly managed field of endeavor.

And to manage software development, in all its aspects, requires a preliminary grasp of the subject – such as it is – of software engineering, and a clearer apprehension of the facts of life regarding software than is normally the case amongst managers and others in companies for which software is a crucial aspect of their business. This can be demonstrated by the question to any manager involved with software development: 'Could *you* evaluate the competence of the exponents and facilities at your disposal?'

13.6.1 Evaluating levels of competence

It should be possible, by now, for managers to evaluate the status of software engineering within their own company. A simple check-list method, as shown in Tables 13.9 and 13.10, should suffice. The examples given are, in this case, from a real company. Extracting the answers is a manager's task in most cases, but one may be extracting them by delegation to a competent software engineer as: (a) the questions might have to be explained and expanded, and (b) the answers might be implausible and require qualification if not justification.

These sources of information are highly revealing. Fairly typical representatives of each of three interview types are combined here, so as to highlight the dramatic differences. The actual people concerned were a young software engineer, about four years into her career in the subject (a graduate in modern languages incidentally), an electronic engineer *circa* 40 years old – perhaps the best product engineer in the firm and, finally, a senior member of the sales group, the 'client representative' for a major part (avionics) in the defense sector of this firm's repetoire, a man in his early 50s with a previous background in physics.

First of all, the education needs of the software engineer are dramatically clear, not least to the practitioner herself. However, she may be wrong in several respects. Sometimes a supposed inadequacy is revealed (to a more experienced person) as, actually, some considerable competence. 'I'm not very good at design' turns out to be a very competent, but unsure, designer. On the other hand, some capabilities might be overstated. 'Yes, I could do a software test strategy' turns out to be only partly true; the next one ends up as a bit of a mess. Still, this practitioner, like almost all others who are *en route* to being The Real Thing, recognizes a need for further improvement, and has the perspective to be self-

TABLE 13.9 Establishing past and present status in a company/division

Previous experience	Practitioners		General managers (and others)
	Software engineers	Amateur programmers	
1. When did you last work on a software task?	Ongoing	Last year	1973
2. What size was the software being developed (source)?	17.5K	0.5K	1K
3. What size was the part you did?	4.5K	0.5K	1K
4. What language was it written in?	Ada	Assembler	Fortran 2
5. Was it developed on a host for use elsewhere?	Yes	No	No
6. Was it an S, P or E type system?	E + P	?	?
7. Did it involve prototypes?	Yes	No	No
8. Was it for a product or project?	Product	Own project	Practice
9. Was the overall development small, medium, large?	Medium	Small	Small
10. Was it a team-based development?	Yes	No	No
11. Have you ever worked on a medium or large system?	Yes – both	No	No
12. Have you ever done a design review?	Not yet	No	No
13. Have you ever done a code reading?	Not yet	No	No
14. Name another language you have used other than in 4.	Pascal, C, Assembler	Basic,	— Assembler
15. Name a graphical design notation you have used.	Mascot, Petrinets		Flowcharts ?
16. Have you ever estimated a software task?	Yes (not well)	No	No
17. Has your software ever been quality assured?	No! – sadly	No	No
18. Have you ever done a beta-test (white-box)?	No	?	?
19. Have you ever quality-assured software documentation?	No, but mine has been	? Ha-ha	No

critical. The 'consolidation' course is called for or, if that is not seen to be sufficient, perhaps the 'preparation' course administered a bit late in the day.

Equally, the need for secondary-skill education of (at least) this product engineer is obvious if only to impress the facts of software-life on what might already be an amateur programmer, or one who tolerates that genus. A course for this purpose should place amateur practitioners in an exposed position, where their *modus operandi* is immediately evident and cannot be explained away behind a plethora of causes and reasons, and – let's face it – excuses. This is possibly the hardest species of education to undertake, from both sides. It is very difficult to enter into the spirit of things if you have an implied label round your metaphorical neck saying 'this chap is part of the problem', and you have put straight onto the tightrope – like Blondin above Niagara – without a balancing pole or a safety net. Reading down the list of this production engineer's answers, in Table 13.10, is a spine-chilling experience. Here is a man who will, almost certainly, find himself managing a composite development at some time – or may have already done so. The most devastating part is the answer to question 31.

The managers (and others) often have none of these inhibitions; theirs is not the reluctance to exposure, so much as a real (or supposed) inability to invest the time to

TABLE 13.10 Evaluating future potential in a company/division

Interest, potential and need	Practitioners		Gen. managers (and others)
	Software engineers	Amateur programmers	
20. Could you do a structured walkthrough?	Yes	?	No
21. Could you do a functional specification?	Have	No	Possible
22. Ditto software taxonomy?	? Yes	?	?
23. Ditto software estimates (±50% accuracy)?	Think so	Why?	No
24. Ditto software design review?	Yes	?	No
25. Ditto program code read (static test)?	Yes	Yes ?	No
26. Ditto software test strategy?	Yes	Yes ?	No
27. Ditto QA beta-test (Black-/white-box)?	? Yes	No	No
28. Ditto QA on deliverable documentation?	Yes	?	No
29. Could you assess software modifiability?	Doubt it	Why?	No
30. Could you define the PSE features your firm needs?	? Yes	?	No
31. Do you need further education in software engineering?	Yes !!	Possibly ??	Yes !!

follow a course in, when all is said and done, a specialist's subject. Our avionics representative, an ancient programmer as we can see, has cheerfully strung together an impressive sequence of negatives in answer to the questionnaire, and a suitably pleasing 'Yes!!' to the prospect of self-improvement. He will get on very well with the young software engineer – even better when they have both done some continuing education, in his case the orientation course (C) described earlier, with a common 'core curriculum'.

Both the senior and very junior operatives may have trouble with the chap in the middle; 40 is a tricky time of life when you are halfway up the greasy pole of management; admitting inadequacy can be the toughest part of your job, then.

13.6.2 The standards' issue revisited

How many of software engineering's problems would fall into the limbo of history if only we had a decent set of universal standards for it? In truth, not many, for that little qualification, 'if', stands in the way.

It is inconceivable that any 'universal standards' could encompass the whole subject, and the possible variants for so rich a variety of circumstances as may arise. Not, that is, without occupying several large rooms in a library.

The search for a global standards set for the generality of software applications is like the search for a philosopher's stone or the elixir of life – perfect in motivation, exciting in execution but somewhat less than likely of achievement. However, proto-chemistry and alchemy do not look so different now, at a distance of a few hundred years.

We must be clear about what are, and are not, suitable topics for standardization. The 'total approach' may be both futile and fatuous, but some partial approaches may be far from either. There are several categories to consider:

1. Management matters. What can, and what cannot, be 'standardized' for managing the software process? Here the answers are very clear; between companies, let alone across

geography, very little. Within companies, just about everything pertaining to managing software development may be (parochially) 'standardized'.

If Ipse development in future is successful enough, and its adoption widespread enough, then the electronic environment will provide the *de facto* standard, and violation of it may put all the lights out, set the sprinkler systems working (to drown a bit of common sense into Fred, no doubt), or lead to some other penalty for the lapse.

2. Technical, and quasi-technical matters. What can, and what cannot, be 'standardized' in the process of specification, design, implementation and validation? We have already seen that several domestic and international standards' agencies are (and have been for a long time) busy with matters in all these areas – and that of the proliferation of terminology too.

In fact, outside the implementation domain (PSE facilities, including languages), it is difficult to see how real standards can have any meaning. What is often conflated with the issue of standards for an object, such as a tool to make programs with, is the issue of guidelines for good practice. The more strongly these are enforced, the more they fall under the categorization of 'management matters' in 1 above.

Outside these areas – parochially expressed management standards, and those imposed by the PSE in use – it is folly to pretend that software engineering can be standardized at the present time. So poor are the developed means and approaches in some areas, such as specification and design, that one would hope that they remain unstandardized, if in standardizing them they were lent a spurious authenticity.

Another area of folly is to pretend that the object, as distinct from process, can have some quality rating affixed to it, based on a standard metric, objectively determined for a class of applications. We cannot rate somebody's operating system at 18.42 on a scale of values, and another at 0.67 on the same scale; there is no scale, and it is unlikely – in the nature of software quality – that there ever will be one.

In speaking of standards, then, we must be certain of what we are speaking as well as what we are saying. That which one can standardize, in the process or its outcome, parochially or otherwise, one may introduce standards for. Otherwise, one should emit guidelines for practice in the process, and helpful means for enhancing confidence in its outcome.

If that if the reality, it is not the subject's failure – nor any other sort of failure. It is the constraint we work under in software development.

EPILOG

It may be thought that this book is an essay in detraction because it fails to give a penny-in-the-slot exposition of software's problems, and an equally economic prescription for them. If so, that is an unavoidable effect.

As all its practitioners know, to their cost, software engineering is a tricky business – so evasive of definition and detail that one sometimes questions if it is a subject at all, or merely:

> Shape without form, shade without colour,
> Paralysed force, gesture without motion;
> > (Eliot: 'The hollow men')

My aim had been to introduce this tricky subject by facing its hard truths. But 'what is truth?' as the most famous handwasher in history asked. One may well enquire 'what is humor?', for without it, as an ingredient in the courses on software engineering that I have promoted, life would have been grim.

A subject without wit is a desolate affair. There is even room for mirth, they tell me, in mathematics, although the ill-named Wittgenstein tended to the lugubrious school. Still, one must not lose hope; I once knew a chap who claimed to have roared his head off through a Wagner opera. Five hours'-worth is a lot of joy. He must have seen the Laurel and Hardy version.

Solemnity and software are sad bedfellows, which is a shame when it happens – for it makes software engineering harder to learn, and software development less easy to do. We have all seen the most awful problems arise it the subject, and have watched poor practitioners, in all fields of endeavor, undergoing the most fearsome stress for a season and a time. Yet, whatever was to follow, a moment arrived when the helplessness and hopelessness dissolved in a small contagion of laughter. But for that redemption, software engineering would be a terrible thing to catch, and one would send flowers and grapes to its victims.

At the start we asked, rhetorically, whether the subject was a creature to be tamed, inferring otherwise by the form of the question. Then, before that zoological moment had fully passed, we described an approach to the problem of explaining software engineering as like fighting a grizzly bear – one could only jump up, grab at the loose fur and climb. Leaving the subject is no easier matter. One cannot declare a draw with the animal, take it

by the arm and go off to the pub for a drink. 'Put that bear down' is not a useful piece of advice if the brute is a slab of brisket twice your size, and half the weight of a locomotive engine. All one can do is to drop from its grasp and limp away at as high a speed as damaged limbs will sustain.

And if that gets the last laugh, have this one – like all the rest – on me.

PART FOUR

APPENDICES

APPENDIX 1

A CONSOLIDATED CASE STUDY

A WORKED EXAMPLE OF SOFTWARE MANAGEMENT, SHOWING EXTRACTS FROM DESIGN

Examples in the text have been harmonized, where possible, by using a common specification. That does not mean that they may be taken together as representative of work from a real development exercise, for their purpose is illustrative only. Further, the examples tend to illustrate specification and design methods more than software management, and this is inevitable across chapters of the text.

Here, we offer a consolidated example, based on exactly the same specification set out in Chapter 5, picking matters up (so to speak) at the outline system design stage, and proceeding into design, implementation and validation. Through all of this, the management aspects are traced, in particular those concerning estimates, activities' plans and quality functions.

Educators of software engineers are urged to use this as an example, or a paradigm for examples of other sorts, on their courses. Instruction and fun can be had, and the combination is an irresistible one. In the modest hope that this will happen, I salute both instructors and instructed, and hope that this worked example serves its purpose, and theirs.

1 EXPLANATION OF CONTENTS, CONTEXT AND METHOD

This worked example is set out in the following way:

1. Explanation
   1.1 context of the 'GAMBIT' application
   1.2 Method
2. Task definition for 'GAMBIT'
3. Extracts from a product development archive – GAMBIT
   3.1 Invitation to tender/user specification – see Example 1 in Chapter 5
   3.2 Functional specification – see Example 2 in Chapter 5
   3.3 Extracts from management archive – set (A): start and management methods
   3.4 Extracts from management archive – set (B): feasibility, plans and schedules
   3.5 Extracts from technical archive – set (C): design at top, intermediate and low levels

The worked example will first be introduced, by means of a brief summary of the context in which the problem was set, and then the method adopted for this worked example will be explained at more length than in the synopsis.

1.1 Context of the 'GAMBIT' application

The specification set out, as a URS first in Chapter 5, has been one of a set of such used as the practical 'backbone' for primary-skill education courses of the type described in Chapter 13. For any help that it might be to other purveyors of courses in this subject, this context is briefly described. It will also serve to show the rather terrible circumstances under which the work to be quoted was done.

The following points define this context:

1. Courses were thirty-five days in duration, continuous except for weekend days, and 'residential' – that is, held at a location distant from both work and domestic environments. Consequently, a 'working day' on the course was a flexible commodity, sometimes in the order of twice the normal duration – i.e. circa fourteen hours as distinct from the seven or so of normal working life.

2. Practicals, such as 'GAMBIT', were attempted by teams, usually made up of four people.

3. As the courses were, in effect, 'master classes' in software engineering, for junior practitioners as well as amateur programmers, teams showed a rich variety of experience-levels.

4. Attendees on courses had a wide variety of applications' experience, covering the three main paradigms defined earlier – computation, data processing, and process type systems. This showed conspicuously in attitudes to design, and language familiarity.

5. Work on a practical was done, in all cases, on a pseudo-contract basis, with the course principal acting as 'client'. This role involved specification, QI/contract management and QA beta-testing functions. Teams acted competitively, an element that was stressed by the 'client'. There was to be a clear 'winner'.

6. Teams arranged their time to work on practicals to be interwoven with a burden of lecture sessions and structured reading, with 'free-form' discussions on chosen topics as an added call on time. From that point of view, the course parted company with the real-life paradigm, and the burden of work was extreme. Nonetheless, high quality software was expected by the implacable 'client'.

7. Teams were required to practice the precepts they were learning, in lectures, con-

cerning 'good software engineering practice'. The contents of this book may be taken as representative of its modalities.

8. Facilities, such as project rooms, adequate PSE and access to it, and ordinary office facilities, were provided. The implementation language was Pascal, and familiarity with this language was achieved by pre-course reading, and lectures during the course.

We will return to this 'context' in Section 4, for a final comment on the education purpose being served by the 'GAMBIT' practical. In the meantime, a brief note on the method of presentation, for this consolidated example, is offered.

1.2 Method

If the context of 'GAMBIT' cannot be advertised as a paradigm for the circumstances under which software should be developed, being interwoven as an endeavor with tutorial activities and beset by exhaustion in the people, the practices employed and their outcome as software were representative of software development in real life. This is particularly true of the non-technical activities required of the implementation teams.

So, in viewing the following, it is not proper to think: 'Oh dear, it's not real. It was just part of role-playing on a course.' The role-playing aspect dropped from sight very quickly, and the endeavor became 'realer than real' to teams, a fact etched in every face by the time we were finished.

The following extracts are taken to highlight management interaction with software implementation teams. No one course from any one firm for which they were given has been raided for this material; it could have come from any one of a large number of sources; in a sense it came from them all.

The team comprised four young software people: Jane, Richard, James and Sarah:

1. Jane was 'chief programmer'; a graduate in mathematics with four years of software engineering experience, mainly developing software for computer aided design, using a SEL-32 computer and Fortran-77; she was about 26 years old at the time.
2. Richard was deputy chief programmer on the team; a non-graduate electrical engineer with about eight years of intermittent experience, such as in Basic for a PC-based engineering computation routine, and in assembler for embedded microcomputer systems (Rockwell hardware) for a 'domicile of the future' product development; age 37 years.
3. James was a junior software engineer; a graduate in music who, lacking employment in that sector, had done a programming course and, at this time, had just less than two years of experience developing Cobol and PL/1 programs on an IBM mainframe for a bank; age, 24 years.
4. Sarah was a graduate entrant, with a degree in computer science; her only implementation experience concerned small, numerical methods applications, written in Modula-2 on a Prime minicomputer; age 21 years.

The team kept an archive, and produced deliverable documentation. The following extracts are taken from these documents. No attempt has been made to make anything

better than it was, although the publisher's professional ethics stop short of replicating the exact state of archive documents – blood and beer-stained, and worse.

As already said, the emphasis is on the management aspects, but important extracts are also taken from design and quality section. What cannot be done is to give any meaningful selections from the code, as this amounted to c. 5,000 source statements of Pascal. Consequently, the archive was a bulky document in its hard-copy form, comprising two comfortably filled files of the ring-binder type. What follows is a 'red-thread' selection, to highlight the main points of this book.

2 TASK DEFINITION FOR 'GAMBIT'

The user requirement was set out in exactly the form given in Section 5.2 in Chapter 5. Some 'bidders meetings' were held, and clarification given – as evidenced in Section 3.3 below.

We pick matters up at the point where the 'GAMBIT' team (their name, for their system) have put a functional specification to the client, for comment or approval. As the archive contains both formal and informal documents, in the contract sense, we have marked them thus, as appropriate. Readers are referred to the specifications, which we recommend are read with sufficient care to make the following intelligible.

3 EXTRACTS FROM A PRODUCT DEVELOPMENT ARCHIVE – GAMBIT

MEMO
From: Client
To: GAMBIT team
Date: D1
File: MA(v) – Formal

3.1 Invitation to tender/user specification – see Example 1 in Chapter 5

Specific and additional instructions to bidder-teams are as follows:

1. 'Offers' are to comprise a full, functional specification – derived from the requirements' specification of the invitation to tender, plus a clear indication of how – in activities' management terms – you will achieve the task in the time stipulated, and with the resources of your team. This evidence in your offer must take the form of an activities' plan, with full explanatory notes as needed.
2. An essential component of your offer must be a quality plan, for which you may assume that the client will perform three structured walkthrough exercises:

(a) on the seventh project day (D7), numbering from the date of authorization of the functional specification;

(b) on project day 18;

(c) immediately before your scheduled alpha-test. Note that your activity plan must show an alpha-test not later than project day 31.

3. The whole project must be performed between project day 1, as defined, and 31 – when a client beta-test will begin; this will be conducted between D32 and 35 inclusive.

4. Deliverable documentation. This must be available on D31, and must comprise:

(a) a user's manual;

(b) a maintenance manual including: summary requirement definition, software design diagrams and text, program structure charts, data dictionary, and code listing, commented meaningfully;

(c) a test record of each stage of integration.

5. You will refer to specifications and their emendations as URS 1, 2, etc., and FS 1, 2, etc. depending on whether you refer to our bidders' document or its variants, or your functional specification or its variants.

6. Change. No change to the specification will be valid, after D1, unless authorized by both parties.

7. The requirements detailed in an agreed and approved functional specification shall comprise the whole of requirements against which compliance will be judged, during beta-tests.

3.2 Functional specification – see Example 2 in Chapter 5

> MEMO
> From: Client
> To: GAMBIT team-leader
> Date: project day one (D1)
> File: MA(v) – Formal

GAMBIT TEAM

You are hereby authorized to implement the specifications now signed-off for this purpose, and known as FS(1). Please note and observe the strictures given in addenda to our invitation to tender concerning changes, schedule and deliverables.

One further note, or rather two:

1. Insofar as your specifications are not specific (i.e. by incorporating the FIDE laws of chess), it is expressly understood that any disputes over compliance in respect of laws will be decided by that exposition of them, and no other. For example, can a side castle if its king has *been* in check. In our conversation, one of your team (James) thought that castling is prevented in this case. Yet there is nothing in FIDE rules to this effect. A side can castle if (a) the path between king and rook is unoccupied, (b) none of the intervening squares is under threat, nor the king's final square, nor the king's departure square, and (c) so long as neither piece has been moved at all before in the game.

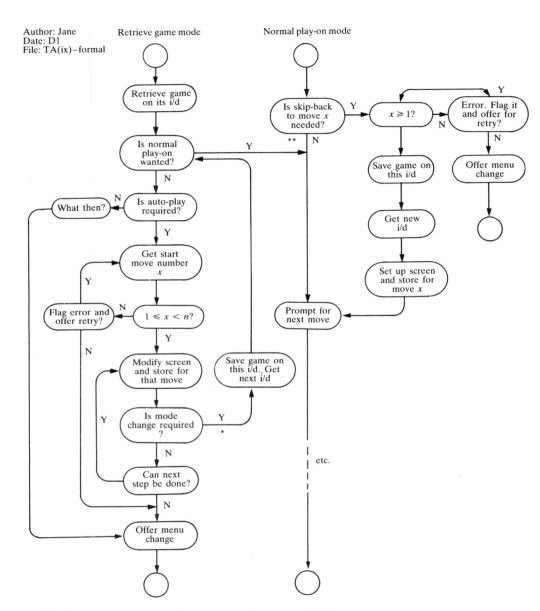

Author: Jane
Date: D1
File: TA(ix)–formal

FIGURE A.1 Clarifications in the functional specification.

2. So far as I can tell, your screen and keyboard features are all right. However, and this is to be taken as a reservation against full authority to proceed, I cannot tell from a piece of paper (FS1) if such things are really adequate. I suggest that you amend your activities' plan (PP1) to include an early prototype through which we may review and revise these formats as necessary. Note though, that you are to proceed on the basis of FS(1) until this document is emended, if at all, after the prototypes.

Signed: *AM-client*

> MEMO
> From: GAMBIT Jane
> To: Client
> Date: D2
> File: MA(v) – Formal

AUTHORIZATION AND PROTOTYPES

We agree to your points 1 and 2 in the memorandum of D1, you to us. A revised activities' plan, PP1*, is being prepared. Could we meet on D4 at 11.00 to discuss this prototype exercise, please?

We still have an outstanding question that remains unanswered. Having recalled a saved-game, do you want to have a perpetual option to jump forward or backward to a nominated move before playing on (forward or backward in accordance with the game as previously played, or with new moves in forward play from the point of choice)? I enclose a sketch of how the requirement would be if affirmative, and otherwise as it may be [Figure A.1]. As you can see, the features could be true for backward-skip in normal mode as well as this mode.

Please indicate which requirement option is the case. Could we have your answer by D4 please?

3.3 Extracts from management archive – set (A): start and management methods

> MEMO
> To: GAMBIT Jane
> cc: Manager
> From: Client
> Date: D2
> File: MA(v) – Formal

The functional specification is amended to FS(1)* = FS(1) + option * (but *not* **) on your logic chart of yesterdate.

A beta-test will begin on D31; walkthroughs will occur on D3, D8 and D29; a meeting on i/o formats is confirmed for D4 at 14.00. Times for all other meetings will be 08.30, and they will be held in the conference room adjacent to my office. Please install a terminal there, with access to your computer development system, so that the beta-test for compliance may be done there too.

Signed: *Client-AM*

MEMO
From: Jane
To: Team
Date: D1
File: MA(v) – Informal

ROLES AND ADMIN.-STUFF

Suggestions to discuss at our team meeting this morning:

1. Who does what.
2. How; in management terms – reporting and that.

I'm sorry two of you don't like meetings, and like memos less – but we are going to have some 'rules of engagement' on this job. If you get too fed up, we'll have to review things, but until then please cooperate. My choices should be yours, and vice versa when we agree.

First of all, we are up against a very tough job. We can only increase time on it by making nights into 'days'. Still, rather than moaning, let's get on with the plan and *make* it work.

First of all, attention to the OSD and the netplan. [For outline system design see Figure 12.6.] Tasks are as defined in PP1* attached below.

Now, we will keep a development archive in the following format:

I. Technical Section (TA)
    (i) Contents of I and II.
    (ii) User requirement specification: Bid invitation; traffic pertaining.
    (iii) Outline systems design: General scheme: software taxonomy.
    (iv) Functional specification.
    (v) Design of GAMBIT: General decomposition; integrand specifications.
    (vi) Quality control: Review and reading schedule; test plan.
    (vii) Code listings.
    (viii) Deliverable documentation: User's manual; maintenance manual.
    (ix) Oddbins: E.g. technical bits and pieces.
II. Management section (MA)
    (i) Activities' plans: PP1* schedules; updates.
    (ii) Status and cost: Status matrices; effort histograms.
    (iii) Quality plan: QI schedule; beta-test.
    (iv) Walkthrough: Minutes.
    (v) Oddbins: E.g. Management and client stuff.

I suggest that we have a full team-meeting, every Monday, in Fred's Pigsty (that's the refectory, Sarah), and Jim can bring his own ginseng tea. And none of this 08.30 nonsense – let's start at the crack of 10.00. This meeting is a must; no sexist excuses for absence (I

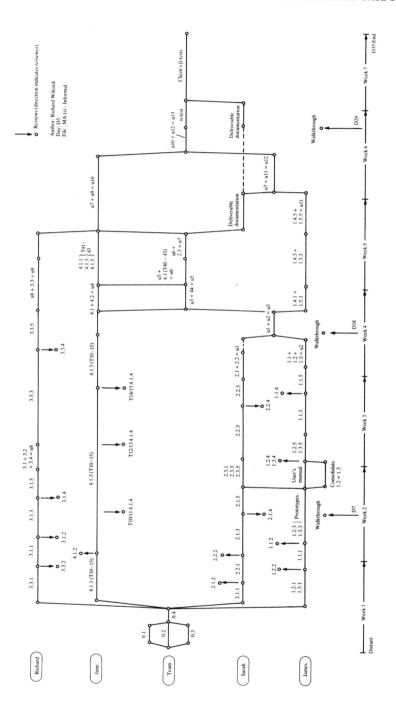

FIGURE A.2 Coded sequence of activities.

TABLE A.1 Task definition and codes – OSD-based

Author: Jane
Date: D2
File: MA(i) – Informal

James	Task 1	1.1 Main scheduler	Code-size = 500 source	OSD tasks 1, 2
		1.2 Screen manager	300	3, 4, 5
		1.3 Menu selection	50	6
		1.4 Index – get & show	150	27, 28
		1.5 Display moves	200 (= 1,200 total)	29, 30, 31
Sarah	Task 2	2.1 Save game	250	32, 33, 34
		2.2 Retrieve game	600	35, 36, 37, 38, 39, 40
		2.3 All place & move errors	50 (= 900 total)	7
Richard	Task 3	3.1 Main setup, play or place	400	8, 9
		3.2 Prompt for place	50	18
		3.3 Check place valid	400	19, 20, 21, 22, 23, 24
		3.4 Message for illicit place	50	25
		3.5 Effect valid placement	100 (= 1,000 total)	26
Jane	Task 4	4.1 Standard start and play	1,500	10, 11, 12, 13, 14, 15, 41, 42, 43
		4.2 Prompt for move	100 (= 1,600 total)	16, 17
			(= 4,700 total)	

Other codes	0.1	Project start and planning
	0.2	Familiarization; chess, PSE and Pascal
	0.3	Complete review of FS, informal detailing & OSD extension
	0.4	Overall systems design
	$x.y.1$	Design of module $x.y$ (e.g. 3.2.1 = Design prompt for place)
	$x.y.2$	Design review of module $x.y$
	$x.y.3$	Code $x.y$ integrands
	$x.y.4$	Code read $x.y$ integrands
	$x.y.5$	Author test integrands in $x.y$ module, and compose into program

liked Richard's try today, if he's got those sort of cramps we should show him in a barrel at the funfare). Seriously, this is not blind bureaucracy – we *must* keep this archive. Sarah and 'dismal Jimmy' need to find out how to administrate a potential fiasco like GAMBIT, to prevent total chaos. We must all walk (not march, Richard) in step.

Full discussion this afternoon please, in the meantime note the following specialist tasks:

Jane: PSE (and 'no', we don't want your PC, Richard).
Richard: FS detail (that means learn it, lad).
Jim: Chess (suggest you make sure we all know the rules).
Sarah: Pascal (get and distribute manuals; what don't we know?).

We will have a librarian of the week in the following rota: me, Sarah, Dismal (Jim), Richie – with me being '*it*' for W1 *and* 2, then Sarah (W3), Dismal (W4), Richie (W5) and back to me in W6. That means I do 50 percent of the dogsbody stuff, so I don't want any grousing about pencil-pushing. D5/W6 = D30, if you hadn't noticed, and I suppose the archive will be dominant during the W7 beta-tests; anyway, 'librarian' can pass to Sarah then as it'll do

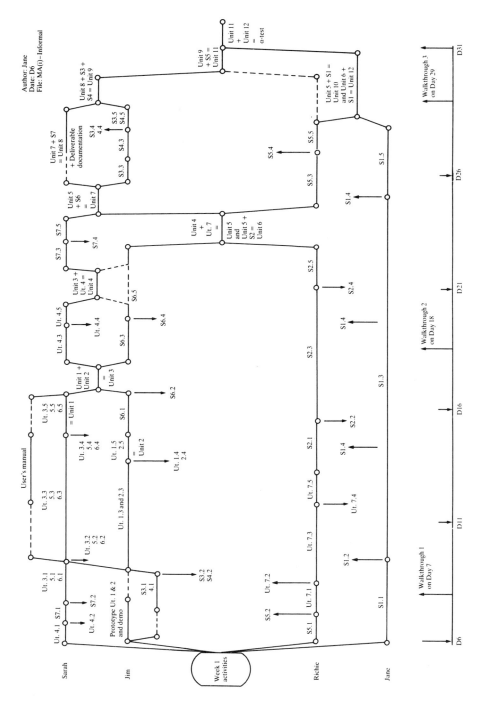

FIGURE A.3 Revised activities' plan – design-based.

TABLE A.2 Revised task definitions and codes for use – design-based

Author: Chief prog.
Date: D6
File: MA(i) – Informal

Code size estimates

		Jim	Sarah	Dick	Self
Utility 1:	350 ss Pascal				
2:	100	Utilities 1, 2	Utility 3/5/6	State 2	State 1
3:	350	(Prototype and	5.1–5.3	2.1–2.9	
4:	150	substantive)	6.1–6.9	Utility 7	
5:	150		Utility 4	7.1–7.3	
6:	200	State 3	State 7	State 5	
7:	350	State 4			
State 1:	1,350	State 6			
2:	500				
3:	250	1,300	1,000	1,300	1,350
4:	350				
5:	450				
6:	250				
7:	150 (=4,950)				

Codes for use: Ut. = utility routine
Un. = unit (e.g. in integration and testing)
S = State routine
0.1 to 0.4 as before
0.0.1 to 0.0.5 as before (e.g. now Ut.$x.y.1$ = design of utility 1)

Note: All estimates are based on the software design, not OSD here.

---

her good to wipe the blood stains off the archive. It's your fault for being youngest, kid. This job should age you.

Signed: *Calamity Jane*

3.4 Extracts from management archive – set (B): feasibility, plans and schedules

[For outline system design, see Figure 12.6]

MEMO
From: Jane
To: Team
Date: D7
File: MA(i) – Informal

Urgent/Note

The activities' plan agreed at yesterday's meeting in appended [Figure A.3], with a new task ascription [Table A.2]. This will *be* the basis for a discussion at today's walkthrough, of the client's revision to quality plan.

3.5 Extracts from technical archive – set (C): design at top, intermediate and low levels

TABLE A.3 GAMBIT software design – architecture

	Author: Jane
	Date: D4
	File: TA(v) – Informal

GAMBIT software architecture

	States	Utilities
Level 1		Ut.1 Main scheduler and controller
		Ut.2 Menu selector
		Ut.3 Screen manager
Level 2	S1. Normal game start and play	Ut.4 Keyboard input handler
	S2. Start by piece placement	Ut.5 Screen states for Ut.3
	S3. Show index	Ut.6 Error messages for Ut.3, and prompts for Ut.2
	S4. Retrieve game	Ut.7 Filing and retrieving data features
	S5. Step (backward or forward)	
	S6. Save game	
	S7. Show game moves	
Level 3	Piece move tests:	Formats:
	S1.1 impeded path	Ut.5.1 for normal board & message states
	S1.2 geometrically valid, per type	Ut.5.2 for games index
	S1.3 *en passant* capture	Ut.5.3 for game moves format
	S1.4 castling	Error and prompt messages:
	S1.5 promotion	Ut.6.1 prompt for i/d
	S1.6 own king check	Ut.6.2 prompt for next move
	S1.7 delivered check or mates	Ut.6.3 prompt for next piece
	Piece place tests at sequence end:	Ut.6.4 prompt for retry after error
	S2.1 number of kings of each color	Ut.6.5 prompt for menu choice
	S2.2 number of pawns of a color	Ut.6.6 syntax error, all contexts
	S2.3 double first move for pawn in e.p.	Ut.6.7 illicit chess, move or place
	S2.4 number of major pieces of a color	Ut.6.8 check delivered, or special game and for mates
	S2.5 K or R on move square, prior move	Ut.6.9 promotion, piece type input needed
	S2.6 multiple checks to a king	Data manager for:
	S2.7 pawn an own first rank	Ut.7.1 board/pieces
	S2.8 full sets of pawns part each other	Ut.7.2 saved games file
	S2.9 unmoved pawns, B, Q, (R) in play	Ut.7.3 index file
Level 4 (virtual mechine)	Computer operating system and executive features (DEC–VMS) Computer hardware = Digital microvax + VT100 Keyboard screens + duplex floppy disk handlers	

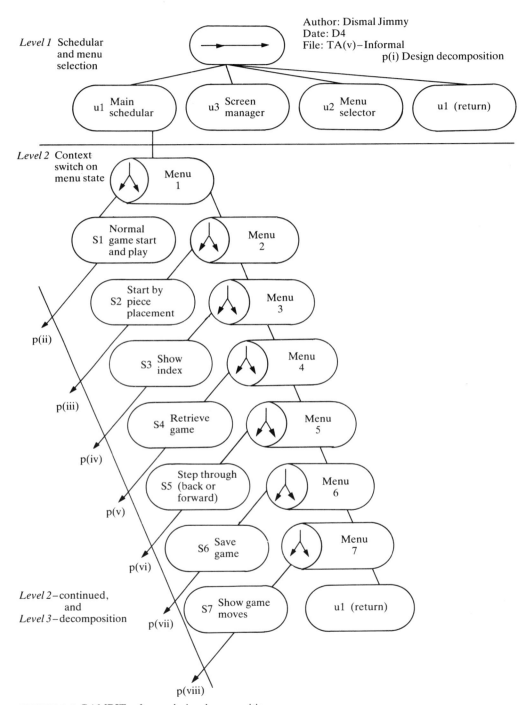

FIGURE A.4 GAMBIT software design decomposition.

Author: Richie
Date: D7
File: TA(v)–Informal
p(iii)

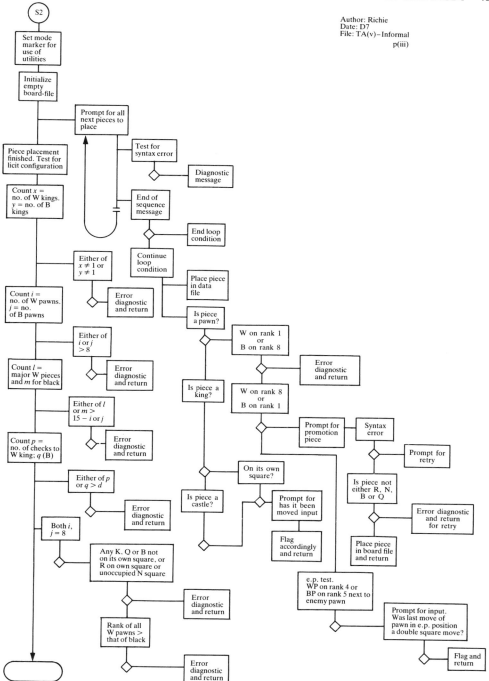

FIGURE A.5 Logic design of S2 = piece placement and test.

Author: RW
Date: D13   p(iii) – 12
File: TA(v) – Informal

Integrand specification
Subroutine S2.5
Name "TESTK/RMOVED"
Entered from S2 on 0–6 (max.) occasions per board setup
Purpose: Prompts for moved indicator, and sets flag as appropriate on board-square
Exits to S2 (main)
Author: Richard Wilcock
Date (absolute): 27 January 1990/D12 relative

```
          begin "TESTK/RMOVED"
                                    entercall "SCREENMGR"
                                    1n: in Promptfield
                                    1n: "Indicate (Y or N key) if . . . previously moved"
                                    1n: insert Piecetype in . . .
                                    return
          if: marker = 0, then:
                                    end
                           else: Board (i,j) = −Board (i,j)
                                    end
                    end
            end
```

Calls: routine "Screenmgr" with prescribed format (1n/1n/1n)
Requires: monitor (u1) keyboard manager to process keyboard input: N = 0; Y = 1
        :   Board-square coordinates to be passed in i = rank/j = column for tested piece
Contributes: *no* new properties in data dictionary ('marker' is used in u1 keyboard manager)

FIGURE A.6 Integrand specification: TEST K/R MOVED.

MEMO
From: Chief Prog.
To: Team
Date: D7
File: MA(i) – Informal

REVISIONS TO SCHEDULE

At our team meeting, it became obvious from the status matrices that we cannot hold to the test plan done on day 4. A revised version is appended, and this is now in operation, and known as the D7 version [Table A.6]. There is a walkthrough today, the client has sent me a revised quality plan to fit into our new activities' plan. Both are attached [for plan, see Figure A.3].

The test schedule is based on the following task concepts:

1. Jim and Sarah will produce the main screen management and keyboard system, which we will use as a 'driver' for all further accretive testing.

3.6 Extracts from technical Archive – set (D): design review and code reading schedule; test plan

TABLE A.4 Schedule for design review and code reading (D3 version) – OSD-based

Day 3/Author: James Hughes
File: TA(vi) – Informal

1. Design reviews

Day	R + Jane	Jane + R	Jane + S	S + Jane	S + James	James + S
			Author/*reviewer*			
4				2.1		
5	3.3					
6		4.1		2.2		1.2
7	3.1					1.1

2. Code reading

Day	R + Jane	Jane + R	Jane + S	S + Jane	S + James	James + S
7			4.1 (part)		2.1	
8	3.1					
11						1.2/1.3
12			4.1 (part)			
13					2.2	
14						1.1
15			4.1 (part)			
17	3.3					

TABLE A.5 Test sequence (D4 version) – OSD-based

Day 4/Author: Sarah Milbay
File: TA(vi) – Informal

Level 1: Author test and compose (u = unit/program or programs)	S + Jim	Level 2: integration		Level 3: full team
		S + Jane	Jane + R	
3.1 + 3.2 + 3.4 = u8				
2.1 + 2.2 = u1				
1.1 + 1.2 + 1.3 = u2				
	u1 + u2 = u3			
4.1 (part) + 4.2 = u4				
		u3 + u4 = u5		
		u5 + 4.1 = u6		
u8 + 3.3 = u9		u6 + 2.3 = u7		
1.4 + 1.5 = u11			u7 + u9 = u10	
		u7 + u11 = u12		
				u10 + u12 = u13
				α-test

TABLE A.6 Revised test sequence (D7 version) – design-based

Day 7/Author: Sarah Milbay
File: MA(vi) – Informal

| Day | Level 1: Author test and compose | | | | James + S | Level 2: Integration James + R | Jane + R | Level 3: full team |
	R	James	S	Jane				
12	Ut.7							
14		Ut.1/2 = u2						
15			Ut.3/5/6 = u1					
17					u1 + u2 = u3			
20			Ut.4.5					
21					u3 + Ut.4 = u4			
22	S2	S6						
24			S7			u4 + Ut.7 = u5		
24						u5 + S2 = u6		
25					u5 + S7 = u7			
26				S1				
27	S5							
27		S3 + 4	u6 + S7 = u8					
28					u8 + S3 + S4 = 49			
29					u9 + S5 = u11		u5 + S1 = u10	
30							u6 + S1 = u12	
31								u11 + u12 = α-test

TABLE A.7 Quality plan, showing QI/QA and beta-test schedules (D4 version) – OSD-based

Day	QI		Int. test	Walkthrough	β-test		
	Design reviews	Code read			B-box	W-box	Doc.
					D4 From: Client (encl. memo) File: MA(iii)		
5	General + 3.3						
6	4.1						
7	1.1 + 1.2 + 2.1 + 2.2	2.1		No.1			
8					[Prototype demo 1.2/1.3]		
11		1.2/1.3					
15		4.1 (part)					
17		3.3					
18				No.2			
23			u6 + 2.3 = u7				
29				No.3			
32					1 + 2		Inspect
33					S1–7		
33–35						Mod.	

2. Richie will do the main data file handling (needed for S2 and S5 anyway), and will integrate it (Ut.7) on the 'driver' as an early activity. This integration produces the total utility as the 'driver'.

3. Main states, developed by myself (play), Richie (place pieces) and Jim (save/retrieve) will be progressively integrated on this driver.

The revised task attributions, and revised code size estimates, are agreed between us [Table A.2].

3.7 Extracts from management archive – set (E): quality plan; QI and QA

MEMO
From: Client
To: GAMBIT team-leader
cc: Jane's manager
Date: D4
File: MA(iii) – Formal

QUALITY

First, who *is* your manager? Sending you his copy seems like asking the felon to hang himself. Herself in your case. I note that you (Jane) signed-off the functional specification for your side.

TABLE A.8 Revised quality plan – D7 version

Author: Jane
Date: D7
File: MA(iii) – Formal

Revised quality plan – agreed with client

Day	QI		Integration tests	Walkthrough	β-test [As before – D4 version]
	Design reviews	Code reading			
5	General				
7				No.1	
8	Ut.1 & 2				
	Ut.3, 5 & 6				
9	S1				
15	S2			No.2	
18					
19		S6			
24			Units 5 & 6		
25		S1			
29			Units 9 & 10	No.3	

Annotation: All activities now refer to design nomenclature (Tables A.2/A.7) – not OSD.

Have you the authority? Your affirmative is no consolation – you'd better get your manager in on the act, and quickly! All this concerns quality, and that concerns *the chop* if it's got wrong, and guess who'll qualify for it, my girl?

I attach a schedule of walkthrough, QI and beta-test activities [Table A.7] for you to add to your revised plan (PP1*), or whatever you want to do with it. As for the beta-tests, I shall *not* (*vide* your question) release their details so that you can dry-run at the alpha-test stage. All I will tell you now is the following:

1. I shall *fully* demonstrate (or fail) all functional features specified, by direct use of the system.
2. I shall evaluate the acceptability of deliverable documentation, in part, by inspection. Item 3 below applies, also, to this test.
3. I shall attempt to make a controlled change to your software *without* recourse to you or your team. You will *not* be informed of this change, but you may know that, by 'controlled', I mean 'known and intended', rather than dropping the system on the floor, or firing bugs at random into it.

I hope all this concentrates your mind to the fact that D32 is some matter of significance. *Bon* as they say, *chance*.

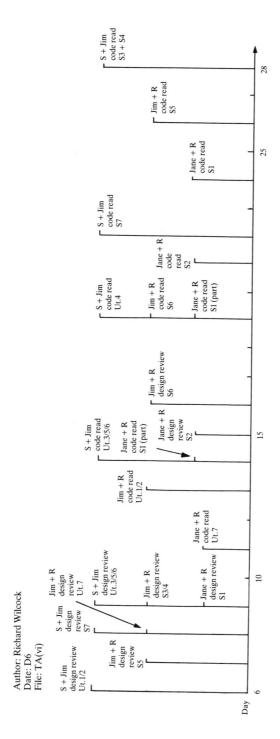

FIGURE A.7 Quality control plan (D6 version) – design-based.

3.8 Extracts from management archive – set (F): updated schedules, status matrices and cost accounting

MEMO
From: Team-leader
To: Team
Date: D6
File: MA(v) – Informal

ADMIN.

Further to mine, to you, dated D1 – and our team meeting that day – and for discussion at our team meeting this p.m. in The Sty:

1. Archive is now set up (me), and this is an entry to it, destined for MA(v) – 'Oddbins'. I will go on as librarian dogsbody this week, then dump it all on the infant prodigy (S).
2. You will have seen the OSD activities' plan PP1* from Richie (thanks, you engineers draw better than we lesser breeds). I shall do a revised version – no, sorry, same end date – by the end of this week, now we have a real design. Note! There will be a change of nomenclature on it, from that of PP1* – except for second decimal place activity types.
3. Incidentally, about the archive, *do* file in proper place. Don't send designs (R and J!) to the management archive, bless you.
4. I will update status matrices at each Monday meeting. A blank specimen is attached. Similarly with 'cost' (effort). I shall take a 'normal' day as *seven* hours. Please account accurately.

Signed: *Your leaderene*

MEMO
From: Chief programmer
To: Manager
Date: D35
File: MA(ii)

COST ACCOUNTING

I am not sure that cost accounting for fixed resources over a fixed time-scale is a really meaningful exercise. However, the 'degree of freedom' is overtime, although none of us would allow the word 'freedom' for an instant, used this way.

I have used a 'basic' day of 7 hours, and this assumes that other activities (class time) did not exceed 1.5 hours per day. Time records were kept, and submitted to me against a task number, weekly. They were well kept records in all cases, and accurate representations. An analysis, for what it is worth in those circumstances shows the following points:

1. The effort overrun was approximately 19.3 percent of the flat base of 7 hours per person per day.

TABLE A.3 Status matrix – week 2 end

Author: Librarian (Jane)
Date: D10
File: MA(ii) – Informal

Requirement / State	F.S.	System design	Part design	Review	Prog. spec.	Code	Code read	Author test	Unit 1	2	3	4	5	6	7	8	9	10	11	12	α-test	D-doc	β-test
Total requirement	+																				−	−	−
Total system		+	0	0	0	0																	
Utility 1/2: Scheduler & menu			+	+	+	0	−	−															
3/5/6: Screen/keyboard			+	+	0	0	−	−															
State 1: Normal game			+	+		0	−	−															
1.1: Impeded path						−	−	−															
1.2: Geometry					+	0	−	−															
1.3: En passant						−	−	−															
1.4: Castling					+	+	−	−															
1.5: Promotion					+	+	−	−															
1.6: Own K check					+	−	−	−															
1.7: Checks/mates				−	−	−	−	−															
2: Place pieces					−	−		−															
2.1: Too many kings																							
2.2: Too many pawns																							
2.3: e.p. pawns																							
2.4: Too many pieces																							
2.5: Castling K/R																							
2.6: Too many checks																							
2.7: P on first rank																							
2.8: All passed pawns																							
2.9: Pieces in play																							
3: Show index																							
4: Retrieve game																							
5: Step																							
6: Save game																							
7: Show game																							
Utility 4: Keyboard input			+	+		−	−	−															
5: Screens			+	+		−	−	−															
5.1: Normal			+	+		−	−	−															
5.2: Index			−	−		−	−	−															
5.3: Moves			+	+		−	−	−															
6: Manages			−	−		−	−	−															
6.1: i/d prompt			+	+		0	0	−															
6.2: Next move						+	+	−															
6.3: Next piece						+	0	−															
6.4: Retry						0		−															
6.5: Menu						+	0	−															
6.6: Syntax error			−	−		+	+	−															
6.7: Illicit chess						+	+	−															
6.8: Check or mate						+	+	−															
6.9: Promotion								−															
7: Data manager			+	+		0	0	−															
7.1: Board/pieces						+	0	−															
7.2: Saved games								−															
7.3: Index						+	+	−															

Integration and testing spans columns 2–12.

Comments: Generally on schedule. Jane and Richard seem to be traveling well, so far. Thank God the dismal one got through the prototype of Ut.1/2. The next week will be a bit tricky. Still better have trouble upstream rather than as we go over Niagara Falls in a leaking barrel. Archive and librarian tasks now pass to the Infant (S). Good luck kid. If in doubt – shout! Jane.

TABLE A.10 Status matrix – week 3 end

Author: Librarian (Sarah)
Date: D15
File: MA(ii) – Informal

	F.S.	System design	Part design	Review	Prog. spec.	Code	Code read	Author test	Unit 1	2	3	4	5	6	7	8	9	10	11	12	α-test	D-doc.	β-test	Comments
Total requirement	+																							Whoopee! Thank God that's over. It's up to you now, Jimmy. And Halleluja – our Richard has found a bug in this matrix format! No row for a pawn on its eighth rank. He'll use 2.7 for that. Why don't we read your stuff more carefully, Jane? Progress seems to be ominously good. Jim has produced unit 1, and my mickey-mice screen and keyboard handlers are all written. Not much news from the big guns (Richard and our revered leaderene), and S1 and S2. Has anyone heard of the two engineering teams drilling a tunnel from opposite directions – good luck, a tunnel; bad luck, two tunnels. Over to you, Dismal. If in doubt, don't shout – panic! Sarah.
Total system		+																						
Utility 1/2: Scheduler & menu **3/5/6**: Screen/keyboard			o	o	o	o	o	o	o	+											−	−	−	
State 1: Normal game			+	+	+	+	+	+																
1.1: Impeded path			+	+	+	+	+	+																
1.2: Geometry					o	o	−	−																
1.3: En passant					+	o	−	−																
1.4: Castling					+	+	−	−																
1.5: Promotion					−	−	+	−																
1.6: Own K check					+	+	+	−																
1.7: Checks/mates					+	+	+	−																
2: Place pieces			+	+	+	+	+	−																
2.1: Too many kings					+	+	−	+																
2.2: Too many pawns					o	o	−	−																
2.3: e.p. pawns					+	+	−	−																
2.4: Too many pieces					+	+	−	−																
2.5: Castling K/R					+	−	−	−																
2.6: Too many checks					+	−	−	−																
2.7: P on first rank					−	−	−	−																
2.8: All passed pawns					+	o	−	−																
2.9: Pieces in play					+	−	−	−																
3: Show index			+	+	−	−	−	−																
4: Retrieve game			+	+	−	−	−	−																
5: Step			+	+	−	−	−	−																
6: Save game			−	−	−	−	−	−																
7: Show game			+	+	−	−	−	−																
Utility 4: Keyboard input			+	+	+	+	+	+																
5: Screens			+	+	+	+	+	+																
5.1: Normal					+	+	+	+																
5.2: Index					+	+	+	+																
5.3: Moves					+	+	+	+																
6: Manages			+	+	+	+	+	+																
6.1: i/d prompt					+	+	+	+																
6.2: Next move					+	+	+	+																
6.3: Next piece					+	+	+	+																
6.4: Retry					+	+	+	+																
6.5: Menu					+	+	+	+																
6.6: Syntax error					+	+	+	+																
6.7: Illicit chess					+	+	+	+																
6.8: Check or mate					+	+	+	+																
6.9: Promotion					+	+	+	+																
7: Data manager			+	+	+	+	+	+																
7.1: Board/pieces					+	+	+	+																
7.2: Saved games					+	+	+	+																
7.3: Index					+	+	+	+																

Note: Columns 2–12 are grouped under the heading **Integration and testing**.

Author: Librarian (Jim)
Date: D20
File: MA(ii) – Informal

	F.S.	System design	Part design	Review	Prog. spec.	Code	Code read	Author test	Unit 1	Integration and testing 2	3	4	5	6	7	8	9	10	11	12	α-test	D-doc.	β-test
Total requirement	+																						
Total system		+	0	0	0	0	0	0													–	–	–
Utility 1/2: Scheduler & menu			+	+	+	+	+	+		+	+												
3/5/6: Screen/keyboard			+	+	+	+	+	+	+		+												
State 1: Normal game			+	+	+	0	0	–															
1.1: Impeded path			+	+	+	0	–	–															
1.2: Geometry		*	0	–	–	–	–	–															
1.3: *En passant*			–	–	–	–	–	–															
1.4: Castling					+	+	+	–															
1.5: Promotion					+	+	+	–															
1.6: Own K check					+	+	+	–															
1.7: Checks/mates					+	+	+	–															
2: Place pieces			+	+	0	0	–	–															
2.1: Too many kings					+	+	–	–															
2.2: Too many pawns					+	+	–	–															
2.3: e.p. pawns					+	+	–	–															
2.4: Too many pieces					+	+	–	–															
2.5: Castling K/R					+	+	–	–															
2.6: Too many checks		*			0	–	–	–															
2.7: P on first rank		*			0	–	–	–															
2.8: All passed pawns					+	+	–	–															
2.9: Pieces in play					+	+	–	–															
3: Show index			+	+	–	–	–	–															
4: Retrieve game			+	+	–	–	–	–															
5: Step			+	+	–	–	–	–															
6: Save game		*	+	+	+	0	–	–															
7: Show game			+	+	–	–	–	–															
Utility 4: Keyboard input			+	+	+	+	+	+															
5: Screens			+	+	+	+	+	+															
5.1: Normal					+	+	+	+															
5.2: Index					+	+	+	+															
5.3: Moves					+	+	+	+															
6: Manages			+	+	+	+	+	+															
6.1: i/d prompt					+	+	+	+															
6.2: Next move					+	+	+	+															
6.3: Next piece					+	+	+	+															
6.4: Retry					+	+	+	+															
6.5: Menu					+	+	+	+															
6.6: Syntax error					+	+	+	+															
6.7: Illicit chess					+	+	+	+															
6.8: Check or mate					+	+	+	+															
6.9: Promotion					+	+	+	+															
7: Data manager			+	+	+	+	+	+															
7.1: Board/pieces					+	+	+	+															
7.2: Saved games					+	+	+	+															
7.3: Index					+	+	+	+															

Comments

In stock market terms, utilities are bullish, but short positions in states are a bit weak. The basic utilities' driver is there – unit 3 in all its glory, and Sarah has the keyboard handler ready to integrate, which will make unit 4 of the driver when we've accomplished it. On the other hand, some of us are slipping on 'states' routines. I have used the spare 'systems design' column to flag the slippages, by asterisk. They are:

State 1: Jane had a nasty shock when our bold Richard found a dreadful problem with 'piece geometry' at a code reading session. Backtracking here, I'm afraid. This has prevented proper progress on 1.1 coding. Midnight oil is called for here – and elsewhere it should be said.

State 2: Richard does not seem quite on schedule and his code reading may slip. Integrands 2.6/2.7 seem to be the trouble, or more accurately, the promotion business in 2.

State 6: I am late in the coding of 'save game'. No real reason, except that I have been keeping to my food and sleep schedules too well. Archive/librarian job goes to Richard now. Note the empty section on deliverable documentation. Sarah knocked my drink over MA(iv). It was rum and orange, and 11.55 p.m. Jim.

TABLE A.12 Status matrix – week 5 end

Author: Librarian (Richie)
Date: D25
File: MA(ii) – Informal

	F.S.	System design	Part design	Review	Prog. spec.	Code	Code read	Author test	Unit 1	2	3	4	5	6	7	8	9	10	11	12	α-test	D-doc.	β-test
Total requirement	+																						
Total system			+	+																			
Utility 1/2: Scheduler & menu		+	+	+	0	0	0	0	0														
3/5/6: Screen/keyboard			+	+	+	+	+	+	+	+	+												
State 1: Normal game			+	+	+	+	+	0			+	+											
1.1: Impeded path					+	+	+	0			+	+											
1.2: Geometry					+	+	+	0															
1.3: En passant					+	+	+	+															
1.4: Castling					+	+	+	+															
1.5: Promotion					+	+	+	+															
1.6: Own K check					+	+	+	–															
1.7: Checks/mates					+	+	+	+															
2: Place pieces		*	+	+	+	+	+	+															
2.1: Too many kings					+	+	+	+															
2.2: Too many pawns					+	+	+	+															
2.3: e.p. pawns					+	+	+	+						–									
2.4: Too many pieces					+	+	+	+															
2.5: Castling K/R					+	+	+	+							–								
2.6: Too many checks					+	+	+	+							–								
2.7: P on first rank					+	+	+	+															
2.8: All passed pawns					–	–	–	–															
2.9: Pieces in play					–	–	–	–															
3: Show index			+	+	–	–	–	–															
4: Retrieve game			+	+	+	+	+	+															
5: Step			+	+	+	+	+	+			+												
6: Save game			+	+	+	+	+	+															
7: Show game			+	+	+	+	+	+															
Utility 4: Keyboard input		*	+	+	+	+	+	+															
5: Screens					+	+	+	+															
5.1: Normal					+	+	+	+															
5.2: Index					+	+	+	+															
5.3: Moves					+	+	+	+															
6: Manages			+	+	+	+	+	+															
6.1: i/d prompt					+	+	+	+															
6.2: Next move					+	+	+	+															
6.3: Next piece					+	+	+	+															
6.4: Retry					+	+	+	+															
6.5: Menu					+	+	+	+															
6.6: Syntax error					+	+	+	+															
6.7: Illicit chess					+	+	+	+															
6.8: Check or mate					+	+	+	+															
6.9: Promotion					+	+	+	+															
7: Data manager		**	0	–	–	–	–	–						–									
7.1: Board/pieces					–	–	–	–															
7.2: Saved games					–	–	–	–															

Comments

A bothersome week, with team trouble being the worst of the bothers. First the good news. States 1 and 2 seem to be effectively implemented – about 40% of the feature specified. The utilities' driver is now about 80% complete, with all scheduler, menu, screen and keyboard facilities integrated.

But there is bad news, and worse. Unit 5 integration failed, and this prevented unit 6 integration, and the integration of states 6 and 7 to form unit 7. Utility 7 had passed a design review with the author of the routines it now seemed to be not compatible with, and had been code read by the chief programmer. A lack of civility developed at the unit 5 integration, and the chief programmer had to arbitrate. Result, utility 7 to be redone. I take this occasion to again object to that decision. I find it depressing to be told I know nothing about file handling by a Cobol plonker.

Anyway, there are all sorts of consequential slippages, including to my own S2 integration, and this affects my work on S5, which affects. . . and so on.

One bright bit of news; Jane recovered from the cockup over piece-move geometry. Let's hope I can do the same. Over and out. Richie.

Author: Librarian (Jane)
Date: D30
File: MA(ii) – Informal

	F.S.	System design	Part design	Review	Prog. spec.	Code	Code read	Author test	Unit 1	2	3	4	5	6	7	8	9	10	11	12	α-test	D-doc.	β-test
Total requirement	+																						–
Total system		+							+	+	+	+	+	+	+	+	0	+	–	+	–	+	
Utility 1/2: Scheduler & menu			+	+	+	+	+	+			+	+	+	+	+	+	0	+	–	+	–		
3/5/6: Screen/keyboard			+	+	+	+	+	+													–		
State 1: Normal game		*	+	+	+	+	+	+	+												–		
1.1: Impeded path			+	+	+	+	+	+													–		
1.2: Geometry		*																					
1.3: *En passant*		*	+	+	+	+	+	+							+					+	–		
1.4: Castling																							
1.5: Promotion																							
1.6: Own K check																							
1.7: Checks/mates																							
2: Place pieces																							
2.1: Too many kings																							
2.2: Too many pawns																							
2.3: e.p. pawns																							
2.4: Too many pieces																							
2.5: Castling K/R																							
2.6: Too many checks																							
2.7: P on first rank																							
2.8: All passed pawns																							
2.9: Pieces in play																							
3: Show index			+	+	+	+	+	+	+		+	+	+	+	+	+	0	+	–	+	–		
4: Retrieve game			+	+	+	+	+	+							+	+	0	+	–	+	–		
5: Step			+	+	+	+	+	+								+	0	+	–	+	–		
6: Save game			+	+	+	+	+	+								+	0		–		–		
7: Show game			+	+	+	+	+	+								+	0		–		–		
Utility 4: Keyboard input			+	+	+	+	+	+	+		+	+	+	+	+	+	0	+	–	+	–		
5: Screens			+	+	+	+	+	+	+		+	+	+	+	+	+	0	+	–	+	–		
5.1: Normal																					–		
5.2: Index																							
5.3: Moves																							
6: Manages																							
6.1: i/d prompt																							
6.2: Next move																							
6.3: Next piece																							
6.4: Retry																							
6.5: Menu																							
6.6: Syntax error																							
6.7: Illicit chess																							
6.8: Check or mate																							
6.9: Promotion																							
7: Data manager			+	+	+	+	+	+							+	+	0	+	–	+	–		
7.1: Board/pieces																							
7.2: Saved games																							
7.3: Index			+	+	+	+	+	+													–		

Comments

Tomorrow will tell all. We have two units, one of which 'works', and the other of which is still being integrated. Unit 12 is the basic game modes 1 and 2, working on the full utilities' driver. That is about two-thirds of the required system. It really looks quite pretty, and we are very braced up about it.

The other part, effectively the whole of the index, save/retrieve, stepthrough and game display features, working on the full utilities' driver, is in integration right now. The first step is to secure S3+S4, and then integrate S5. We are very hopeful.

It all goes well, we will do full integration (α-) test on D31 afternoon. Sarah has done the deliverable documentation and even integrated Jimmy's 'Save game' feature to save him time. She has also helped to dissolve the animosity over utility 7 and now that S1 is in unit 12, I am more available than before. The archive/librarian now passes to our blessed infant. Good work, Sarah! Here's looking at you kid. And thanks, team. Jane.

TABLE A.14 GAMBIT staff, time records

Author: Jane
Date: D35 (end)
File: MA(ii) – Informal

Day		Jane		Richard		James		Sarah	Comments
	Time	Task	Time	Task	Time	Task	Time	Task	
1	4	0.1	3	0.1	4	0.1	4	0.1	
2	3	0.1	3	0.2	3	0.2	3	0.2	
3	5	0.2	4	0.2	2	0.2	4	0.2	
4	5	0.1/0.2	3	0.3	3	0.3	4	0.3	
5	4	0.4	3	0.4	4	0.4	4	0.3	Week total = 72 hours
6	5	S1.1	6	S5.1	6	Ut.1/2 Pt	4	Ut.4.1	
7	6	S1.1	6	Ut.7.1	4	S3/4.1	6	S7.1	
8	7	S1.1	6	Ut.7.2	8	Ut.1/2 Demo	7	Ut.3/5/6.1	
9	8	S1.2	7	Ut.7.3	4	S3/4.2	7	Ut.3/5/6.1	
10	7	S1.3	7	Ut.7.3	6	Ut.1/2.3	7	Ut.3/5/6.2	Week total = 124 hours
11	10	S1.3	8	Ut.7.4	6	Ut.1/2.3	8	Ut.3/5/6.3	
12	10	S1.3	10	Ut.7.5	7	Ut.1/2.3	7	Ut.3/5/6.3	
13	10	S1.3	10	S2.1	7	Ut.1/2.4	7	Ut.3/5/6.3	
14	10	S1.4 (part)	10	S2.1	7	Ut.1/2.5 = u2	7	Ut.3/5/6.4	
15	10	S1.3	10	S2.2	7	S6.1	7	Ut.3/5/6 = u1	Week total = 168 hours
16	10	S1.3	10	S2.3	6	S6.2	7	u1.5	
17	10	S1.3	10	S2.3	4	unit 3.5	7	unit 3.5	
18	10	S1.3	10	S2.3	6	S6.3	7	Ut.4.3	
19	10	S1.4 (part)	10	S2.3	7	S6.4	7	Ut.4.4	Code read – fault in S1
20	12	S1.3 (bt)	10	S2.3	8	S6.5	7	Ut.4.5	Week total = 168 hours
21	10	S1.3 (bt)	10	S2.4	6	unit 4.5	8	unit 4.5	
22	10	S1.3 (bt)	10	S2.5	4	S6.5	10	S7.3	
23	12	S1.3	12	unit 5.5	8	unit 5.5	10	S7.5	Integration failure = u5
24	12	S1.3	12	Ut.7.1 (bt)	10	S3.3	10	Doc.	
25	12	S1.4	12	Ut.7.3 (bt)	11	S3.5	8	u4 + S6	Week total = 197 hours
26	10	S1.4	14	Ut.7.5 (bt)	12	S4.3	8	Doc.	
27	12	S1.5	14	Ut.7.5 + u4	12	S4.5	9	u4 + S6 + S7	
28	12	S1.5	14	S5.3	14	u4 + Ut.7 = u5	10	u4 + S6 + S7	
29	14	u4 + S1	14	S5.5	14	unit 7.5	12	unit 7.5	
30	10	units 10/12.5	13	units 10/12.5	14	unit 8.5	14	unit 8.5	Week total = 246 hours
31	14	α-test	14	α-test	14	units 9/11.5	14	units 9/11.5	
32	10	β-test	10	β-test	8	β-test	8	β-test	
33	9	β-test	11	β-test	10	β-test	8	β-test	
34	9	β-test	9	β-test	9	β-test	9	β-test	

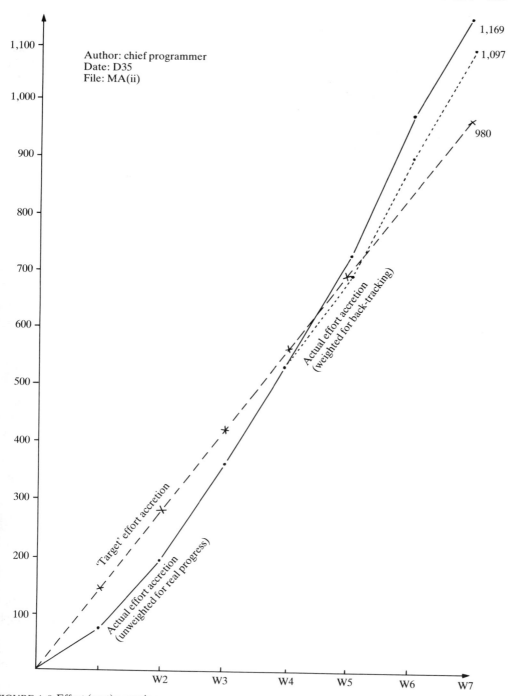

Author: chief programmer
Date: D35
File: MA(ii)

FIGURE A.8 Effort (cost) accretion.

2. We took some time to get going. After two weeks, we had spent only 70 percent of the 'target' effort of 280 hours for that period. The rate of overrun gradually increased, peaking on D31 (predictably), when we were running round like the proverbial chickens with a fox in the coop. The effort to base ratios, per week, were as follows: 51; 88; 120; 120; 140; 175; and 140 percent. On D31, we hit a ratio of 200 percent!

3. Two major problems arose, causing back-tracking. This 'cost' about 74 hours, or about 6.3 percent of the total effort expended. Perhaps we were lucky.

Cost accretion graphs are attached. However, the impression remains that this is not a true or really representative picture, given the 'degrees of constraint' on time-scale and effort. We literally had to get a gallon into a pint pot.

Signed: *Jane*

3.9 Extracts from management archive – set (G): walkthrough minutes

MEMO
From: Client
To: GAMBIT Manager
cc: Chief programmer
Date: D1
File: MA(iv) – formal

During the development of the chess-playing systems, I intend to undertake structured walkthrough reviews at regular intervals. It is currently my plan to hold three such, on days 7, 18 and 29 – but this may change if the activities' plan, currently in development, changes.

The meetings will take about an hour, unless major snags arise, and I shall hold them 'one on one' with Jane, who will minute the proceedings for you, me and the team's archive. Jane may co-opt as she wishes. I may co-opt as I wish.

An agenda will comprise, simply, the following:

1. Changes or additions to requirements.
2. Status of each system component, based on design nomenclature.
3. Review of any major slippages or problems.
4. Other matters.

As it is none of my business, I shall not enter the territory of cost (effort), nor that of staff motivation. I shall require Jane to bring the technical archive she is keeping, but only such parts of the management equivalent as pertain, e.g. MA(i).

If exigencies require it, I shall flag a need for you and I to meet, by means of these minutes. However, I expect no such dire event, and I look forward to a very competent implementation.

1. MINUTES OF FIRST WALKTHROUGH MEETING

Date: D7
Present: Client/Jane
Venue: CP's office

Agendum

0. *Style*: Minutes to be kept in synoptic form other than for any matter needing amplification.
1. *Changes*: No changes to specification suggested by either side.
2. *Status*: The following activities are complete:
   0.4 Overall software design.
   Design of: utilities 4.1 and 7.1, and state 5. Design reviews have been done for all, and the client attended one such, for the overall design.
   The following actions are in progress and on schedule:
   Design of: utilities 3, 5, 6 and 7; and state 1, 3 and 4 routines. The prototype versions of utilities 1 and 2 is well advanced, and the client reported good progress, having rejected some suggested formats so far.
3. *Plan.* The client questioned the dependency between utilities' prototypes, and 3/5/6 implementation. The answer is that, at the design review of Ut.3/5/6, Jim will give the definitive results from his prototypes to Sarah, for her integrand specifications, and for the user's manual. This raised the subject of the user's manual, and the client pointed out that this is a missing activity on the D6 netplan (now added, at top). *Sarah* should note that the user (client) must be content with this by D16.

   The client also questioned two concatenations on the plan. First, why are states 3 and 4 concatenated; and second, why are units' 5 and 6 integrations apparently done in parallel? The answers were forthcoming, and accepted. (i) S3 and 4 are, like some other issues (Ut.1/2, Ut.3/5/6) very contiguous subjects, that can and should be done together; (ii) units 5 and 6 require the same resources – Jim and Richard – who therefore, between them, 'resource constrain' the plan. (It is not dangerous, but about one day might prove too optimistic to do both integrations.) Then, Jim takes the competence of the unit 5 integration into his collaboration with Sarah, and Richard takes his competence in the unit 5 integration into his (future) collaboration with Jane. Thus, it is a logical nexus.
4. *Other.* None.
   The client inspected the technical archive and passed no comment othe than: 'It's a bit thin, still it's early days'.

2. MINUTES OF SECOND WALKTHROUGH MEETING

Date: Day 18
Present: Client/CP
Venue: Client's office
File: MA(iv) – Formal

Agendum

1. *Changes*. The client requested that a change to screen format be made in the feature concerning screen overflow for index moves display. This was discussed and agreed.
2. *Status*. The D15 status matrix was discussed. Since then, the following actions have been completed:
S6 design review; unit 3 integration.
Currently, the following are in progress and on schedule:
Implementation of Ut.4, S6, S1 and S2.
The client reported that a user's manual had been drafted, discussed, agreed and produced. It was 'a bit late' (D17), but not critically so.
The activity status was generally very satisfactory, but the chief programmer pointed out that the major concatenations of events was due imminently, and decorous progress might not be so easy to achieve then. Another problem is noted in 3 below.
3. *Plan*. Jane reported that she and one other (Jim) had been affected by a computer failure around D14. She had lost a whole program file from working store, and had had to fall back on a hard copy version that was rather out of date. Jim had been caught without access, when testing Ut.1/2, for six hours! There is apparently an intermittent electrical fault on a hard disk unit head, that brings the whole system down. Fortunately, it was not so critical this time. But if it hits around D28–31, chaos will ensue. Her manager has been informed.
4. *Other*. None.

The client inspected the technical archive in full, and management archive (i) and (ii) – status matrices. Client found TA satisfactory as evidence of good practice, and is encouraged to see a volume of design documents appearing, as well as 'a cubic meter' of code listings. Thinks the status matrices are 'good' but 'of uneven level of detail' – for example, items in S1 average about 200 statements, those in (e.g.) Ut.6 about 20 statements. CP pointed out that this definition in Ut.5/6 particularly had been because its author is the least experienced team member, and 'status' seemed an important consideration. Client said that the lower half of the status matrix looks like 'Flanders field', with crosses 'row on row' as far as the eye can see; suggests we drop the ancillaries when the substantive routine has paused 'author test'. Agreed.

Client suggested next meeting on D30, not 29, as 'being just before scheduled alpha-test'. Jane asked to keep D29, as 'D30 might be a bit of a scramble, with lots of contingency planning needed'. Agreed.

3. MINUTES OF THIRD (UNSCHEDULED) WALKTHROUGH

Date:	Day 25
Present:	Client/CP plus James/(Richard)
Venue:	Jane's office
File:	MA(iv) – Formal

0. *Event*. The client arrived, at 11.30 a.m., and requested an impromptu walkthrough.
1. *Changes*. None.

2. *Status*. A new status matrix is due (from R) today, so that from D20 was used as the basis, in the meeting, for an update.

All activities due for completion before D20 had been completed on schedule, except: Part of S1 (routine 1.2 'geometry') and part of S2 ('promotion'). Jane reported that both S1 and S2 were now back on schedule. She had had to back-track for three days(!) in the period D20–22.

As for the progress since D20 status matrix, the following is reported. On schedule: S7 is implemented, code read and tested.
S6 is finished testing.
S2 is code read, and finished testing.
S1 is code read, and begun testing.

Against this, it must be reported that a major hitch has occurred in unit 5 integration. Jim, asked to be present for this purpose, reported. A fundamental discrepancy existed betweent the understanding, by he and Sarah, he could not speak for others it might affect, of how the data and file handling of utility 7 was intended to work, and how it had been implemented. This had some effect in utilities 1/2 (for imaging), but had severe impact on the design and implementation of the history/ retrieve/step/index routines. Jim pointed out it must also have potential effect in S2, where all board image and storing is done for both play (S1) and placing (S2). However the same author has done both S2 and Ut.7, so they may have been made compatible. In fact, in his view, the discrepancy has come about because of this; the needs of S2 have affected Ut.7 implementation *after* the design review of Ut.7 on day 7. Jane said that, from her investigation, this seemed likely. The original design of Ut.7 had, after the review, been perfectly competent. It must be realized that Jim is very experienced in data management problems, and had 'added value' to that design. So, Jane had instructed Richard to redo utility 7, adhering to the original design, and the design requirements of S3, 4 and 6 currently. This has caused great difficulty, but would be done. The client asked about consequences to the plan. . . .

3. *Plan*. Jane said she was awaiting Richard's suggestions, perhaps he should be co-opted? The client concurred, but said that Jim's presence may then be provocative. All agreed, and Jim withdrew to get Richard.

Richard began by saying he would 'lose' three days through this. He had started to change Ut.7 yesterday, and would finish on Monday (D26). The effect to S2 would not take more than half a day, but his work to S5 was delayed. He refused to say how his routines Ut.7 and S2 should now be integrated with the basic driver.

Jane said that she intended, around D27, to 'chair' an integration – by Richard and Jim – of unit 5 (the basic utility routines 1–6, and the redone 7), and that she would then help Richard to integrate unit 6 (the full basic driver routines, plus S2). This would affect her testing S1, but she would make that up. Richard is now on a hypercritical path because of the need for S5 by the Jim/Sarah team. They (J/S) are hypercritical too, because of the lack of unit 5 for the units 7 and 8 tests. Oddly, this hypercriticality would leave them underoccupied for a couple of days (27–28). Jim would use the time to test S3/4 most assiduously; Sarah would do 'stubbed' integration of S6 (for Jim) and S7, using the unit 4 driver, and a 'stub' for utility 7; she would also get the deliverable documentation in shape.

The client congratulated Jane on this planning. All depended on the promptness and quality of the new utility 7. Richard is, indeed, the hypercritical path, and others' future hypercriticality is contingent. It could get much worse. Paracriticality?

Jane expressed her confidence. The team is working very well under stress. Richard agreed, and said he'd 'stopped buggering about' – a technical expression, apparently.

4. *Other*. None.

Jane asked the client 'if there would be any more unexpected walkthroughs, and he replied 'by definition, not'. The meeting ended baffled, but amused.

4. MINUTES OF THE FOURTH WALKTHROUGH

Date: D29
Present: Client/GAMBIT team
Venue: Project office
File: MA(iv) – Formal

0. Client requested all team to be present. Agreed.
1. *Changes*. Client said he had noticed, at the code reading of S1, after the walkthrough on D25, that a curious feature of pawn promotion had been implemented. If the pawn move reveals the opposing king to check, this is not signified until after the promotion is effected, when the message could, surely, be thought to refer to the new piece, whether that too delivers check, or not. It is not a big point, but could it be changed? Jane replied that the change would be straightforward, and would be done before beta-testing started.

The client voiced another problem. He had asked for samples of code, before this meeting, from each team member: Sarah – Ut.3 (full routine); James – S6; Richard – S2 (routine 4); Jane – S1 (routine 2). He asked an expert software engineer for a view on the quality of code, as apparent from the listings. That person's comments were:

Sarah: Excellent in all respects; good page layout, indenting, superscription text defining integrands; good parameter naming and not much use of globals; limited parameter exporting and, therefore good localization; single functional decision per integrand; good 'structure' with few unconditional transfers.

Jim: Well structured code, but rather large integrands – one of just over two pages. Good, but not exceptional readability, rather a lot of text per page, in-line comments not too useful, but very good superscription text; good limitation of globals and very good rules for limited parameter passing; some parameter names baffling.

Richard: Rather worrying. Algebraic names for variables, even when obvious ones available (K, Q, etc.). Evidence of a strange concept for the board data as a three dimensional array (rank, file, occupancy), with a 'magic field' for special attributes of a piece, such as for *en passant* capture and castling. Congested pages in documentation, no superscript text but very many in-line comments in places, few in others. Free use of global variables, and para-

meter passing, and rather a lot of unconditional transfers. Large program units (one of over three pages).

Jane: Excellently structured and documented code – with one, rather grave exception. Why, other than that you are a mathematician, did you opt for an entirely algebraic naming system? The excellent lexicon is not enough. It is still a bugbear to have to find out what 00A47 refers to.

Now, the client asked, what was to be done? The software expert said that there would be a medium scale problem in maintaining the software done by Jim and, to a lesser extent, Jane. There would be a very substantial problem, at any time, to modify Richard's code, and the expert said that he personally would not risk it.

Jane replied that, in the time available she could only suggest the improvement of deliverable documentation on Richard's code, better superscription texts, better partitioning, better comments. On her own code, she would write a small 'back assignment' routine to convert the names in the lexicon to better ones, then run her code as an operand of this program. That should solve that problem.

The client agreed, but repeated that the code reading must have failed, in some way, for Richard's code. Jane replied that code reading had concentrated on categorical error, not 'style', and perhaps this had been a mistake. Richard remarked that he was not happy about these comments. Coming on top of others recently, he found them demotivating. Sarah pointed out that time had been a crucial factor; she had had a smaller task than others – Richard a rather difficult mixture of states and utilities. Jim said he had code read Richard's S5 routine, and had no trouble at any level, in fact they had managed to find two errors in it, which proved the point. He thought Richard's code clearer than his own in many respects.

The client expressed reservations.

2. *Status*. The current status was reported as 'roughly on schedule' (Jim suggests a comma after 'roughly'). Unit 9 is in preparation by Sarah and Jim; Richard has done unit 6, and is currently testing S5 and running it, with stubs, in unit 5; Jane had produced unit 10. The deliverable documentation is done – *pace* the previous comments.

This represents a considerable recovery from the position on D25. Jane and Richard had worked very well to produce unit 5, and James joined them for some time – hence unit 7.

The client congratulated the team, but again warned of the effect of this hiatus on quality. Had utility 7 been properly code read? Jane said that she had stood her own work down to support Richard, and that utility 7 – not a large suite – was high quality software for which she would take responsibility.

3. *Plan*. Two days remained before beta-tests. Unit 12 would be compiled – all the game-playing and piece place validation, operating on the driver – and unit 11 also (all the 'history' features, working on the driver). This would occupy D30. Then, on D31, the two fundamental units would be run together, and 'benevolently' tested in all their modes of operation. Some known bugs exist (e.g. in S5, S6 and S7), and the mutual interaction of S1 and S2 is likely to show up errors of incompatibility. However, the situation is 'on schedule', if one could schedule a voyage into the unknown.

The client thanked the chief programmer. He said how struck he was by the logical

accretion of integrated units, and hoped we would be spared 'superbug', the software engineer's nemesis, when everything goes haywire at once.

4. *Other*. The client spoke of the beta-tests to be. He referred to his note on D4 (see MA(iii)), and its point 3 – controlled changed. His tame software engineer, Herr Werner Winkel, would make a controlled change to the software, between D32 and D34. The following will be required:

(a) A GAMBIT system's disk, and operator's guide.

(b) Full user and maintenance documentation.

(c) Access to *one* person on the team, neither Jane for Sarah, for clarification. On the spin of a coin, this person had been chosen to be – our tame musician Jimmy! Let's hope he can arpeggiate a bit of sense into the software.

Herr Winkel will report his findings in a brief memorandum, and a team meeting has been convened, at 10.00 a.m. on D35, to hear this, and the client's view on quality. James enquired how well Herr Winkel understands English, and was rewarded by the client's crisp rejoinder: 'Well enough, my lad. Nice try!'

The client made a final inspection of the project archive, and expressed the view that, although he would not be prepared to eat his dinner off it, it was very comprehensive, well formatted, had obviously been very useful, and was almost readable in places. Richard remarked that the file glowed in the dark, the ambient conditions under which the job had been done, and answered to the name of 'Fred'. He was teaching it to sing 'Drink, puppy, drink'.

3.10 Extracts from management archive – set (H): tests and quality report

Test record: File MA(iii) – Formal
Author: Client
Date: D32–33

1. CHANGE TO PRESCRIBED BETA-TEST STRATEGY

I began by springing a change in method on the unhappy team. I would do the black-box tests, unaided except for access to one team member – Richard Wilcock. During this time, surprise surprise, the GAMBIT team will be required to effect their own change to the software, specified by me. Thus, *three* levels of testing will be proceeding in parallel; my black-box testing, in two parts (D32 will be testing of S1 and S2; D33 will be testing of S3–7 features); and white-box testing in two parts – those due to the team, and to Herr Winkel respectively. As for the white-box tests, these can be summarized as follows:

WBT1: The team will implement the following changes:
1. Suppress the error message after each illicit piece placement in S2, and present a composite list of illegalities after the end of sequence code, with screen overflow facility.
2. Add a feature to the 'stepthrough' option. On menu request, the system will effect 'autostep', forward or back, with a ten second delay between steps. The keyboard will be an autonomous device (Herr Winkel has a version of the operating system allowing this), and 'autostep' may be interrupted by entry to

menu states S1 or S2 only, with possible exit from them as defined in the functional specification.

3. Add a 'find mate' feature to be entered from S2 or S4, to compute a checkmate from a fixed position, and show the moves needed to do it. Menu exit will be as normal from S7.

WBT2: Herr Winkel will perform the following:

1. He will 'seed' the software with known errors of own devising, in S1, S2, S6/4, S5, and Ut.2, 3 and 7.
2. He will attempt to effect WBT1(b) as defined.
3. He will attempt to change keyboard input formats in Ut.3/6, and screen message formats in Ut.3/5.

The results are summarized as follows: section 2 = my black-box test; 3 = team's reported experience with WB1; 4 = Herr Winkel's report.

2. BLACK-BOX TESTS

This went remarkably well. I exercised the menu options (permutation of routing), and S1/S2 features, for four hours on D32, playing several games, but not storing, retrieving, filling the index and showing it, or using the step features at all. The results were successful except for the following:

2.1. The optional double first move for a pawn does not test for impeded path on the intermediate square (error in S1).
2.2. A null i/d is not tested for (error in Ut.4).
2.3. The sequence: place rook on own square, indicate previously moved, delete rook, place rook on own square, indicate not moved; seems to lead to illicit error messages (error in S2).

On day 33, I spent happy hours testing S1/2 in combination with S3–7. Again, things stood up remarkably well. Richard appeared with a system disk in which errors 2.1, 2.2 and 2.3 had been corrected!! And I thought they'd used up or drunk all their 'midnight oil'.

This time, the following errors were found:

2.4. Changing to back-step after the sequence back-forward, seems to lose the 'in range' check; an entry $n = 1$ produced very curious effects (error in S5).
2.5. A sequence: show index/show overflow/show overflow/show index seems to get the software in a tangle for some reason (error in S3/Ut7 perhaps?).
2.6. An error appeared, somewhere between menu states 1 and 2, that I later could not repeat.

Going from S1 to S2, to alter the board during a game, produced a 'ghost' piece, where none had been before, when S1 was resumed. The good news is that it was a legal placing (e.g. not a pawn on its own first rank). Even better news is that Richard was there when it happened. His diagnosis was both anatomical and blasphemous. For the record, it was a phantom bishop – appropriately, in the light of the disagnosis.

That was it, six rather obscure 'failures of compliance' thrown up by about ten hours of

very extensive and convoluted use. At the time of writing, 2.1–2.5 inclusive have been corrected, demonstrably. Error 2.6 has not recurred, and is not fixed therefore.

The acceptance will be qualified for 2.6.

3. WHITE-BOX TESTS (TEAM)

The attempt to make a new version of GAMBIT (called GAMABITMORE) produced the following:

3.1. WBT1(a) – effected and demonstrated.

3.2. WBT1(b) – partly effected; the interrupt feature not yet successful.

3.3. WBT1(c) – effected and demonstrated.

The client asked team members for their best 'objective' opinion of other's software, e.g. do they think it easy to correct/emend?

> Sarah (on Richard and Jane): Jane's software is very easy to follow, and its documentation also. I would tackle it, but not Richard's. I feel this is too complex and unclear to change unless you know it well. I obviously know Jim's stuff too well to be objective.

> Jim (on Richard and Jane): I don't follow other people's lines of thinking well in any event. I find it difficult to get into Jane's mind by looking at her code, and the documentation is rather intimidatingly functional to me. Richard's stuff is a bit like mine, sloppy and human, and I had no trouble with myself, i.e. wanting to understand it. He uses some very bizarre ways of doing things – he's an engineer – but they work. I guess his stuff is hardest to fix, but fun.

> Richard (on the other three): Sarah's stuff is OK. Her's were straightforward jobs, and anyone could fix or change the programs. Jane's stuff is like algebra, perfect but terrifying. Anyway I know it well enough. Jim writes everything like Cobol, he even uses Pascal like Cobol. It's easy to follow, but horrible. I'd throw it away and redo it, or – better – get Jane to redo it.

> Jane (on the other three): Sarah is a first class junior software engineer who wrote very good code, to equally good design, and well documented. We had no trouble here. Richard's code is idiosyncratic, but we could all follow it, even though itching to do it better; this will be a comprehension problem, in future, for changes. Jim writes big blocks of code – too big. We were playing 'tag' across pages of code every time we came near his stuff; having Richard do his code reading was a mistake on my part.

The overall impression of the team was that Herr Winkel did not stand 'a winkle's chance in hell' of changing GAMBIT. In effect, to use Jane's words: 'We passed our system as being modifiable by us, but failed it on behalf of everyone else. We've learned . . .'.

4. QUALITY REPORT – MODIFIABILITY

Author: Werner Winkel
Date: D34
File: MA(iii) – Formal

Summary of results:

4.1. WBT2(a) – seeding. First, a confession. I began by spending some hours 'black-box' operating all the features, and browsing through all the documentation, until I had a good 'feel' for the system. Then I began to fire corruptions into the routines named (see 3 above), using one of a set of GAMBIT system disks, copied for the purpose. Two main facts emerged. First, none of the 'seeds' disappeared without trace – a very upsetting thing when it happens. Second, none of the seeds caused chaos, with transfer of control unpredictably around the programs. The overall impression from this was that the software was (is) well structured. My confidence in Jane's team, not low to start with, rose.

4.2. WBT2(b) – addition. After much ado, I implemented *all* these features, and demonstrated them to the client. I was very difficult to do – too difficult. I found that the quality of implementation was very low in places (S5 particularly), and some of the deliverable documentation was execrable – Sarah's part excepted. Still, the task *was* in range of someone unfamiliar with the software, thus it is difficult to fail it on QA grounds.

4.3. WBT2(c) – the format changes were trivially easy; the code was very clear and its documentation, at all levels, accurate. I, too, found the i/d range error (2.2 above).

I conclude by recommending that the GAMBIT software is assigned a positive QA status, with the following qualification: that Sarah Milbay is required to review, revise and produce deliverable documentation for all work done by James Hughes and Richard Wilcock.

5. VERIFICATION AND VALIDATION, BY CLIENT

I conclude as follows:

5.1. The software development process was very competently undertaken in both technical and management senses. The whole process was properly archived, from which it was clear that team-meetings were regularly held, as were design reviews and code reading exercises. Even when things got sticky, around D25–30, these good practices were maintained. A most convincing feature of QC was the test plan for integration around a basic utilities 'driver' – a plan that was carried into practice exactly, even though things got displaced from the planned sequencing a little, during the hiatus.

The competence of team members was demonstrated adequately, and that competence was much higher at the end than originally.

The process of software development may be said to have been *verified*, therefore.

5.2. The GAMBIT system was compliant, with the exception of a spectral bishop appearing after the S1/S2/S1 sequence.

Equally, GAMBIT is modifiable, albeit with difficulty.

The conclusion is that the software is valid in these respects, with the reservation that the documentation of S2, 3, 4, 5 and 6, and Ut. 1, 2 and 7 is entirely reworked, by Sarah Milbay, reporting to the chief programmer. This must be completed by D37.

6. ACCEPTANCE AND QUITTANCE

The client herewith accepts GAMBIT, subject to the qualifications in 5.2 above. This acceptance will be withdrawn, with contractual consequences as defined, if either the S1/S2 compliance fault is not identified and cured by D37, or the deliverable documentation is not redone, as specified, by that date.

Signed: *Client*

4. SUMMARY COMMENTS ON THE WORKED EXAMPLE

1. The first thing to strike one is how incredibly well they did, this Rag, Tag and Bobtail crew of mathematicians, engineers and defrocked musicians. Put to work together for the first time, in a very abbreviated time-scale, *and* with coursework intervening, they produced a just about good enough system, although clearly qualified for modifiability.

    On the question of productivity, the team's effort of 1,169 hours must be incremented by the amount they spent on the FS/OSD before D1 of the development. This was, in fact, 56 hours – 2 team days. Productivity, from FS to the end of beta-test was, therefore:

    $$(4{,}950 \times 7)/1{,}225 = 28.3 \text{ source statements per person, per equivalent day.}$$

    It is perhaps instructive to see that the expectation had been a productivity of:

    $$4{,}950/(35 \times 4 + 8) = 33.4 \text{ source statements per person, per assumed day}$$

    Preposterous, of course.

2. The behavior of the team is interesting.

    Jim and Sarah obviously worked well together, and Jane had a 'mother-hen's' care for Sarah; it is doubtful if anyone really related to poor Richard, who seems to have been an amateur programmer at heart, and a not-very-good choice as deputy chief programmer. However, despite quite clear evidence of a row between the men, the team reacted to defend each other at the final walkthrough.

    We would like to meet Sarah; in seven years or so she should be a great chief programmer. Austere Jane should bend her own algebriac ways a bit, although she put out her wing to protect the embattled Richard, who was having a thin time of it in that fraught and desolate season, D25–35. Perhaps it had taken her five weeks to bridge that eleven years' age gap.

    Dismal Jimmy seems on the edge of a nexus in his career; forward into the wild world of software engineering, or back to the database world and a life of over-configured mainframes. Perhaps the only thing worse than being thought a 'Cobol-plonker' is being one.

3. Some task assignments seem a little quixotic in retrospect; everyone had a nicely integrated set of requirements to do, except Richard – the one who might be thought most in need of such. Jane had *the* most integrated set, S1 alone. Did she expect the men to be better software engineers than the women? If so, she was wrong.

4. One great virtue was clearly the integration planning, with accretion over thirteen steps. Another advantage was the very good design decomposition. It is useful to see

how relatively un-useful ('useless' is too strong), the concepts based on the OSD were. The incorporation here of OSD and design-based tasks and plans is for that purpose. The difference can be said to be the 20 percent difference between the first plan and the actual effort.

5. Aren't the status matrices fun, and aren't they revealing?

6. And didn't the 'client' get up to some devilment, with his unscheduled walkthrough – just as the males were squaring off at each other in shortsleeve order, puce in the face – and then his 'do it yourself' white-box test at the end. I can see him chuckling into his beer, the rat.

   The virtues of the walkthrough are clearly evident, but I'll bet the last two took more than an hour each.

7. Crafty client again, for his external QA agency – Herr Werner Winkel. And how well *he* did in the circumstances, making the lunatic WBT2(b) work. We'd like to see his copy of the operating system that lets terminals act as unbuffered, autonomous devices – still, it's an innovative world is that of the PSE.

8. The effort-profile in the D35 analysis shows software development as it really is. Against a comfortable, rectangular effort expenditure (100 percent per week), we find a profile more parabolic, for the first weeks, then linear.

   Done propely, the GAMBIT software should, minimally, have occupied four software engineers, working six to ten hours a day, for about fifty days – i.e. an 'overrun' of about 63 percent! That is the degree of compression involved here. Why did the job not become infeasible? For 63 percent is much greater than the 25 percent guideline in Chapter 12. The answer is that the GAMBIT team produced 'a miracle at a pauper's price'. That must be credited to the austere Jane; I have seen people take the poker to each other for less reason.

   Another point is that quality was only 'good' in a qualified sense, and the qualifications on modifiability were serious ones. The very high productivity achieved was done at a price in quality.

   Interestingly, the 'minimal' time-scale and effort quoted above would assume a productivity of equivalent to twenty source statements per person per seven-hour day. A more reasonable expectation.

9. It may be questioned whether the validation was not rather excessive for a computer game – all those levels of black- and white-box tests. In fact, the effort spent by client, Herr Winkel and the team, between D32–35, was 188 hours. Furthermore, the QC activities of design review, code reading and testing, amounted to 405 hours – making a total 'quality effort' of 593 hours over all tasks. To see this in context, one has to consider the total effort. To the total team effort of 1,225 hours, including FS/OSD stages, we must add two client days (fourteen hours) for the URS, and fifty hours for the QA time expended by the client and Herr Winkel. Thus, the effort due to QA alone was:

$$(188 \times 100)/1{,}289 = 14.6 \text{ percent}$$

whilst the total quality 'cost' was:

$$(593 \times 100)/1{,}289 = 46 \text{ percent}$$

Nearly 50 percent for quality in a computer game! Excessive, surely? Yet, this aspect of good software engineering practice was exactly the reason that Calamity Jane's ramshackle gang delivered a miracle at a robber's price. *Sic probo*, as damned Faustus would cry – 'So I prove!'

But would you travel on the space-shuttle?

APPENDIX 2

SPECIMEN QUESTIONS

There follows a specimen examination paper. This is for non-specialists in software engineering, and for new entrants to the profession – 'trainees' – assuming that both populations have completed a short orientation course in the subject, such as might be represented by the contents of this book.

The author respectfully suggests that the questions can be put to the following uses:

1. In their current form, as a set paper for examinations on courses in the subject. To course organizers and lecturers I would say: 'Try it. You may get revealing results.'
2. In their current form, or as disaggregated questions, to measure the scope of subject awareness in a department of (e.g.) 'amateur pro-grammers' (or even software engineers, come to that), and the range of that awareness.
3. In their disaggregated form, for use as individual questions requiring short, written answers at interviews – the 'literacy test'; personnel officers please note!

I have used this, and many other similar question papers, in all these ways – with splendid results, although this might not be unanimously viewed by the unfortunates on the receiving end of it all.

Some question are slightly off-center concerning the material in this book. Software engineerng is like that – almost always presenting the unexpected, and often the unwelcome it must be said, and education in the subject should prepare one appropriately. Question 7.1 is an almost perfect instance of this; I have seen it cause a classful of the brightest and best to emulate an ostrich swallowing a brass door-knob.

To those distant students in their time, and any future miners at the seams of knowledge, I offer my last, and lasting, tribute.

EXAMINATION: A THREE HOURS' WRITTEN PAPER IN SOFTWARE ENGINEERING ORIENTATION

Questions carry the following maximum scores: question 1 = 5 marks; question 2 = 8; question 3 = 15; question 4 = 10; question 5 = 24; question 6 = 12; question 7 = 6; question 8 = 6; question 9 = 4; question 10 = 10.

Note: it is possible to score 49 percent by answering perfectly all the questions bearing possible scores of 10 or less. It is also possible to spend three hours on question 5 and fail the paper catastrophically.

Question 1 See how easy number-base manipulation really is:

1.1 Express the following binary-base bit pattern by (a) its decimal number equivalent, and (b) its octal equivalent:

100 011 001 111

1.2 The following are numbers in octal (base eight): 5, 2, 4, 6. Express them as (a) their binary equivalents, and (b) their decimal equivalents.

1.3 Express the following hexadecimal numbers as (a) their binary, and (b) their octal equivalents: f, a, d, b.

1.4 Express the hexadecimal number 2f61 as its equivalent in septal (number-base seven).

1.5 111 and 11 are numbers in bases seven and two respectively. Express their ratio (111 : 11) as a number in base five.

Question 2 The following assertions contain fallacies; identify them, and explain briefly why they are fallacies:

2.1 'Software development is the theoretical basis for software engineering, and concerns research into standard ways of making software.'

2.2 'Software engineering is that part of computer science concerning research into programming methods.'

2.3 'Software engineering is the set of adequate management techniques for software development – no more, no less.'

2.4 'Software development is like electronic assembly, and should be done on the basis of circuit diagrams in standard notations, and using basic functional "software components".'

Question 3 Figure A.9 purports to be a rudimentary life cycle depiction of a software product development task:

3.1 Are 'Passes 1(1) and 1(2)' examples of prototype activity with software development, so far as one can see from the diagram? If not, explain why you hold the view, and suggest a better expression to describe 'Passes 1(1) and 1(2)'.

3.2 Identify the categorical error in 'Pass 5' concerning the overall task description, and give a brief explanation of your answer, indicating how the diagram should be emended.

3.3 The total development budget, set during URS 1, was equivalent to 87.3 person-years of effort, and an 'opportunity window' for the product development of three years was estimated as the maximum lead-time to get the product to market. Completion of FS5 finds the company with an estimate to develop of 32.2 person-years of effort in eighteen elapsed months, and residuals on original budgets of 15.1 person-years and fourteen months respectively. Advance three

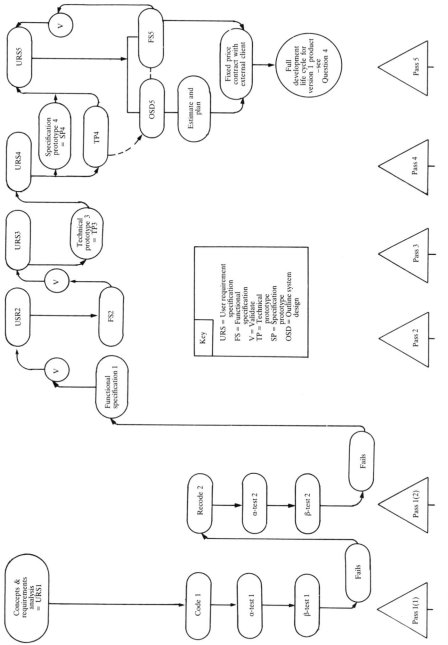

FIGURE A.9

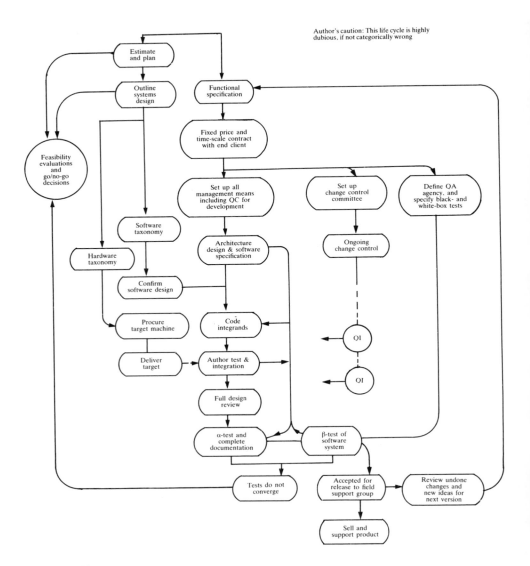

Author's caution: This life cycle is highly dubious, if not categorically wrong

FIGURE A.10

fundamental arguments why the company should not try to save time and cost by predicating 'Implementation 5' on the prototypes TP3 and SP4, and the code from 'Implementation 1(2)'.

3.4 Assuming a cubic relationship in $E \propto T^z$, what would be the expected effort to

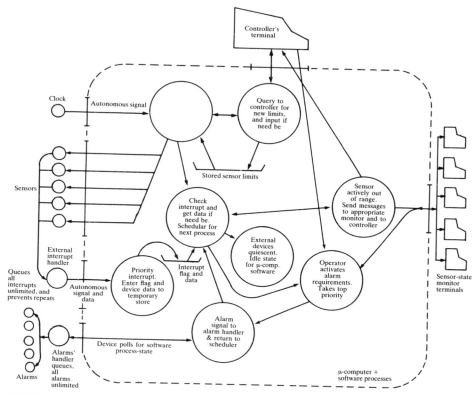

FIGURE A.11

do the substantive 'Pass 5' development in (a) the fourteen months available, and (b) nine months?

3.5 Assuming the resources to be available for option (b) in 3.4, outline arguments why it should not be attempted.

Question 4 Figure A.10 purports to be a simplified life cycle scheme for the substantive product development at 'Pass 5' of the previous example.

4.1 The scheme incorporates several major categorical errors, or at least highly questionable aspects, some being errors of commission and one being a serious error of omission consequent on one of the errors of commission.

Define these apparent anomalies, and explain the probable consequences flowing from them.

4.2 Comment on the apparent schedule for a full design review between completion of authors' integration tests, and their full-scale alpha-testing of the system.

4.3 Where on the schematic would you expect to see the 'user's manual' written?

Question 5 Figure A.11 is a simple depiction, in Mascot-ACP notation, of sensor-based process applications with interrupt and polling features.

5.1 Write a short functional specification for the software requirements within the microcomputer, in the following format: a brief, but complete systems description so far as can be deduced; assumptions; a definition of the processes, suggesting additional detail where possible; a definition of input and output messages both between processes, and across the exogenous interface.

5.2 In the scheme as shown, it is possible that interrupts may be lost by arriving more quickly than the microcomputer software can handled them. Redraw the Mascot diagram to solve this problem by software (process) means.

5.3 The following events occur at the times indicated in seconds:

Clock initiates reset sensor limits (0.0); interrupt from sensor 4 (0.005); interrupt from sensor 1 (0.007); manual input query to controller (0.04); affirmative response from controller (2.8); alarm on sensor 4 state (0.63); interrupt from sensor 5 (2.719); state output to monitor for sensor 4 (1.62); state output to monitor for sensor 1 (6.7) controller manual input of critical ranges (6.2–38.1); interrupt from sensor 2 (6.7); alarm on sensor 5 state (3.0).

Draw a timing diagram showing these events, and indicate their connectivity by cross-bars (horizontal connecting lines).

5.4 What 'granularity of time' applies in the process system defined; explain how you arrive at the conclusion.

5.5 Use data-flow notation to depict the activities in the Mascot/ACP diagram (Figure A.11).

5.6 In a small essay (half of an A4/5 page, say), explain why you think data flow is either suitable or otherwise for the purpose in 5.5, and use your previous answer to illustrate this.

Question 6 One author gives the following formula concerning software reliability (Shooman 1983):

$$\text{Availability} = T(\text{up})/[T(\text{up}) + T(\text{down})]$$

where $T(\text{up})$ = sum of all up times (t_{iu}) over i identical configurations; $T(\text{down})$ = sum of all down times (t_{id}) similarly; 'up time' is when the (software) system is working properly; 'down time' is when it is not.

Now, the production made at 'Pass 5' of Questions' 3 and 4 life cycle, is sold to five clients. Over the first year, the statistics given in Table A.15 are collected by the field maintenance group (in all cases, 'down time' is caused by software failure alone; up and down times are expressed as percentages; relative intensity/variety of use are factors measured on an agreed scale of values).

6.1 What value for availability would you derive from Schooman's formula as it stands? Do you take this value as a fair/plausible measure of reliability? If so, advance arguments why, as though to convince a non-subject specialist; if not, likewise.

6.2 Two alternative formulae are put forward relating the following quantities:

TABLE A.15

Client	(days)	Period of measurement (%)	(%)	Relative intensity	Relative variety of use
A	50	98	2	0.5	0.2
B	150	48	52	1.0	0.8
C	5	100	0	1.0	1.0
D	300	87	13	0.7	0.1
E	50	100	0	0.6	0.7

n = sample size (5 in this case).

d = period over which measurement was taken; sum of all d is total of such over the sample.

$t(up)$ = up time expressed as a fraction, e.g. 0.98 in case A above.

$i + v$ = relative intensity + relative variety of use; sum $(i + v)$ is total of such over the sample.

iv = product of intensity and relative variety of use; sum (iv) is total of such over the sample

Formula (b)

$$\text{reliability} = n \text{ (for all } i \text{ sum } (d_i/\text{sum } (d_i) \times t_i(\text{up}) \times (i_i v_i)/\text{sum } (i_i v_i))$$

Formula (b)

$$\text{reliability} = n \text{ (for all } i \text{ sum } (d_i/\text{sum } (d_i) \times t_i(\text{up}) \times (i_i v_i)/\text{sum } (i_i v_i))$$

Using the values in the table, compute reliability according to these formulae.

6.3 Are either, both, or neither values from 6.2 more plausible than that from 6.1? State your arguments in full.

6.4 As a client, what stance would you adopt toward your supplier on the basis of the availability/reliability figures from 6.1 and 6.2? How would you justify it?

Question 7 Conceptions in software engineering often require lateral thought.

7.1 What physical demonstration, from any field of endeavor, could you offer for the legitimacy of the arithmetic convention:

$$-(-1) = +1$$

Your answer should say enough to show that it really fits the question.

7.2 In what aspect of software development is that arithmetic convention espoused? Describe how this is essential to the process, in a short essay of about one A4/A5 page.

Question 8

8.1 Define the following terms: white box tests; synchrony; type; maintenance manual; algorithm; Petrinet; global variable; static test; verification; code reading.

8.2 What relationship do the following bear toward each other: editor, configuration management system, PSE, database management system, program linker/loader, Ipse, Ada compiler.

8.3 What is the essential difference between validation and certification of a software system?

Question 9 Programming matters

9.1 List the main criteria in choosing a programming language, assuming that you have a set of substantial and well defined applications to be undertaken for the first time, and a computer of adequate properties – however acquired – but no programming languages and their associated tools, as yet.

9.2 Rank the following in order of decreasing importance for program readability:

not more than twenty lines of print per page; extensive and detailed in-line comments; structured (goto-less) code; minimal global variables; language statements allowing extended syntax; lack of magic numbers; indenting of text; address naming as distinct from numbering, superscript 'essay' text defining purpose and access means.

9.3 Specify an integrand, by means of a structured flowchart using the three basic constructs for iteration, sequence and choice, to describe how you solved Question 1.5. (If you have not attempted that question yet, you had better do so now.)

Question 10 Management techniques

10.1 How would back-tracking be depicted on: (a) a cumulative cost (effort) graph over time; (b) an activity plan; (c) a status matrix? Draw simple diagrams in each case to illustrate your answers.

10.2 Which of the following are best viewed as formal documents, and which may be viewed as informal ones: (a) effort and time estimates for life cycle phase 1 activities; (b) proceedings of the change control committee; (c) QI deficiency reports; (d) functional specification; (e) the result of prototype TP3 in the Question 3 life cycle?

Justify (or qualify) your answer as necessary in each case.

10.3 By replicating a part of the Question 4 life cycle, indicate the stage at which general comprehensibility of issues becomes specialist comprehensibility.

10.4 Are software systems above the level of small, S programs, likely to be categorically provable? If so indicate by what means; if not, indicate why not – in either case, a half page essay (A4/5) will suffice.

10.5 What documents would you require access to in order to conduct a management structured walkthrough of a software development?

10.6 Indicate the most likely matching of terms in the following lists – note, only one correspondence (the 'most likely') is called for.

List A	*List B*

List A
1. Company payroll
2. Digital telephone switch
3. Multi-station word processor
4. PC-game 'FRAAK'
5. On-board satellite control

List B
1. User input error diagnostic
2. *n*-order, hot standby, with election
3. Security access system with i/d card
4. Dictionary and lexical analyzer
5. Warm standby allowing some message-loss

Postscript: Deciding to proctor this examination once, I watched students turn over the paper – and change color. One at a time they slowly raised their eyes to mine, each pair having a hunted look. No one spoke, for that was disallowed under examination rules, except I:

'Oh yes it can', I said stoutly, 'but not if you waste any more time trying to stare me to death.'

I was right, and I have a set of their completed papers to prove it – one scoring as high as 90 percent and all better than a halfway score. Courage then, and success.

APPENDIX 3

GLOSSARY OF TERMS

Apology

This glossary was planned from the start, and is not an afterthought tacked on to avoid criticism of unexplained terms. The alternative was thought to be either too cumbersome, a repetitive definition of terms, or too abrupt and inaccessible – such as a single amplification wherever a term is first used.

It will undoubtedly fall short of expectation, where that is seen as the sum total of all its possible uses, for one would need at least another volume for that; thus compendia such as the *Dictionary of Computing* (Glaser *et al.* 1983) are available – and highly recommended – for general reference purposes. This is a little concentration of some rare, and not-so-rare, terms that the reader might find useful not only in reading this work and others in the series, but for general usage. It begins with a summary of abbreviations in frequent use, usually derived from late Latin. As for what we might call 'subject-specific' terms, a lexical interpretation is offered.

To give two examples from the preceding sentences: lexical: pertaining to the use of words (OED); OED: Oxford English Dictionary.

In the following, to avoid a plethora of cross-referencing amongst terms in the glossary, only forward-referencing to hitherto undefined terms is used.

Abbreviations

cf.	Lat., imperative of *conferre* (to compare)	compare
e.g.	Lat., *exampli gratia*	for example
FIDE	Féderation Internationale des Échecs	World Chess Federation
ibid.	Lat., *ibidem*	in the same place
i.a.	Lat., *inter alia*	amongst other things
i.e.	Lat., *id est*	that is
Lat.		Latin (source)
n.b.	Lat., *nota bene*	note well
OED		Oxford English Distionary
op. cit.	Lat., *opere citato*	in the work quoted

passim	Lat., past participle of *pandere* (to spread out)	scattered throughout
q.v.	Lat., *quod vide*	which see
seriatim	Lat.	serially; in order
sic	Lat.	so

Other, non-abbreviated terms – understood meanings

a fortiori:	Lat. 'from strong(er) reason'
a posteriori:	Lat. 'from later reasons'
a priori:	Lat. 'from prior reasons'
ex post facto:	Lat. 'from after the fact'
locus quem:	Lat. 'the point from which'

Synoptic definition of terms

Activity plan Logically ordered, resources-constrained schedule of necessary actions to achieve a defined objective; often depicted graphically in one of a variety of notations within methods such as CPM (critical path method) and PERT (project evaluation and review technique).

Adaptive A type of application in computer use embodying rule-based decisions and their adaptation through acquired experience; comprises the fields of advanced expert systems and simulated ('artificial') intelligence.

Algorithm Any set of defined rules for solving a problem; often, but not necessarily, mathematical or logic-based. Algorithms and associated data-definitions are what make up integrand (q.v.) specifications.

Alpha-test The most comprehensive level of testing undertaken by the author-team (q.v.) during software development; part of quality control comprising dynamic black-box (q.v.) tests to demonstrate the compliance (q.v.) of the software system. When other system components are to be tested in combination with developed software, the most comprehensive level of this testing is the system's alpha-test.

Amateur programmer A person whose active engagement in software development is intermittent within some other field of vocational specialism, such as electronic engineering; as a result, there is diminished opportunity for empirical learning in the subject, and the consolidation of experience into a framework of 'good software engineering' practice.

Archive An ordered, historical record of a software development over all stages of the 'life cycle' (q.v.) from earliest system concepts, to delivery, maintenance and evolution of the software artefact; initiated and maintained by the author-team (q.v.) as part of good software management practice.

Author-team One or more people engaged directly in software development activities such as specification, design and implementation.

Batch The way in which a software system is performed, in this case as a task within a sequential 'batch' of such; the connotations are that the output results are not required

with urgency but, say, within hours or even days of the task being presented for operation on the computer.

Behavior space The total permutation of eventualities within a system, software plus hardware in this case, for all possible usages of it arising from foreseen ('licit') inputs and accidental inputs of all forms. With licit and illicit human usage, limited by input means, a behavior space may still be a very large number of possible eventualities.

Beta-test The independent dynamic (q.v.) testing of a software system to determine its compliance (q.v.) by means of black-box (q.v.) testing, and its modifiability (q.v.) by means of white-box (q.v.) testing. The activities are seen as quality assurance, and include the status of the deliverable documentation (q.v.); the 'independence' is achieved by beta-tests being undertaken by competent software engineers not part of the author-team.

Big-bang An ill-advised testing practice, the exact converse of a recommended practice of accretive testing embodied in the precept to 'build a bit, test a bit; build a bit more, test a bit more'; the whole, or a large part of software, is dynamically tested in complex combination for the first time. The behavior space of possible eventualities is, therefore, very large at a time when confidence in the software to work as required is, inevitably, very low.

Black-box As in 'black-box testing'; a practice within dynamic alpha- and beta-testing to determine the compliance of a software system operating on its intended computer configuration, whereby the software is treated as a unity defined by its legitimate inputs, and its expected outputs consequential on these inputs – plus the expected behavior (output) in the event of illicit input according to the definition of legitimacy.

Bottom up (a) Design. The notion or approach to program design that sees requirements in terms of details of program or integrand (q.v.) features in the first place, and proceeds 'upward' by progressive aggregation, to a point where (it is hoped) the collection of detailed designs fits the requirements.

(b) Testing. Progressive, accretive dynamic (q.v.) testing of program parts, programs, program aggregates and so on, with the test environment being incremented for each additional program component involved.

Bottom up testing should be planned, and not haphazard or merely circumstantial.

Certification The practice of operating a software system in its real-world environment, as distinct from testing it otherwise, however exhaustively and plausibly, in order to enhance confidence in its compliance (q.v.). The software system being so 'certified' would not be contractually accepted until this stage is satisfactorily completed.

Cohesion The degree of single purposefulness of programs or program parts; a low level design concept closely related to that of information hiding (q.v.). The degrees of cohesion are graduated from 'coincidental' (low) to 'functional' (high). See also *coupling* for an associated concept in good design.

Complexity A compound feature of (software) systems on which many issues such as estimating, management in general of the development process, testing, maintenance and evolution are dependent. The aggregate effect comprises the following elements: complexity of intention through specification; complexity of implementation through design and programming; and complexity of interaction – basically the behavior space problem, concerning the dynamic behavior of software.

Compliance The 'fit' between dynamic behavior of a software system and its required properties as specified by 'hard', management requirements in the functional specification (q.v.). This 'fit', which may be seen as an absence of misfit (Alexander 1964), tends to be positively demonstrated through 'black-box' alpha-testing by the author-team; a failure to falsify this positive demonstration by independent 'black-box' beta-testing leads to the conclusion that software is compliant, so far as is known.

Component A program or program part developed with design reuse in mind, to serve purposes across a set of specifications for which it is functionally suitable. Although far from unknown, software component development is relatively rare in the totality of software development.

Computation A type of application in computer use embodying high order arithmetic and logic operations on low order aggregates of data, via numerical methods and other algorithms and formulae comprising the functions of programs and program parts.

Computer science Research into, and study of, computer systems in general, their means of use (languages) and applications. Properly seen as a subject in applied mathematics, computer science provides the formal foundations for software engineering (q.v.), and research into improvements in practical methods.

Concurrent Happening at the same time; concurrent features are often properties of distributed systems in process- (q.v.) oriented systems that are designed for real-time (q.v.) applications.

Configuration The duplex of programs and data comprising a software system and the relevant deliverable documentation (q.v.), between which there should be a one-for-one correspondence. Configuration control concerns the management of this correspondence during the evolutionary history of software versions (q.v.); synonyms are configuration control, configuration management, version control and version management.

Coupling A term in program design associated with the concepts of cohesion and information hiding (q.v.); meaning the degree of connectedness of programs or program parts. As with cohesion, there is a spectrum-scale of coupling encompassing 'data-coupled' (generally low order), 'control-coupled' (average) and 'common-coupled' (high order) instances. An object of good design is to achieve low order coupling/high order cohesion. Data-coupled elements pass data via argument lists; control-coupled elements effect decisions across the interfaces by means of signals; common-coupling is a feature of systems with globally defined data areas.

Data processing A type of application in computer use in which low order arithmetic or logical operations are performed on high order aggregates of data whose ordering and structure are, therefore, important for the efficiency of the process.

Design As in 'software design'; the progressively detailed conceptualization of a system of programs ('solution') whose dynamic execution on defined computer and ancillary equipment will serve a set of explicitly defined requirements. In many contractual cases, software design cannot be incorporated in specification, as might seem ideal, due to the technical limitations of users' defining requirements, and their need to authorize specifications.

Documentation As in 'deliverable documentation'; the minimal, necessary and sufficient definition of the system of programs developed to supply an explicitly specified set

of requirements. Deliverable documentation – so called because it is due to users/ operators of the system, and to agencies nominated to maintain it – usually comprises a user's/operator's manual and a maintenance manual (q.v.). The sufficiency of maintenance documentation, involving version control, is crucial to maintenance and evolution of programs; even so, maintenance documentation is a representation of the static state (programs), whereas the real issue (software) is a dynamic matter.

Dynamic As in 'dynamic testing'; the attempted execution of programs on the equipment-type for which they were developed. Dynamic testing stands in contradistinction to static testing (q.v.), which concerns the inspection of programs to detect errors.

Education As in 'software engineering education'; more properly seen as craft-oriented training in which practical experience is a prerequisite in a sequence of minimal training – doing – failing – doing – succeeding – consolidating. Education, in these terms, is the amplification of empirically gained knowledge, and its extension then, into a framework of good practice.

Efficiency Of programs, usually expressed in terms of space – i.e. bytes of programmable store occupied by the translated programs – or the time it takes for them to execute (q.v.) on defined equipment. Achieving efficiency objectives should not be allowed to occlude good design principles other than knowingly (i.e. after a good design has been implemented), and within limits. Otherwise, modifiability (q.v.) is likely to be reduced.

Estimate The management concept in software development involving derivation of effort and time-scale resources required to undertake the defined task; these values are normally derived from an activities' plan for the development, done on the basis of an outline design or an actual software design.

Execute The dynamic behavior of programs, translated into a working state for defined equipment; synonyms in this context are 'run' and 'operate'.

Formal As in 'formal methods'; in fact, a slight misnower since 'methods' carries the connotation of certainty of use. Formal means concerns the research into, and progressive use where appropriate, of abstract languages in order (a) to reduce the ambiguity of specification in natural language, and (b) to reduce the possibility of divergence from specification through transliteration into design notations and computer languages. In the limiting case, this concerns the formal computation of correctness (program proof) at steps of transliteration – another research topic.

Functional specification The base-line document that, when authorized by requirement and solution authorities, acts as the definition against which a software system will be developed, and against which its compliance will be validated by black-box beta-tests. For these purposes, the functional specification must be the necessary and sufficient information about requirements, unambiguously expressed.

Heuristic Literally, 'finding out'. Applied in the context of rule-based applications, such as so-called 'expert' systems and in simulated intelligence research, for optimal or best-search algorithms.

Hobbyist A computer programmer who practices for self-instruction or entertainment, but not as a part of working occupation; thus is even more unlikely than an amateur

programmer to acquire real software engineering skills, or produce good quality software. A subspecies is the 'hacker' who employs specialist, acquired knowledge of computers, programming and communication technology to violate security/integrity of developed systems.

Host A computer configuration, hardware, software and ancillaries, for software development as distinct from its intended execution, for which the defined target (q.v.) configuration is required.

Implementation The activities for detailed definition of algorithms and data for programs, coding programs in a defined language, and testing them by static and dynamic means at author level, with progressive, logical accretion of programs in the dynamic testing stage, up to alpha-test. Incorporated in this author-team implementation activity is the continuation and completion of documentation.

Information hiding A concept, due to Parnas and of use in low level design of integrands (q.v.) and programs, in which the localizing of function for cohesion is accompanied by that of access (single entry/single exit), and availability of data and parameters, which are locally not globally defined. The concept of cohesion fits with that of information hiding which, if achieved, produces low order coupling.

Information technology (IT) A generic term of wide-ranging and uncertain scope, generally taken to mean any and all things concerning computer hardware and software, and their applications in the widest sense, and those incorporating other technologies such as communications, electronics in the widest sense and production engineering. IT is seen, correctly, since about 1975 as constituting a new industrial revolution.

Integrand The smallest part of program structure directly accessible by assigned name, apart from data; generally, an integrand incorporates a single function or decision, or a limited set of such, and embodies the principles of design cohesion and information hiding. An integrand may be a few statements of code, several dozen, or anything up to a hundred or so, but is unlikely – give the purpose of cohesion – to be larger. Integrands are linked into larger units of addressable code, programs and program packages, and their accretive testing is known as integration – from which they derive their names.

Integration A dynamic testing method, in which developed programs, or program parts, are tested in logical combination with each other on a planned and purposive basis, toward the assembly of the total system and its trial to alpha-test level without 'big bang' effects.

Integrity The avoidance of, or detection/recovery from, accidental corruption or loss of programs or data.

Ipse Integrated project support environment. The combination of (host) hardware and software facilities on which software development is done in the technical sense of specification, design, implementation and validation, and the whole process is supported by management tools within the electronic environment.

Large As in 'large software system'; generally taken to be any combination of programs comprising *circa* 100,000–1,000,000 source statements of code.

Lehman types A loose but serviceable classification of (software) systems on the basis of their specification characteristics. Thus; S systems are ones whose specification can be

formally expressed and will be invariant; P systems are precisely specifiable at a high generic level, but only approximately at more detailed levels of analysis where suitable algorithms will be liable to change over time; E systems are ones whose specifications will tend to change over time, as requirements in the real world evolve.

Life cycle A directed graph, normally in box and arrow notation (q.v.), of main activities in software development. Generally used as a management model of the process, conceptually adequate if not oversimplified.

Manuals As in deliverable documentation. There are usually considered to be three such for necessity and sufficiency; (a) the user's manual describing what the system does, and not necessarily how it does it or how to get it to do so; (b) the operator's manual describing how to use the system, i.e. start/stop, restart and recover, with details of diagnostics for faulty use and corrective actions required; (c) the maintenance manual comprising extracts from the functional specifications, software designs, high quality code listings and test data and results.

Medium As in 'medium sized software system'; generally taken to be any combination of programs comprising *circa* 2,000–100,000 source statements of code.

Method An explicit and generally accepted way of doing something. Specifically, in software design a method will comprise a procedure to be adopted, and a notation (or language) for depicting the result. Either or both, or neither, of the procedure and notation may be elaborate, relatively simple, or even quite trivial.

Methodology A term used loosely to mean 'method', or the procedure of a method. Its proper meaning concerns the science and study of methods.

Model As in 'software estimating model'; more properly, parametric cost/time estimating model. The formula relationship between effort (E), time (T) and task properties (P_t) and environment properties (P_e); of the general from $F(E, T, P_t, P_e) = 0$.

Modifiability The relative ease or difficulty experienced in changing a software system, and the relative likelihood of decreased reliability after so doing. Software may be difficult to change owing to structural properties at the level of programs or data, or inadequacy of documentation, or both.

Modifiability and compliance comprise the two mandatory criteria of software quality (q.v.), and subsume reliability.

Module A very imprecise term, generally used in its adjectival form 'modular' to denote 'non-monolithic', as in 'modular design' and 'modular programming'. Design modules are whatever parts of a design are being described, and may be at high or low level of detail; program modules, likewise, may be large aggregates of statements, or small functional units comprising few statements. A 'load module' may be a set of programs linked for purposes of translation to machine executable code, or for presentation to a target (q.v.) machine for execution.

Notation A term to distinguish graphical design languages, comprising a vocabulary (of symbols) and a syntax (rules) for their use, from other types of language such as: (a) natural language, (b) abstract languages for use in formal means and (c) programming languages.

On-line The way in which a software system performs, in this case interactively with human users whose response requirements will determine response characteristics of the software (else it is non-compliant).

OSD Outline system design. A notional design exercise in which elements in the functional specification are seen in terms of their possible solution as hardware or software; details of notional hardware and software systems are developed as catalogs or taxonomies (q.v.) to act as the basis for feasibility and estimating exercises.

Paradigm An especial example with a connotation of shared experience.

Peer-group CPT Peer-group chief programmer team. A small sized group of task-oriented software engineers, typically three to six in number and of various skill levels, who define, estimate and do the whole or part of a software development task. The value of good software engineering practice including strong, stage-wise quality control (q.v.) is stressed within a highly motivated, professional ethos.

Process Concerning events or activities ongoing over a duration; in software engineering (q.v.), the type of systems in which time is a major determinant in compliance, either concerning synchrony (q.v.), or limited allowable response delay to stimuli as in applications containing so-called real-time (q.v.) properties.

Program A set of statements in a computer language that, when translated into executable form, will regulate the equipment's circuitry to perform specified tasks in a required way. A program may be a small number of such statements, or a larger aggregation up to any size. In good practice, however, large monolithic programs are avoided in order to segment the behavior space problem in testing and repair. Generally, a program comprises a set of generically related integrands, each incorporating algorithms and data.

Proof In the context of software development, proof concerns the categorical correctness of program statements to bring about a prescribed state (the 'post-condition') from an original state ('pre-condition'). The result is a static proof of a program or program part; any inference that this is a correctness-status for the software of which it is a part must be qualified for its dependency on other factors such as the virtual machine on which programs are dynamically executed, as well as the consistency of the program's post-condition with real requirements.

Prototype An original pattern or model effected to increase knowledge. Thus the activity to make a prototype is seen as an exercise in 'buying information'; in software development this can be about one of two things particularly: (a) scope of specifications, or their detail; (b) technical means to bring about a (software) solution.

PSE Programming support environment; the technical support tools for software development and, thus, properly seen as a subset of the Ipse. Such tools may be primitive or elaborate, not integrated or highly integrated. The ideal, which tends to be expensive, is for extensive (as required) integrated tool-sets, whether within an Ipse or not.

Quality (a) Of software in general. The properties of compliance and modifiability, qualification of either leading to concomitant reservation on software quality. Reliability (q.v.) is not overlooked, being subsumed in the two, named, mandatory quality criteria.

(b) Quality control (QC). The activities directed by the author-team for achieving high quality software. These include (*inter alia*) the use of good software engineering practices in general, appropriate PSE tools, code reading and design review practices, and a sufficiency of planned testing within a rational integration policy – all of which presume the relevant competence of 'authors'. The end objects of QC are the code as it is brought into being, and its documentation, but the QC process should be seen as operating on all stages of the life cycle from specification to alpha-test.

(c) Quality inspection (QI). The independent monitoring of QC activities and provisions to ensure that such are undertaken and are competent.

(d) Quality assurance (QA). The independent determination of compliance and modifiability, by means of black- and white-box beta-tests, of the software and its documentation. This is generally best done by the same independent agency as does QI.

Real-time An impressive term, often too loosely assigned for the good of its possible, more precise use. Properly seen as the property of applications that requires software to behave in a manner corresponding to events in the external world and, to some degree, synchronized with them. An instance would be critical response to stimuli. Consequently, the execution time of a program becomes a critical feature of compliance, and software systems for real-time applications may take on highly complex structures with concurrency features, and highly elaborate devices to achieve a required response time.

Reliability Properties of a software system concerning its two fundamental criteria of quality:

(a) In compliance; the tendency of the system to go on working as specified if operated properly, improperly or under accidental conditions; the construction of the system in the interest of its integrity is the foundation for its degree of reliability in this regard.

(b) Of modifiability; the degree of confidence a qualified person may have to effect serious modification to a software system. The construction of the system for these purposes – such as rationally decomposed design, and the structured coding of 'cohesive' integrands with low coupling via information hiding – is the foundation for its degree of reliability in this regard, and its maintenance documentation is equally important.

Reuse A desideratum in software development, concerning the increased possibility to develop software components for use across a requirements set. The difficulties of defining commonality tend to outweigh any technical difficulties to make multi-usable integrands or programs, and the degree of real reuse, as distinct from multiple execution, remains relatively low in software development.

Security The avoidance or detection of unauthorized, purposive access to programs or data, through the use of software keys, encryption and special hardware devices.

Software (a) Software system. The dynamic behavior of programs, in their lowest order translated state (i.e. highest degree of abstractness), on the computer and ancillary equipment for which they were developed.

(b) Software development. The set of activities in specification, design, implementation, validation and emendation required to produce programs to satisfy explicit requirements when executed as software.

(c) Software engineering. The corpus of knowledge, from computer science and empirical practice, whereby software development may be done best.

(d) Software engineer. A person versed in software engineering and skilled in its enactment, as distinct from a hobbyist/hacker or an amateur programmer.

State As in 'finite state'; a concept based on a notional automaton or 'machine' in which, for a duration, its state is defined by the input functions that have brought it about, the output functions to which it will give rise, and the changed state function that will alter its properties for a next duration. The simplest, and most common, example in software development is that of a menu-driven system.

Static testing Error detection in program code/data, by inspection ('reading') as distinct from dynamic execution.

Status matrix A tabular 'snapshot' through an activities' plan concerning software design, implementation and testing activities, showing the state of activities for parts in development at that time; states are: not started ($-$), started but not complete (**0**), or completed ($+$). Back-tracking, e.g. from $+$ to **0** or $-$, is possible to depict and detect easily this way.

Structured As in 'structured coding'; the use of single entry/single exit concepts for integrand design, and simple, standard design concepts for algorithms within them based on standard structures for sequence, iteration and choice. Properly applied, structured code – along with cognate notions of cohesion, coupling and information hiding – act to contain gratuitous complexity of implementation at the coding level.

Synchrony The quality of being coincidental in time.

Target Machine; the computer configuration – hardware and software – and ancillary equipment on which programs are designed to execute as software, as distinct from any other configuration on which they were developed ('host').

Taxonomy A catalog of generically related items for which a specialized nomenclature exists; thus a hardware taxonomy, tools taxonomy and notional software taxonomy in the outline systems design.

Top down An approach to detailed definition, e.g. in the design of programs, in which high level, generic statements of requirements are considered in parts (decomposition) and progressively defined to greater levels of solution detail, with associated decomposition at these levels. The term stands in contradiction to 'bottom up'. Few exercises in design are ever either one or the other entirely.

URS User requirements specification. The result of systems analysis and systems engineering to elicit requirements. The results are often insufficient to act as base-line for implementation/validation, and a 'clean-up' exercise, involving abstraction and the avoidance of ambiguity to produce a functional specification, is generally required.

V & V Verification and validation activities in QI/QA to establish software quality. The process of software development is said to be verified as competently undertaken by the QI independent (non-author-team) agency; the software systems are said to be valid if they successfully survive attempts to falsify their compliance by beta-test undertaken by the QA independent (non-author-team) agency. Where greater surety in quality is

required, a certification may be undertaken – and the whole process is then known as VV & C.

Version The generation of a software system before (further) changes are made to it, either for corrective maintenance or emendation reasons. It is crucial to relate the versions of a software system to an accurate representation of its static state (program documentation) through a configuration management system.

Virtual As in 'virtual computer'; the combination of computer and ancillary hardware, operating and PSE (or Ipse) software comprising a host or target.

Walkthrough Alternately, 'structured' walkthrough; a purposive review for one of two distinct reasons, or both at the same time – i.e. technical considerations of design, implementation or testing; and management planning resource allocation and control. The two purposes will be strongly interdependent, but walkthrough activities for technical review purposes should be held as separate events to those for resource management purposes.

White-box As in 'white-box testing'; part of beta-testing, but this time more to form a judgmental view of modifiability than to validate compliance. The software is seen as a holistic aggregation of program and program parts, and white-box testing effectively judges the quality of its design in the sense of cohesion, coupling and structure. This, it must be said, may be a relatively straightforward matter for computation and data processing applications, although in the latter case program structure is not the whole of the matter as the modification of data structures may be a limiting issue. However, the whole issue of white-box testing of process-oriented systems for real-time requirements may be very far from straightforward.

The methods of white-box testing include error-seeding, and attempts to make controlled changes to code; and these are usually undertaken by the independent QA agency.

APPENDIX 4

REFERENCES

Abrahams, P., 'What is computer science?', *Communications of the ACM*, Vol. 30, No. 6 (1987), pp. 472–3.

ACARD, *Software – a Vital Key to UK Competitiveness* (report) (HMSO, 1986).

Agrawal, J.C., and Zunde, P. (Editors), *Empirical Foundations of Information and Software Science* (Plenum Press, 1984).

Akiyama, F., *An Example of Software Debugging*, proc. IFIP Congress '71 (Ljubljana) (American Federation of Information Societies, 1971).

Alexander, C., *Notes on the Synthesis of Form* (Harvard University Press, 1964).

Allworth, S.T., *Introduction to Real-time, Software Design* (Macmillan Computer Science Series, 1981).

Ansoff, H.I., and Brandenberg, F.G., 'A language for organizing design', *Management Science*, Vol. 17, No. 12 (1971), pp. 705–31.

Balzer, R., and Swartout, W., 'On the inevitable intertwining of specification implementation', *Communication of the ACM*, Vol. 25, No. 7 (1982), pp. 438–40.

Balzer, R., Cheatham, T.E., and Green, C., 'Software technology in the 1990's using a new paradigm', *IEEE Computer Journal* (Nov. 1983), pp. 39–45.

Barnes, J.G.P., *Programming in Ada* (Addison-Wesley, 1982), pp. 271–2.

Belady, L.A., and Lehman, M.M., 'A model of large program development', *IBM Systems Journal*, Vol. 15, No. 3 (1976), pp. 225–52.

Belady L.A., and Lehman, M.M., 'The characteristics of large systems', in P. Wegner (ed.), *Research Directions in Software Technology* (MIT Press, 1979), pp. 106–38.

Benington, H.D., *Production of large computer programmes*, Proc. ONR 1956; Symposium on Advanced Programming Methods; pp. 15–27.

Bergland, G.D., 'A guided tour of program design methodologies', *IEEE Computer Journal* (Oct. 1981), p. 19.

Birrell, N.D., and Ould, M.A., *A Practical Handbook for Software Development* (Cambridge University Press, 1985).

Blank, J., and Krijger, M.J. (Editors), *Software Engineering, Methods and Techniques* (Wiley/Interscience, 1983).

Blum, B.I., 'The Lifecycle – a debate over alternate models', *ACM Sigsoft, Software Engineering Notes*, Vol. 7, No. 4 (1982), pp. 18–20.

Boehm, B.W., 'The high cost of software', in Horowitz *et al.*, *Practical Strategies for Developing Large Software Systems* (Addison-Wesley, 1975).

Boehm, B.W., *Software Engineering Economics* (Prentice Hall, 1981).

Boehm, B.W., 'Software technology in the 1990's using an evolutionary paradigm', *IEEE Computer Journal* (Nov. 1983), pp. 30–7.

Boehm, B.W., 'A spiral model of software development and enhancement', *ACM Sigsoft, Software Engineering Notes*, Vol. 11, No. 4 (1986), pp. 14–23.

Booch, G., *Software Components with Ada* (Benjamin/Cummings, 1988).

Bott, M.F., and Wallis, P.L.J., 'Ada and software re-use', *IEE/BCS Software Engineering Journal* (Sept. 1988), pp. 177–83.

British Standards Institution, *Guide to Structure Diagrams for Use in Program Design – BS 6224 DSD* (BSI, 1987). With the permission of Nederlandse Normalisatie Institute, Delft.

Brooks, F.P., *The Mythical Man-month* (Addison-Wesley, 1976).

Brooks, F.P., 'People are our most important product' (Keynote speech at the Software Education workshop at Carnegie-Mellon, 1986). Reported in Gibbs and Fairly (1987), pp. 1–15.

Butcher, J. (MP), Chairman, *Information Technology Skills Shortages*, first report of committee proceedings (HMSO, 1984).

Buxton, J.N., *Requirements of Ada PSE (Stoneman)* (US Dept of Defense, OSD/R&E, 1980).

Buxton, J.N., Naur, P., and Randall, B. (Editors), *Software Engineering Techniques* (Proc. NATO, Conference, Rome, 1969) (Scientific Affairs Division, NATO, 1969).

Codd, E.F., 'A relational model of data for large shared data banks', *Comm. ACM*, Vol. 13 (1970), pp. 377–87.

Constantine, L.L., and Yourdon, E., *Structured Design* (Prentice Hall, 1979).

Conte, S.D., Dunmore, H.E., and Shan, V.Y., *Software Engineering Metrics and Models* (Benjamin/Cummings, 1986).

DeMarco, T., *Controlling Software Projects* (Yourdon Press, 1982).

Deutsch, L.P., 'Project Support in the Smalltalk-80 integrated environment'; in J. McDermid (ed.), *Integrated Project Support Environments* (Peter Peregrinus, 1985), Ch. 10.

De Wolf, B., *Requirements Specification and Preliminary Design for Real Time Systems*, Computer Software and Applications Conference, Charles Stark Draper Labs. (Nov. 1977).

Dolotta, T.A., *Data Processing in 1980–85* (Wiley, 1976).

Dunsmore, H.E., and Gannon, 'Data referencing: an empirical investigation', *Computer* (December 1979), pp. 177–83.

Geary, K., 'The practicalities of introducing large-scale software re-use', *IEE/BSC Software Engineering Journal* (Sept. 1988), pp. 172–6.

Gehani, N., and McGettrick, A.D. (Editors), *Software Specification Techniques* (Addison-Wesley, 1986).

Gibbs, N.E., and Fairley, R.E., *Software Engineering Education* (Springer-Verlag, 1987).

Gladden, G.R., 'Stop the lifecycle, I want to get off', *ACM Sigsoft, Software Engineering Notes*, Vol. 7, No. 2 (1982), pp. 35–9.

Glaser, E.L., Illingworth, V., and Pyle, I.C., *Dictionary of Computing* (Oxford Science Publications, 1983).

Glass, R.L., *ACM Sigsoft, Software Engineering Notes*, Vol. 7, No. 4 (1982), pp. 3–13.

Guttag, J.V., and Horning, J.J., *Formal Specification as a Design Tool*, ACM Seventh Annual Symposium on Principles of Programming Languages (1980), pp. 251–61.

Hall, J.A., Hitchcock, P., and Took, R., 'An overview of the ASPECT architecture', in J. McDermid (ed.), *Integrated Project Support Environments* (Peter Peregrinus, 1985), Ch. 7.

Halstead, M.H., *Elements of Software Science* (Elsevier, 1977).

Herd, J.R., Polsa, J.N., Russel, W.E., and Steward, K.R., *Software Cost Estimation – Study Results* (RADC-TR-77220, Vol. 1, Doty Assoc., June 1977).

Horning, J.H., 'Letter from Jim Horning', *ACM Sigsoft, Software Engineering Notes*, Vol. 10, No. 3 (1985), pp. 2–3.

Horowitz, E., and Munson, J.B., 'An expansive view of reusable software', *IEEE Transactions on Software Engineering*, SE-10 (Sept. 1984), pp. 477–87.

Jackson, M.A, *System Development* (Prentice Hall, 1983).

Jensen, R.W., *Estimating Software Costs* (Institute of Dataprocessing Management, Rome lecture, 1984).

Kemmerer, C.F., 'An empirical validation of software cost estimation models', *Comm ACM*, Vol. 30, No. 5 (1987), pp. 416–29.

Kernighan, B.W., 'The Unix system and software re-usability' *IEE Trans. on Software Engineering*, SE-10 (1984), pp. 513–18.

Lawrence, M.J., *An Examination of Evolution Dynamics*, Proc. 6th International Conference on Software Engineering (Sept. 1982), pp. 188–96.

Ledgard, H.F., *Programming Practice* (Addison-Wesley, 1987).

Lehman, M.M., *Programs, Programming and the Software Lifecycle* (Dept. of Computing and Control, Imperial College, London, 1980).

Lehman, M.M., 'Approach to a disciplined development process – the ISTAR integrated project support environment', *ACM Sigsoft, Software Engineering Notes*, Vol. 11, No. 4 (1986), pp. 28–30.

Lehman, M.M., and Turski, V.M., 'Essential properties of Ipses', *ACM Sigsoft, Software Engineering Notes*, Vol. 12, No. 1 (1987), pp. 52–5.

Lehman, M.M., Stenning, V., and Turski V.M., 'Another look at software design methodology', *ACM* Sigsoft, *Software Engineering Notes*, Vol. 9, No. 2 (1984), pp. 38–53.

Levy, L.S., *Taming and Tiger* (Springer Verlag, 1987).

McCabe, T.J., 'A Software complexity measure', *IEEE Trans. on Software Engineering*, Vol. 2, No. 12 (1976), pp. 308–20.

McCracken, D.D., and Jackson, M.A., 'Lifecycle concepts considered harmful', *ACM Sigsoft, Software Engineering Notes*, Vol. 7, No. 2 (1982), pp. 29–32.

McDermid, J. (Editor), *Integrated Project Support Environments* (Peter Peregrinus, 1985).

Macro, A., and Buxton, J.N., *The Craft of Software Engineering* (Addison-Wesley, 1987).

Malengé, J.P., *Critique of Software Science* (University of Nice, France; trans. by M. Marcotty at General Motors, Detroit, 1980).

Marcotty, M., *Software Implementation* (Prentice Hall; 1990 (in preparation)).

Martin, J., and Kleinrock, L., 'An information system manifesto', *Communications of the ACM*, Vol. 28, No. 3 (1985), pp. 252–62.

Mathis, R.F., 'The last 10 percent', *IEEE Transactions on Software Engineering*, Vol. 12, No. 6 (1986), pp. 705–12.

Metzger, P.W., *Managing a Programming Project* (Prentice Hall, 1981).

Michee, D., and Bratko, I., 'An advice program for a complex chess programming task', *Computer Journal of the British Computer Society*, Vol. 23, No. 4 (1980), pp. 353–76.

Miles, T., and Ahlberg, R., *A Competitive Assessment of the United States Software Industry* (US Dept. of Commerce, Feb. 1985).

Nelson, R.A., Haibt, L.M., and Sheridon, P.B., 'Casting Petri-nets into programs, *IEEE Software Engineering*, Vol. 9, No. 5 (1983), pp. 590–602.

Norden, P.V., 'Useful tools for project management', in B.V. Dean (ed.), *Operations Research in R&D* (Wiley, 1963).

Ottestein, L.M., 'Quantitative estimates of debugging requirements', *IEEE Trans. on Software Engineering*, Vol. 5, No. 5 (1979), pp. 504–14.

Oviedo, E.I., 'Control flow, data flow, and program complexity', *Proc. IEEE Computer Software and Applications* (conference, Nov. 1980), pp. 146–52.

Perlis, A.J., De Millo, A., and Lipton, R.J., 'Social process and proofs of theorems and programs', *Communications of the ACM*, Vol. 25, No. 5 (1979), pp. 271–80.

Popper, K., *Conjectures and Refutations* (Routledge & Kegan, 1963/72).

Prather, R.E., 'An axiomatic theory of software complexity metrics', *Computer Journal*, Vol.

27, No. 4 (1984), pp. 340–7.

Putnam, L.H., 'Software Cost Estimating and Lifecycle Control (IEEE Catalog, 1982).

Reiffer, D.J., *Increasing Software Productivity* (Institute of Dataprocessing Management, London Conference, 1982).

Riddle, W., 'Eighteen plus or minus three', *ACM Sigsoft, Software Engineering Notes*, No. 2 (1984), pp. 21–37.

Ross, D.T., 'Structured analysis for requirements definition', *IEEE Trans. on Software Engineering*, Vol. 3, No. 1 (1977), pp. 19–34.

Royce, W.W., *Managing the development of large systems: concepts and techniques*, Proceedings, Wescon (August 1970).

Russell, B., *A History of Western Philosophy* (George Allen & Unwin, 1946), p. 778,

Salter, K.G., 'A methodology for decomposing system requirements into data processing requirements', in *Proc. 2nd International Conference on Software Engineering* (IEEE Computes Society Press, 1976), pp. 91–101.

Selby, R.W., Basili, V.R., and Baker, F.T., 'Cleanroom software development: an empirical evaluation', *IEEE Trans. on Software Engineering*, Vol. 13, No. 9 (1987), pp. 1027–37.

Shannon, C., and Weaver, W., *The Mathematical Theory of Communication* (University of Illinois Press, 1975).

Shepperd, M., 'A critique of cyclomatic complexity as a software metric', *IEEE/BCS Software Engineering Journal*, Vol. 3, No. 2 (1988), pp. 30–36.

Shooman, M.L., *Software Engineering* (McGraw-Hill, 1983).

Smedema, C.H., Medema, P., and Boasson, M., *The Programming Languages Pascal, Modula, Chill and Ada* (Prentice Hall, 1985).

Sommerville, I., *Software Engineering* (Addison-Wesley, 2nd edition, 1985).

Sommerville, I., Welland, R., and Beer, S., 'Describing software design methodologies', *British Computer Society Journal*, Vol. 30, No. 2 (1987), pp. 128–33.

STARTS, *The STARTS Purchasing Handbook* (National Computing Centre, 1987).

Stepney, S., and Lord, S., 'Formal specification of an access control system', *Software – Practice and Experience*, Vol. 17, No. 9 (1987), pp. 575–93.

Stevens, W.P., *Using Structured Design* (Wiley Interscience, 1980).

Thayer, T.A., Lipton, M., and Nelson, E.C., *Software Reliability* (North-Holland, 1978).

Tracz, W., 'Software re-use myths', *ACM Sigsoft, Software Engineering Notes*, Vol. 13, No. 1 (1988), pp. 17–21.

Ullman, J.D., *Principles of Database Systems* (Computer Science Press, 2nd edn, 1982).

Walston, C.E., and Felix, C.P., 'A method of program measurements and estimation', *IBM Systems Journal*, Vol. 16, No. 1 (1977), pp. 54–73.

Weinberg, G.M., *The Psychology of Computer Programming* (Van Nostrand Reinhold, 1971).

Weiner-Erlich, W.K., Hamrick, J.R., and Rudolfo, V.F., 'Modeling software behaviour in terms of a lifecycle curve', *IEEE Software Engineering*, Vol. 10, No. 4 (1984); pp. 376–83.

Weizman, C., Distributed micro-computer systems (Prentice Hall, 1980).

Wirth, N., 'Program development by stepwise refinement', *Communications of the ACM*, Vol. 14 (1971), pp. 221–7.

Wolk, S.R., and Luddy, W.J., *Legal Aspects of Computer Use* (Prentice Hall, 1986).

Zave, P., 'An operational approach to requirement specification for embedded systems', *IEEE Trans on Software Engineering*, Vol. 8, No. 3 (1982), pp. 250–69.

Zipf, G.K., *The Psycho-biology of Language: an Introduction to Dynamic Philology* (MIT Press, 1965; reprint of 1935 original).

INDEX